AMNESTY
INTERNATIONAL
REPORT
1994

This report
covers the period
January to December
1993

Amnesty International is a worldwide voluntary movement that works to prevent some of the gravest violations by governments of people's fundamental human rights. The main focus of its campaigning is to:

– *free all prisoners of conscience.* These are people detained anywhere for their beliefs or because of their ethnic origin, sex, colour or language – who have not used or advocated violence;

– *ensure fair and prompt trials for political prisoners;*

– *abolish the death penalty, torture and other cruel treatment of prisoners;*

– *end extrajudicial executions and "disappearances".*

Amnesty International also opposes abuses by opposition groups: hostage-taking, torture and killings of prisoners and other deliberate and arbitrary killings.

Amnesty International, recognizing that human rights are indivisible and interdependent, works to promote all the human rights enshrined in the Universal Declaration of Human Rights and other international standards, through human rights education programs and campaigning for ratification of human rights treaties.

Amnesty International is impartial. It is independent of any government, political persuasion or religious creed. It does not support or oppose any government or political system, nor does it support or oppose the views of the victims whose rights it seeks to protect. It is concerned solely with the protection of the human rights involved in each case, regardless of the ideology of the government or opposition forces, or the beliefs of the individual.

Amnesty International does not grade countries according to their record on human rights; instead of attempting comparisons it concentrates on trying to end the specific violations of human rights in each case.

Amnesty International has more than 1,100,000 members, subscribers and regular donors in over 150 countries and territories. There are 4,349 local Amnesty International groups registered with the International Secretariat and several thousand school, university, professional and other groups in over 80 countries in Africa, the Americas, Asia, Europe and the Middle East. To ensure impartiality, each group works on cases and campaigns in countries other than its own, selected for geographical and political diversity. Research into human rights violations and individual victims is conducted by the International Secretariat of Amnesty International. No section, group or member is expected to provide information on their own country, and no section, group or member has any responsibility for action taken or statements issued by the international organization concerning their own country.

Amnesty International has formal relations with the United Nations (UN) Economic and Social Council (ECOSOC); the United Nations Educational, Scientific and Cultural Organization (UNESCO); the Council of Europe; the Organization of American States; the Organization of African Unity; and the Inter-Parliamentary Union.

Amnesty International is financed by subscriptions and donations from its worldwide membership. No funds are sought or accepted from governments. To safeguard the independence of the organization, all contributions are strictly controlled by guidelines laid down by the International Council.

AMNESTY INTERNATIONAL REPORT

1994

Amnesty International USA
322 Eighth Avenue
New York, NY 10001

First published 1994
by Amnesty International Publications
1 Easton Street, London WC1X 8DJ, United Kingdom

© Copyright Amnesty International Publications 1994

ISBN: 0-939994-89-5
AI Index: POL 10/02/94
Original language: English

Typesetting and page make-up by:
Accent on type, 2-4 Tysoe Street, London EC1R 4QR

Printed by: John D. Lucas Printing Co.
1820 Portal Street, Baltimore, MD 21224

Cover design: John Finn, Artworkers

Cover photograph: Anti-racist demonstration in Italy, November 1992
© Luigi Baldelli/Contrasto/Katz Pictures

This report documents Amnesty International's work and its concerns throughout the world during 1993. The absence of an entry in this report on a particular country does not imply that no human rights violations of concern to Amnesty International have taken place there during the year. Nor is the length of a country entry any basis for a comparison of the extent and depth of Amnesty International's concerns in a country. Regional maps have been included in this report to indicate the location of countries and territories cited in the text and for that purpose only. It is not possible on the small scale used to show precise political boundaries. The maps should not be taken as indicating any view on the status of disputed territory. Amnesty International takes no position on territorial questions. Disputed boundaries and cease-fire lines are shown, where possible, by broken lines. Areas whose disputed status is a matter of unresolved concern before the relevant bodies of the United Nationas have been indicated by striping only on the maps of the country which has *de facto* control of the area.

CONTENTS

CONTENTS

CONTENTS

APPENDICES

INTRODUCTION

Human rights activists under fire

There was a lot of official talk about human rights in 1993. The noise reached a crescendo in June when government representatives met at the United Nations (UN) World Conference on Human Rights. But even as they were making worthy declarations, the people at the sharp end – the activists who daily defend human rights – were being threatened, imprisoned, tortured and gunned down.

Human rights activists are often victimized because their work undermines the facade of respectability created by their governments. They are the lawyers, teachers, doctors, journalists, peasant leaders, students, relatives of victims and many others who stimulate understanding of human rights, monitor government actions and collate information about human rights violations. They take legal action against perpetrators, provide assistance to victims and mobilize their communities in campaigns to stop the violations. In short, they work to protect the weak and hold the powerful to account.

Their contribution has rarely been more needed than it is today. In a world experiencing rapid political change, they could help create an atmosphere in which the promises of new governments and the "new world order" could be realized. Yet in many countries it has been the human rights activists who have been among the first victims in times of tension.

Paradoxically, it is the governments who are guilty of such actions that are often among the loudest in declaring their support for human rights, as was apparent at the World Conference in Vienna. South Korea's Minister of Foreign Affairs, for example, declared: "I am happy to report to you that human rights have finally come of age in Korea. I stand before you representing a nation and a people who can proudly say that truth, freedom and democracy have at last triumphed in their country."

A few weeks later South Korean police arrested Noh Tae-hun, one of the most prominent human rights activists in South Korea and an organizer of the Korean human rights groups' participation at the World Conference. He was interrogated for 10 days, during which he was threatened and deprived of sleep. He was held in prison until October, when he was released after being given a one-year suspended prison sentence under a law whose sole aim is to curtail free speech. He was convicted of possessing and distributing pamphlets and books written by former political prisoners with the aim of "praising" and "siding with" North Korea. The publications are freely available in South Korea.

Noh Tae-hun is not alone in being victimized for his human rights work. Thousands of such men and women – the very

Noh Tae-hun

people who are in the forefront of creating a more just world – suffer the most appalling persecution for their beliefs. They "disappear" after making inquiries about others who have "disappeared". They are assassinated for protesting against state violence. They are put behind bars for demanding prisoners' rights.

In Guatemala, those brave enough to stand up for human rights are aware that others like them have paid for their courage with their lives. In a country where violations have been a daily reality, particularly for indigenous Indian communities, organizations which try to protect the most vulnerable find that they themselves are then in the firing line. Since the foundation of the Council of Ethnic Communities "We Are All Equal" (CERJ) in 1988, 17 of its members have been extrajudicially executed by the security forces and seven have "disappeared". Among them was Tomás Lares Cipriano, who was shot dead in April 1993 by civil patrollers armed by the security forces, the day after he organized a demonstration against the military presence in his local area, Joyabaj, El Quiché. He was under permanent surveillance by the military at the time because of his human rights activities and had been repeatedly threatened with death.

In countries where state officials feel free to act with impunity, human rights activists are often the only force standing between the mass of ordinary people and the unbridled power of the state. No one else would take up the cases of peasants wrongly evicted from their land. No one else would petition the courts to obtain the release of those unlawfully imprisoned. No one else would try to find out what had happened to the men and women who have "disappeared".

Human rights activists on the ground are a crucial source of data about what is really happening in any particular country. International organizations, whether they be non-governmental like Amnesty International or intergovernmental institutions like the UN, are heavily dependent on that information. It is clear that governments which are responsible for human rights violations cannot be trusted to provide the whole truth, and without the local and independent sources, they would get away with far more than they do at the moment.

At first glance it would seem that few countries take human rights more seriously than Tunisia. A Tunisian was President of the UN Commission on Human Rights in 1993 and there are Tunisian members on five of the international and regional committees which monitor the implementation by governments of human rights treaties. Tunisia has ratified nearly all UN human rights instruments, sends its reports to the relevant committees on time and in late 1992 hosted the Africa regional meeting of the World Conference on Human Rights. It is the seat of the Arab Institute of Human Rights and the government has instructed that all police stations keep on hand the Universal Declaration of Human Rights.

Yet a closer look inside the country reveals a blatant contempt by the authorities for the human rights of its citizens. In recent years thousands of suspected government opponents have been arbitrarily arrested, held in illegally prolonged incommunicado detention, tortured and imprisoned after unfair trials. Those who have publicized these violations and spoken out against them have been punished with the same abuses.

In 1992 the government closed down the Tunisian Human Rights League, one of the oldest human rights organizations in the Arab world. After the arrest and torture of left-wing government opponents, 18 local human rights activists announced on 2 February 1993 the formation of a national committee to defend prisoners of conscience. Two days later the police hauled them in for questioning. The committee's coordinator, Salah Hamzaoui, was held for two weeks; the others were released. All 18 were charged with forming an unauthorized organization, distributing leaflets and spreading false information. They have yet to be tried.

With such intimidation and repression of human rights activists on the ground, it will become increasingly difficult to monitor the real human rights situation in Tunisia. In circumstances such as these, it is even more imperative that human rights groups around the world work together to support human rights activists who are under fire.

Rosa Pu Gómez, a member of CONAVIGUA, *the National Coordinating Committee of Widows of Guatemala, is one of many human rights activists who have been threatened or attacked in recent years. In October 1993, for example, her name appeared on a list signed by a shadowy "anti-communist" group, believed to be linked to the security forces, which threatened 20 people with death unless they left the country within 72 hours. Rosa Pu is fully aware of the danger she is in: she has already lost several close relatives who have "disappeared".*

AMNESTY INTERNATIONAL REPORT 1994

4

International organizations have to take collective responsibility for the defence of human rights activists in all corners of the globe. They must work to create the space for human rights activism in countries where it remains virtually impossible today. Those who can operate in relative safety must protect those who are most vulnerable. More effective links must be forged between individuals who risk their lives or liberty if they speak out and those who are able to publicize human rights issues and apply pressure on repressive governments.

This is particularly important at a time when the world is changing so rapidly. The end of the Cold War has led to new democratic institutions being formed for the first time in generations in many countries. Human rights groups have sprung up in dozens of places where they could not operate openly before. The new freedoms, however, are proving to be fragile. Many of these countries are now teetering on the edge of violence and disintegration, with human rights being sacrificed in the pursuit of power and privilege.

Such is the case in some of the countries which have emerged from the former Soviet Union. In Uzbekistan, for example, the authorities have been busy promising new freedoms and rights – while their security forces have been busy using the methods of old. In August 1992, for instance, a small explosive device blew in the front door and started a fire at the Tashkent apartment of Mikhail Ardzinov, the deputy chairman of the Human Rights

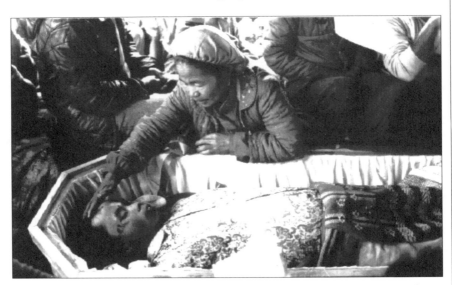

In the Philippines, where government and government-backed forces have maimed and slaughtered their perceived enemies for many years, human rights activists have often been high on the hit lists. Among the victims in 1993 was Chris Batan, a 26-year-old human rights activist, seen here being mourned by his mother. He was shot dead in February by members of a government-backed militia. He had spent much of his short adult life campaigning for the rights of indigenous people.

Society of Uzbekistan. Two nights earlier, an identical attack had taken place on a flat with the same number in an adjacent block. When Mikhail Ardzinov confronted the Interior Ministry about the two attacks, an officer reportedly acknowledged the first attack, saying it had happened because Mikhail Ardzinov had "given the wrong address" during a police interrogation. Later in the year, in December, the Uzbek secret police abducted the chairman of the Human Rights Society of Uzbekistan, Abdumannob Pulatov, from a human rights conference in Kyrgyzstan and took him back to Uzbekistan. He was convicted of slandering the Uzbek President, although he was immediately granted an amnesty and released.

The role of human rights activists is key in countries going through major reforms or transitional periods. They help create the space in which the institutions of civil society can be built and within which the right to peaceful dissent can be exercised and protected. Their ideas can contribute to establishing new laws and institutions that can better protect the rights of all, and their actions can help ensure that those responsible for human rights crimes in the past and present are held to account. Yet all too often, the authorities see such activists as a problem rather than part of the solution for creating a better future.

In Nigeria human rights activists were among the first to be arrested following the military government's decision to annul the result of a presidential election held in June 1993. The authorities claimed that the election was invalid owing to malpractices. In early July, human rights activists Beko Ransome-Kuti, Femi Falana and Chief Gani Fawehinmi, all prominent members of the Campaign for Democracy, were arrested after the Campaign for Democracy called for a week of protest against the government's decision. All three had been arrested several times before. On 12 July they were charged with sedition and conspiracy and remanded in custody until 30 September. On 28 July bail was granted and the conditions of bail met, but the authorities refused to release them. They were eventually freed on 29 August shortly after an interim government took power. In October Beko Ransome-Kuti was rearrested and charged after further peaceful demonstrations. His trial was adjourned until 1994.

In South Africa, where the political reform process to end *apartheid* has been accompanied by increasing levels of violence, the security forces have on many occasions trampled on human rights in the name of maintaining law and order. Among the victims have been community activists who have been trying by peaceful means to defend human rights. Louis Sibeko, for example, the general secretary of the Thokoza Civic Association and a man who has worked tirelessly on behalf of victims of human rights violations, was arrested in a pre-dawn police raid at his home on 17 August 1993. He was threatened with assault by his interrogators and held for a month at Boksburg Prison under emergency regulations which allow the police to hold a

Dr Fernando Gomes, a founder and president of the Guinea-Bissau Human Rights League, has faced persistent threats to stop him working for human and democratic rights. The threats took an ominous turn in May 1993 when the President of Guinea-Bissau alleged in a broadcast that the League had known about an attempted coup in March. In September Fernando Gomes was ordered to go the headquarters of the Public Order Police for interrogation. He refused to answer any questions and was released, but remains fearful for his safety.

person without charge or trial for up to 30 days. Before his arrest, armed men had been keeping him under surveillance and had threatened him with death.

Governments that victimize human rights activists almost invariably have a great deal to hide. If they cannot tolerate people speaking out for the most basic rights of their fellow citizens, it is highly likely that they will not tolerate dissent and must therefore rely on fear and violence to maintain their power.

In Saudi Arabia, where the government allows almost no public criticism of its policies, human rights activists face intimidation and abuses by the security forces. On 15 June 1993, for instance, Dr 'Abdullah al-Hamed, a university professor and one of six founding members of the Committee for the Defence of Legitimate Rights, was arrested at his home by members of the General Intelligence and taken to an unknown destination. He was held incommunicado without charge or trial until his release in late September or early October. During his detention he was allegedly deprived of sleep for long periods.

In Colombia, where the regular security forces or paramilitary organizations operating with their support have extrajudicially executed thousands of people in recent years, human rights activists have been increasingly targeted. Since 1992, for example, three members of the Magdalena Medio Regional Human Rights Committee (CREDHOS) have been assassinated. There has also been a systematic attempt by military authorities to discredit leading human rights organizations by falsely accusing them of having links with armed opposition groups. Many human rights lawyers and activists have felt forced to abandon their activities and seek refuge in other areas of the country or abroad. As a result, those who remain are even more isolated and at risk.

The Indonesian authorities have been equally determined to silence those standing up for human rights. A recent victim was Ahmad Jauhari, a 28-year-old lawyer and human rights activist. On 6 October 1993, 10 men came to his home while he was away and, while his wife and newly born child were inside, wrecked his house. A note left behind by the attackers read: "Leave Rancamaya now, or be ready to die like a dog!" The attack appeared to be motivated by his work on behalf of farming communities in the Bogor area of West Java, and the way it was carried out raised suspicions of police involvement or complicity. Less than two weeks before the attack, Ahmad Jauhari had been detained and interrogated by the police for three days after a peaceful demonstration about a land dispute in Bogor.

One reason governments turn on human rights activists is that they know how damaging the effective monitoring of abuses can be in terms of their international image. This is particularly true when activists are trying to publicize violations in territories seeking independence or occupied by foreign forces.

Such is the case in the Tibet Autonomous Region, where the Chinese authorities continue to hound those advocating independence for Tibet and, more recently, human rights activists. On 13 May 1993, for example, one of Tibet's best-known tourist guides, Gendun Rinchen, was arrested after the security forces raided his home and found documents describing the state of human rights in Tibet, including information about prisoners. He had been planning to give his notes to a delegation of European ambassadors due to arrive in Lhasa on 16 May. He was held in Seitru Detention Centre until mid-January 1994 facing charges of "stealing state secrets" and "engaging in separatist activities" – charges which are punishable by a minimum sentence of 10 years' imprisonment and can be interpreted to warrant the death penalty.

In Rwanda, several activists who helped an international commission of inquiry into human rights violations committed in the country since 1990 were themselves threatened with death by various security and government officials in 1993. One man, known as Muhikira, was reportedly forced to commit suicide. On 13 January armed gangs reportedly surrounded his house in Mutura district, Gisenyi prefecture, and ordered him to come out and be killed or commit suicide. The gangs were said to be accompanied by local police. Muhikira was apparently targeted because his son, Eustache Mupenzi, acted as an interpreter to the commission of inquiry.

In countries where the human rights situation is rapidly deteriorating, it is especially vital that human rights monitors are able to operate freely. Without them, it becomes easier for the international community to turn its back on those most in need.

In the Federal Republic of Yugoslavia, many human rights monitors and organizations have found themselves under fire. In July 1993, for example, Sami Kurteshi, a member of the Council for the Defence of Human Rights and Freedoms in Priština, was

© TIN

Gendun Rinchen

© Howard J. Davies

Koigi wa Wamwere was among eight possible prisoners of conscience held in 1993 in Kenya for campaigning for human rights and peacefully criticizing the government. They were arrested by police in September and accused of being in possession of "seditious publications", including material produced by the National Democratic and Human Rights Organization, and illegal weapons. All eight were released on bail within a few days or weeks, but Koigi wa Wamwere was arrested again in November and charged, with four others, with violent robbery. He faces a possible death penalty. He denied being involved in an armed attack on a police station and was apparently arrested for his non-violent political and human rights activities.

beaten and arrested during a raid on the Council's offices by the police. The police confiscated materials documenting human rights abuses committed against ethnic Albanians in Kosovo by the police force, which is largely Serbian. Sami Kurteshi was released within a few days but reportedly needed medical treatment for injuries inflicted on him by the police during his arrest and detention.

The hostility of the Yugoslav Government to human rights monitoring had already been shown earlier in the year when it refused to allow the UN Special Rapporteur on the former Yugoslavia to base staff in the Federal Republic of Yugoslavia. In July the government forced the long-term monitoring mission in Kosovo, the Sandžak and Vojvodina regions, established by the Conference on Security and Co-operation in Europe, to leave the country. Two months later Amnesty International was refused permission to visit Kosovo province.

This annual report exposes the enormous gap between the rhetoric and the reality – what governments say about human rights and what they actually do. It could not have been put together without the contribution of the thousands of human rights activists who are standing up for human rights in their communities; many of them have had to risk their lives or defy their governments to search for the truth.

Human rights activists around the world have all too often been left to stand virtually alone, surviving only through sheer

In Cuba, freedom of expression, association and assembly remains severely restricted. Among the hundreds of prisoners of conscience currently held is 61-year-old Sebastián Arcos Bergnes (left), the Vice-President of the unofficial Comité Cubano Pro Derechos Humanos (CCPDH), Cuban Committee for Human Rights. He was arrested in January 1992 with two other leading CCPDH members – his brother Gustavo (centre) and Jesús Yanes Pelletier (right). While the two others were released 24 hours later, Sebastián Arcos was tried in October that year and sentenced to four years and eight months' imprisonment for spreading allegedly false information about human rights abuses.

grit and courage. The international community, as represented by governments, has singularly failed to do what is needed to protect them. For more than eight years governments at the UN Commission on Human Rights have been unable to reach agreement on the text of a basic declaration aimed at recognizing and protecting the rights of human rights defenders. Meanwhile, those defenders continue to be tortured, imprisoned and gunned down. Amnesty International urges the world's governments to agree on a strong text for this declaration on human rights defenders and to adopt it as a matter of urgency. This would be a first step. Then governments must ensure that they fully implement its provisions and protect the activities of human rights workers in every country. We urge the UN and regional bodies to work more closely with non-governmental human rights organizations. These organizations offer the genuine commitment to human rights that is vital if progress is to be made.

We also believe that the international community of non-governmental human rights organizations must forge stronger links to protect its members and isolate guilty governments behind "walls of shame".

The hope for humanity lies with the millions of men and women who have committed themselves in one way or another to defending human rights. We must do all we can to protect them now and keep them alive.

Mobilizing in defence of human rights

Actions speak louder than words. While diplomats and officials proclaimed their support for fundamental freedoms at the UN World Conference on Human Rights, Amnesty International activists were out on the streets of Vienna, campaigning to stop torture, campaigning to save lives.

On a busy street near the heart of the city, Amnesty International members from Germany, Austria and many other countries set up a stall to help individuals in danger of detention, "disappearance", torture or execution. Five fax machines were set up to send urgent appeals to the governments responsible, to the people with the power to stop human rights violations. The cases of the victims were printed on large posters for all to read. Passers-by, attracted by the sight and sound of the machines, were encouraged to join in.

More than 25,000 faxes were sent from the "Urgent Action" stall during the two weeks of the Conference in mid-June. They called for action by governments on behalf of people in many countries, including Tunisia, China and the United States of America (USA). And they had an effect. One set of appeals was for a journalist in Peru, known for his reports on police brutality. He had received numerous death threats, so that when he was detained there were fears that he would be killed in custody. Three days after the opening of the Conference, he was released.

The Urgent Action stall was just one of hundreds of events organized by Amnesty International members at the time of the World Conference on Human Rights. In Vienna itself, on one day alone, members from Norway and the Philippines ran a series of workshops on human rights education; the Dutch Section organized an event on the role of non-governmental organizations in countering political killings and "disappearances"; and members from Tunisia and Switzerland held a symposium on Human Rights and Islam. Every day of the fortnight was similarly packed with activities.

Elsewhere, Amnesty International members used the opportunity to raise their vision of a better world in their own communities. In the Philippines, a theatre caravan toured poor urban districts with a play about human rights. In Colombia, Amnesty International worked with other Colombian human rights groups to organize a series of press conferences, each highlighting a different aspect of the issues raised at the World Conference.

The determination not to stay silent in the face of human rights violations unites Amnesty International members all over the world. When Amnesty International was born in 1961, it worked for the release of prisoners of conscience. Since then its members have decided to campaign on behalf of victims of torture and unfair political trials, those who have "disappeared" or have been extrajudicially executed, and all those who face the death penalty. The movement has also decided to confront abuses by armed opposition groups.

Prisoners of conscience remain central to Amnesty International's concerns, and the release of a prisoner of conscience is always a source not only of great joy, but also of great encouragement. However, when Vera Chirwa, Africa's longest serving known prisoner of conscience, was released after more than 11 years, the joy was tinged with sadness. Her husband, Orton Chirwa, had died in prison three months earlier. "Every day of freedom is like a miracle to me. If it had not been for Amnesty International, I would not be standing before you today", she said soon after her release.

Vera and Orton Chirwa were abducted from Zambia by Malawian agents in 1981. They were taken back to Malawi, where they were convicted of treason on fabricated charges and sentenced to death. The death sentences were commuted to life imprisonment after a massive international appeal on their behalf. For 11 years the two were held in the same prison, but they saw each other only once, three weeks before Orton Chirwa's death.

Amnesty International members around the world campaigned long and hard for the Chirwas. In the early 1980s, when their executions appeared imminent, urgent appeals for their lives were sent by tens of thousands of men and women from many countries. Once their death sentences had been commuted, Amnesty International members concentrated on trying to win their freedom. In Germany and the United Kingdom, countries with long-standing aid and trade links with Malawi, members urged government ministers and officials to apply pressure

The traditional Chinese Lion Dance vividly illustrates a human rights theme in Hong Kong. First the lion is tied up in chains, helpless. When the chains are broken, the lion dances to freedom. Amnesty International members in Hong Kong use dance, theatre and music to raise human rights awareness.

AMNESTY INTERNATIONAL REPORT 1994

Vera Chirwa was released in 1993 after 11 years as a prisoner of conscience in Malawi's notorious Zomba prison. Together with her husband Orton, who died in prison in 1992, she was sentenced to death after a grossly unfair trial: the sentence was commuted to life imprisonment after widespread international protests. "I was released" she told an Amnesty International audience, "because of all your good work, and because of the pressure from you friends at Amnesty International."

on the authorities to release them. Lawyers had a special role, since both the Chirwas were lawyers (Orton Chirwa had been the first African barrister in Malawi). At an Anglo-French legal conference, empty chairs with the Chirwas' names gave silent witness to their plight. After Orton Chirwa's death, leading British lawyers joined a wreath-laying ceremony outside the Malawi High Commission in London. The efforts of local Amnesty International groups included mass letter-writing to the Malawi authorities, and publicity. One result was that a rope-making company refused to supply special hemp ropes, apparently destined for hangings, to Malawi.

Amnesty International members in Nigeria and Japan were also prominent in the efforts to win the Chirwas' freedom. They raised the issue in the media, and with officials, judges, religious groups, academics and the medical profession. According to Vera Chirwa herself, "My freedom is due entirely to the international outcry about our case. I shall never be able to thank Amnesty International enough for fighting for Orton and myself ... Although my husband is gone, his blood has watered the spirit of the Malawian people – his fight for human rights will never be forgotten."

The campaign to free the Chirwas illustrates a few of the many different ways in which Amnesty International members try to achieve their aims. There are now over a million Amnesty International members, donors and subscribers in more than 150 countries in every region of the world. Many are organized in local groups, which meet regularly in 94 countries. In 53 of these countries, the groups have established Amnesty International sections to coordinate efforts at a national level. Special networks of people such as lawyers, medical workers, students and trade unionists are also organized to use their connections and influence to aid human rights.

The patterns of human rights abuses that Amnesty International seeks to combat have become more and more complex in recent years. The hopes for peace and justice raised by the end of the Cold War have not been fulfilled. A spate of local wars, often accompanied by the virtual disintegration of state authority, have spread turmoil and terror. On different continents, some new (or newly revived) democracies have made a shaky but promising start; others have descended into political chaos. Nationalist, ethnic and religious conflict, famine and repression have led to massive movements of refugees. More and more countries, especially wealthy ones, have closed their doors to people who need and deserve sanctuary.

These horrific events illuminate the interdependence and indivisibility of human rights more powerfully than any abstract argument. In this increasingly volatile human rights environment, Amnesty International offers a structure for people from all continents to campaign for human rights and influence events worldwide as well as in their own regions. Amnesty International is determined to adapt to the evolving realities by adjusting its responses. It must play its role within the broader human rights movement. And it must transcend its Western roots and continue to develop as a truly international, multicultural human rights movement.

Efforts to build an effective Amnesty International organization in every area of the world were pursued with tenacity and determination during 1993.

Members in the Asia and Pacific region continued their steady growth in numbers, organization and influence. There are now nine sections in the region: sections in Bangladesh, Nepal and South Korea were formally recognized during the year.

The Hong Kong Section has been lobbying for many years to abolish the death penalty in Hong Kong. This was finally achieved in April to the delight of the section's members. In March 1993 representatives from Japan, the Philippines and Thailand took an active part in a regional meeting in Bangkok preparatory to the UN World Conference on Human Rights.

Members of the Karachi group, Pakistan, celebrated the release of prisoner of conscience Mohammad Nasheed, a journalist from the Maldives. While he was in prison the group had sent greeting cards to his relatives and had organized a campaign in Sindh province for his release. Members across Pakistan organized conferences, poster exhibitions and musical evenings to raise human rights awareness throughout the country.

In Africa, there are sections in seven countries. During 1993 a national committee was set up in South Africa to coordinate the work of the new Amnesty International groups in the country. In September a meeting of Amnesty International campaign coordinators from West African sections and groups was held in Benin: the first-ever meeting of its kind in Africa.

In Nigeria, about 800 people are involved in an Urgent Action network which responds rapidly to reports of people at risk of human rights violations around the world. However, financial hardship and escalating postal costs mean that most of them cannot afford to post letters abroad on behalf of human rights victims. The volunteer network coordinators – a university researcher and a lawyer – have come up with a solution: writers who cannot afford to mail letters or cards forward them to the Amnesty International section office. The network coordinators then deliver them to the relevant country embassy in the capital, Lagos. If there is no embassy or country representative, then they are posted in one package. The difficulties of raising funds beset many sections in the countries of the South and East, and much energy and time goes into devising ways of collecting money for Amnesty International's work.

In the Middle East, political violence made 1993 a difficult year for Amnesty International development. In particular, the upsurge of religious and political strife in Algeria and Egypt led to political polarization in which those campaigning impartially for human rights came under great pressure from both sides.

Despite the problems, Amnesty International succeeded in establishing new groups in the Israeli-occupied territories of Gaza and the West Bank, as well as in Yemen. Sections in Israel and Tunisia persisted in their work despite the difficult circumstances. National coordinating committees in Egypt, Kuwait and Jordan made headway. Human rights education was one area of progress. Members in Tunisia established long-term human rights education projects at the national level with support from Amnesty International's Teaching for Freedom project. In Jordan members also began work in this area.

In Latin America and the Caribbean, there are 12 sections, three national coordinating structures and groups in another five countries. There is an organized Amnesty International presence in 20 countries throughout the region. During 1993 the first Amnesty International group was established in Jamaica; the organization's presence in Bolivia and Paraguay went from strength to strength and the Colombian Section was recognized. A concerted effort was launched across the whole region to agree strategies and coordinate activities. It resulted in the formation of a group to lobby for human rights concerns at the regional level, at the Organization of American States.

Members in some long-standing sections had to face difficult arguments in the face of escalating violence and social instability. In Peru, members worked to counter the proposed reintroduction of the death penalty. In the Caribbean and Colombia too, the death penalty was one of the main issues to be tackled.

In Chile, members explored how they might find new ways of working within their own community to address human rights issues without putting Amnesty International's impartiality into question or reducing international solidarity. The Uruguayan Section collaborated with other local human rights groups to campaign against "disappearances" around the world. The production of human rights materials in local languages such as Brazilian Portuguese was given a high priority during the year.

In the field of human rights education, the Brazilian Section ran a course for members of the police force and the Puerto Rico Section helped prepare teaching materials to be used in primary and secondary schools. Sections in Guyana and Ecuador reached agreement with their governments' education ministries to develop human rights courses for the national education curriculum. A network of Amnesty International medical groups in Ecuador successfully pressed for the introduction of a human rights teaching component in all faculties of medicine in the country. In Argentina, Venezuela, Peru and Mexico, human rights education materials produced by Amnesty International members were distributed widely to schools and to non-governmental organizations. The sections in Chile and Uruguay began human rights education projects with marginalized sectors of society, such as the homeless.

Five years ago there were no Amnesty International groups in the countries of the former Soviet bloc. By 1993, there were members in 26 of the 27 countries of the region: the sole exception was Tadzhikistan. About 70 local groups meet regularly in 17 of the countries, from Albania to Kyrgyzstan. In Poland, Slovenia and the Czech Republic, coordinating committees have opened offices and are making progress towards becoming fully fledged sections.

In November, a meeting was held for members from across

Several hundred thousand postcards, sent from all around the world, were made into a giant patchwork covering the Stephansplatz in the historic heart of Vienna to mark the opening of the UN World Conference on Human Rights in June. While governments excluded human rights activists from key discussions, this symbolic action sent a clear message from ordinary people to diplomats and officials to remember that it's "Our World, Our Rights".

"Ukraine was almost unknown to the outside world, but very well represented in the Gulag archipelago. I was one of those prisoners of conscience, and in addressing you today, I would like to express my sincere gratitude to all those members of Amnesty International who cared about us and worked in favour of our freedom." The convener of the first-ever Ukrainian group, Myroslav Marynovych, served 10 years in prison and internal exile for his belief in democracy and freedom. In 1993 he spoke to Amnesty International's International Council Meeting.

Ukraine. The convener of the first ever Ukrainian Amnesty International group, Myroslav Marynovych, is a former prisoner of conscience. He served 10 years in prison and internal exile for his belief in democracy and freedom: he was one of many people detained for monitoring Ukraine's compliance with the Helsinki Agreement. In mid-1993 he addressed Amnesty International's International Council Meeting (ICM) in Boston, USA: "In 1991, a Ukrainian branch was grafted on the Amnesty tree ... There is too much against us for carefree optimism: first and foremost, political instability, economic collapse, and other hardships so typical of the post-communist world. And yet I remain an optimist, and I firmly believe that the flame of Amnesty's candle will continue to burn in Ukraine."

The 1993 biennial ICM – Amnesty International's supreme policy making body – was the most internationally representative ever. First-time delegates came, not only from Ukraine, but also from the West Bank and Gaza and from South Africa.

The ICM demonstrated a clear desire to move forward and explore change, while building on Amnesty International's strengths and safeguarding its unique contribution. It reaffirmed that Amnesty International is a campaigning organization. Our specific contribution to the global human rights movement is international activism against the violation of certain civil and political rights. Amnesty International also collaborates with others to promote the values of the Universal Declaration of Human Rights – which covers a far wider spectrum of human rights – through human rights education, and promoting international standards.

The ICM emphasized the need to strengthen the worldwide coverage and reporting of human rights violations. It also called for more innovative campaigning and rapid crisis response in increasingly volatile human rights situations. The ICM stressed that the development of the broader human rights community is fundamental to the long-term prevention of violations. The ICM

Participation in the Kuwait Book Fair has become one of the regular activities of Amnesty International groups in Kuwait, generating significant interest from the general public in the organization's human rights reporting.

also stated clearly that Amnesty International members around the world must have the confidence and expertise to plan and carry out effective actions appropriate to their own cultures, systems and resources.

Those actions are based on information carefully researched and analysed by the staff at the International Secretariat in London, where over 290 people, drawn from more than 50 countries, work. The information is sent out in reports, the monthly *Amnesty International Newsletter* and campaigning documents; once a year it is summarized in this annual report.

Top of the agenda for Amnesty International's members and supporters in the coming decade is a worldwide campaign against political killings and "disappearances". The campaign, launched in October 1993, confronts governments head-on about one of the greatest threats to human rights in the 1990s: the ever-growing number of killings and "disappearances" at the hands of the state.

Increasingly, these human rights crimes have happened in countries that are supposedly committed to human rights. Long-standing democracies such as India, or more recent ones such as the Philippines, have talked about human rights on the international stage even as their people were gunned down or abducted. In countries such as Brazil and Colombia, whose governments know that a poor human rights record damages their international relations, "death squads" have committed the crimes. Governments claim they have no control over these killers, but the trail of responsibility leads back to the authorities.

In the former Yugoslavia, several of the republics of the former USSR, Somalia and Zaire, the toll of the dead and "disappeared" runs into thousands. And in a world of growing instability, armed political opposition groups have also been responsible for deliberate and arbitrary killings or have abducted or held hostage their opponents, as in Algeria, India, Liberia, Peru, Sri Lanka and the Sudan.

18

This is the first major international campaign where Amnesty International clearly condemns such abuses by those groups – abuses which are outlawed even in war and fly in the face of international humanitarian principles.

All over the world, from Australia to Albania, from Mexico to Mauritius, Amnesty International members used their creativity and imagination to launch the campaign. In Côte d'Ivoire, Ivorian musician Waby Spider released a cassette tape of songs about human rights. The songs are intended to let people in Africa know and understand more about their rights and the African Charter on Human and Peoples' Rights. Amnesty International members in Africa plan to use music as a major part of their campaign, especially as radio is so important across the continent. Waby Spider embarked on a concert tour around West Africa to promote the campaign against political killings and "disappearances", with all money from the sales of cassettes going to Amnesty International's Ivorian Section. Music was used elsewhere too: in Poland, the Gdánsk Amnesty International group organized a concert tour with a Latin American band.

In many sections, former "disappeared" prisoners and relatives of the "disappeared" or murdered proved the most powerful advocates for action against these abuses. For example, the Bourequat brothers, who were released after having "disappeared" for 18 years in Morocco, went to Sweden to help launch the campaign. Their testimonies reduced seasoned journalists to tears, and ensured wide media coverage and renewed inspiration and energy for Amnesty International members themselves.

Amnesty International members launched many other campaigns during 1993 – too many to list here. In a concerted effort to bring to an end the gross human rights violations in Chad,

Human Rights Day 1993: Amnesty International members in Mauritius campaign against political killings and "disappearances", among the gravest human rights threats of our age.

'Ali 'Abdul-Fattah Hashim, a prisoner of conscience, was released in June. He had been held in prison in Yemen for over a year. A writer and teacher, he had been detained and tortured on previous occasions because of his political activities.

Amnesty International sections and groups in West Africa were especially active. In Côte d'Ivoire, the section organized a public meeting attended by around 140 people, including journalists and the Chadian Consul in Côte d'Ivoire. Together with other non-governmental organizations, Amnesty International members gathered signatures for a petition to be forwarded to the Government of Chad. In Ghana, members lobbied doctors, lawyers, journalists, teachers and Muslim organizations. In Benin, appeals and information were sent to the embassies of Chad, France (the former colonial power), Nigeria (where many Chadian refugees had fled) and the USA (which, with France, had armed and trained the Chadian armed forces). In Sierra Leone, a photo exhibition displayed in a central library was visited by various prominent people, including foreign diplomats. Members contacted religious and children's groups and produced a special calendar for the campaign. In Cameroon, the groups used the occasion of the 30th anniversary of the Organization of African Unity to have a radio program broadcast on human rights – featuring Chad.

There were new as well as long-standing issues that inspired members to action. Against the background of a frightening rise in racism and neo-Nazism, Amnesty International produced material about racist ill-treatment by police in Europe, and groups all over the world took up the question.

In response to the carnage in the former Yugoslavia, Amnesty International members from around the world sought different ways to put pressure on the parties involved to remember basic human values. In January, over half a million postcards appealing for human rights to be respected arrived in Geneva as high-level talks among the combatants were in progress. In May a caravan of peace travelled from a former execution yard in an Irish jail to the borders of Yugoslavia. The "Witness for Yugoslavia – Caravan of Conscience" carried the message: "Stop the torture, stop the rape, bring those responsible to justice".

Members who have campaigned for many years against the death penalty in the Caribbean celebrated when the final court of appeal in London, United Kingdom, ruled that two men who had been on death row in Jamaica for over 13 years could not be

"I want to place on record my profound gratitude and deepest appreciation ... for all your innumerable efforts to get me released." Chief Gani Fawehinmi, a prominent human rights lawyer and democracy activist in Nigeria, was arrested in July and charged with conspiracy and sedition. He had criticized the annulment of presidential election results by the military authorities. He was released in late August after worldwide appeals on his behalf.

put to death. The ruling may save the lives of over 100 others who have been on death row for years in parts of the Caribbean.

These campaigns were just a few of dozens taken up enthusiastically by Amnesty International members during 1993. Others included major initiatives on Burundi, Brazil, China, Myanmar and the Sudan. Human rights violations against women and trade unionists across the world were also highlighted.

As government repression and bitter civil conflict threaten large parts of the world, it is becoming increasingly clear that humanity's best hope lies with the millions of ordinary people involved in the worldwide human rights movement. We are proud to be a part of this movement, and urge all readers to join us in action.

The death penalty: a gross violation of human rights

Amnesty International is unconditionally opposed to the death penalty and works for its worldwide abolition. Through its constant campaigning against this violation of fundamental human rights, the organization seeks to save the lives of those facing the ultimate form of cruel, inhuman and degrading punishment. It also works strenuously to raise awareness among both politicians and the general public about the arbitrary and irrevocable nature of the death penalty – emphasizing how it is often used as a tool of political repression or disproportionately imposed on the poor and the powerless. In its campaigns and publications, Amnesty International exposes the bankruptcy of the argument that the death penalty has any real deterrent effect on rates of crime or political violence in a society. The organization monitors death sentences and executions around the world and appeals for clemency whenever it learns of an imminent execution.

The good news in 1993 was the addition of four countries to the list of nations that are abolitionist. Guinea-Bissau's National Assembly amended the Constitution in February to abolish the death penalty for all crimes. Before the amendment, military courts were empowered to impose the death penalty for aggravated murder and offences against state security. Hong Kong's Legislative Council voted to abolish the death penalty for all crimes in April. The same month, the Gambia's House of Representatives also voted to abolish the death penalty for all crimes. Lastly, in December, Greece abolished the death penalty for all crimes, both in time of war and in peacetime.

Other positive developments included a judgment in November by the Judicial Committee of the United Kingdom's Privy Council (JCPC), the final court of appeal for many Commonwealth countries. The JCPC ruled that executions carried out on prisoners who had been held for more than five years after receiving a death sentence amounted to inhuman and degrading punishment. It also stated that anyone held for more than five years after being sentenced to death should have their sentence commuted to life imprisonment. It is believed that the ruling, which related to the cases of two Jamaican men who had spent more than 14 years awaiting execution, will have a significant impact in at least 16 Commonwealth countries. The commutation of the death sentences of more than 100 prisoners in Jamaica alone is expected to result from the ruling.

Far less encouraging was a judgment by the US Supreme Court in January. It ruled that a death-row prisoner who presents belated evidence of innocence is not normally entitled to a new hearing in a Federal Court before being executed. The Supreme Court stated that in a capital case a "truly persuasive" demonstration of actual innocence made after trial would render the execution of a defendant unconstitutional, but "because of the very disruptive effect that entertaining claims of actual innocence would have ... the threshold showing for such an assumed right would necessarily be extraordinarily high". Leonel Herrera, the Texas prisoner who had presented the appeal, was executed on 12 May. During the year, 38 people were executed in the USA, including 17 in Texas alone. Four of these 38 were juvenile offenders who were aged only 17 at the time of the crime for which they were sentenced to death. The execution of juvenile offenders, which is extremely rare worldwide, is prohibited by numerous international treaties.

Amnesty International regretted the decisions taken to restore or extend the scope of the death penalty in the Philippines and Peru. In December the death penalty was restored in the Philippines for a range of criminal offences, including murder, drug-trafficking, rape and arson. The country's 1987 Constitution had abolished the death penalty for all offences.

In September the Peruvian Congress approved the final draft of a new Constitution. This extended the scope of the death penalty to include the crime of "terrorism". The Constitution, which was approved by Peruvian voters in a referendum, violates Article 4(2) of the American Convention on Human Rights, which Peru ratified in 1978. The Convention states that the death penalty "shall not be extended to crimes to which it does not presently apply".

Amnesty International expressed great concern over the decision by the Japanese authorities to resume executions in March after a period of over three years. One of the three prisoners hanged that month was suffering from mental illness. By the end of the year, seven people had been executed in Japan – the highest number of executions in a single year since 1976. Executions also resumed in Kuwait in May when an Iraqi national was hanged after being convicted of "collaboration" with Iraqi forces during the 1990/1991 occupation of the country. It was the first recorded judicial execution to have been carried out by the Kuwaiti authorities since 1989. Amnesty International expressed concern that a further 22 people sentenced to death in Kuwait since April 1992 after being convicted of "collaboration" were at risk of imminent execution following trials which did not conform to international standards for fair trial.

Amnesty International also expressed grave concern about the resumption of executions in Algeria after a period of three years. Twenty-six people were executed there during the year and over 300 people were sentenced to death after grossly unfair trials. Elsewhere in the region, Amnesty International recorded an increase in the number of executions in Egypt and Saudi Arabia, where 33 and 87 people were executed in 1993 respectively. At

Frederick Lashley sent this picture and note to his family and friends while on death row in Missouri, USA. He was executed in July 1993 for a crime he committed when a juvenile, aged 17. The USA is one of only five countries reported to have carried out such executions in the past five years. The other countries are Iran, Iraq, Saudi Arabia and Yemen.

least 77 people were executed in Iran in 1993 although the true number of executions there was thought to be much higher. The death penalty continued to be used on a massive scale in China, where over 1,400 people (possibly many more) were executed in 1993.

During the year, Austria, Ecuador, Gambia, Mozambique, Panama, Slovenia, Uruguay and Venezuela acceded to the Second Optional Protocol to the International Covenant on Civil and Political Rights, aiming at the abolition of the death penalty.

By the end of the year, 47 per cent of countries in the world had abolished the death penalty in law or practice. Fifty-three countries had abolished the death penalty for all offences and 16 for all but exceptional offences, such as wartime crimes. A further 21 countries and territories, while retaining the penalty in law, had not carried out any executions for at least 10 years.

During 1993, 1,831 prisoners are known to have been executed in 32 countries and 3,670 were sentenced to death in 61 countries. These figures include only cases known to Amnesty International: the true number is certainly higher. As in previous years, a very few countries accounted for the majority of the executions recorded.

Protecting refugees

The world's refugee population continued to grow in 1993. By the end of the year, the Office of the United Nations High Commissioner for Refugees (UNHCR) estimated the total number of refugees who had been forced to abandon their homes at almost 20 million. The vast majority fled to neighbouring countries; others went further afield. Many of the countries where large refugee populations sought protection are among the world's poorest.

Behind these movements of people whose lives have been irrevocably disrupted lie histories of persecution and brutality. Many refugees have fled in fear of arbitrary detention, "disappearances", torture or extrajudicial executions committed by governments cracking down on dissent or targeting specific ethnic or religious groups. Others have been forced to seek sanctuary abroad because their countries are racked by armed conflict in which government forces or armed opposition groups have shown blatant disregard for human rights.

It became evident during 1993 that a number of states are becoming less and less committed to the fundamental principles of international refugee law which have been built up since the Second World War. In recent years the importance of the right to asylum – set out in the Universal Declaration of Human Rights

Refugees from the Sudan seek sanctuary in Kenya. Nearly three million people have been displaced by the civil war in the Sudan. Both government and rebel forces have attacked and killed unarmed civilians to gain military advantage. Among the refugees are tens of thousands of vulnerable children.

in 1948 – has been increasingly treated as subsidiary to other political or economic concerns. Some countries where refugees have tried to find sanctuary have attempted to deflect the responsibility for dealing with them on to other countries. In some cases, they have made token gestures of assistance and protection to people under threat in an effort to persuade them to remain in their own countries or to return there precipitately. At the same time, the human rights violations which are so often the cause of refugee movements have been allowed to continue unchecked.

Maintaining commitment to fundamental principles

In October 1993 Amnesty International raised these concerns with the intergovernmental Executive Committee of the Pro- gramme of the UNHCR. Forty-six states take part in the Executive Committee, which has over the years developed and elaborated the basic principles set out in treaty law for the protection of refugees. In a paper submitted to the Executive Committee Am- nesty International argued that measures being taken by promin- ent states to restrict the access of asylum-seekers to their territories were undermining basic international standards. As examples of this tendency, Amnesty International drew attention to the policy of the Government of the USA of forcibly returning Haitian asylum-seekers, and to restrictive asylum policies being pursued by member states of the European Union (EU).

These developments were by no means the only instances in which the protection of refugees and asylum-seekers was threat- ened. For example, Amnesty International was concerned about unfair asylum policies in Japan, reports of forcible return of refugees from Saudi Arabia to Iraq, and the lack of protection for Indonesian asylum-seekers in Malaysia. But Amnesty Interna- tional believed that the developments in the USA and the EU were critically important because of the threat they pose to the inter- national system for the protection of refugees.

The new administration of President Bill Clinton maintained the previous US Government's policy of forcibly returning direct to Haiti all Haitian asylum-seekers intercepted at sea outside US territorial waters, without any examination of their asylum claims. In June 1993 the US Supreme Court ruled that the policy did not violate US or international law. The US Government maintains that the prohibition on *refoulement* (forcible return of refugees to countries where their life or freedom is at risk), set out in the 1951 Convention relating to the Status of Refugees, is not binding on the US outside its territorial jurisdiction and that therefore the US Coast Guard can return asylum-seekers inter- cepted in international waters. This amounts to saying that, while governments are obliged to protect refugees who have already arrived within their country's territory, they may inter- cept fleeing refugees before they arrive at the border and return

Afghan asylum-seekers in Denmark who have sewed up their mouths in protest after the Danish authorities forcibly returned an Afghan asylum-seeker to Kabul in August 1993. They were also protesting at the authorities' refusal to grant asylum to other Afghans.

them to face the risk of arbitrary imprisonment, torture, or death. This is clearly contrary to the underlying purpose of the 1951 Convention – the protection of refugees from persecution.

European governments, particularly those of the EU, continued to develop common policies towards asylum-seekers. They moved towards a shared approach on returning asylum-seekers to "third countries" – countries they had passed through since fleeing their homes – on the grounds that they should seek asylum there. They also took steps towards a common approach on "screening out" from the normal asylum procedures people with certain types of asylum claims, such as those considered to be "manifestly unfounded", or those made by people coming from countries considered "safe". European governments also worked together on developing a common interpretation of the refugee definition set out in the 1951 Convention. Many aspects of these issues have already been dealt with in past years by the UNHCR Executive Committee. For example, the Executive Committee has concluded that "asylum should not be refused solely on the ground that it could be sought from another state" and, at the request of the Executive Committee in 1977, the UNHCR issued detailed and authoritative guidelines for governments on the interpretation of the refugee definition.

Amnesty International warned that European cooperation on these issues is leading to policies falling short of established standards developed by the UNHCR Executive Committee. Like the US policy towards Haitian refugees, these moves threaten to undermine the international system for refugee protection. In particular, the policy of returning asylum-seekers to third countries without examining their asylum claims would lead to third countries outside the EU being required to accept back many thousands of asylum-seekers. This could put in jeopardy those asylum-seekers who might not be assured of effective and durable protection in those countries. Furthermore, this policy undermines the principle of international solidarity and cooperation among states in refugee protection, because certain countries, in restricting access to their territories by refugees and asylum-seekers, are placing a burden on other countries which took no part in formulating the policy.

Amnesty International appealed to the UNHCR Executive Committee to take steps to support the international system of refugee protection in the face of these developments. As well, a number of states attending the Executive Committee voiced concerns similar to those which Amnesty International had raised. Regrettably, Amnesty International's recommendations for action by the Executive Committee were, for the most part, not taken up, and the conclusions adopted by the meeting did little to counter the threats to refugee protection.

Policies for transferring asylum-seekers to "safe" third countries require a multilateral approach involving all affected countries and must ensure that asylum-seekers will only be sent to countries where they will be assured of effective and durable protection. At a minimum there must be guarantees that asylum-seekers returned to third countries have access to a full and fair asylum procedure which accords with international standards. States should therefore work with the UNHCR to develop a common international agreement on minimum standards for asylum procedures to ensure that all asylum-seekers receive a fair and satisfactory hearing. Amnesty International called for the development of such an agreement, and during 1993 similar calls were made in a resolution on human rights adopted by the European Parliament in March and a resolution adopted in September by the Council of Europe Parliamentary Assembly.

Hundreds of thousands of people fled from appalling human rights abuses in the territories of the former Yugoslavia, leading to a continuing refugee crisis. Amnesty International repeatedly expressed concern about the policy of EU governments – a policy also followed by other European governments – that refugees should be encouraged to stay in the nearest safe areas to their homes. Amnesty International believed that this policy could prevent them from leaving areas where they might be at risk, and prevent them from exercising their right to seek asylum – a right which is set out in the Universal Declaration of Human Rights. EU member states omitted any reference to the right to seek asylum from their conclusion on people displaced by the conflict in the former Yugoslavia, adopted in November 1992. Furthermore, over the past two years, one European country after another has imposed a visa requirement on nationals of Bosnia-Herzegovina. By the end of 1993 almost all EU member states and many other European states had such a visa requirement – which in most cases had been imposed after the war started there and people began to flee. These exclusionary measures clearly meant that many refugees were forced to stay in countries where they were at risk, such as Croatia, which continued to forcibly return Bosnian Muslim refugees to Bosnia-Herzegovina (see **Croatia** entry).

There is no forum in Europe where all affected states, UNHCR

28

and non-governmental organizations and other agencies can meet to discuss refugee issues in the region and ensure that the protection of those at risk remains the cornerstone of government policies. Amnesty International therefore called on the Conference on Security and Co-operation in Europe (CSCE) – the intergovernmental grouping comprising the largest number of states in the region – to establish such a forum with a view to developing a coordinated and comprehensive response to the refugee crisis in Europe. At the CSCE Human Dimension Implementation meeting in Warsaw (see **Working with international organizations**), Amnesty International called for a regional response to the refugee crisis in Europe, reiterating its concern about restrictive measures by EU member states and their effect in countries of central and eastern Europe. The Council of Foreign Ministers meeting in Rome in December confirmed the recommendation made by the meeting in Warsaw that the CSCE political decision-making bodies should address this issue.

Individual countries

Amnesty International's work for refugees at the national level is largely carried out by Amnesty International members based in the countries where people seek protection. The deteriorating conditions described above were reflected in many of those countries. Asylum-seekers' access was often restricted by the practice of returning them to third countries, and of denying a

© P. Harvey

Refugees from Iraq. Thousands of marsh Arabs fled to southern Iran in the second half of 1993, after the Iraqi Government drained large stretches of marshland, destroying the local economy, and attacked unarmed civilians.

full hearing to asylum-seekers whose claims were deemed "manifestly unfounded" or who came from supposedly "safe" countries.

In Germany, where until 1993 the Constitution had given all asylum-seekers the right to a full examination of their claims, Amnesty International opposed a constitutional amendment (which finally came into effect in July 1993) which restricts the right to asylum for people who have come from countries of origin deemed to be "safe" or who have travelled to Germany through "safe" third countries (see **Germany** entry). Amnesty International's French Section also raised concerns about a constitutional change in France, which came into effect towards the end of the year, allowing the French authorities to return asylum-seekers to certain other European countries without any examination of their asylum claims.

In March Amnesty International published a report on refugee protection in Japan detailing the many deficiencies in Japanese policy and practice and setting out a number of recommendations to the government. Amnesty International's Japanese Section campaigned actively throughout the year, in cooperation with other Amnesty International groups around the world, to persuade the Japanese Government to implement these recommendations (see **Japan** entry).

In July Amnesty International's British Section issued a report

© Howard J. Davies

A Cambodian refugee returning from a camp in Thailand under a UN repatriation program. In spite of the presence of UN human rights monitors, political killings, threats and intimidation were reported from almost every part of Cambodia during the course of 1993.

about cases where the authorities in the United Kingdom had returned asylum-seekers to so-called "safe" third countries, citing several cases where this practice had resulted in inadequate protection for those returned.

In many other countries, including Australia, Austria, the Czech Republic, Finland, the Netherlands, Norway, Portugal, Switzerland and the USA, Amnesty International members and bodies made representations to their national authorities or parliaments about policies affecting asylum-seekers or proposals to amend asylum legislation. In almost all cases, proposed changes in legislation would put restrictions on the right to seek asylum.

However, there were also some positive developments. In Belgium, in a case brought by Amnesty International and other groups, the *Cour d'Arbitrage*, arbitration court, in March 1993 ruled unconstitutional a controversial legislative provision under which certain types of asylum claims were deemed inadmissible. In Iceland and in Ireland, following campaigning undertaken by Amnesty International's local sections, steps were being taken, for the first time, to introduce specific legislation dealing with the rights of asylum-seekers who seek protection.

Working with international organizations

The UN World Conference on Human Rights

The year under review – 1993 – was a historic year for human rights at the UN with the convening of the first global conference on human rights for 25 years, followed by the decision of the General Assembly to establish a High Commissioner for Human Rights as a new high-level official with principal responsibility for all human rights activities within the UN system. The UN World Conference on Human Rights was held in Vienna from 14 to 25 June 1993. The Conference was beset by political difficulties throughout and did not, by itself, achieve the far-reaching results expected of such an event. However, it did raise the profile of human rights within the UN and focused international attention on these issues. It also set in motion the process which resulted in the landmark decision in December to create, at long last, a UN High Commissioner for Human Rights. The objectives of the World Conference were to review progress in the human rights field since the adoption in 1948 of the Universal Declaration of Human Rights and to evaluate the effectiveness of the UN's human rights activities, standards and mechanisms. Its stated aim was to assess how these might be improved and how to ensure adequate resources for the human rights program. It also examined the link between human rights, democracy and development.

The Conference was preceded by four largely unproductive Preparatory Committee sessions, the last of which took place in April 1993; three regional meetings for Africa (Tunisia, 1992), Latin America (Costa Rica, 1993) and Asia (Thailand, 1993), each of which produced regional Declarations; an inter-regional expert meeting under the auspices of the Council of Europe; and scores of other satellite and expert meetings. Governments, UN human rights experts and other bodies, the specialized agencies, other intergovernmental organizations, national institutions and thousands of non-governmental organizations (NGOs) from all regions of the world produced documents and proposals.

The official preparations were marked by difficult and often highly divisive debates between governments over issues such as universality of human rights, national sovereignty, aid and conditionality, the feasibility and impartiality of new methods and mechanisms for human rights protection and the role of NGOs. These divisions frequently threatened to undermine the existing framework of human rights protection. The Conference eventually adopted by consensus the Vienna Declaration and Programme of Action. This is an uneven document which narrowly avoided being a step backwards for human rights but does contain some positive elements and recommendations to enhance the promotion and protection of basic human rights.

The Vienna Declaration and Programme of Action strongly reaffirms the universality, indivisibility and interdependence of all human rights. It recognizes that the promotion and protection of all human rights is a priority objective of the UN and a legitimate concern of the international community, and reaffirms the duty of all states to respect human rights, regardless of their political, economic and cultural systems. Its provisions cover a wide range of particular groups, such as women, children, indigenous peoples, minorities, refugees and the internally displaced, migrant workers and the disabled. It brings women's rights firmly into the mainstream as an integral part of the UN's human rights activities and endorses the proposed appointment by the Commission on Human Rights of a new Special Rapporteur on violence against women. It deals with a range of specific violations, including torture, "disappearances", racism, discrimination, genocide and "ethnic cleansing"; and related issues such as democracy, the rule of law and the administration of justice, impunity, development, poverty and human rights education. It calls for governments to take steps at the national level to improve human rights protection, including universal ratification of international human rights instruments.

The Vienna Declaration's recommendations for strengthening the international supervisory and implementation mechanisms are weak. However, it did take one very significant step forward in this respect by its call to the 1993 General Assembly to take up the question of the establishment of a High Commissioner for Human Rights as a matter of priority. It also calls for increased coordination and cooperation on human rights issues throughout the UN system; increased resources for the UN Centre for Human Rights as the focal point of this system; human rights officers to be assigned to regional UN offices to provide information, training and other assistance to requesting states; recognition of the important role of human rights components in peace-keeping operations; an expanded program of advisory services and technical assistance; the further development of individual complaints procedures linked to existing treaties; preventive mechanisms such as that envisaged in the draft Optional Protocol to the Convention against Torture to be set up; and the development of an international penal court.

Although the Conference did little more than pay lip-service to the role of NGOs in the field of human rights, and effectively excluded them at the Conference from the drafting process of the Vienna Declaration, representatives of well over 1,000 NGOs attended the Conference. They participated in a huge NGO Forum, which made formal proposals to the Conference, and in a lively program of parallel activities. The coming together of the NGO community on this scale was one of the highlights of the Conference. For the first time NGOs active at the international level – those with consultative status with the UN – collaborated with a host of national and regional NGOs who do not normally have access to UN meetings. Amnesty International participated throughout the preparatory process and at the Conference itself, as well as in the NGO Forum.

The UN General Assembly endorsed the Vienna Declaration and Programme of Action and called on all states and relevant UN bodies to ensure the full implementation of its recommendations. It also requested the Secretary-General to report to it annually on implementation and decided to review this each year under a new standing agenda item. However, it agreed to only a minimal increase in resources for the realization of the Vienna recommendations, far below the necessary budgetary provision identified by the Centre for Human Rights, which has sharply called into question the commitment of the international community to genuine and concrete measures to translate the words of Vienna into reality.

The High Commissioner for Human Rights
The proposal to establish within the UN system a High Commissioner for Human Rights has been considered from time to time over many years. However, the proposal was not actively pursued once the other UN human rights mechanisms began to be established. The proposal was revived during preparatory discussions for the World Conference and was supported by several governments and a large number of NGOs. Amnesty International made this proposal its priority objective for action by the World Conference and in 1992 submitted a substantial paper on the need for and the role of a High Commissioner. Although the proposal gained considerable support in the run-up to the Conference in June, it remained highly controversial with some governments. However, the Vienna Declaration and Programme of Action did call on the General Assembly at its 1993 session to consider the question as a matter of priority.

After prolonged procedural discussions that threatened to end in stalemate, the Third Committee of the General Assembly set up a working group to consider the Vienna recommendations, taking up the High Commissioner as its first priority. Amnesty International monitored the deliberations of the working group very closely and attended those sessions which were open to NGOs. Discussions were protracted and difficult but eventually resulted in the adoption, by consensus, of a resolution to establish a High Commissioner for Human Rights.

The High Commissioner's mandate includes promoting and protecting all human rights, including the right to development; playing an active role worldwide in removing obstacles to the full realization of human rights and in preventing violations; enhancing international cooperation in this field and engaging in dialogue with governments; coordinating all human rights activities throughout the UN system; providing advisory services and technical assistance and coordinating education and public information programs in the human rights field; rationalizing, adapting and strengthening the UN human rights machinery to improve its efficiency and effectiveness; and carrying out other tasks assigned by the competent UN bodies, such as the Commission on Human Rights, and making recommendations to these bodies to improve human rights promotion and protection.

The mandate of the High Commissioner for Human Rights does not explicitly cover all the elements that human rights activists had hoped for. The development of a proactive and effective role for the High Commissioner, particularly in the area of protection of rights, will depend very much on the individual to be appointed to this new post. However, the status and profile of human rights within the UN has been raised considerably by the establishment by the General Assembly itself – one of the highest political organs of the UN – of a senior official at the rank of Under-Secretary-General with responsibility and oversight system-wide for all human rights activities.

Peace-keeping and peace-building

In 1993 the UN's role in the field of peace-keeping and peace-building continued to evolve, despite growing difficulties and frustrations. The UN's objectives and methods came under close scrutiny as new problems seriously impeded the execution of many peace-keeping operations. The heavy drain on resources to meet the massive financial costs and provide the large numbers of personnel required for these operations, the political difficulties and confrontations which undermined an increasing number of them, and growing attacks on UN personnel all posed tough questions for the future of peace-keeping. This also led to an increasing reluctance by UN member states to undertake new peace-keeping or peace-building operations. Following the October coup and widespread killings in Burundi, for example, the UN Security Council issued a statement of concern but took no steps towards a full-scale UN operation there, leaving the main role to the under-resourced Organization of African Unity.

Attacks on UN military and civilian personnel led to an important initiative in the Sixth Committee of the General Assembly where discussions opened on a draft Convention on the status and safety of UN personnel in the context of peace-keeping operations. However, equally pressing concerns relating to the responsibility of UN personnel for human rights abuses, and the need for troops to be properly trained and equipped to respond to attacks without inflicting unnecessary civilian casualties, were not adequately addressed.

These concerns were particularly acute with respect to the second phase of the UN operation in Somalia, UNOSOM II, which began in April. Incidents in which UNOSOM and US troops – themselves the target of a series of attacks and killings – were reported to have killed unarmed Somali civilians were not adequately investigated, and were not explicitly included in the mandate of a Commission of Inquiry set up by the Security Council in November to investigate attacks on UN personnel. Furthermore, UNOSOM failed to respect UN standards and safeguards relating to detention: a number of detainees held by UNOSOM were denied access to lawyers and families and detained without any prospect of judicial review of their detention or of being charged and brought to trial. Amnesty International urged all UN personnel to observe international humanitarian, human rights and criminal justice standards and called for an explicit binding commitment to this effect by the UN.

Amnesty International continued to call on the UN to pay more attention to the promotion and protection of human rights in its peace-keeping operations. A number of operations were gravely deficient in measures to address human rights concerns. It was not until August that the UN took some steps towards including a human rights component in the operation in Somalia, but even these measures did not appear to be operational by the end of the year. They included an Office of Human Rights to investigate alleged violations and to assist in the establishment of a Somali human rights committee, as well as international advisers to assist in the re-establishment of the judicial and criminal justice systems.

In the context of the UN operation in Mozambique, ONUMOZ, Amnesty International called for measures to ensure the impartial and effective investigation of human rights violations and for full and public reporting of human rights concerns. It also urged the UN to deploy a proposed team of UN police monitors and to support local human rights institutions and NGOs. The Liberia peace agreement signed in July entailed an implementation role for the UN, the Organization of African Unity and the Economic Community of West African States. Amnesty International deplored the absence of provisions to ensure respect for human rights and to bring to justice those responsible for past violations. The organization called for mechanisms for human rights monitoring and investigation to be set up and for civilian human rights advisers to provide human rights training and to assist in establishing an institutional framework to ensure respect for human rights. It was also disappointing that another new operation, established in 1993 for Rwanda, failed to address human rights concerns adequately.

An important and more encouraging innovation was the General Assembly's authorization of the International Civilian Human Rights Monitoring Mission in Haiti (MICIVIH). This joint mission between the UN and the Organization of American States, involving some 266 civilian human rights monitors, was to verify respect for human rights, based on the Haitian Constitution and the international instruments to which Haiti is a party. The monitors could receive allegations of violations, interview anyone freely and privately, and visit any place, including prisons and detention centres, throughout the country. Under the subsequent Governor's Island Agreement, the monitors were to be supplemented by military and police personnel (UNMIH) whose tasks would have included verifying respect for human rights by the security forces and training the new police force. However, by October a sharp upsurge in political killings and hostility to the UN on the part of Haiti's military rulers led to the collapse of these initiatives and the withdrawal of the monitoring mission. There was no clear decision on its future prospects by the end of the year.

Even where a human rights component was incorporated into peace-keeping operations, the UN showed itself ill-equipped to ensure adequate follow-up to secure the long-term protection of human rights. In Cambodia, as the massive UN operation UNTAC prepared for withdrawal following the May election, calls for a continued UN presence with a monitoring and investigatory role went unheeded. In March the Commission on Human Rights called only for a program of technical assistance and advisory services and support for institution-building coordinated by a Representative of the Secretary-General. By the end of the year, administrative delays meant that the program was barely starting. In El Salvador, the human rights division of ONUSAL continued to carry out human rights verification but, notwithstanding calls by the Security Council and the Secretary-General, it was only right at the end of the year that the first steps began to be taken to follow up the recommendations of the UN-appointed Truth Commission.

War crimes and the international court

For the first time since the Nuremberg and Tokyo war crimes tribunals more than 40 years ago, an international tribunal was set up to try individuals responsible for war crimes committed in the former Yugoslavia. The UN Security Council took this historic decision in February and in May adopted the Statute of the International Tribunal for the prosecution of persons responsible for serious violations of international humanitarian law committed in the territory of the former Yugoslavia since 1991. The 11 judges who will sit on this *ad hoc* tribunal were elected by the UN General Assembly in September and, following months of deadlock, the Security Council appointed the chief prosecutor in October. The tribunal, which is based in The Hague, held its inaugural meeting in November and began to formulate its rules of procedure.

When the tribunal was proposed, Amnesty International expressed its concern that *ad hoc* tribunals often lacked real independence and impartiality and risked being no more than token political gestures to satisfy the short-term interests of states. It urged that this tribunal should be the first step towards setting up a permanent international court competent to try grave violations of humanitarian and human rights law wherever they occur. Before the tribunal was established the organization also submitted to the UN detailed recommendations aimed at ensuring that the tribunal would be just, fair and effective.

The UN International Law Commission, an expert body working for the progressive development and codification of international law, submitted to the General Assembly a revised draft statute for a permanent international criminal court; a final draft is expected in 1994. Under the revised draft the court would have jurisdiction over war crimes and crimes against humanity, but only if states parties to the statute consented, except in cases submitted by the Security Council. The draft contains a number of important safeguards for defendants, such as the right to silence, and, like the tribunal for the former Yugoslavia, a prohibition of the death penalty. However, it still falls short of international fair trial standards in a number of other respects.

Action on countries and human rights issues

The Commission on Human Rights adopted an unprecedented number of new resolutions during its January to March session and established several new country or theme mechanisms, including a Special Rapporteur on racism and xenophobia, a Special Rapporteur on freedom of opinion and expression, and a 15-member Working Group on the right to development. However, without any corresponding budgetary increase these new steps threatened to stretch to breaking point the grossly inadequate resources of the Centre for Human Rights. In December the General Assembly finally agreed to what amounted in practice to only a modest increase in the resources for the Centre for Human Rights which does not fully address the pressing need for adequate resources to carry out all its new responsibilities.

For the first time, both the Commission and its Sub-Commission on Prevention of Discrimination and Protection of Minorities adopted resolutions on East Timor, although the Sub-Commission took no action on another draft resolution on Aceh, Indonesia. The Commission took stronger measures in respect of Sudan and Zaire, moving them from the confidential "1503 procedure" to the public agenda and appointing a Special Rapporteur on Sudan. Another new rapporteur was appointed in respect of the Israeli-Occupied Territories. The Commission adopted for the first time a resolution on Bougainville (Papua New Guinea) and one on Togo, while the Sub-Commission adopted resolutions on Chad and Peru, although the latter was regrettably very weak.

Much attention was paid to the former Yugoslavia with Commission resolutions on the general human rights situation and on rape and abuse of women and children. The Sub-Commission adopted a resolution on the worsening human rights situation in Kosovo and another on Bosnia-Herzegovina, which rejected any partition resulting from ethnic cleansing. It also adopted a statement denying the validity of any peace agreement obtained under duress. The General Assembly also adopted a strong resolution condemning human rights violations throughout the former Yugoslavia and another on the rape and abuse of women which calls for a report on this subject in January 1994.

In an important move, the Commission endorsed the proposal of the Special Rapporteur on Iraq to send human rights monitors to the country, reinforcing support already expressed for such an initiative by the General Assembly in 1992 and reiterated subsequently at the Assembly's 1993 session. However, the Iraqi Government remained firmly opposed to this and no further action was taken by the UN to implement the proposal.

It was particularly disappointing that both the Commission and Sub-Commission failed yet again to take action on China, including Tibet. As in 1992, the Commission adopted a procedural motion to take no action when faced with a draft resolution on

Countries under scrutiny by the UN

(Item 12 of the agenda of the UN Commission on Human Rights)

* Afghanistan	* Israeli-Occupied Territories
Bougainville	* Myanmar
* Cuba	South Africa
East Timor	Sri Lanka
El Salvador	* Sudan
* Equatorial Guinea	Tadzhikistan
* Haiti	Togo
* Iran	* former Yugoslavia
* Iraq	Zaire

* A Special Rapporteur or Representative has been appointed to scrutinize human rights in these countries

Countries under the Advisory Services and Technical Assistance Program of the UN

(Item 21 of the agenda of the UN Commission on Human Rights)

Albania	Romania
Cambodia	Somalia
Georgia	

Agenda item to be decided

El Salvador	Guatemala

China, and the Sub-Commission took no action on a draft concerning Tibet.

The mandates of all existing country experts and rapporteurs were renewed by the Commission. Equatorial Guinea was moved from the advisory services program and the Expert on Equatorial Guinea was upgraded to Rapporteur. As usual, most of the rapporteurs were also required to report to the 1993 General Assembly which adopted its own resolutions on these country situations. Statements by the Chairperson of the Commission continued to be used in some instances as an alternative to tougher action in the form of a resolution. Such statements were issued about the human rights situation in Latvia/Estonia, Sri Lanka and Tadzhikistan. The General Assembly subsequently adopted a resolution on Estonia and Latvia, calling on the Secretary-General to report on the human rights situation there.

The Commission decided to transfer examination of Albania and Romania to the advisory services and technical assistance program, and called for an evaluation of the need for technical assistance in Georgia. It established advisory services programs for Cambodia and Somalia and called on the Secretary-General to appoint country experts to work with the UN peace-keeping operations in both those countries. The General Assembly subsequently requested the Commission to consider establishing an on-site human rights monitoring mission in Somalia once political stability was restored. Once again no clear decision was taken by the Commission as to whether El Salvador and Guatemala should be taken up under advisory services or under the agenda item on violations.

The Commission formalized its procedures for special sessions, held for the first time in 1992 on the situation in the former Yugoslavia, but took no decisive action on another form of emergency procedure proposed by Austria. More attention was paid to the links between refugee flows and human rights protection: a new sub-item on mass exoduses and the displaced was established and issues of preventive diplomacy and early warning were included in the brief for a report to the 1994 Commission. The mandate of the Special Representative on the internally displaced was renewed for two years. A resolution was adopted on the human rights of women, indicating that the Commission will consider appointing a Special Rapporteur on violence against women in 1994. Both the Commission and the General Assembly adopted resolutions on street children and children in armed conflict. The Sub-Commission undertook new studies on humanitarian intervention and on the recognition of gross human rights violations as an international crime.

Standard-setting
A new human rights text, the Declaration on the Elimination of Violence against Women, transmitted by the Commission on the Status of Women, was adopted by the UN General Assembly in

December. The Declaration requires all governments to adopt preventive and other policies to eliminate violence, to investigate and punish violence against women, and to ensure the protection of women.

Amnesty International attended the Working Group of the Commission on Human Rights on a draft Declaration aimed at the protection of the rights of human rights defenders. The final text was expected to be transmitted to the 1994 session of the Commission. Amnesty International also attended the second session of the Commission's Working Group which is drafting an Optional Protocol to the UN Convention against Torture, aimed at establishing a system of preventive visits by UN experts to places of detention. The Sub-Commission's Working Group on Indigenous Populations, also attended by Amnesty International, was asked to complete consideration of the contentious draft Declaration on indigenous people at its 1994 session. This instrument may be given a higher profile following the proclamation by the General Assembly of an International Decade of the World's Indigenous People to commence in December 1994.

Regional intergovernmental organizations

The Organization of American States (OAS)

Amnesty International continued to submit information to the Inter-American Commission on Human Rights (IACHR) relating to its concerns in member states of the OAS, including Brazil, Colombia, Guatemala and Peru.

In February the Inter-American Court of Human Rights ruled on the Peruvian Government's preliminary objections in the Cayara case, submitted to it in 1992. This case concerns the killing of at least 31 people by the army in the Cayara region, Ayacucho, in May 1988 (see previous *Amnesty International Reports*). The Court ruled that the IACHR had filed the case after the time limit allowed by the American Convention had expired, and ordered that the case be dismissed. As a result, strong evidence of the government's responsibility for the massacre could not be considered. Subsequently, the IACHR submitted a full report on the Cayara case to the OAS General Assembly, but the Assembly took no action to secure the government's compliance with the recommendations of the IACHR.

In June Amnesty International again attended the OAS General Assembly in Managua, Nicaragua, as a "special guest", together with other NGOs. A progress report on the draft Inter-American Convention on the Forced Disappearance of Persons was submitted to the General Assembly by the OAS Permanent Council. Some improvements were made to the seriously flawed text, notably the elimination of a "due obedience" clause that would have exonerated those committing "disappearances" while obeying orders. However, the draft still fails to provide for the operation of special emergency procedures by the IACHR in cases involving "disappearances". The General Assembly asked the Permanent Council to consider the draft urgently and submit a final text to the next Assembly session.

The Organization of African Unity (OAU)

In a six-point program submitted to the OAU Assembly of Heads of State and Government in Egypt in June, Amnesty International called on the OAU to take stronger measures to promote and protect human rights. It called for more action in election monitoring and conflict resolution, and urged OAU members to be more vigorous in implementing the African Charter on Human and Peoples' Rights and in supporting its expert monitoring body, the African Commission. The organization also submitted detailed proposals for reform of the African Charter aimed at strengthening the African Commission.

The Assembly adopted a declaration with only a general commitment to strengthening human rights. The Assembly also established a Mechanism for the Prevention, Management and Resolution of Conflict. Its first action was to demand that those responsible for the attempted coup in Burundi "respect the sanctity of human life" and to decide to send a peace-keeping mission to that country, but it had not been deployed by the end of the year.

Amnesty International participated in both of the African Commission's regular sessions. The Commission considered the periodic reports on the implementation of the African Charter of Nigeria and Togo (in April) and that of Ghana (in December). It remained a matter of concern, however, that in six years the African Commission has not transmitted to the Assembly any one of more than 100 communications submitted under Article 55 of the African Charter. In an oral statement at the December meeting Amnesty International called for a thorough public discussion of this procedure, with a view to making it effective. The organization also called on the Commission to take specific measures to address extrajudicial executions and to develop a procedure for emergency cases, but no action was taken on these proposals.

The Council of Europe

In an attempt to deal with the rising tide of racism and minority conflicts in Europe, the Council of Europe's 32 heads of state met for the first time in the organization's 44-year history at an October Summit in Austria. They agreed to draft two new conventions on minority rights and adopted a program of action against racism, xenophobia and anti-semitism. The Summit also confirmed that the European Commission of Human Rights and European Court of Human Rights will be merged into a single court to tackle the current huge delays in the hearing of cases.

Before the Summit, Amnesty International urged the Council also to deal with other challenges, including the failure of the

Council's political organs to tackle patterns of grave and systematic human rights violations in member states and the fact that much of the Council's work is carried out in secret.

The number of member states increased from 26 to 32 with the admission of Estonia, Lithuania and Slovenia in May, the Czech Republic and the Slovak Republic in June and Romania in October. The newly admitted members signed, and two ratified, the European Convention on Human Rights and four signed the European Convention for the Prevention of torture and Inhuman or Degrading Treatment or Punishment (see **Appendix** VII).

The Council continued work on a draft Protocol to the European Convention on Human Rights on the rights of persons deprived of their liberty, but it was seriously flawed. Amnesty International submitted a memorandum on its concerns regarding the text and urged states not to accept it. In November it was sent back to an expert body for redrafting.

The European Committee for the Prevention of Torture made seven periodic visits, to Greece, Iceland, Ireland, Liechtenstein, Luxembourg and Norway, and one *ad hoc* visit to the United Kingdom (visiting Northern Ireland). Finland, France, Germany, Luxembourg, the Netherlands, Sweden, Switzerland and the United Kingdom agreed to the public release of reports relating to earlier visits by the Committee, which would otherwise remain confidential. A Protocol to the European Convention for the Prevention of Torture was opened for signature, enabling ratification of this treaty by non-member states.

The European Union (EU)[1]

A paper prepared on behalf of the EU for the UN World Conference on Human Rights addressed the interrelationship between human rights, democracy and development, the need for implementation of human rights standards and support for the establishment of a High Commissioner for Human Rights. The Council of Ministers of Development Cooperation adopted a separate statement on human rights, democracy and development in May. The EU adopted declarations on the human rights situation in various countries including Chad, China/Tibet, Haiti, Malawi, Myanmar and the former Yugoslavia. It also continued to work towards the harmonization of EU asylum policy (see **Refugees**).

In January the EU Commission announced that a human rights clause would be inserted in every EU cooperation and association agreement. Human rights were raised in EU Council meetings including the EU-Central America Council Meeting in February, the EU-ASEAN Council Meeting in July and Council meetings dealing with agreements with countries in central and eastern Europe where the EU Commission also decided

[1] The European Community was renamed the European Union on 1 November 1993 when the Treaty on European Union came into force.

to support 52 projects aimed at promoting democracy and human rights.

The European Parliament called for an EU-wide system of human rights protection in its first annual report on human rights within the EU and for a more coherent external policy in its report on human rights in the world. It organized a number of hearings on human rights issues, including racism, rape and sexual abuse in Bosnia-Herzegovina, and on accession of the EU to the European Convention on Human Rights. Urgent resolutions were adopted on a wide range of countries including Brazil, Cuba, East Timor, Iraq, Morocco, Rwanda, Turkey, the USA and the former Yugoslavia. Reports on the interrelationship of human rights, democracy and development were adopted separately by the European Parliament and the Joint Parliamentary Assembly of the EU and the African, Caribbean and Pacific states.

Amnesty International urged the institutions of the EU to take effective action on a range of human rights issues including racist ill-treatment by police in EU member states. It called on them to support the strengthening of UN mechanisms, including the establishment of a High Commissioner for Human Rights, and to support action in individual countries, including international monitoring in the former Yugoslavia. Amnesty International also expressed support for the accession of the EU to the European Convention on Human Rights.

The Conference on Security and Co-operation in Europe (CSCE)

Conflicts or simmering tensions in the former Yugoslavia, the Caucasus, the central Asian republics and the Baltic states dominated CSCE deliberations. The CSCE continued to implement major reforms in an attempt to turn itself into a peace-maker and peace-keeper in Europe.

The first-ever Human Dimension Implementation Meeting was held in Warsaw, Poland, in September and October. It examined the human rights record of participating states and made recommendations on the strengthening of CSCE human rights mechanisms. NGOs enjoyed unprecedented access to observe and speak at every session and Amnesty International actively participated. While the meeting failed to recommend concrete CSCE action to deal with serious violations in particular states, it did recognize that the protection of human rights should be an important part of CSCE attempts to deal with conflicts in Europe. It also recommended that the CSCE should play a role in developing a common regional plan to tackle the current refugee crisis in Europe. These recommendations were endorsed at the December meeting of the Council of Ministers in Rome, Italy. Amnesty International also participated in an expert seminar on refugee issues held in April.

The CSCE is increasingly establishing long-term missions in countries to monitor the human rights and political situation and to encourage dialogue between parties in conflict. Such missions were set up during 1993 in Estonia, Latvia, Moldova, and Tadzhikistan, and existing missions were maintained in Georgia and the Former Yugoslav Republic of Macedonia, as well as in the Federal Republic of Yugoslavia until the mission was forced to leave in July. Amnesty International urged that every long-term mission should have a strong human rights component.

The first CSCE High Commissioner on National Minorities, appointed in December 1992, offered governments advice on minority issues in Albania, Estonia, Hungary, Latvia, Lithuania, Slovakia, Romania and the Former Yugoslav Republic of Macedonia. The High Commissioner is not expressly a human rights mechanism, but is mandated to prevent minority disputes erupting into violent conflict by trying to conciliate such tensions at an early stage.

The number of CSCE participating states increased to 53 with the admission of the Czech Republic and the Slovak Republic as of 1 January 1993. In practice only 52 states participated, as the Federal Republic of Yugoslavia continued to be suspended from all CSCE activities. Admission of the Former Yugoslav Republic of Macedonia, currently an observer, was blocked by opposition from Greece, Albania and Cyprus.

The Francophone Summit

The fifth biennial Conference of heads of state and government of francophone countries, the theme of which was human rights and development, took place in Mauritius in October 1993. The Declaration of Mauritius stated that the francophone countries are dedicated to justice, democracy and respect for human rights, and another final document affirmed that the primary responsibility of governments is to promote and protect these rights. A resolution on Africa welcomed progress in implementing human rights but regretted difficulties encountered in certain countries in establishing the rule of law and democracy. None of these documents were a significant advance on the weak Declaration of Chaillot adopted at the 1991 Conference (see *Amnesty International Report 1992*), but the Conference also approved a program for human rights promotional activities. In November, in a significant advance, the Permanent Francophone Council condemned those responsible for the killings during and after the attempted coup in Burundi.

Amnesty International urged the francophone states at the Conference to take effective steps to promote and protect human rights, to tackle grave human rights violations and to end the impunity of those responsible.

The Commonwealth

The biennial Commonwealth Heads of Government Meeting (CHOGM) took place in Cyprus in October 1993. The final communique reaffirmed a commitment to democracy, fundamental rights, the rule of law, the independence of the judiciary and just and honest government as essential ingredients of the Commonwealth's fundamental values. The Cyprus communique called on all 50 member governments to ratify the International Covenants on Civil and Political Rights and on Economic, Social and Cultural Rights by 1995. It also stated that the Commonwealth would assist in the promotion of human rights in South Africa and that the Commonwealth Observer Mission to South Africa would remain there until after the 1994 elections, when its role would be reviewed in consultation with the new government. The CHOGM strongly condemned the attempted military coup in Burundi on the opening day of the meeting, but took no further action. It was agreed to admit Cameroon as a member of the Commonwealth in 1995 provided that a democratic system consistent with the Harare Declaration was then in place.

The CHOGM welcomed measures taken by the Commonwealth Secretariat to promote human rights, including providing advice on law reform, election monitoring and human rights education and training. It called for more resources to be allocated to this and for increased practical cooperation between the Secretariat and non-governmental organizations. Before the CHOGM Amnesty International again called on the Commonwealth to do more to promote and protect human rights.

Amnesty International submissions to specialized agencies in 1993

INTERNATIONAL LABOUR ORGANISATION

Bangladesh	Myanmar
Brazil	Pakistan
Colombia	South Africa
Cuba	Syria

INTER-PARLIAMENTARY UNION
Committee on the Human Rights of Parliamentarians

Senegal

UNESCO
Committee on Conventions and Recommendations

Yemen
Morocco

Ratification of major international human rights treaties in 1993

Treaty	Ratification/accession/ succession by
International Covenant on Civil and Political Rights (ICCPR)	Armenia Bosnia-Herzegovina Cape Verde Czech Republic Dominica Ethiopia Malawi Moldova Mozambique Nigeria Slovakia
Optional Protocol to the ICCPR	Armenia Czech Republic Germany Guinea Guyana Romania Slovakia Slovenia
Second Optional Protocol to the ICCPR, aiming at the abolition of the death penalty	Austria Ecuador Ireland Mozambique Panama Slovenia Uruguay Venezuela
International Covenant on Economic, Social and Cultural Rights (ICESCR)	Armenia Bosnia-Herzegovina Cape Verde Czech Republic Dominica Ethiopia Malawi Moldova Nigeria Slovakia

UN Convention against Torture and Other Cruel, Inhuman or Degrading Treatment or Punishment	Antigua and Barbuda Armenia Bosnia-Herzegovina Barundi Costa Rica Czech Republic Morocco Slovakia Slovenia South Africa
UN Convention relating to the Status of Refugees	Armenia Azerbaydzhan Bahamas Bosnia-Herzegovina Czech Republic Russian Federation Saint Vincent and the Grenadines Slovakia Tadzhikistan

COUNTRY
ENTRIES

AFGHANISTAN

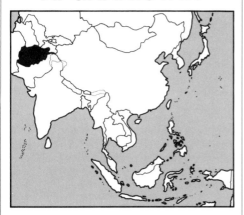

Hundreds of civilians were deliberately killed by government forces and by those of other Mujahideen groups in Kabul and elsewhere. Others, including children, were imprisoned and in some cases tortured or ill-treated. Some were reportedly raped; and deaths under torture were reported. Some of those detained were missing and unaccounted for at the end of the year. Several people were executed after they were apparently sentenced to death after unfair trials before Islamic law courts.

An accord, signed by most Mujahideen groups in March and guaranteed by Pakistan, Iran and Saudi Arabia, confirmed President Burhannudin Rabbani, leader of the *Jamiat-e-Islami*, Society of Islam, in office for 18 months. It also laid down a schedule for general and presidential elections. In May Mujahideen groups agreed on a new cabinet headed by Prime Minister Gulbuddin Hekmatyar of the *Hesb-e-Islami*, Party of Islam. It took office in June. A constitutional commission set up by the government presented a draft interim Constitution to the cabinet in September; its provision to introduce the Hanafi school of Islamic law was opposed by the country's Shi'a minority.

Government control remained restricted to parts of the capital, Kabul. The rest of the country was controlled by provincial warlords, who set up local administrations loosely affiliated to factions of the government but were not held accountable to it. Some provincial authorities were believed to have established Islamic courts in their territories.

The scale of political instability and security problems made human rights information gathering extremely difficult during 1993. Details of individual cases were frequently incomplete and impossible to verify.

Throughout the year there were violent clashes between rival Mujahideen groups represented in the government who were competing for control over administrative institutions and territory. Hundreds of people died and thousands were injured in the fighting. The worst violence was reported from Kabul and the southern provinces. In May over 1,000 people were killed and more than 5,000 injured in the capital as the forces of the *Hesb-e-Islami* and troops loyal to the President bombarded each other's positions.

Between 60,000 and 90,000 Muslims from Tadzhikistan sought refuge in the northern provinces of Balkh, Kunduz and Takhar. An agreement was signed with Tadzhikistan in August to provide for the voluntary return of refugees under the supervision of the Office of the UN High Commissioner for Refugees.

Approximately 130,000 Afghan refugees reportedly returned from Pakistan and over 300,000 from Iran but some 1.4 million refugees remained in Pakistan and 2.2 million in Iran at the end of the year. However, thousands of people became new refugees or were displaced by the factional fighting, and almost half of Kabul's population left the city. Educated women, members of the former government, liberal members of the professions and members of ethnic and religious minorities were particularly at risk of human rights violations: many sought asylum abroad.

Against the background of widespread factional fighting, human rights abuses were committed with impunity and there was a virtually total absence of the rule of law.

All Mujahideen groups and the central government were reported to have imprisoned political rivals, frequently to be held for exchange with prisoners of their own faction, or for money. Repeated cease-fire agreements referred to releases of prisoners, but few releases appeared to have taken place.

Torture, including rape, was widely reported both in official detention centres and those run by the different Mujahideen groups. The victims included members of

52

rival political factions and their families as well as civilians not associated with any particular group. According to reports received in May, female inmates of a mental asylum in Kabul had been repeatedly raped by Mujahideen of different factions in previous months. In September Nasir Khan, the brother of Shomali Khan, the deputy governor of Nangahar province (see below), was allegedly tortured to death by the local council authorities in Jalalabad.

Hundreds of deliberate and arbitrary killings were perpetrated by government forces and Mujahideen groups but often in circumstances which made it impossible to determine who was responsible, given the security and other obstacles to effective human rights monitoring. The victims included former and current government officials, members of rival Mujahideen groups, unarmed civilians and members of ethnic minorities.

General Abdul Haq Ulomi, a member of the previous government, was killed in Kabul in March. In Ghazni province, dozens of members of the Watan Party, which was formerly in government under President Najibullah, were reportedly deliberately and arbitrarily killed between April 1992 and the end of 1993, including 14 members of the party's *Parcham* faction who were killed in July. Other victims included some 200 suspected supporters of the *Khalq* faction of the Watan Party in Helmand province who were reportedly killed in mid-1993 by forces under the joint command of the governors of Herat and Kandahar, affiliated to President Rabbani's *Jamiat-e-Islami* group. Also in mid-1993, some 20 people, including Rozi Khan, a member of the Afghan Socialist Party, and several former government officials, were reportedly extrajudicially executed in Jalalabad after being detained by members of the *Jamiat-e-Islami*.

Several officials and civilians were among those deliberately and arbitrarily killed. Nasrollah Mansoor, the governor of Paktia province, was killed in February near Gardez. The same month four UN relief workers were killed near Jalalabad. In September Shomali Khan, the deputy governor of Nangahar province, was shot dead in Jalalabad: members of the local administration reportedly claimed responsibility for the killing.

Deliberate and indiscriminate bombings of homes, hospitals and mosques in Kabul left hundreds of people dead and thousands injured, among them children. Members of particular ethnic and religious groups were frequently targeted by various groups, including government troops loyal to the President, Mujahideen groups supporting the government and those opposed to it.

Such victims included civilians belonging to the Shi'a minority who were attacked in Kabul's Afshar district in February by troops loyal to President Rabbani and members of the *Ittehad-e-Islami*, Islamic Alliance, apparently in retaliation for earlier attacks by Shi'a on Pashtuns and Tajiks. Men were extrajudicially executed in front of their families, women and children were detained. The following day, several women were raped and dozens of homes were set on fire.

Civilians were reportedly also targeted in attacks in the provinces; dozens of women and children were said to have been deliberately killed by forces of the *Jamiat-e-Islami* and the *Hesb-e-Islami* in Argandab near Kandahar in August.

Several of those reported by their families to have been detained by various armed Mujahideen groups were missing and unaccounted for at the end of the year, raising fears for their safety, but few details were available.

Both in Kabul and in certain provinces Islamic law courts were said to have sentenced people to death after unfair trials. In one case in May, a man convicted of murder was reported to have been publicly executed in Kunar by the father of the victim. The same month two men were publicly executed by firing-squad in Maidanshah, Wardak province, after a local court found them guilty of killing a commander of a rival faction.

Amnesty International urged both the central government and those in effective control of other parts of the country to take all possible steps to bring an end to the cycle of gross human rights abuse, and to ensure that their forces were clearly instructed to observe human rights and basic humanitarian standards. Amnesty International also urged the international community to use its influence with the various parties to the conflict to ensure respect for human rights in Afghanistan.

In September Amnesty International issued a report, *Afghanistan: Political crisis and the refugees*, which expressed concern about the hundreds of Afghan asylum-seekers in Europe, North America and in other countries who were in danger of being deported to Afghanistan where they could face serious human rights violations.

ALBANIA

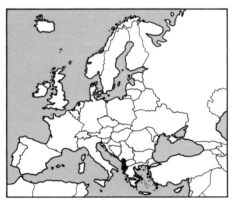

At least 16 prisoners of conscience served prison sentences of between 15 days and four months. In December, 10 former communist party officials received prison sentences of between six and eight years for "violating the equality of citizens". On a number of occasions police beat or otherwise ill-treated anti-government demonstrators. Three men died as a result of ill-treatment in police custody. A police officer shot dead an unarmed man who was fleeing from him. At least two men were executed for murder.

In March a constitutional amendment was adopted by parliament which provided that fundamental human rights should be guaranteed.

In November parliament reduced the number of capital offences; murder, treason, espionage and terrorist acts continued to be punishable by the death penalty.

Two prisoners of conscience were imprisoned for newspaper articles they had written. In March Aleksandër Frangaj, editor of *Koha Jone* (Our Time), was placed under house arrest for five weeks on charges of "spreading false information liable to cause panic". He had reported that dozens of tanks had recently been transported towards the country's northern border. At his trial in May the prosecution withdrew the charges against him and he was released. In June Idajet Beqiri, the leader of an opposition political party, the

National Unity Party, was placed under house arrest after the party's newspaper, *Kombi* (The Nation), published an article by him which the prosecution said was insulting to the President of Albania, Dr Sali Berisha. In July Idajet Beqiri was sentenced to six months' imprisonment. The sentence was confirmed on appeal and he was sent to Tirana prison. However, he was released early, in October. Neither Aleksandër Frangaj nor Idajet Beqiri had advocated violence.

At least 16 men were sentenced to prison terms of between 15 and 45 days on charges of taking part in unauthorized demonstrations in July and August in Tirana and Laç. Although it was reported that some demonstrators had been violent, it appeared that at most two of those who were brought to trial were charged with using or advocating violence. Fatmir Kumbaro, a leading member of the main opposition party, the Socialist Party, was charged with organizing an unauthorized demonstration on 30 July in Tirana and sentenced to four months' imprisonment. He denied the charges against him and claimed he had been wrongly identified in a photograph of demonstrators which was produced as evidence at the trial. Police witnesses reportedly made statements in court differing from those they had previously given at a police station. On appeal, his sentence was reduced to two months' imprisonment.

In December, 10 former communist party officials received prison sentences of between six and eight years for "violating the equality of citizens" by granting themselves privileges during the time they were in power. At the opening of the trial, the court banned all press reporting on the grounds that this was "in the interest of public order, national security, morality and the privacy of the accused". The ban was lifted at the end of the trial.

On a number of occasions police beat with truncheons or otherwise ill-treated people taking part in anti-government demonstrations, most frequently those organized by the Socialist Party. In some cases demonstrators were peacefully exercising their right to freedom of assembly and expression. In others, where there were clashes between police and demonstrators, police sometimes used excessive force in controlling or detaining demonstrators and failed to distinguish between

54

violent and peaceful demonstrators.

On 25 June police beat between 10 and 15 members of the Greek ethnic minority, including several elderly women, in Gjirokastër during a protest against the expulsion from the country of a Greek Orthodox priest, a Greek citizen. On 30 July police beat dozens of anti-government demonstrators in Tirana when an authorized Socialist Party rally developed into a mass march to the city's main square following the arrest of the party's leader, Fatos Nano, on charges of abuse of office. Engjëll Petriti was among those beaten; he was arrested by plainclothes police who put him in a police car and hit him with truncheons causing severe bruising to his face and body.

Three men died in separate incidents after being arrested and beaten by police. One of them, David Leka, died in August after being beaten in police custody in Laç; he had been arrested on suspicion of having knifed a police officer during a brawl.

Romeo Gaçe was shot dead in May in Korça by a plainclothes police officer who had attempted to arrest him and was pursuing him. The authorities investigating the case later stated that Romeo Gaçe had not committed any crime and was unarmed at the time. Investigations were opened into this case and the deaths in police custody, but no one had been brought to trial by the end of the year.

Two men sentenced to death in 1992 for murder were executed in September. According to a press report more than 20 people were on death row during the year.

Amnesty International called for the release of prisoners of conscience and the commutation of death sentences. In July the organization wrote to President Sali Berisha about incidents in which police were alleged to have beaten demonstrators or protesters; at the end of the month an Amnesty International delegate visited the country to investigate these allegations and other concerns.

In October Amnesty International published a report, *Albania: Human rights abuses by police*. The organization called on the authorities to set up a mechanism for the impartial and independent investigation of complaints against the police; to take steps to ensure that police officers were informed of and required to observe international guidelines for law enforcement; and to review legislation governing

the right to public assembly and demonstration. In December Amnesty International urged that 10 former communist party officials on trial be given a fair and public hearing and that a ban on press reporting of their trial be lifted.

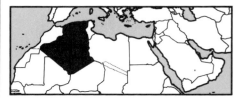

ALGERIA

Thousands of suspected supporters of Islamist groups were arrested and tried on terrorism charges; most were sentenced to prison terms by three newly constituted special courts after trials which violated international fair trial standards. Some were possible prisoners of conscience. Over 1,000 people arrested in 1992 remained administratively detained without charge or trial. Political detainees were routinely tortured and ill-treated to extract confessions; at least 12 were alleged to have died as a result. Suspected members of armed Islamist opposition groups were extrajudicially executed. Over 370 people were sentenced to death, most of them by special courts, and 26 were executed. Twelve asylum-seekers were forcibly returned to their countries. Armed Islamist opposition groups also committed grave human rights abuses; they deliberately killed over 150 civilians including foreign nationals.

Algeria continued to be run by a five-member *Haut Comité d'Etat*, Higher Council of State, headed by Ali Kafi. Multi-party elections which had been cancelled in 1992 were not rescheduled (see *Amnesty International Report 1993*). In February the state of emergency declared a year earlier was renewed indefinitely, in breach of the Constitution. A curfew imposed on three provinces in December 1992 was extended to seven other provinces and remained in place throughout the year. The authorities intensified the crack-down on armed Islamist opposition groups, applying emergency regulations and an anti-terrorist legislative decree of September 1992 which gave the security forces increased powers (see *Amnesty International Report 1993*). According to official sources, over 700 people were killed by the security forces in armed clashes with Islamist groups and raids on suspected safe houses. Unofficial sources said the death toll was significantly higher and that some of the victims had been extrajudicially executed.

After the renewal of the state of emergency in February, Islamist opposition groups such as the *Mouvement islamique armé* (MIA), Armed Islamic Movement, and the *Groupe islamique armé* (GIA), Armed Islamic Group, stepped up their armed opposition to the government. They were responsible for grave human rights abuses, including deliberate killings of civilians, in some cases after kidnapping. Many of the victims were intellectuals who had criticized the political agenda of Islamist opposition groups and had openly condemned their use of violence. Over 300 members of the security forces, including off-duty officers, were also killed by Islamist opposition groups during the year in clashes and armed attacks.

Thousands of members and suspected supporters of Islamist opposition groups were arrested and tried on terrorism charges by three special courts in Algiers, Oran and Constantine. The trials violated international fair trial standards. The special courts, set up under the anti-terrorist decree of September 1992, provide for secret and accelerated trials of people accused of terrorist offences. The decree had extended the scope of the death penalty, doubled sentences for terrorist offences and lowered the age of criminal responsibility in such cases to 16 years. It had also limited the right of appeal and broadened the definition of "terrorist or subversive acts" to include offences such as reproducing or distributing "subversive" literature. The decree was applied retroactively. Cases begun before its promulgation were transferred to the special courts and defendants in such cases who were convicted were subject to the increased penalties which had been introduced after they committed the offences.

Detainees were routinely held for longer than the maximum legal period of *garde à vue* (incommunicado) detention, which was extended to 12 days under the anti-terrorist decree. Confessions extracted under torture were routinely used in the special courts, and were often the sole basis for conviction. The courts systematically ignored defence lawyers' requests that defendants who alleged torture in *garde à vue* detention should be medically examined and there were no independent investigations into torture allegations.

Defence rights were seriously curtailed in the special courts. Defence lawyers were given insufficient time to prepare their case, were given access only to part of their client's file and were often not allowed to call defence witnesses. In April the anti-terrorist decree was amended to provide for the expulsion from the special courts and suspension for up to one year of lawyers whose behaviour the court considered objectionable. Scores of lawyers refused to plead in the special courts because of such constraints.

The composition of the special courts remained secret, so the independence of those presiding could not be assured. There is no right of appeal although the Supreme Court, which can rule only on procedure and does not re-examine the evidence, may review convictions. However, should the Supreme Court annul a special court verdict, the case must be sent back to the same special court "differently composed" or to another special court for retrial. Such limited form of appeal does not safeguard the accused's right to defence.

A trial known as the "Amir Noe Trial" from the *nom de guerre* of the group's leader, Abdennour Allam, was held in March before the Algiers Special Court. Fifty-one defendants, including 11 *in absentia*, were accused of murder, possession of arms and theft. The charges related to the period 1990 to 1992, before the promulgation of Decree 92-03 under which they were tried. Several lawyers refused to participate, stating that they had not had access to their clients' files. Many court-appointed lawyers also then withdrew for the same reason. The defendants had wounds and bruises when they appeared in court; they had reportedly been beaten by guards inside and outside the lawcourts. They were examined by doctors who stated that they were fit to stand trial. The prosecutor urged the court to sentence six of the defendants to death; in fact, the judge sentenced seven to death. The other defendants were sentenced to long prison terms. All the death sentences were confirmed by the Supreme Court in August.

56

Pleas for clemency were submitted, but the prisoners were executed in October, before lawyers and families had been told the result of the pleas.

Over 1,000 people remained in administrative detention without charge or trial in Ain M'Guel and other camps, beyond the maximum one-year period allowed under state of emergency regulations. Conditions of detention remained harsh and the remote location of the camps in the south of the country meant that many detainees received no family visits (see *Amnesty International Report 1993*). About 2,000 administrative detainees were released during the year and several camps were closed.

Lieutenant Lembarek Boumaarif, who was arrested and accused of the assassination of President Mohamed Boudiaf in June 1992, had not been brought to trial by the end of the year.

The dramatic increase in torture and ill-treatment recorded in 1992 continued. Detainees were routinely tortured and ill-treated by members of the police, gendarmerie, national guard, and military security officials in police stations and detention centres, particularly when held in incommunicado detention for interrogation. Many detainees were also reportedly beaten at the time of arrest and by prison guards. The most common method of torture reported was the so-called *chiffon* (cloth), whereby the victim is tied to a bench and partially suffocated with a cloth soaked in dirty water or chemicals. Other methods used were the *chalumeau* (blowlamp), whereby a blowlamp is held near the victim's face and other parts of the body causing burning; cigarette burns; electric shocks; sexual abuse with bottles and other objects; beatings with bars, sticks and wires, especially on the genitals; and death threats.

Yassine Simozrag, who was arrested on 23 July and held in illegally prolonged *garde à vue* detention at the police station in Chateauneuf, was allegedly deprived of food for several days, tortured with the *chiffon* and the *chalumeau*, and severely beaten until he lost consciousness. His family and lawyer were unable to ascertain his whereabouts until 18 August, when they learned from the family of another detainee that he was in the prison in El Harrach. His lawyer's request for an independent medical examination was ignored

by the authorities. At the end of the year he was still imprisoned awaiting trial.

There were reports of at least 12 deaths in custody as a result of torture. Mohamed Lamana, who had been arrested in December 1992, was held incommunicado for 40 days, during which he was allegedly tortured. He was released but rearrested in February by the same security force members. There was no news of him until his family was informed on 10 March that he had died. According to a death certificate dated the day of his rearrest, he died of asthma. However, relatives who saw his body said there were bruises on the head and neck. No official investigations were known to have been carried out into this or other cases of deaths in custody.

Extrajudicial executions of people posing no threat to the lives of the security forces were reported. For example, in June Mohamed Lecheb was allegedly shot dead by police wearing hoods when he opened the door of his parents' flat in El Harrach in answer to a police raid.

Twenty-six people were executed by firing-squad, the first death sentences to be carried out since 1989. Six people sentenced to death by a military court were executed in January and February: they had been convicted of carrying out attacks on a border post and the Navy Headquarters in 1991 and 1992 respectively. Seven people sentenced to death by the special court in Algiers in May were executed in August. They had been convicted of having planned and carried out the bombing of Algiers airport in August 1992. Some of them had confessed to the bombing on television, but all retracted their confessions in court saying they had been extracted under torture. Thirteen others, sentenced to death in the "Amir Noe Trial" and by the special courts in Constantine and Oran, were executed in October. Their families were not informed in advance of the executions.

More than 370 people were sentenced to death (more than half *in absentia*), most of them after unfair trials before the special courts. All the death sentences imposed by the special courts and referred to the Supreme Court for review were upheld. The only remaining recourse was a plea for clemency to the President of the *Haut Comité d'Etat*. Six death sentences were commuted by the President in October. In December the authorities announced that executions were suspended.

Ten Tunisian and two Moroccan asylum-seekers, all recognized as refugees by the UN High Commissioner for Refugees, were forcibly returned to their countries despite fears that they would be at risk of human rights violations. The Tunisians, in fact, were detained upon arrival in Tunisia and allegedly tortured while in illegally prolonged incommunicado detention (see **Tunisia** entry).

Over 150 civilians, including foreign nationals, were killed in attacks believed to have been carried out by armed Islamist opposition groups. The victims included Djilali Belkhenchir, a paediatrician at the Bir Traria Hospital in Algiers and Vice-President of the *Comité algérien contre la torture*, Algerian Committee against Torture, who was killed by three armed men in the hospital courtyard in October. He may have been targeted because he was a member of the *Comité national pour la sauvegarde de l'Algérie*, National Committee to Save Algeria, which had called for the cancellation of the second round of elections after the *Front Islamique du Salut* (FIS), Islamic Salvation Front, gained a large majority in the first round of national elections in December 1991. At least 10 individuals (most of them foreigners) were reportedly kidnapped by armed Islamist opposition groups: the majority were subsequently killed in captivity, although some were released.

Amnesty International appealed to the government to end the use of prolonged incommunicado detention and torture and ill-treatment of prisoners. It called for all those charged with politically motivated offences to be given fair trials and criticized the procedures of the special courts. Amnesty International also called for the commutation of all death sentences.

In March Amnesty International published a report, *Algeria: Deteriorating Human Rights under the State of Emergency*, and a further report, *Algeria: Executions after Unfair Trials: a Travesty of Justice*, in October. In April, during a visit to Algeria, Amnesty International's Secretary General met the Foreign Minister to discuss human rights and also called publicly for an end to abuses by both the government and opposition groups.

Amnesty International condemned the deliberate killings of civilians by Islamist opposition groups and urged all those responsible to call a halt to such killings.

ANGOLA

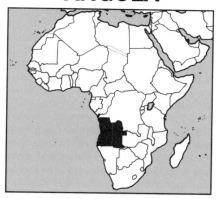

Hundreds, possibly thousands, of suspected opponents of the government were detained without trial, including prisoners of conscience. Some prisoners "disappeared". A wave of extrajudicial executions by government forces, which started in 1992, continued into 1993 bringing the total killed into the thousands. Gross human rights abuses were also committed by the armed opposition, including hundreds of deliberate and arbitrary killings.

By January 1993 outright civil war had resumed. Hostilities began in late 1992 after the *União Nacional para a Independência Total de Angola* (UNITA), National Union for the Total Independence of Angola, led by Jonas Savimbi, rejected the results of Angola's first multi-party elections, redeployed its army and began occupying territory and killing government supporters. The conflict intensified after the government, alleging that UNITA was planning a coup, launched an attack on UNITA offices and homes in Luanda in late October 1992, killing and imprisoning thousands (see *Amnesty International Report 1993*). By late 1993 the United Nations Angola Verification Mission (UNAVEM II), which monitored the 1991 peace agreement, estimated that well over 100,000 people had died as a direct or indirect result of the fighting. The government retained control over most of the country along the coast and several cities in the interior, to which UNITA laid siege. After a fierce nine-week battle, UNITA gained control of Huambo, Angola's second city, in March. Cuito, east of Huambo, and other cities remained under siege at the end of the year. In September, when UNITA

AMNESTY INTERNATIONAL REPORT 1994

58

declared a unilateral cease-fire, the intensity of fighting reduced, allowing aid agencies to deliver food and medicines by air to the cities besieged by UNITA as well as to UNITA-controlled areas.

Attempts to end the fighting included several rounds of talks organized by the UN Secretary-General's Special Representative for Angola. Various member states of the Organization of African Unity and prominent individuals also made diplomatic efforts to promote peace. UN-brokered talks failed in February and again in May. In September the UN Security Council declared that the situation in Angola constituted a threat to international peace and security and imposed arms and fuel sanctions against UNITA. Another round of talks in Zambia had not concluded by the end of the year.

The government reintroduced conscription in March for men aged between 20 and 45 years. Each side accused the other of using mercenaries. Both shelled towns and residential areas, killing civilians. Each tried to prevent deliveries of food aid to areas occupied by the other. The UN, the International Committee of the Red Cross and local church representatives repeatedly condemned violations of humanitarian law by both sides.

Eleven of the 70 UNITA members who had been elected to the 220-seat National Assembly in the 1992 elections took their seats in February. They had been arrested when fighting broke out in Luanda in October 1992 and held in what the government termed "protective custody". Gradually they were given some freedom of movement but reportedly continued to be monitored by security agents. Two were refused permission to travel and two others went into exile while travelling abroad. A parliamentary human rights commission was set up. It inspected prisons in Luanda in June and protested at the poor conditions but it apparently undertook no investigations into reports of politically motivated human rights violations.

Arrests of suspected UNITA supporters, which had begun in October 1992, continued in 1993. Those detained included UNITA officials, soldiers and supporters. Many of those held were prisoners of conscience: they had not taken up arms and were arrested either because they had revealed themselves during the year's cease-fire to be UNITA supporters or because they

were members of the Ovimbundu ethnic group, from which UNITA draws wide support. They were held without charge or trial in prisons, military barracks and police stations. Over 100 were released in mid-January. They included Godfrey Nangonya, a leading member of the Angolan Civic Association, who, although a UNITA supporter, had denounced deliberate killings and other abuses committed by UNITA. In August a government representative said that no suspected UNITA supporters remained in government custody. Most of those held in military installations were reportedly released but many who could not return to their homes because of the fighting were lodged in what was called a "transit camp" outside Luanda. UNITA, however, maintained that hundreds of its supporters remained in government custody.

Hundreds of UNITA supporters were detained in January when government soldiers and police and government-armed civilians attempted to expel UNITA from over a dozen towns in the south and west including Benguela, Lubango, Menongue and Namibe. Some 500 arrested in the southwest, including women and children, were reportedly held in Bentiaba prison camp in Namibe province. In the following months, as the war intensified, dozens more UNITA members or supporters were said to have been detained but few details were available and corroboration was difficult. Those held reportedly included Maria Fátima Ruth, who was detained in January in Cuando Cubango province, and Ruth Chavanga, detained in Huila province in July. Maria Fátima Ruth was subsequently released but Ruth Chavanga was believed to be among those still held without charge or trial at the end of the year.

Some of those detained reportedly "disappeared", including Linda Calufele and her husband, Carlos Calufele, following their detention in Lobito by police in January.

Hundreds of people were reported to have been extrajudicially executed in January when government forces tried to expel UNITA supporters from towns under government control. As in Luanda in November 1992, after a first wave of killings had taken place the authorities publicly urged restraint but took no effective action to halt the killings or bring those responsible to justice. Those killed in Benguela city included at least two lawyers, Belchior

Rodrigues and Manuel Elemina, and at least two members of the Evangelical Congregational Church, Agostinho Canjila, a minister, and Constantino Chitwe, a lay member, who were reportedly dragged out of their houses and shot. In Lubango, when government soldiers shelled UNITA's main office two young men emerged with their hands raised: they were thrown to the ground and sprayed with machine-gun bullets.

On 22 January dozens of members of the Bakongo ethnic group were killed by armed civilians in open-air markets in Luanda: police reportedly did nothing to stop the violence. Police said they had recorded about 20 deaths but unofficial sources said that scores were killed, many others were injured and women were raped.

The killings occurred after UNITA, allegedly with assistance from the neighbouring Republic of Zaire, occupied Soyo in northwestern Angola. The Bakongo ethnic group spans both countries and Bakongo people are often referred to in Angola as "Zairians". The National Assembly called for an inquiry but none was reported to have been carried out. Several people were reportedly arrested in connection with the attacks but released uncharged within a few weeks.

Details continued to emerge about extrajudicial executions carried out in November and December 1992 indicating that killings which the government had said were retaliation by angry civilians for earlier killings by UNITA had actually been committed with the involvement of the security forces, who had recruited civilians to help them. This was consistent with reports of people being taken out of prisons at night, of mass executions and of mass graves. Thousands were said to have been executed in Luanda alone, including Anastácio Franco Dungue, a teacher, who was reportedly shot dead by police and civilians in Cazenga suburb in November 1992, and Kanjundo Pinheiro, an aircraft mechanic who was killed in Sambo suburb in December 1992. Many other people were executed in Viana, a town near Luanda, including Madalena Georgina Kapamba, a member of the Roman Catholic women's movement.

UNITA was responsible for gross human rights abuses, including widespread deliberate and arbitrary killings. UNITA also held a number of prisoners, including some who should have been released before the 1992 elections, as required by the 1991 peace agreement (see *Amnesty International Report, 1993*), and scores of others detained in 1993. Those arrested in Huambo in March after UNITA took control of the city included Joaquim Tavares, a judge, and Valdemar Peres da Silva, a Portuguese national, who was reportedly tortured in custody. There were frequent reports of civilians being captured and forced to be soldiers or porters for UNITA's army.

People fleeing from UNITA-controlled areas gave graphic accounts of ill-treatment of civilians and summary executions but it was impossible to verify the accuracy of most of these reports. Nevertheless, a pattern emerged of systematic deliberate and arbitrary killings of young men of military age and traditional leaders in areas where support for the government was strong.

In May UNITA troops in Huila province ambushed a train which they said was carrying soldiers and then bayoneted some of the survivors, including women and children.

In July UNITA reportedly murdered seven people in Cabuta, Kwanza Sul province: a survivor said that the dead included four men who were beheaded, two women who were raped and a child. In October after government soldiers recaptured Balombo in Huila province, they said they found the bodies of 30 government soldiers and police who had been executed.

In May, when UN-sponsored peace negotiations between the government and UNITA were taking place in Côte d'Ivoire, Amnesty International wrote to the UN Secretary-General to urge that increased protection for human rights be included in the agreement which was then being prepared. It proposed mechanisms to ensure that abuses were independently investigated and properly remedied, so that the cycle of impunity for those responsible for killing and torture could be stopped.

In August Amnesty International published a report, *Angola: Assault on the right to life*, which described the political killings which had taken place since October 1992. The organization appealed for the release of prisoners of conscience and sought information about the cases of dozens of individuals who were detained, or who were reported to have "disappeared" or been killed in custody by both sides.

ARGENTINA

Journalists, students and human rights activists critical of the government were subjected to death threats and attacks by unknown assailants believed in many cases to be linked to the ruling political party. There were allegations of human rights violations by police in several provinces, including torture and ill-treatment of detainees. A student was believed to have "disappeared" and there was no progress in the investigation into the fate of four people who had "disappeared" in custody in previous years. The whereabouts of hundreds of children who "disappeared" in custody during the years of military government, many of whom are probably alive, remained unknown. One possible extrajudicial execution was reported.

The ruling Peronist party won parliamentary elections in October. In December Congress passed a law declaring the need for a constitutional reform that, among other changes, would allow President Menem to stand for re-election. Also in December thousands of workers demanding payment of their salaries sacked and burned government buildings in the northern province of Santiago del Estero.

According to the Argentine Press Workers' Federation, between March 1992 and the end of August 1993, over 100 cases of death threats and assaults on journalists were recorded. No one was brought to justice for these attacks and there were widespread allegations that people associated with the ruling Peronist party were responsible for at least some of them. In one case, Hernán López Echague, a reporter on the Buenos Aires daily *Página 12*, was twice violently attacked by unidentified men. He had published articles linking leading members of the ruling Peronist party with people who attacked journalists on 14 August at a farm fair addressed by President Menem. On 25 August Hernán López Echague was attacked by two unidentified men outside his home in Buenos Aires. The assailants hit him and slashed his face with a knife. On 8 September two unidentified men attacked him in the streets in Buenos Aires Province and forced him into a car. Inside the vehicle other men allegedly hit him and warned him to stop publishing such things or that next time they would kill him.

In September the government appointed a special attorney to investigate the attacks on journalists but no apparent progress had been made by the end of the year.

Students and human rights activists also received death threats believed in many cases to be sent by people involved with the ruling party. In July two student leaders – Andrés Petrillo and Mario Insúa – of the University of Buenos Aires were beaten by two unknown people. On 5 August several unidentified individuals visited the home of Hebe de Bonafini, president of the human rights organization *Madres de Plaza de Mayo*, Mothers of Plaza de Mayo, in La Plata, Buenos Aires Province. They told her: "If you do not shut your mouth we will shut it with bullets."

Police in several provinces were reported to have tortured or ill-treated detainees. In September Diego Ponce, aged 16, was reportedly severely beaten by the police in Comodoro Rivadavia, Chubut Province. As a result of the beatings he had emergency surgery which revealed extensive damage to his abdominal organs. A judicial inquiry was opened into this case, but no results were known by the end of the year.

Miguel Bru, a student, was alleged to have "disappeared" in August. He was last seen near the coastal resort of Punta Blanca, Buenos Aires Province. Miguel Bru had filed a complaint against members of La Plata 9th Police Station, who had earlier raided his house without a search warrant. No progress was reported in investigations aimed at establishing his whereabouts and identifying those responsible for his apparent "disappearance".

There was also no progress reported in investigations into the reported "disappearances" of Pablo Cristian Guardatti in

May 1992 and three others in 1990 (see *Amnesty International Report 1993*).

An official commission set up in 1992 to investigate the fate of hundreds of children who "disappeared" during the so-called "dirty war" of the 1970s and 1980s continued its work. It reported that no new "disappeared" children had been identified in 1993. In December the Executive sent to Congress for approval a list of military promotions which included the promotions to very senior navy posts of two officers accused of serious human rights violations during the "dirty war".

Police officers were responsible for what appeared to be a possible extrajudicial execution. The victim, Carlos Ibarra, aged 17, was mortally wounded by police in May during an escape attempt at the Aráoz Alfaro II Institute for young offenders near La Plata, Buenos Aires Province. He was apparently mortally wounded while posing no threat to police officers. In the same institution, in August, a group of prison guards conducted a dawn search during which a number of young offenders were allegedly beaten. According to the director of the Institute, who was dismissed after denouncing the raid, 11 youths were injured in the incident, including one whose hip was broken.

Evidence emerged about a possible extrajudicial execution by police in 1991. Abel Solís was alleged to have "disappeared" in Corrientes in September 1991. His body was found a week later on the outskirts of the city. He had been shot in the back of the head at close range. At the time of his death Abel Solís, who had a criminal record for petty theft and other offences, was being sought by the Corrientes police. He had reportedly told relatives that he had received death threats from the police and that he was afraid of being tortured if taken into police custody, as had happened in the past. Relatives of Abel Solís alleged that an official investigation into his murder was not conducted thoroughly: they said that crucial witnesses had not been interviewed and that a postmortem examination had been inadequate. Antonio Velozo, a friend of Abel Solís who had campaigned for a full investigation into his death, had reportedly been detained without warrant in June 1992 by police officers from the Investigations Brigade in Corrientes, then taken to their headquarters, beaten, tortured and warned he would meet the same fate as Abel Solís if he did not cease campaigning.

In November the Supreme Court of Justice of Buenos Aires Province confirmed a lower court sentence of life imprisonment on three police officers convicted of the extrajudicial execution of three youths in March 1987.

During the year Amnesty International repeatedly expressed concern to the government about the attacks and death threats against journalists and others, and urged the authorities to take all possible steps to safeguard them and their families. The organization also called on several provincial authorities to investigate reports of "disappearances", possible extrajudicial executions, torture and ill-treatment in police custody and urged them to take steps to prevent such abuses.

ARMENIA

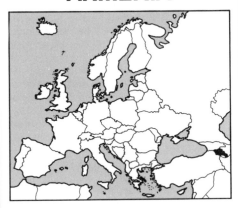

Seven prisoners under sentence of death awaited the outcome of their appeals for clemency.

A new draft constitution was published for discussion in July, but had not been adopted by the end of the year. Its provisions included establishing the post of a Defender of Human Rights, responsible among other things for ensuring that all laws comply with international standards. Talks continued on resolving the conflict over Karabakh (see **Azerbaydzhan** entry), with a meeting in September between President Levon Ter-Petrosyan and his Azerbaydzhani counterpart.

In June Armenia acceded to the four Geneva Conventions of 1949 and their 1977 Additional Protocols, and to the International Covenant on Civil and Political

62

Rights and its (First) Optional Protocol. The following month it acceded to the 1951 Convention relating to the Status of Refugees and its 1967 Protocol.

As a result of the Karabakh conflict several Azerbaydzhani civilians were said to be held hostage in private hands, but with the apparent complicity of the authorities, on Armenian territory. For example, unofficial sources reported that Yolchu Akhmed ogly Gyoyushov and his relative Ramazan Gasym ogly Mamedov were taken hostage by ethnic Armenians while tending cattle in the neighbouring republic of Georgia in September. They were taken across the border to Armenia, where they were said to be held pending an exchange for hostages held in Azerbaydzhan.

According to press reports seven men sentenced to death were awaiting execution at the end of the year. This number was believed to include two of the three men sentenced to death in 1990 (see *Amnesty International Report 1993*). The third, Vagarsh Ovanyan, was said to have been murdered in November by another death-row inmate. The reports stated that no executions had been carried out for four years owing to a lack of facilities. Previously, prisoners had been sent for execution to a neighbouring republic of the former Soviet Union.

Amnesty International urged the authorities to investigate all allegations of hostage-taking in Armenia; to take all necessary steps without delay to identify any people who might be so held; to ensure their immediate, safe release; and to bring to account anyone found responsible.

In the light of continuing allegations of hostage-taking and deliberate and arbitrary killings by ethnic Armenians and other parties to the conflict over Karabakh in Azerbaydzhan, Amnesty International continued to urge the authorities to exert all influence possible to ensure that international human rights and humanitarian principles were observed by all those associated with the conflict.

Amnesty International also urged the government to commute all pending death sentences and to take concrete measures towards total abolition of the death penalty in line with worldwide trends.

AUSTRALIA

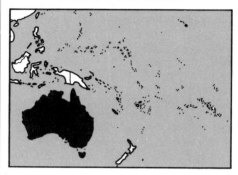

Two Aboriginal prisoners died in custody allegedly after being ill-treated by police.

In July the Australian Government informed the UN Working Group on Indigenous Populations that it had appointed an Aboriginal and Torres Strait Islander Social Justice Commissioner. The Commissioner is to report annually to the government on Australia's performance in the area of indigenous rights, both nationally and internationally.

Five Aboriginal prisoners died in custody during 1993, two of them after they were allegedly ill-treated by police. Barry Raymond Turbane died in April at the Arthur Gorrie Remand and Reception Centre in Brisbane, Queensland, within a week of being arrested for alleged unlawful use of a motor vehicle. He was found hanged from socks tied above his cell door. His wife alleged that he had been beaten by police officers at the time of his arrest and other relatives alleged that police had beaten him in jail, and they accused prison authorities of negligence. In November Daniel Yock died in police custody after allegedly being severely beaten by police officers in Brisbane. Investigations were opened into both deaths but had not concluded by the end of the year.

In February Amnesty International issued a report, *Australia: A criminal justice system weighted against Aboriginal people*. It expressed concern that conditions in certain detention facilities may amount to cruel, inhuman or degrading treatment and might have contributed to a high rate of deaths in custody among Aboriginal prisoners, who continued to be imprisoned in grossly disproportionate numbers. It urged the Australian authorities to closely examine the patterns of incarceration of

Aboriginal people, and to give particular consideration to elements of the criminal justice system which appear to discriminate against Aboriginal people and contribute to their high levels of imprisonment.

In April the Chief Minister of the Northern Territory responded at length to the report, saying that "persons are taken into protective custody only if they are seriously affected by liquor or refuse to comply with police direction regarding their drinking in public". In May John Fahey, the Premier of the State of New South Wales, indicated to Amnesty International that the New South Wales Summary Offences Act 1988 – one of the laws Amnesty International had asked the authorities to examine – was under review.

In 1992 Amnesty International had appealed for the repeal of sections of the Tasmanian Criminal Code Act which allow for the prosecution and imprisonment of consenting adults who engage in homosexual acts in private (see *Amnesty International Report 1993*). In June Ray Groom, the Premier of Tasmania, informed Amnesty International that there was insufficient consensus in the community for the repeal of those sections but that prosecutions under the provisions were rare.

In November Amnesty International wrote to the state governments of Queensland and Victoria and inquired about the nature and results of the official investigations into the deaths of Aboriginal prisoners including Barry Turbane and Daniel Yock.

In an oral statement to the UN Working Group on Indigenous Populations in July, Amnesty International included reference to its concerns in Australia.

AUSTRIA

Allegations were received of ill-treatment of detainees by police and prison officials. One conscientious objector to military service served a prison sentence; he was considered a prisoner of conscience.

In March Austria ratified the Second Optional Protocol to the International Covenant on Civil and Political Rights, aiming at the abolition of the death penalty.

In November the UN Committee against Torture, in its first ruling on an individual submission, found that the Austrian authorities had violated the Convention against Torture. Qani Halimi-Nedzibi had alleged that a police officer from the Lower Austria Drugs Squad had beaten him about the head, punched him in the stomach and forced his head into a bucket of water to force him to sign a false confession (see *Amnesty International Report 1992*). Although Qani Halimi-Nedzibi made these allegations before an investigating judge in December 1988, no inquiry was launched until March 1990. Although the committee found insufficient evidence to sustain Qani Halimi-Nedzibi's allegations of ill-treatment, it concluded that the delay of 15 months before an investigation into the allegations was launched was unreasonably long and violated Article 12 of the Convention.

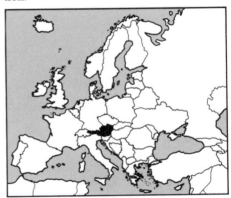

A number of reports were received that people had been ill-treated in police custody. For example, Rudolf Reumann, who was arrested for riding a bicycle while under the influence of alcohol, alleged that he had been beaten in the street and struck with batons at a police station in Salzburg in August 1992. His injuries included a perforated ear-drum, bruising and a broken finger. Rudolf Reumann himself was accused of resisting state authority and of causing aggravated bodily harm to two police officers.

In June the Vienna Independent Administrative Tribunal ruled that excessive force had been used by police officers in arresting Werner Hirtmayr (see *Amnesty International Report 1993*). Werner Hirtmayr had suffered torn ligaments to his right knee necessitating surgery.

Several allegations were received that prisoners in Vienna Provincial Court prison had been ill-treated by prison officers. In March Ahmet S. alleged that he

64

had been hit in the face, kicked and struck with a rubber truncheon by a prison officer.

Helmut Hejtmanek spent a total of four months in prison for failing to report for military duties after his call-up in 1989 and for refusing to obey military orders following his call-up in 1986. He had previously received a suspended prison sentence for the second offence. Helmut Hejtmanek's original application for conscientious objector status had been rejected by the authorities in 1985. He then refused to perform both military and alternative service. He was arrested in January following a routine police identity check.

In January Amnesty International called for the release of Helmut Hejtmanek. The organization does not normally adopt total objectors as prisoners of conscience. However, in cases where people have applied to perform alternative service on sincere grounds of conscience it will adopt them if their applications are turned down, even if subsequently, and often precisely because of this rejection, they decide to become total objectors.

In February Amnesty International asked the authorities about the investigation into Rudolf Reumann's allegations of ill-treatment. The organization was informed in September that the Salzburg Public Procurator had brought charges against two police officers under Article 312 ("tormenting or neglecting a detainee") of the Penal Code. The trial of the two officers began in December.

In May Amnesty International asked the authorities about the steps taken to investigate Ahmet S.'s allegations of ill-treatment. In September the organization was told that an investigation by the Vienna Public Procurator had resulted in charges being brought against four officers of Vienna Provincial Court prison.

In August Amnesty International asked the authorities whether an earlier decision not to bring charges against the officers accused of ill-treating Werner Hirtmayr would be re-examined in the light of the decision by the Vienna Independent Administrative Tribunal. In December Amnesty International was informed by the authorities that the evidence presented at the Tribunal's hearings had not clarified the circumstances which led to Werner Hirtmayr's injuries. It had therefore not been possible to charge or discipline any of the officers involved.

AZERBAYDZHAN

After a change of government in June scores of possible prisoners of conscience were arrested or briefly detained under administrative procedures. Scores of prisoners were reportedly held as hostages on grounds of their ethnic origin in the conflict over the disputed Karabakh region: some were released in exchanges sanctioned by the Azerbaydzhani Government and the ethnic Armenians controlling Karabakh. Dozens of people alleged that they had been ill-treated in police custody. At least 12 death sentences were reported, of which five were commuted, but there were no known executions.

In June over 30 people died when government troops unsuccessfully tried to disarm a mutinous military unit in the city of Gyandzha. President Abulfaz Elchibey left the capital, Baku, later that month following a rebellion led by the unit's head, Suret Guseynov, who then became Prime Minister. Most senior government officials were replaced and some were arrested. In August a referendum returned a vote of no confidence in President Elchibey; Geydar Aliyev was elected President after a nationwide vote in October.

Fighting continued over the disputed region of Karabakh (see *Amnesty International Report 1993*), and over 100,000 civilians were displaced when ethnic Armenian forces from Karabakh occupied other large areas of Azerbaydzhani territory.

Azerbaydzhan acceded to the 1951 Convention relating to the Status of Refugees and its 1967 Protocol in February, and to the 1949 Geneva Convention in June.

Following the fall of President Elchibey, scores of possible prisoners of conscience were arrested or briefly detained under administrative procedures. Many supporters of President Elchibey were held for short periods for taking part in demonstrations, forbidden under the state of emergency then in force, or for other expressions of political dissent. For example, four members of the opposition Musavat Party – Yashar Tyurkazar, Rizvan Gumbatov, Rushdi Magomedli and Mamed Amrakhov – were sentenced to 15 days' administrative detention at the end of July for distributing leaflets in a tea-house in Baku. At the end of the year at least three former government officials remained in detention in connection with the events in Gyandzha. Ikhtiyar Shirinov, former Procurator General, Gabil Mamedov, former Deputy Interior Minister and Sulkheddin Akperov, former Deputy Security Minister, had travelled to Gyandzha to oversee attempts to disarm the mutinous military unit and were detained there on 4 June by forces loyal to Suret Guseynov. They were subsequently transferred to Baku and charged with exceeding their authority and using armed force against the Azerbaydzhani people.

In the context of the Karabakh conflict there were continued reports of hostage-taking on grounds of ethnic origin, with the complicity of the authorities. For example, around 40 ethnic Azeris, including many elderly civilians and children, were taken to the Karabakh regional capital of Khankendi (Stepanakert) in April following an offensive by ethnic Armenians in the Kelbadzhar district. They were said to be held there pending exchange. However, dozens of other people reportedly held as hostages were released in exchanges sanctioned by the Azerbaydzhani authorities and the ethnic Armenians controlling Karabakh. Four possible prisoners of conscience were among a group of 29 people handed over by the Azerbaydzhanis in August. They included Vilik Oganesov and Artavaz Mirzoyan, ethnic Armenian citizens of the Republic of Georgia, who had been held without charge following their arrest in 1992 while in transit through Baku (see *Amnesty International Report 1993*).

There were reports of ill-treatment in police custody under both administrations. For example, Zardusht Alizade, a journalist, reported being kicked and beaten when he was arbitrarily detained on 27 March in Baku by, among others, the then Interior Minister, who was said to have found some articles in his newspaper politically unacceptable. Later in the year the three former officials named above were reportedly severely beaten – one of them, Sulkheddin

Akperov, to the point of unconsciousness – in the first weeks of their detention in Gyandzha.

At least 12 death sentences were reported, although in the absence of official statistics, the real total, which may have been higher, was not known. Unofficial sources reported in December that 48 people were awaiting execution on death row. Five death sentences, which had been passed in May without right of appeal on five soldiers of the Russian Army stationed in Armenia, were commuted. Servicemen Vladislav Kudinov, Konstantin Tukish, Yaroslav Yevstigneyev, Andrey Filippov and Mikhail Lisovoy were convicted of taking part in an attack on Azerbaydzhani forces in Karabakh, but in September parliament voted to hand the men over to the Russian authorities.

No executions were reported, although five men were believed to face imminent execution after their petitions for clemency were turned down by the President in October. Kurban Babayev, Ali Guliyev, Dzhulagay Mamedov, Kingiz Pashayev and Sirudin Rufulayev had been sentenced to death for murder and banditry in November 1990.

Three men on death row died in custody: Sergey Grebenkov, of Russian and Armenian descent, was found hanged in his cell in Gyandzha in February, and Arno Mkrtchyan and Armen Avanesyan, both ethnic Armenians, died in a Baku prison in September and October respectively.

Throughout the year Amnesty International urged all parties involved in the conflict over Karabakh to refrain from detaining civilians as hostages and from holding people solely on grounds of their ethnic origin.

Amnesty International sought further information on possible prisoners of conscience following the events in Gyandzha. The organization welcomed any efforts by properly constituted legal authorities to investigate the deaths there, but expressed its hope that no one would be imprisoned for lawfully exercising their legitimate authority. Amnesty International also urged the authorities not to imprison anyone for the legitimate exercise of their right to freedom of expression.

Amnesty International continued to urge the authorities to commute all pending death sentences and to take steps towards abolition of the death penalty.

BAHAMAS

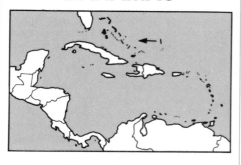

At least eight people were sentenced to death. No executions were carried out; the last execution took place in 1986. At the end of the year there were 32 people on death row. A constitutional challenge to the death penalty was still pending a final decision.

In September the Bahamas acceded to the 1951 Convention relating to the Status of Refugees and its 1967 Protocol.

Eight men convicted on murder charges were sentenced to death, bringing the total number on death row to 30 men and two women. A decision by the Judicial Committee of the Privy Council (JCPC) in the case of two Jamaican prisoners – that execution more than five years after sentencing would constitute "inhuman or degrading punishment or other treatment" and that sentences should be commuted to life imprisonment – was applicable to at least nine prisoners in the Bahamas (see **Jamaica** entry). However, no final decision to commute their sentences had been made by the end of the year.

In January the Court of Appeal dismissed the appeal of Anthony Neely and Jeremiah Poitier who had challenged the constitutionality of the death penalty on the ground that neither the Constitution nor any other law specifies the method of execution (see *Amnesty International Report 1991*). A final appeal to the JCPC in London, the final court of appeal for the Bahamas, was still pending at the end of the year.

Amnesty International appealed to the authorities to commute all death sentences and to amend the country's legislation to bring it into line with international standards by abolishing corporal punishment as it constitutes cruel, inhuman and degrading treatment or punishment.

BAHRAIN

Around 40 political prisoners, including possible prisoners of conscience, continued serving long prison terms imposed after unfair trials in previous years. Thirty-three political prisoners benefited from amnesties. Sporadic arbitrary arrests took place, principally of members of the majority Shi'a community. Scores of Bahraini nationals were forcibly exiled from the country, although some were allowed to return after years abroad.

In January the newly created Consultative Council held its first session. The council has no legislative powers and its 30 members (15 Sunni and 15 Shi'a Muslims) were appointed by the Amir of Bahrain, al-Sheikh 'Isa Bin Salman Al Khalifa. The 1974 State Security Measures, which permit administrative detention without charge or trial for up to three years, as well as provisions governing trial procedures for security cases, remained in force. Such legislation falls far below international human rights standards. No moves were made to introduce basic safeguards for detainees into law and practice.

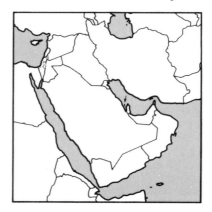

Approximately 40 political prisoners, including possible prisoners of conscience, continued to serve long prison terms imposed after unfair trials in previous years. Most prisoners were held because of their alleged association with banned Islamic groups such as the Islamic Front for the Liberation of Bahrain and *Hizbollah*, Party of God. Some had been sentenced following an alleged coup attempt in 1981. Long-term prisoners included Mohammad Jamil 'Abd al-'Amir al-Jamri and Salah al-

Khawaja (see *Amnesty International Report 1993*), who were serving 10-year and seven-year prison sentences respectively for offences including membership of an unauthorized organization.

Three amnesties for political prisoners and victims of forcible exile were declared by the Amir, in March, May and December: 33 prisoners benefited, including some who had been serving long prison terms. Among them were 'Abd al-Karim Bahar, a student, and 'Abd al-Hussein al-Moussawi, an electrician, both of whom were serving sentences of 15 years' imprisonment in connection with the alleged coup attempt.

Reports continued to be received of sporadic arbitrary arrests of members of the Shi'a community. For example, al-Sayyid 'Alawi al-Sayyid Muhsin al-'Alawi was detained twice, apparently following religious commemoration ceremonies. He was held for six weeks following his arrest in August and was rearrested in December. Al-Sayyid Dhiya' al-Sayyid Yahya al-Moussawi was reportedly arrested and detained after delivering a sermon in a Manama mosque in September. Both were believed to be prisoners of conscience.

Scores of Bahraini nationals were denied entry when they attempted to return to Bahrain after periods of residence abroad. 'Ahmed Hussein 'Akbar 'Abbas was forcibly exiled from Bahrain in 1982 when he was stripped of his Bahraini papers and expelled to Iran. On his return to Bahrain in September with his Lebanese wife and four children, he was reportedly interrogated and beaten. He was then forcibly expelled to Lebanon, where he was also refused entry and returned to Bahrain. He was again expelled by the Bahrain authorities to Lebanon, where he was given temporary residence.

Bahraini nationals who returned to Bahrain with expired passports after an absence of some years abroad were often issued with new one-year Bahraini passports, sometimes valid only for two or three countries, before being forcibly exiled from the country. Dr 'Abd al-'Aziz Rashid al-Rashid, a doctor, attempted to return to Bahrain in November. In the course of one week he was expelled from Bahrain four times, but repeatedly refused entry by other countries. He was finally issued with a new Bahraini passport, valid for one year, before being sent to the United Arab Emirates. However, several Bahrainis who had been forcibly exiled from the country for long periods were allowed to return to Bahrain in 1993, although for some it had taken more than one attempt.

Amnesty International expressed concern to the government about arbitrary arrests and cases of forcible exile, and called on the authorities to respect international human rights standards. The organization welcomed the releases as a result of the amnesties. In December Amnesty International issued a report, *Banned from Bahrain: Forcible exile of Bahraini nationals*, and called on the government to end its policy of forcible exile by issuing a public declaration on Bahrain's national day that all Bahraini nationals were entitled to return there.

In response to appeals on behalf of Mohammad Jamil 'Abd al-'Amir al-Jamri, the Minister of the Interior denied that he had been tortured and said he had received a fair trial. Amnesty International's request for information regarding any investigation into Mohammad al-Jamri's alleged torture and a copy of the court's judgment remained without response. The Minister also informed Amnesty International of the release of two detainees whose cases it had raised in 1992 and denied that Hassan Medan had been forcibly exiled in December 1992. The Minister said that he had arrived in Bahrain with no travel documents and had been refused entry in accordance with normal international practice. The response failed to take into account the obligation of all states to readmit their own nationals.

BANGLADESH

Hundreds of critics and opponents of the government were detained without charge or trial under the Special Powers Act (SPA) and an anti-terrorism law. They included prisoners of conscience. Torture in police custody continued to be reported, resulting in at least four deaths. Dozens of people were reported to have been killed by the security forces in suspicious circumstances. At least three people were sentenced to death, one *in absentia*. Three men were executed.

Thousands of people were injured and hundreds arrested by the security forces during anti-government demonstrations. In

68

clashes between the security forces and university students affiliated to the major political parties, including the ruling party, over 30 students were killed and some 2,250 were injured by September.

Trials of former government members continued and several further arrests were made. Former Air Vice Marshal Mamtazuddin Ahmed was arrested in October on corruption charges. Former President Mohammad Ershad and his wife Raushan were each sentenced to another seven years' imprisonment for illegal transfer of assets.

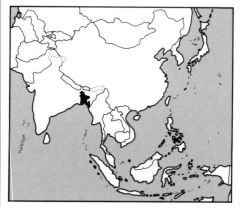

In June the Law Minister announced the creation of a Law Commission to undertake law reform, but it had not been established by the end of the year.

Several rounds of talks between representatives of the tribal population of the Chittagong Hill Tracts and the government took place, but no political solution was found to end years of strife. Cease-fire agreements and amnesties for tribal militants who surrendered to the authorities were periodically extended. In May an agreement was signed with India for the repatriation of over 50,000 tribal refugees from camps in Tripura. The refugees refused to leave when the Bangladeshi Government failed to provide guarantees for their safety or for international supervision of the repatriation process.

By September some 48,000 of 260,000 Burmese Muslim refugees had returned to Myanmar. The repatriation process was interrupted in mid-January, but resumed in February after the UN High Commissioner for Refugees was permitted to interview refugees in the transit camps preparing to return. Amnesty International received reports that Bangladeshi security forces kicked, raped and beat some of the refugees with sticks to make them "volunteer" for repatriation. Hundreds of Burmese Muslim refugees who were detained without charge or trial at the end of 1992 under the SPA or the Curbing of Terrorist Activities Act were released, but some 500 refugees still remained in detention in March 1993. Some new arrests took place; some newly arriving refugees were charged with "loitering" when they could not produce valid documents.

The SPA was reportedly used to detain hundreds of people, including prisoners of conscience. The SPA empowers the authorities to detain without charge or trial for an indefinitely renewable period anyone suspected of committing a "prejudicial act" likely to endanger public safety or order. In most of the cases which reached the High Court such detention was declared unlawful. Khaledur Rahman Tito, the secretary of the opposition Jatiya Party, detained in December 1992 under the SPA, was released in May after the order for his detention was ruled illegal. Sanchoy Chakma, a tribal student leader, was arrested without warrant on 16 March; police interrogated him about human rights training he had received abroad. Eight days later he was served with a 120-day detention order under the SPA. He was a prisoner of conscience. On 6 April he was informed that he was being charged with "being a spokesman of an anti-state people". However, he was released uncharged and untried on 25 May after the government revoked his detention order.

By June some 1,300 people had been arrested and 90 people, including members of opposition parties and dozens of trade unionists, had been tried and sentenced under the Curbing of Terrorist Activities Act, which had been passed in November 1992 (see *Amnesty International Report 1993*). Seven trade unionists were reportedly each sentenced in their absence to 10 years' imprisonment. Many of the trials may have been unfair (see *Amnesty International Report 1993*).

Torture in police custody continued to be reported. In July a 13-year old streetchild, Mohammad Shawkat, was allegedly raped by two police constables in Dhaka. The constables were suspended, but no charges were brought against them. Also in July, four men who had been arrested on criminal charges were allegedly tortured with electric shocks in Saturia police station. No official action was known to have been taken.

At least four people died in custody reportedly as a result of torture. In January Rustam Ali died in a police station in Sylhet allegedly following torture; he had been arrested the same day and was reportedly in good health. No investigation was known to have been undertaken.

The government failed to take adequate action when the first cases of arbitrary punishments, including public flogging and the death sentence, imposed without legal authority by the *salish*, village arbitration councils, were reported. The *salish* try, convict and sentence individuals using a form of Islamic law which contravenes the civil law in force in Bangladesh. In January a 21-year-old woman sentenced to death by stoning in Chatakchara survived the stoning but died apparently after committing suicide. Another woman was publicly burned to death in Dokhin Sripur in June following a *salish* verdict. A 14-year-old girl in Dohar Thana was sentenced to 100 lashes in April after she was allegedly raped by an influential villager. The *salish* acquitted the alleged rapist but took her pregnancy as evidence of illicit sexual intercourse. In one case only was action known to have been taken: seven members of the *salish* in Chatakchara were charged with murder. The case was still pending at the end of the year.

Dozens of people were reported to have been killed by the security forces in suspicious circumstances. In January naval staff of the Essa Khan naval base near Chittagong reportedly attacked residents of Bandartila and Halishahar, two nearby villages, following a quarrel. Hundreds of people were injured and thousands rendered homeless when their homes were set on fire by the naval staff. Police stated that 10 people had been killed, but local human rights groups reported between 17 and 30 dead. An official inquiry was set up but its report had not been made public by the end of the year. Naval officials reported that several naval personnel had been dismissed and five officers and eight sailors were to be tried by court-martial for their direct involvement in the incident. It was not known whether the court-martial had concluded by the end of the year.

Nine men were reported to have been extrajudicially executed in two separate incidents by the paramilitary Bangladesh Rifles (BDR). In April four men were shot dead in cold blood by the BDR at Kolar Haat village and in July five men were killed in Zakiganj, in Sylhet district, when the BDR opened fire on peacefully demonstrating villagers who were demanding that the local authorities open a dike.

In the Chittagong Hill Tracts violations of tribal people's human rights continued to be reported. Dozens of tribal people were arbitrarily detained under the SPA. Several people were believed to have been extrajudicially executed on 17 November in Naniarchar, in Rangamati district, when a demonstration organized by tribal students was attacked by Bengali settlers and the army opened fire on the demonstrators. Officials said 13 people died, including 12 tribal people, but local human rights groups said that over 20 people had been killed. The Home Minister announced that an inquiry commission would investigate the incident but there had been no progress by the end of the year.

Amnesty International learned that disciplinary action had been initiated against seven police officers for their involvement in an attack on journalists in July 1992 (see *Amnesty International Report 1993*); the report of the official inquiry was not made public. In July the government said that criminal proceedings had been initiated against eight people, including members of the paramilitary forces, for their alleged participation in the killings in April 1992 in Logang (see *Amnesty International Report 1993*); one member of the paramilitary BDR who had been involved in the Logang incident was dismissed for "mishandling the excited non-tribals", according to an official report.

At least three people were sentenced to death, one of them *in absentia*. Home Ministry sources said in August that 115 people were then on death row. Three people were executed during the year after being convicted of murder.

In April Amnesty International published a report, *Bangladesh: A summary of human rights concerns*, which described unlawful detention of political prisoners, torture, extrajudicial executions and the use of the death penalty in 1992 and 1993. The government stated that it would investigate Amnesty International's allegations. However, there was no information to indicate that the government had taken any action by the end of the year.

When an agreement to repatriate refugees to the Chittagong Hill Tracts was signed with India in June, Amnesty International expressed its concern that insufficient measures had been provided to protect the human rights of returning refugees. In October Amnesty International published two reports: *Bangladesh: Thirteen-year-old boy raped by police in custody – other children illegally detained, held in shackles or tortured*; and *Bangladesh: Taking the law in their own hands – the village salish*. Amnesty International called on the government to investigate the reported extrajudicial killings at Naniarchar.

In a written statement to the UN Working Group on Indigenous Populations in July, Amnesty International described its long-term concerns regarding killings of defenceless tribal villagers by government forces in the Chittagong Hill Tracts. In an oral statement to the UN Sub-Commission on Prevention of Discrimination and Protection of Minorities in August, Amnesty International included reference to its concerns in Bangladesh.

BARBADOS

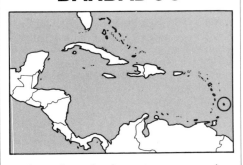

At least four death sentences were imposed but there were no executions. There were at least 19 people under sentence of death at the end of the year.

The coroner's inquest into the death of 17-year-old Ryan Jordan, who died as a result of injuries allegedly sustained while under interrogation in police custody in April 1992, had concluded by the end of the year but a decision was still pending. The procedures – started in November 1992 – were interrupted several times. Ryan Jordan's mother made submissions to the High Court about the conduct of the inquest, stating, for example, that conditions and procedures required by law during an inquest were not being observed. In March a Supreme Court judge ordered the Coroner to conduct the inquest proceedings according to law; however, according to the family's lawyer, the order had not been complied with as of September. At the end of the year, proceedings on this action were continuing in the High Court. Although the four policemen involved in the interrogation were initially suspended, they later returned to full duties.

At least four men were sentenced to death on conviction of murder. No executions were carried out; the last execution took place in 1984. The appeal of Peter Bradshaw and Denzil Roberts, who were scheduled for execution in May 1992, was dismissed by the Barbados Court of Appeal in April (see *Amnesty International Report 1993*). They appealed to the Judicial Committee of the Privy Council (JCPC) in London, the final court of appeal for Barbados, where the case was pending at the end of the year.

A decision by the JCPC in the case of two Jamaican prisoners – that execution more than five years after sentencing would constitute "inhuman or degrading punishment or other treatment" and that sentences should be commuted to life imprisonment – was applicable to three prisoners in Barbados, including Peter Bradshaw and Denzil Roberts. However, no final decision to commute their sentences had been made by the end of the year.

Amnesty International called for the commutation of death sentences and urged government authorities and legislators to abolish corporal and capital punishment.

BELARUS

Dozens of prisoners alleged that they had been ill-treated by, or with the complicity of, prison guards.

Tensions continued in parliament between those seeking greater ties with the Commonwealth of Independent States (CIS), formed after the break-up of the Soviet Union, and those wishing to pursue a different line on economic and political reform. Parliamentary Chairman and Head of State Stanislav Shushkevich lost a confidence vote in July after opposing ratification of a CIS collective security treaty, but remained in office as the session was inquorate.

Male homosexual activity remained illegal under Article 119 of the criminal code which punished such activity both between consenting adults and if committed by use of force or against a minor. According to the Ministry of Justice, 15 people were sentenced under Article 119 during the first six months of the year, but it was not revealed how many of these sentences were for adult consensual homosexual activity.

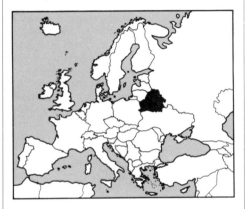

Dozens of convicted criminal prisoners, mainly from Grodno prison in the west of the country, reported that guards had beaten them or allowed them to be ill-treated. One prisoner said that guards kicked him and beat him with rubber truncheons after he refused food in protest at prison conditions. Others alleged that guards had placed them in a special cell where they faced rape by other prisoners, in an attempt to make them cooperate with the authorities.

The death penalty was abolished in July for four economic crimes. According to the Minister of Justice, a new draft criminal code under discussion in parliament proposed exempting women from the death penalty, and further reducing the number of offences carrying a possible death sentence to eight: preparing and conducting an aggressive war, terrorist acts against a representative of another state, international terrorism, genocide, premeditated murder, treason, sabotage, terrorist acts and conspiracy to seize power. No statistics were known to have been published on the application of the death penalty in 1993.

Amnesty International sought further information throughout the year on the allegations of ill-treatment in detention. Representatives from the organization visited the country in February but were refused access to Grodno prison on grounds of security. Amnesty International sought clarification on whether men engaging in adult consensual homosexual activity were among those sentenced during the year.

Amnesty International welcomed the abolition of the death penalty for economic offences, and continued to urge moves towards total abolition. The organization also called on the government to commute any pending death sentences and publish full statistics on the application of the death penalty.

BELIZE

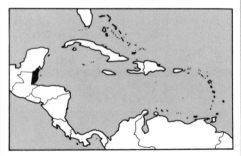

Two people were sentenced to death and three people remained on death row. One death sentence was commuted. No executions were carried out.

In June Prime Minister George Price of the People's United Party was defeated in general elections and was succeeded by Manuel Esquível of the United Democratic Party.

Alfred Codrington and Lindsbergh Logan were sentenced to death in February. An appeal on behalf of Lindsbergh Logan was dismissed outright by the Court of Appeal in September, without a hearing. He remained on death row and an application for clemency was submitted to the Advisory Council which advises the Governor General. Alfred Codrington was awaiting an appeal hearing before the Judicial Committee of the Privy Council (JCPC) in London, the final court of appeal for Belize.

Dean Edwardo Vásquez and Catalino O'Neil remained on death row, awaiting an appeal hearing before the JCPC scheduled for 1994. They had been sentenced to

72

death for murder in 1991, but were granted leave to appeal days before the scheduled execution in October 1992 of Dean Vásquez (see *Amnesty International Reports 1992* and *1993*). Ellis Taibo also remained on death row, awaiting an appeal to the JCPC. He had been convicted and sentenced to death in August 1992 for rape and murder (see *Amnesty International Report 1993*).

In February the Belize Court of Appeal reduced the previous murder conviction of Francisco Conorquie to manslaughter and commuted his death sentence to 10 years' imprisonment (see *Amnesty International Report 1993*).

In February Amnesty International appealed to the Governor General and the Prime Minister on behalf of the prisoners under sentence of death, expressing concern about the possible resumption of executions in Belize after eight years and urging that no further warrants of execution be issued. Amnesty International called for the abolition of the death penalty.

BENIN

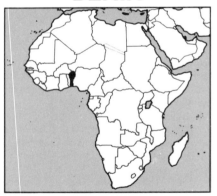

Three possible prisoners of conscience continued to be held, apparently without charge or trial, throughout 1993. A journalist was jailed, five months after being sentenced *in absentia*, apparently because he had criticized the authorities. Other possible prisoners of conscience received suspended prison sentences or were held without trial. Seven people were sentenced to death *in absentia* but there were no executions.

Three members of a farmers' union, *Migbe Aya* (We Reject Poverty), who had been arrested in December 1992, were detained throughout the year, apparently awaiting trial on criminal charges. However, they appeared to be prisoners of conscience, arrested solely because of the advice they had given to an individual wanting to lodge a complaint about an attempted armed robbery in which two gendarmes (paramilitary police officers) were implicated. For the first two weeks of their detention and perhaps for as long as two months, they were reportedly held in chains. Throughout the year they were held in the prison of Athiémé, a town in southern Benin, and were denied access to their lawyer.

As in 1992 several prison sentences were imposed in an apparent attempt to deter criticism of the authorities. Edgar Kaho, a journalist, was arrested and imprisoned in May, enforcing a one-year prison sentence imposed on him in December 1992. He had been convicted *in absentia* of libel on account of an article he had written about alleged bribery of an industrialist by a former government minister. The sentence was enforced apparently in response to another article published in Edgar Kaho's newspaper, which implied that President Nicéphore Soglo and his wife had been involved in corruption. He appeared to be a prisoner of conscience.

In August a Senegalese lawyer, Elimane Kane, was sentenced to 18 months' imprisonment and four Beninois lawyers were given suspended prison sentences after they were convicted of libel in relation to statements they had made in court. They had apparently alleged that two people, a lawyer and a Ministry of Justice adviser, had promised their client, Amadou Mohammed Cissé, an adviser to former President Mathieu Kérékou (see *Amnesty International Report 1993*), that he could go free if he agreed to pay a large sum of money. More than half the money was to be paid to the Minister himself. However, Elimane Kane, normally resident in Senegal, was not known to have been taken into custody by the end of the year.

The situation of 16 people arrested for their suspected involvement in an unsuccessful coup attempt in May 1992 (see *Amnesty International Report 1993*), remained unclear. They had been charged with offences against the security of the state. However, it appeared that some or all were among a number of prisoners who escaped from Ouidah jail in March.

Jean N'Tcha, who had been held without trial since August 1991 on charges of murder and theft in connection with his activities as a security official under the previous government (see *Amnesty International Reports 1992* and *1993*), was released on bail in April. Fousséni Seïdou Gomina, who had been arrested at the same time for similar reasons, remained held awaiting trial because he faced charges relating to the coup attempt in May 1992.

In March, seven prisoners were released on the President's orders: they included at least two people sentenced to terms of imprisonment following protests during the presidential elections in March 1991 (see *Amnesty International Reports 1992* and *1993*).

Limited progress was made in prosecuting those believed to be responsible for torture. A national commission on torture submitted its conclusions to the government in February. It had been set up in 1991 to compile information about cases of torture, primarily those reported under the government of President Mathieu Kérékou, and to establish the circumstances in which some prisoners had died. Its findings were not made public, apparently because of disagreement within the government. In April the Minister of Justice told Amnesty International that the procuracy in Cotonou was investigating at least two individual complaints which could result in the prosecution of alleged torturers, but no verdicts had been reached by the end of 1993. In December the government agreed to allocate some money to compensate torture victims.

In response to inquiries about the death in March 1992 of Gbea Orou Sianni, apparently as a result of torture (see *Amnesty International Report 1993*), the authorities said they were satisfied by a medical report which concluded that he had died of acute hypoglycaemia. However, they did not clarify whether torture had caused this medical condition.

Seven people were sentenced to death *in absentia* in May. They had escaped from prison two months previously. They were found guilty of various criminal offences, including armed robbery and possession of firearms.

Amnesty International expressed concern about the detention without trial of the three farmers, calling for them to be released or brought to trial, and urged the authorities to investigate allegations that they had been held in chains, indicating that this constituted a form of cruel, inhuman or degrading treatment.

BHUTAN

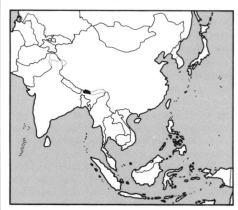

A prisoner of conscience, a former adviser to the King, was sentenced to life imprisonment in November, then pardoned but not released. Hundreds of Nepali-speaking people who had been arrested in 1993 and previous years remained in detention without charge or trial throughout the year. They included possible prisoners of conscience. The use of torture and ill-treatment by the security forces continued to be reported.

At least 10,000 Nepali-speaking people from southern Bhutan fled to Nepal, bringing the total who had fled since 1990 to 85,000. Many had left as a result of unrest due to the government policy of national integration on the basis of northern Bhutanese traditions and culture and the continuing census operations which were being conducted in the south of the country to identify Bhutanese nationals (see previous *Amnesty International Reports*). Among them were many refugees who had been classified as illegal immigrants during the census.

Some refugees said that although they had been classified as Bhutanese citizens in the census, local authorities had deliberately taken various measures to force them into exile. Some reported being threatened by local government officials and coerced into signing a migration form which stated they had agreed to accept compensation for

74

their land and leave the country willingly. Some said they had been forced to leave by the authorities because they already had relatives living in refugee camps in eastern Nepal, others because they were relatives of political prisoners being held in Bhutan. Many refugees said that their Bhutanese citizenship identity cards and other papers had been confiscated by the Bhutanese authorities before they left the country. The houses of some refugees were reportedly dismantled by order of the authorities after they had left the country.

Attacks on civilians in southern Bhutan, including incidents of armed robbery during which villagers were beaten or stabbed and sometimes killed, continued to be reported throughout the year and were attributed by the government to members of opposition groups, termed "anti-nationals".

The governments of Bhutan and Nepal reached an agreement in October that the refugees would be screened and classified into four different categories. Discussion on the mechanism for verification and what would happen to the four categories of refugees was deferred until February 1994. As the local Bhutanese authorities in the south reportedly continued to pressurize Nepali-speakers to leave the country, Bhutan's Head of State, King Jigme Singye Wangchuck, apparently sought to counter this by himself visiting villages in the south to try and dissuade the people from leaving. The King also reportedly instructed district administrators not to accept emigration applications without first checking to see whether those submitting them genuinely wished to emigrate. The King also reportedly continued to reject proposals made by some members of the National Assembly that suspected government opponents should be expelled from the country.

Tek Nath Rizal, a prisoner of conscience, was convicted in November on four out of nine charges under the National Security Act, 1992, and sentenced to life imprisonment, after a trial lasting 10 months. He had been arrested in 1989 for allegedly initiating unrest among the Nepali-speaking population in the south, after he had petitioned the King over his concerns about the 1988 census and had campaigned against the government's policy of national integration. In a royal decree issued in November, the King

pardoned Tek Nath Rizal but said he would only be released after the governments of Nepal and Bhutan had resolved the refugee problem.

Hundreds of other suspected government opponents continued to be detained without trial. Some had been held for more than two years. Deo Datta Sharma had completed more than three years in detention without trial by the end of 1993 and many of some 170 or more untried political detainees at Chemgang detention camp had been held for more than two years by the end of 1993. At least 20 other political prisoners were tried during the year but details of the charges, the proceedings and the outcome of their trials were not known.

Former political detainees reported that after the International Committee of the Red Cross first visited Chemgang detention camp in January their shackles had been removed and conditions had improved. There were new reports of torture and ill-treatment at police stations and prisons in the south but these were fewer than in previous years. In one case, a former detainee said that he had been beaten on the soles of the feet while in custody at Geylegphug police station and kept handcuffed for eight months while in detention at Lodrai Jail in Geylephug District.

There were allegations of abuses by "anti-nationals", but details were difficult to verify.

In January Amnesty International told the government that it wished to send an observer to the trial of Tek Nath Rizal, but the authorities refused to permit this. Amnesty International continued to call for his immediate and unconditional release, and for all other political prisoners to be promptly and fairly tried or else released. Amnesty International also sought information about the case of Deo Datta Sharma: in response, the government informed Amnesty International of his place of detention but did not disclose the charges against him or whether his trial had begun.

BOLIVIA

A 16-year-old boy died after allegedly being beaten in police custody. The trial of a former president and 55 co-defendants charged with offences including human rights violations ended, with sentences of

up to 30 years' imprisonment being imposed after the majority were convicted of various offences.

In August Gónzalo Sánchez de Lozada of the *Movimiento Nacional Revolucionario* (MNR), National Revolutionary Movement, succeeded Jaime Paz Zamora of the *Movimiento de la Izquierda Revolucionaria* (MIR), Revolutionary Left Movement, as President of Bolivia, at the head of a coalition government.

There were widespread strikes and demonstrations in protest at economic measures implemented by both governments, and against the new government's policy of "rationalization", which led to the dismissal of many workers from state-owned companies. Dozens of demonstrators, including trade unionists and students, were detained for short periods.

In March Javier Ramirez Melchor, a 14-year-old student, was killed during violent clashes between trade unionists, students and members of the police and the army in Potosí. He allegedly died after being hit by a tear-gas canister. Several demonstrators and members of the armed forces were injured and dozens of students were arrested and subsequently released.

Reports of ill-treatment of detainees by the police continued. In June, 16-year-old Ramiro González Torrico was arrested in Oruro by the police on suspicion of committing a mugging. He was detained at the headquarters of the *Policia Criminalística*, Criminal Investigation Police. According to his relatives, he was beaten in police custody to make him confess to the crime. A week later he was transferred to hospital where he subsequently died, reportedly as a result of head injuries. In July the President of the *Comisión de Derechos Humanos*

de la Cámara de Diputados, Human Rights Commission of the Chamber of Deputies, reportedly stated that the commission would request a thorough investigation into the incident, in order to safeguard and improve the deteriorating image of the police force. However, no such investigation had reportedly been initiated by the end of the year.

The authorities also failed to investigate cases of ill-treatment and torture of political detainees in previous years (see *Amnesty International Reports 1989* to *1993*) and allegations of extrajudicial executions in 1990 (see *Amnesty International Reports 1991* to *1993*).

The *Juicio de Responsabilidades* (responsibilities trial), in which former President Luis García Meza, his Minister of Interior and 54 co-defendants were accused of crimes including human rights violations (see *Amnesty International Reports 1985* to *1993*), concluded in the Supreme Court in April. All were tried *in absentia*, but 11 were detained for sentencing. In an unprecedented action, the Supreme Court convicted 47 of the accused: six defendants were absolved of various economic crimes, and three had died between the start of the trial in 1986 and its conclusion in 1993. Luis García Meza was sentenced *in absentia* to 30 years' imprisonment without a right to pardon and 46 others to sentences ranging from one to 30 years' imprisonment. The defendants were convicted of various crimes, including killings and torture of government opponents, during the period of military rule between July 1980 and August 1981 (see *Amnesty International Reports 1981* to *1983*). By the end of the year, only nine of those sentenced by the Supreme Court were serving their sentences.

In April Amnesty International sent an observer to the final stages of the *Juicio de Responsabilidades* (responsibilities trial).

An Amnesty International delegation which visited Bolivia in May met the Minister of Interior, Migration and Justice and expressed concern both about reported extrajudicial executions, torture and ill-treatment of prisoners since 1989 and the authorities' failure to investigate these allegations.

In November Amnesty International published a report, *Bolivia: Cases of torture and extrajudicial executions allegedly committed by the Bolivian security forces,*

76

which it submitted to the new government and urged the new authorities to ensure that all allegations of extrajudicial executions, torture and ill-treatment were fully investigated and that those responsible for such abuses were brought to justice. The organization also called on the authorities to introduce safeguards to protect all detainees from torture and ill-treatment.

BOSNIA-HERZEGOVINA

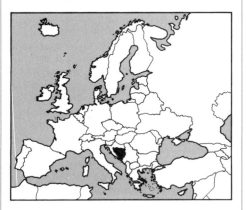

Hundreds of deliberate and arbitrary killings by all three sides in the conflict were reported. Thousands of civilians were detained; most of them were believed to be prisoners of conscience. All three sides were responsible for holding detainees, but Bosnian Croat forces appeared to hold the majority. Many detainees and prisoners of war were reportedly tortured or ill-treated. There were reports of rape and "disappearance" perpetrated by all sides. Mass expulsions of populations took place, mostly of Muslims or Croats under Bosnian Serb control and Muslims under Bosnian Croat control. Two Serbs were sentenced to death in Sarajevo after being convicted of war crimes.

The war became three-sided in the spring with the almost complete breakdown of the fragile alliance against the Bosnian Serbs between the Bosnian Croat forces – the *Hrvatsko Vijeće Obrane* (HVO), Croatian Defence Council – and the largely Muslim *Armija Bosne i Hercegovine* (*Armija BiH*), Army of Bosnia-Herzegovina. In August Mate Boban, the leader of the *Hrvatska Demokratska Zajednica* (HDZ),

Croatian Democratic Union, which is closely linked to the ruling party in Croatia, and other HDZ politicians withdrew HDZ participation from the Bosnian Government and Presidency. They declared the area they controlled, previously a self-proclaimed "community", a Republic: the *"Hrvatska Republika Herceg-Bosne"*, "Croatian Republic of Herzeg-Bosna". Bosnia's state President, Alija Izetbegović, a Muslim, who had previously been accused by nationalist Bosnian Serb and Croat politicians of representing only Muslims, was left still more closely associated with the Muslim nationality alone, as were the Bosnian Government and armed forces. Another Muslim politician, Fikret Abdić, declared an autonomous province in a pocket of territory in western Bosnia-Herzegovina. This was followed by clashes with forces loyal to President Izetbegović within the area. Radovan Karadžić, leader of the rebel Serbs, and his party, the *Srpska Demokratska Stranka* (SDS), Serbian Democratic Party, had announced a self-proclaimed *"Republika Srpska"*, "Serbian Republic", in 1992 in Bosnian territory controlled by rebel Serbs.

Both Croatia and the Federal Republic of Yugoslavia were involved politically and militarily in the war in Bosnia-Herzegovina. Both Croatian and Yugoslav army units were reported to be inside Bosnia-Herzegovina fighting alongside the HVO and Bosnian Serb army respectively.

Fierce fighting continued throughout the year on various fronts. The siege of Sarajevo by the *Vojske "Republike Srpske"* (VRS), the Army of the "Serbian Republic", persisted throughout the year. There was also intense fighting between the VRS and the *Armija BiH* around the northern rim of government-controlled territory, particularly around Brčko and Doboj. In the spring Bosnian Serb forces launched offensives against government-controlled pockets in eastern Bosnia. Fighting between the HVO and *Armija BiH* took place in central and southern Bosnia-Herzegovina. In Mostar the HVO besieged around 50,000 Muslims, mainly civilians, in the east of the town.

All sides accused the others of breaches of international humanitarian law. The complex military situation, with restricted access for international observers and the frequent reluctance of witnesses to give testimony, made it difficult to monitor human rights abuses.

The distribution of humanitarian aid, particularly to Muslims and Croats in central Bosnia, became increasingly problematic as all sides sought to use aid as an instrument of political or military tactics and hindered or prevented aid reaching civilians on the other sides.

International efforts, led by the UN and the European Union (EU), to negotiate a peace settlement based on the division of the state into a confederation of three republics continued with interruptions, but without success, throughout the year. In May the UN established an *ad hoc* international tribunal to try perpetrators of grave breaches of humanitarian law in the former Yugoslavia since 1 January 1991 (see **Working with international organizations**).

The UN Protection Force in Bosnia-Herzegovina (UNPROFOR), which had first been mandated to protect humanitarian aid distribution, was also given a mandate to protect demilitarized "safe areas" for Muslims besieged by the VRS in several areas of eastern Bosnia. There was criticism of UNPROFOR's effectiveness, including its failure to properly protect the "safe areas".

Deliberate and arbitrary killings were widespread and committed by all sides. For example, in February HVO soldiers evicted a group of people, predominantly Serbs, from a block of flats in Mostar. They were made to cross the front line to Serb positions near Stolac. HVO soldiers or military police reportedly fired at them as they crossed the front line killing two women, Elvira Savić and Draginja Borozan, and injuring an 85-year-old woman. In April Muslim soldiers, apparently paramilitaries, reportedly shot dead at least nine Croatian men, including civilians and disarmed HVO soldiers, after taking control of the village of Trusina near Konjic. Earlier in the attack two Croatian children were injured as a Muslim soldier fired indiscriminately into a room. The same day in Ahmići, near Vitez, HVO forces ambushed and shot 20 unarmed Muslim civilians who were trying to flee. Most of the Muslim houses in the village were razed, apparently with the intent of killing the occupants, and 89 bodies, mostly of elderly people, women and children, were later recovered. In July, 12 civilians who were queuing for water in the Dobrinja district of Sarajevo were killed by a shell deliberately aimed at them by Serbian forces. More than 35 Croats, mostly civilians, were killed by *Armija BiH* forces in the village of Uzdol near Vitez in September; most of them were burned in their homes. The bodies of six more Croats were found in the neighbouring village of Križ. HVO forces attacked the lightly defended Muslim village of Stupni Do near Vareš on 25 October. After the village fell, the HVO soldiers reportedly killed and mutilated the Muslim inhabitants. Three days later, UN peace-keeping forces discovered the charred and mutilated bodies of 25 Muslims, most of whom they reported to be civilians.

Although many places of detention were undeclared and many prisoners not registered by the International Committee of the Red Cross, at least 3,000 prisoners, mostly male, were known to be detained by all sides at the start of the year. They included many civilians who had not used or advocated violence and had been detained solely on account of their nationality or political or other beliefs and who had been taken into detention during 1992. Many more civilians were detained for similar reasons during the year. Although many releases took place (largely in exchanges), at the end of December the HVO and *Armija BiH* were reported to be holding 1,600 and 1,300 detainees respectively. The VRS was reported to be holding 500 detainees at the end of October. Most of the new detentions took place in the context of the Croat-Muslim conflict. The HVO carried out large-scale actions throughout the area it controlled in which Muslim families were forced out of their homes, men were frequently detained and women and children were forced to cross into Bosnian Government-controlled territory, often at gunpoint. The UN Special Rapporteur on the former Yugoslavia estimated that at the peak of these actions, in late July, around 15,000 men were being detained by the HVO. Although most were Muslims, he reported that Serbs and Roma had also been detained.

The conditions of detention in HVO detention centres often amounted to cruel, inhuman or degrading treatment and in some cases prisoners were reportedly tortured. There were allegations of ill-treatment and appalling conditions in Bosnian Government-controlled camps. Many of the detainees taken by all sides were apparently held as hostages for exchange with another side. People were also reportedly imprisoned for desertion or for attempting to avoid mobilization into the contending armed forces. Large numbers of men were known to have sought asylum abroad because of their objections to service in one or other of the armies; many may have refused on conscientious grounds. Conscientious objectors may have been among 1,000 deserters reported to have been sentenced to suspended prison sentences, or up to five years' imprisonment, by the Bosnian Serb military court in Banja Luka between January and August. As well as prosecuting men from their own national group, on occasion all sides also reportedly either forcibly mobilized men of the opposing national groups who were under their control, or made detainees undertake work close to front lines.

All sides held trials or initiated investigations against individuals for alleged "war crimes", although only defendants of an opposing national group were tried, usually in conditions which precluded the possibility of a fair trial. Individuals who had been convicted or were under investigation for alleged "war crimes" were reportedly included in exchanges.

Poor communications and the large number of individual detainees, who were often held in unacknowledged detention or exchanged a long way from where they had originally been detained, made it difficult to estimate the incidence of "disappearances". However, a number of cases were documented, such as that of a Serb, Dragan Ilić, who was taken from his home in Bosnian Croat-controlled Mostar in March by uniformed men and not seen again.

Many thousands of people were forcibly expelled from their homes during the year. Many people were frightened into leaving by fear of further human rights abuses. Among the victims were an estimated 20,000 Muslims who were forced from their houses in Bosnian Croat-controlled territory and then made to cross to Bosnian Government-controlled territory, in some cases under fire.

Tens of thousands of Muslims and Croats who remained in areas controlled by the Bosnian Serbs sought to leave amid reports of a range of human rights abuses continuing in these areas and other acts, including the destruction of important buildings such as mosques. Individuals seeking to leave faced obstacles such as having to pay large sums in foreign currency to the Bosnian Serb authorities and for visas for travel to or through Croatia.

Two Serbs, Borislav Herak and Sretko Damjanović, were sentenced to death by a Bosnian Government military court in Sarajevo in March on charges of genocide, rape and looting. The main evidence for their conviction reportedly came from Borislav Herak's testimony in which he incriminated both himself and Sretko Damjanović. There was apparently little corroborating evidence. The legality of the conviction of Borislav Herak, solely on the basis of his own confession and in the light of his mental state, was challenged by his defence lawyer. Sretko Damjanović withdrew his own confession which he claimed had been extracted under torture. A court-appointed doctor reportedly concluded that he had scars consistent with his allegations. The sentences were not reported to have been carried out by the end of the year.

Throughout the year Amnesty International appealed to all sides within Bosnia-Herzegovina and to the authorities in the Federal Republic of Yugoslavia and in Croatia to prevent human rights abuses, to investigate all reports of abuses and to ensure that perpetrators were brought to justice. It appealed for the protection of Muslims and Croats in Bosnian Serb-held areas, calling for the investigation of and the prevention of a range of abuses including deliberate and arbitrary killings. In March it appealed for investigations into the "disappearance" of around 25 men from a railway train near the Yugoslav border (see **Federal Republic of Yugoslavia** entry). In the same month it appealed for the commutation of the death penalties imposed on Borislav Herak and Sretko Damjanović. In April the organization appealed for the release of Serbian villagers detained by Croats in Raščani and for investigations into the "disappearance" of Dragan Ilić in Mostar. From April onwards it appealed on behalf of civilians in central and southern Bosnia-Herzegovina, victims of both the Bosnian Croat and Bosnian Government forces, calling for the investigation of deliberate and arbitrary killings, the release of civilian detainees and the prevention of these and other human rights abuses. In July Amnesty International wrote to Radovan Karadžić, the representative of the Bosnian Serbs, calling on him to investigate the shelling of the water queue in Sarajevo in July, to ensure that those responsible were brought to justice and to prevent the recurrence of such abuses.

In January Amnesty International published two reports: *Bosnia-Herzegovina: Rana u duši – A wound to the soul,* and *Bosnia-Herzegovina: Rape and sexual abuse by armed forces.* In May and July the organization addressed the UN on the establishment of the *ad hoc* international war crimes tribunal (see **Working with international organizations**). In July it expressed its concern about the situation of refugees from Bosnia-Herzegovina in European countries in the report, *Bosnian refugees: A continuing need for protection* (see **Croatia** entry).

BRAZIL

As in previous years hundreds of adolescents, street children and other people were killed by the police and death squads in the major cities; others "disappeared". Peasants and indigenous people continued to be extrajudicially executed or to "disappear" in rural areas and the Amazonian rain forest. There were further reports of torture and ill-treatment in police custody. Human rights workers received death threats.

By the end of the year the country was in deep political and economic crisis, with inflation running at over 35 per cent a month and widespread allegations of corruption against several leading members of Congress.

Hundreds of adolescents, street children and adults were killed by the police and death squads, which often included off-duty police officers, in Rio de Janeiro and other cities. According to official figures, 328 children and adolescents were killed

in Rio de Janeiro state alone during the first half of 1993.

In July, eight street children and young people aged between 10 and 20 were killed when hooded men fired on a group of over 50 street children sleeping rough in the vicinity of Candelária church, in the centre of Rio de Janeiro. Four boys died instantly, a fifth was killed as he ran away and two others were shot dead in nearby gardens. Another youth, Marcos Antonio Alves da Silva, died of his wounds four days later. Following a national and international outcry, three military police officers were charged with the killings. They had not stood trial by the end of the year.

In November two youths, Marcos José do Espírito Santo, aged 17, and Hemisfério Peres Ferreira, aged 16, were apparently extrajudicially executed in the town of Várzea Grande, Mato Grosso state. According to testimonies, the two youths were taken in a police car, together with two other boys, to a lake near the town where they were shot dead and their bodies thrown into the water. The two other boys, who witnessed the killings, were later released unharmed. Although a civil and a military police inquiry were opened into the killings, by the end of the year nobody had been charged with the murders and the police officers suspected of the crime continued on active duty.

In January Edméia da Silva Eugenio and a friend, Sheila da Conceição, were shot dead in broad daylight by two men in downtown Rio de Janeiro. Edméia da Silva Eugenio was the mother of Luiz Henrique da Silva, one of 11 youths abducted in July 1990 from a farm in Magé, Rio de Janeiro, allegedly with the involvement of civil and military police officers, and whose fate was unknown (see *Amnesty International Report 1991*). She had been campaigning for an investigation to locate the youths and had received repeated death threats.

In March Reinaldo Silva was extrajudicially executed by a group of over 40 uniformed military police officers who stormed the hospital in Corumbá, Mato Grosso do Sul state, and shot him in his hospital bed. He was under police guard and receiving treatment for a bullet wound sustained in a gun battle in which he had allegedly killed an off-duty police officer.

Also in March a local councillor was extrajudicially executed. Renildo José dos Santos was abducted from his home in

80

Coqueiro Sêco, Alagoas state, by a group of heavily armed men believed to be off-duty military police officers. His headless body, which bore marks of torture, was found two days later on waste ground. Renildo José dos Santos had repeatedly denounced death threats which he had been receiving since 1989. He attributed the threats to political differences with local politicians and to his homosexuality which he had publicly acknowledged.

In August, 21 people were killed when over 30 hooded and heavily armed men attacked the shanty town of Vigario Geral, Rio de Janeiro, for two hours during which they shot indiscriminately at local residents. Among the dead were seven men playing cards in a bar and eight members of a family, including a 15-year-old girl. Twenty-eight military policemen, three civil policemen and two members of the state public security department were charged with the killings but had not been brought to trial by the end of the year. The attack was reportedly committed in revenge for the killing two days earlier of four military police officers, allegedly by drug traffickers based in the shanty town.

Also in August Jorge Carelli, an employee of the state-owned Oswaldo Cruz Medical Foundation, "disappeared" after witnesses reportedly saw him being beaten and then detained by police during a raid in the shanty town of Varguinha, Rio de Janeiro. The police denied that they had detained him and his whereabouts remained unknown.

During the year some action was taken by the authorities in relation to killings in previous years. In March a military court charged 120 members of the São Paulo military police with homicide, attempted homicide and causing injuries while on active duty. The charges related to the killing of 111 prisoners in October 1992 during a disturbance at the House of Detention prison in São Paulo (see *Amnesty International Report 1993*). None of those charged had been brought to trial by the end of the year. The national and international outcry caused by the prison massacre was followed by a sharp fall in the number of people killed by the military police in São Paulo city, from an average of 114 a month in the first five months of 1992 to an average of 27 a month over the same period in 1993.

In May the courts upheld a 21-year prison sentence given to a man convicted of acting as an intermediary in the killing of lawyer and former state deputy Paulo Fontelles de Lima in June 1987 in Pará state (see *Amnesty International Report 1988*). In September and December a police investigator and a prison guard were respectively sentenced to a total of 516 years' and to 45 years' imprisonment for ordering 51 prisoners to be locked in a nearly airless punishment cell in a São Paulo prison, causing 18 deaths, in February 1989 (see *Amnesty International Report 1990*).

Peasants and indigenous people were killed in rural areas and the Amazonian rain forest; others "disappeared". The abuses continued against a background of government failure to investigate past or current violations or to take action to protect those in danger.

In January Márcia Maria Eugenio de Carvalho, a lawyer who frequently defended rural workers in labour suits against local landowners, was killed by unknown gunmen who ambushed her car near Recife, the state capital of Pernambuco. A friend travelling with her was also killed.

In February Antonio Inacio Faria and Luis Rodrigues dos Santos "disappeared" in the municipality of Conceição de Araguaia, Pará state. They were among a group of peasants who had occupied land on a local estate. They "disappeared" on 9 February shortly before the peasants and local rural union representatives were due to meet to discuss the protest. Friends who went to meet the two men at Luis Rodrigues dos Santos' hut found an unfinished meal and signs of struggle, as well as prints of boots similar to those used by the military police.

In March Diniz Bento Teixeira da Silva, a leader of the *Movimento dos Trabalhadores Sem Terra* (MST), Landless Peasants' Movement, in Campo Bonito, Paraná state, was reportedly extrajudicially executed after surrendering to military police. He had been wanted by the police for allegedly killing three military policemen.

In June Amancio Francisco Dias, president of the Rural Workers' Union of Belém de Maria, Pernambuco state, was killed in circumstances indicating that he may have been extrajudicially executed. He was reportedly shot dead in his home in Belém de Maria by two men who claimed they wanted advice on labour matters. He had allegedly received several death threats in the weeks prior to his killing. According to the Roman Catholic Church's Land Pastoral Commission, Amancio Francisco Dias was the seventh rural worker to have been assassinated in Pernambuco in 1993.

In July and August at least 16 Yanomami Indians were killed during a series of attacks by gold prospectors (*garimpeiros*) on the village of Haximu. In early July, four Yanomami men were killed and one wounded by the *garimpeiros*. Yanomami Indians subsequently killed two *garimpeiros* in separate incidents. In retaliation, on 22 or 23 July, *garimpeiros* killed 12 Yanomami women, teenage girls, children and an old man collecting fruit while the Yanomami men were away visiting another village. A police investigation revealed that the killings had occurred on the Venezuelan side of the border, but arrest warrants were issued for 19 Brazilian *garimpeiros* who had illegally invaded the Yanomami reserve. To Amnesty International's knowledge, of 16 cases of killings of Yanomami Indians recorded between 1984 and 1992 in which police investigations were actually opened, not one had resulted in a conviction.

The Assistant Attorney General of the Republic reportedly stated that his office was investigating 173 cases of rural murder involving paid gunmen. Of these, the office found that 72 cases involved military policemen and eight involved members of the civil police. In almost no cases of killings of peasants and rural leaders recorded over the years have the alleged perpetrators been detained or tried. In three trials that finally did take place – for the murder of indigenous leader Marçal de Souza Guaraní in 1983 (see *Amnesty International Report 1984*), and the 1988 murders of trade union president José Francisco Avelino and of two Macuxi Indians, Damião Mendes and Mario Davis – the accused were all acquitted.

In February Darci Alves da Silva and Darli Alves da Silva, respectively convicted of and charged with the murder of the rubber tappers' leader Francisco "Chico" Mendes (see *Amnesty International Reports 1989* to *1991*), escaped from jail in Rio Branco, Acre state. This was the latest in a number of similar escapes over the years by people imprisoned in connection with serious human rights violations.

There were new reports of torture and ill-treatment in police custody. In April in Fortaleza, Ceará state, a commission of inquiry into torture in police stations came across police officers torturing Antônio Ferreira Braga, a criminal suspect, in a police station. It also found a stock of instruments of torture. The local branch of the Brazilian Bar Association subsequently published a dossier containing 26 well-documented cases of torture, including two deaths in custody in the state. This revealed a disturbing pattern of impunity: police officers previously implicated in torture had been allowed to remain in office and the Public Ministry had failed to mount proper investigations. Following the commission of inquiry's initial findings, the local police chief and four police officers were suspended, the state Secretary of Public Security was dismissed, the Civil Police Statute was altered and a new State Security Council was set up.

In September Osório Barbosa de Barros, a rural worker, was taken to the police station of Xinguara, Pará state, to be interrogated as a witness to a murder. He alleged that during four days of questioning he was beaten, suffocated and given electric shocks. He was then released but was unable to work for nearly three weeks owing to the injuries he had sustained.

Human rights workers were harassed and threatened with death. In April Pedro Horacio Caballero, a priest who worked with street children in the Cathedral Square, São Paulo, was verbally abused, threatened and beaten by military police when he attempted to stop them beating a street child. In July sister Elsa Rosa Zotti and other Franciscan nuns who work with indigenous people in Escondido, Mato Grosso state, reportedly received death threats. The threats were believed to have been initiated by local landowners and agents of lumber companies, because of the nuns' defence of Indian rights, and the authorities made no attempt to bring those responsible to justice.

Amnesty International repeatedly expressed concern to the government about alleged extrajudicial executions, "disappearances", torture and threats against human rights workers and others.

In January Amnesty International published a report, *Brazil: 'We are the land' – Indigenous peoples' struggle for human rights*. In May the organization issued another report, *Brazil: 'Death has arrived' – Prison massacre at the Casa de Detenção, São Paulo*. The report concluded that there

82

was compelling evidence to show that military police had killed prisoners in cold blood, the vast majority of them after surrender. In June the Secretary of Justice of São Paulo visited Amnesty International's International Secretariat in London to present the state government's formal response to the report. The reply did not contest the report's contents but argued that the state government had done everything in its power to investigate the case. In September Amnesty International urged President Itamar Franco to review the entire structure of the Brazilian police forces and to end the persistent violations committed by the military police in almost all states.

Amnesty International also repeatedly urged the government to ensure the safety of child witnesses in what had become known as the "Candelária massacre" of street children in July (see above).

In an oral statement to the UN Working Group on Indigenous Populations in July, Amnesty International included reference to its concerns in Brazil.

BULGARIA

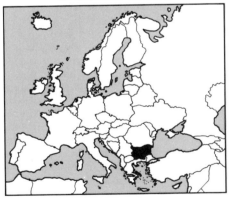

There were reports of torture and ill-treatment by the police. One man died in detention in suspicious circumstances. Two death sentences were passed but there were no executions.

In August Bulgaria ratified the 1951 Convention relating to the Status of Refugees and its 1967 Protocol. Bulgaria signed the European Convention for the Prevention of Torture and Inhuman or Degrading Treatment or Punishment in September but had not ratified it by the end of the year.

Suspected perpetrators of past human rights abuses continued to be brought to justice. In August five police officers from Razgrad were charged with illegal detention and use of force against ethnic Turks who had applied for passports to leave Bulgaria in August 1989. The trial of four former officials of Lovech labour camp charged with the killing of 14 prisoners (see *Amnesty International Report 1993*) was postponed in September following the death of one of the accused. The defendants remained at liberty.

There were reports that among approximately 6,000 men who did not report for military service during the year, there were some who had conscientious objections. Although the right to perform an alternative service is recognized by Article 59 of the Constitution, no such alternative was available in Bulgaria.

The prosecution of former Prime Minister Andrey Lukanov and 21 other former state and party officials, who were charged in August with misappropriation of state funds, appeared to be politically motivated. The trial had not begun by the end of the year. The defendants remained at liberty.

There were reports of torture and ill-treatment by the police; the victims' ethnic origin appeared to be a factor in most cases. Members of the Roma community were particularly targeted, with many being assaulted in public. In March Khristo Nedialkov Khristov, suspected of attempting to steal copper wire, was beaten with truncheons and kicked by police in front of his home in Stara Zagora. Several of his ribs were broken and he required surgery to have a part of his lung and a kidney removed.

In April, around 60 police officers attacked Roma in Novi Pazar, claiming to be in search of criminal suspects. They broke into homes and reportedly beat indiscriminately men, women and children. No official inquiry into this incident was known to have taken place. At the end of the year the government had still not disclosed the results of its investigation into a similar attack on Roma which took place in Pazardjik in June 1992 (see *Amnesty International Report 1993*).

In April dozens of ethnic Macedonians, many of them members of *Obedinena Makedonska Organizatsiya "Ilinden"*, the United Macedonian Organization "Ilinden", were beaten by the police. When they attempted peacefully to visit Rozhen Monastery, special police forces assaulted them with truncheons and rifle butts. Some who managed to escape to their cars had their windows broken, were dragged out and knocked to the ground.

One man died in detention in suspicious circumstances. Zaharie Stefanov was arrested in Dubovo in June and reportedly beaten by police in front of the railway station and in the mayor's office. The beatings continued in his home and at another house where he was taken to identify objects he had allegedly stolen. Two days later Zaharie Stefanov died; the police reportedly said he had jumped from a third-storey room in Kazanluk police station, where he was being interrogated.

One man was sentenced to death in June after being convicted of murder and another in August. In October a government official disclosed that 10 people had been sentenced to death since the introduction of a moratorium on executions in July 1990. There were no executions.

Amnesty International repeatedly urged the authorities to investigate reports of torture and ill-treatment. In May the organization published a report, *Bulgaria: Torture and ill-treatment of Roma*. In July Amnesty International urged the government of Prime Minister Lyuben Berov to take steps towards abolition of the death penalty. Amnesty International urged President Zelyu Zhelev in October to suspend all prosecutions of conscientious objectors until a law on alternative service had been adopted.

In June an investigation by the Director of National Police concluded that Khristo Nedialkov Khristov had not been ill-treated by police and that he had no injuries when released from the police station. Amnesty International questioned the composition of the investigation commission and the methods used.

BURUNDI

The newly elected President and other leading figures were brutally killed by soldiers who tried to seize power in October. This sparked off widespread intercommunal violence and political killings in which tens of thousands of people, including children, were killed and hundreds of thousands became refugees. Many of the victims were executed extrajudicially by the army. Earlier, there were arrests of suspected government opponents in the first half of the year, and others were brought to trial, some being sentenced after apparently unfair trials. However, all those still held were among some 500 political prisoners who were released as part of a general amnesty in September. Those freed also included 91 political prisoners sentenced after unfair trials in 1992. There were no executions: all death sentences were commuted under the September amnesty which also, however, gave immunity from prosecution to perpetrators of past human rights violations.

In February Burundi acceded to the UN Convention against Torture.

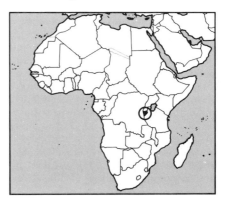

At the start of the year a multi-party electoral process began, raising hopes of an end to massive human rights violations which had been committed during 28 years of one-party military rule. However, there were violent incidents between supporters of the then ruling party, the *Union pour le progrès national* (UPRONA), Union for National Progress, and the main opposition party, the *Front pour la démocratie au Burundi* (FRODEBU), Front for Democracy in Burundi. In January the Minister of the Interior threatened to ban FRODEBU, accusing it of inciting violence and being a front for the banned *Parti pour la libération du peuple hutu* (PALIPEHUTU), Hutu People's Liberation Party.

President Pierre Buyoya, a member of the minority Tutsi ethnic group which dominates the armed forces, was defeated in presidential elections on 1 June. He had come to power in a coup in 1987. He was replaced by Melchior Ndadaye, a former

84

prisoner of conscience and the first member of the majority Hutu ethnic group to become President. National Assembly elections on 29 June were won by FRODEBU. President Ndadaye said the new government was committed to the promotion of human rights and would abolish the death penalty. In a move apparently designed to foster national unity, he appointed a Tutsi member of UPRONA as Prime Minister to head a government which included Tutsi ministers. However, there were demonstrations by Tutsi students and UPRONA supporters against the transfer of power to a Hutu-dominated government.

On 21 October the President and other senior officials were killed by soldiers who attempted to overthrow the government. Other members of the government took refuge in the French Embassy. Those responsible for the coup, Tutsi members of the army, announced the formation of a National Public Salvation Council with Hutu former minister François Ngeze as its President. However, their actions were condemned by the UN, the Organization of African Unity (OAU) and governments around the world, and received a hostile reaction from the majority Hutu population. After several days the army's commanders said that the coup had been carried out by low-ranking soldiers and asked surviving members of the government to return to power.

The attempted coup, and the murder of the President and others, sparked off a wave of intercommunal violence which engulfed the country for the following month. Tens of thousands of civilians, including children, were killed in violence between Hutu and Tutsi. Hutu attacked Tutsi and Hutu supporters of UPRONA to avenge the killing of Hutu leaders by Tutsi soldiers. Tutsi civilians killed Hutu either in self-defence or in revenge attacks for the killing of Tutsi. Members of the security forces carried out reprisal attacks on Hutu villagers or failed to intervene to stop the violence. Approximately 700,000 refugees fled to neighbouring countries, and some 250,000 people were displaced within Burundi.

Surviving members of the government called on the UN and the OAU to help them put an end to the violence, set up a commission of inquiry to establish responsibility for the coup and related human rights abuses, and bring those found responsible to justice. In December the government

headed by Prime Minister Sylvie Kinigi appointed a commission of inquiry headed by the Procurator General to investigate the human rights abuses which had occurred after the October coup attempt. However, the commission of inquiry had not started its work by the end of the year because of objections to its appointment from the opposition. The UN said it would send a team to Burundi to investigate the execution by soldiers of President Ndadaye and other government officials and to complement the work of the government's commission of inquiry, and the OAU offered to send soldiers to protect ministers, but none had been deployed by the end of the year.

No steps were known to have been taken by the military high command to identify those involved in the coup attempt and the killings and other violations linked to it. The government refused to agree to an amnesty for the killers of President Ndadaye and other senior officials and for those responsible for the coup attempt. Eight soldiers suspected of involvement in the October coup attempt were arrested in the days after the attempt. They were still held without charge or trial at the end of the year. Other soldiers suspected of having had a leading role fled the country. In December the Burundi Government demanded the extradition of two of these soldiers from Uganda.

In addition to President Ndadaye, the President and Deputy President of the National Assembly, the Minister of the Interior, the head of the security police and other officials were killed by soldiers during the coup attempt, as were the wife of a government minister and that of a National Assembly member. The President was reportedly stabbed to death with bayonets at a military barracks in Bujumbura, the capital, on 21 October. The same day, soldiers opened fire on people taking part in a peaceful demonstration in Bujumbura to protest against the attempted coup, killing about 10.

Elsewhere in the country, in the days and weeks following the coup, Hutu local government officials and supporters of the murdered President killed thousands of defenceless Tutsi civilians. For example, on 22 October a local government official in Mututa commune, Kayanza province, reportedly organized the execution of 90 Tutsi at Mungara trading centre. In reprisal for killings of Tutsi, serving and former members of the security forces attacked Hutu civilians. In some cases members of the security forces distributed arms to Tutsi civilians to use against Hutu. For instance, in Ruyigi province Tutsi students from a local secondary school, who had been armed by a Gendarmerie commander, attacked Hutu civilians at Ruyigi bishopric, killing about 70. The governor of Ruyigi province, who attempted to stop the killings, was imprisoned for a week by the local military commander.

Earlier, about 50 government opponents were arrested between January and May but none of these had been tried when the new National Assembly passed a general amnesty for all political prisoners. Most of those detained were members of FRODEBU accused of inciting violence or of involvement in killing political opponents. Seven others were alleged members of PALIPEHUTU who the authorities said were insurgents who had entered the country from neighbouring Rwanda.

On 3 July, seven army officers were arrested in connection with an alleged coup attempt and detained on the orders of the military procurator. They included Lieutenant-Colonel Sylvestre Ningaba, former President Buyoya's Principal Private Secretary. They had not been brought to trial when they were freed by other soldiers at the time of the October coup attempt.

Eight soldiers, including Major Hilère Ntakiyica, who had been arrested in connection with the alleged coup attempt in July and freed in October, were rearrested by military authorities at the end of October. They were held in Mpimba prison and accused of attempting to murder the Head of State but it remained unclear at the end of the year whether they had been formally charged.

About 500 political prisoners and detainees arrested during the previous two years were released in September, along with some 4,000 criminal prisoners, following the ratification by the National Assembly of a general amnesty. Death sentences were also commuted. Those released included about 400 prisoners who had been accused of involvement in attacks by Hutu insurgents at the end of 1991 (see *Amnesty International Report 1993*). The amnesty also applied to members of the security forces who were thereby given immunity from possible prosecution for tens of thousands of past human rights violations, including extrajudicial executions, which remained uninvestigated.

There were several trials of people who had been arrested in 1991 and 1992 in connection with political violence at the end of 1991, but some were still in progress in September when most political prisoners were released under the amnesty. Those tried included about 140 civilians whose trial began in May 1992 before the Court of Appeal in Ngozi. The prosecution reportedly failed three times to provide evidence to the court that the defendants had been involved in the violence, which had not directly affected northern Burundi where the defendants lived. In March the Court of Appeal submitted the case to the High Court in Ngozi, which subsequently convicted about 60 people who had been arrested in Kayanza province: the court ruled that they had been involved in planning the 1991 violence. They were sentenced to between five and 20 years' imprisonment. However, the impartiality of the court was in question: it was alleged that the defendants were convicted after unofficial consultation between the court and government officials. Trials were subsequently suspended and about 80 defendants remained untried in custody until their release in September.

Earlier, about 30 people were brought to trial in March before the Court of Appeal in Bujumbura. They included Alexandre Sindakira, a PALIPEHUTU leader, who denied involvement in or advocating violence. Defence lawyers alleged that most of the defendants had been tortured to make them confess (see *Amnesty International Report 1993*). The trial was adjourned and had not resumed by the time of the September amnesty, when they were released.

Other trials in connection with an alleged coup attempt in early 1992 began in March and April. The defendants included Cyprien Mbonimpa, a former Minister of Foreign Affairs, and more than 100 soldiers (see *Amnesty International Report 1993*). The soldiers were tried by court-martial: 60 were convicted and sentenced to between one and 20 years' imprisonment and the others were acquitted. Cyprien Mbonimpa appeared before the Supreme Court in April and his trial had not resumed when he was released in July. Other soldiers and civilians had been released without trial in previous months.

All prisoners sentenced to death before

86

mid-1993 were released or had their sentences commuted as a result of the general amnesty in September. No new death sentences were reported and there were no executions.

Amnesty International was greatly concerned by the mass killings sparked off by the October coup attempt and murder of the President and others. An Amnesty International delegation was in Bujumbura at the time of the coup to discuss human rights with government officials, including the problem of impunity. Both before and after the October events, Amnesty International called on the authorities to ensure that all human rights violations were fully and impartially investigated, and that those responsible for perpetrating torture, extrajudicial executions or other grave violations were brought to justice.

CAMBODIA

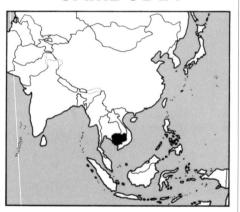

Hundreds of people were killed in political violence before elections in May, some of them victims of extrajudicial executions. At least four people "disappeared". There were new political arrests during the year. Prisoners were subject to torture or ill-treatment: at least seven were extrajudicially executed after an escape attempt. Forces of the *Partie* of Democratic Kampuchea (PDK or Khmer Rouge) committed grave human rights abuses, including deliberate and arbitrary killings.

The UN Transitional Authority in Cambodia (UNTAC) continued to register voters for elections under the terms of the Paris Peace Agreement, which was signed in 1991 by the State of Cambodia (SOC) government and the three other main political factions: the PDK; the National United Front for an Independent, Neutral, Peaceful and Co-operative Cambodia (FUNCINPEC); and the Khmer People's National Liberation Front (KPNLF) (see *Amnesty International Report 1992*). In spite of the presence of UNTAC human rights monitors, political killings, threats and intimidation were reported from almost every province, and more than 10 UNTAC personnel were killed. The PDK refused UNTAC access to areas of the country under its control, and attacked UNTAC personnel and property. In April the PDK withdrew from the Supreme National Council (SNC) and its representatives left Phnom Penh.

Elections for the 120-member constituent assembly were held in May, despite threats from PDK forces to disrupt polling. FUNCINPEC won 58 seats, while the Cambodian People's Party (CPP), which had formed the previous SOC government, won 51 seats. The PDK boycotted the elections and fielded no candidates. The CPP initially refused to accept the election result, and an attempt at secession in Cambodia's eastern provinces, led by prominent CPP members, resulted in a further wave of political violence, primarily against FUNCINPEC members and supporters. However, the secessionist movement quickly collapsed, and a national provisional government was formed. Cambodia's Head of State, Prince (later King) Norodom Sihanouk appointed his son, Prince Norodom Ranariddh, the leader of FUNCINPEC, as First Prime Minister, and Hun Sen, the leader of the CPP, as Second Prime Minister.

A new national army was formed, which launched an offensive against the forces of the PDK in August. Limited hostilities continued from that time, and hundreds of members of the PDK armed forces defected to the side of the new government. PDK forces attacked civilian targets, including trains and villages, particularly in the second half of the year.

The provisional government formed a committee which drew up a new Constitution during July and August. UNTAC's mandate came to an end in September with the promulgation of the Constitution of the Kingdom of Cambodia, and the coronation of King Sihanouk. The two Prime Ministers of the provisional government retained their posts in the new government. Under the terms of the new Constitution, the Kingdom of Cambodia recognizes and respects human rights as defined in the UN Charter, the Universal Declaration of Human Rights, and all human rights treaties and conventions. All existing laws remain in force until new laws or regulations are promulgated to replace them. The UN maintained a Human Rights Centre in Phnom Penh to continue the human rights education work started by the UNTAC Human Rights component.

More than 200 people were killed and over 330 injured in politically motivated attacks during the two months preceding the May elections. There were numerous attacks on opposition political party offices and serious acts of harassment and intimidation during this period, such as death threats and destruction of property. UNTAC identified CPP forces as responsible for at least 20 attacks on opposition party personnel which resulted in grave human rights violations, including extrajudicial executions and "disappearances". Dozens of FUNCINPEC members were extrajudicially executed by SOC police and armed forces, and at least 10 others were killed by unidentified assailants. In February FUNCINPEC reported that six of its members had been arrested by members of the Cambodian People's Armed Forces (CPAF, the SOC army) in northwest Cambodia. Investigations by UN civilian police revealed that one had been released, one had escaped, and four had been killed. In the same month, four FUNCINPEC workers, who had recently returned from refugee camps on the Thai-Cambodian border, were abducted by CPAF soldiers in Battambang province. The CPAF soldiers denied all knowledge of the incident and, by the end of the year, the four remained "disappeared".

The seven remaining known political prisoners held by the SOC were released in January. They included Ben Sophari and U Sakhun, and were all members of the Liberal Democratic Party, which at the time of their arrests in 1990 and 1991 was the political wing of the KPNLF.

Evidence of detention without charge or trial on political grounds of adults and children was found throughout the year. CPAF troops arrested 52 civilians in February, in Siem Reap province, and held them without adequate food and water. The civilians were accused of associating with the PDK. Nine of them were detained for more than four days. An UNTAC human rights officer found three secret jails, one military and two civilian, in the first four months of 1993. Two 14-year-old boys were found in PJ prison in Phnom Penh where they had been held since September 1992. Despite applications by UNTAC human rights officials, the boys were not brought to trial by the authorities.

Torture and extrajudicial execution of prisoners continued to be reported. Under special powers of arrest and prosecution granted by the UN in January, UNTAC human rights officers arrested two SOC prison officials in July on charges of torture, ill-treatment of prisoners and murder. The deputy director of Prey Veng prison was charged with murdering seven prisoners who had pleaded for mercy on their hands and knees after being recaptured by prison officials following an escape attempt in May. The seven inmates were shot in the head, neck and chest. Other escapees who were recaptured were subjected to severe torture, including beatings and strangulation. The second deputy director of Battambang prison was arrested by UNTAC in July and charged with torture of prisoners by burning, beatings and other methods. Both men were taken to the UNTAC Phnom Penh prison to await trial.

A third prisoner held by UNTAC on charges of gross human rights violations died in custody, reportedly of a heart attack. Than Theuan was a former member of the PDK armed forces and had been charged in connection with the murder of 16 ethnic Vietnamese civilians in Kompong Chhnang province in 1992. A SOC police officer charged with the murder of an opposition party member was in UNTAC custody at the end of September, after SOC authorities had refused to bring him to trial prior to the elections.

At the end of UNTAC's mandate, the three surviving prisoners remained in custody without trial, because UNTAC's Human Rights component had apparently been unable to find a competent judge to hear the cases. The new Cambodian Government agreed to take the two former prison officials into custody and to arrange for their trial. They were transferred to a Cambodian prison, and UNTAC documentation of witnesses' testimonies was passed to the Ministry of Justice. The case of the former police officer was referred directly to a court hearing by the Ministry of Justice. The judge ordered an immediate provisional release. None of the cases had

88

reached a conclusion by the end of the year.

Cruel, inhuman or degrading treatment was reported in Cambodian prisons. Seventy prisoners were discovered shackled in T-3 prison in Phnom Penh. On a routine visit to the prison in June, UNTAC human rights officials found the prisoners held in leg-irons. Shackles had previously been banned from Cambodian prisons, but were reintroduced in T-3 prison after a mass escape. Following UNTAC's visit, the Ministry for National Security agreed to have the shackles removed. One prisoner starved to death in August. Chhay Narith had been held in T-3 prison without trial for almost a year, on charges of stealing a motorcycle. He was given inadequate food and no medical care, and was only transferred to hospital at the insistence of UNTAC personnel, too late to save his life.

The PDK was responsible for grave abuses of human rights. Scores of civilians were deliberately killed in attacks by the forces of the PDK against members of the Vietnamese ethnic minority. More than 30 ethnic Vietnamese, including at least eight children, were killed in an attack on a fishing village in Siem Reap province in March. PDK soldiers attacked the village of moored houseboats, shooting into a video parlour. Later that month eight ethnic Vietnamese civilians, including three children, were killed by PDK soldiers in Kompong Chhnang province. Most of the victims were shot at close range, while two were hit with an axe or spear. Thousands of ethnic Vietnamese fled to Viet Nam. Following the May elections, the provisional government refused to allow these civilians to return to Cambodia, on the grounds that their safety could not be guaranteed. PDK attacks on ethnic Vietnamese civilians who remained in the country continued. In August, two adults were killed and eight ethnic Vietnamese children were held hostage by suspected PDK soldiers in Kompong Chhnang province. The children were released after a ransom was paid. Neither SOC nor provisional government officials apparently took any measures to protect the rights of the ethnic Vietnamese population.

In April, three Bulgarian UNTAC soldiers were shot dead by PDK forces in Kompong Speu province, and three more were injured. Three PDK soldiers had been invited to share a meal with the UN platoon. After eating, two of the PDK soldiers left the tent, and returned with 10 armed men, who fired on the Bulgarian soldiers, killing three of them. PDK forces also apprehended UNTAC personnel for short periods, following a pattern which began in 1992 (see *Amnesty International Report 1993*).

In February Amnesty International published a report, *Cambodia: Human Rights concerns, July to December 1992*. This report drew attention to human rights violations that occurred despite UNTAC's extensive operation in Cambodia, notably extrajudicial executions by the SOC government and killings by the PDK. A second report, *Cambodia: Arbitrary killings of ethnic Vietnamese*, was published in September. This drew attention to the killing of ethnic Vietnamese civilians in politically motivated attacks, most of which were attributable to the forces of the PDK. Amnesty International expressed concern that provisions for human rights protection in the new Constitution would not be effective unless the arbitrary use of police powers was prevented, and an independent and well-trained judiciary put in place. Amnesty International called on the government, the PDK and other Cambodian political parties, and the 18 signatories to the 1991 Paris Peace Agreement, to take all steps to end attacks on ethnic Vietnamese. An Amnesty International delegation visited Cambodia in July to discuss these and other concerns with the then Prince Norodom Sihanouk, representatives of the provisional government and UNTAC officials.

CAMEROON

Hundreds of government opponents were detained for short periods without charge or trial. Most were prisoners of conscience. Political detainees and criminal suspects were tortured and ill-treated; at least two people died from their injuries. In March, two people were killed and more than 20 others injured when security forces opened fire on a peaceful demonstration. There were reports of extrajudicial executions by government forces during security operations in the north of the country.

Opposition political parties who had united in a coalition, the Union for Change, continued to campaign against the government of President Paul Biya, who had narrowly defeated John Fru Ndi of the Social Democratic Front (SDF) in 1992 in presidential elections marked by widespread fraud.

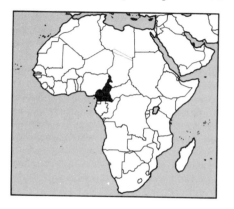

A new draft constitution was submitted to a government-appointed committee in May and a second draft was completed in June but a final draft had not been submitted to the Head of State by the end of the year. The draft constitution would restrict the powers of the President, proscribe one-party rule and envisaged that Cameroon should remain a unitary state: this led to protest from the English-speaking community, which favours a federal system of government and greater autonomy for English-speaking regions.

Dozens of people died in continued intercommunal fighting in the far north; in September leaders of the Shua Arab and Kotoko communities signed a peace agreement but fighting continued. The agreement specified that members of the security forces responsible for maintaining order in the Department of Logone and Shari should be from other parts of the country.

Critics and opponents of the government, including opposition political party leaders and journalists, were harassed and detained without charge or trial, usually for short periods but in some cases exceeding the legal limit of 72 hours in police custody before referral to a judicial authority. Most were prisoners of conscience.

In early March the Union for Change called for weekly demonstrations throughout the country urging, among other things, new presidential elections. Dozens of people were briefly detained following demonstrations in the capital, Yaoundé,

and Douala, Bafoussam and Bamenda. Over 100 supporters of the opposition *Union des forces démocratiques du Cameroun* (UFDC), Union of Cameroon Democratic Forces, were arrested on 31 March when security forces raided the party's headquarters in Yaoundé. The day before, the Minister for Communications had announced that all demonstrations involving a risk of violence were banned. Those arrested included UFDC president, Dr Victorin François Hameni Bieleu, and secretary general Dr André Kekuine. Dr Hameni Bieleu had been held briefly, together with other opposition leaders, two weeks earlier. On 1 April, a further 50 supporters of opposition parties, including the SDF, were arrested. The detainees were held in the Presidential Guard's barracks at Ekounou, outside Yaoundé. They received no food or water until 2 April and were denied visits from lawyers and families until their release on 8 April. The authorities claimed that the UFDC had been planning a violent demonstration.

On 14 October Jean-Michel Nintcheu, president of the opposition *Rassemblement pour la patrie* (RAP), Rally for the Nation, and a leading member of the Union for Change, was taken into custody by police in Douala for questioning, but subsequently escaped and went into hiding. The police held his wife, Clothilde Nintcheu, and seven other family members hostage, in an attempt to make him give himself up. They were held until 22 October.

Also in October, the leader of another party, Mboua Massock, was detained for a week without charge after the *Programme social pour la liberté et la démocratie* (PSLD), Social Program for Freedom and Democracy, published a document cataloguing grievances against the government, including its failure to pay public employees' salaries.

Although most government opponents were detained without charge or trial, Jean-Baptiste Nkouemou, a member of the opposition *Union des populations du Cameroun* (UPC), Union of Cameroonian Peoples, was charged after being held incommunicado in police custody for three weeks. Normally resident in France, he had attended the UN World Conference on Human Rights in Vienna in June as a representative of a non-governmental human rights organization based in France, the *Ligue camerounaise des droits de l'homme,*

90

Cameroon Human Rights League. Jean-Baptiste Nkouemou was arrested on 1 September on his arrival from France at Douala airport, because he was in possession of leaflets denouncing human rights violations in Cameroon. He was charged with dissemination of false information, incitement to hatred and revolt against the government but was freed when a court dismissed the case against him on 13 October.

Thirty-two supporters of the SDF and five journalists were detained overnight on 3 November after police dispersed a meeting in Yaoundé. At least 15 journalists were detained during the year. For example, in January Martin Ayaba, a journalist working for the independent *Cameroon Post*, was arrested in Douala, stripped, beaten and held for 10 hours. Pius Njawe, editor of an independent newspaper, *Le Messager*, was arrested in May following an article critical of President Biya. He was released uncharged the following day but arrested again in August, tried and convicted with two other journalists on charges relating to the publication of confidential documents; he received a six months' suspended sentence. François Borgia Marie Evembe, political columnist of *Le Messager*, was arrested by police in Yaoundé in August also because of an article critical of President Biya. He was released after four days but rearrested by police at his home the following day and held for a further week before being released uncharged. He was again arrested on 3 November.

At least nine students from Yaoundé University arrested in June were detained for almost six months without charge or trial. They were arrested because of their membership of an organization called the Students' Parliament which had opposed increases in student fees announced in January. The government said that the Students' Parliament was responsible for the death of a student at Yaoundé University in April. However, students said that he had been killed by the security forces. The Minister of Education announced that the death would be investigated but no findings had been made known by the end of the year.

At least 15 people were reported to be held illegally on the orders of a traditional ruler, known as the *lamido*, in Rey Bouba in the Department of Mayo Rey in Northern Province. Some of those detained were arrested in May while others had been held since 1992; they were reported to be supporters of opposition political parties. They were held in the private residences of the *lamido* and other local dignitaries. In May the *lamido* was reported to have ordered some 300 armed men under his control to open fire on the inhabitants of Mbang Rey following protests against the removal from office of a local chief by the *lamido*; about 10 people died and several others were wounded. Despite complaints to the government by opposition members of the National Assembly from the Department of Mayo Rey about these detentions and killings, there was no official investigation and it appeared that the *lamido* acted with the tacit approval of the authorities.

Political detainees and criminal suspects were routinely beaten following arrest. They were often stripped, held in filthy and overcrowded conditions and denied food and water. Two people were known to have died as a result of torture, but other deaths in custody may have occurred.

Louis Abondo Langwoue was arrested by gendarmes on 16 March in Diang, Eastern Province, after being accused of theft by his employer. He died four days later. Gendarmes who took his body to the Provincial Hospital in Bertoua for an autopsy claimed that he had died from poisoning. However, a senior doctor concluded that death had resulted from severe and prolonged beating. The doctor was subsequently dismissed from the hospital.

Cyprian Tanwie Ndifor, who worked at a Catholic pastoral centre, was arrested on 15 December with a friend, apparently suspected of theft. They were taken to gendarmerie headquarters in Bamenda, North-West Province. Although visited in detention on the day of their arrest, subsequent visits were refused. Three days later gendarmes admitted that Cyprian Tanwie Ndifor was dead. He had apparently died on the night of 15 December after being severely beaten.

During his detention in March, Dr Hameni Bieleu was beaten and denied medication to treat diabetes. On 1 August Peter Ndoh, a businessman, was arrested by police in Bamenda for illegal possession of firearms and taken to Douala, where he was tortured while held incommunicado in police custody. He was reported to have been beaten while suspended from a tyre and received serious injuries including a broken shoulder blade. Initially denied medical treatment, he was finally admitted to hospital at the end of August before being returned to prison. SDF supporters detained in Yaoundé in November were beaten and kicked by police; one woman subsequently required treatment in hospital. In none of these cases was any action taken by the authorities against those responsible.

Two people were killed after security forces fired on peaceful demonstrators in Bamenda in March. Gendarmes initially used tear-gas to disperse the demonstration, organized by the Union for Change, but when this failed they opened fire, killing two men and injuring more than 20 others. Prime Minister Simon Achidi Achu denounced the killings and said there would be an inquiry. A commission of inquiry, reported to have been composed entirely of government security officials, concluded that the gendarmes had fired in self-defence and no member of the security forces was prosecuted in connection with the shootings.

The security forces were reported to have arbitrarily arrested and killed members of the Shua Arab community in June during military operations ordered by the Ministry of Defence against armed bandits in the Department of Logone and Shari in the far north. There has been long-running conflict between the Kotoko community and Shua Arabs which has claimed hundreds of lives in recent years. Shua Arabs were apparently indiscriminately accused of banditry by the Kotoko. The security forces reportedly attacked several Shua Arab villages, rounding up and beating the inhabitants. At least seven men were reported to have been extrajudicially executed and another to have died as a result of torture. Sixty-two men were reported to have been arrested and held without charge in Makari before being transferred to Kousséri. They were subsequently released.

In May, 10 soldiers and gendarmes accused of extrajudicial executions of Shua Arabs in Kousséri in January 1992 were tried by a military tribunal in Yaoundé (see *Amnesty International Report 1993*). Six were convicted; two received sentences of death, the others terms of imprisonment ranging from 10 to 15 years. The other four were acquitted. Appeals against the convictions and sentences were still pending at the end of the year.

No other death sentences were known to have been passed and there were no executions.

Amnesty International called for the release of prisoners of conscience and criticized the detention of government opponents beyond the legal limit. It called for impartial investigation of all reports of torture and ill-treatment, for those responsible for such abuses to be brought to justice and for all prisoners to be safeguarded against torture or ill-treatment.

In March Amnesty International called for Dr Hameni Bieleu to be allowed medical treatment and in August it urged that Peter Ndoh be admitted to hospital for treatment of injuries sustained under torture. Amnesty International also called for thorough investigation of all killings by the security forces and for those responsible for extrajudicial executions to be brought to justice. However, there was no response from the government.

CENTRAL AFRICAN REPUBLIC

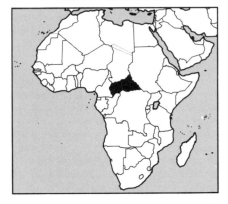

At least three people were shot dead by members of the security forces in circumstances suggesting that they may have been executed extrajudicially and others were reportedly beaten or ill-treated in custody.

There were widespread strikes and demonstrations protesting against the postponement of elections originally scheduled for October 1992 and the non-payment of

92

government employees' salaries and student grants. Persistent demands by government opponents for political change culminated in the electoral defeat of President André Kolingba when the first round of presidential elections was held in August. In the second round former prisoner of conscience Ange Patasse was elected President. The outgoing President declared a general amnesty shortly before leaving office in September. All prisoners were released, including former Head of State Jean-Bedel Bokassa (see *Amnesty International Report 1989*).

At least three people were killed by the security forces in circumstances suggesting they may have been extrajudicially executed. In April, 17-year-old Ibrahim Zouibele-Guinguissa was reportedly shot at point-blank range by a gendarme as he gathered together goods he had been selling in a market in the capital, Bangui. The market was the scene of violent clashes between gendarmes and demonstrators which left at least one other person dead and more than 30 injured.

In May Hermine Yakite, a pregnant woman on her way to hospital to give birth, was shot dead by a member of the Presidential Guard when she resisted attempts to commandeer her car. Soldiers of the Presidential Guard had staged a mutiny to demand payment of their salary arrears by surrounding the presidential palace and occupying the government-owned radio station in Bangui for several hours. In June another person was killed and two were injured when the security forces used sticks, leather whips and, reportedly, firearms to break up a banned march by women protesting against pay arrears, school closures and lack of health facilities.

None of these incidents were known to have been investigated by the government of President Kolingba or the government of President Patasse which replaced it, nor was any action taken against the soldiers responsible.

Also in June, at least 15 students were detained following a protest at the authorities' failure to pay their grants and were reported to have been severely beaten in custody. One woman student arrested with her three-month-old baby was reportedly forced to strip by male police. The students were held for four days, charged with destruction of state property and illegal imprisonment, but then released. They were not brought to trial.

The authorities did not take any further action to investigate the death in custody of Dr Claude Conjugo in 1992 (see *Amnesty International Report 1993*).

Amnesty International appealed to the Central African authorities to ensure that all members of the security forces acted in full accordance with international standards on the use of lethal force, to investigate whether extrajudicial executions had occurred and to bring to justice any soldiers or others responsible for human rights violations. The authorities did not respond.

CHAD

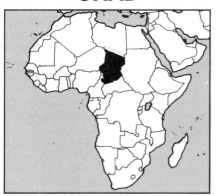

Hundreds of unarmed civilians were extrajudicially executed by government forces, some in areas affected by armed conflict and scores of others when soldiers fired automatic weapons and rockets at demonstrators. More than 220 opponents of the government were arrested and detained without trial. They included prisoners of conscience. Most detainees were held incommunicado; many were tortured or ill-treated. Several detainees "disappeared" in security force custody. Two soldiers convicted of murder in 1992 remained under sentence of death, but no executions were reported.

The government of President Idriss Déby faced repeated challenges to its authority, both from armed opposition groups and from popular protests against the state of the economy and human rights violations.

Armed conflict continued in several parts of the country between government forces and various armed opposition groups. One rebel leader, former minister Abbas Koty, who returned to Chad in August 1993 after he and the government signed a peace agreement, was shot dead in October in the capital, N'Djamena. The authorities said he was killed while resisting arrest for plotting to overthrow the government. Unofficial sources said he was extrajudicially executed. He had defected from the government in June 1992 and left the country. He had been detained for several months in Cameroon before he escaped to Libya in early 1993 (see *Amnesty International Report 1993*).

Armed clashes between government forces and the *Mouvement pour la démocratie et le développement* (MDD), Movement for Democracy and Development, continued intermittently in the western Lake Chad region. In the east of the country, armed rebels loyal to Abbas Koty carried out sporadic raids. In the south there were repeated armed clashes between government troops and rebels loyal to Moïse Ketté, a former senior official of President Déby's *Mouvement patriotique du salut* (MPS), Patriotic Movement for Salvation.

Members of armed opposition groups were reported to have carried out abuses against known or suspected government supporters. For example, in southern Chad rebels loyal to Moïse Ketté were reported to have been deliberately killed or abducted Muslim civilians from the north. The rebel action sparked off intercommunal violence in several southern towns. There were also attacks on civilians by armed gangs, some of them thought to be rebels, in the eastern prefecture of Ouaddaï. In one such attack on 4 August, about 80 members of the Ouaddaï community at Chokoyam, 100 kilometres east of Ouaddaï's capital, Abéché, were killed.

More than 800 prominent Chadians, including representatives of human rights groups and other non-governmental organizations, attended a sovereign National Conference in N'Djamena from mid-January to early April to debate Chad's political future and introduce measures to engender respect for human rights. The conference was called by various political parties and convened by the government. It elected a transitional National Assembly to supervise the government's implementation of the conference's decisions during a one-year period to precede a multi-party general election. The National Conference ended with the election of a new Prime Minister, Dr Fidel Moungar, previously Minister of Education.

The National Conference adopted a number of resolutions on human rights. It demanded the immediate release of all political prisoners and compensation for victims of human rights abuses, as well as an end to arbitrary arrests, unlawful detentions, "disappearances" and extrajudicial executions. The conference called for all members of the security forces responsible for human rights violations to be brought to justice and for commissions of inquiry to be set up to investigate such crimes and establish responsibility.

The National Conference also called on the transitional government to give greater support to the judiciary, assist non-governmental human rights groups and ratify all major human rights treaties and ensure their implementation.

Some recommendations, such as the abolition of special courts and of the security police, known as the *Centre de recherche et de coordination de renseignements*, Centre for Research and Coordination of Intelligence, were implemented in May and June. However, no political prisoners were released and the security forces continued to violate human rights with impunity. The Prime Minister, who was nominally officially responsible for the administration and management of the security forces, was in practice unable to exercise such powers.

Within months of the end of the National Conference a power struggle had developed between President Déby and Prime Minister Moungar. It culminated in November with the replacement of the Prime Minister by Delwa Kassiré Coumakoye, then Minister of Justice.

Hundreds of unarmed civilians were extrajudicially executed by the security forces. In the south of the country, where rebels loyal to Moïse Ketté were active, the security forces killed at least 300 unarmed men, women and children in the first half of the year. In January, at least 45 civilians were indiscriminately killed by members of the Republican Guard, an army unit directly responsible to President Déby. The wave of killings began on 21 January, in Goré, a town in Logone Oriental prefecture, after an unsuccessful attempt by the army to capture Moïse Ketté. Soldiers reportedly burned several villages to the ground and

94

killed entire families. Among the dead was Matthieu Ndotoloum, a Protestant pastor. In February a government commission of inquiry investigated the killings but concluded that the army was not responsible. A request by the Chairman of the National Conference that a new commission composed of government officials and National Conference representatives be sent to the area was rejected by the government without explanation.

In February four soldiers and a local pastor, Jacques Diedje, were arrested near Doba. Jacques Diedje died on 22 February as a result of beatings; the four soldiers "disappeared". On 23 February four unarmed men were gunned down by soldiers near Goré. On 16 March soldiers using heavy weaponry and rockets killed 26 people in the village of Bebou.

On 5 April a further group of at least 100 civilians was massacred in three villages in Logone Oriental prefecture. In one village soldiers separated the men from the women and children, on the pretext of carrying out a population census, then shot them. In another village soldiers shot or cut the throats of 18 people. In a third village the military surrounded people in the market and opened fire – apparently without provocation.

In mid-April the government established after the National Conference sent a new commission of inquiry to investigate reports of atrocities committed by the army since January. The commission was composed of government and security officials, including the Minister of Defence, members of independent human rights groups and journalists. The commission's official report confirmed that at least 300 extrajudicial executions had occurred. It said that local people blamed the Republican Guard for the killings but did not confirm that the unit was responsible. However, a report published by human rights groups which participated in the inquiry put most of the blame on the Republican Guard.

The commission recommended that those responsible for the killings be brought to justice and army units be replaced by the gendarmerie. However, no soldiers had been brought to justice by the end of the year, although some commanders were reportedly removed from the area.

Political violence was not confined to the south of the country. In Ouaddaï, there

were repeated reports of killings, looting and other human rights violations by the security forces, directed against members of the local Ouaddaï community.

On 8 August more than 60 demonstrators were killed by the security forces during clashes at a demonstration by members of the Ouaddaï community in N'Djamena. The demonstrators were protesting at the government's failure to protect ordinary people from killings and other abuses. Soldiers attacked the demonstrators, some of whom were armed, using automatic weapons and rockets. Some civilians not involved in the demonstration were reportedly shot in their homes.

A pattern of incommunicado detention of political detainees, none of whom were brought to trial, continued during 1993. For example, Moussa Ben Moussa, a nurse, was arrested in March in the southern town of Moundou. He was accused of links with Moïse Ketté and taken to N'Djamena, where he was held incommunicado in the presidential palace. He was freed in May without having been referred to the judicial authorities.

At least 220 people, including 30 youths aged between 14 and 17, were arrested and held for several weeks in the aftermath of the 8 August demonstration. Many were reportedly held at the gendarmerie headquarters, although a substantial number were held incommunicado at an unknown location. On 10 August, three well-known representatives of the Ouaddaï community in N'Djamena – Outhman Issa, Imam Ahmat Abaker and Mahamat Zalba – were arrested. They and others arrested appeared to be prisoners of conscience. They were released without charge or trial before the end of the month.

At least 30 civilians and soldiers accused of supporting Abbas Koty were detained in October and still held incommunicado without trial at the end of the year. Those detained included Ibrahim Kossi, a businessman, who had previously been detained for five months in 1992 after Abbas Koty defected (see *Amnesty International Report 1993*).

It was unclear whether political detainees arrested during 1992 were still held at the end of 1993. The authorities did not reveal whether suspected supporters of Abbas Koty, including Captain Amine Youssouf Oumar, were released when Abbas Koty returned to Chad (see *Amnesty*

International Report 1993).

Torture and ill-treatment of detainees, most of whom were held incommunicado, were widespread. No allegations of torture were independently investigated. Reports from former detainees and other sources indicated that most detainees were routinely beaten at the time of their arrest and during interrogation. Some were reportedly given electric shocks or subjected to a method known as *arbatachar*, where the victim's arms and legs are tied behind the back, causing extreme pain and leading to open wounds and gangrene in some cases. For example, Mahamat Saleh Issakha, a member of the Ouaddaï community, who was arrested without warrant by members of the Republican Guard on 12 July and held for 48 hours, said he had been subjected to beatings and *arbatachar*. After his release he reported that he had seen six unidentified detainees in custody. The authorities did not reveal the identities or the legal status of these detainees and they were believed to be still held incommunicado at the end of the year.

Several detainees "disappeared" in military custody. Among them were four soldiers arrested in the vicinity of Doba in February, including Lieutenant Sérayohim Doyo, and four women taken away by soldiers near Goré, also in February.

Two soldiers convicted of murder in 1992 remained under sentence of death. The court martial which convicted them, and the Special Court of Justice, both of whose procedures did not satisfy international fair trial standards, were abolished in June as recommended by the National Conference. No judicial executions or further death sentences were reported.

In January Amnesty International made a public appeal to National Conference delegates and the government to take immediate action to protect human rights. The appeal was broadcast on national television and radio and published by Chad's leading national newspaper.

In April Amnesty International published a report, *Chad: Never again? Killings continue into the 1990s*, and launched an international campaign against continuing human rights violations in Chad. The report documented violations committed since 1990 and drew attention to the failure of President Déby's government to end the brutal legacy inherited from the dictatorship of Hissein Habré. The report contained a series of recommendations to the government, urging it to take immediate steps to end three decades of grave human rights violations. It also called on foreign governments which assist Chad's security forces – particularly France – to press for an end to the killings and for public accountability.

Later in April, after learning of a new wave of killings by the army, Amnesty International published a report, *Chad: Amnesty International calls for a full inquiry into army killings in the South in 1993*. Throughout the year the organization urged the government to investigate extrajudicial executions and to bring those responsible to justice.

In April Amnesty International submitted information about its concerns in Chad for UN review under a procedure established by Economic and Social Council Resolutions 728F/1503, for consideration of communications about human rights violations.

In an oral statement to the UN Sub-Commission on Prevention of Discrimination and Protection of Minorities in August, Amnesty International included reference to its concerns in Chad.

CHILE

There were reports of torture and ill-treatment of criminal suspects by police. Two journalists and a former naval officer were briefly imprisoned. At least 10 political prisoners convicted under the former military government continued to be held. The Supreme Court continued to approve the transfer of investigations into past human rights violations to the military

96

courts; most cases remained unresolved and in only one case were convictions obtained. One prisoner on death row had his sentence commuted to life imprisonment and another recommended death sentence was also commuted to life imprisonment.

There was rising tension between the government and the military over issues relating to past human rights violations. This culminated with a military show of force at the end of May, when troops in combat uniform remained on the streets of the capital, Santiago, for several hours.

In August President Patricio Aylwin presented a draft law to Congress to speed up investigations into pending cases of human rights violations committed under the former military government. The proposal provided for the protection of the identity of those with information leading to the clarification of these cases and left in place the 1978 Amnesty Law (see *Amnesty International Report 1978*), thus allowing those responsible for past abuses to go unpunished. The bill, which lacked Congressional support and was vigorously condemned by local human rights groups, was withdrawn in September.

The second presidential elections in more than 20 years were held in December. Eduardo Frei of the Christian Democratic Party was elected President.

The *Corporación Nacional de Reparación y Reconciliación*, National Corporation for Reparation and Reconciliation, which was established in 1992 (see *Amnesty International Report 1993*), was informed of over 900 cases in which people had "disappeared" or had been killed by the security forces under the former military government. The Corporation's mandate was extended until January 1994.

The proposal to extend the scope of the death penalty introduced in January 1992 was still being considered by Congress at the end of the year.

There were several attacks by armed opponents of the government. In October a prison guard was killed, apparently by the *Frente Patriótico Manuel Rodríguez* (FPMR), Manuel Rodríguez Patriotic Front, and several people were killed in a gun battle between police and members of the *Fuerzas Rebeldes y Populares Lautaro* (FRPL), Lautaro Popular Rebel Forces.

There were at least 30 reported cases of torture and ill-treatment of criminal suspects by the police. Tania María Cordeiro Vaz was arrested with her 12-year-old daughter in March by the investigations police in Rancagua and taken to Santiago. During the first week of her 18 days in incommunicado detention, Tania Cordeiro was reportedly raped, subjected to electric shocks, beaten and kicked. Her daughter, who was held for five days, was threatened with her mother's death. Tania Cordeiro presented a formal complaint to the courts, but those allegedly responsible were not taken into custody. Eight members of the investigations police were charged in November with her illegal arrest but not her torture. At the end of the year, she remained in detention.

Hugo Bernardo Mülchi Cocio, aged 17, was also arrested in March by the investigations police in Santiago. He was reportedly forced into a vehicle, subjected to mock executions and punched in the stomach while being interrogated for six hours. No one had been charged with any offences in connection with his allegations by the end of the year.

Two journalists were held briefly as prisoners of conscience. Juan Andrés Lagos, director of *El Siglo* magazine, and Francisco Herreros, a journalist on the magazine, who had both been arrested and charged with publicly accusing the police of corruption in 1992, were rearrested in January and charged with offending the judiciary by criticizing the transfer of a case to the military courts. They were held for 15 days on the orders of the Santiago Appeals Court before being released on bail. They were still awaiting trial at the end of the year.

A former naval captain, Humberto Palamara, was arrested in March in Punta Arenas, southern Chile, following the confiscation of a book he had written on the intelligence service, and accused of failing in his military duties and of disobedience. He was released 10 days later and was awaiting trial at the end of the year.

The case against Juan Pablo Cárdenas, a director of the magazine *Análisis*, was dismissed by the Supreme Court in June. He had been accused of "offending the armed forces" in 1991 after he published a letter about the discovery of a clandestine mass grave at Pisagua containing the remains of victims of extrajudicial executions carried out under the former military government. However, at least nine other journalists continued to face legal proceedings in the military courts on charges that could lead to their imprisonment as prisoners of conscience.

Thirteen political prisoners convicted under the former military government were released. However, at least 10 others were still in prison at the end of the year, despite repeated announcements by the authorities that they intended to resolve the cases of those arrested under the former government whose trials were marred by serious irregularities.

The military courts continued to claim jurisdiction over human rights cases in civilian courts and to close cases covered by the 1978 Amnesty Law (see *Amnesty International Report 1992*).

For example, an investigation into the 1974 abduction, torture and "disappearance" of Alfonso Chanfreau Oyarce (see *Amnesty International Report 1993*) was closed by a military court in August. The Supreme Court continued to support the transfer of investigations from civilian courts to military courts.

In December the Supreme Court refused to apply the 1978 Amnesty Law to the cases of three people who had "disappeared" in 1974 and 1975, allowing further investigations. However, also in December, a special investigating judge designated by the Supreme Court to investigate the 1976 killing by the DINA of Carmelo Soria, a Spanish citizen, confirmed the application of the 1978 Amnesty Law by a military tribunal and closed the case. The Spanish authorities had protested against the transfer of the case to military jurisdiction in November and had requested the appointment of a special investigating judge.

Progress was reported in some cases of past human rights violations not covered by the 1978 Amnesty Law. Two former high-ranking officers of the disbanded *Dirección de Inteligencia Nacional* (DINA), Directorate of National Intelligence, who had been charged in 1992 with having planned the 1976 murder of Orlando Letelier (see *Amnesty International Report 1993*), were convicted by a special investigating judge in November. Manuel Contreras, former director of the DINA, was sentenced in the first instance to seven years' imprisonment and Pedro Espinoza, former deputy director, to six years. Their cases were referred to the Supreme Court on appeal.

Seventeen policemen and one civilian were charged in September with the murder of three communists in 1985 (see *Amnesty International Report 1986*). Carlos Herrera, a former agent of the disbanded *Central Nacional de Informaciones* (CNI), the state security police, was awaiting extradition from Argentina at the end of the year in connection with the killings of union leader Tucapel Jiménez in 1982 and of carpenter Juan Alegría in 1983 (see *Amnesty International Report 1993*).

The bodies of at least 24 people exhumed in 1991 in a Santiago cemetery were identified (see *Amnesty International Report 1993*). Human remains found in a clandestine grave in Cuesta Barriga, between Santiago and Valparaiso, in 1984 were identified as those of Juan Orellana Catalán, a member of *Juventudes Comunistas*, Communist Youth.

The prosecution called for the death penalty for four members of the FRPL convicted of participating in an incident in 1990 in which four police officers were killed. Sentence had not been passed by the end of the year.

Juan Domingo Salvo Zúñiga, who had been sentenced to death for murder in 1992, had his death sentence commuted to life imprisonment. A recommended death sentence against Hugo Gómez Peña, a political prisoner who had been convicted of the 1986 killing of a police officer, was also commuted to life imprisonment (see *Amnesty International Report 1992*).

Amnesty International continued to call for full investigations into past and recent human rights violations and for those responsible to be brought to justice. However, no substantive response to communications sent to the government was received.

In March Amnesty International published a report, *Chile: Torture and ill-treatment continue*. It detailed 15 cases of alleged human rights violations by the police and called for full investigations to be carried out and for the authorities to ensure that those responsible for human rights violations were brought to justice. Amnesty International also called for steps to be taken to bring an end to torture and ill-treatment by the police.

CHINA

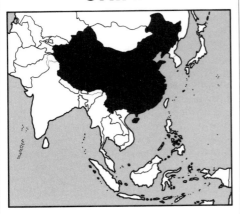

Hundreds of political activists and members of religious or ethnic groups were arrested. Scores of them, including prisoners of conscience, were held without charge or sentenced to terms of imprisonment after unfair trials. Over a dozen prisoners of conscience were released from prison, but not unconditionally. Thousands of political prisoners, including hundreds of prisoners of conscience arrested in previous years, remained imprisoned. Torture and ill-treatment of prisoners were widely reported. The death penalty continued to be used extensively.

Political opposition continued to be repressed by the authorities and the police continued to exercise extensive powers of arbitrary arrest and detention. In October a government official publicly sought to justify the prosecution of individuals for "counter-revolutionary" acts and stated that the number of convicted "counter-revolutionaries" imprisoned was over 3,300 – a figure far below the total number of political prisoners.

In September the authorities called for a "resolute" crackdown on "separatists" in Tibet. Similar statements were made about Muslim nationalists in other regions of western China. During September a large number of troops were moved into Kashgar, Xinjiang Autonomous Region, apparently in response to bomb attacks allegedly carried out by Muslim nationalists. Large-scale arrests were reportedly carried out. In October the authorities crushed protests by tens of thousands of Muslims in Xining, Qinghai province, by storming a mosque occupied by the protesters and arresting

over a dozen Islamic leaders. Arrests related to ethnic unrest were also believed to have been carried out in other areas, but few details were available.

Widespread arrests of suspected government opponents continued throughout the year. Some people were released without charge, but others remained held. Between April and June over a dozen dissidents were detained in Shanghai, including veteran pro-democracy campaigners Fu Shenqi and Zhang Xianliang. They were sentenced in July to three years of "re-education through labour", a form of administrative detention imposed without charge or trial. Both had previously spent several years in prison for writing articles advocating democracy.

Hundreds of people were detained because of their religious views or for taking part in unauthorized religious activities, including Protestants, Roman Catholics, Buddhists and Muslims. Some were released but others remained in detention without charge or trial. Among those particularly targeted were Christians in Shanxi, Henan, Shandong, Shaanxi and Anhui provinces. Many were arrested following police raids on religious meetings held in private homes. Often, they were beaten during raids or in police custody. Most were held without charge for a few days or up to several months and were freed only after paying heavy fines. Some were still held without trial at the end of the year.

Information emerged during the year about Christians imprisoned in previous years, including 37 members of a Protestant group called the Jesus Family in Shandong province, who were sentenced in 1992 to terms of imprisonment or "re-education through labour" for their peaceful religious activities.

At least 160 Tibetans were reported to have been detained in Tibet for activities in support of Tibetan independence or for monitoring human rights. Of these, 123 were known to be still detained at the end of the year, mostly held without charge or trial.

Gendun Rinchen, a tourist guide, and Lobsang Yonten, a former monk, were arrested in May shortly before the arrival in Lhasa, the capital of the Tibet Autonomous Region (TAR), of a delegation of European Community (EC) diplomats on a human rights fact-finding tour. The two men had been monitoring human rights and planned to contact the delegation. They were accused of "stealing state secrets" and engaging in "separatist activities". Both prisoners of conscience, they were believed to be held in Seitru Detention Centre in Lhasa at the end of the year.

Following the EC delegation's visit, large protests took place in Lhasa on 24 and 25 May, during which demonstrators stoned government buildings, resulting in casualties on both sides. Many Tibetans were arrested. Further arrests were reportedly carried out later when small groups of Tibetans attempted to stage peaceful protests. Among those detained were 12 nuns from Garu, near Lhasa, including Gyaltsen Pelsang, a 15-year-old novice. In May and June around 50 Tibetans were arrested in villages where a series of pro-independence protests took place. In early July hundreds of Chinese soldiers reportedly surrounded a group of villages in southern Tibet and arrested around 35 lay people and monks following pro-independence demonstrations. Later in July around 60 Tibetans were arrested in the provinces of Qinghai, Sichuan and Gansu which border the TAR, on suspicion of preparing pro-independence leaflets for distribution.

Over a dozen prisoners of conscience were freed during the year in an apparent concession to international pressure. In February a number of students jailed for their role in the 1989 protests in Beijing, such as student leaders Wang Dan and Guo Haifeng, were released on parole. Several Roman Catholic clergy and lay members were released, including Zhang Weiming and Bishop Yang Libo (see *Amnesty International Report 1993*), as well as Bishop Wang Milu (see *Amnesty International Report 1989*).

Other prisoners of conscience released on parole included three prominent dissidents who had been imprisoned for over 12 years: Wang Xizhe, who was freed in February; Xu Wenli, who was released in May; and Wei Jingsheng, who was released in September, six months before his 15-year sentence was due to expire.

Many former prisoners of conscience, however, remained under police surveillance and were liable to further punishment if they engaged in unauthorized activities. Ma Shaofang, a former student leader who had been released in mid-1992, was reportedly arrested in Beijing in April and banished to his home province of Jiangsu because he had contacts with foreign journalists.

While a few political prisoners were released, thousands of others, including hundreds of prisoners of conscience arrested after the 1989 pro-democracy protests, remained in jail. The fate of thousands of others remained unknown (see *Amnesty International Reports 1990* to *1993*).

One among the thousands who remained in jail was Jigme Sangpo, a 65-year-old Tibetan former primary school teacher, who had spent more than 23 years in jail since 1964 for supporting Tibetan independence. Wang Wanxing, who was arrested in Beijing in 1992 for unfurling a banner commemorating the June 1989 massacre (see *Amnesty International Report 1993*), remained confined in a psychiatric hospital run by the police.

Over 30 pro-democracy activists secretly detained since mid-1992 for their suspected involvement in underground dissident activities were due to go on trial at the end of the year. At least 15 of those held in Beijing were reportedly served with indictments in or around September. However, no trial was known to have taken place by the end of the year. Those held in Beijing included Kang Yuchun, a doctor detained since early June 1992. Nearly 18 months later, his parents had still not been formally notified of their son's arrest and continued to be denied permission to see or write to him.

Trials continued to fall far short of international fair trial standards. Extreme limitations were placed on the right to defence and confessions – often extracted under duress or torture – were used as evidence. Defendants had no right to call witnesses and had inadequate time and facilities to prepare a defence. In political cases, verdicts and sentences were routinely decided by the authorities before trial.

Dozens of political dissidents were believed to have been tried, although only some cases were known. Liao Jia'an, a postgraduate student at Beijing's People's University, was sentenced in August to three years' imprisonment on "counter-revolutionary" charges. Detained since June 1992, he was accused of circulating leaflets and hanging up a banner at the university campus to commemorate the 1989 massacre in Beijing. His family reportedly had difficulty finding a defence lawyer as the

Beijing judicial authorities had allegedly warned law firms in the city not to defend him. Zhang Minpeng, a democracy activist from Wuhan in Hubei province who had previously been jailed for three years for publishing an unauthorized magazine, was sentenced in August to five years' imprisonment for organizing a "counter-revolutionary" political group, the Republican Party. Twelve other members of the group were due to be tried separately, but no information was available about their trials.

Several people were also tried in secret on charges of leaking or selling "state secrets" to foreigners, although this usually referred to information that would not be considered a state secret in other countries. They included Bao Weiji, a former Foreign Ministry employee, who was sentenced in May to 10 years' imprisonment for giving "national secrets" to a foreign journalist. He was tried in secret together with several other defendants. Others were arrested on similar charges, but had not been tried by the end of the year.

Torture and ill-treatment of prisoners were frequently reported throughout the country. The most common methods cited were severe beatings, the use of electric batons and shackles, deprivation of sleep and food, and exposure to extremes of cold or heat.

In April Chinese Government representatives stated before the UN Committee against Torture that all cases of torture were "rigorously" investigated. However, few reports of investigations were made public, and in many cases no investigations were known to have taken place.

In March, during a police raid on a religious meeting in Xungyang county, Shaanxi province, a group of about 30 Christians were reportedly severely beaten. Five of them, including two women, were said to have been partly stripped, suspended by the arms and beaten until they lost consciousness. One of the men, Lai Manping, died a few days later, apparently as a result of the injuries he sustained. Despite photographic evidence of the injuries sustained, the authorities denied that the beatings had occurred.

Information came to light during the year about at least 10 people who had died as a result of torture in police custody since 1992. One of them was a villager from Beigang township, Jiangxi province, who had died under torture in March 1992.

The man was said to have been shackled with his hands tied behind his back, suspended by the arms, whipped, and repeatedly beaten and kicked until he died. No investigation into his death was known to have been initiated.

Many other cases of torture were reported, including those of several political prisoners at Hanyang prison, Hubei province, who had been brutally beaten on several occasions since their imprisonment in 1989 and who in 1993 were still being held in cruel and inhuman conditions. Their complaints were either ignored by the prison authorities or resulted in further ill-treatment.

Prison conditions were often harsh and many prisoners were reportedly seriously ill as a result. Both political and criminal prisoners were subjected to prolonged periods in solitary confinement, often resulting in physical or psychological disorders. Medical care was usually inadequate. Liu Gang, a student leader imprisoned in northeast China, was reported in April to be seriously ill owing to repeated torture and harsh prison conditions. In August the authorities denied that he had been tortured but gave no indication that the allegations of torture had been formally investigated.

A former prisoner of conscience, Han Dongfang (see *Amnesty International Report 1993*), was forcibly exiled. He was refused entry to China in August when he returned from the USA where he had received medical treatment. His passport was revoked, leaving him stateless.

The dramatic increase in the use of the death penalty which began in 1990 (see *Amnesty International Reports 1991* to *1993*) continued. The number of ·people sentenced to death for non-violent economic crimes appeared to be increasing. Many executions for alleged corruption were recorded after the authorities launched a campaign against corruption in August. At least 2,564 death sentences and 1,419 executions were recorded by Amnesty International, but the actual figures were believed to be far higher. Many prisoners were executed after summary trials. Some were publicly displayed shortly before execution at mass sentencing rallies or in parades through the streets. These "execution parades" are illegal and officials denied they took place, but photographs of such events were publicly displayed.

Throughout the year Amnesty International urged the authorities to release prisoners of conscience, ensure fair and prompt trials for other political prisoners, investigate torture allegations and safeguard prisoners from ill-treatment, and commute all death sentences. The government did not respond. In October Amnesty International wrote to the government proposing that an Amnesty International delegation should visit China to discuss human rights with government officials and others. However, the government had not responded by the end of the year.

In oral statements to the UN Commission on Human Rights in February and to its Sub-Commission on Prevention of Discrimination and Protection of Minorities in August, Amnesty International included reference to its concerns in China.

Amnesty International published several reports on China including: in April, *China: Torture and ill-treatment*; in June, *Persecution of Christians in China*; in July, *China: Victims in their thousands – the death penalty in 1992*; and in August, *China: Appeal for Gendun Rinchen*.

COLOMBIA

Many hundreds of people were extrajudicially executed by the armed forces and their paramilitary agents. Over 120 people "disappeared" after being seized by the security forces or paramilitary groups. "Death squad"-style killings of people regarded as "disposable" in urban areas continued. Over 1,000 people were tried for alleged "terrorist" offences; some were possible prisoners of conscience. Some political detainees were tortured or ill-treated. The armed forces continued to evade accountability for thousands of extrajudicial executions and "disappearances" in recent years. Armed opposition groups committed grave human rights abuses: several hundred people were held hostage and scores more were deliberately and arbitrarily killed.

In March negotiations opened between the government and the Socialist Renewal Current, a small, dissident wing of the *Ejército de Liberación Nacional* (ELN), National Liberation Army, an armed opposition group. The dialogue was interrupted in September after two of the group's negotiators were killed by the army in circumstances suggesting that they had been extrajudicially executed. In December an agreement to start a formal peace process was signed. The principal remaining guerrilla organizations, including the majority faction of the ELN, the *Fuerzas Armadas Revolucionarias de Colombia* (FARC), Revolutionary Armed Forces of Colombia, and the *Ejército Popular de Liberación* (EPL), Popular Liberation Army, maintained their campaigns of armed opposition throughout the year.

In June Congress approved a law regulating states of emergency. The law allows the security forces to carry out arrests and raids without warrant and gives the government powers to impose press censorship, restrict the right to strike, redefine crimes, increase sentences and modify penal procedures.

The state of "internal commotion" introduced in November 1992 was lifted in August. However, most of the emergency measures were extended for a further 90 days.

Many measures introduced by the government under the state of "internal commotion" were incorporated in a Public Order Bill presented to Congress for conversion into permanent legislation. The bill, which gives broad powers to the government to deal with public order issues, was passed by Congress in December.

In November Congress approved a bill designed to penalize those responsible for "disappearances" with sentences of up to 30 years' imprisonment. It had not become law by the end of the year.

Intense counter-insurgency activities continued in several areas of the country, particularly the central Magdalena Medio region and the departments of Cesar, North Santander and Meta. The armed forces and

102

paramilitary groups operating under their command or with their support continued to commit extensive human rights violations, including torture, extrajudicial executions and "disappearances".

Growing numbers of extrajudicial executions and "disappearances" were attributed to the army's counter-insurgency Mobile Brigades. In January several men from San José del Tarra, North Santander department, were detained by troops from Mobile Brigade No. 2. Most were released after a few hours in custody, during which they were tortured, but four detainees – Ramón Villegas, Gustavo Coronel, Luis Alfonso Ascanio and Wilson Quintero – were not released. The military denied having detained them. Days later, the local Mobile Brigade commander handed over to the police several bodies of men he claimed had been "killed in combat". Three were identified as Gustavo Coronel, Wilson Quintero and Luis Alfonso Ascanio. Several days later, 15-year-old Luis Ernesto Ascanio "disappeared" as he was returning home. In May his body was identified among 14 that were exhumed from the cemetery in the nearby town of Ocaña. Another of the bodies exhumed was believed to be that of Ramón Villegas.

Members of human rights organizations were again repeatedly threatened and publicly accused by senior military commanders of links with guerrilla organizations, although no evidence was provided to back the allegations. The government failed to take action to prevent or punish such accusations, which appeared clearly to place those targeted at risk of human rights violations. Members of the Magdalena Medio-based Regional Human Rights Committee (CREDHOS) were threatened by the military in July after the committee's lawyers had denounced the torture of political prisoners held by the army's *Nueva Granada* Battalion in Barrancabermeja.

In December Jesús Montoya, a human rights lawyer, was shot dead by gunmen in Cali. Jesús Montoya worked with the *Comité de Solidaridad con Presos Políticos* (CSPP), Political Prisoners' Solidarity Committee, and also represented a group of trade unionists claiming compensation for their arbitrary arrest and torture by the army in 1990. Another of the trade unionists' lawyers, Alirio de Jesús Pedraza Becerra, "disappeared" in July 1990. His whereabouts remained unknown (see

Amnesty International Reports 1991 and *1993*).

Members of legal left-wing political parties continued to be targets for political killings. José Miller Chacón, a member of the Executive Committee of the *Partido Comunista Colombiana* (PCC), Colombian Communist Party, was shot dead by unidentified men in Bogotá, the capital, in November. In July leaders of the PCC and the Patriotic Union (UP) had complained to the Attorney General about what they alleged was a military operation to murder UP and PCC leaders, including José Miller Chacón. Amnesty International knew of no investigation into the complaint.

The majority of victims of extrajudicial execution were people with no known political connections. In June troops attached to the army's V Brigade broke into the home of Marlene Varón Espinosa as she slept with her three young children and a friend. The soldiers allegedly beat Marlene Varón to death when she failed to answer questions about the whereabouts of alleged guerrillas.

Members of indigenous communities continued to be targeted by both government forces and some guerrilla organizations. In April soldiers from the army's *La Popa* Battalion pursued three armed men to the Arsario indigenous community of Maracaso in the Sierra Nevada mountains. The soldiers shot at Gregorio Nieves and three other Indians who were working in the fields, wounding Gregorio Nieves; they then shot him through the head at point-blank range. The other three Indians were interrogated and tortured by the soldiers before being released.

Paramilitary forces, declared illegal by the government in 1989, continued to commit widespread human rights violations in several areas of the country. Scores of peasant farmers were threatened with death, extrajudicially executed or "disappeared" at the hands of army and paramilitary forces in the municipalities of Carmen and San Vicente de Chucurí in the central Magdalena Medio region. In May a bus travelling between El Carmen and San Vicente de Chucurí was stopped at a road-block mounted by paramilitary forces, who seized Ramiro Pinto Ladino, a peasant farmer. His dead body was found days later.

Over 120 people "disappeared" while in the custody of the security forces or their paramilitary allies. In April Delio Vargas, a member of the UP and president of a regional human rights group, "disappeared" after being abducted from a street in Villavicencio, Meta department. A Public Ministry investigation led to the arrest of the driver of the vehicle used in the abduction, who was identified as a retired army sergeant working for an army intelligence unit in Villavicencio. He was not known to have been tried by the end of the year.

The killing of so-called "disposables" by "death squads" with links to the National Police continued in many cities and towns. In September a senior council official in Cali accused the police of murdering 12 youths in a three-month period in an attempt to undermine a council initiative to disarm and rehabilitate members of juvenile street gangs. The official subsequently received death threats.

In August posters appeared in Bogotá inviting the public, in the name of "industrialists, shopkeepers and civic organizations", to attend the funerals of "delinquents". Miguel Angel Martínez, a popular poet who lived on the streets of Bogotá, was beaten to death by police officers in September. Although a number of police agents were dismissed from service for their involvement in "social cleansing" killings, little progress was made in bringing those responsible to justice.

Anti-terrorist legislation, ostensibly introduced to combat drug-trafficking offences and insurgent forces, was increasingly used to suppress social protest. In February, 13 workers from the state-owned telecommunications company Telecom were charged with terrorist offences in connection with a strike in April 1992. In April a further three were charged. In October the workers were released on bail when the Appeals Court modified the charges of "terrorism" to "disruption of telecommunications", an offence under the ordinary penal code.

Some political detainees were tortured by the security forces. Ramón Pérez Vargas was detained in November with two other men in Cúcuta, North Santander department, by army personnel. The three men were taken to the outskirts of Cúcuta where they were interrogated and tortured by being beaten on the head and testicles and nearly drowned in an irrigation canal. One of the detainees, Gerardo Lievano García, died as a result. Military officials denied

that the three were in detention. Ramón Pérez was released without charge two days later.

In April the Procurator General reported that the Public Ministry had received 2,618 complaints of human rights violations by state agents during 1992, affecting 3,099 people. The complaints covered 74 massacres, 403 homicides and 370 reported "disappearances".

In some cases investigations led to disciplinary measures. The Procurator General's office announced in April that an army corporal, four soldiers and two civilians were under investigation for the killing of 17 people who were forced off a bus and shot dead near Los Uvos, Bolívar municipality, Cauca department, in April 1991. Four members of a counter-insurgency patrol of the José Hilario López Battalion had confessed to participating in the massacre.

However, in other cases those implicated in serious human rights violations were exonerated despite strong evidence of culpability. In July the Procurator Delegate for Human Rights dropped charges against two police officers, including the local police commander, implicated in the murder of 20 Paez Indians in Caloto, Cauca department, in December 1991. Eye-witnesses had testified that a group of approximately 18 police agents, including the commander, had carried out the killing, with a number of civilian gunmen. Rafael Barrios, a lawyer acting for the relatives of the victims, received repeated death threats (see Amnesty International Report 1993).

In at least one case, the failure of the Public Ministry to bring to justice those responsible for human rights violations led to further abuses. In April the Procurator General overturned the decision of the Procurator Delegate to the Armed Forces to seek the dismissal of three army officers, including Lieutenant Colonel Luis Felipe Becerra Bohórquez, for their part in a series of massacres in Urabá, Antioquia department, in 1988 (see Amnesty International Reports 1988, 1992 and 1993). In October troops from the Palacé Battalion under the command of Lt Colonel Becerra killed 13 peasant farmers in the community of El Bosque, municipality of Riofrío, Valle de Cauca department. Eye-witnesses said that a group of 20 armed and uniformed men tortured and shot seven members of the Ladino family, five members of the Molina family and Hugo Cedeño. The victims, whose ages ranged from 15 to 75, included five women, one of whom, Carmen Emilia Ladino, was a Gregorian nun. Lt Colonel Becerra claimed the victims were ELN guerrillas who had died in a confrontation with his troops. This version was soon discredited by judicial investigators who established that the victims were unarmed peasant farmers. In November the government announced that Lt Colonel Becerra had been discharged from the army.

Armed opposition groups were responsible for grave human rights abuses. In March the ELN deliberately killed Eustorgio Colmenares Baptista, director of *La Opinión* newspaper in Cúcuta. In a communique the ELN said it was responsible for the killing and criticized the newspaper's coverage of counter-insurgency actions. The ELN also admitted responsibility for the killing of Liberal Party Senator Dario Londoño Cardona in Medellín in November. Senator Londoño had promoted the executive's Public Order Bill in Congress. Yesid Ducuara Villabon, a leader of the Guaipá Centro Indigenous community in Coyaima, Tolima department, was shot dead by FARC guerrillas in March.

EPL guerrillas murdered Javier Cirujano Arjona, parish priest of San Jacinto in Bolívar department. The EPL said they had killed the priest for "collaborating with paramilitary groups". The priest's body was found in July. Former members of a faction of the EPL guerrilla organization which demobilized in 1991 and set up a new political group were particular targets for assassination in the Urabá region of Antioquia department, apparently as a result of conflict with the faction of the EPL which continued in armed opposition. Trade union leader Jesús Alirio Guevara was abducted and killed by EPL guerrillas in Apartadó, Urabá, in January. The EPL claimed that they killed him because he had links with civilian militia accused of a series of massacres in the area.

Amnesty International condemned abuses by armed opposition groups, including deliberate and arbitrary killings.

Amnesty International repeatedly appealed to the government to ensure full and impartial investigations into all reported extrajudicial executions and "disappearances" and torture cases and called for those responsible to be brought to justice. It continued to urge the government to dismantle paramilitary forces and to take measures to ensure that human rights monitors and others were able to carry out their legitimate activities in safety.

In oral statements to the UN Commission on Human Rights in March, to the UN Sub-Commission on the Prevention of Discrimination and the Protection of Minorities in August, and to the Sub-Commission's Working Group on Indigenous Populations in July, Amnesty International included reference to its concerns about continuing human rights violations in Colombia.

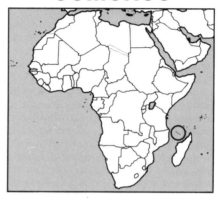

COMOROS

Opposition members of the National Assembly were detained. More than 70 soldiers arrested in 1992 remained in detention without charge or trial and some were reportedly held incommunicado. Nine people (including four *in absentia*) were sentenced to death and five others received lengthy prison terms after an unfair trial at which they were convicted of offences against state security. However, the death sentences on those in custody were commuted and prison terms on others were reduced. Some of the prisoners were subjected to harsh prison conditions and ill-treatment.

The political situation remained unstable, as the opposition-dominated National Assembly repeatedly voted down governments appointed by President Saïd Mohamed Djohar, until the President dissolved the Assembly in June and ordered new elections to take place in December.

No investigations were carried out into reports of torture and extrajudicial executions during 1992 (see *Amnesty International Report 1993*).

Two opposition members of the National Assembly, Maître El Bak and Cheikh Ali Bakar Cassim, were arrested in June after they had publicly criticized President Djohar's dissolution of the National Assembly. They were detained in the capital, Moroni, and released two days later without charge. They were prisoners of conscience. The independent local radio station which broadcast their criticisms was temporarily closed down by the authorities. The two men were arrested again in November, but released without charge on the same day, after electoral meetings by government candidates were disrupted.

Violence erupted on the island of Anjouan, after members of opposition parties were elected following the first round of legislative elections on 12 December. Ahmed Mohamed Fouad, an opposition deputy, and seven of his colleagues were arrested by members of the gendarmerie, the day after his election victory was announced. They were first held at Koki prison in Mutsamudu where some of them were allegedly ill-treated, then transferred to Moroni prison. It was unclear whether they were charged.

Two people were reportedly shot dead and secretly buried by members of the gendarmerie after rioting in Anjouan on the eve of the second round of the legislative elections on 20 December.

More than 70 soldiers were reportedly held incommunicado throughout the year, apparently without charge or trial. At least 50 were held at Moroni's Kandani military barracks; about 27 others, all members of the Presidential Guard, were held at Moroni Prison. All those held had been among dozens of members of the security forces who had been arrested in late 1992 in connection with a coup attempt in September 1992 and the mutiny that followed (see *Amnesty International Report 1993*).

Most civilians arrested in 1992 in connection with the coup attempt were reportedly freed without trial early in the year.

Sixteen people, four *in absentia*, were tried in April by the State Security Court on charges related to the 1992 coup attempt. Two former ministers, Dr M'Tara Maecha and Omar Tamou, and seven soldiers, four tried *in absentia*, were sentenced to death. The soldiers included two sons of former President Mohammed Abdallah, Lieutenant Abdallah Ahmed Cheik and Lieutenant Abderahmane

Ahmed Abdallah, both of whom were present in court. Five other defendants received prison sentences of between 10 and 20 years and two others were acquitted.

The trial was unfair: defence lawyers had limited access to the defendants and their case dossiers; the independence of the court was in question as the judges and assessors were appointed by the government for renewable one-year terms and may not have been adequately trained in law; and there was no right of appeal.

In April Dr M'Tara Maecha and Omar Tamou went on hunger-strike at Moroni Prison in protest against their sentences and being denied regular visits by their relatives, who brought them food. They gave up their hunger-strike after a week and were then transferred to hospital.

The three imprisoned soldiers under sentence of death were reportedly held in cramped, humid and poorly ventilated cells without sanitary facilities at Kandani barracks, given inadequate food and denied regular visits by their relatives and medical care. Former President Abdallah's sons were said to have been singled out for particularly harsh treatment.

In May the government commuted the death sentences on the five prisoners in custody to life imprisonment and reduced the prison sentences that had been imposed to two years with hard labour. In September a further reduction in sentences was announced, the life sentences being reduced to 20 years' imprisonment.

Amnesty International urged President Djohar to ensure that all reports of torture and ill-treatment of detainees, including the alleged ill-treatment of Hassan Arouna (see *Amnesty International Report 1993*), were thoroughly and urgently investigated, and that those responsible for such abuses were brought to justice. It called for an impartial inquiry to be initiated into alleged extrajudicial executions in October 1992.

Amnesty International also expressed concern about the prolonged incommunicado detention of those held in connection with the 1992 coup attempt and urged that they should either be brought to trial promptly and fairly or released. Following the State Security Court trial, Amnesty International appealed for the commutation of death sentences and urged that all those convicted should be given a retrial in accordance with international standards for fair trial.

CONGO

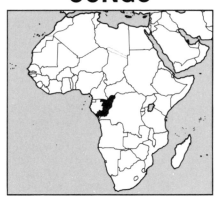

Several dozen government opponents, some of whom may have been prisoners of conscience, were detained without charge or trial for a few weeks. Some were reportedly tortured. Government opponents were reported to have been executed extrajudicially by members of the security forces. At least four people remained under sentence of death but there were no reports of executions. Armed opposition supporters captured, tortured and killed government supporters.

There was continued political instability which resulted in fighting both in the middle of the year and in November and December between government and opposition supporters. At least 160 people were killed and scores injured.

New elections for the National Assembly, which had been dissolved by President Pascal Lissouba in October 1992, took place in May and June and resulted in parties allied to the President remaining in power. However, an opposition party coalition led by Bernard Kolelas disputed the results and demanded fresh elections. When the government rejected this, opposition supporters set up barricades and road-blocks across the capital, Brazzaville, and began a campaign of civil disobedience and violent opposition to the government. Following clashes between members of different political and ethnic groups, the government declared a state of emergency in mid-July, giving wide powers of arrest to local security officials. However, in an attempt to defuse the crisis, President Lissouba asked the Supreme Court to decide whether electoral irregularities had occurred: the court ruled that the elections had been flawed. The state of emergency was lifted in August after international mediation temporarily ended violence between the government and the opposition. A second round of voting took place in October in which the government won three of the 11 seats contested.

In November, however, there was further violence after several government supporters were abducted by armed supporters of the opposition. In response, members of the security forces used automatic weapons and rockets against the opposition strongholds of Bacongo and Makélékélé, suburbs of Brazzaville. Violent clashes between government and opposition supporters persisted to the end of the year.

A general amnesty bill announced in 1992 by President Lissouba to protect the country's past leaders from prosecution for offences including human rights violations had not been submitted to the National Assembly by the end of 1993 (see *Amnesty International Report 1993*). The only reported inquiry into past human rights violations was an investigation into the killing of several demonstrators by the security forces in December 1992. The results of the inquiry were not published but, according to unofficial sources, the inquiry concluded that the security forces had been ordered by the government to open fire on the demonstrators. No action was taken against those implicated.

Several dozen opposition supporters were detained for up to a few weeks by government forces during the political disturbances in June and July. Twenty-three government opponents were freed in July, apparently uncharged, in exchange for 17 government supporters held by the opposition. Some detainees said that they had been tortured, including with electric shocks, and some that they had been made to throw the dead bodies of other detainees into the River Congo. However, no official investigation into these allegations was initiated.

Among those reportedly tortured was Jacques Koyo, a musician. He was arrested by members of the Presidential Guard and accused of acquiring arms for the opposition. He subsequently alleged that he had been taken to the Presidential Palace and tortured. He said he had been stabbed with bayonets, the tendons in his legs had been cut and that burning objects had been placed on his back. The authorities failed to take any steps in response to these allegations.

In February, two students were killed when the security forces used firearms to disperse a student demonstration in the southwestern town of Pointe-Noire. They appeared to be victims of extrajudicial executions. The students were protesting at the death in a traffic accident of a fellow student. The authorities took no action to establish whether the killings were lawful or not.

Dozens of people were reported to have been killed, some of them executed extrajudicially, by the security forces during the political violence between government and opposition supporters, yet the authorities took no measures to prevent or denounce unlawful killings, to ensure that killings by the security forces were thoroughly investigated or to establish clearly the circumstances in which the security forces could legitimately use lethal force. Among those killed was the Libyan Ambassador, who was shot dead by soldiers in June at a military road-block.

Four people convicted of criminal offences in 1989 remained under sentence of death. No new death sentences or executions were reported.

Opposition supporters who took up arms and resorted to violence were themselves responsible for abuses. In June Dr Roger Moukoumba, a World Health Organization official, and another man who was an aide to the Minister of Interior and Security, were shot dead, reportedly by members of the armed opposition. Fortified houses of opposition leaders were used as prisons to hold abducted government supporters who were allegedly subjected to torture. Some government supporters freed by the opposition at the end of July claimed that they had been held at the house of an opposition leader where they were subjected to beatings and torture, including cigarette burns. As many as 14 others held by the opposition were reportedly severely tortured and "disappeared".

Amnesty International appealed to the government to investigate reports of extrajudicial executions and other human rights violations, to bring to justice those found responsible for such violations, and to issue clear guidelines to all members of the security forces regarding the use of lethal force, in conformity with relevant UN standards. The government failed to respond. Amnesty International also appealed to the opposition to abide by international humanitarian standards.

CÔTE D'IVOIRE

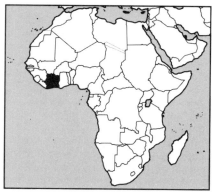

More than 40 students were arrested and sentenced to terms of imprisonment, and a teacher was held incommunicado for over 40 days: all were possible prisoners of conscience. At least 100 prisoners died in the main prison in Abidjan as a result of extremely harsh conditions. Four people were sentenced to death but there were no executions.

In December Henri Konan Bédié, President of the National Assembly, became President of the Republic following the death of Félix Houphouët-Boigny. During the first half of the year the government faced pressure, including demonstrations and public meetings, from students and teachers' trade unions after it changed the qualifications necessary to enter university. In August more than 20 students went on hunger-strike for 15 days. The protest ended when the government promised to satisfy most of the students' demands.

On 19 April more than 40 students were arrested following a public meeting called by the *Fédération estudiantine et scolaire de Côte d'Ivoire* (FESCI), Ivorian Federation of Students and School Pupils, at the University of Cocody in the capital, Abidjan. The meeting started peacefully but violence erupted when the security forces intervened to break up the meeting, which they claimed had been banned. Student leaders stated that they had obtained permission to hold the meeting on the campus. Cars and other property were damaged during the violence. Although the perpetrators of the damage were not clearly identified, 44 students were arrested shortly after the protest. On 9 May Angenor Gballou, FESCI's Information Secretary, was arrested on the grounds that he had organized the 19 April meeting.

The 45 students were charged with assault and wilful destruction of public property and vehicles. They were the first people to be charged under a new law introduced in 1992 which provides for the prosecution of anyone who calls or leads a gathering that becomes violent, irrespective of whether they are personally responsible for inciting or perpetrating violence. The use of similar legislation in the past has led to the conviction of prisoners of conscience (see *Amnesty International Report 1993*).

The 45 students were provisionally released on 22 May and tried in September. Only one received a court summons, however, and was in court; the 44 others were tried *in absentia*. The 44 were sentenced to heavy fines and a term of imprisonment which corresponded exactly to the time they had already spent in prison although the prosecution did not establish individual responsibility for specific acts of violence. They subsequently lodged an appeal. The one student who was present in court was acquitted for lack of evidence. It appeared that the controversial new law of shared responsibility was not invoked.

In a related case, a teacher arrested in late April was detained incommunicado for 43 days although the maximum period allowed by law is a total of no more than 96 hours. Koné Bakary, an activist of the *Syndicat national des Enseignants du Secondaire de Côte d'Ivoire*, National Union of Secondary School Teachers, was held at the *Direction de la sécurité territoriale* (DST), the security headquarters in Abidjan, apparently because he was suspected of helping to organize the 19 April students' meeting. A prisoner of conscience, he was eventually referred to an examining magistrate who decided that he had no case to answer and ordered his immediate release. Koné Bakary was reportedly harassed after his release by members of the security forces.

Sylvain Gokou, another student, may also have been a prisoner of conscience although he was arrested in July at a meeting on the Cocody University campus in Abidjan which became violent. There was no evidence to suggest that he was involved in the violence. He was sentenced to two months' imprisonment for allegedly resisting arrest but provisionally released in early September.

As in past years, a large number of common law prisoners held at the *Maison d'Arrêt et de Correction d'Abidjan* ("MACA"), the main prison in Abidjan, died as a result of extremely harsh prison conditions. During the year, at least 100 prisoners died apparently as a result of gross medical neglect, poor hygiene and malnutrition. An average of about 3,500 prisoners were held in the jail, around a third of whom had been awaiting trial for long periods.

In June Bakary Sidibé was sentenced to death after being convicted of murder; three Liberian refugees were sentenced to death after being convicted of cannibalism. No executions were carried out.

Amnesty International expressed concern to the government about the arrest in April of students who had not used or advocated violence and called for the immediate and unconditional release of all prisoners of conscience. It once again expressed concern that if the authorities were to hold peaceful demonstrators responsible before the law for the violent actions of others, they would effectively be violating the right to freedom of association. No response was received from the government.

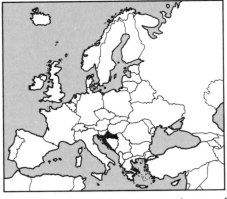

CROATIA

One government critic was a prisoner of conscience and two others who were convicted for exercising their right to freedom of expression appeared likely to be prisoners of conscience if imprisoned. Trials or investigations of Serbs and others accused of "undermining the territorial unity of Croatia by force" or similar offences continued. Some may not have received fair trials. A number of people were reportedly ill-treated by civilian or military police. Muslim refugees were forcibly returned to Bosnia-Herzegovina. A number of Serbian civilians may have been extrajudicially executed by Croatian soldiers. There were reports of human rights abuses by rebel Serbs, including deliberate and arbitrary killings, in the areas which they occupied.

In January and September the Croatian Army launched offensives to recover small areas of Croatian territory occupied by rebel Serbs in or adjoining one of the UN Protected Areas (UNPAs), known as Sector South. Attacks on targets spread over larger areas followed. In the January offensive the populations of several predominantly Serb villages were displaced. This was followed by the expulsion by rebel Serbs of some of the remaining Croats in Sector South. The UN Security Council called upon Croatia to withdraw its forces from the UNPA.

Little progress was made towards implementing the UN peace plan agreed when a cease-fire came into force in January 1992. Approximately 250,000 people remained displaced within Croatia and few were able to return to their home areas during the year. During the fighting in January, rebel Serb forces took back some of their heavy armaments which they had handed over to the UN under the disarmament provisions of the peace plan.

The Croatian Government stated that around 13,000 people were missing as a result of the 1991 war. New refugees, both Muslims and Croats, continued to arrive from all areas of Bosnia-Herzegovina.

The mandate of the UN peace-keeping force, UNPROFOR (UN Protection Force), was renewed three times. The Croatian Government threatened to veto the extensions. On each occasion it expressed dissatisfaction with the lack of progress in implementing the peace plan and argued that UNPROFOR should be given greater powers to enforce the plan.

In May the UN Security Council established an *ad hoc* international tribunal to try perpetrators of serious violations of humanitarian law – war crimes – in the former Yugoslavia, including those committed in Croatia since 1 January 1991 (see **Working with international organizations**). In response, the Government of Croatia established a commission to collect evidence for the tribunal.

In November exhumations of two mass graves in UNPAs began. The exhumations were initiated by a UN Commission of Experts to provide possible evidence for the war crimes tribunal. Rebel Serb authorities in the UNPAs were reportedly willing to cooperate with the Commission in the investigation of crimes committed against Serbs, but prevented the exhumation of a grave believed to contain Croatian victims.

Political opponents of the government of President Franjo Tudjman and minority groups such as Serbs and Muslims continued to face harassment and ill-treatment initiated or apparently tolerated by the authorities. For example, tenants of flats formerly owned by the Yugoslav National Army (JNA) were evicted by soldiers or military police, sometimes violently, in favour of members of the Croatian Army.

In November leaders of the ultra-right *Hrvatska Stranka Prava*, the Party of Rights, which had formed a paramilitary wing which was later incorporated into the Croatian Army, were acquitted of charges of "violently destroying the constitutional order" and terrorism.

There was compelling evidence of direct Croatian Army involvement in Bosnia-Herzegovina, including sightings of Croatian Army tanks by international observers. President Tudjman, during a press conference in September, admitted aiding the *Hrvatsko Vijeće Obrane*, Croatian Defence Council, in Bosnia-Herzegovina.

Three people charged with "spreading false information" appeared likely to become prisoners of conscience if convicted and imprisoned. Two were prosecuted a second time for the same offence, in violation of international law. In June Jasna Tkalec, a journalist, was sentenced to three months' imprisonment under Article 197 of the Criminal Code for writing an article in the publication *Nokat* in 1991, in which she accused the Croatian authorities of supporting *ustaša* (the Second World War Croatian fascist movement) and neo-fascist aims. At the end of the year she remained free pending appeal. In September Stjepan Kralj was imprisoned for 15 days under Article 16 of the Law on Petty Offences against Public Law and Order, after accusing a government minister of corruption in March. The real reason for his prosecution may have been other allegations he had

110

made, which were included in a later indictment under Article 197, that the same minister had protected the assassins of a Serbian trade unionist. In November the trial of Stjepan Kralj on criminal charges was postponed owing to the defendant's ill-health. Milovan Škorić, a Serb, was sentenced to 60 days' imprisonment in June under Article 16 after alleging that Serbs were being held in detention camps in Croatia. He had not served the sentence by the end of the year. In September he was sentenced under Article 197 to six months' imprisonment, suspended for two years, for the same act.

Serbs and Croats returning to Croatia were subject to investigation by civilian or military police when they were suspected of having been in Serbia, Montenegro or rebel Serb-controlled areas of Croatia. In some cases these investigations resulted in criminal charges. In March Nenad Mišković, a Serb who had returned to his family in Zagreb from Belgrade in December 1992, was sentenced to 12 years' imprisonment after being convicted of war crimes committed in 1991. He may not have received a fair trial. In July he was exchanged against his will for a prisoner held by the Government of the Federal Republic of Yugoslavia. A Croatian woman, Milica Ćuk, was sentenced to 10 years' imprisonment by a military court in Osijek in April for "armed rebellion against the Republic of Croatia". Some months after returning from Serbia to Croatia she was accused of having pointed out individuals who had been seized by Serbian paramilitaries and who had "disappeared" when the JNA took control of Vukovar in November 1991. The weak and contradictory evidence which was presented raised concerns about the fairness of her trial.

The civil and military police were both reported to have ill-treated people in their custody, either following arrest or while evicting tenants from ex-JNA flats. A number of Muslims from Bosnia-Herzegovina who were arrested for allegedly having invalid residence or identity documents, or for offences which might be used to justify their deportation, were reportedly beaten in custody.

In September UNPROFOR soldiers discovered the charred and dismembered corpses of more than 50 Serbs killed during the Croatian offensive in the villages of Medak, Divoselo, Čitluk and Počitelj. At least nine of these were believed to have been extrajudicially executed. The Croatian authorities reported that their investigation found that all those killed were combatants.

In the areas under the control of rebel Serbs, especially UNPAs, Croats and other non-Serbs were the target of politically motivated killings and other abuses. Information was difficult to verify, as witnesses were generally unwilling to speak and reports were sometimes contradictory. The information that was available indicated that the perpetrators were mostly uniformed local Serbs. Local Serbian police reportedly failed to provide protection and UNPROFOR soldiers and civilian police were also unable to effectively deter such abuses and were denied access to some areas. A wave of incidents followed the Croatian offensive in January. For instance, on 22 January, the day following the start of the Croatian offensive, neighbours discovered the bodies of Ante and Anela Vuksan, both aged about 80, in their bedroom in the village of Šopot. Reportedly both had been shot in their bed from inside the room. No one had seen the perpetrators. A number of similar killings were reported to have occurred in the areas of Benkovac and Obrovac between January and March.

Rebel Serbs were believed to have held Muslim and Croat prisoners in Glina prison. Some may have been civilians held solely on account of their ethnic or national group after being detained by rebel Serbs in Bosnia-Herzegovina in 1992 or 1993.

There were continuing reports that the Croatian authorities were forcibly returning male Bosnian refugees of military age to Bosnia-Herzegovina despite repeated objections by the office of the UN High Commissioner for Refugees (UNHCR) in Zagreb. Also, Bosnians in Croatia who did not have proper documentation were arrested and threatened with forcible return to Bosnia-Herzegovina; in most known cases the returns were averted after the intervention of the UNHCR. Although the Croatian authorities insisted that only those Bosnians "illegally" in Croatia were arrested, they did not acknowledge the difficulties many Bosnians faced in registering as refugees. Muslim refugees fleeing Bosnia-Herzegovina continued to face difficulties in entering Croatia. They were required to obtain entry or transit visas in advance which were only issued on the production of letters from guarantors in Croatia or a third country. The visas explicitly excluded any possibility that the person could apply for protection as a refugee in Croatia. In contrast, it appeared that Bosnian Croats, such as a group of 4,000 who fled Muslim-Croat fighting in Travnik in June, were allowed to enter Croatia without such advance clearance.

In July Amnesty International published a report, *Bosnian refugees: A continuing need for protection in European countries*, in which it expressed concern about the policies of the Croatian Government and those of other European countries towards Muslim refugees from Bosnia-Herzegovina. In October, as part of its worldwide campaign against "disappearances" and political killings, the organization called for the establishment of a UN commission to investigate "disappearances" in the former Yugoslavia. In September Amnesty International appealed to the Croatian authorities for the immediate and unconditional release of Stjepan Kralj. The organization also appealed to President Tudjman and the Croatian Defence Minister to stop Croatian forces committing human rights abuses in Bosnia-Herzegovina. Amnesty International called on all parties to the conflict to take action to investigate and prevent "disappearances" and extrajudicial executions.

CUBA

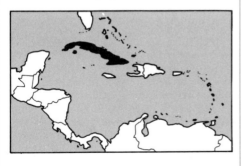

At least 500 prisoners of conscience were believed to be serving prison terms. Scores of non-violent government opponents were arrested and harassed. Detention and trial procedures in all political cases fell far short of international standards. Reports were received that prisoners were subjected to ill-treatment, on occasion amounting to torture, leading to at least two deaths in custody. Four people died in circumstances suggesting they may have been victims of extrajudicial executions. At least one man may have been executed and at least six others were known to be appealing against death sentences.

The government of President Fidel Castro was faced with serious economic problems resulting from the political changes in the former Soviet Union and Eastern European countries, formerly its principal trading partners, compounded by the US trade embargo in place since 1962. It initiated economic reforms but resisted pressure, mainly from abroad, to alter its political system. In February the first direct elections for representatives of the country's parliament, the *Asamblea Nacional de Poder Popular*, National Assembly of People's Power, took place. The *Partido Comunista de Cuba*, Communist Party of Cuba, continued to be the only legal party, although non-party members were permitted to stand for election as individuals.

In August the authorities blamed "counter-revolutionaries" for a wave of vandalism and anti-government protests during prolonged electricity black-outs, particularly in Havana, the capital, and vowed to crack down heavily on those found guilty of serious economic and terrorist offences.

The government insisted that limitations on civil liberties had to be maintained as long as the US Government continued its hostile policy and Cuba remained the target of armed opposition groups. In November the mainly US-based armed opposition group, Alpha 66, threatened to kidnap foreigners visiting Cuba.

Independent human rights monitoring was again severely limited. No independent human rights monitors were known to have been allowed to visit the country officially. The government continued to refuse to cooperate in any way with the UN Special Rapporteur on Cuba, arguing that Cuba had been unfairly singled out for scrutiny by the UN Commission on Human Rights as the result of a US-led campaign against it.

It was therefore difficult to estimate the number of prisoners held either as prisoners of conscience or for other offences of a political nature. However, at least 500 prisoners of conscience were believed to be held, some serving sentences as long as 13, or in one case 15, years' imprisonment.

112

Most prisoners were members of unofficial political, trade union or human rights groups although scores, possibly hundreds, of others were believed to be held for trying to leave the country illegally.

Peaceful political and human rights activists were frequently subjected to intimidation by the security forces and sometimes also by members of the *Destacamentos Populares de Respuesta Rápida*, People's Rapid Response Detachments, set up in 1991 to counter signs of dissent (see *Amnesty International Reports 1992* and *1993*). Dozens of people reported being regularly taken in for questioning about their activities and warned that if they did not desist or leave the country, they would be arrested. In September Rolando Roque Malherbe and Félix Bonne Carcacés of the unofficial *Corriente Cívica Cubana*, Cuban Civic Current, were detained for several days in connection with a party organized by the group at Rolando Roque's house to which foreign diplomats and dissidents were invited. Officials and pro-government crowds gathered outside to try to prevent the event from taking place.

Arrests of prisoners of conscience took place throughout the year. They included Joel Mesa Morales, Vice-President of the unofficial *Comisión Nacional de Derechos Humanos "José Martí"*, "José Martí" National Human Rights Commission, who was arrested in January. He was brought to trial in September, together with the group's president, Amador Blanco Hernández, who had been arrested on 10 December 1992, on a charge of "enemy propaganda". They were accused of "carrying out a propaganda campaign to discredit the Cuban Revolution by compiling numerous false reports" that were sent abroad to be transmitted back to Cuba by "subversive" US-based radio stations. They were convicted: Amador Blanco was sentenced to eight years' imprisonment and Joel Mesa to seven years. Prisoner of conscience Rafael Gutiérrez Santos, president of the unofficial *Unión Sindical de Trabajadores de Cuba* (USTC), Workers' Trade Union of Cuba, was arrested in Havana in February and held at the headquarters of the *Departamento de Seguridad del Estado* (DSE), Department of State Security, without access to a lawyer. He was released in August, apparently for health reasons, but still faced trial on charges of "acts against state security". No further action had been taken against him by the end of the year.

In August teacher Domiciano Torres Roca, vice-president of the unofficial *Partido Cívico Democrático*, Civic Democratic Party, was assaulted by police on a Havana street and arrested. His family were later informed that he was to be transferred to prison to await trial for "enemy propaganda". Reports were subsequently received that, before being sent to El Pitirre Prison, he had been transferred to the Havana Psychiatric Hospital.

Between August and November, apparently in response to a crime wave, particularly in Havana, some 2,500 people were reportedly imprisoned for "dangerousness" (*"peligrosidad"*). Defendants were sentenced after summary hearings to prison terms of up to four years if they were considered to have behaved in an anti-social fashion or it was feared that they had a "special proclivity" to commit crime. Such "anti-social behaviour" ranged from refusing to work to being drunk or getting involved in fights. It was feared that in some cases this procedure was being used as a pretext for imprisoning political opponents of the government, with at least six political activists reportedly imprisoned under it. Luis Felipe Lorens, president of the unofficial *Organización Juvenil Martiana*, Martí Youth Organization, was reportedly arrested in September after going to a Havana police station to inquire about his brother who had been detained for "dangerousness". He himself was tried two days later for "dangerousness" and sentenced to four years' imprisonment, apparently for not working.

Hundreds of people tried to leave the country illegally by sea. While some had been unable to leave the country legally because they had been unable to obtain visas to enter other countries, others had been refused exit visas by the Cuban authorities. Some 3,600 reached the USA by sea while others reached other nearby countries, but an unknown number died in the attempt and still others were caught by Cuban coastguards. Writer Norberto Fuentes and others were captured by coastguards while trying to depart by boat on 10 October. Norberto Fuentes, who had been refused official permission to leave, was held in the DSE headquarters for 20 days before being released. It was not clear whether he was still to face trial for attempting to leave the country illegally.

Reports were received that the authorities were putting pressure on some political prisoners to accept early release on condition they went into exile. Prisoner of conscience Sebastián Arcos Bergnes (see *Amnesty International Report 1993*) was said to have been threatened that his family visits would be terminated, his sentence extended or reprisals would be taken against relatives if he refused to go into exile. At the end of the year he remained imprisoned.

Several prisoners of conscience were released during the year. They included María Elena Cruz Varela, José Luis Pujol Irizar and Marco Antonio Abad, all released in May; three members of the unofficial *Movimiento Cristiano "Liberación"*, Liberation Christian Movement, released in June (on condition that they left Cuba – they went to Spain); and Jorge Crespo Díaz, who was released in September (see *Amnesty International Report 1993*). All were released several months (or, in the case of the three who went to Spain, several years) before their sentences were due to expire.

Detention and trial procedures continued to fall far short of international standards. Prisoners accused of offences against state security, which include "enemy propaganda", were held under investigation by the DSE for several weeks or months without access to lawyers. It was feared that psychological pressures during this period were such that some detainees may have been coerced into confessing to the charges against them.

At the trial of Amador Blanco and Joel Mesa in September (see above), their defence lawyer was reportedly prevented from presenting witnesses on their behalf. Prisoner of conscience Adriano González Marichal, arrested in January 1992, was detained for 21 months before being tried in September on a charge of "enemy propaganda", convicted and sentenced to 10 years' imprisonment. He was reportedly not permitted to speak in his own defence at the hearing.

Cases involving "dangerousness" (see above) are tried in municipal courts, often within days of a person's arrest. Contrary to other cases tried in these courts, the law states that a lawyer must participate. However, reports indicated that in some cases defendants had no opportunity to appoint a lawyer of their choice and had no contact with the lawyer assigned to them by the court prior to the trial hearing.

Reports were received that prisoners were sometimes beaten by prison guards or held in so-called "punishment cells" in conditions amounting to cruel, inhuman or degrading treatment or, in some cases, torture. Some prisoners were punished for protesting about lack of food, medicines, water and other essentials, of which there were reportedly serious shortages. Those punished had sometimes been involved in hunger-strikes or committed other breaches of prison discipline, but others had simply written to the authorities complaining about the conditions.

In May prisoner of conscience Luis Alberto Pita Santos and Jesús Chambes Ramírez, a possible prisoner of conscience, were reported to be held handcuffed and with chains on their ankles for 14 hours a day in Camagüey Special High Security Prison, apparently because they had refused to wear prison uniforms and gone on hunger-strike. Luis Alberto Pita was also said to have been injured in April when guards forcibly dressed him.

Jorge Luis Alvarez Antunes, another possible prisoner of conscience serving a 10-year sentence for "enemy propaganda", who was called as a state witness at the trial of Amador Blanco and Joel Mesa in September, alleged in court that guards had beaten him with rubber hoses and set dogs on him.

At least two people were alleged to have died as a result of torture. In March Rogelio Carbonell Guevara died after he was apparently beaten by police at the time of arrest. The authorities were said to have taken action against those responsible, although the nature of this was not clear. Luis Quevedo Remolina died in October when coastguards caught him and three others trying to leave the country. The authorities said he had been shot dead after refusing to obey an order to halt but other sources alleged that he died from injuries caused by beatings received after he was detained.

At least four people died in circumstances suggesting they may have been victims of extrajudicial executions. Three men, all apparently unarmed, were killed in Cojímar in July when the security forces fired on people trying to board a boat that had arrived illegally from the USA to help them flee the country. Other people were injured. The authorities were believed to

114

be carrying out an investigation into the incident but no further news was received. Vladimir León Aballí was reportedly assaulted and shot dead by police in Havana in December after being stopped and asked for his identity card.

At least one man may have been executed and at least six others were known to be appealing against death sentences. Nelson Baez Jorge had his death sentence for murder confirmed by the Council of State in early December but it was not known whether he had been executed by the end of the year. In February, two men were reported to be on death row in Boniato Prison after having been sentenced to death for murder in late 1992, but no further news of them was received. Four others were sentenced to death in October and November, all for murder, and were believed to be awaiting the result of appeals to the Supreme Court.

Amnesty International appealed to the authorities to release prisoners of conscience, to ensure that detention and trial procedures conformed to international standards, to investigate allegations of ill-treatment or torture and possible extrajudicial executions, and to commute death sentences. Little substantive response was received to requests for information.

In an oral statement to the UN Commission on Human Rights in February, Amnesty International included reference to its concerns in Cuba regarding arbitrary detention.

CYPRUS

At least 10 prisoners of conscience, all Jehovah's Witnesses, were held for refusing on conscientious grounds to perform military service or reservist exercises. Two Somali asylum-seekers were reportedly ill-treated.

Glafcos Clerides succeeded George Vassiliou as President following elections in February.

Legislation passed in 1992 recognized the right to conscientious objection to military service and provided for "unarmed military service" inside and outside military camps (see Amnesty International Report 1993). However, its provisions fall short of international standards in several respects: the length of alternative service –

42 months as against 26 months of ordinary military service – is punitive; and the right to transfer to alternative service from military service would be suspended during periods of emergency or general mobilizations. Moreover, the alternative service appears not to be entirely civilian and individuals must enlist before applying to do it: this may have deterred conscientious objectors from applying for alternative service. No conscientious objectors were known to have been offered the option of "unarmed military service" by the end of the year.

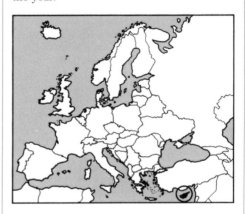

At least 10 conscientious objectors continued to serve prison sentences of up to 15 months, including Georgios Anastasi Petrou who was sentenced to six months' imprisonment in July for refusing to carry out the reservist exercises. This sentence, later reduced to one month by the Cyprus Appeal Court, was his fourth term of imprisonment for refusing to perform military service.

One conscientious objector was also prosecuted by the Turkish Cypriot authorities in northern Cyprus. Salih Askeroğul was arrested in September and in November was sentenced to three months' imprisonment for failing to enlist for military service, and a further three years for "making propaganda against the armed forces" after he made a public statement on his reasons for refusing to perform military service.

Two foreign nationals, Martin Handke and Andreas Rabl, who visited northern Cyprus to monitor the trial of Salih Askeroğul and were distributing leaflets on the case, were arrested together with a local photographer, Ahmet Serdar Gül, and held for nine days.

Allegations of ill-treatment in police custody were received. In January two Somali brothers, Abdukarim and Abdukahnan Mohamed Ibrahim, who had sought asylum on their arrival in Cyprus from Saudi Arabia, were reportedly ill-treated at Larnaca International Airport. They were allegedly punched, kicked and slapped by airport police who failed to provide them with food or a place to sleep while they were held. The brothers were returned to Saudi Arabia, apparently without the authorities obtaining any assurances that they would receive effective and durable protection there against being forcibly returned to Somalia.

Amnesty International received no response from the Cypriot authorities concerning the trials of two police officers charged with ill-treating Dimos Dimosthenous in April 1992 (see *Amnesty International Report 1993*).

Amnesty International called for the immediate and unconditional release of all imprisoned conscientious objectors. It repeatedly urged the government to bring its legislation on conscientious objection fully into line with international standards.

Amnesty International also addressed the Turkish Cypriot authorities in northern Cyprus, calling for the immediate and unconditional release of Salih Askeroğul, Martin Handke, Andreas Rabl and Ahmet Serdar Gül.

In March Amnesty International expressed concern to the government that Antonis Damianos could face imprisonment for refusing to perform military service, despite having been declared medically unfit for military service. In April the authorities replied that he had been exempted from military service on grounds of ill-health.

Amnesty International expressed concern to the government about the allegations of ill-treatment of asylum-seekers by police and called for an impartial investigation into the case. It urged the authorities not to return the two Somali brothers to Saudi Arabia in the absence of satisfactory assurances that they would not be forcibly returned from Saudi Arabia to Somalia, but received no response.

DENMARK

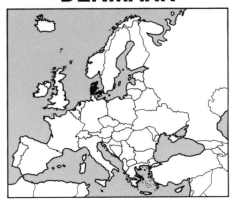

At least 11 people were wounded in disputed circumstances when police shot into crowds during a violent demonstration. There were several reports of ill-treatment by police.

The police shootings occurred at the time of a violent demonstration in Copenhagen, the capital, on 18 May, following the second Danish referendum on the Maastricht Treaty. The circumstances in which the police resorted to lethal force were disputed. The government, after first refusing to do so, initiated an official inquiry, but the findings had not been reported by the end of the year.

There were several reports of ill-treatment by police. In May a 50-year-old woman, Helle Cordsen, was allegedly hit and denied food and water while detained in a police station in a suburb of Copenhagen. Several other people alleged during the year that they had been beaten, thrown on the ground and handcuffed behind their backs by police conducting searches for drugs in and around Christiania, a former military base in Copenhagen which was settled by squatters in the early 1970s. Some of them were injured by having their feet forced back and up under the handcuffs. The case of Benjamin Schou, who suffered cardiac arrest and severe brain damage allegedly as a result of ill-treatment by police when arrested in 1992, was the subject of a civil claim against the police, which had not come to court by the end of the year.

In July, in a parliamentary report following a judicial investigation into the ill-treatment of Babading Fatty and Himid Hassan Juma (see *Amnesty International*

116

Reports 1991 and *1993*), the Minister of Justice said that the authorities' actions in those cases were "unfortunate", and "unsatisfactory", although not due to "mistakes" or the negligence of any individual. He stated that measures taken and planned in relation to the reception and treatment of foreigners by the prison service and Copenhagen police would contribute to the prevention of such incidents in the future. He specifically called on the National Commissioner of Police to consider improving the training of officers involved in immigration control.

In May Amnesty International wrote to the government about its continuing concerns in the cases of Babading Fatty and Himid Hassan Juma. These included the judicial inquiry's limited definition of physical ill-treatment as treatment which is "deliberate and intended to frighten or to compel one to make a confession", the failure to initiate formal disciplinary proceedings against any of the police officers or prison guards involved, and the failure to pay compensation to the victims.

Also in May, Amnesty International urged the government to initiate an independent inquiry into the police shootings on 18 May and to make the findings public.

In June an Amnesty International delegate visited Denmark to inquire into the police shootings and allegations of ill-treatment. She met the Attorney General, who was conducting an investigation into the events of 18 May based on information gathered by the police.

In September Amnesty International wrote to the government concerning the imprisonment of Greenlanders in Denmark for prolonged indefinite periods, after conviction for serious crimes in Greenland. The organization noted that the European Committee for the Prevention of Torture and Inhuman or Degrading Treatment or Punishment had confirmed allegations that the alienation of these prisoners from their country and culture was so extreme that it could cause psychological disorders. Amnesty International therefore expressed concern that the possible serious effects on their mental health could amount to cruel, inhuman or degrading treatment or punishment. It urged the government to work with appropriate agencies in Denmark and Greenland to resolve this problem. The organization was informed by a member of the Greenland Home Rule Government that it intended to form a joint commission with the Danish Government which would address the imprisonment of Greenlanders in Denmark.

DJIBOUTI

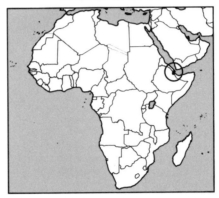

One prisoner of conscience, a human rights activist, was imprisoned for two months for criticizing human rights violations by the army. Eleven other prisoners of conscience, held since 1991 and serving prison sentences imposed after an unfair trial in 1992, were released in December 1993. There were new reports of torture, including rape and ill-treatment, and of dozens of extrajudicial executions by government soldiers. The only death sentence was commuted.

President Hassan Gouled Aptidon was re-elected for a fourth six-year term in May. His government continued to face armed opposition from the *Front pour la restauration de l'unité et de la démocratie* (FRUD), Front for the Restoration of Unity and Democracy. Killings and other abuses by the army led to tens of thousands of members of the Afar ethnic group, from which the FRUD drew support, fleeing to Ethiopia, and many more were displaced within the country.

Mohamed Houmed Soulleh, president of the non-governmental human rights group, the *Association pour la défense des droits de l'homme et des libertés* (ADDHL), Association for the Defence of Human Rights and Liberties, was arrested in the capital, Djibouti, in September. Initially held incommunicado, he was charged with defaming the Defence Minister and publishing false information. The ADDHL had published reports of recent killings and other human rights violations by the army, including the killing of Mohamed Houmed Soulleh's brother (see below). The charges related to the ADDHL's accusation that soldiers had shot at members of an independent inquiry investigating the killings. The government had denied the soldiers were responsible and blamed the shooting on the rebels. Mohamed Houmed Soulleh, who was a prisoner of conscience, continued to be detained despite a magistrate's order for his provisional release, and went on hunger-strike in protest. In late October, after a trial which appeared to fall short of international standards, he was convicted and sentenced to three months' imprisonment and a fine. He was provisionally released in mid-November pending the judgment on his appeal, which had not been given by the end of the year.

Ali Aref, a former head of government, 10 other prisoners of conscience, and two other prisoners, continued to serve long prison terms imposed after an unfair trial in July 1992 (see *Amnesty International Report 1993*). The Cassation Court rejected their appeal in June. Also in June they went on hunger-strike to demand improvements in prison conditions, which were granted. One detainee, Mohamed Hassanleh Abakari, a police lieutenant, died in custody in August after an operation. On 15 December Ali Aref and all the 12 remaining prisoners in the same case were given a presidential pardon and released.

There were reports of torture and ill-treatment by the security forces. The victims included criminal prisoners, Ethiopian refugees detained in Djibouti town and Afar civilians who were suspected of links with the FRUD in areas affected by armed conflict. Afar women and girls were reported to have been raped by soldiers. Over 100 people arrested in different parts of the north in early September were reported to have been tortured at a military post near Lake Asal by having burning pieces of paper and plastic placed on their bodies.

Extrajudicial executions and other human rights violations by the army during operations against FRUD forces were reported in February in Tadjourah district, and again in September in Tadjourah, Mabla and Obock districts in the north, and Dhikil district in the southwest. Kamil Houmed Soulleh, a postal worker and brother of Mohamed Houmed Soulleh (see

above), was arrested with another man in Randa town on 5 September: both were found dead the next day. Over 60 other Afar civilians were reportedly extrajudicially executed by soldiers in rural areas in the north in mid-September.

In June the President commuted the death sentence imposed on Adouani Hamouda Ben Hassan in 1991 for a bomb attack four years earlier. He had been the only person condemned to death in Djibouti since independence in 1977.

Amnesty International appealed for the release of human rights activist Mohamed Houmed Soulleh, and Ali Aref and other prisoners of conscience held with him. It called for a thorough and impartial inquiry into reports of extrajudicial executions and torture, including rape, by the security forces and for steps to be taken to prevent further violations by government forces.

DOMINICAN REPUBLIC

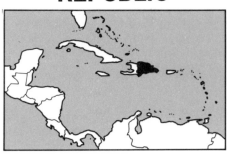

At least one political prisoner continued to be imprisoned despite judicial orders for his release. Several prisoners were reported to have been tortured or ill-treated.

President Joaquín Balaguer's government stated in April that it planned to establish a human rights centre to investigate allegations of human rights violations and to promote awareness of human rights standards. However, the centre was not apparently in operation by the end of the year. According to a government representative, 70 per cent of the prison population were awaiting trial because of shortage of resources in the judiciary, leading to long delays in trials, including political trials.

At least 54 prisoners were deliberately denied their freedom, many apparently for political reasons, despite completing their

118

sentences or obtaining judicial orders for their release. President Balaguer reportedly announced in September that 54 prisoners said to be held illegally in the National Penitentiary of La Victoria should not be released.

In one case, the police continued to refuse to comply with three judicial decisions, including one issued in August 1992 by the Supreme Court of Justice, ordering the release of Luis Lizardo Cabrera, a political activist. He had been detained since 1989 on suspicion of having planted a bomb (see *Amnesty International Reports 1990* to *1993*).

There were new allegations of torture and ill-treatment of prisoners. At least 20 of the prisoners said to be illegally held were reportedly beaten by members of the National Police after they had gone on hunger-strike in August in protest at their continued detention in the National Penitentiary of La Victoria. Two inmates, Luis Lizardo Cabrera and Víctor Manuel Penaldo Almonte, required hospital treatment as a result. Despite a complaint to the authorities by an independent human rights organization, no known investigation into this incident was conducted.

In July Juan Díaz Ulerio, a peasant from Mata de Palma, Hato Mayor Province, was reportedly beaten by police officers, then drenched in gasoline and set alight by a tradesman who was accompanying the police. The assault took place during a police operation to evict peasant families from land they had occupied. Juan Díaz was hospitalized with severe burns. No investigation was apparently initiated into the incident.

In September one police captain was sentenced to six months' imprisonment and another was suspended without pay for 30 days for the torture of Felipe de Jesús Medrano García (see *Amnesty International Report 1993*).

Amnesty International urged the authorities to investigate the alleged torture of Juan Díaz Ulerio. In October the organization wrote to the Procurator General about the continued illegal imprisonment of Luis Lizardo Cabrera and 53 other prisoners. The organization also requested a full and independent investigation into the alleged ill-treatment of at least 20 of these prisoners. The authorities had not replied to Amnesty International's communications by the end of the year..

ECUADOR

There were new reports of torture and ill-treatment of suspects by the police. One possible "disappearance" was reported. The authorities failed to account for victims of "disappearances" in previous years. Eight people were killed by the security forces in circumstances suggesting that they may have been victims of extrajudicial executions. A Bolivian political activist was forcibly returned to Bolivia despite fears for his safety there.

The authorities continued to invoke Decree Law 86, issued by the new government of President Sixto Durán Ballén in 1992. The law allows the armed forces to be used for the control of common crime thought to constitute "a serious state of internal unrest". In March, 100 intellectuals publicly criticized anti-crime operations in which they claimed the security forces "first kill and then ask". During June indigenous groups organized demonstrations in Quito, the capital, in protest against a newly drafted agrarian law; during one of these demonstrations an indigenous leader was killed in circumstances which the authorities had not clarified at the end of the year.

Officials of the *Tribunal de Garantías Constitucionales* (TGC), Tribunal of Constitutional Guarantees, inspected a police centre run by the *Oficina de Investigación del Delito* (OID), Crime Investigation Office, in Quito. Following the visit, the president of the TGC wrote to the Minister for Government and Police stating that the TGC had found torture instruments in the centre and had no doubt that torture was practised there. As a result, a number of officers were dismissed. A newly appointed commander general of the police was reported as saying in September that the investigative work of the police would be based on respect for human rights. He added that a judicial police force was to be created (see *Amnesty International Reports 1992* and *1993*).

In February Ecuador acceded to the Second Optional Protocol to the International Covenant on Civil and Political Rights, aiming at the abolition of the death penalty.

Numerous cases of torture and ill-treatment of detainees, mostly by police, continued to be reported. José Ignacio Chauvín, aged 17, who had participated in demonstrations on behalf of the "disappeared", was twice detained and tortured by the police in Quito. On 15 January he was reportedly hooded, forced inside a van, kicked and beaten, and subjected to electric shocks to his genitals. He was released after a uniformed police officer ordered the beatings to stop. He was detained a second time on 14 February, taken to a police building, again tortured, and then released. A police investigation into his allegations stalled, apparently because José Ignacio Chauvín was too frightened to appear before the inquiry.

Luis Olmedo Aguilera López, a peasant leader from the province of Pichincha, was reportedly severely beaten by members of the OID in Quito. He was detained at his home on 24 February and first taken to a police provisional detention centre, where, according to a police report, he was admitted "without beatings or bruising on his body". The following day he was transferred to the headquarters of the OID. Relatives who saw him there say he appeared to have been severely beaten and was unable to walk. On 2 March he was transferred back to the detention centre, and then to a hospital, where he died the following day. A report by a police doctor indicated that the "probable cause of death" was a generalized infection, but that his body revealed extensive bruising. The authorities did not apparently order an independent investigation into the allegations.

Official investigations into cases of torture and ill-treatment were carried out by the same bodies reported to be responsible for the violations. The Ministry of Foreign Affairs stated in April that it had requested the appropriate authorities to conduct detailed and thorough investigations into the alleged torture in 1992 of Víctor Hugo Cadena and of five young artists, and the death in custody of Felipe Moreira Chávez (see *Amnesty International Report 1993*).

One possible "disappearance" was reported. On 16 January Nixon Alcides Pacheco Guijarro was recruited into the army. Between February and May his mother repeatedly attempted but failed to contact him, despite being told by the military that her son was fulfilling his duties. However, in June the Ministry of National Defence (MND) stated that Nixon Pacheco had deserted in January. In September Nixon Pacheco's mother was approached by two men who claimed to be attached to the MND and told to desist from her inquiries and to look for her son "in the morgue".

The vast majority of "disappearances" since the change of government in 1985 remained unresolved. Judicial investigations continued to no avail into the "disappearances" of Marco Antonio Romero Carrasco, detained in 1992, (see *Amnesty International Report 1993*) and Consuelo Benavides Cevallos, detained in 1985 (see *Amnesty International Reports 1987*, *1990*, *1991* and *1993*). Trial proceedings before the Supreme Court against the former commander general of the police and at least eight other officers implicated in the "disappearance" and subsequent killing of the Restrepo brothers had not reached a conclusion by the end of the year (see *Amnesty International Reports 1992* and *1993*).

Eight people were killed in circumstances which suggested they may have been extrajudicially executed. Five of the victims – Wilmer Zambrano Vélez, brothers José Miguel and Segundo Olmedo Caceido, Fernando Calderón Chico, and Antonia Mera de Molineros – were killed in March in three separate incidents which occurred during efforts by police and army to control organized crime in Guayaquil city. The authorities said that the victims had all died as a result of armed confrontations with the security forces, but relatives alleged they had been extrajudicially executed. For instance, the husband of Antonia Mera de Molineros alleged that the police forcibly entered his home, held him at gunpoint, and then shot his 65-year-old wife in cold blood as she emerged from her room.

Three brothers, Orestes, Enrique and Fredy Cañola, were arrested on 12 April in

120

the town of Viche, Esmeraldas province, following a fight involving a policeman who later died. The brothers were taken to the police station in Viche, and then put into a vehicle to be taken to a police station in Esmeraldas town. However, they never arrived: their bodies were found in a cemetery at Esmeraldas, reportedly with bullet wounds and bruising. By the end of the year the authorities were not known to have made public the results of any investigations into the manner, causes, and circumstances of these eight deaths.

Despite fears that he might be tortured or ill-treated if returned to Bolivia, the Ecuadorian authorities forcibly returned a Bolivian political activist, Luis Alberto Zalles Cueto, in March. Five months later, the TGC resolved that his deportation had been unconstitutional and ordered his return.

Amnesty International appealed to the government to ensure the prompt and impartial investigation of the possible "disappearance" of Nixon Pacheco and of allegations of torture and ill-treatment of prisoners and extrajudicial execution. The authorities informed Amnesty International that various investigations had been initiated but gave few details and failed to provide satisfactory information about their outcome. Amnesty International urged the authorities not to forcibly return Luis Alberto Zalles Cueto to Bolivia on the grounds that he would be at risk of serious human rights violations there.

In October Amnesty International submitted information about its concerns regarding torture in Ecuador to the UN Committee against Torture, pursuant to Article 20 of the UN Convention against Torture.

EGYPT

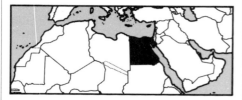

Thousands of people, most of them members or sympathizers of banned Islamist militant groups, were detained under state of emergency legislation. Many were held without charge or trial but hundreds of

others, almost all civilians, received unfair trials before military courts. Torture of political detainees was routine. At least 61 people were sentenced to death and 43, including 15 sentenced in previous years, were executed. Dozens of people were killed by the security forces in circumstances suggesting that some had been extrajudicially executed. Armed opposition groups also were responsible for grave human rights abuses, including deliberate killings of dozens of civilians.

The state of emergency, in force since 1981 (see previous *Amnesty International Reports*), continued. Administrative detention without charge or trial of political suspects, permitted under emergency legislation, remained widespread.

In October President Hosni Mubarak was re-elected, unopposed, for his third term of office. Throughout the year the President continued to refer civilians charged with terrorist offences for trial by military courts. In January the Constitutional Court rejected a challenge to this practice and ruled that the President was empowered to issue special decrees for this purpose.

There were further violent clashes between members of banned Islamist militant groups and the security forces, resulting in deaths on both sides. A number of civilians were killed in circumstances suggesting they had been extrajudicially executed, as they posed no serious threat at the time they were shot. These included eight people killed when police stormed a mosque in Aswan in early March.

Numerous bomb and other attacks were carried out by armed opponents of the government, including *al-Gama'a al-Islamiya*, Islamic Group, and *Gihad* (Holy War). Dozens of civilians were deliberately killed in such bomb attacks; others, including foreign tourists and Copts, were victims of targeted killings. Those deliberately killed by *al-Gama'a al-Islamiya* and other armed opposition groups included Mohsen Maurice Yassa, a Christian shopkeeper, and Nash'at Fawzi, a doctor, who were both shot dead in Dayrut, Upper Egypt, in July and October respectively. Three government ministers and numerous police officers were assassinated or targeted by armed Islamist militants.

Thousands of members or sympathizers of banned Islamist militant groups were detained under state of emergency regulations. Some were arrested after violent clashes with the security forces, particularly in Upper Egypt, Alexandria and parts of Cairo, the capital, but many were arrested as suspected sympathizers, including some possible prisoners of conscience.

Hundreds of people were arrested in the first three months of the year, with some 290 suspected supporters of banned Islamist groups arrested throughout the country on 11 February alone. They included 'Abd al-Mun'im Gamal al-Din 'Abd al-Mun'im, a journalist, and Magdi Mohammad Mohammad Salim, a university graduate, both of whom were detained in Cairo by the Giza branch of the State Security Intelligence (SSI) and reportedly tortured. Both had been arrested several times previously but never convicted of a criminal offence. They were among more than 240 detainees referred to a military court some months later (see below).

Also in February, four foreign nationals and an Egyptian were arrested and charged with "exploiting religion to foment sectarian sedition". They were detained in Istiqbal Tora prison for over two months before their release in early May. The foreigners were deported to their respective countries; the Egyptian was placed in a mental hospital where he remained, apparently against his will, until the end of the year. His legal situation remained unclear.

Four supporters of the opposition Labour Party were briefly detained in October. Dr Mohammad Hilmi Mourad, a 74-year-old writer and the party's deputy leader, 'Adel Hussain, its secretary general, and two journalists at al-Sha'ab, the party newspaper, were held for up to three days, then released on bail, apparently in connection with the publication of articles critical of President Mubarak. They had not been tried by the end of the year.

The authorities revealed few details of arrests and detentions but at most points in the year at least 2,000 people were believed to be held under emergency legislation. They included hundreds arrested in 1992 or before, among them many of the 700 or more people arrested in Imbaba, Cairo, in December 1992 (see Amnesty International Report 1993).

The authorities continued to move many political detainees to remote police stations or detention centres, apparently in order to prolong their detention. They also continued to serve new detention orders, often repeatedly, on detainees who had obtained court orders for their release. Consequently, some detainees had been held for up to three years without charge or trial. For example, Hassan al-Gharbawi Shehata, a lawyer, reportedly remained in administrative detention, despite many court orders for his release and despite being acquitted at his trial. Another 18 lawyers remained in detention at the end of the year.

In October General Sa'd al-Din al-Shazli, a former ambassador and commander of the armed forces who had been arrested on his return to Egypt in 1992 (see Amnesty International Report 1993), was released under a presidential amnesty.

Hundreds of civilians charged with membership of militant Islamist groups and violent political offences had their cases referred to military courts by order of President Mubarak, and appeared in mass trials. The procedures of the military courts fell far short of international fair trial standards: the judges, military officers, were not independent, and defendants were denied adequate time to prepare their defence and had no right of appeal to a higher court. Before coming to trial defendants were routinely held in prolonged secret incommunicado detention and tortured to extract confessions. Between April and the end of October, military courts sentenced 30 people to death, including four in absentia, 12 of whom were hanged in July, five more in November and nine in December; 175 people received sentences ranging from life imprisonment to one-year prison terms and 122 defendants were acquitted.

Two trials began in August before the Supreme Military Court in Cairo, involving respectively 55 and 66 civilians charged with membership of Talai' al-Fatah, The Vanguards of the Conquest, a banned Islamist militant group, and calling for the overthrow of the government and the Constitution. Some defendants also faced murder, attempted murder or other charges.

Defendants at both trials testified that they had been tortured while secretly detained by state security police in Cairo. They said they had been blindfolded, suspended in painful positions and given electric shocks to make them confess. Medical reports indicated that many of the defendants had scars which were consistent with their torture allegations.

Judgment in both trials, the proceedings of which had been attended by Amnesty International observers, was given in October. Eight people were sentenced to death, including two *in absentia*, and six were executed in December. Seventy-six defendants received prison sentences ranging from one year to life imprisonment, and 37 were acquitted. Those acquitted were not released but were served with new detention orders and were still held at the end of the year.

Torture of political detainees was frequently reported, particularly in police stations, at the headquarters of the SSI in Cairo, and at the premises of the *Firaq al-Amn* (security brigades) and SSI branches throughout the country. The most common methods alleged were beatings, suspension by the wrists or ankles, burning with cigarettes, electric shocks and psychological torture. Several detainees died apparently as a result of torture. Ahmad Farouq Ahmad, who was accused of participating in the attempted assassination of the Minister of the Interior, General Hassan al-Alfy, in late August, died within 24 hours of his arrest early in September, reportedly following torture. It was reported that Mohammad Hamidou and Yasser 'Abd al-Rahim had died as a result of torture in late December 1992; they had been among hundreds of people arrested earlier that month in Imbaba, Cairo.

Lawyers and human rights organizations lodged hundreds of formal complaints of torture with the Procurator General's Office, but the latter apparently took no action to investigate them.

Twenty-four defendants accused of involvement in the assassination of the Speaker of the People's Assembly, Dr Rifa'at al-Mahgoub, in October 1990 (see *Amnesty International Reports 1991* to *1993*), were acquitted in August after the civilian Supreme State Security Court ruled that some defendants had been tortured to make them confess. Some, however, received prison terms for other offences while others, such as Safwat 'Abd al-Ghani, were also on trial for involvement in the murder of the writer Farag Foda in June 1992 (see *Amnesty International Report 1993*), even though they were in prison at the time of the murder. Judgment in this trial was given in late December: one person was sentenced to death, three to prison sentences ranging from three to 10 years (two of them *in absentia*) and eight were acquitted, including Safwat 'Abd al-Ghani.

There was a dramatic increase in the use of the death penalty. At least 61 people were sentenced to death: 32 of them, including four *in absentia* (see above), for politically motivated offences, and at least 29 after being convicted of murder. Forty-three people were executed: of these, 28 had been sentenced to death by military courts in 1993 and had had no right of appeal (see above). Fourteen others had been convicted of murder in previous years and Mohammad 'Abd al-Salam 'Ali al-Shahid, who was hanged in June, had been sentenced to death by a military court in Cairo in May 1992 after being convicted of espionage.

Amnesty International strongly condemned the deliberate and arbitrary killings of civilians by armed opposition groups and called on them to abide by international humanitarian standards.

Amnesty International repeatedly appealed to President Mubarak to commute death sentences and called for an end to trials of civilians before military courts and for all political prisoners to receive trials which conformed fully to international fair trial standards. Amnesty International also criticized the long-term detention without charge or trial of political detainees, called for all prisoners to be safeguarded against torture or ill-treatment, and for urgent, thorough and impartial investigations into all allegations of torture and extrajudicial executions.

In June an Amnesty International delegation, led by the Secretary General, visited Egypt and met senior government officials, including the newly appointed Minister of Interior. The Minister undertook to prevent the use of torture, but no specific steps were reported to have been taken by the end of the year.

Amnesty International published two reports: in May, *Egypt: Grave human rights abuses amid political violence*; and in October, *Egypt: Military trials of civilians, a catalogue of human rights violations*. In response to the first report, the authorities acknowledged that isolated abuses had taken place, but said these were the exception rather than the norm and were not the result of any policy to abuse human rights. The response referred to the high level of violence against the state – more than 80 attacks on police officers in 12 months – and the legal provisions which exist to safeguard human rights. However, it failed to give adequate information on the cases and concerns raised by Amnesty International. In their response to the second report, the authorities maintained that civilians received a fair trial before military courts and that the use of the death penalty was justified. They failed to respond to Amnesty International's specific criticisms. In August Amnesty International issued a statement expressing concern about deliberate and arbitrary killings by armed opposition groups.

In March and again in October Amnesty International submitted information about its concerns regarding torture in Egypt to the UN Committee against Torture, pursuant to Article 20 of the UN Convention against Torture.

EL SALVADOR

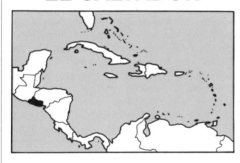

The process of human rights reform was undermined by an amnesty law protecting human rights violators. There was a series of killings of members of the former armed opposition and dozens of other killings which appeared to have been carried out by "death squads" linked to the armed forces. Numerous figures identified with the opposition received death threats. Ill-treatment of detainees by the police was widespread.

Implementation of the 1992 peace accords, which ended 12 years of armed conflict between the government and the *Frente Farabundo Martí para la Liberación Nacional* (FMLN), Farabundo Martí National Liberation Front, made faltering progress. The accords had provided for the FMLN's demobilization and the implementation of a host of military, judicial and socio-economic reforms aimed at promoting democratization and respect for human rights. However, the agreed timetable for implementation was rarely adhered to and many human rights commitments had not been complied with by the end of the year.

The FMLN was supposed to have demobilized in 1992, to allow its reorganization as a political party ahead of elections scheduled for 1994. However, in May 1993 arms caches allegedly belonging to the FMLN were found in Nicaragua, and subsequently in El Salvador and Honduras. Nevertheless, in August UN monitors certified that the FMLN's military apparatus had been fully dismantled. There were also delays in the restructuring and *"depuración"* ("purging") of the government's armed forces. By July the government had removed 102 military officers whose dismissal had been recommended in 1992 by an *Ad Hoc* Commission created under the accords (see *Amnesty International Report 1993*).

At the end of the year the new National Civilian Police had not been fully deployed and there was concern that many ex-members of disbanded security force units with a long history of responsibility for human rights violations had joined existing police bodies.

A number of judicial reforms arising from the accords were initiated during the year. Nevertheless, many deficiencies remained. There were numerous indications of the judiciary's resistance to reform and there were death threats against the newly appointed *Consejo Nacional de la Judicatura* (CNJ), National Council of the Judiciary, charged by the accords with evaluating the competence of all judges.

There were serious setbacks in implementing agreements on socio-economic reform, such as those concerning land transfers. Against a backdrop of widespread economic hardship, labour conflicts and demonstrations were frequent and the security forces responded in at least one incident with excessive force. In the face of rising crime, army troops were deployed to fulfil police functions and the ruling *Alianza Republicana Nacionalista* (ARENA), Nationalist Republican Alliance, proposed in February that the death penalty should be reintroduced for certain offences. This proposal was defeated shortly after by the Legislative Assembly.

The UN observer mission in El Salvador, ONUSAL, continued to monitor compliance with the peace accords. Its Human Rights

124

Division reported in October that many of its recommendations to the government had not been heeded. The *Procuraduría para la Defensa de los Derechos Humanos* (PDDH), Office of the Counsel for the Defence of Human Rights, created by the accords and due to assume many of ONUSAL's functions on its departure, consolidated its work, voicing particular concern at increasing political killings and violations of due process. However, the judicial, military and police authorities frequently failed to comply with the PDDH's recommendations on individual cases.

March saw the publication of the report of the *Comisión de la Verdad* (Truth Commission), established by the accords to investigate some of the worst human rights abuses by government and FMLN forces committed since 1980 and to make recommendations to prevent their recurrence, recommendations which both parties had formally agreed to abide by in the accords. The Commission's report confirmed that the army, police and paramilitary groups were responsible for massacres, killings, torture and "disappearances" on a massive scale. It concluded that "death squads" linked to state structures had systematically eliminated political opponents and said that the judiciary bore great responsibility for the impunity with which abuses had been committed. Ninety-five per cent of the abuses reported to the Commission were attributed to government forces or "death squads", but the FMLN was also held responsible for scores of killings and abductions. The Commission presented findings on 32 cases which it had selected for in-depth investigation from the 22,000 reported, and made some 40 recommendations, including the removal and banning from office of military, judicial and FMLN officials named in the report, compensation for victims and relatives, an urgent investigation into "death squads", judicial reforms and implementation of ONUSAL's recommendations. The institutions most criticized, the military and judiciary, rejected the Commission's conclusions and recommendations, accusing it of bias and defamation. By the end of the year, many key measures recommended by the Commission had yet to be implemented.

The government took prompt action to grant impunity to those accused in the Commission's report. Days after its publication, the Legislative Assembly approved the *Ley de amnistía general para la consolidación de la paz*, General Amnesty Law for the Consolidation of Peace, which protected from prosecution all those responsible for carrying out or covering up human rights abuses during the civil war, including judicial officials. Salvadorian human rights organizations challenged the law as unconstitutional before the Supreme Court, but in April the court ruled that it did not have jurisdiction to consider the appeal.

The law resulted in the release in March of a colonel and lieutenant convicted of murdering six Jesuits, their cook and her daughter in 1989. They had served 14 months in prison. Also freed were: a major accused of ordering the killing of 10 peasants in San Sebastián in 1988 (see *Amnesty International Report 1989*); César Joya Martínez, an army deserter, who had testified about army "death squad" operations after fleeing the country, and who was forcibly returned from the USA to El Salvador in 1992 to stand trial for two killings in 1989; political prisoner Jorge Miranda, sentenced in 1992 for the 1987 killing of human rights activist Herbert Anaya, after an unfair trial (see previous *Amnesty International Reports*); and three members of the FMLN accused of killing two US military advisers in 1991 (see *Amnesty International Report 1993*). An FMLN member, William Rivas Bolaños, convicted in 1991 of killing US marines in Zona Rosa in San Salvador, the capital, in 1985 was not released; the judge in his case argued that the killing of individuals with diplomatic status was excluded from the amnesty law. Amnesty International was concerned about serious irregularities in his trial.

Although evidence of past abuses continued to come to light, the amnesty law blocked investigations to identify those responsible and bring them to justice. Despite exhumations at the sites of two massacres committed in the early 1980s in El Mozote, Morazán department, and the Sumpul River, Chalatenango department, judicial proceedings into these cases stalled.

Reports of political killings increased during the year. There was a series of murders of leaders and other members of the FMLN and its electoral ally, the *Convergencia Democrática* (CD), Democratic Convergence. Most of the cases were not investigated and the pattern of killings, which intensified in the weeks before the official start of the electoral campaign in November, suggested the involvement of government forces or agents linked to them.

Fredy Fernández Torres Portillo, FMLN leader in the city of Mejicanos, was shot dead in February. ONUSAL identified a member of the National Police as responsible, but this suspect was released within days of his detention by the National Police in March. ONUSAL concluded that the police's actions and the disappearance of records of the investigation indicated a possible police cover-up.

Oscar Grimaldi, an FMLN member prominent in the demobilization process, was shot dead in August by unidentified individuals in a bar in San Salvador. He had been released from prison in 1992 under a previous amnesty.

In October Francisco Véliz, a member of the FMLN's National Council and parliamentary candidate, was shot dead as he took his baby daughter to a crèche in San Salvador. The government immediately condemned the killing and requested international assistance in investigations, but the case remained unresolved. On 8 November the body of Manuel de Jesús Alvarado, a local FMLN activist and husband of the party's electoral affairs secretary, was found on a rubbish dump, with signs of torture and his hands tied behind his back with barbed wire.

This and dozens of other unclarified killings recalled the *modus operandi* of the so-called "death squads". Although the identity of the killers was difficult to establish, their methods and the lack of official action strongly suggested the continued existence of clandestine government "death squads". The Truth Commission had highlighted the need for a special inquiry into the phenomenon of the "death squads" because of the threat these still posed to society. There was renewed UN pressure for such an inquiry following the October killings and the release of US intelligence documentation implicating senior Salvadorian government officials, including the Vice President and ARENA's presidential candidate, in past "death squad" activities. In December the government announced the creation of a commission to investigate the existence of illegal armed groups. Known as "*Grupo Conjunto*" (Joint Group), it consisted of ONUSAL, the PDDH and two government lawyers.

In May CD member Gregorio Mejía Espinoza was bundled into a vehicle by armed men in plain clothes in a manner reminiscent of "death squad" abductions common in the past. He was interrogated about the FMLN's election plans and tortured with lighted cigarettes. Blindfolded and with his hands tied behind his back, he was driven to a deserted roadside, where his captors attempted to shoot him, but he managed to escape when the gun failed to go off. Gregorio Mejía Espinoza had previously received death threats from the "death squad", *Ejército Secreto Anticomunista*, Secret Anticommunist Army. In October the PDDH expressed concern that the judicial investigation into the case had still not produced any results.

In the run-up to the electoral campaign, the FMLN presidential and vice-presidential candidates received death threats, as did numerous other FMLN and CD members, as well as lawyers, journalists and members of non-governmental organizations identified with the opposition.

The systematic use of torture, widespread in the past, was no longer reported. However, there were many complaints of ill-treatment by National and Municipal Police agents, in some cases apparently motivated by the victim's political affiliation. In February Cruz René Morales Escobar and his brother Veito were arrested by about 10 National Police agents who burst into their home in Ilobasco, Cabañas, without a warrant. Handcuffed and with their hands tied behind their back, they were punched, kicked and beaten with rifle butts before being taken to the local mayor's office, and accused of being FMLN guerrillas and possessing weapons. The courts subsequently found no reason for their detention, but they were not released until June.

Several deliberate and arbitrary killings of police and army officers were attributed to former FMLN combatants and armed groups allegedly composed of ex-combatants from both the army and FMLN. The killing in November of a local ARENA politician and several other killings were attributed to such groups.

Amnesty International called repeatedly on the government to investigate cases of apparent political killings, attacks and death threats. It campaigned against the amnesty law on the grounds that passing such a law before those responsible for

126

human rights abuses had been brought to justice was unacceptable under international standards. It also urged the Legislative Assembly in February to oppose reintroduction of the death penalty. Amnesty International called for a special inquiry into "death squad" killings, following statements by President Cristiani that "death squads" were a phenomenon of the past, and again following the killings in October and November. The inquiry, Amnesty International said, should include examination of links with state institutions and review the role of the intelligence services within the newly reformed armed forces. It repeatedly urged the government to comply with the recommendations of the Truth Commission, stressing the need to bring to justice those responsible for human rights violations. It also called on the government to implement fully the judicial reforms recommended by ONUSAL and others. Amnesty International urged measures to prevent further political violence in the run-up to the elections.

President Cristiani replied to Amnesty International's concerns regarding the amnesty law, arguing that it was necessary for national reconciliation. Amnesty International reiterated its concern that, far from promoting reconciliation, the law prevented justice in thousands of cases, went against the accords' intention to end impunity and thus laid a dangerous foundation for the future.

EQUATORIAL GUINEA

Hundreds of suspected government opponents were detained, including at least 40 prisoners of conscience, and held without charge or trial, for periods ranging from a few days to several months. Fourteen other people sentenced to prison terms in two unfair trials were also prisoners of conscience. Torture was routinely used and three political prisoners reportedly died as a result. Two people were extrajudicially executed by the security forces. One person was sentenced to death and publicly executed.

In January an electoral law was passed which, like the 1992 laws governing political activity (see *Amnesty International Report 1993*), severely restricted civil

and political rights. It required all parties except the ruling *Partido Democrático de Guinea Ecuatorial* (PDGE), Equatorial Guinea Democratic Party, to obtain official permission for any political gathering, a process which, in practice, took months, and to seek government approval for campaign speeches and party propaganda. In March the government and representatives of opposition parties signed a National Pact, according to which the government undertook to allow the free exercise of civil and political rights, to punish all arbitrary acts by public officials and to release political prisoners. A joint commission was established to monitor implementation of the National Pact. However, although some prisoners were released, the other reforms had not been implemented when, in July, President Obiang Nguema scheduled legislative elections for September. In August negotiations between the government and opposition broke down and the opposition said it would boycott the elections. These were then rescheduled for November, when six opposition parties participated. The elections were won by the ruling PDGE.

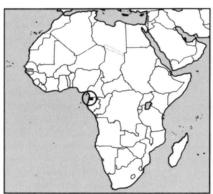

Moroccan troops, which had been seconded to Equatorial Guinea under a bilateral agreement with the Kingdom of Morocco in 1979, were withdrawn in mid-August following international pressure. In previous years they had been implicated, together with Equatorial Guinean security personnel, in human rights violations (see *Amnesty International Report 1990*). They were replaced by a new paramilitary group, commonly known as *Antorchas* (Torches), drawn from the ranks of the youth movement of the PDGE, which was armed and had powers of arrest.

Hundreds of political activists and

suspected government opponents were arrested. Small groups were detained between January and July and at least 130 were detained from August onwards. Most were held without charge or trial; some were restricted to their villages; and a few were charged and brought to trial. Many of those held were released after a few weeks or months but dozens apparently remained detained or restricted to their villages at the end of the year.

There were two amnesties leading to releases of political prisoners: one in March after the signing of the National Pact, and one in October to mark the 25th anniversary of the country's independence (see below).

Several leading members of opposition parties were arrested in January and briefly detained in Bata, the capital of the mainland province of Río Muni, when they were meeting to discuss the electoral law. In February, two members of the *Partido del Progreso de Guinea Ecuatorial* (PPGE), Equatorial Guinea Progress Party, were reportedly detained briefly for listening to a tape-recording of party propaganda.

Political repression increased sharply in August after opposition parties said they would boycott the elections, and as Moroccan troops were being withdrawn. Dozens of soldiers and former soldiers were arrested in August in Malabo, the capital on Bioko island, apparently on suspicion of plotting against the government. Some were confined to their villages in Río Muni.

On Annobon island, 670 kilometres southwest of Bioko, over 20 people were arrested in August following an argument between a group of people and two government officials. The detainees were accused of rebellion and imprisoned in Bata. In the past the authorities had severely punished anyone who accused the government of neglecting the interests of the island's inhabitants or called for independence for Annobon.

In late August, Francisco Engomo Micué and his cousin, José Ramón Obama, were arrested in Bata by police who were looking for the former's son, Father José Luis Engomo. A Roman Catholic priest, Father Engomo had gone into hiding two days earlier after criticizing the government in a sermon. Father Engomo came out of hiding after the authorities indicated that he would not be arrested and four days later his father and cousin were released.

There were two political trials, both of which failed to satisfy international standards for fair trial. Both took place before military courts using summary procedures, which curtail the right to adequate defence and deny any right of appeal. In September over 20 people who had been arrested on Annobon island in August were tried in Bata. Eight were convicted of secession and an attempt against the security of the state, but the others were acquitted and released. Orlando Cartagena and Francisco Medina were both sentenced to 28 years' imprisonment; the other six received 20-year prison terms. However, all eight, who were prisoners of conscience, were released in the October amnesty.

The second trial took place in October when six of the soldiers and former soldiers arrested in August in Malabo were tried in secret. One was acquitted but the five others were convicted of conspiracy, incitement to rebellion and slander. Sergeant Jacinto Nculu was sentenced to 24 years' imprisonment; the other four were each sentenced to prison terms of three years and one day, although these sentences were reduced by half at the time of the October amnesty. Jacinto Nculu's sentence was reduced to eight years. He and the four others were prisoners of conscience. Amnesty International believed the charges against them were false.

Seven soldiers, all possible prisoners of conscience who had been accused of belonging to the PPGE and detained without trial since September 1992 (see *Amnesty International Report 1993*), were reported to have been freed in the March amnesty. Those released in the October amnesty included Paulino Oná Obiang, local organizer of the *Convergencia para la Democracia Social* (CPDS), Convergence for Social Democracy, in Akurenam, in the south of Río Muni, who had reportedly been detained in August for telling people not to attend celebrations to mark President Obiang Nguema's accession to power.

Most of those detained during the year were reportedly tortured or ill-treated by being beaten on the soles of their feet with truncheons or having the bones in their hands broken. Three members of the opposition *Unión Popular* (UP), Popular Union, who were among five people arrested in Nsok Nsomo, Río Muni, in June following a dispute over the siting of a health

128

centre, were tortured by having their arms broken in detention. One of the five, Gaspar Oyono Mba, died in hospital in July reportedly as a result of torture. The other four continued to be ill-treated in detention until they were released, untried, in October.

Former Lieutenant Tobías Obiang Nguema was arrested in August in Malabo and severely tortured before being restricted to his village in Río Muni. He was rearrested in early September and taken to Malabo where he was forced under torture to sign a statement implicating himself in a plot to overthrow the government. He was tried in October and acquitted.

Two other members of the UP died in detention, reportedly as a result of torture. Dámaso Abaga Nve died in Ebebiyín police station in late March. He had been arrested two days earlier for allegedly insulting the PDGE. The commission set up to monitor the National Pact began an investigation into his death, but it had not concluded its work when negotiations between the government and opposition parties broke down in August. Former Lieutenant Pedro Motú Mamiaga, who had been a prisoner of conscience from December 1990 to January 1992, died in custody in August. He had been arrested a day earlier after visiting the leader of the UP who had just returned from exile. He was said to have been severely tortured at a military camp in Malabo. The authorities announced that he had committed suicide and accused him of plotting to overthrow the government.

In August two people were reported to have been extrajudicially executed on Annobon island by the security forces who had been called to the scene of an argument (see above). Soldiers fired indiscriminately and then pursued people who fled. Manuel Villarrubia, who was wounded while attempting to escape, was pursued into the sea by a soldier who was said to have shot him at close range. Simplicio Llorente was reportedly deliberately killed outside his house by the same soldier. There was no official investigation into the killings and no one was brought to justice.

One person, Romualdo Rafael Nsogo, was sentenced to death for murder and executed: he was convicted of murdering a youth in a brawl. Although he was a civilian he was tried before a military court and had no right of appeal against his conviction or sentence. He was publicly executed the day after his trial on a beach outside Bata.

Amnesty International repeatedly appealed for the release of prisoners of conscience and for the introduction of effective safeguards against torture and ill-treatment of prisoners. It urged the government to set up a full and impartial inquiry into all reports of extrajudicial executions and deaths in custody and to abolish the death penalty. In January the organization published a report, *Equatorial Guinea: Political reform without human rights*, which described the human rights violations which had occurred at the same time as the introduction of a multi-party political system.

In February the UN Commission on Human Rights discussed Equatorial Guinea and decided to appoint a Special Rapporteur to investigate the human rights situation in the country.

ERITREA

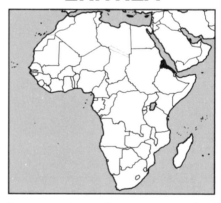

Three returning exiles were arrested and remained in detention without charge at the end of the year. The fate or whereabouts of several people reportedly detained in the previous two years remained unknown. All death sentences were commuted in August.

Eritrea became formally independent from Ethiopia on 24 May after a UN-supervised referendum in April resulted in a 99.8 per cent vote in favour of independence. The Eritrean People's Liberation Front (EPLF) forces had defeated Ethiopian President Mengistu Haile-Mariam's army in May 1991 after 30 years' armed struggle for independence. For the two-year interim period Eritrea had been governed by the

EPLF Provisional Government, led by its Secretary General Issayas Afewerki, who became President when Eritrea gained independence.

Three members of an Eritrean lowlands group known as the Jaberti were detained on 6 January. They had returned to Eritrea the previous week after many years' exile in Saudi Arabia, for talks with the provisional government. They were arrested at Asmara airport as they were about to return to Saudi Arabia. They remained in detention without charge or trial at the end of the year. They were prisoners of conscience, held on account of their criticism of the government and their demands for special political status or representation for the Jaberti people.

There was little other information about political arrests or about political prisoners detained during the previous two years.

The authorities announced an amnesty in August, under which 250 untried detainees were released and sentences for other prisoners reduced. However, no details about the prisoners concerned were disclosed by the authorities so it was not possible to establish if they included any political prisoners. In particular, it was not possible to establish if any of the 200 or more members of the previous Ethiopian administration or security forces who had been arrested in May 1991 or later for alleged crimes or human rights violations were among those freed.

The fate or whereabouts of several "disappeared" opponents of the EPLF remained unknown. They included people who, in previous years, had been abducted in Addis Ababa, the Ethiopian capital, or arrested in Kassala refugee camp in Sudan, and who were reported to have been secretly detained in Eritrea (see *Amnesty International Report 1993*).

All death sentences were commuted in the August amnesty. However, the authorities did not disclose how many people had been under sentence of death, or any details about their offences or trials.

Amnesty International wrote to President Issayas Afewerki welcoming Eritrea's new membership of the UN and urging swift ratification of international and regional human rights instruments. It asked for details of the August amnesty and continued to inquire about "disappeared" or detained government opponents, but received no response.

ESTONIA

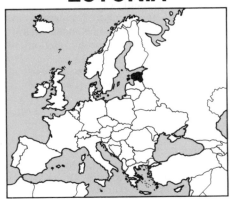

Two people were sentenced to death.

Estonia became a member of the Council of Europe in May and signed the European Convention for the Protection of Human Rights and Fundamental Freedoms and its Protocol No. 6 concerning abolition of the death penalty. It had not ratified either instrument by the end of the year.

Two people were sentenced to death, both for the crime of aggravated murder. Both men were believed to be still under sentence of death at the end of the year. Two people under sentence of death at the end of 1992 had their sentences commuted to life imprisonment by President Lennart Meri. The last execution took place in September 1991.

Amnesty International appealed for commutation of the death sentences and urged the authorities to consider the complete abolition of the death penalty.

In January Amnesty International published a report entitled *The Baltic States: Time to abolish the death penalty*.

ETHIOPIA

Several thousand suspected government opponents were detained without charge or trial, including prisoners of conscience: some were reported to have been tortured or to have "disappeared". Over 2,000 others who had been detained in 1991 or 1992 continued to be held without charge or trial: they included both suspected government opponents and officials of the former government suspected of human rights violations. However, over 20,000

130 other suspected government opponents **arrested in 1991 and 1992, and over 1,000 former government officials, were released. Some government opponents were reportedly killed in circumstances suggesting that they had been the victims of extrajudicial executions.**

The Transitional Government, headed by President Meles Zenawi, extended its rule for a further six months up to early 1994, beyond the two-year transitional period which followed the overthrow of former President Mengistu Haile-Mariam's government in May 1991. Eritrea, formerly part of Ethiopia, proceeded to full independence after a UN-supervised referendum in April (see **Eritrea** entry). A commission started work on a new Constitution. There was fighting in some Oromo-populated areas between government forces and the Oromo Liberation Front (OLF), which had left the government in June 1992. There were also intercommunal conflicts and violent incidents between government soldiers and alleged opponents in other areas.

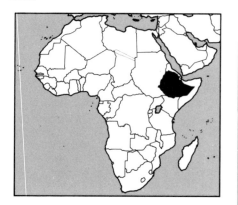

In June Ethiopia acceded to the International Covenant on Civil and Political Rights (but not its Optional Protocols) and the International Covenant on Economic, Social and Cultural Rights.

Government opponents with a wide range of political affiliations were arrested. Although over 70 political groups, mostly ethnic-based, were either represented in the Council of Representatives (the interim parliament) or allowed to operate openly, critics of the government were often interrogated by the police, or detained. Many suspected supporters of the OLF and other opposition political groups, including some based abroad, were arrested.

Nearly all those arrested for political reasons were detained without charge or trial. Some were taken to court and remanded virtually indefinitely for investigation into alleged criminal offences. Others were provisionally released after periods of up to several months, but many of these detentions appeared to be illegal.

In January up to 100 students from Addis Ababa University were arrested and one killed during a demonstration against the UN-supervised referendum in Eritrea, in which the security forces fired on students (see below). There were further arrests at the university in April, when students demonstrated against the authorities' dismissal of certain academic staff and expulsion of student activists. Some of the students were still held without charge or trial at the end of the year.

Also in January, several officials of the All-Amhara People's Organization (AAPO) were arrested for allegedly inciting interethnic violence at a political rally. All denied the offence and were released on bail after a few days. In July Asrat Woldeyes, chairperson of AAPO and a professor of medicine, and Sileshi Mulatu, another AAPO official, were arrested and detained in connection with an AAPO meeting in 1992. Professor Asrat Woldeyes was released on bail six weeks later, but Sileshi Mulatu and four others remained in detention at the end of the year with no date set for their trial. They appeared to be prisoners of conscience.

At least 2,000 members of the Oromo ethnic group were detained for suspected links with the OLF. They included farmers in Bale region in the south and Hararghe in the east, teachers in Ambo and Dembi Dollo, and businessmen in Addis Ababa. In October, all 15 staff of the Oromo Relief Association office in Dire Dawa were arrested – most were released after a few days but two were still detained at the end of the year.

In many cases, it seemed that Oromo prisoners were arrested solely because they were known to have supported the OLF when it was a legal political organization between May 1991 and June 1992, and had not been involved in subsequent armed opposition. They were all detained without charge or court order; many of them were held in large so-called "re-education." centres for OLF members in Dedessa, Hurso and Agarfa.

Many government critics were detained for questioning by the police and security forces but later provisionally released. In most cases, there were no further judicial proceedings but those concerned were subjected to restrictions on their movements. Among these was Professor Mesfin Wolde-Mariam, chairman of the Ethiopian Human Rights Council, whose conditions of release prevented him from travelling to the UN World Conference on Human Rights in Vienna in June. Ashenafi Abaje, a journalist accused of links with the banned Ethiopian People's Revolutionary Party (EPRP), was arrested in May and released on bail in September without being charged. Fifteen publishers and journalists of newly permitted independent magazines were arrested in October and held for up to a month – two were later rearrested and charged with political offences for which they had not been tried by the end of the year. Yilma Chamola, vice-chairman of the opposition Sidama Liberation Movement (SLM), a southern political group, who was arrested with other SLM officials in Awassa in August, and Makaddin Mohamed Ali, an official of the Ogaden National Liberation Front (ONLF), who was arrested near Harar in June, remained in detention without charge or trial at the end of the year.

In December some opposition exiles were arrested on their return to Ethiopia from the USA, France and Sweden for a Conference on Peace and Reconciliation. Seven were charged with armed rebellion and other political offences related to the activities of the organizations to which they belonged, including the OLF and the US-based Coalition of Ethiopian Democratic Forces (COEDF). The COEDF denied that it had advocated violence and some of those arrested appeared to be prisoners of conscience.

In many cases secrecy surrounded political arrests and details were difficult to obtain. This applied to the reported detentions in early 1993 of several senior military, political and intelligence officials of the ruling Ethiopian People's Revolutionary Democratic Front (EPRDF), who seemed to have been arrested for opposing President Zenawi's policies. Information was also deficient on reported mass round-ups in early 1993 of government opponents in Gojjam region, where an armed rebel group was active and where there were grievances about regional boundary changes.

There were also few available details of large-scale arrests of demonstrators and rioters in Gondar town in September after a church demonstration (see below).

Daniel Tessema and five other former army officers, who had been arrested in early 1992 and charged with a plot to overthrow the government, were still detained without trial at the end of the year.

Large numbers of political detainees arrested in the previous two years were released. In February and March over 20,000 suspected members of the OLF, including members of militias and civilians, among them children, who had been detained in the months following the OLF's move to armed opposition in June 1992, were released uncharged. In addition, some 1,100 officials of the former government, armed forces and the former ruling Workers Party of Ethiopia (WPE) were provisionally released as a result of habeas corpus applications or on the orders of the Special Prosecutor's Office which had been set up in 1992 to investigate crimes by officials of the former government. Nine hundred armed forces officers captured in Eritrea by the Eritrean People's Liberation Front (EPLF) in May 1991, and handed over to the Ethiopian government in August 1992, were also released.

Some 1,500 former government officials remained in detention throughout the year, accused of human rights crimes, war crimes or other unspecified criminal offences. None had been formally charged, and their continuing detention without trial appeared to be illegal. They were allowed regular family visits and access to the International Committee of the Red Cross.

Many government opponents held since 1991 or 1992 remained in detention without charge or trial, without observance of legal formalities or safeguards, and in many cases incommunicado. They included several hundred suspected OLF members held since mid-1992; several members of the EPRP; and Hagos Atsbeha, abducted from Sudan and held incommunicado since 1988 by the Tigray People's Liberation Front (TPLF), whose members head the present government (see Amnesty International Report 1993).

Torture and ill-treatment, particularly of Oromo political detainees, were reported from secret detention centres in many areas, including Addis Ababa. Details were difficult to obtain: victims were reportedly

132

threatened with reprisals if they spoke about their imprisonment. Torture methods included tying the victims' arms together tightly behind their backs with plastic strips, depriving them of food, death threats and mock executions. Torture, including rape of women, was said to be frequently used to punish or deter suspected OLF sympathizers in rural areas where OLF forces were operating, such as Wollega region in the west and Hararghe in the east.

Scores of government opponents, particularly suspected OLF members, "disappeared" after being arrested. They were believed to be held in secret security detention centres where torture was reported. Wakuma Soboka, a bank security guard in Addis Ababa, "disappeared" in May after being arrested by police. There was no news either of Yosef Ayele Bati, a teacher and OLF supporter previously tortured and detained for nine years under the Mengistu government, who "disappeared" after being arrested in Addis Ababa in November 1992.

Killings of civilians by the security forces which appeared to be extrajudicial executions were reported on several occasions. In January the security forces fired on a peaceful demonstration by students from Addis Ababa University, killing one student. A public inquiry was established, headed by the President of the Supreme Court, but its report had not been made public by the end of the year. Many civilians in Hararghe region suspected of supporting the OLF were reportedly killed by security forces in the second half of 1993. In September the police shot dead 13 people in Gondar during a demonstration against an attempt by the security forces to arrest a dissident Ethiopian Orthodox Church preacher who had criticized the government in a church sermon. The authorities said the shootings were in response to violent opposition but refused to establish an independent inquiry.

Amnesty International appealed for the release of prisoners of conscience and urged that all political detainees be either charged with a recognizably criminal offence and tried within a reasonable time, or released. Amnesty International welcomed the government's stated commitment to bring to justice those officials of the former government accused of human rights violations, but it was concerned by the long

delays in processing the cases of individual detainees and the failure to formally charge and bring to trial those being held. It was concerned too that, if convicted, some might be sentenced to death and executed. Amnesty International called for urgent and impartial investigation of all reports of "disappearances", torture and extrajudicial executions, and for steps to be taken to prevent such violations.

Amnesty International representatives visited Ethiopia in July and November and discussed the organization's concerns with government officials and others, including human rights activists. Officials denied that there were any prisoners of conscience or illegally held detainees, or that torture, "disappearances" or extrajudicial executions had occurred.

FRANCE

Hundreds of conscientious objectors to the national service laws were considered prisoners of conscience. There were numerous allegations of ill-treatment of detainees by police. There were reported shootings of unarmed people by police.

In January the European Committee for the Prevention of Torture, charged under the European Convention for the Prevention of Torture and Inhuman or Degrading Treatment or Punishment with examining the treatment of people deprived of their liberty, published its report on its visit to France in late 1991 and the government's response. It concluded that " ... a person deprived of his liberty by the forces of order runs a not inconsiderable risk of being ill-treated". Complaints were made of punching and slapping, blows to the head with telephone directories, psychological pressure, insults and deprivation of food and medicines. The Committee observed that foreigners and young people appeared to be a "preferred target". The Committee recommended strengthening the guarantees against ill-treatment through informing third parties of arrests, allowing lawyers access to people in police custody and improving doctors' conditions of access to detainees.

In March a new Code of Penal Procedure came into force. This introduced, *inter alia*, radical improvements to the procedures governing police custody. Lawyers were granted access to detainees at stipulated points during police custody, depending on the suspected offence under investigation; detainees were given greater rights regarding medical examinations; and family or friends would be informed of the arrest.

General elections were held in March; in September the new government introduced significant amendments reducing the effect of the March reforms.

There was still no right to claim conscientious objector status during military service and the alternative civilian service available to recognized objectors remained twice the length of ordinary military service.

Conscientious objectors refusing to conform to the national service laws continued to receive prison sentences. The vast majority were Jehovah's Witnesses. According to unofficial estimates, over 700 Jehovah's Witnesses were imprisoned during the year for refusing to perform military service. They had not applied for conscientious objector status because they also rejected, on religious grounds, the option of civilian service.

Christophe Lascaray, from the Basque region, based his objection to military service on his anti-militarist and political beliefs. He did not apply for civilian service because, among other objections, he considered its length to be punitive. He was released in June after serving over seven months of a 13-month prison sentence.

There were numerous allegations of ill-treatment of detainees by police throughout the year. Many of the most serious cases concerned members of ethnic minorities.

In January Nzungu Nkanza, a Zairian, was arrested in Paris during an identity check. He alleged that the police handcuffed him, threw him to the ground and beat him unconscious. Nzungu Nkanza alleged that officers stamped and spat on him and racially insulted him in the police station. He received medical treatment in a hospital before being released without charge.

Two cases of alleged ill-treatment by police in previous years were pursued in the courts. In May Amnesty International was informed that, following a judicial inquiry into the alleged ill-treatment of Lucien Djossouvi in Paris in 1989, two police inspectors and an investigating officer had been charged with acts of violence (see *Amnesty International Reports 1990* to *1993*). Four years after the original complaint had been lodged, the trial had still not opened.

In May a court in Strasbourg convicted two police officers of injuring two motorists in a police station. Sukhder Parek, an Indian, and Veejayvan Jaganathan, a Mauritian, had been arrested for drunk driving in October 1991. They alleged that officers had punched and hit them with a metal ruler, causing head injuries and a perforated ear-drum to Veejayvan Jaganathan and a broken finger to Sukhder Parek. The officers received fines and suspended prison sentences of two months and one month respectively.

There were reports of police shootings of unarmed people in circumstances indicating an excessive and illegal use of force. In April there were several killings by the police. Eric Simonté was shot in the head near Chambéry by an officer taking him into custody. He had reportedly been attempting to steal car tyres.

Rachid Ardjouni, a 17-year-old of Algerian origin, was shot and fatally wounded by a police officer in Wattrelos. According to press reports, the officer, suspected of being drunk, was kneeling over Rachid Ardjouni, who was lying face downwards on the ground, when he shot him.

Makomé M'bowole, a 17-year-old Zairian, was killed in a police station in Paris. An inspector shot him through the head while he was questioning him about a suspected petty theft. The inspector reportedly claimed that he had merely wished to intimidate him with the gun.

Following the killing of Makomé M'bowole there were demonstrations, accompanied by civil disturbances, in Paris, the capital. Numerous allegations of ill-treatment by police were made. Philippe Gibes and Salim Hadjadj were arrested by four or five police officers in the vicinity of one of the demonstrations, but they claimed that they had not participated in it. Philippe Gibes alleged that he was hand-cuffed, punched, kicked and beaten with a truncheon. Salim Hadjadj stated that officers racially abused him and repeatedly hit him until he lost consciousness. In the police station they were both allegedly forced to kneel for one and a half hours, handcuffed and facing the wall. Salim Hadjadj was transferred to hospital for treatment.

Yves Zaparucha, who had earlier taken part in a demonstration, was arrested by police officers on his way home. He alleged that he was beaten while on the ground and then repeatedly kicked, punched and hit with truncheons while being dragged to the police station. In the station he was handcuffed and made to kneel facing the wall. Yves Zaparucha was later transferred to another police station where he alleged that he was again hit and racially insulted before being admitted urgently to hospital.

Judicial inquiries were opened into all the cases of alleged ill-treatment of detainees and the reported shootings of unarmed people by the police.

Amnesty International continued to call for the release from prison of conscientious objectors whom it considered to be prisoners of conscience. Amnesty International considered that because of its punitive length, civilian service did not provide an acceptable alternative to military service. It also considered that individuals should be able to seek conscientious objector status at any time.

Amnesty International sought information from the authorities about the progress of investigations into allegations of ill-treatment. In August the organization wrote to the Ministers of the Interior and Justice regarding its concerns over deaths in custody, shootings and allegations of ill-treatment by police. No replies had been received from the authorities by the end of the year.

During a meeting with Amnesty International representatives in April, President François Mitterrand expressed his severe disapproval of reported violence in police stations.

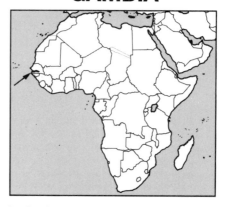

GAMBIA

The death penalty was abolished.

In April Parliament voted overwhelmingly in favour of a bill abolishing the death penalty.

The proposal to abolish the death penalty had been made by the President, Sir Dawda Jawara, who had previously publicly stated his personal opposition to the punishment. At the UN World Conference on Human Rights held in Vienna in June he stated that "the death penalty is increasingly difficult to reconcile with evolving human rights standards ... it has no value, no useful purpose in relation to crime prevention and control".

The government also announced that the Gambia would accede to the Second Optional Protocol to the International Covenant on Civil and Political Rights, aiming at the abolition of the death penalty.

Since independence in 1965, 87 people had been sentenced to death, but only one execution had been carried out. It was not clear whether anyone was under sentence of death when the death penalty was abolished.

In August Amnesty International published a brief report, *The Gambia: President abolishes the death penalty*. Amnesty International welcomed the decision to abolish the death penalty as a clear indication of the country's commitment to human rights.

GEORGIA

Both sides to the conflict in the disputed region of Abkhazia were said to have deliberately and arbitrarily killed non-combatant civilians. The scope of the death penalty was widened to include two new offences, and a decree authorizing summary executions in certain cases was introduced. At least 13 people were reportedly executed.

The political situation remained unstable. The government resigned in August and the following month parliament suspended its activity for eight weeks during a state of emergency declared by Head of State Eduard Shevardnadze. In the disputed region of Abkhazia, in the northwest of the country, hundreds of people were reportedly killed in September when Abkhazian forces broke a July cease-fire, attacking and eventually taking the Georgian-held regional capital of Sukhumi. Tens of thousands of refugees fled the region, almost all of which quickly fell under Abkhazian control. The situation in Georgia was further complicated by the return in September of former president Zviad Gamsakhurdia, who had been ousted in January 1992. He called for the government to be overthrown, and his supporters briefly took control of large areas in the west of the country before either fleeing or surrendering.

In September Georgia acceded to the 1949 Geneva Conventions and their Additional Protocols of 1977.

There were dozens of reports that both sides to the conflict in Abkhazia had carried out deliberate and arbitrary killings of non-combatant civilians, although the state of emergency and other factors connected with the fighting in the region made it difficult to investigate the reports.

Allegations against Georgian troops continued (see *Amnesty International Report 1993*) while they controlled Abkhazia. For example, in April five Abkhazian members of the Gabunia family, including two aged over 80, were reportedly killed in their house in the village of Adzyubzha.

After Abkhaz forces captured Sukhumi in September, soldiers were said to have sought out Georgian civilians, tortured and killed them because of their ethnic origin. For example, it was reported that a 67-year-

old Georgian man was detained in his apartment in Sukhumi by two armed men belonging to the Abkhaz forces, taken on to the balcony and beaten to death.

At least one person said to have been detained solely on grounds of his ethnic origin was released during the year. Garri Pilia, an ethnic Abkhazian, had reportedly been detained by Georgian forces in August 1992 and held hostage because he was related to an opposition Abkhazian member of parliament. He was released in April. The fate of at least seven other non-Georgians said to have been detained at about the same time because of their ethnic origin was still unclear at the end of the year.

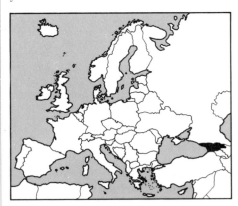

Throughout the year supporters of Zviad Gamsakhurdia alleged that many of their number were imprisoned solely for their peaceful political opposition to the government, although official sources stated that they were held in connection with violent attacks which had involved loss of life.

Despite official reports that the death penalty had been abolished when the 1921 Constitution was restored in 1992 (see *Amnesty International Report 1993*), it emerged that the criminal code had not in fact been amended: at the beginning of the year it still retained 10 offences carrying a possible death sentence. Two further offences were added to those punishable by death: mercenary activity in armed conflicts and genocide. In November Eduard Shevardnadze issued a decree authorizing, on a temporary basis, measures including summary execution for cases of banditry and looting in areas of combat activity.

At least 13 people were reportedly executed. According to unofficial sources,

136

N. Gelashvili, D. Maysuradze, V. Nikolaevili and D. Dartsmelidze were executed at Dranda prison on 19 April for attempting to seize an aircraft at Sukhumi airport. Five days after the decree on summary executions was introduced two armed supporters of Zviad Gamsakhurdia and seven local inhabitants were reported by the Interior Ministry to have been shot dead in Zugdidi for looting. Later that month the commandant of the capital, Tbilisi, was reported as saying that "several" people had been summarily executed during a curfew after refusing to present identification papers. No complete official statistics were known to have been published on the application of the death penalty in 1993.

During the year Amnesty International sought further information on allegations that opposition figures were imprisoned solely for their political beliefs, and on reports that both sides to the conflict in Abkhazia had murdered non-combatant civilians. The organization also appealed to all parties to the conflict to respect human rights and basic humanitarian standards.

Amnesty International expressed regret that the death penalty had not been abolished in law, in line with constitutional provisions, that its scope had been extended, and that a decree permitting summary executions had been introduced. The organization urged that this decree be rescinded, and that any other pending death sentences be commuted.

No substantive replies from the Georgian authorities had been received by the end of the year. In November the Abkhazian authorities informed Amnesty International that around 40 people had been arrested and charged in connection with offences against the civilian population when their forces took control of the region.

GERMANY

There was a marked increase in the number of reports of police ill-treatment; most of the victims were foreign nationals. Police officers were also accused of failing to protect the victims of racist attacks in previous years. At least one prisoner detained under anti-terrorist legislation was held in prolonged isolation. One person was shot in disputed circumstances. An amendment to the Constitution and a new law on asylum procedures came into force, severely restricting the right to seek asylum in Germany.

The Federal Republic of Germany acceded to the (First) Optional Protocol to the International Covenant on Civil and Political Rights in August.

In September the Berlin Regional Court sentenced three former senior East German officials—former Defence Minister Heinz Kessler, his deputy, Fritz Streletz, and district Communist party leader Hans Albrecht—to prison sentences of between four and a half and seven and a half years for their part in killings at the border between the two Germanies before 1989. Proceedings against other senior figures, including former East German head of state Erich Honecker, were stopped earlier in the year on grounds of ill-health.

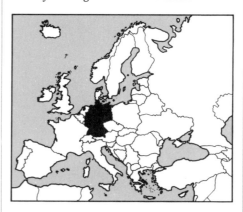

There was a marked increase in the number of reports of police ill-treatment; most of the victims were foreign nationals. In January Habib J., an Iranian student who had been granted asylum in 1988, alleged that after being assaulted by a bus driver in Berlin he was violently arrested by the police and later taken to a police station where he was hit and racially abused by officers. A witness confirmed that she had seen the bus driver assault Habib J. and also seen officers violently throw the victim into the back of a police van.

In September the Bremen prosecuting authorities rejected a complaint lodged by Mehmet S., a 14-year-old Turkish Kurd, that he had been ill-treated by police in March 1992 (see *Amnesty International Report 1993*). According to the Bremen Ministry of Justice, the investigation into Mehmet S.'s complaint had failed to establish how his injuries had occurred or who had been responsible for them. Mehmet S. successfully appealed against the decision to close the investigation and it was reopened in November.

Police officers were also accused of failing to protect victims of racist attacks. In January it was alleged that the police in Rostock had withdrawn from the scene of racist attacks on an asylum hostel in August 1992, following negotiations with rioters, despite being aware that over 100 Vietnamese housed next to the hostel would be left in danger. During the police withdrawal rioters set fire to the hostel forcing those inside to escape on to the roof of the building. These allegations were made during an inquiry into the events of August 1992 by the parliament of Mecklenburg-West Pomerania.

In March three police officers, who had failed to intervene during a racist attack on Amadeu Antonio Kiowa, an Angolan national, in November 1990 (see *Amnesty International Report 1993*), were charged with causing him bodily harm leading to his death.

In February two German victims of police ill-treatment were awarded compensation by the Hamburg Regional Court. Lutz Priebe had alleged that in August 1989 officers at Station 16 in the St Pauli district of Hamburg had struck his face against the edge of a counter, breaking his nose. Frank Fennel had alleged that in July 1991 officers from the same station had punched, kicked and hit him with batons; as a result he was in hospital for a week. No criminal charges were brought against any of the police officers involved in the two incidents.

At least one prisoner detained under anti-terrorist legislation was held in prolonged isolation. Such isolation may have serious physical and psychological effects on prisoners and may constitute cruel, inhuman or degrading treatment. Birgit Hogefeld was arrested in June in Bad Kleinen in northern Germany during a police operation in which suspected Red Army Faction member Wolfgang Grams and a police officer died. In July she was transferred from Frankfurt to Bielefeld prison where she reportedly had no contact with her fellow prisoners. A decision of the Federal High Court in July prohibited Birgit Hogefeld from participating in church services or any other communal activities.

In the same police operation, Wolfgang Grams was shot dead following a gun battle with members of the GSG-9 anti-terrorist unit at Bad Kleinen railway station. According to eye-witness reports, Wolfgang Grams was shot in the head at close range by a member of the unit as he lay motionless on the ground.

On 1 July an amendment to the German Constitution (*Grundgesetz* or Basic Law) and a new asylum law came into effect. Prior to this date anyone claiming asylum had the right to receive a full examination of their claim with rights of appeal in the courts. Since 1 July people who travel to Germany through countries where they could have claimed asylum are denied the right of asylum in Germany. These so-called "safe" third countries include the member states of the European Union (EU) and other specified countries which are party to and apply the 1951 Convention relating to the Status of Refugees and the European Convention for the Protection of Human Rights and Fundamental Freedoms, including all countries which share borders with Germany. The measures also restrict the right to asylum in Germany for people who have come from countries of origin (listed in the law) where they are presumed not to risk human rights violations. Asylum-seekers can rebut this only in an accelerated asylum procedure which has limited appeal rights and which does not contain all the safeguards necessary to ensure the protection of those at risk.

In June Amnesty International asked the Berlin authorities whether charges had been brought against the officers accused of ill-treating Habib J. In the same month, the organization was informed that investigations were still continuing into complaints brought against the police officers involved, against the bus driver and against Habib J. himself.

In February Amnesty International wrote to the Minister of Justice of Mecklenburg-West Pomerania expressing concern that police officers may have failed in their duty to protect Vietnamese citizens during the Rostock riots. It urged that a thorough and speedy investigation take place into allegations about their actions; some of those allegations had been made for the first time during a parliamentary inquiry. In May the organization was informed that an investigation into the actions of the minister responsible during the riots and of

138

senior police officers was continuing.

In October Amnesty International wrote to the Minister of Justice of Brandenburg expressing concern about the delay in judicial proceedings against the three officers accused of failing to come to the assistance of Amadeu Antonio Kiowa. Charges against the officers had been brought more than six months previously. In December the Minister of Justice of Brandenburg informed Amnesty International that a Berlin court had ordered further investigations to be conducted by the prosecuting authorities before it could decide whether the officers in question should be tried.

In a letter to the Hamburg authorities in March Amnesty International expressed concern about reports it had received that officers based at Station 16 had ill-treated people in their custody. In May it asked whether, following the rulings by the Hamburg Regional Court, charges would be brought against the officers who ill-treated Lutz Priebe and Frank Fennel. In the same month Amnesty International was informed that the rulings in the two cases would be examined to find out whether there were grounds for reopening investigations. Later in the year the organization learned that this re-examination had not resulted in charges being brought against the officers who had assaulted Lutz Priebe and Frank Fennel.

In December Amnesty International wrote to the Federal Ministry of Justice about the prolonged isolation of Birgit Hogefeld. The organization asked whether the restrictions on her association with other prisoners remained in force and whether a review of them was planned. Amnesty International also asked what measures the prison authorities had taken to alleviate the physical and psychological effects of prolonged isolation on Birgit Hogefeld.

In a letter to the Schwerin Public Procurator in July, Amnesty International expressed concern about the circumstances surrounding the shooting of Wolfgang Grams. The organization noted that many of the statements made by government, justice and police officials following the incident had been confusing and in some cases contradictory. The organization pointed out the relevant international standards regarding the use of force and the deprivation of life and urged that the inquiry into the death of Wolfgang Grams

be as wide-ranging as possible. The Schwerin Public Procurator informed Amnesty International that he was unable to give any details about the investigation into Wolfgang Grams' death.

In March Amnesty International appealed to members of the *Bundestag* (the lower house of parliament) not to adopt the amendment to the Constitution and the new asylum law. The organization expressed concern that countries which had serious deficiencies in asylum procedures, or which still had fragile systems for refugee protection, had been specified as "safe" third countries. It also expressed concern about the systematic use of a list of "safe" countries of origin and that asylum-seekers from such countries would have their claims examined in an inadequate and accelerated procedure.

In June Amnesty International published a report, *The alleged ill-treatment of foreigners in the Federal Republic of Germany: A summary of recent concerns.*

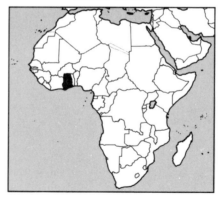

GHANA

Six demonstrators were detained briefly following a peaceful, unauthorized demonstration. One prisoner of conscience was released after completing a prison sentence. Several students were assaulted and two were shot and wounded by police following demonstrations. Three prisoners were sentenced to death and 12 executed.

The 1992 Constitution came into force in January and President J.J. Rawlings swore in a civilian government in March. Most ministers were former members of the Provisional National Defence Council (PNDC), the military government which seized power under Flight-Lieutenant

Rawlings in 1981.

Under the new Constitution the Public Order (No. 2) Law, PNDC Law 288 of 1992, was automatically repealed. This law allowed 28 days' administrative detention without charge or trial on the authority of the Minister of the Interior with no recourse to the courts. The new Constitution provided for any detainee to be brought before a court within 48 hours of arrest.

In July Parliament abolished the National Public Tribunal, the highest in a system of special courts created in 1982 which were not independent of the executive and whose procedures did not guarantee a fair trial. Appeals from lower Public Tribunals can now be made to the higher courts in the ordinary court system. Public Tribunal chairpersons have to have the same qualifications as High Court judges and the judiciary was given the main responsibility for their appointment.

Also in July, the government established a Commission on Human Rights and Administrative Justice to investigate allegations of human rights violations in Ghana.

There were public protests at the renewed government employment of Warrant Officer Salifu Amankwah, convicted of murder and sentenced to death in 1987 but granted an amnesty in 1988 by the Head of State before his appeal had been heard. It was widely alleged that his release so soon after conviction was due to his close relationship with the government. Salifu Amankwah had been in charge of a traffic police task force which in many cases had illegally arrested and beaten suspects, and had been convicted of beating and killing a retired accountant. Warrant Officer Amankwah was returned to his former post. The family of the murdered man had not received any compensation from the government.

Six men were arrested and reportedly beaten following a peaceful demonstration in February against the government's economic policies. Charged with holding an unauthorized demonstration, they were released on bail the next day. Charges brought against them under the 1972 Public Order Decree were withdrawn in March. In July the Supreme Court ruled that parts of the Public Order Decree were inconsistent with the right to demonstrate without police permit, granted by the 1992 Constitution.

One prisoner of conscience was released in May at the end of his sentence. George Naykene, editor of the *Christian Chronicle* newspaper, had been sentenced in April 1992 to 18 months' imprisonment after being convicted of libel (see *Amnesty International Report 1993*).

In July Eben Quarcoo, editor of the *Free Press* newspaper, was reportedly detained briefly following his publication of allegations of corruption against a government minister and the President's wife.

In response to an application for *habeas corpus* in February, the High Court in Accra ordered the authorities to produce 10 prisoners in court. The application failed when the prison authorities refused to produce the prisoners on the grounds that they had been lawfully imprisoned following conviction for offences against the security of the state between 1983 and 1987. Some were political prisoners. All had been convicted by Public Tribunals.

In February Hadi Tahidu Damba, and three others who were not in court, were convicted by the National Public Tribunal on various charges of conspiracy and causing criminal damage, in connection with bomb attacks in Accra and Tema in 1992 (see *Amnesty International Report 1993*). Hadi Tahidu Damba was convicted of conspiracy and sentenced to six months' imprisonment; the others were sentenced *in absentia* to between two and 10 years' imprisonment.

The trial of Professor Albert Adu-Boahen, leader of the opposition New Patriotic Party, and Kwesi Pratt, a journalist and former prisoner of conscience, had not been completed by the end of the year. They had been charged in December 1992 with refusing to testify in the case against Hadi Tahidu Damba and others: they disputed the jurisdiction of the National Public Tribunal. In June the Supreme Court ruled that their trial had not started before the National Public Tribunal, and the Chief Justice, under the transitional provisions of the new Constitution, reassigned the case to the High Court. The defendants appealed against a High Court ruling that new charges could be brought, and the case had not proceeded by the end of the year.

In February six newspaper sellers in Accra were reportedly arrested and beaten by security officers at Osu Castle, the seat of government. They apparently had their heads forcibly shaved and their takings seized for selling newspapers in the wrong

140

place. They included two boys, aged 14 and 16.

Following demonstrations in Accra on 22 and 23 March in support of increased loans to students, a number of students were assaulted and three female students were shot and wounded by police in their hall of residence. In June an internal committee of inquiry reported that the police had "over-reacted" and that there had been no justification for the use of force against the students. The Minister of the Interior said that injured students would be compensated. By the end of the year, the students had not received any compensation, and no official action had been taken against the police involved: they were not brought to justice.

Three men were sentenced to death by the National Public Tribunal in February after being convicted of armed robbery. Twelve prisoners were executed by firing-squad in July, in the first executions since February 1990. They had been convicted on various charges of murder or armed robbery, and some for both.

In May a Togolese opposition group based in exile in Ghana reportedly detained a Togolese national, Vincent Coco Adote Akouete-Akue, and killed him in captivity. He was apparently suspected of betraying the group.

Amnesty International expressed concern at the resumption of executions, and appealed for the commutation of all death sentences and for the abolition of the death penalty.

GREECE

About 400 conscientious objectors to military service were held: all were prisoners of conscience. More than 15 people were prosecuted for peacefully exercising their right to freedom of expression. Conscientious objectors in military camps continued to face harsh prison conditions. There were further reports of torture and ill-treatment. The death penalty was completely abolished. Two Albanian citizens were feared to have "disappeared".

Following elections in October, Andreas Papandreou, leader of the *Panellinio Sosialistiko Kinima* (PASOK), Panhellenic Socialist Party, succeeded Constantine Mitsotakis as Prime Minister.

In December parliament officially abolished the death penalty in peace and wartime.

There is no alternative civilian service for conscientious objectors to military service. Some 400 conscientious objectors, the vast majority of them Jehovah's Witnesses, were imprisoned for refusing to undertake military service. Most were serving four-year sentences which they could reduce to about three years by working in prison.

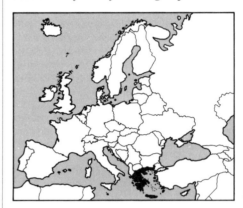

A Jehovah's Witness minister, Charalambos (Babis) Andreopoulos, was threatened with imprisonment for refusing to perform military service on conscientious grounds. Although Greek law provides for automatic exemption from military service for all religious ministers, the military authorities refused to exempt Charalambos Andreopoulos because they considered that the Jehovah's Witness Watchtower Society "is not a religion, but rather a business of economic and political nature". In March the Ministry of National Defence, on the basis of an emergency provisional ruling from the Council of State, granted Charalambos Andreopoulos a postponement from military service pending a final ruling which had not been given by the end of the year.

At least 15 people were tried for criticizing government policies on ethnic minorities and foreign affairs. In April Christos Sideropoulos and Anastasios Boulis were both sentenced to five months' imprisonment for comments they had made to a magazine calling for the recognition of a Macedonian minority in Greece (see *Amnesty International Report 1993*). Their sentences were suspended pending an appeal which had not been heard by the end of the year.

The appeal of four members of the *Antipolemiki Antiethnikisti Syspirosi*, Anti-War Anti-Nationalist movement, including Stratis Bournazos, who had been sentenced to 19 months' imprisonment in May 1992 (see *Amnesty International Report 1993*), had not been heard by the end of the year. The defendants were not remanded in custody.

Two further appeals against convictions for public declarations of opposition to government policy on Macedonia were still pending. Michail Papadakis, a 17-year-old high-school pupil, had been arrested in December 1992 after handing out leaflets about the Macedonian question during a demonstration. He was convicted of incitement and carrying a weapon – no corroborative evidence was produced for the second charge – and sentenced to one year's imprisonment. The other appeal concerned five members of the *Organosi gia tin Anasingrotisi tou Kommunistikou Kommatos Elladas* (OAKKE), Organization for the Reconstruction of the Communist Party, who had been arrested in 1992 while putting up posters in Athens, the capital. They were convicted of incitement and illegally posting bills although the law on posting bills has rarely, if ever, been enforced. They were sentenced to six and a half months' imprisonment in January 1992, but were released pending an appeal which was not heard during the year.

Reports continued to be received that conscientious objectors were being held in military camps in conditions which amounted to cruel, inhuman or degrading treatment or punishment. In February, two conscientious objectors, Pavlos Kyriakou and Petros Manthou, were transferred to hospital in Kozani suffering from pneumonia. They had apparently been held in disciplinary cells in sub-zero temperatures without heating or blankets.

There were further reports of torture and ill-treatment, including several which involved riot police. In February Nikitas Papanastassatos, a photographer for the newspaper *Eleftherotypia*, was reportedly seized by riot police officers after he had taken photographs of them beating a reporter from another newspaper. He alleged that he was held handcuffed in a police van where he was beaten by 15 police officers and that his face was slapped while riot police officers attempted to force him to hand over his film.

Amnesty International also received a large number of allegations of ill-treatment during the expulsion of tens of thousands of Albanian nationals in mid-1993. In most cases the allegations were that soldiers, police and border guards beat, kicked or punched those being expelled. Gëzim Cani, from Çerme, Lushnjë in Albania, was arrested by Greek border guards after crossing the border into Greece illegally in May. Gëzim Cani was allegedly beaten with truncheons by the soldiers who arrested him and forced to run alongside a moving military vehicle while soldiers held him by the hair.

Two cousins, Tom and Roberto Natsis, apparently "disappeared" in March. Both ethnic Greeks with Albanian citizenship, they were last seen being arrested by an armed police officer in Zagora. Despite initial confirmation by the police in Zagora that they were holding the cousins, police later gave conflicting information as to where the cousins had been taken and denied any knowledge of their whereabouts. By the end of the year, no further information had been received concerning the whereabouts of the two men.

In January Amnesty International published a report, *Greece: Violations of the right to freedom of expression – further cases of concern*. It called for the quashing of the convictions of prisoners of conscience and for the conviction of Michail Papadakis to be reviewed.

In February Amnesty International called on the government to ensure impartial investigations into allegations of ill-treatment of conscientious objectors by soldiers and military police and also into the conditions in which conscientious objectors were being held in military camps. The government gave no information about investigations into dozens of cases of torture and ill-treatment raised in 1992 (see *Amnesty International Report 1993*), other than about Süleyman Akyar, who died in January 1991 apparently as a result of being tortured by police officers. In a letter in September the Greek authorities stated that "the investigation remained inconclusive".

In March Amnesty International published a report, *5,000 years in prison: conscientious objectors in Greece,* which drew attention to the failure of successive governments to bring Greek legislation on conscientious objection into line with international standards.

142

In June Amnesty International urged the authorities to take urgent steps to trace Tom and Roberto Natsis. In their reply the authorities denied that the cousins had ever been arrested by police, but gave no details of any investigation into their alleged "disappearance". In December Amnesty International again wrote to the authorities expressing concern about torture and ill-treatment in police stations and prisons.

Amnesty International continued to urge the government to release all prisoners of conscience and to introduce legislation on conscientious objection which fully reflects international standards.

GUATEMALA

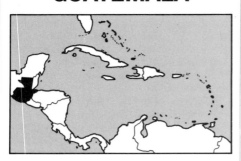

Extrajudicial executions continued to be carried out with almost total impunity by the security forces and their civilian agents, including so-called "civil patrols" – civilian militias in which Guatemala's largely indigenous peasants are forced to serve. Several people "disappeared". There were reports of excessive use of lethal force by members of the security forces and civilian militias, resulting in possible extrajudicial executions. Human rights activists and suspected government opponents were subjected to harassment and death threats. The Supreme Court confirmed the death sentence on a soldier for killing four peasants in 1992, but it was commuted.

Talks to end long-term armed conflict between government forces and the armed opposition broke down in May. They remained stalled on issues such as the scope of negotiations; whether the UN could mediate and verify accords without agreement by both parties; the establishment of a Truth Commission to examine past abuses; abolition of the civil patrols; the reincorp-

oration into Guatemalan life of refugees and displaced persons; and the terms of any eventual amnesty for government and opposition combatants.

Unrest swept the capital, Guatemala City, in May as students and trade unionists demonstrated against cost of living increases and government policies.

On 25 May President Jorge Serrano, the first elected civilian president to succeed an elected civilian president in Guatemalan history, announced that he would rule by decree. He was apparently pressed by elements within the security forces who feared that a Truth Commission would challenge military impunity and were determined to oppose demands from refugees and internally displaced peasants living outside military control in so-called "communities in resistance" (CPRs). President Serrano suspended the Supreme and Constitutional Courts, the offices of the Attorney General and the Human Rights Procurator, and certain constitutional guarantees; Congress was dissolved and arrest orders issued for several top officials including the Human Rights Procurator, Ramiro de León Carpio. However, within days, an unprecedented alliance of more moderate sectors of the army, opposition parties, business leaders, human rights groups and popular organizations reversed the attempted *"auto-golpe"* ("self-coup"). Both President Serrano and Vice President Gustavo Espina were forced into exile abroad. Widespread discontent at corruption allegedly involving high-level officials, including former President Serrano, and international pressure contributed to the reversal of the attempted coup.

On 6 June Congress elected former Human Rights Procurator Ramiro de León Carpio as President. He promised to improve Guatemala's human rights situation and to end corruption and impunity. The Presidential High Command, implicated in recent human rights violations, was restructured and its intelligence gathering functions removed. However, reports of abuses persisted, as did rumours of plots to overthrow the new President, apparently because of his repeated unsuccessful attempts to purge corrupt officials.

Extrajudicial executions by the security forces and their civilian agents were reported both before and after the change of government. By August, Guatemalan human rights groups claimed that 149 extrajudicial executions had occurred during 1993. Some victims were shot outright in the presence of witnesses; others were abducted by armed men in civilian clothes believed to be security force members, then tortured and murdered.

Apparent extrajudicial executions reported under President Serrano included that of Luis Arturo Alvarez Concoa, a law student who "disappeared" after leaving the *Universidad de San Carlos* (USAC), University of San Carlos, in Guatemala City in March. His mutilated body was found in April. Staff and students of USAC, which was characterized by successive governments as a "centre of subversion," have long been targets of government abuse.

In April Tomás Lares Cipriano, a Quiché member of the indigenous peasant organization *Comité de Unidad Campesina* (CUC), Committee for Peasant Unity, and the indigenous rights group *Consejo de Comunidades Étnicas "Runujel Junam"* (CERJ), Council of Ethnic Communities "We are all Equal", became the 17th CERJ member known to have been killed since CERJ's founding in 1988. He was shot dead the day after organizing protests against the presence in his area of military and civil patrols. The Public Ministry said it had summoned members of the civil patrol allegedly responsible to testify, but there was no further news on the case.

One street youth, Henry Yubani Alvarez Benítez, was known to have been killed by the police in 1993: he was shot dead in Guatemala City by an officially licensed private security policeman. No one was apparently brought to justice for his death.

In February trade union leader Carlos Ranferi Gómez survived an apparent extrajudicial execution attempt when four heavily armed hooded men stopped a bus on which he was travelling, singled him out and shot him. His assailants seized material he had just gathered from CPRs and returned refugee settlement sites.

Apparent extrajudicial executions reported after President de León came to office included those of his cousin and long-term political ally, Jorge Carpio Nicolle, two members of Jorge Carpio Nicolle's political party and a member of his security guard. They were all killed in El Quiché department, weeks after the new President's inauguration. Jorge Carpio Nicolle was the owner and publisher of an influential newspaper. Initially, witnesses blamed the armed opposition; later, officials suggested the victims died during a robbery. However, discrepancies between information released by the police and the military and the fact that the victims were not robbed led relatives to conclude that Jorge Carpio was extrajudicially executed because of his prominent role in the alliance which drove former President Serrano from office. They rejected army efforts to implicate CUC member Tomás Pérez Pérez, as the killers did not have peasant accents. According to the CUC, documents were planted at Tomás Pérez' home and he was tortured to make him sign statements that the CUC and the opposition were involved. Jorge Carpio's wife reported receiving death threats because of her campaign for genuine inquiries into the murders.

The indiscriminate use of lethal force by the security forces and their agents was reported, resulting in possible extrajudicial executions. The army continued aerial bombings of CPRs in which non-combatant civilians were reportedly wounded. In August Juan Pablo Chanay was killed and several others wounded when civil patrollers from Colotenango, Huehuetenango department, indiscriminately fired upon villagers peacefully protesting against harassment by the army and patrollers. President de León promised that those responsible would be prosecuted, but no proceedings were known to have been initiated.

"Disappearances" reported after President de León came to office included that of indigenous activist Tomás López Chitic, who was detained in October by armed men in plain clothes at his home in Suchitepéquez department. There was no further news of him.

Others who were initially reported to have "disappeared" later reappeared; many had been tortured in custody. Elizabeth Recinos Alvarez de León and Eluvia de Salam, two trade union leaders, were abducted in Guatemala City on 17 June by men in civilian clothes. Eluvia de Salam was released the following day, but Elizabeth Recinos was found unconscious in the street on 23 June, with two broken ribs. She had been beaten, kicked and drugged while being interrogated about her allegations of congressional corruption.

In October, Marco Choco Damas, a Quekchí literacy promoter with the *Consejo Nacional de Desplazados de Guatemala* (CONDEG), National Council for

144

the Displaced of Guatemala, "disappeared" after being detained by soldiers in Baja Verapaz department. There were fears that he had been killed or forcibly recruited by the army, but he was freed without explanation in November from the Baja Verapaz army base.

Suspected opponents of the government and human rights activists were subjected to intimidation, including death threats. Guillermo Armando Estrada Quezada, a student leader in the May demonstrations against the cost of living, and Amílcar David Montejo García, who criticized President Serrano's education policies on television, both received death threats. In September, a bomb exploded in the offices of the *Grupo de Apoyo Mutuo* (GAM), Mutual Support Group, a group attempting to clarify the fate of the "disappeared". A few hours later, members of FAMDEGUA, another group of relatives of the "disappeared", received a telephone call threatening that they too would be bombed if they did not close their office.

An anonymous communique in October warned indigenous leader Rigoberta Menchú, the 1992 Nobel Peace Prize winner, and Héctor Rosada, head of President de León's official delegation to the peace talks, and 20 others that their days "were numbered" because of supposed links with the armed opposition.

Also in October, President de León commuted the death sentence, which had been upheld by the Supreme Court, on a soldier, Nicolás Gutiérrez Cruz, for the January 1992 killings of four displaced indigenous people in Sololá department, despite apparently widespread domestic support for his execution.

Tens of thousands of past human rights violations remained uninvestigated, while those involved in inquiries suffered threats and abuses. In April a 30-year sentence was upheld on Noel de Jesús Beteta, formerly with the Presidential High Command, for the 1990 murder of anthropologist Myrna Mack (see *Amnesty International Reports 1991* to *1993*). However, the institute where she had worked was entered on several occasions in 1993 by unidentified men in plain clothes who threatened those involved in the case, particularly the victim's sister, and twice attacked institute staff. In October, two former soldiers sentenced to long prison terms for the 1990 murder of a US citizen,

Michael Devine (see *Amnesty International Reports 1992* and *1993*), said that they, and several others including Noel de Beteta, were willing to name superior officers who had ordered "death squad" killings. However, they withdrew their testimonies, allegedly after threats from the military high command. Subsequently, five prisoners were found dead in their cells, one of them a close friend of Noel de Beteta. Initially, the government claimed all had committed suicide, but the toxicology department of USAC found that all had been drugged and murdered.

Those sentenced in 1993 for human rights abuses included two civil patrollers convicted of the murder of a father and son in 1991; a senior police chief and four other officers who had violently broken up a peaceful demonstration of indigenous people in Guatemala City in July 1992; and a number of military agents convicted of killing Julio Cuc Quim, a student, in 1992, although the case against the commander of the unit responsible was left open (see *Amnesty International Report 1993*). However, a one-year suspended sentence against a member of the Mobile Military Police for the beating of two street youths in January 1991 was overturned and he was unconditionally released.

Other inquiries into reported violations failed to make significant progress owing to lack of official cooperation. In March, two former combatants who claimed to have escaped from unacknowledged detention by the Guatemalan military made detailed allegations to the UN Commission on Human Rights (UNCHR) and the Organization of American States (OAS). They testified that they had seen or heard of other unacknowledged prisoners, including Efraín Bámaca Velásquez, an opposition commander who the army claimed had died in combat in 1992. In August a body exhumed from the grave where the army claimed he was buried proved not to be his. However, there were no official efforts to locate either Efraín Bámaca or others allegedly held in secret detention. Similarly, the official response to the exhumation of the remains of some 150 people at Rio Negro, Baja Verapaz department, was to claim that they had been killed by "guerrillas". However, in 1982, Amnesty International had recorded allegations that some 170 villagers had been killed there by the army.

Amnesty International repeatedly called on the government to investigate all reported human rights violations and to bring those responsible to justice. In May it published a report, *Guatemala: Impunity – a question of political will*, in which it said that the security forces and their auxiliaries must obey national and international laws and cooperate fully with human rights investigations. Also in May an Amnesty International delegation visited Guatemala to manifest concern that President Serrano's attempted coup represented an unacceptable risk to human rights protection. Following the reversal of the coup attempt, Amnesty International's delegation pressed the newly inaugurated President to move decisively to end abuses.

In March Amnesty International submitted a written statement to the UN Commission on Human Rights (UNCHR) in which it insisted that investigation of past violations was vital to halt abuses. A new UN Expert on Guatemala was appointed in November after prolonged government efforts to delay ratification by the Economic and Social Council of the UNCHR's March resolution on Guatemala. After a September visit to Guatemala, the Inter-American Commission on Human Rights of the OAS recommended that because of "continued friction and violations of human rights", the civil patrols should be disbanded or transformed into institutions "appropriate to a democratic society."

In an oral statement to the UN Working Group on Indigenous Populations in July, Amnesty International included reference to its concerns in Guatemala.

GUINEA

Dozens of people were shot dead and many more injured by the security forces during demonstrations, but the government took little or no action to curb the killings. A prisoner died after reportedly being tortured. Two political detainees were held without charge or trial.

Following its postponement of multiparty elections in December 1992, the government of President Lansana Conté faced renewed pressure from the opposition which culminated in September in a series of demonstrations calling for the establishment of a government of national unity.

These demonstrations were suppressed using force and at least 18 people were killed. The presidential election in December, in which President Conté was returned to power, was marred by violence in which 12 people died, and was criticized by international observers and opposition parties as unfair.

In June Guinea ratified the (First) Optional Protocol to the International Covenant on Civil and Political Rights.

Dozens of people were shot dead and others wounded by the security forces who repeatedly opened fire on demonstrators and were permitted to do so with impunity. As in previous years, the government failed to hold the security forces accountable for human rights violations and most killings were not even investigated. In one case only did the authorities announce that soldiers had been arrested for shooting demonstrators and then no further action was reported.

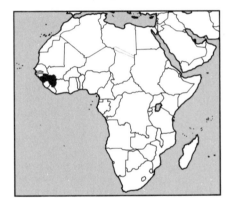

In February four women were reportedly killed in Faranah, 500 kilometres northeast of the capital, Conakry, when security forces fired at demonstrators protesting against alleged corruption in army recruitment and calling for the release of two people who had been arrested at a related demonstration. The authorities accused opposition leaders of responsibility for the violence but no investigation into the killings was known to have taken place.

In Conakry, two people were killed during a violent demonstration in May: some sources suggested that people loyal to the President had instigated the violence which led to these deaths, but this could not be confirmed. After the demonstration, six political party leaders were summoned for questioning by the gendarmerie: this led to further protests in which two government supporters were reportedly killed by opposition activists in Dinguiraye and at least three opposition supporters were reportedly shot dead by soldiers in Kankan in early June.

Two other people were reportedly shot dead by soldiers at Dinguiraye in June, after a dispute between the local governor and religious officials about the correct date of the Muslim Tabaski ('Id al-Kabir) festival. The shootings occurred after local people refused to obey an order banning the celebration of the festival on 1 June.

The largest number of killings occurred in late September, when some 30 opposition political parties organized a rally to demand a government of national unity. Three demonstrators were shot dead when the rally, on 28 September, which had begun peacefully, became violent. Further demonstrations followed and by 30 September official figures reported 18 people dead and nearly 200 injured. An eyewitness reported seeing 40 corpses at the main morgue in Conakry, all with bullet wounds. Following the killings on 28 September the authorities announced the arrest of two soldiers, but no subsequent action was reported. President Conté's response to the killings was to publicly accuse opposition leaders of exploiting inter-ethnic tension and to impose a two-month ban on street demonstrations.

In July a suspected murderer, Mamadou Keita, was reportedly summarily executed by soldiers in Kissidougou. Suspected of killing a relative, he gave himself up to the authorities after a crowd threatened to take revenge on his mother. In the face of continued public unrest, the military apparently overruled a judicial decision to guarantee his security and reportedly executed him by firing-squad in front of a large crowd. The authorities took no action against those responsible.

One detainee was alleged to have died as a result of torture. Almamy Liman Kourouma, a criminal suspect, died in August at the central police station in the Commandanyah area of Conakry the day after his arrest. A forensic doctor reportedly concluded that his death was due to a heart attack, but people who saw his body said it bore signs of torture. An official inquiry was reportedly initiated but its outcome was not known.

Jean Soumaoro, a newspaper director, was sentenced to three months' imprisonment in February, after being convicted *in absentia* of libel. He had apparently accused an army captain of ordering soldiers to open fire on demonstrators in October 1991 in Kankan (see *Amnesty International Reports 1992* and *1993*). The court issued a warrant for his arrest but apparently he remained at liberty.

Amadou II Diallo and Amirou Diallo, arrested in October 1992 in connection with an alleged assassination attempt against President Conté, were held without charge or trial throughout the year. It emerged that the brief detention of opposition leader Amadou Oury Bah in October 1992 (see *Amnesty International Report 1993*) occurred after he was implicated in the assassination attempt by Amadou II Diallo.

In December about 20 people, mostly local traders, were killed in three villages around Macenta, close to the border with Liberia, by members of a Liberian rebel force, the United Liberation Movement for Democracy in Liberia (ULIMO), who raided villages suspected of harbouring opponents from the National Patriotic Front of Liberia (NPFL).

Amnesty International expressed concern to the government about killings by the security forces, calling for them to be thoroughly investigated and for those responsible for human rights violations to be brought to justice. Amnesty International also urged the government to instruct all members of the security forces that lethal force may only be used strictly in accordance with international standards, in particular, the UN Basic Principles on the Use of Force and Firearms by Law Enforcement Officials.

GUINEA-BISSAU

Dozens of soldiers and two civilians were arbitrarily detained after an alleged coup attempt in March. Ten were released in June, apparently pending trial. Sixteen were formally charged and were to be tried in January 1994. Those arrested included two possible prisoners of conscience who were briefly redetained in August. Other political activists were detained during the year and reportedly

beaten in police custody. The death penalty was abolished.

In February the National Assembly approved a package of constitutional amendments to move the country to a multi-party political system, a process which started in 1991. The reforms were proposed by a multi-party commission preparing for Guinea-Bissau's first multi-party elections. President João Bernardo Vieira announced in July that elections would be held in March 1994. The reforms, which strengthened human rights protection, included the rights not to be arbitrarily arrested or subjected to torture or unfair trials. All the opposition parties and a significant number of members of the ruling *Partido Africano para a Independência de Guiné e Cabo Verde* (PAIGC), African Party for the Independence of Guinea-Bissau and Cape Verde, supported abolition of the death penalty which was abolished when the revised Constitution was published in early June.

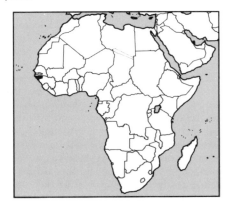

Dozens of soldiers and two civilians were arrested after an incident on 17 March in which a senior military officer was killed and several army units briefly mutinied. The detainees were held incommunicado while they were questioned by a military Commission of Inquiry set up to investigate the incident. The authorities ignored a Supreme Court order for one of the civilian detainees, João da Costa, to be brought before a judge within 48 hours so that the legality of his detention could be tested. The non-governmental *Liga Guineense dos Direitos do Homem*, Guinea-Bissau Human Rights League, expressed concern that extracts of statements made before the Commission of Inquiry were broadcast on television, thereby prejudicing the right of those accused to be presumed innocent until proved guilty. Concern was also expressed that detainees had been denied access to lawyers and relatives. The League's president, Fernando Gomes, subsequently received death threats.

In mid-June, 10 of the detainees were released, apparently pending trial. They included two possible prisoners of conscience: João da Costa, a former government minister and president of the opposition *Partido da Renovação Democrática*, Democratic Renewal Party, and Tagmé Na Waié, a member of the *Resistência da Guiné-Bissau-Movimento Bafatá* (RGB-MB), Guinea-Bissau Resistance-Bafatá Movement. Neither they nor, apparently, the eight others had been charged with any offence. However, under the terms of their release both were prohibited from leaving Bissau, the capital, and from engaging in political activities, although there appeared to be no basis in law for such a prohibition. Other detainees were reportedly released during the year but some remained in detention.

In early August João da Costa and Tagmé Na Waié were rearrested by soldiers after publicly criticizing the government in defiance of their bail conditions. They were held in a military prison for four days before being released without charge. In December they and 14 others were charged and committed for trial by the Military Court in January 1994.

Police were reported on several occasions to have ill-treated political activists and others. They included Fô Na Nsofa and four others, some of whom apparently belonged to the RGB-MB, who were detained in late June and early July in the south of the country and reportedly beaten in police custody. Four remained in detention without charge or trial until August. Fô Na Nsofa was released on bail in late October or early November.

Mussa Baldé, an RGB-MB official, was among several people briefly detained and beaten with rifle butts by police in August. They had been unable to produce identity cards and tax certificates when stopped by police.

In mid-May the procurator of the Regional Military Court of Bissau formally charged seven police officers, who had been arrested in late 1992, with complicity in the death in September 1992 of

148

Ussumane Quadé (see *Amnesty International Report 1993*). The Interior Minister, who was apparently not arrested, was charged with failing to take appropriate action after receiving allegations that Ussumane Quadé had died as a result of torture. However, those arrested in connection with the case were released in July and the eight accused had not been brought to trial by the end of the year.

In May Amnesty International published a report, *Guinea-Bissau: In defiance of the law*, and called publicly for all those detained after the 17 March incident to be properly charged and given a fair trial, or released. The organization said that the proceedings of the Commission of Inquiry were so flawed that any findings should be totally excluded as evidence at the trial.

Amnesty International expressed concern about the rearrest in August of João da Costa and Tagmé Na Waié, who appeared to be prisoners of conscience. Amnesty International also appealed on behalf of Fô Na Nsofa and the four men detained with him.

Amnesty International welcomed the abolition of the death penalty.

GUYANA

There were new reports of torture and ill-treatment of suspects by police, who also shot dead two men in suspicious circumstances. At least four people were sentenced to death for murder and some 24 people were under sentence of death at the end of the year. No executions were carried out.

In May Guyana ratified the (First) Optional Protocol to the International Covenant on Civil and Political Rights.

There were new reports of torture and ill-treatment of suspects by police. Criminal suspects were reportedly beaten and held in inhumane conditions at Kitty police station, near Georgetown, the capital, in July. Also in July, Bissoon Sukhdeo, an employee of an East Bank Demerara sawmill, alleged that he was assaulted, threatened with a gun and immersed in the Demerara River by a party of attackers who claimed to be police officers, one of whom was in police uniform. He was taken to the local police station and charged with an earlier attack on a neighbouring firm with whom the sawmill was in dispute.

In October more than 10 youths who had been arrested in connection with a murder investigation alleged that they were beaten with pieces of wood, punched, deprived of food and coerced by threats into signing statements while detained in Mahaica police station in Demerara-Mahaica province. A woman arrested with them alleged that she too was beaten and that two army officers threatened to rape her.

In September Rickey Samaroo and Joseph "Dingo" Persaud were shot dead by police while allegedly attempting to rob the Licence Revenue Department in Georgetown. Initial police reports stated that the men were shot after one of them fired at the police. However, the men's relatives questioned the killings as Joseph Persaud was a key witness in a case brought against the police for the murder of another suspect, Michael Teekah, in 1988.

Michael Teekah had been arrested with Joseph Persaud in May 1988 and allegedly died after he and Joseph Persaud were forcibly immersed in a canal by officers from the Criminal Investigation Division (CID) at Eve Leary police headquarters in Georgetown; both men were allegedly handcuffed, and had bags tied over their heads, when they were repeatedly immersed in the water.

Before his death, Joseph Persaud had testified in a civil action brought against several officers accused of involvement in Michael Teekah's death. The case was due to resume hearing but was reportedly abandoned after Joseph Persaud's death. The Guyana Human Rights Association cited what they termed a "host of suspicious circumstances" surrounding Joseph Persaud's killing, including discrepancies between police accounts and relatives' reports that he had been shot in the mouth. Police were reported to be investigating the shootings.

Following Joseph Persaud's death, a second witness to Michael Teekah's killing, George Bacchus, wrote to the Minister of Home Affairs, alleging that his life had been threatened by the officers involved.

At least four people were sentenced to death for murder and some 24 people were under sentence of death at the end of the year. No executions were carried out.

Five men awaiting trial since 1990 for treason, a capital offence, had the charges against them dropped in May. Three of the accused who were still in prison were released (see *Amnesty International Reports 1993* and *1991*).

In December Amnesty International wrote to the Minister of Home Affairs urging that a full and impartial investigation be carried out into the shooting of Joseph Persaud and Ricky Samaroo. Amnesty International also expressed concern that a second witness had allegedly received death threats from officers involved in the killing of Michael Teekah (see above). Amnesty International urged that the government order a full, independent inquiry into the circumstances of Michael Teekah's death and that steps be taken to ensure the physical safety of witnesses in the case.

Amnesty International also asked if inquiries had been conducted into alleged police involvement in the assault on Bissoon Sukhdeo and the allegations of ill-treatment of suspects at Mahaica police station.

The organization reiterated its requests for information on earlier cases, including a number of cases in which unarmed suspects had been shot dead by the police in disputed circumstances (see *Amnesty International Report 1993*).

In February the Ministry of Home Affairs responded to Amnesty International's inquiry about the alleged ill-treatment of Hardath Ramdass and the alleged rape of a woman by police in 1992 (see *Amnesty International Report 1993*), stating that it would look into the cases and that its findings would be communicated. However, no further information had been received from the government by the end of the year.

HAITI

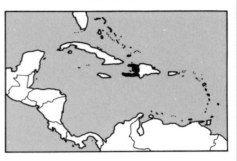

Hundreds of real and suspected supporters of President Jean-Bertrand Aristide were detained unlawfully with many of them being held without charge for longer than the legal limit. Torture and ill-treatment of detainees was widespread, and several detainees reportedly died as a result of torture. Prison conditions were extremely harsh and also resulted in deaths. Hundreds of people "disappeared" or were extrajudicially executed.

In February the first group of civilian human rights monitors appointed by the UN and Organization of American States (OAS) arrived in Haiti as part of the *Misyon Sivil Entènasyonal an Haïti* (MICIVIH), International Civilian Mission to Haiti. The mission was mandated by the UN General Assembly and the OAS, at the request of President Aristide, to verify respect for human rights.

In June the UN Security Council imposed restrictions on the movement of arms, petroleum and finance to Haiti in an effort to force the Commander-in-Chief of the Armed Forces, General Raoul Cédras, to accept the return to Haiti of President Aristide, who had been deposed in 1991 (see *Amnesty International Report 1992*).

On 3 July President Aristide and General Cédras signed an accord, brokered by the UN and the OAS, under which President Aristide would return to office on 30 October. Both parties pledged to cooperate fully to ensure a peaceful transition to a democratic society which would guarantee respect for human rights. Other measures included in the agreement were the suspension of sanctions once a new Prime Minister was installed; an amnesty to be granted by President Aristide; the creation of a new police force under a chief to be appointed by the President; the early

AMNESTY INTERNATIONAL REPORT 1994

retirement of General Cédras; and the nomination of a Prime Minister by the President.

Robert Malval was subsequently nominated by President Aristide and installed as Haiti's new Prime Minister on 30 August. A new Cabinet was sworn in on 2 September. On 4 October President Aristide granted an amnesty for political crimes committed between 29 September 1991 and 3 July 1993, although the precise crimes to which it was to apply remained unclear.

Violence accelerated as the date of President Aristide's agreed return drew nearer, as his opponents took steps to thwart his return. On 11 October, for example, opponents of President Aristide orchestrated a violent demonstration in order to prevent the docking of a US ship carrying some 200 US soldiers, the first contingent of some 1,300 foreign troops and police whom the UN planned to deploy in Haiti to train the police and army. The 200 troops then returned to the USA. By mid-October, in the face of rising violence, the 250-strong group of UN and OAS civilian human rights monitors was withdrawn from Haiti, and on 18 October worldwide oil and arms sanctions were reimposed by the UN. President Aristide did not return to power on 30 October as stipulated in the 3 July accord, nor did General Cédras or Chief of Police Michel François step down.

Hundreds of people were arrested without warrant by the military, the police or *attachés* (armed civilian auxiliaries to the security forces). Many were held without charge for longer than the 48-hour limit specified in the Constitution and many were asked to pay money to gain release or avoid ill-treatment. Most were released without charge or any form of judicial proceedings. Victims included political activists supporting President Aristide, members of grassroots organizations, peasants, trade unionists, members of the Catholic Church and journalists, as well as people apparently considered potential supporters of President Aristide simply because they lived in working-class areas.

In one case in January, Gisèle Saint-Firmin, Raymond Azazan, Maxime Horacius and six others, all supporters of President Aristide, were arrested in Les Cayes, South Department, by the security forces. All were released in early February. However, Gisèle Saint-Firmin, the mother of Marie-Josée Saint-Firmin, previously the local branch secretary of the *Organisation Politique Lavalas*, *Lavalas* Political Organization, which supports President Aristide, was only provisionally released. She could be recalled at any time to face charges of possessing subversive materials. She was reportedly beaten in custody.

Also in January, Yves Jean-Noel, a member of a local grassroots organization, was detained in Nouvelle Cité, Grande-Anse Department, accused of distributing photographs of President Aristide. He was beaten in detention at the Miragôane military barracks; he was released in April.

In February Corlson Dormé, a radio correspondent for Radio Tropic FM, was detained in Port-au-Prince, the capital, while reporting a demonstration protesting against the arrival of UN Special Envoy Dante Caputo. Corlson Dormé was detained for six days, during which he was beaten and warned to stop collaborating with *Lavalas*.

Torture and ill-treatment of detainees were widespread. In January Jean-Emile Estimable, a journalist for Radio Cacique, was severely beaten while held at the home of the *chef de section* (rural police chief) in the Marchand Dessalines locality of Artibonite Department, before being taken to the local prison. He was later transferred to St Marc prison where he was beaten again and received the *kalot marassa* – simultaneous blows to both ears – and was forced to pay money in order to stop the beatings. He was provisionally released by the criminal court in St Marc in February. Direct Jean-Baptiste, who was also detained in January near Marchand Dessalines, was ill-treated while held at the local military barracks: he was hit on the stomach with a club, his testicles were squeezed and he was slapped around the face. He was released the same day.

Manistin Caprien, president of *Lavalas*, was arrested on 30 March by the military in Môle St Nicolas, North-Western Department. He was reportedly beaten on the ears and stomach in the local military barracks while being interrogated about his organization. He was also allegedly forced to eat photographs of President Aristide, and subjected to further beatings and humiliations, including being forced to eat his own hair. When brought before a judge he fell unconscious and the judge ordered him to be treated in hospital. There, he was reportedly kept under police surveillance and threatened to the point where he felt obliged to flee despite his poor health.

Ricardo Chéry, founder of the *Union des jeunes démocrates nationalistes des Gonaïves*, Union of Young Nationalist Democrats of Gonaïves, was arrested by soldiers in April and taken to a detention centre in Gonaïves, where he was beaten and questioned about his connection with UN/OAS civilian monitors. He was then taken to a prison where the telephone number of the OAS was found in his pocket. Apparently as a result, he was subjected to the *djak* (a baton is wedged under the knees and over the arms while the prisoner is beaten repeatedly all over the body). After nine days he was released uncharged.

Trade union members Cajuste Lexius, Phabonor StVil and Saveur Aurélus of the *Centrale générale des travailleurs* (CGT), General Workers' Union, were arrested on 23 April by police belonging to the 30th Company in Port-au-Prince and severely beaten. On 26 April they were transferred to the *Service d'investigation et de recherches anti-gang*, Anti-gang Investigation Service. Cajuste Lexius, who was unconscious for two days as a result of the beatings, had to be transferred to a military hospital where he received treatment for kidney failure and for multiple open sores on his buttocks. He was finally released from hospital on 21 May. Phabonor St.Vil and Saveur Aurélus also required medical attention when they were released on 29 April.

In June Gabriel Tigen and Anaciase Pierre, both members of the *Mouvman Peyizan Papay* (MPP), a peasant grassroots organization, were arrested by police and taken to the office of the *chef de section* in Hinche, Central Department, where they were both subjected to the *djak*. They were accused of distributing pro-Aristide material, but released four days later, after paying a bribe.

Fritz Charlot, a member of the *Syndicat des travailleurs agricoles de Savanette*, Union of Agricultural Workers of Savanette, was abducted in August and driven blindfolded to a house. He was then interrogated about distributing photographs of President Aristide and was beaten and pushed to the floor; his abductors pounded his head against the ground. After two days he was dumped in the street and warned that "next time" he would be killed.

Several people were reported to have died as a result of torture, including Oriol Charpentier, who died in April while held at the military barracks in Thiotte, South-Eastern Department. The military authorities, the doctor who signed the death certificate and prisoners gave contradictory accounts of the circumstances and cause of his death. Georges Mathias died in May while in prison in Terrier Rouge, North-Eastern Department. He had been arrested in April when he was reportedly beaten by an *attaché*.

Conditions in prisons and detention centres continued to be extremely harsh, with ill-treatment, overcrowding, malnutrition, poor sanitation and a lack of adequate medical treatment. Several deaths of prisoners reportedly occurred as a direct result of such conditions.

Dozens of people were known to have "disappeared"; the true figure may have been much higher. Joseph Winy Brutus, the Treasurer of the *Parti national démocratique et progressiste d'Haïti*, National Democratic and Progressive Party of Haiti, reportedly "disappeared" in May. He had previously received death threats, apparently because of his political activism and because he had testified abroad about human rights violations in Haiti. Jéhovah Jean Louis, the brother of a parliamentary deputy, was abducted by armed men in September; his fate and whereabouts were still unknown at the end of the year, as were those of Fritz Dérose, who "disappeared" in April 1992 (see *Amnesty International Report 1993*).

At least 200 people were extrajudicially executed by the army or *attachés*, including at least 60 in September. In May the mutilated body of Mrs Souffran, an active member of *Ti Legliz*, a grassroots church group which supports President Aristide, was found in the village of St Antoine, North-Eastern Department. In August Germéus Deshommes, an active member of a peasant movement in Ravine Desroches in North Department, was arrested and accused of putting up posters of President Aristide. He was reportedly severely beaten by the local *chef de section*; his dead body was later found on the street.

In a particularly blatant case on 11 September, Antoine Izméry, a businessman and prominent supporter of President Aristide, was forced out of a church in Port-au-Prince and shot dead in the street by *attachés* while military and police

152 personnel in the area made no attempt to intervene. He had been attending a mass to commemorate the fifth anniversary of an attack on Father Jean-Bertrand Aristide while saying mass at St John Bosco Church (see *Amnesty International Report 1989*). Antoine Izméry's brother, Georges Izméry, was shot dead in May 1992, apparently after being mistaken for his brother (see *Amnesty International Report 1993*). In all, 12 bodies were found on 11 September. Another of the victims was retired army colonel Fritz Jocelyn, a known supporter of President Aristide, who was shot dead by armed men while at a petrol station in Pétionville.

Guy Malary, who had been appointed Minister of Justice by President Aristide in August, was shot dead by armed men on 14 October, together with his bodyguard and driver. Prior to his murder, he had taken a leading part in planning new legislation to separate formally Haiti's army and police, a proposal opposed by the military leadership. He had also previously been involved in inquiries into certain high-profile human rights cases and had received death threats.

In another case, Orelia Joseph, a nanny working for a prominent supporter of President Aristide, was dragged from her home in Cité Soleil in Port-au-Prince by *attachés* and beaten in front of her daughters. She was taken away and next day her severed head and legs were found in different places; the rest of her body was not found.

The army, police and *attachés* also made indiscriminate use of lethal force. For example, in September *attachés* killed five people and injured at least 30 others outside the City Hall in Port-au-Prince following a ceremony to reinstate Evans Paul as mayor.

Amnesty International repeatedly appealed to the authorities to investigate cases of human rights violations and to bring those responsible to justice. In October Amnesty International published a report, *Haiti: Human rights gagged – attacks on freedom of expression*.

Amnesty International urged the international community to use all appropriate means to promote and protect human rights in Haiti.

HONDURAS

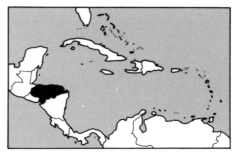

Evidence came to light early in the year implicating the security forces in a series of extrajudicial executions. A Nicaraguan citizen "disappeared" in the custody of the Honduran police: he was subsequently found to have been executed. Two soldiers were jailed for the rape and murder of a student in 1991. The police and armed forces were also believed to be responsible for numerous threats against journalists, human rights workers and others. A government report found former and current government officials responsible for "disappearances" during the 1980s.

Several former police agents gave testimony implicating the police and army in unlawful killings, drug-trafficking, corruption and other crimes. In February a former agent of the *Dirección Nacional de Investigaciones* (DNI), National Directorate of Investigations, the intelligence branch of the security forces, accused the DNI of involvement in a string of killings of union and business leaders in the northern city of San Pedro Sula in preceding months. He also alleged that the former *Batallón 3-16*, 3-16 Battalion, a military intelligence body which the government said had been disbanded following allegations that it was responsible for killings and "disappearances" in the early 1980s, was still intact and had collaborated covertly with the DNI in these abuses.

The national and international reaction to these events prompted the government to set up the *Comisión Ad Hoc de Alto Nivel*, High Level *Ad Hoc* Commission, to propose measures for the reform of the DNI, the police, the judiciary and the Attorney-General's office. In mid-March the Commission recommended the formation of an arbitration commission to review DNI personnel, to implement safeguards against torture and ill-treatment and to place those responsible for abuses before the courts. The Commission's final recommendations were published in April. It urged the creation of an autonomous Public Ministry empowered to initiate investigations and judicial proceedings and to discipline public officials where appropriate. It called for the transfer of the DNI's functions to a new *Departamento de Investigación Criminal* (DIC), Criminal Investigation Department, within the Public Ministry. In July the arbitration commission reported progress in the review of the DNI, and said reports of abuses had decreased. Legislation creating the Public Ministry was approved in December and the creation of the DIC was pending at the end of the year.

The armed forces proved reluctant to relinquish their control over the police and their traditional immunity from prosecution for human rights abuses. Although publicly supportive of the transfer of the DNI to civilian control, the armed forces High Council opposed moves by Congress to issue a clear interpretation of Articles 90 and 91 of the Constitution concerning the jurisdiction of military courts. Investigations into alleged human rights violations by army personnel had frequently been blocked by the military's claim for jurisdiction over all cases involving its members (see *Amnesty International Report 1993*). Congress approved legislation in April restricting the scope of military jurisdiction.

The *Partido Liberal*, Liberal Party, led by Carlos Roberto Reina, defeated the ruling *Partido Nacional*, National Party, in presidential elections in November. Both main parties strove to implicate each other in over 100 "disappearances" which occurred in the 1980s until the *Comisionado Nacional de Protección de los Derechos Humanos*, National Commissioner for the Protection of Human Rights, announced that his office would report on the "disappeared" by the end of the year. The report, published on 29 December, found former and current military and civilian officials responsible for the "systematic, clandestine and organized" "disappearance" of 184 individuals throughout the 1980s. Among the officials cited in the report as responsible were two former presidents and the current head of the armed forces. It also stated that military advisers from the USA and Argentina were involved in these crimes. The Commissioner recommended

that those named in the report be brought before the courts with a view to punishing those responsible, despite the 1991 amnesty law (see *Amnesty International Report 1992*). It also called for efforts to locate clandestine cemeteries where the "disappeared" were alleged to be buried, and for the disclosure of military archives relating to military counter-insurgency operations.

Several former armed opposition groups participated in the elections after renouncing armed struggle and reorganizing as political parties. A number of attacks were carried out in the name of former rebel groups, such as the *Frente Patriótico Morazanista* (FPM), Morazanist Patriotic Front, but there was compelling evidence that some such attacks, in fact, were carried out by members of the armed forces trying to discredit opposition groups.

On 29 January television journalist Eduardo Coto witnessed the killing of Eduardo Piña Van Tuyl, a businessman, in San Pedro Sula and filmed the three killers as they fled on a motorbike. A communique issued in the name of the FPM claimed responsibility. However, Eduardo Coto identified the killers as members of the army: this was subsequently confirmed by the *Comité para la Defensa de los Derechos Humanos en Honduras* (CODEH), Committee for the Defence of Human Rights in Honduras, whose investigations linked the killers to the 3-16 Battalion, alleged to be operating from the 105 Infantry Brigade in San Pedro Sula. After receiving threats, Eduardo Coto went into hiding at the home of the editor of the opposition newspaper *Tiempo*, which was then the target of a bomb attack. Eduardo Coto then left the country.

The killing of Eduardo Piña Van Tuyl was one of seven killings since November 1992 which the former DNI agent said in February had been committed by members of the army in San Pedro Sula. He also said that the 1992 killing of electricity workers' union leader Rigoberto Borjas (see *Amnesty International Report 1993*) and the killing of Guillermo Agurcia, a businessman, and his fiancée, Lourdes Enamorado, on 5 January had been carried out by a drug-trafficking and extortion network within the armed forces. After making these allegations the former DNI agent was taken under the protection of the National Human Rights Commissioner and the government undertook to mount exhaustive

154

investigations. Four DNI officers were temporarily confined to barracks at the 105 Brigade headquarters in February pending their appearance before a court, but judicial proceedings did not appear to have progressed by the end of the year.

In December Juan Pablo Laguna Cruz, a Nicaraguan citizen, was detained by Honduran police near the border town of El Triunfo. Despite a *habeas corpus* petition, the Honduran authorities denied detaining him. He was subsequently found to have been killed.

A significant step towards overcoming impunity was taken in July when an army colonel and a sergeant were sentenced to 16 and 10 years' imprisonment respectively after being convicted of the rape and killing in 1991 of a 16-year-old student, Riccy Mabel Martínez (see *Amnesty International Reports 1992* and *1993*). The family of the victim lodged an appeal against the sentence, arguing that the officers should have been convicted of murder rather than the lesser crime of homicide, for which they were given minimum sentences. A test case of the military's accountability before the law, the trial was obstructed by threats against the judge and the prosecutor, and attempts by the military to have the accused tried before a military court, countered by intense pressure from fellow students and human rights campaigners.

A civilian court was also granted jurisdiction in the case of the army massacre at the El Astillero cooperative in Agua Caliente, Atlántida department, in 1991 (see *Amnesty International Report 1992*). Proceedings against a colonel accused of ordering the killings had been opened before a military court. However, the Supreme Court upheld a complaint by CODEH that military jurisdiction in this case was unconstitutional and the case was continuing before a civilian court at the end of the year. Those allegedly responsible for other human rights violations by the army in previous years, including the killings of Juan Humberto Sánchez in 1992 and of Manuel de Jesús Guerra in 1991 (see *Amnesty International Report 1993*), remained free, the corresponding investigations having apparently stagnated.

A series of threats and attacks were directed at figures critical of abuses by the armed forces. In March Lucy Cantarero, the wife of a former armed forces chief, Arnulfo Cantarero López, said she had received death threats after her husband made public statements about the existence of 3-16 Battalion and army corruption. In April anonymous leaflets appeared in the capital, Tegucigalpa, accusing CODEH and the *Comité de Familiares de Detenidos Desaparecidos de Honduras* (COFADEH), the Committee of Relatives of the Disappeared, of bribing the opposition press and others such as Lucy Cantarero to mount a campaign to discredit the armed forces. Others who received threats throughout the year included several witnesses, lawyers and relatives involved in investigations into human rights abuses by the army.

Following the intervention of the Commissioner, two DNI agents were detained in March in connection with the torture of three detainees in police custody in Jesús de Otero, Intibucá department, in December 1992. Jesús Arquímides Monzón Mejía, Miguel Angel Montoya and Benjamín Manzanares Castro had been beaten, kicked and nearly suffocated with a *capucha* (hood) at a local police station, in order to make them confess to a robbery they denied having committed. They had been released two days later for lack of evidence. The two DNI agents were dismissed from service, but no judicial proceedings were initiated against them.

A police officer who beat a 15-year-old boy in front of numerous witnesses in a Tegucigalpa bar in July was given 30 days' detention and dismissed from the police in October, following investigations by the *Oficina de Responsabilidad Profesional*, Office of Professional Responsibility, which had been set up in 1991 to carry out internal investigations into security force abuses. However, the authorities did not appear to have investigated other cases of alleged ill-treatment of street children by security forces in Tegucigalpa – for example, the alleged ill-treatment of four children in May by security force agents in Colonia Cerro Grande. The security forces were also reported to have ill-treated people when forcibly recruiting young people into the army and in responding to strikes and demonstrations.

Amnesty International urged the government to ensure full investigation of the alleged killings and torture by the DNI and expressed concern about the lack of progress in investigating the killings of Juan Humberto Sánchez, Manuel de Jesús

Guerra and others in 1992 (see *Amnesty International Report 1993*). In September Amnesty International wrote to the National Commissioner for the Protection of Human Rights about the cases of the "disappeared" to express disquiet at the way in which their cases had been dealt with during the election campaign and to call for a full and proper investigation to clarify the fate and whereabouts of the victims. In December Amnesty International welcomed the Commissioner's report and called on President-elect Reina to bring those responsible for these and more recent abuses to justice.

HONG KONG

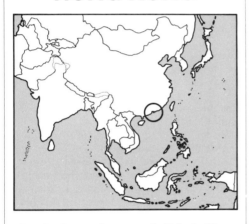

The death penalty was abolished. Thousands of Vietnamese remained in detention after being denied asylum or pending a decision on their asylum applications.

Preparations for the transition to Chinese sovereignty in 1997 dominated political debate. Successive rounds of Sino-British negotiations held during the year failed to resolve sharp criticism by China of political reform proposals made by Governor Christopher Patten in October 1992 (see *Amnesty International Report 1993*). Some of the proposals, which centred on widening the electoral base for members of the Legislative Council (Legco) to be elected in 1995, were submitted to Legco in December, despite Chinese objections.

In June the People's Republic of China announced that it had set up a committee to prepare for the establishment in 1997 of the Hong Kong Special Administrative Region. The committee adopted working rules banning unauthorized disclosure of its discussions.

In July Legco approved without dissent a motion to establish an independent Human Rights Commission, but by the end of the year the proposal had not been approved by the Governor. Proposals for the Commission's functions included receiving and investigating complaints, advising individuals who allege that their rights have been violated, recommending reform of laws which conflict with the 1991 Bill of Rights, assuming an educational role on human rights, and exercising an adjudication role subject to review by the courts.

The death penalty was abolished in April. It had applied to murder and other offences but had not been used for 27 years. Legco had passed a motion in favour of abolition in 1991 and the Governor had committed himself to abolition in an October 1992 policy statement.

At the end of the year, about 34,000 Vietnamese asylum-seekers remained in detention, of whom more than 30,000 had been denied refugee status ("screened out"); the rest were awaiting a decision on their applications for asylum. Several thousand Vietnamese voluntarily returned to Viet Nam during 1993; a further 435 were forcibly returned. Asylum-seekers still did not have the right to appear in person when appealing against refusal of refugee status. There was no mechanism for detained Vietnamese asylum-seekers to have the legality of their detention reviewed, as required by international standards.

In April Amnesty International wrote to Governor Patten to welcome the abolition of the death penalty. In October Amnesty International representatives met government officials to express concern about the continuing detention of Vietnamese asylum-seekers. An Amnesty International delegate also discussed with government officials, Legco members, legal scholars and human rights activists proposals for an independent Human Rights Commission and for broadening human rights education. Amnesty International said that a Human Rights Commission should improve the implementation of the Bill of Rights and international human rights standards by ensuring that victims of human rights violations had access to an affordable and effective complaints mechanism and by undertaking independent monitoring of human rights violations.

156

HUNGARY

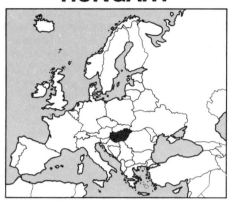

There were reports of torture and ill-treatment of Roma and foreign nationals in detention.

In February Hungary signed the European Convention for the Prevention of Torture and Inhuman or Degrading Treatment or Punishment but had not ratified it by the end of the year.

Members of the Roma community were allegedly ill-treated by law enforcement officers, apparently because of their ethnic background. In one such incident on 21 May, police surrounded the Roma neighbourhood in Örkény. They searched several houses, reportedly looking for thieves. They were then said to have attacked about 20 people using truncheons, tear-gas sprays and police dogs. Some officers allegedly shouted threats such as: "Stinking Gypsies, we will make soap of you and finish off what Hitler started!" Nine Roma were injured and one was hospitalized following this apparently unprovoked attack.

Police in Budapest allegedly tortured and otherwise ill-treated 12 foreign nationals in separate incidents on 30 and 31 December 1992 and 6 January. The 12 men were taken to the 5th District Police Station and interrogated for their suspected involvement in illegal foreign currency transactions. They were ordered to strip in front of other detainees, beaten and subjected to racist verbal abuse by officers. Mohammed Walid Fouvel was reportedly detained and beaten twice. Five of the victims subsequently had medical examinations which found injuries consistent with their allegations of torture and ill-treatment.

On 28 April Haiszam Mzaik was beaten in his coffee house in Budapest by two police officers who asked for his identity card because his car was parked illegally. The officers reportedly knocked him to the ground, twisted his hands behind his back and kicked him all over his body. A representative of Amnesty International saw Haiszam Mzaik in Budapest Police Headquarters shortly after the incident. He was no longer bleeding, but his shirt was bloodstained and he had bruises and cuts on his face, arms and back.

Six refugees from Bosnia-Herzegovina were reportedly beaten by police in the Nagyatád Refugee Camp. On 2 August, after returning from the nearby town of Tarany, the six men were taken to the camp's administrative building for questioning about allegations of disorderly conduct. The officers were alleged to have handcuffed and then beaten Damir Salihović, who was hitting his head against the wall in an apparent state of hysteria. They also handcuffed and beat Nisvet Safetović after he tried to assist Damir Salihović. The police then sprayed tear-gas into the room and locked the door. The following day the six refugees were taken to the police station in Nagyatád and later transferred to another camp in Kaposvár.

None of the reports of torture or ill-treatment was independently and impartially investigated. In July the UN Human Rights Committee expressed its concern "about the use of excessive force by the police, especially against foreigners residing in Hungary and asylum-seekers held in detention".

Amnesty International wrote to the government of Prime Minister József Antall in April and May urging it to initiate an independent and impartial inquiry into all allegations of torture and ill-treatment by police officers in Budapest. The government replied in July and October denying excessive use of force by police officers while attempting to carry out body searches. Amnesty International asked the authorities for full details of their investigations, particularly about the methods used.

In September Amnesty International urged the Minister of the Interior to investigate allegations of ill-treatment of six refugees in the Nagyatád Refugee Camp. No reply had been received by the end of the year.

In December Amnesty International wrote to the Minister of the Interior about allegations that in different incidents members of the Roma community had been ill-treated by police officers.

INDIA

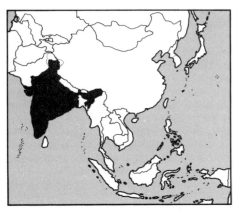

Tens of thousands of political prisoners, including prisoners of conscience, were held without charge or trial under special or preventive detention laws. Torture of detainees was routine throughout the country and scores of people died in police and military custody as a result. Scores of political detainees "disappeared". Hundreds of people were reported to have been extrajudicially executed by the security forces. At least three people were executed. Armed opposition or separatist groups committed numerous abuses, including deliberate killings of civilians and taking hostages.

The government faced violent political opposition in several states, notably in Jammu and Kashmir, Punjab, Andhra Pradesh, Assam and the other northeastern states.

Jammu and Kashmir remained under direct rule by central government throughout the year, as did Uttar Pradesh, Madhya Pradesh, Himachal Pradesh and Rajasthan until November.

In September the government established a National Human Rights Commission with the stated objective of improving India's human rights record. However, the Commission's mandate effectively excludes investigation of particularly widespread violations committed by the army and paramilitary forces operating in Jammu and Kashmir and the northeastern states. Moreover, when investigating other

alleged violations it must rely on state investigative agencies, which may have a vested interest in covering up human rights violations.

No legal reforms were implemented to safeguard detainees or to limit the arbitrary powers granted to the security forces under special legislation such as the Armed Forces (Special Powers) Act and the Terrorist and Disruptive Activities (Prevention) Act (TADA). The TADA, which was in force in 22 of India's 25 states, was extended in May for a further two years. In March the Supreme Court ruled that victims of abuses are entitled to compensation if the state fails to protect human rights guaranteed under the Constitution.

Tens of thousands of political prisoners were held without charge or trial under the special laws. According to official figures released in February, for example, 52,268 people were being held under the TADA nationwide. Many were apparently held on suspicion of committing ordinary criminal offences in states where there is no organized armed opposition violence, but others were clearly held for political reasons. Hundreds of petitions challenging the constitutionality of the TADA were pending before the Supreme Court: some had been pending for nine years.

Several newspaper editors and journalists were among those detained in 1993, including Parag Kumar Das, Krishna Barua and Nripendra Sarma, respectively editor, publisher and printer of the Assam newspaper *Budbhar*. Apparently prisoners of conscience, they were detained under the TADA in February, reportedly because of an article commemorating the death of an opposition leader. The government said they had advocated "disruptive activities" but they were released on bail in March to await trial. Several other prisoners of conscience were held throughout the year, including Shabir Ahmed Shah, leader of the Jammu and Kashmir People's League, who had been arrested in 1989 and remained in detention without charge or trial (see *Amnesty International Report 1993*).

Hundreds of suspected political activists were also detained without charge or trial under the National Security Act and, in Jammu and Kashmir, the Public Safety Act.

Torture of detainees in police and military custody was routine in every state. Torture methods most frequently cited were

158

beatings, often with *lathis* (canes), and, less frequently, suspension by the wrists or ankles, electric shocks and rape. Most victims were criminal suspects, although many were political detainees suspected of supporting armed opposition or separatist groups. Victims often came from under-privileged and vulnerable sections of society, particularly the scheduled castes and tribes. For example, Buhiben, a villager from Antras in Gujarat State, was seized in April by police searching for her husband. She was reportedly stripped, beaten with sticks and raped by two police officers.

Senior police officials frequently participated in covering up torture and prosecutions of police were rare. Amnesty International identified 484 deaths in custody allegedly resulting from torture between January 1985 and June 1993. In only six of these cases were police officers known to have been convicted. In April the Ministry of Home Affairs stated that it had verified 230 of the cases with the relevant state governments, and that in 85 of these there was evidence to justify further action against police officers.

In Delhi, the capital, there was an apparent increase in the number of deaths in custody allegedly caused by torture, rising to nine during 1993. Satyavan, a truck driver, was arrested with two friends in March. All three were reportedly beaten in Najafragh police station until Satyavan collapsed and died. One police officer was subsequently transferred and one suspended, but no independent investigation was ordered.

In Punjab, officials continued to falsely attribute deaths under torture to "encounters" between armed militants and the police or to "escapes". For example, Gurdev Singh Kaonke, a former Sikh religious leader, died in early January, allegedly as a result of torture. The police said he had "escaped", but he never returned home. Punjab's Chief Minister said in February that the police in the state would not be "screened and cleaned up" as it would hamper "anti-terrorist operations". No prosecutions for human rights violations took place in Punjab.

In Jammu and Kashmir, torture by the security forces was reported almost daily. Police records reportedly showed 132 deaths in custody in 33 days during March and April alone. One victim, Manzoor Ahmed Ganai, a farmer, had to have both legs amputated after prolonged torture by the army's Bihar regiment. This reportedly included hanging him upside-down by his ankles for several days and burning the back of his thighs with lighted paraffin. He died in February apparently as a result of the injuries he had sustained under torture.

A rare survivor of torture and attempted extrajudicial execution in Jammu and Kashmir, Masroof Sultan, a student, was beaten, shot five times and left for dead by the paramilitary Border Security Force (BSF) in April. He was found by the police who had been told by the BSF to collect the bodies of "militants killed in an exchange of fire".

Scores of political detainees "disappeared" during the year. Most were young men suspected of having links with armed secessionist groups. Many were taken into custody solely because they lived in areas where armed separatist groups were active. Few "disappearances" were clarified. Sometimes officials eventually admitted that an arrest had been made, only to claim later that the "disappeared" person had "escaped" or was killed in an "encounter".

In Jammu and Kashmir, the army and paramilitary forces were responsible for scores of "disappearances". Ashiq Hussain Ganai, a student, was arrested by an army unit in March. His relatives were given conflicting reports on his fate by various officials but he remained "disappeared".

In Punjab, most "disappearances" were carried out by the police. Victims included 65-year-old Budh Singh and his son, Tejinder Singh, who were arrested by police in mid-May. They were both apparently held in Lada Kothi detention centre and tortured. Budh Singh was last seen there; Tejinder Singh was released provisionally then detained again in July, following which he too "disappeared". The police denied all knowledge of their whereabouts.

Hundreds of people were reported to have been extrajudicially executed by security forces. At least 53 people were killed in the town of Sopore, Kashmir, by members of the BSF on 6 January. Witnesses said that soldiers fired indiscriminately into a crowded bazaar, dragged people from their homes and shot them at point-blank range, and burned others to death. The killings were apparently in retaliation for the death of a BSF member in a clash with Kashmiri separatists. The dead included a 70-year-old shopkeeper, Ghulam Mohammed

Sheikh; a woman and her two children who were burned alive in their car; and a bus driver and at least 15 passengers who were forced off a bus and shot. A judicial inquiry was ordered but had not concluded by the end of the year.

Extrajudicial executions in Jammu and Kashmir continued throughout the year. Fifty-one people were arbitrarily shot dead in Srinagar and Bijbehara on 22 October, most by the BSF, during an apparently peaceful protest against an army siege of the Hazratbal shrine.

In Bombay, a judicial investigation continued into the deaths of 1,788 people during riots between members of the Hindu and Muslim communities in December 1992 and January 1993 following the destruction of the mosque at Ayodhya (see *Amnesty International Report 1993*). The investigation, which was still in progress at the end of 1993, investigated reports that the police had sided with Hindu mobs during the rioting.

An official committee reported in July that police had colluded in killings during anti-Sikh riots in 1984, after the assassination of Prime Minister Indira Gandhi, in which almost 3,000 people died. Police had failed to intervene and subsequently failed to register reports, allowing those responsible to escape punishment. The committee's report indicted 298 police officers and two senior Congress Party leaders but they had not been brought to trial by the end of the year.

At least three people were executed; the three were all members of the same family who had been convicted of multiple murder.

Armed opposition groups committed grave human rights abuses, including hostage-taking, torture and deliberate and arbitrary killings. The victims included officials, politicians, relatives of members of the security forces, and suspected informers. For example, on 2 March separatist militants in Jammu and Kashmir killed former assistant commissioner Ghulam Nabi Baba. In Punjab, although violence declined in 1993, officials and Hindu civilians continued to be targeted by armed opposition groups. In Andhra Pradesh, members of the Naxalite People's War Group were reportedly responsible for torturing and killing many people whom they suspected of being police informers. Armed groups in Assam, Andhra Pradesh

and Jammu and Kashmir were reported to have taken hostages.

Amnesty International called on the government to release prisoners of conscience and to ensure that all other political prisoners were brought to trial promptly and fairly, or released; to investigate impartially all allegations of torture and deaths in custody and to bring to justice those responsible for torturing or ill-treating prisoners; and to implement safeguards outlined in a 10-point program to halt torture.

Amnesty International repeatedly expressed grave concern about continuing reports of deaths in custody and of extrajudicial executions. In April it published *India: Sopore – a case study of extrajudicial executions in Jammu and Kashmir*, which appealed to both the authorities and armed opposition groups to stop human rights abuses. In October Amnesty International called for an investigation into the killings by the BSF of 51 people in Srinagar and Bijbehara. Throughout the army siege of the Hazratbal mosque, Amnesty International urged the government to instruct the security forces to act with restraint and urged armed separatists to safeguard the lives of civilians trapped inside the mosque. It welcomed the peaceful ending of the siege.

In December Amnesty International published *India: "An Unnatural Fate" – "Disappearances" and Impunity in the Indian States of Jammu and Kashmir and Punjab*, which documented 208 alleged "disappearances" since January 1990. It urged the government to establish the fate or whereabouts of the victims and implement detailed recommendations to halt "disappearances". Amnesty International appealed for the commutation of death sentences and the abolition of the death penalty.

Amnesty International welcomed reports that plans to forcibly repatriate some 30,000 tribal refugees from Tripura State to the Chittagong Hill Tracts of Bangladesh were not to be implemented. The organization called for assurances that no refugees would be repatriated against their will.

Amnesty International also welcomed the establishment of a National Human Rights Commission but criticized the severe limitations placed on its powers, mandate and methodology.

Amnesty International renewed its long-

160

standing request to conduct independent research in various Indian states. The government allowed Amnesty International representatives to visit Bombay but authorization for access to Jammu and Kashmir had not been granted by the end of the year.

In oral statements to the UN Commission on Human Rights in February, the Working Group on Indigenous Populations in July and the Sub-Commission on Prevention of Discrimination and Protection of Minorities in August, Amnesty International included reference to its concerns in India.

Amnesty International condemned deliberate and arbitrary killings and other abuses by armed opposition groups and urged them to respect basic standards of humanitarian law and release all hostages immediately.

INDONESIA AND EAST TIMOR

More than 200 suspected government opponents were prisoners of conscience or possible prisoners of conscience, including 33 people arrested or sentenced during the year. An estimated 250 other political prisoners continued to serve lengthy sentences imposed after unfair trials. Hundreds of people were arrested and held without charge or trial. The fate of possibly hundreds of Acehnese and East Timorese who "disappeared" in previous years remained unknown. Torture and ill-treatment of political detainees, peaceful protesters and criminal suspects was common, resulting in some deaths. Reports of extrajudicial executions continued. At least 32 prisoners were under sentence of death, two of whom were sentenced during the year. No executions were known to have been carried out.

President Suharto was elected unopposed for a sixth term as President in March. The army's continued dual role in national security and politics was debated openly during the year. The government continued to face both armed and peaceful opposition from groups seeking independence for Aceh, East Timor and Irian Jaya. There were some allegations of abuses by armed opposition groups, but details were difficult to verify.

A personal envoy of the UN Secretary-General visited East Timor in April to examine the implementation of recommendations made the previous year concerning the November 1991 massacre in which the security forces killed at least 100 and possibly as many as 250 people (see *Amnesty International Report 1992*). On three occasions between January and June, the International Committee of the Red Cross (ICRC) felt obliged to suspend visits to political prisoners in East Timor because of restrictions placed on the organization by the government.

Two resolutions, of the UN Commission on Human Rights in March and of the UN Sub-Commission on Prevention of Discrimination and Protection of Minorities in August, expressed concern about persistent human rights violations in East Timor and urged the Indonesian Government to allow access to the territory by humanitarian and human rights organizations.

In June a national human rights commission was established, but its members were not appointed until December. Access to East Timor and parts of Indonesia continued to be restricted, making effective human rights monitoring almost impossible. Hundreds of thousands of former members of the Indonesian Communist Party (PKI), banned since 1965, remained subject to heavy restrictions affecting their freedom of movement and basic civil rights.

The perpetrators of human rights violations were rarely brought to justice: a small number of police officers and prison officials were convicted of killing or torturing criminal suspects but they generally received very short sentences.

Lukas Luwarso and Poltak Ika Wibowo, university students from Semarang, Central

Java, were sentenced to four months' imprisonment in November for taking part in a cultural event which criticized the country's electoral process and urged young people to boycott the 1992 national elections. Both were prisoners of conscience.

Cheppy Sudrajat, a farmer and a prisoner of conscience, received a 10-month prison term for organizing a peaceful demonstration over land issues in West Java in September. The following month, there were suspicions of police complicity in death threats and in an attack on the house of Ahmad Jauhari, a human rights lawyer.

Eleven East Timorese prisoners of conscience sentenced to long prison terms after unfair trials in 1992 remained in prison at the end of the year. Two of them, Carlos dos Santos Lemos and Bonifacio Magno Pereira, had their sentences reduced by two years. Four others, Gregorio da Cunha Saldanha, Fernando de Araujo, João Freitas da Camara and Virgilio da Silva Guterres, had their final appeals rejected by the Supreme Court. Their lawyer said that he had been unable to file appeals on their behalf within the allotted time because he had not been supplied promptly with copies of court decisions concerning his clients.

At least 50 alleged supporters of the armed pro-independence group *Aceh Merdeka*, sentenced after unfair trials in 1990, continued to serve prison terms. Two others were sentenced during the year, including Usman bin Muhammad Ali. A possible prisoner of conscience, he was sentenced to five years' imprisonment in July after being convicted of channelling funds to *Aceh Merdeka*.

Over 100 political prisoners from Irian Jaya, including at least 59 prisoners of conscience, remained in jail for advocating Irian Jaya's independence. Most had been sentenced after unfair trials in 1989 and 1990 to terms of between five and 20 years for planning or participating in peaceful demonstrations. Eight of the prisoners were released during the year, after completing their sentences.

At least 50 out of more than 150 Islamic activists, imprisoned for subversion and serving sentences of up to life imprisonment, were also prisoners of conscience. At least 11 Islamic activists were conditionally released, including prisoner of conscience Andi Mappetahang Fatwa, who had been sentenced in 1985 to 18 years'

imprisonment for subversion.

More than 30 prisoners sentenced in the 1960s after unfair trials for alleged involvement in a 1965 coup attempt or for PKI membership remained in prison. Most of them were believed to be prisoners of conscience. Seven were on death row, one of whom, Iskandar Subekti, died in custody in August after 25 years in prison, most of them on death row.

Political trials failed to meet international standards of fairness or to conform to Indonesia's Code of Criminal Procedure. East Timorese resistance leader Xanana Gusmão was sentenced to life imprisonment for rebellion and illegal possession of firearms in May after a blatantly unfair trial. He had been held incommunicado for the first 17 days of his detention and there were fears that he may have been tortured. In August his sentence was reduced to 20 years.

Hundreds of alleged government opponents were detained without charge or trial and denied access to relatives and lawyers. More than 200 villagers in North Sumatra, including women and children, were arbitrarily detained in March and held incommunicado for up to two months, following a confrontation with security forces concerning a land dispute. Dozens of people, possibly many more, were arrested in East Timor before US and Swedish officials visited the area in September. Apparently the arrests were made in order to prevent pro-independence demonstrations.

The fate of possibly hundreds of Acehnese and East Timorese who "disappeared" in previous years remained unknown (see *Amnesty International Reports 1992* and *1993*).

Torture and ill-treatment of political detainees continued to be widespread. At least 17 students who had taken part in a peaceful protest in support of farmers from Belangguan, East Java, were reportedly tortured or ill-treated during interrogation by military intelligence authorities in East Java in January. The students were said to have been forced to undress, hit with metal rods and punched, and at least 11 of the 17 were reportedly given electric shocks. The authorities denied that any ill-treatment had occurred and no investigation into the case had been undertaken by the end of the year.

Criminal suspects were also tortured and ill-treated, resulting in some deaths. A construction worker, his wife and their nine-year-old child were reportedly tortured by police in West Java in January in order to extract a confession that they had stolen a wallet. The father, Sudarmono, died as a result of torture; his wife, Dasmen, had to be hospitalized after falling into a coma while under interrogation; and their son, Junyonto, suffered injuries to his legs. Under pressure from local residents five police suspects were reportedly detained for questioning. However, to Amnesty International's knowledge, none of the suspects had been charged or brought to trial by the end of the year.

Extrajudicial executions continued to be reported. In East Java, a young factory worker was raped, tortured and then murdered in May because of her role as a labour activist. In November it was announced that a local military commander was among 10 people due to be tried in connection with her death. Despite evidence of his involvement in her abduction, it was reported that he was charged with a disciplinary offence only. He was to be tried in a military court, closed to the public. Four members of an outlawed religious group, *Haur Koneng*, were killed when government forces stormed their meeting place in West Java in July. Despite the findings of national human rights organizations that security forces had used excessive force and had deliberately killed group members, no member of the security forces had been detained or charged by the end of the year. By contrast, by the end of the year at least eight *Haur Koneng* members had been tried on various charges and sentenced to between four months and one year's imprisonment. The trials of other members of the community continued.

In September, four people were killed and three injured when security forces opened fire on about 500 peaceful demonstrators in East Java who were protesting over the building of a dam. Four police and military officers were removed from their posts after public protests, but the government and military authorities insisted that there was no need for an independent investigation.

At least 2,000 civilians were reportedly extrajudicially executed by Indonesian soldiers in Aceh between 1989 and early 1993, but no official investigations into any of the killings had been initiated by the end of the year. Most of the victims were ordinary villagers living in areas of suspected rebel activity. Nearly two years after completing its investigation, the government had yet to identify the vast majority of the up to 250 civilians believed to have been killed during and immediately after the 1991 massacre in East Timor. More than 200 people who reportedly "disappeared" after the massacre remained unaccounted for.

At least 17 criminal suspects were shot dead in Jakarta as part of a continuing "shoot-on-sight" policy instigated by the city's police chief in 1989. Despite claims by police authorities that proper procedures were followed, most died in suspicious circumstances and some may have been extrajudicially executed.

At least 32 people were in custody and under sentence of death at the end of 1993. Six were political prisoners, all elderly men sentenced for involvement in the 1965 coup attempt or PKI membership. In April former army sergeant Robert Suryadarma, accused of supporting *Aceh Merdeka*, was sentenced to death *in absentia* for subversion. At least one person was sentenced to death for murder. In January lawyers submitted a second request for presidential clemency on behalf of Kamjai Khong Thavorn, sentenced to death for drug-smuggling in 1988. The President's decision had not been announced by the end of the year, but there was deep concern that the execution was imminent. No executions were known to have taken place but in September President Suharto announced that there were no grounds for granting a stay of execution for Sukatno, a former parliamentarian and PKI member, and that he would have to be executed in accordance with the law.

In June and July a group of seven East Timorese asylum-seekers who entered the Finnish and Swedish embassies in Jakarta were turned away despite inadequate guarantees for their safety. They were allowed to leave the country in December.

Amnesty International appealed throughout the year for the release of prisoners of conscience, for the fair trial or release of other political prisoners, for urgent government action to halt torture, extrajudicial executions, "disappearances" and the use of the death penalty. The organization continued to call for investigations into past violations.

In January an Amnesty International

delegate attended the second UN Asia-Pacific Workshop on Human Rights Issues in Jakarta, the first time in 15 years that the organization had been allowed to visit Indonesia. The government, however, limited the delegate's visa to five days.

In July Amnesty International issued a report, *Indonesia: "Shock Therapy" – Restoring Order in Aceh, 1989-1993*, which documented evidence of human rights violations in Aceh and called for urgent action to tackle the pattern of gross human rights violations in the province. References to Amnesty International's concerns in Indonesia and East Timor were included in an oral statement to the UN Commission on Human Rights in March. In July Amnesty International outlined its human rights concerns in East Timor in an oral statement to the UN Special Committee on Decolonization as well as referring to its concerns in Indonesia in a separate oral statement.

IRAN

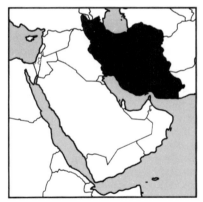

Political arrests, torture, unfair trials and summary executions were reported throughout the country. Prisoners of conscience were among those detained or serving long prison terms after unfair trials. Judicial punishments of flogging and amputation of fingers continued to be implemented. At least 93 people were executed, including political prisoners. Several government opponents were abducted or killed outside Iran in circumstances suggesting that they may have been victims of extrajudicial executions involving Iranian officials.

President 'Ali Akbar Hashemi Rafsanjani was elected to a second four-year term

of office. His government continued to face armed opposition from the Iraq-based People's Mojahedin Organization of Iran (PMOI), and organizations such as the Kurdistan Democratic Party of Iran (KDPI) in Kurdistan and Baluchi groups in Sistan-Baluchistan. Government forces raided opposition targets inside Iraq, and the PMOI claimed responsibility for attacks on various installations within Iran.

There were continuing reports of arbitrary arrests, as well as the detention, torture and execution of suspected government opponents. Those arrested included current and former officers of the armed forces and security police who were detained in October. Among them were Colonel Nasrollah Tavakkoli Nayshaboury. The precise reasons for their arrest were unclear. Some reports stated that those detained were connected with a critical open letter addressed to the government and the Islamic Consultative Assembly earlier in the year, others suggested that they may have been involved in a coup attempt. They were believed to have been released in November. Other political prisoners were serving long prison terms following unfair trials: they included supporters of the PMOI; at least 24 followers of Dr 'Ali Shari'ati; members of left-wing organizations such as the *Tudeh* Party, *Peykar* and *Razmandegan*; supporters of Kurdish organizations such as the KDPI and *Komala*; and members of other groups representing ethnic minorities such as Baluchis and Arabs.

In August *Resalat* newspaper reported a senior prison official as stating that a total of 99,900 prisoners were held during the Iranian calendar year ending in March 1993. However, no figures were made public regarding the number of political prisoners nor the number of prisoners executed.

Members of the Shi'a and Sunni clergy continued to be subject to harassment and arrest. At least five followers of Ayatollah Hossein 'Ali Montazeri were reportedly arrested in February, after he had publicly criticized the authorities. Their fate remained unknown at the end of the year.

Journalists continued to be imprisoned, among them 'Abbas 'Abdi, editor-in-chief of *Salam* newspaper, who was reportedly held in prolonged incommunicado detention following his arrest in July. In December, after a secret trial before an Islamic

164

Revolutionary Court, he was given a one-year prison term and a suspended sentence of 40 lashes. He was allegedly charged with offences against national security. Naser 'Arabha, a journalist sentenced in 1992 to six months' imprisonment for violating press laws (see *Amnesty International Report 1993*), was released. However, Manouchehr Karimzadeh, a cartoonist for the science magazine *Farad*, had his one-year prison term overruled by a second court and increased to 10 years' imprisonment on account of his caricature depicting a football-playing amputee who allegedly resembled the late Ayatollah Khomeini. He was reportedly convicted of insulting the former leader. He was believed to be a prisoner of conscience.

Other political prisoners and prisoners of conscience, some arrested many years before, remained in prison. They included Mehdi Dibaj, a prisoner of conscience held since 1984, apparently for converting from Islam to Christianity. He was reportedly sentenced to death on charges of apostasy in 1986. After the case was examined by other courts it was referred to Criminal Court No. 1 in Sari, which reportedly confirmed the death sentence for apostasy in December 1993. He was given 20 days in which to appeal against the sentence. Approximately 10 members of the Baha'i faith were also imprisoned. Three were believed to have received death sentences. One of the three was subsequently released and the others, Behnam Mithaqi and Kayvan Khalajabadi, appealed against their sentences to the Supreme Court, but no final decision had been reached by the end of the year.

Several amnesties were declared during 1993. On 1 April, for example, on the occasion of Islamic Republic Day, 1,682 prisoners convicted by public, military and Islamic Revolutionary courts had their prison terms reduced by Ayatollah Khamene'i, the spiritual leader of the Islamic Republic. No further details were made available, and it was not known whether political prisoners were among those who benefited. Arasto Shabani, arrested in 1990 (see *Amnesty International Report 1993*), was reportedly released from prison in November but was sentenced to a five-year term of internal exile.

Political trials continued to fall far short of international standards for fair trial. Trial hearings were almost always held *in camera*, inside prisons. Proceedings were summary with hearings often lasting only a few minutes. Reports consistently indicated that political detainees were denied access to legal counsel at any stage of judicial proceedings, despite official assurances to the contrary.

Torture and ill-treatment of prisoners continued to be reported to extract confessions or statements to be used as evidence at trial. Methods most commonly used were beatings, particularly on the back and on the soles of the feet, and suspension. Former political prisoners consistently reported being kept blindfolded in incommunicado detention for prolonged periods, and subjected to beating with cables and batons.

Amputation and flogging as judicial punishments remained in force. In December seven people convicted on repeated counts of theft had the fingers of their right hands amputated in the province of Gilan. In June, during a nationwide crack-down on "vice and moral corruption", a number of women were reported to have been sentenced to flogging. The punishment laid down by law for infringing the dress code is 74 lashes. They were among hundreds of women who were reported to have been arrested in Tehran for allegedly failing to conform to the strict dress laws of the Islamic Republic. Flogging was frequently imposed for a wide range of other offences, often in conjunction with prison sentences.

At least 93 people were executed, some of whom were hanged in public. In previous years many executions for non-political offences, such as drug-trafficking and murder, were reported in the Iranian press. These figures alone amounted to hundreds each year. In 1993, however, far fewer executions were reported by the Iranian news media, apparently as a result of government directives designed to prevent such reports being used by the UN Special Representative on Iran and other human rights bodies in criticism of Iran's use of the death penalty. Over 20 Baluchis were reported in the press and by unofficial sources to have been executed between December 1992 and February 1993. Some were said to have been detained without charge or trial for over a year; others had reportedly been charged with drug-trafficking, armed robbery or counter-revolutionary activities. No information was available about their trials. In December a 15-year-old girl, Mitra Zahraie, was sentenced to death and 20 lashes, having been convicted of murder and other offences by a court in Qazvin. Among the prisoners executed on political grounds was Mohsen Mohammadi Sabet, who was executed in Rasht Prison in August after being held incommunicado in solitary confinement for about 10 months.

Salim Saberniah and Mustafa Ghaderi, two alleged members of *Komala* who had been convicted of undertaking activities against the Islamic Republic, were reportedly sentenced to death and had their sentences confirmed by the Supreme Court in March. They were held in Tabriz Prison. By the end of the year no further information had come to light regarding their situation.

There were further reports of government opponents being abducted or killed outside Iran in circumstances suggesting that Iranian officials or people acting on their behalf were responsible (see *Amnesty International Report 1993*). In May 1993 German prosecutors investigating the murder in Berlin in September 1992 of Sadegh Sharafkandi, the Secretary General of the KDPI, and three other Iranians (see *Amnesty International Report 1993*) stated that the ringleader of the Berlin attack was an agent of the Iranian secret service and that he had received orders from his superiors in Tehran to carry out the killings. The Iranian authorities continued to deny categorically accusations of involvement in any of the killings. Trial proceedings began in Germany at the end of October and were still in progress at the end of the year.

The pattern of attacks on opposition activists suggested that at least some might have been victims of extrajudicial executions by Iranian government agents. On 16 March Mohammad Hossein Naghdi, representative of the National Council of Resistance of Iran and former Chargé d'Affaires at the Iranian Embassy in Rome, Italy, was killed by two gunmen in Rome. Also in March, two members of the Naroui tribe, Haibat and Dilavar, were killed outside their home in Karachi, Pakistan. In June Mohammad Hassan Arbab (also known as Mohammad Khan Baluch), a PMOI activist, was assassinated in Karachi. In August Mohammad Ghaderi, a former member of the KDPI, was abducted from his home in Kirshahir, Turkey. His badly mutilated body was discovered 10 days later.

Also in August Bahram Azadifar, a KDPI member, was killed in his home in Turkey, reportedly by two men dressed as Turkish policemen. There were reports that people arrested in connection with the abduction in Turkey of 'Abbas Gholizadeh in December 1992 (see *Amnesty International Report 1993*) had confessed to his abduction, adding that they had been instructed several months later to bury his body. There was no further information by the end of the year.

Swiss authorities investigating the murder of Kazem Rajavi in Geneva in 1990 (see *Amnesty International Report 1991*) had sought the extradition from France of two Iranian nationals in connection with his murder. Their investigation had reportedly revealed evidence of Iranian officials' involvement in the killing. Although the French court of appeal agreed with the request, the French authorities announced in December that the two men had been returned to Iran.

The threat of extrajudicial execution extended to many Iranian nationals abroad, as well as to non-Iranians such as the British writer Salman Rushdie and individuals involved in publishing or translating his novel, *The Satanic Verses*, which provoked a *fatwa* (religious edict) calling for his killing in 1989.

Amnesty International continued to press for the release of all prisoners of conscience. It urged the government to introduce safeguards to ensure that political detainees would receive fair and prompt trials and expressed grave concern about the continuing reports of torture. Throughout the year Amnesty International appealed for an end to executions.

The government replied to certain inquiries, although most of Amnesty International's requests for information on particular cases failed to produce a substantive response. The authorities again denied that any of Dr Shari'ati's followers were in prison.

In November Amnesty International published a report, *Iran: Victims of human rights violations*, highlighting a number of individual cases and calling on the authorities to bring its human rights law and practice fully into line with international standards.

Amnesty International had planned to discuss its concerns with government and judicial officials in Tehran in January 1993,

166

but was unable to go ahead owing to government objections. By the end of the year, there was no change in this situation, despite repeated public statements by Iranian officials suggesting that Amnesty International had been invited to visit the country.

In a written statement to the UN Commission on Human Rights in February, Amnesty International described its concerns in Iran, including mass executions, unfair trials, torture and the detention of prisoners of conscience. The Commission voted to extend the mandate of the UN Special Representative on the situation of human rights in Iran: however, he was denied access to the country by the Iranian authorities for the second consecutive year.

The UN Human Rights Committee continued its examination of Iran's second periodic report regarding implementation of the International Covenant on Civil and Political Rights in April and July. It deplored the high number of executions, particularly after unfair trials, and also condemned the *fatwa* imposing a death sentence on the British writer Salman Rushdie.

IRAQ

Thousands of suspected government opponents were detained and tens of thousands of others who had been arrested in previous years continued to be held. Many of them were prisoners of conscience. Torture remained widespread. Hundreds of detainees "disappeared" and the cases of more than 100,000 people who "disappeared" in previous years remained unresolved. Hundreds of judicial and extrajudicial executions were reportedly carried out. Human rights abuses were committed in areas of Iraqi Kurdistan under Kurdish control, including torture, executions and deliberate and arbitrary killings.

Economic sanctions against Iraq imposed by a UN Security Council cease-fire resolution in April 1991 remained in force. Two "air exclusion zones" over northern and southern Iraq continued to be imposed (see *Amnesty International Report 1993*). A UN-sponsored Memorandum of Understanding, which expired in March, was not formally renewed but the distribution of humanitarian relief under its terms continued on a reduced scale.

The scope of the death penalty was extended to cover three additional offences, including trading in banned goods.

Kurdish opposition groups retained control of parts of the northern provinces of Duhok, Arbil, Sulaimaniya and Kirkuk. These areas continued to be administered by the Council of Ministers for Iraqi Kurdistan. The economic blockade imposed on the region by the Iraqi Government in October 1991 remained in force. In January a Law on Judicial Authority came into effect in Iraqi Kurdistan, which stressed the independence of the judiciary, established the principle of public trials and defined the areas of jurisdiction for nine types of civil courts. In October the Kurdistan National Assembly passed a Law on Political Parties, requiring groups wishing to function as political parties to apply for authorization to the Kurdish Ministry of the Interior. Existing political parties were expected to comply with the law within three months of its coming into effect.

Widespread arrests of suspected opponents of the government of President Saddam Hussain were carried out throughout the year as part of the government's continuing crackdown on the Shi'a Muslim population. Most arrests took place in southern towns and villages, including in the southern marshes region, particularly between August and December. People suspected of assisting anti-government "saboteurs" or of having participated in the March 1991 uprising (see *Amnesty International Report 1992*) were especially targeted. Many of those detained were tortured while held for short periods in al-Radwaniyya and al-Ramadi garrisons, Abu Ghraib Prison near Baghdad or other places. Some were released only after making large cash payments to the authorities. Others were transferred to unknown destinations and there were fears that many of them were later extrajudicially executed (see below).

At least seven foreign nationals arrested between April and August and convicted of illegal entry into Iraq were held in Abu Ghraib Prison. Five of them were released between October and December. Five foreign nationals who had been detained in 1992 on similar charges remained held, but six others also arrested in 1992, a Filipino, two British and three Swedish nationals, were released in October and December (see *Amnesty International Report 1993*).

In August scores of prominent Sunni Arabs were arrested in Baghdad and other places by security and intelligence personnel. The fate and whereabouts of many of them remained unknown; it was feared that some may have been extrajudicially executed. They included retired army officers, economists, lawyers and former government officials. Among them were 'Abd al-Karim Hani, a former Minister of Labour and Social Affairs, and Rajeh al-Tikriti, a military doctor. Both were executed in November.

Thousands of government opponents and their relatives arrested in previous years remained held throughout 1993, among them prisoners of conscience. They included Arabs, Kurds, Assyrians and Turcomans arrested during the late 1970s and throughout the 1980s as well as thousands of others arrested since the March 1991 uprising. Several hundred Kuwaitis and other nationals arrested by Iraqi forces during the 1990 to 1991 occupation of Kuwait were believed to be still held in Iraq, although the Iraqi Government continued to deny holding such detainees. The Kuwaiti Government estimated that some 650 Kuwaitis had not been repatriated from Iraq after the cease-fire agreement. Among those believed to be still held in Iraq were two Kuwaitis – Faisal al-Sane', an entrepreneur and former parliamentarian, and Samira Ma'rafi, a university student.

Numerous new reports of torture and ill-treatment of detainees were received. The majority of victims were Shi'a Muslims from southern cities and the marshes region. They were held in al-Radwaniyya Garrison, the headquarters of the 4th Army Corps in al-'Amara city and other detention centres where torture was routine and systematic. Detainees were reportedly subjected to prolonged beatings, electric shocks, breaking of limbs, burning of the skin and mock executions. Scores of detainees reportedly died in custody during the year as a result of torture.

A Shi'a Muslim peasant was beaten with cables and given electric shocks while in detention in al-'Amara in April. He was then transferred to al-Radwaniyya where, he alleged, several detainees suffered critical burns after being pushed into a fire during interrogation. In another case, a Shi'a Muslim said he had been tortured for several days in al-Radwaniyya. He testified that he had been suspended by an arm and a leg from the ceiling, given electric shocks to his genitals, beaten with cables and burned with cigarettes. He was released after paying 30,000 Iraqi dinars. He also said that while he was in al-Radwaniyya, two fellow detainees had died under torture.

More than 100,000 "disappearance" cases from previous years remained unresolved. New details were received about scores of such victims, including information about Kurdish families who "disappeared" during the 1988 "Anfal operations" in Iraqi Kurdistan and Shi'a Muslim Arabs who "disappeared" between 1979 and 1985 (see previous *Amnesty International Reports*).

Several hundred people were reported to have been executed for alleged criminal or political offences. In most cases it was not possible to determine whether these were judicial or extrajudicial executions. The victims included four suspected members of the Syrian Ba'th Party whose bodies were returned to their families in October; among them was Walid al-'Ubaidi, a former employee of Iraq's Ministry of Oil. Two of the others were said to have had their eyes gouged out.

Mass executions of suspected government opponents held in prisons were reported, in particular in al-Radwaniyya Garrison where several thousand Shi'a Muslims arrested since the March 1991 uprising were held. Many former detainees reported that executions were carried out regularly throughout the year, with scores of people executed in September and October alone. Some were said to have been executed by firing-squad and buried in mass graves inside the garrison; others were allegedly burned to death. The mutilated bodies of others were returned to their families, who were forbidden from mourning

168

AMNESTY INTERNATIONAL REPORT 1994

in public. Scores of detainees were reportedly executed in Abu Ghraib Prison; their relatives were instructed to collect the bodies, some of which were allegedly mutilated. Scores of military personnel were reportedly executed in September and October after two alleged coup attempts: no further information about these cases could be obtained by the end of the year.

Scores of non-combatant men, women and children were extrajudicially executed during attacks by government forces on civilian targets in the southern marshes. The attacks were part of the government's efforts to secure control of the vast marshlands area located between Basra, al-'Amara and al-Nasiriyya which has traditionally served as a hiding place for government opponents and army deserters. Up to 8,000 people had fled the southern marshes by the end of the year as a result of military attacks on villages, the draining of large stretches of marshland and the destruction of the local economy. Scores of refugees confirmed that the government was continuing its policy of deliberately targeting non-combatant civilians, particularly in villages in the southern al-Hammar marshes. Several hundred people, many of them civilians, were reportedly killed or injured on 26 September during military attacks in the 'Ulaiwi and Abu Zargi marshes. The villages targeted included Abu al-Sanadij, al-Ghatra and al-Ghag. A UN team which visited the area in November announced subsequently that it could not confirm allegations that chemical weapons were used in these attacks.

Kurdish opposition groups and the Kurdish authorities in control of parts of Iraqi Kurdistan committed human rights abuses, including torture and deliberate and arbitrary killings. Most of the 13 political detainees who had been arrested in 1992 during a demonstration in Arbil (see *Amnesty International Report 1993*) alleged they had been beaten during interrogation by the *Asayish* (security) forces. Some said they had been given electric shocks. All were released in January. Scores of other detainees were allegedly beaten or otherwise ill-treated during interrogation. They were among hundreds of detainees held in prisons under the jurisdiction of the police and *Asayish* forces in Arbil, Sulaimaniya and Duhok, the vast majority for alleged criminal or security offences. In September, two Kurds accused

of murder needed intensive care treatment in al-Jumhuri Teaching Hospital in Arbil after being tortured at Azadi police station. One of them, Muhsin Hamad Ibrahim, died a week later from renal failure. Two policemen were subsequently arrested and arrest warrants were issued for four others.

Scores of deliberate killings were carried out in Duhok, Arbil and Sulaimaniya regions between April and August, some of which were politically motivated. Three political parties appeared to be implicated in the killings – the Kurdistan Democratic Party (KDP), the Patriotic Union of Kurdistan (PUK) and the Islamic Movement in Iraqi Kurdistan (IMIK). Among the victims were Qais Muhammad Ahmad, a member of the Central Committee of *Zahmatkeshan*, Kurdistan Toilers' Party, and Ra'uf Kamel 'Aqrawi, one of the 13 political detainees released in January (see above). In December, four unarmed demonstrators were killed in Sulaimaniya following clashes between the KDP and forces of the Kurdistan Socialist Party-Iraq (KSP-I). Also in December, hundreds of IMIK members and supporters and scores of PUK members were arrested following armed clashes between the two groups in a number of Kurdish towns and cities. Deliberate and arbitrary killings were carried out by both sides, as well as the torture and execution of detainees. Official investigations into many of these incidents were set up by the Kurdish authorities but had not been concluded by the end of the year.

At least seven people were sentenced to death by the Sulaimaniya and Arbil criminal courts, all after being convicted of premeditated murder. Three people who had been convicted of similar offences in 1992 were executed in Arbil after their death sentences were upheld by the Court of Cassation and, in the absence of a head of state, ratified by the Speaker of the Kurdistan National Assembly.

Amnesty International appealed to the Iraqi Government to halt human rights violations, including the detention of prisoners of conscience, unfair trials, "disappearances" and executions. In April Amnesty International published a report, *Iraq: "Disappearance" of Shi'a clerics and students*. It urged the government to clarify the 106 cases highlighted in the report. No substantive response was received. In September the organization published a further report, *Iraq: Secret detention* of Kuwaitis and third-country nationals, which called on the government to account for several hundred detainees still missing after the end of the Gulf conflict. In November the government denied holding these detainees but stated its willingness to investigate 625 cases referred to it by the Kuwaiti Government through the International Committee of the Red Cross. Also in November, Amnesty International publicly expressed its concern about gross human rights violations in the southern marshes region, and called on the UN General Assembly to request the UN Secretary-General to provide the necessary resources for establishing a human rights monitoring operation for Iraq.

In October Amnesty International raised its concerns about human rights abuses committed in Iraqi Kurdistan with Kurdish political leaders and officials during a visit to the area. In December Amnesty International expressed its concern to the Council of Ministers and to leaders of the KDP, PUK and IMIK about reports of deliberate and arbitrary killings that month (see above). The organization urged that impartial and thorough investigations be conducted into all politically motivated killings, and called for measures to protect detainees from torture. A response was received from the KDP leader, Mas'ud Barzani, stating, among other things, that KDP forces had not been responsible for the killing of four unarmed demonstrators in Sulaimaniya.

In a written statement to the UN Commission on Human Rights in February, Amnesty International drew attention to its grave concerns about human rights violations in Iraq, and in an oral statement urged the Commission to take up the recommendation of the UN Special Rapporteur on Iraq that a human rights monitoring operation be established in the country. The Commission adopted a resolution extending the Special Rapporteur's mandate for a further year and requesting the UN Secretary-General to take the necessary measures to implement the Special Rapporteur's recommendation. In an oral statement to the UN Sub-Commission on Prevention of Discrimination and Protection of Minorities in August, Amnesty International urged the implementation of the Commission's resolution in view of the continuing human rights violations in Iraq. The human rights monitoring operation had not been set up by the end of the year.

In December the UN General Assembly adopted a resolution requesting the UN Secretary-General to cooperate with the Special Rapporteur on Iraq in setting up a human rights monitoring operation for Iraq.

IRELAND

Information was received about the alleged ill-treatment of asylum-seekers by immigration and police officers in late 1992.

In June a law was passed legalizing homosexual acts between people aged 17 and over.

Inquiries begun in 1992 into the alleged ill-treatment of a group of asylum-seekers continued during the year. Twenty-seven Turkish Kurds, who had sought asylum when they arrived at Shannon Airport in November on a flight from Cuba to Moscow, were allegedly assaulted and verbally abused by immigration and police officers. The Irish immigration authorities allegedly refused them permission to apply for asylum and denied them access to a lawyer, an interpreter, or a representative of the Office of the UN High Commissioner for Refugees. When they refused to board the flight to Moscow, the police and immigration authorities tried to force them onto the aeroplane. During the ensuing struggle the Kurds were allegedly kicked, punched, beaten with batons, pulled by the hair and dragged along the ground. Eventually, they were sent to Canada, where their asylum claims were being considered. In December legal proceedings on behalf of the Kurds were started against government authorities claiming damages for assault, battery,

170

unlawful removal and breach of constitutional rights.

In January Amnesty International called on the Irish Government to initiate an independent and impartial inquiry into the incident. In August Amnesty International was informed that the Minister of Justice had requested the Commissioner of the Gardai (police) to carry out an investigation and report back to the Minister. No information about the findings of this investigation had reached Amnesty International by the end of the year.

Amnesty International wrote to the government in June welcoming the proposed new legislation governing sexual offences which would decriminalize consensual homosexual acts between adults in private.

ISRAEL AND THE OCCUPIED TERRITORIES

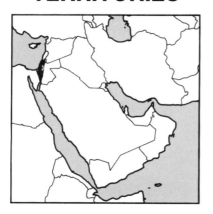

Approximately 13,000 Palestinians were arrested on security grounds. About 300 were held in administrative detention without charge or trial and over 15,300 were tried before military courts. About 1,000 prisoners and detainees were released in May and October. At the end of the year about 10,400 remained held, including over 140 administrative detainees. Palestinian and Israeli prisoners of conscience, including conscientious objectors to military service, were among those held during the year. Palestinians were systematically tortured or ill-treated during interrogation. Three died in custody in cases in which medical negligence may have been a contributory factor. **About 150 Palestinians were shot dead by Israeli forces, some of them in circumstances suggesting extrajudicial executions or other unjustifiable killings. Palestinian armed groups committed human rights abuses, including torture and deliberate and arbitrary killings.**

In January the parliament repealed legislation in force since 1986 which prohibited unauthorized contacts with the Palestine Liberation Organization (PLO) and had previously been used to imprison prisoners of conscience. In September the government and the PLO signed a Declaration of Principles on Interim Self-Government Arrangements. Under the arrangement, the government was due to transfer administrative responsibilities to a newly established Palestinian authority in the Gaza Strip and the Jericho area in the West Bank in December. The implementation of this arrangement had not started by the end of the year.

The number of attacks by armed Palestinians increased. Some 35 Israeli civilians and 25 members of the security forces were killed in such attacks, as were over 100 Palestinian civilians (see below).

The authorities frequently used massive firepower against houses in which Palestinians sought for arrest were believed to be hiding. Such operations resulted in extensive damage and may have been intended also as collective punishment. In March the West Bank and Gaza Strip were closed off after an increase in the number of attacks against Israelis. Palestinian residents subsequently required special authorization to enter East Jerusalem and Israel.

The Palestinian deportees who had remained stranded in south Lebanon since their expulsion from Israel in late 1992 (see *Amnesty International Report 1993*) were all allowed to return by December, although 18 chose to remain. Some of those who returned were arrested and held in administrative detention, such as Dr 'Abd al-'Aziz al-Rantisi, spokesman for the deportees. Thirty other deportees expelled in previous years were allowed to return in April and May.

About 300 Palestinians were held during the year under renewable administrative detention orders of up to six months. They included prisoners of conscience. A two-step judicial appeal process with legal counsel was available to detainees. However, legal safeguards were undermined:

crucial evidence about the reasons for detention was almost always withheld from detainees and their lawyers, although it was available to the presiding judges.

Prisoners of conscience held in administrative detention during the year included Ahmad Muhareb, a leading activist in *Fatah*, the main faction of the PLO. He was freed in September after a six-month order imposed in August was reduced on appeal. The appeal judge stressed that there was no evidence linking Ahmad Muhareb to violence.

Israeli prisoners of conscience included conscientious objectors to military service. Among them was Fu'ad Mu'addeh, a Druze from Yarka aged 18, who served two 28-day terms of imprisonment starting in August and October for refusing to be conscripted in protest at the occupation of the Occupied Territories. Other objectors included Eran Paz, who served a 28-day sentence in March for refusing to do reserve duty in the Gaza Strip.

At least 20 Lebanese nationals taken prisoner in Lebanon between 1986 and 1989 remained held, apparently in administrative detention. The authorities said that they were "being held legally" and that their detention was "subject to continuous judicial review". Among those held were Shaikh 'Abd al-Karim 'Ubayd, a Shi'a Muslim leader who had been abducted in Lebanon in 1989, and six Lebanese Shi'a Muslims who had been taken prisoner in Lebanon by the Lebanese Forces militia in 1987 and secretly transferred to Israel in 1990, where they remained held in incommunicado detention (see *Amnesty International Report 1993*).

Over 200 detainees were held at any one time in the Khiam detention centre in an area of south Lebanon controlled by Israel and the South Lebanon Army. They were held incommunicado outside any legal framework (see **Lebanon** entry).

Over 15,300 Palestinians were tried by military courts on charges including violent acts. Adults were frequently held for up to 18 days before appearing before a judge, and were denied access to lawyers and relatives for longer periods. Confessions were often obtained during these periods of incommunicado detention. The use of plea bargains remained prevalent and long delays continued to occur.

In October Ahmad Qatamesh, allegedly a senior official of the Popular Front for the Liberation of Palestine (PFLP), was eventually released on bail but placed in administrative detention while trial proceedings against him continued. He had been arrested in September 1992 (see *Amnesty International Report 1993*) and his trial had been postponed several times.

Palestinians under interrogation continued to be systematically tortured or ill-treated. Common methods included beatings, hooding with dirty sacks, sleep deprivation, solitary confinement (including in closet-sized dark cells), and prolonged shackling to a small chair. For example, Nader Qumsieh received injuries to his testicles while held under interrogation in May in the Dhahiriyyah detention centre. One medical report claimed that Nader Qumsieh said he had fallen down stairs, whereas he repeatedly stated he was injured as a result of torture. He was released from interrogation but remained held in administrative detention until July. A government investigation into his treatment was apparently continuing at the end of the year.

In April Ayman Nassar died in Barzalai Hospital 13 days after his arrest during a military operation in Deir al-Balah in which a "smoke bomb" was used. He was reportedly beaten immediately after arrest. According to a Danish pathologist who attended the official autopsy, Ayman Nassar died from "pneumonia due to ruptured lung blisters ... presumably due to irritating smoke ... and possibly influenced through beating on the chest". The pathologist believed Ayman Nassar might have survived had adequate medical treatment been provided earlier. A coroner's inquest was initiated. In August and October two other prisoners died in custody. Medical negligence also appeared to have contributed to their deaths.

In May a confidential "medical fitness form", apparently used in interrogation centres, was publicized by the *Davar* newspaper. Doctors allegedly used the form to certify whether a detainee could withstand solitary confinement, tying-up, hooding and prolonged standing during interrogation. In June the Israeli Medical Association announced that it would forbid doctors to use the form. The authorities suggested the form had been a mistake.

In August the High Court of Justice rejected a 1991 petition aimed at obtaining a ruling on the legality of the existing secret

172

guidelines for interrogation by the General Security Service (GSS) and their publication. The guidelines, allowing "the exertion of a moderate measure of physical pressure", were first drawn up in 1987 by the Landau Commission of Inquiry. Following a review in April, the authorities said that methods of interrogation involving food and drink deprivation, denial of access to a toilet and exposure to extreme temperatures were not permitted.

Mordechai Vanunu remained held in solitary confinement for the seventh consecutive year (see *Amnesty International Reports 1988 to 1993*), a situation considered by Amnesty International to be cruel, inhuman and degrading treatment. During the year it was disclosed that Avraham Klingberg, a 75-year-old physician and university professor, had been imprisoned since 1983 on spying charges and apparently held in solitary confinement until 1991.

About 150 Palestinians were shot dead by Israeli forces. Some were killed during clashes with the army or border police, or during operations ostensibly aimed at arresting them. Others were killed while apparently not involved in any violent activity and they may have been victims of extrajudicial executions or other unjustifiable killings. Najah Abu Dalal died in April reportedly after being shot in the head by a soldier stationed on a building in the Nusayrat refugee camp in the Gaza Strip. She was in a private courtyard when she was shot. Fares al-Kurdi, aged 18 months, was shot in the chest and killed in May, apparently while sheltering in a shop doorway with his father during clashes in the Jabalia refugee camp, also in the Gaza Strip. In October the High Court of Justice rejected a 1990 petition against the existing guidelines on the use of firearms.

According to the authorities, 35 Israeli soldiers were tried for violating military orders. A soldier was sentenced in May to one year's imprisonment, half to be served doing military labour. He had been convicted of causing death by negligence after the killing in November 1992 of Amjad Jaber, a 12-year-old Palestinian, in al-Ram near Jerusalem. The Military Appeals Court accepted an appeal by the prosecution and ruled that the entire sentence be served in prison. The Supreme Court rejected in May an appeal by the prosecution against the acquittal of a Border Police officer for the killing of Fadi Zabaqli in 1989 (see *Amnesty International Report 1993*). Amnesty International learned in March that the State Attorney had recommended that disciplinary measures should be brought against a medic and a GSS officer in relation to the death in custody of Mustafa 'Akkawi in February 1992 (see *Amnesty International Report 1993*).

In September John Demjanjuk was deported after his acquittal on appeal by the Supreme Court in July. The Supreme Court overturned his conviction and death sentence passed in 1988, citing doubts as to whether he was the "Ivan the Terrible" guilty of crimes against humanity (see *Amnesty International Reports 1989 to 1993*). No other person was under sentence of death.

Palestinian armed groups committed grave human rights abuses, including torture and deliberate and arbitrary killings. In October some 12 men were shot in the legs by alleged members of *Fatah*, apparently as punishment for acts such as burglary in Gaza. Israeli civilians were deliberately killed in attacks for which the Islamic Resistance Movement (*Hamas*), the Islamic Jihad, the PFLP and the Democratic Front for the Liberation of Palestine claimed responsibility. Among the victims was Ian Feinberg, an Israeli lawyer killed in Gaza in April in an attack claimed by the PFLP. *Hamas* took responsibility for the capture and subsequent killing of two Israeli soldiers in August and October. Members of Palestinian groups also killed over 100 Palestinians, most of them suspected "collaborators" with the Israeli authorities. Some may have been killed because of their political activities.

Amnesty International called on the government and the PLO to ensure that strong human rights safeguards were integral to any peace settlement.

Amnesty International sought the immediate and unconditional release of prisoners of conscience and the return of Palestinian deportees. It called for administrative detainees to be tried promptly and fairly, or be released. It also called for an end to the use of interrogation methods amounting to torture or ill-treatment and for full compliance with international standards on the use of firearms and impartial investigations of related abuses. Amnesty International's delegates repeatedly visited the country during the year.

In response to Amnesty International's specific concerns about killings of children, the authorities said that because of an increase in attacks by Palestinians, "soldiers have had to open fire more frequently in self-defence" and therefore there were more situations in which children were "liable to be killed accidentally or wounded". The authorities added that in some cases the Israeli army "was not aware of their presence".

The army promised to provide Amnesty International with the findings of investigations into several cases of killings raised by the organization in May, but had not done so by the end of the year.

Amnesty International expressed concern about attacks carried out on houses where suspects might have been hiding. The army denied that such attacks were a punitive measure. It stressed that those sought for arrest were given the opportunity to give themselves up and that residents whose houses were damaged could apply for compensation. However, the authorities did not clarify the specific evidence presented by Amnesty International suggesting that explosives were used after the storming of houses.

In oral statements to the UN Commission on Human Rights (UNCHR) in February and to its Sub-Commission on Prevention of Discrimination and Protection of Minorities in August, Amnesty International included reference to its concerns in the Israeli-Occupied Territories, including south Lebanon.

In March the UNCHR decided to appoint a Special Rapporteur in respect of the Israeli-Occupied Territories.

Amnesty International condemned torture and deliberate and arbitrary killings by Palestinian groups and appealed to them, including the PLO and *Hamas*, to end human rights abuses, particularly attacks on civilians.

In October PLO Chairman Yasser Arafat stated to an Amnesty International delegation in Tunis that the PLO was committed to respect and incorporate into Palestinian legislation all internationally recognized human rights standards.

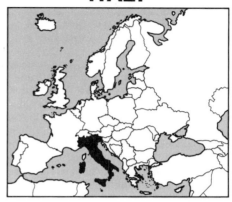

ITALY

There were new allegations of ill-treatment of detainees and prisoners by law enforcement and prison officers. Several inquiries were under way into such allegations.

A series of judicial investigations begun in 1992 into political corruption implicated over 3,000 people, including former prime ministers and government ministers, discrediting all the major political parties which had participated in government since 1945. In April a national referendum voted to reform the electoral system and, at the request of the President of the Republic, Oscar Luigi Scalfaro, the Governor of the Bank of Italy, Carlo Azeglio Ciampi, took office as Prime Minister and formed a new government.

Responsibility for a series of bomb attacks which took place in Florence, Milan and Rome during the year, killing 10 people, was claimed by *Falange Armata*, Armed Falange. Little was known about this group. However, there was widespread speculation that *Falange Armata* was a cover name for a secret alliance of elements within state and public institutions working in collaboration with organized crime to impede the process of political and institutional reform resulting from the judicial investigations into corruption. Extremist political groups were also suspected of involvement in the bombings and other apparent attempts to destabilize the country.

After repeated delays parliament re-examined a bill reforming the existing system of conscientious objection to compulsory military service. The bill had been approved by parliament in January 1992 but rejected by the then President of the

174

Republic, who had returned it for further consideration. At the end of the year a new text, substantially similar to the 1992 text, had been approved by the Chamber of Deputies (the lower chamber of parliament) and was awaiting consideration by the Senate.

In February a majority of the Chamber of Deputies put forward a bill, whose terms had been drawn up with input from Amnesty International, proposing the elimination of the death penalty from the Wartime Military Penal Code, thus abolishing the death penalty for all offences. The Chamber of Deputies approved the bill in July and at the end of the year an analogous bill was awaiting examination by the Senate.

Numerous allegations of ill-treatment by prison officers were made by prisoners held in connection with common criminal offences, including Mafia-related activities; some of the allegations related to incidents in 1992. They were frequently accompanied by reports of severe overcrowding, poor sanitation, inadequate medical assistance and increased tension within the prisons. The most common forms of ill-treatment alleged were repeated kicks and punches as well as sustained beatings with batons, sometimes inflicted on groups of prisoners.

From late 1992 onwards lawyers, newspapers, parliamentary deputies and a parliamentary committee for prison affairs reported receiving allegations from inmates at Secondigliano prison, Naples, who said that they were subjected to "systematic beatings and gratuitous ill-treatment" by prison guards. In April the commandant of the prison guards and five superintendents were temporarily suspended from duty in connection with possible criminal charges, including abuse of authority, striking prisoners and committing perjury. The commandant had allegedly instigated the beating of inmates by prison guards, opened prisoners' outgoing letters and threatened them with violence if they failed to remove passages referring to ill-treatment. It was reported that by June over 100 guards were under investigation in connection with the alleged ill-treatment.

There were also further allegations of ill-treatment by law enforcement officers, often concerning people of non-European ethnic origin.

Mahrez Chanouf, a Tunisian, and Salim Sfouli, an Egyptian, were arrested by Milan police on 19 August after a car chase which ended when they ran into a police car and crashed into a tree. Anonymous callers to a local radio station, who claimed they had witnessed the arrests, alleged that the two men had been dragged from a car, handcuffed and repeatedly kicked and punched for around 20 minutes while on the ground by over a dozen male and female police officers. When Mahrez Chanouf and Salim Sfouli appeared in court the following day accused of stealing a car and resisting arrest, they reportedly displayed cuts and bruises and alleged that they had been repeatedly kicked and punched by numerous police officers, both on the street and later in the police station. A forensic examination confirmed their injuries but was apparently unable to determine their cause.

At a further hearing on 25 August, four officers who had participated in the car chase and had been the first at the scene of arrest told the court that the detainees had tried to assault them and escape. A witness testified in court that she had seen the two detainees being beaten by the police and that they had made no attempt to escape. The court found that the statements made by the police officers contained clear contradictions and were unreliable. Mahrez Chanouf and Salim Sfouli were acquitted of resisting arrest and the charge of car theft was apparently dropped. The affair was referred to the Public Prosecutor's office for further investigation regarding possible charges against Mahrez Chanouf and Salim Sfouli of insulting the police and damaging property, and regarding possible charges against the four police officers of abusing their authority and committing perjury.

Amnesty International made inquiries throughout the year about official steps being taken to investigate allegations of ill-treatment and about the progress and outcome of inquiries opened into such allegations. The authorities supplied no information concerning allegations of ill-treatment made during 1993 but the Ministry of the Interior informed Amnesty International that Daud Addawe Ali, a Somali citizen who alleged he had been ill-treated by police in Rome in 1992 (see *Amnesty International Report 1993*), had violently resisted arrest. The Ministry denied that he had been ill-treated or suffered injuries and stated that the case had been passed to the judicial authorities. These authorities did not respond to Amnesty International's requests for further information.

Amnesty International welcomed the reforms contained in the proposed legislation on conscientious objection but expressed concern that the text made no provision for conscientious objection developed after joining the armed forces. It reiterated its belief that conscientious objectors to military service should be able to seek conscientious objector status at any time. It also welcomed the moves taken towards abolishing the death penalty.

JAMAICA

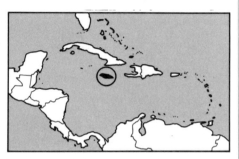

About 80 prisoners had their death sentences commuted as a result of changes to the law and more commutations were expected as a result of a landmark judicial ruling. At the end of the year about 160 people were under sentence of death. At least six new death sentences were passed but there were no executions. Four prisoners were killed by prison warders at St Catherine's District Prison; they may have been summarily executed. There were further cases in which people were killed by police in disputed circumstances.

The People's National Party won a large majority in the general election held on 30 March; Percival J. Patterson was confirmed as Prime Minister.

The implementation of the Offences against the Person (Amendment) Act, which became law in October 1992, continued in early 1993. The act differentiates between capital and non-capital murder: only the first category carries a death sentence on conviction (see *Amnesty International Report 1993*). The law was applied retroactively to all prisoners under sentence of death. Nearly 40 per cent of the death-row population benefited by having

their sentences reduced to prison terms. Those whose death sentences were confirmed had the right to appeal. However, there were grave concerns about the fairness of the appeal process. The law stipulates that prisoners should have 21 days to apply for a review of their classification by three judges from the Court of Appeal whose decision is final, and that prisoners should also be able "to appear or be represented by counsel". However, in most cases the prisoners had not had an adequate opportunity to consult legal counsel. At the time they were notified, in December 1992, few of the 85 prisoners concerned had lawyers; there is no legal aid for representation after trial and direct appeal. The government later agreed to grant legal aid to these prisoners.

In February Albert Huntley, a death-row prisoner sentenced in 1983, whose case had been classified as capital, filed a constitutional motion on the grounds that the classification process contravened his right to protection under the law and to a fair hearing. He said he had not been given the opportunity to be heard or to have legal representation of his choice during the classification review proceedings. The Court of Appeal agreed in February to stay the review of all cases classified as capital, pending a final decision on the motion. In April the Supreme Court ruled against Albert Huntley and in November the Court of Appeal dismissed his appeal.

In late June the Judicial Committee of the Privy Council (JCPC) in London, the final court of appeal for Jamaica, started hearing an appeal from Earl Pratt and Ivan Morgan, two death-row prisoners, after the Court of Appeal dismissed their constitutional motion that delay in execution is inhuman and degrading punishment (see *Amnesty International Report 1993*). The two men had both been under sentence of death since 1979. On 2 November the JCPC issued a landmark decision: it granted their appeal, finding that for them to be executed more than five years after they were sentenced would constitute "inhuman or degrading punishment or other treatment". It said that "the delay in this case is wholly unacceptable and this appeal must be allowed", and ordered that the death sentences be commuted to life imprisonment. The JCPC also stated that "petitions to the two human rights bodies [the UN Human Rights Committee and the Inter-American

Commission on Human Rights] do not fall within the category of frivolous procedures". This decision should affect cases in all Commonwealth countries which retain both the death penalty and the JCPC as their final court of appeal. As a result of the decision, 110 Jamaican prisoners became eligible for commutation of their death sentences.

At the end of the year the number of prisoners on death row had decreased to around 160, from a high of over 270, as a result of the reclassification process. However, the JCPC decision had not been implemented by the end of the year, except in the cases of Earl Pratt and Ivan Morgan. There have been no executions since 1988.

On 31 October, four death-row prisoners were killed at St Catherine's District Prison in Spanish Town. They were allegedly shot dead after they tried to take prison guards hostage, but this was contradicted by reports that two of those killed had received death threats from warders and by other circumstances suggesting that the shootings may have been summary executions. Another three prisoners were injured as well as three prison warders. Amnesty International received allegations of ill-treatment from several prisoners, who complained about beatings, destruction of property and death threats.

There were further cases in which people were killed by police officers in circumstances suggesting that they had been shot dead when they could have been apprehended. In one such case, two suspected robbers were shot in July by members of the Anti-Crime Investigation Detachment (ACID). According to police reports, Leroy Chin and Alfredo Bell had been killed in a shoot-out with the police at the Nuttall Hospital grounds. However, this was disputed by eye-witnesses who reportedly stated that one of the men (who was unarmed) had been shot in the head by police while face down on the ground. The Director of Public Prosecutions (DPP) ruled that a police officer should be charged with murder but the case was still pending at the end of the year.

Several policemen were charged in connection with killings of civilians in previous years. A police constable was charged with capital murder for the death of Fitzgerald Polson who was shot in a New Kingston street in September 1992 (see *Amnesty International Report 1993*). The

trial was still pending at the end of the year.

In March the DPP ruled that five senior police officers should be charged with manslaughter following the deaths of three suspects in the Constant Spring Police Station in October 1992. The three men had suffocated after being placed in a small, overcrowded cell (see *Amnesty International Report 1993*). The officers appeared in court but were released on bail.

In June the DPP also decided that two policemen should be charged with manslaughter in connection with the death of John Headley in November 1992, allegedly as a result of beatings while in police custody (see *Amnesty International Report 1993*). The trial was delayed by the unavailability of witnesses and it had not taken place by the end of the year.

In January Amnesty International wrote to the Minister of Justice and National Security and the Attorney General regarding the reclassification of death sentences. The organization expressed concern that the classification appeal process did not appear to be working. For example, prisoners were not in practice enabled to appear or be represented by counsel before the review panel, and many prisoners were unable to comply with the 21-day deadline to submit an appeal. The organization said that the quality of the evidence and the adequacy of legal representation at the time of a trial should also be taken into account in the review process. Amnesty International also expressed concern that six prisoners' offences had been reclassified as "capital murder" despite a recommendation by the UN Human Rights Committee that their sentences be commuted or that they be released on the grounds that their rights under the International Covenant on Civil and Political Rights had been violated. Amnesty International reiterated its appeal for clemency for all those on death row.

In late January Amnesty International wrote to the Minister of Justice and National Security to express concern about reports of torture or other ill-treatment of suspects in custody, and the apparently high incidence of killings resulting from the alleged unjustified use of lethal force by the police, including four deaths in two police stations in late 1992. Amnesty International listed 13 victims, including a 10-month-old baby girl who had been shot by police in highly questionable circumstances, and requested information on the procedures for investigating police shootings. It urged that the international standards on the use of force by police be fully incorporated into police codes of practice and training programs, and that appropriate disciplinary proceedings be instituted whenever such standards are violated.

In November Amnesty International wrote to the Minister of National Security and Justice about the killing of four prisoners in October, and in December published a report, *Jamaica: Proposal for inquiry into deaths and ill-treatment of prisoners in St Catherine's District Prison.* Amnesty International called for a full, impartial inquiry into the four deaths and other reports of ill-treatment of prisoners at St Catherine's District Prison, and for proper safeguards against torture and ill-treatment to be introduced urgently.

There was no response from the authorities by the end of the year.

JAPAN

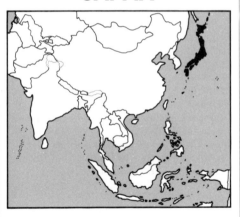

A *de facto* three-year moratorium on executions ended in March when three prisoners were hanged. Four others, including a 70-year old man, were executed in November. Fifty-five others were awaiting execution, some in conditions of detention amounting to ill-treatment, and some 40 others were under sentence of death. Conditions of detention in some police cells amounted to ill-treatment. The government failed to fulfil its international obligations adequately to protect refugees and asylum-seekers.

An eight-party coalition government took office in August, following elections to the Diet (lower house of Parliament) in which the Liberal Democratic Party lost its majority. The new Prime Minister, Hosokawa Morihiro, pledged to implement wide-ranging political reforms. The Minister of Justice, Mikazuki Akira, stated at his inaugural press conference that he would sign execution orders for prisoners whose death sentences had been approved by the Supreme Court, implicitly criticizing some of his predecessors who had blocked the execution process by not signing such orders.

A *de facto* moratorium on executions in force since November 1989 ended in March when three men who had been on death row for between 13 and 23 years were executed after then Minister of Justice Masaharu Gotoda signed their execution orders. They included Kawanaka Tetsuo, who was hanged before all avenues for review or commutation of his sentence had been exhausted. His mental condition had reportedly deteriorated in the months preceding his execution: according to a doctor at Osaka Detention Centre, he was hallucinating and "on the verge" of becoming schizophrenic.

Following established practice, the March executions were carried out in secret. Executions are never announced publicly and even the families or lawyers of the prisoners concerned are not informed of impending executions. Prisoners themselves may not be informed until a few hours before execution takes place. In practice they are unable to meet relatives or a lawyer after being informed of their impending execution.

Those executed in November included Deguchi Hideo, aged 70, and Sakaguchi Toru, who were held at Osaka Detention Centre. They were executed after spending nine years on death row. Also executed were Kojima Tadao, who was held in Sapporo, and Seki Yukio, held in Tokyo. They had both been on death row since 1978.

Approximately 90 prisoners were reported to be under sentence of death at the end of the year, including some 55 whose sentences had been confirmed by the Supreme Court. At least three had spent more than 25 years on death row. Among them were Okunishi Masaru, aged 67, imprisoned since 1961, and Tomiyama Tsuneki, aged 76, imprisoned since 1963 and sentenced to death in 1971.

Prisoners sentenced to death continued to be subjected to arbitrary restrictions on their right to have contact with the outside world. As a general rule, they were only allowed to meet close relatives – and their lawyer if they had one. The authorities justified this practice by stating that it helped to keep the prisoners emotionally "stable". Prison wardens appeared to exercise wide discretion over the degree of isolation imposed on death row prisoners. In some prisons, condemned prisoners were held almost permanently in solitary confinement.

There were new reports of police ill-treatment of suspects. Huang Yuwei, a Chinese resident, alleged that he was punched and beaten with clubs by six police officers while held for 24 hours in June in a Tokyo police station on suspicion of being an illegal immigrant. The police denied that he was beaten and said he had had to be subdued by police officers because he refused to go to the police station. He was released after police confirmed that he was a legal resident. The investigation into his complaint, which was lodged in October, had not been completed by the end of the year.

In October three police officers from the Kawasaki District Police were given suspended prison terms and fined following a complaint by Hayakawa Yoshimitsu, a day labourer. He alleged that he was severely beaten, burned and threatened by the three officers while detained for several hours on 30 December 1992. The police initially denied the claim that severe burns and contusions suffered by Hayakawa Yoshimitsu had resulted from ill-treatment in custody.

Conditions of detention in police custody amounted in some instances to ill-treatment. Police detention facilities, known as "substitute prisons" (*daiyo kangoku*), continued to be used instead of the detention centres administered by the Ministry of Justice to hold criminal suspects for up to 23 days prior to indictment (see *Amnesty International Reports 1991* and *1992*). Interrogators in "substitute prisons" were in practice allowed unlimited access to detainees and were able to deny them adequate rest and access to the outside world for weeks on end – with the exception of short meetings with a lawyer and, at the discretion of police authorities, visits by a doctor. Several former inmates of "substitute prisons" alleged that they had been forced or threatened into signing confessions admitting to crimes they did not commit. Methods of coercion used reportedly included detaining suspects in a "substitute prison" cell together with one or more other inmates who had been instructed to "advise" the suspect to confess. Former inmates reported receiving blows to the head, being deprived of sleep and rest during daily 10-hour interrogation sessions over periods of up to several weeks, and having interrogators shout into their ears.

Protection for refugees and asylum-seekers remained inadequate (see *Amnesty International Report 1993*). Procedures were secretive, arbitrary and often obstructive. Some asylum-seekers, despite clearly being entitled to refugee status, had their applications refused and were kept in a legal limbo on visas which had to be renewed every 30 days. This meant they faced the constant threat of deportation. Restrictive rules and procedures were compounded by a lack of guidance and advice for asylum-seekers. Immigration officials appeared to lack knowledge about international standards relating to refugees, and seemed not to have ready access to reliable information on human rights conditions in applicants' countries of origin.

In February Hong Jianbing, a Chinese asylum-seeker and a well-known political dissident who was at risk of serious human rights violations if returned to China, was forced to leave Japan. His claim for refugee status had been rejected on appeal in October 1992 despite the fact that the UN High Commissioner for Refugees had recognized him as a refugee. In January he was informed by the Japanese authorities that he would be deported to China if he did not leave Japan. He travelled to Europe and was eventually accepted as a refugee by Canada.

In March Amnesty International published a report, *Japan: Inadequate Protection for Refugees and Asylum-Seekers*, which drew attention to the cases of several asylum-seekers, including Hong Jianbing. Amnesty International urged the authorities to establish an independent advisory body composed of impartial members with recognized expertise to review the entire system of refugee protection in Japan, and to ensure that all asylum-seekers have effective access to a fair and satisfactory asylum procedure. It also urged the authorities not to detain asylum-seekers other than in cases of absolute necessity, in accordance with relevant international standards. In response to the report, the Ministry of Justice disputed many of the organization's findings and stated that existing procedures met Japan's international obligations.

In May an Amnesty International representative visited Japan and met officials of the Ministry of Justice and the National Police Agency to discuss safeguards for human rights in "substitute prisons", the use of the death penalty, and conditions on death row. Amnesty International expressed concern that there was inadequate separation of authority between those responsible for the interrogation and those responsible for the custody of suspects held in "substitute prisons", and about the harsh disciplinary regime for death-row prisoners.

In August, following the inauguration of the new government, Amnesty International published an open letter to Prime Minister Hosokawa and called on his government to give urgent attention to human rights in Japan. In October Amnesty International issued two reports, *Japan: Resumption of Executions and Ill-Treatment of Prisoners on Death Row*, and *Japan: The "Substitute Prison" System: a Source of Human Rights Violations*, which it submitted to the UN Human Rights Committee prior to its consideration of the Japanese Government's report on implementation of the International Covenant on Civil and Political Rights (ICCPR). The Human Rights Committee expressed concern at the "number and nature" of crimes punishable by death in Japan and stated *inter alia* that "undue restrictions on visits and correspondence" with prisoners on death row, and the failure of the authorities to notify relatives of executions are "incompatible" with the ICCPR. It recommended reforms to pre-trial procedures, including the "substitute prison" system.

JORDAN

About 270 security detainees were arrested during the year and held almost invariably in prolonged incommunicado detention. They included possible prisoners of conscience. Almost all of those arrested were released uncharged. Up to 13 (including two *in absentia*) were brought to trial before the State Security Court. There were allegations of torture of detainees in the custody of the General Intelligence Department and the police. At least 12 prisoners were executed, the highest number of executions recorded over the past two decades. At least four people were expelled to countries where they risked human rights violations.

National elections for the 80-member Lower House of Parliament, the first in which political parties were formally allowed to participate since 1956, took place in November. By then over 20 political parties had been officially registered in compliance with the Law on Political Parties in force since October 1992. The elections were held under an electoral law amended in August by the government of Prime Minister Dr 'Abd al-Salam Majali, who had taken over in May from Sharif Zeid Ben Shaker. Also in November, King Hussein bin Talal appointed a new 40-member Senate. Prime Minister Majali formed a new government in December.

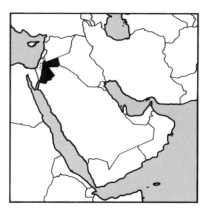

In May an amendment to the law on the State Security Court, introducing a right of appeal before the Court of Cassation, entered into force. The amendment had been originally proposed by the government of Prime Minister Taher Masri in 1991. Members of parliament Leith Shubeilat and Ya'qub Qarrash called for an investigation into their trial by the State Security Court in 1992 (see *Amnesty International Report 1993*), maintaining that the case against them had been fabricated. The government and Parliament debated the issue at a closed session in March but took no further action.

Also in May a new Law on Press and Publications entered into force. It affirms

180

AMNESTY INTERNATIONAL REPORT 1994

the right to freedom of opinion and expression, but Article 8 requires the press to "refrain from publishing anything contradicting the principles of freedom, national responsibility, human rights, respect for the truth and the values of the Arab and Islamic nation". Article 40 forbids the press from publishing "news harmful to the King or the royal family", "articles which may harm national unity" and "articles or information containing a personal insult to heads of Arab, Islamic or friendly states". Breaches of these provisions can be punished by fines. Starting in September, six journalists were charged with offences under this and other legislation for articles they had written and were awaiting trial at the end of the year.

In February King Hussein set up a committee to establish a Centre for Studies on Freedom, Democracy and Human Rights in the Arab World. In October the committee finalized a draft law setting out the Centre's aims and working methods. These included investigating human rights violations in Jordan, making relevant recommendations and reporting annually to the King, Parliament and Cabinet. The draft was presented to Parliament before the end of the year.

Some 270 security detainees were held by the General Intelligence Department (GID), almost invariably in prolonged incommunicado detention. They were held without judicial review and almost all of them were released without charge or trial. The 1961 Code of Criminal Procedure allows public prosecutors to renew indefinitely the detention of suspects for periods of up to 15 days at a time. It also allows public prosecutors to deny access to detainees by lawyers and relatives, for an indefinite period, "in a situation of urgency" or when deemed "necessary to discover the truth". These provisions were routinely used by GID officers acting as public prosecutors. Detainees included over 30 alleged members of Islamic organizations. Among them were 'Ata Abu al-Rushta, Official Spokesperson of the Liberation Party in Jordan (LPJ), and Bakr al-Khawalidah, President of the LPJ's Cultural Committee. They were arrested in May and accused of conspiring to change the Constitution by illegal means, including violence. Both detainees maintained that the LPJ did not advocate violence in pursuit of its aims. They were held without access to lawyers

until their release in November. The LPJ, which seeks the establishment of an Islamic state encompassing Jordan, did not apply for official registration as it opposes some of the conditions imposed by the Law on Political Parties.

Detainees brought before the State Security Court included five military cadets and three others charged with conspiring to kill King Hussein during a graduation ceremony at Mu'ta University in June; working to change the Constitution by illegal means; and membership of the LPJ. Two other defendants were tried *in absentia*. The defendants had been arrested between April and June and held by the GID without access to lawyers until August, when they were moved to Zarqa military prison and brought to trial. In court, they retracted their confessions saying they had been extracted under torture but the court allowed the confessions to be used as evidence and did not allow them to be examined by doctors of their choice. Their trial was continuing at the end of the year. In October an Amnesty International observer attended sessions of the trial, meeting military judges and GID officers as well as lawyers and relatives of the defendants.

In September Ramadan al-Rawashidah, a journalist for the newspaper *al-Ahali*, was detained for five days in Jweidah prison and then released on bail after he published an article in which he said that the State Security Court was delaying the medical examination of the defendants in the above case. He was accused, together with *al-Ahali*'s editor, Jamil al-Nimri, of slandering the court and violating Article 42 of the Law on Press and Publications, which prohibits the publication of minutes of an ongoing trial without the court's authorization. The trials of the two journalists were pending at the end of the year.

There were allegations of torture by the GID and the police. The eight alleged members of the LPJ tried before the State Security Court said that when held in the GID Headquarters' detention centre in Amman they were tortured with methods including *falaqa* (beatings on the soles of the feet) and threats of sexual assault. One of them, Husayn al-Jidi, sustained an injury over his left eyebrow which he said was caused by beatings, while the prosecutor suggested it was the result of an attempt at suicide by banging his head in his cell. The authorities denied torture and informed Amnesty

International in October that the GID detention centre is an official prison, therefore subject to supervision by the prosecuting authorities. However, such supervision is carried out by GID officers in their capacity as public prosecutors. In a separate case relating to drug offences, Ahmad Mustafa was reportedly beaten severely while held in police custody in Ma'an in February and required hospital treatment. His lawyer requested an investigation and compensation but received no answer from the authorities.

At least 12 prisoners were executed during the year, the highest number recorded by Amnesty International over the past two decades. Ten were convicted of murder. Two, who were executed in August, had been convicted by the State Security Court of spying for Israel. They did not have the right of appeal, contrary to international safeguards in death penalty cases. The upsurge in executions followed a year in which no executions had taken place.

At least four detainees were expelled to countries where they risked abuses such as torture. They included Muhammad Bilbaisi, a Palestinian handed over in July to the Israeli authorities who reportedly illtreated him and put him on trial for violent offences, and three Sudanese asylum-seekers from southern Sudan, who were sent back to Sudan in December.

Amnesty International raised several cases of concern with the authorities and received prompt responses from the GID. Amnesty International welcomed the introduction of the right of appeal from the State Security Court. It remained seriously concerned, however, about the continued practice of prolonged incommunicado detention, which facilitates torture and illtreatment and compromises the right to a fair trial. It called for the release of any prisoner of conscience; for the urgent introduction of safeguards for detainees such as prompt access to lawyers and judges; and for the supervision of detainees held in GID custody to be carried out by a separate agency. Amnesty International deeply regretted the resumption of executions during the year and continued to call for clemency to be exercised in all death penalty cases. It also called for adequate procedures to be followed in order to ensure that no one was expelled to a country where he or she could be at risk of human rights violations.

KAZAKHSTAN

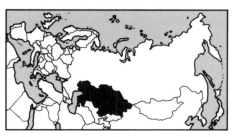

A former prisoner of conscience faced renewed prosecution on a charge of slandering the President. An unknown number of people were executed.

A new Constitution entered into force in January. It incorporates a number of human rights guarantees found in the principal international human rights instruments.

Karishal Asanov, a writer and academic who spent three months in pre-trial detention in 1992 before being acquitted of "infringement upon the honour and dignity of the President" (Article 170-3 of the criminal code – see *Amnesty International Report 1993*), was tried again on this charge in May after the Supreme Court upheld a protest by the procurator against the original trial verdict. At the retrial Karishal Asanov was convicted and given a three-year suspended prison sentence. He appealed against this verdict to the Supreme Court, which in July overturned it on the grounds of violations of the right to legal defence. The Supreme Court ordered a second retrial, but in December the case was dropped.

No death sentences were reported but it was officially announced in September that an undisclosed number of people had recently been executed.

Amnesty International called for further proceedings against Karishal Asanov under Article 170-3 to be dropped. It also called for the criminal code provision under which he was charged to be repealed as it appeared to place unwarranted restrictions on freedom of expression. Throughout the year Amnesty International continued to press for abolition of the death penalty.

In January Amnesty International wrote to President Nursultan Nazarbayev concerning a decree he had issued in December 1992, which provides for deserters from the armed forces and men evading conscription to face criminal prosecution.

182

The organization called for the introduction of an alternative civilian service for conscientious objectors to military service. In March the head of the department of law enforcement organs in the President's office replied that legislation on military service exempts men from conscription if they have taken holy orders or have "work duties" with a registered religious faith. There were no reports of people being imprisoned for refusing conscription on grounds of conscience.

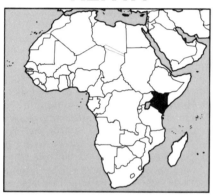

KENYA

Dozens of peaceful protesters, human rights activists and government critics were detained for short periods. Many were prisoners of conscience. Most were released uncharged but others were charged with political offences then freed on bail. Treason charges against five government opponents arrested in 1990 and 1991 were withdrawn and they were freed, but some were rearrested on new charges and remained in prison at the end of the year. There were reports of torture, including rape, and ill-treatment of prisoners. Scores of people were killed in ethnic clashes allegedly instigated or condoned by the government, many of them apparently victims of extrajudicial executions. Some 400 people were under sentence of death, including over 30 convicted during 1993, but no executions were reported.

Many people died in continued interethnic clashes. Between late 1991 and the end of 1993, over 1,500 people were killed and tens of thousands displaced. The violence was in part alleged to have been instigated by the government of President Daniel arap Moi or by the ruling Kenya African National Union (KANU) party and to have been carried out by groups recruited by them. Those protesting against government involvement in the violence were frequently arrested or threatened.

Koigi wa Wamwere, a former member of parliament and political prisoner, who had been arrested in 1990 (see *Amnesty International Report 1993*), was released on 19 January when the prosecution withdrew treason charges. Three others held with him, including lawyers Mirugi Kariuki and Rumba Kinuthia, were also released. However, Koigi wa Wamwere was rearrested on 18 September in Burnt Forest town in the Rift Valley, together with Mirugi Kariuki, his lawyer, and six others. Initially held incommunicado, they were charged with possessing weapons and seditious publications, including documents of the National Democratic and Human Rights Organization, founded by Koigi wa Wamwere, and with illegally entering a restricted security zone – all of which they denied. Members of the Release Political Prisoners (RPP) campaigning group were also arrested. All were released on bail within a few days or weeks, but Koigi wa Wamwere was arrested again on 5 November in Nakuru and charged, with 14 others – including two relatives previously imprisoned with him – with attempted violent robbery, punishable by a mandatory death penalty. He seemed to have been arrested for his non-violent political activities. All 15 denied the allegations of involvement in an armed attack on a police station. Their trial, set for December, was adjourned. Among others held for several days in other arrests of suspected government opponents in Nakuru was Dr S.W. Mwangi, who was providing medical treatment to political prisoners.

Although opposition political parties operated openly and freely, opposition members of parliament, human rights activists, journalists and other government critics were arrested and detained for short periods in connection with peaceful demonstrations, speeches, publications or investigations into human rights abuses.

Some government critics were accused of sedition. John Makhanga, a pharmacist and human rights activist involved in relief work for victims of the ethnic clashes, was arrested in Nairobi on 25 February, beaten up by masked police officers, and taken to an unknown destination. In court a few days later he was charged with sedition but was freed on bail after two weeks in cûstody. In February and again in June, Njehu Gatabaki, editor of *Finance* magazine, was held briefly for alleged sedition. The Reverend Jamlick Miano, editor of *The Watchman*, and people selling his newspaper were arrested on two occasions when the newspaper criticized President Moi. Dominic Martin was held briefly in May for printing an allegedly seditious opposition magazine, and his printing press was damaged by unidentified assailants. Njenga Mungai, an opposition member of parliament, was arrested three times for publicly accusing the government of instigating ethnic clashes in his constituency in Molo. The General Secretary of the Central Organization of Trade Unionists (COTU), Joseph Mugalla, was arrested on 1 May after calling for a general strike: he was charged with inciting disobedience to the law but freed on bail. Sheikh Khalid Salim Balala, an Islamic Party of Kenya (IPK) activist arrested in 1992 for alleged treason and freed in January, was rearrested in May after threatening violence against the government; he was charged with treason but released on bail.

In all these cases, those arrested – who were mostly prisoners of conscience – were released on bail or without charge after a few days or weeks. Charges against some of them were later dropped. Sedition charges with penalties of up to 10 years' imprisonment, which had been brought in 1992 against several non-violent government critics, including Pius Nyamora and other *Society* magazine journalists (see *Amnesty International Report 1993*), were also withdrawn, although sedition charges brought in 1992 and 1993 against Njehu Gatabaki were left pending.

Cases of torture and ill-treatment of prisoners were reported. In January Koigi wa Wamwere's food was allegedly poisoned in Kamiti prison. Rumba Kinuthia continued to be kept chained in custody in hospital until his release on 19 January. Several prisoners testified in court that they had been tortured by police to make them confess to crimes. Some suspected government opponents arrested with Koigi wa Wamwere in September and November were allegedly tortured by police, at least one of them suffering serious injuries.

Police assaulted peaceful demonstrators on several occasions. Refugees, especially those fleeing civil war in Somalia, were frequently ill-treated and there were many reports of police raping Somali women refugees.

In April a court awarded Wanyiri Kihoro, a former prisoner of conscience, compensation for torture and unlawful detention between 1986 and 1989 (see *Amnesty International Report 1989*).

Scores of people were killed by government supporters or armed pro-government groups during 1993, particularly in areas near Burnt Forest, Molo and Nakuru towns in Rift Valley Province and near Mount Elgon in Western Province, many of them apparently victims of extrajudicial executions. In particular cases as in Londiani in June and Molo in August, the violence was carried out by organized groups, known as "Kalenjin warriors", armed with bows and arrows and composed of as many as 300 members of the Kalenjin ethnic group to which President Moi belongs. Police failed to protect victims or investigate complaints. Most victims, who were perceived as supporting opposition parties, belonged to other ethnic groups, particularly the Kikuyu, although Kalenjins also suffered violent reprisals in some areas. In September the government designated some of the disturbed areas as restricted security zones: this resulted in the blocking of independent investigations and relief activities by Kenyan church groups and others. Police arrested and prosecuted over 1,000 people for alleged involvement in the violence but often failed to stop or prevent violence by pro-government or Kalenjin elements.

The full facts of the alleged extrajudicial execution of former Foreign Minister Robert Ouko in 1990 were still unclear. The trial of former District Commissioner Jonah Anguka, who was accused of his murder, was continuing at the end of 1993.

Over 30 people were sentenced to death by the courts after being convicted of armed robbery or murder, with an estimated total of some 400 people under sentence of death. There were no reports of executions.

Amnesty International criticized the frequent arrests and short-term imprisonment of prisoners of conscience, and the use of charges such as sedition – or even violent robbery, in Koigi wa Wamwere's case – to punish and restrict peaceful political activities. The organization called for independent investigations into reports of torture

184

by police officers, including rape and beatings, and also for thorough and impartial investigations into ethnic killings where any sort of involvement by the government, ruling party or security forces was suspected. Amnesty International urged commutation of all death sentences.

KOREA
(DEMOCRATIC PEOPLE'S REPUBLIC OF)

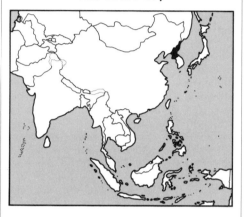

New information emerged about prisoners of conscience who appeared to have been detained for years, sometimes decades, without trial or after unfair trials. They included relatives and children of alleged government opponents. Hundreds of political prisoners were reported to be in unacknowledged detention. Former prisoners stated that conditions of detention were harsh and that ill-treatment of prisoners was common. Reports suggested that executions had taken place, including some in public.

The Democratic People's Republic of Korea (DPRK) remained largely isolated, partly because foreign travel by North Koreans and access to the country by foreign nationals were severely limited by the government. The authorities did not allow independent observers to visit places of detention or to investigate reports of human rights violations.

In March a three-week state of "semiwar" was declared by the government during joint exercises close to the country's border by armed forces of the Republic of Korea (South Korea) and the USA. In April Kim Jong Il, son of President Kim Il Sung,

was elected by the Supreme People's Assembly (SPA) as chairman of the National Defence Commission, succeeding his father. In December the ruling Workers' Party of Korea (WPK) stated that planned economic objectives failed to be achieved "due to world events and the difficult situation [these] created in [North] Korea". The WPK also anounced that Kim Il Sung's younger brother, Kim Yong Ju, had been elected to the party's political bureau.

In January Amnesty International learned that an Institute for Research into Human Rights had been created in 1992 in Pyongyang, headed by Li Chang Ha, a member of the Standing Committee of the SPA. The scope of the Institute's work was unclear but the government stated that it would be responsible for replying to a memorandum submitted by Amnesty International in 1992 detailing its concerns about the human rights situation in the DPRK. However, by the end of the year no response had been received.

In June Paek In Jun, a Vice-Chairman of the SPA, led the DPRK delegation to the UN World Conference on Human Rights in Vienna. He stated that "the problem of human rights of the citizens in each country is a matter to be solved by each sovereign state" and opposed "interfering" and "putting unreasonable pressure" on states. He made no reference to specific allegations of human rights violations in his country.

New information emerged about prisoners and possible prisoners of conscience. They included people accused of "crimes against the state", relatives of people who had sought political asylum abroad and people accused of illegal contacts with foreigners. According to unofficial sources, a woman was sentenced to four years' "re-education through labour" in March because she had had contacts with a foreign student which she failed to report to the authorities. It was unclear whether she had been tried or was given a term of administrative detention, imposed without trial.

Shibata Kozo, a Japanese national imprisoned since 1964, was also believed to be a prisoner of conscience. Having served a 20-year sentence for allegedly encouraging Japanese women resident in Pyongyang to protest after they were denied permission to visit their families in Japan, he should have been released in 1984. However, he continued to be held despite poor health and in late 1990 was being detained in Sungho village near Pyongyang. Since then there has been no news of him: he was not known to have been released. Two other prisoners who had been arrested in December 1982 with their two children, apparently by officials of the Ministry of State Security, were also said to be still detained for political reasons and to have been denied permission either to see or correspond with their relatives.

An unknown number, believed to be many hundreds, of political prisoners were held without trial in unacknowledged detention. Whole groups of North Koreans were believed to have been taken into custody for "re-education" after returning from studies abroad, but details were not available. Those reportedly held included children and young people, among them Oh Hae Won, aged 18, and Oh Kyu Won, aged 15. They were believed to have been detained since 1986 with their mother Shin Sook Ja, after their father sought asylum abroad. They were reportedly held in a "re-education through labour" detention camp in Yodok, Hamgyong South Province, and were prisoners of conscience.

Some political prisoners were reportedly held without trial, others after grossly unfair trials. The latter were believed to have been sentenced by tribunals whose judges were apparently required to carry out the policies of the WPK. Lawyers were said to have virtually no access to prisoners before they came to trial. In certain cases, the authorities apparently imposed periods of administrative detention on individuals accused of less serious offences which did not warrant a full trial. In such cases, the accused reportedly had no access to legal counsel and no effective opportunity to present a defence.

Political prisoners in "re-education through labour" detention camps were reportedly held in extremely harsh conditions. Former prisoners said that in previous years many inmates had died of cold, hunger or untreated illnesses, and that those in the camps were deprived of all rights. Some camps were reported to hold "special" categories of prisoners and to receive virtually no food or other supplies, with the inmates expected to produce their own food to survive.

Some North Korean forestry workers were also reportedly held in makeshift prisons in camps run by North Korean officials and located in the far east of the Russian Federation. Those who attempted to leave the camps, set up for forestry working by agreement between the DPRK and the former Union of Soviet Socialist Republics (USSR), were reportedly detained for indefinite periods. Concern over the detentions, and the poor working conditions in the camps, reportedly led the Russian authorities to decide to close the camps by the end of 1993.

Unofficial sources suggested that the death penalty is widely used, including for political offences. The 1987 Criminal Law describes the death penalty as one of the two kinds of "basic penalties" to be imposed on criminal offenders. This provides a mandatory death penalty for activities "in collusion with imperialists" aimed at "suppressing the national-liberation struggle" and the "revolutionary struggle for reunification and independence". The death penalty is also mandatory for "acts of betraying the Nation to imperialists", and discretionary for offences including "extreme cases" of "betrayal of the country"; participation in a plot to overthrow the Republic or in acts of revolt; acts of "terrorism" against the WPK and government "cadres and patriotic people"; and murder, in particularly serious cases. The precise nature of some of these offences is not defined in the Criminal Law.

DPRK officials told Amnesty International in 1991 that the death penalty was used only "in rare circumstances", but they refused to provide detailed information. They said that statistics on the use of the death penalty were collected but were not then available. However, witnesses at public announcements of death sentences, former detainees and visitors to North Korea reported in 1993 that the death penalty is used frequently, with dozens of prisoners executed each year, including people convicted of economic offences. In one case in November 1992, according to a government statement in October, Chu Su Man, a 30-year-old man officially described as an "habitual violent offender" and convicted of murder, was publicly executed "at the request of the crowd". In other cases in 1992, prisoners under sentence of death had been displayed at public meetings attended by workers and students, including school-age children. Executions were reportedly carried out in front of such meetings. Detainees were also reportedly executed in

186

front of assembled inmates in detention centres.

Amnesty International again sought information from the government about people reportedly held for political reasons and about the use of the death penalty, but there was no response to these inquiries. In October Amnesty International published a report, *North Korea: Summary of Amnesty International's Concerns*. This drew attention to the cases of prisoners of conscience and other political prisoners, allegations of ill-treatment and the use of the death penalty. The report also criticized the inadequate human rights safeguards in the Constitution, which fail to meet the requirements of the International Covenant on Civil and Political Rights, to which the DPRK acceded in 1981, and other human rights standards. Amnesty International expressed particular concern that certain provisions of the Criminal Law are so vague that they can result in imprisonment for the peaceful exercise of fundamental rights – those convicted of being "in revolt" can be imprisoned for up to 10 years, and those who "encourage others to attempt … the undermining of the Republic" for up to seven years.

When publishing the report, Amnesty International called on the government to release all prisoners of conscience immediately and unconditionally; to ensure that all other political prisoners were given fair and prompt trials or released; to safeguard all prisoners against ill-treatment; and to commute all death sentences and abolish the death penalty. Amnesty International also called for the introduction of effective human rights safeguards and their implementation in practice. The organization also reiterated its call to the government to open the country to independent human rights monitors.

The government responded to Amnesty International's report: it "categorically rejected" its contents, describing them as "either utterly groundless or far from the fact". However, the government provided no information about individual prisoners of conscience and others whose cases had been cited in the report. Referring to Amnesty International's criticism of the Criminal Law, the authorities said that provisions relating to "crimes against the state" have "crime-preventive significance and are rarely applied". They denied too that North Korean-run camps in Russia

were used to hold prisoners: they had "only education rooms" to "educate workers to properly observe the Russian laws". The government's response also said that the death penalty was rarely imposed and that no one had been sentenced to death for political reasons. However, it confirmed the use of public executions.

Amnesty International repeatedly informed the government of its wish to visit the DPRK to obtain further information about human rights but there was no response.

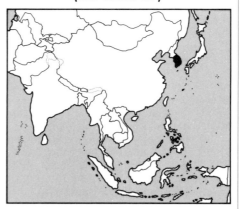

KOREA
(REPUBLIC OF)

Dozens of government opponents were detained on political charges, including prisoners of conscience. Many were tortured or ill-treated during interrogation. Some 250 other political prisoners arrested in previous years, including prisoners of conscience, continued to be held. The majority had been tried and convicted under the National Security Law (NSL), which restricts the rights to freedom of expression and association, and some had been convicted after trials which were believed to have been unfair. Some 50 prisoners were under sentence of death. There were no executions.

In his inaugural speech in February President Kim Young-sam promised greater freedom and democracy. The new government initially expressed a willingness to amend the NSL but reversed this position soon after taking office. In December the National Assembly adopted legislation limiting the powers of the Agency for National Security Planning (ANSP) to arrest and interrogate political suspects and providing for the punishment of ANSP agents found guilty of abuse of authority.

Under the amended law, the ANSP will no longer be permitted to investigate the activities of those suspected of "praising" North Korea or failing to inform the authorities about alleged North Korean spies, although such suspects may still be prosecuted without ANSP involvement. The amendment also provided for the National Assembly to exercise a degree of scrutiny over the ANSP's budget.

In March the International Labour Organisation said that the ban on third party intervention in labour disputes, under which several prisoners of conscience have been held, was a "serious restriction" on the free functioning of trade unions. In May the government said it would amend Article 13(2) of the Labour Dispute Mediation Act to remove the ban, but in August it reversed this decision following a series of strikes.

In June the government announced its intention to ratify the UN Convention against Torture. It had not done so by the end of the year.

In March, 144 political prisoners were released in an amnesty to mark the inauguration of the new President. They included dissidents, students, workers and also six elderly prisoners serving life terms. However, dozens of people were arrested during the year on political charges, many of whom were prisoners of conscience. Most were held under the NSL, which prohibits "anti-state" activities and contacts with "anti-state" organizations and North Korea.

Over 30 people were arrested and charged under the NSL with belonging to or supporting *Sanomaeng*, the Socialist Workers' League, which the authorities considered an "anti-state" organization. Some of those held, who included prisoners of conscience, had no connection with *Sanomaeng* and others said that they had sought to establish a socialist political party through legal and non-violent means. The prisoners of conscience included Professor Cho Kuk, an open critic of the NSL, and nine others arrested in June on suspicion of belonging to the Socialist Academy, alleged to have links with *Sanomaeng*. Some 60 real or alleged members of *Sanomaeng* arrested since 1990 remained in prison at the end of the year. Most of them were prisoners of conscience (see *Amnesty International Reports 1992* and *1993*).

Hwang Suk-yong, a writer detained by the ANSP in April as he returned to South Korea after a period of self-imposed exile, was also a prisoner of conscience. In October he was sentenced to eight years' imprisonment for making an unauthorized visit to North Korea in 1989 and accepting "operational" funds from the North Korean Government which, he said, were the copyright fee for permission to make a film of his book *Jangkilsan*.

Human rights activist Noh Tae-hun was arrested in July; the police tried to make him confess to meeting North Korean spies in Japan, but he denied this. He was charged under the NSL for possessing and distributing books and pamphlets which the authorities said benefited North Korea, but which were publicly available in South Korea. Noh Tae-hun's human rights work appeared to be the real reason for his arrest. He had helped former long-term political prisoners and had also coordinated the participation of South Korean non-governmental organizations in the UN World Conference on Human Rights, held in Vienna in June. He was released in October after receiving a suspended prison sentence.

In July eight former army conscripts were arrested. They had deserted from the military and made "declarations of conscience", in some cases as long ago as 1989, advocating reform of the military and expressing concern at the political and human rights situation in South Korea. Most had been assigned to the riot police and required to perform duties they opposed on grounds of conscience. As the right to conscientious objection is not recognized, no alternative civilian service was available to them. Four of the eight were sentenced to prison terms ranging from one-and-a-half to three years: they were prisoners of conscience. The others were given suspended prison sentences but faced the possibility of being sent back to the army or riot police to complete their military service.

Trade union leaders continued to face arrest for violating the prohibition on third party intervention in labour disputes. In July leaders of the Korean Trade Union Congress (KTUC), including its President Dan Byung-ho, went into hiding when arrest warrants were issued on the grounds that they had given advice to trade unions about wage negotiations and about strike

188

procedures. Dan Byung-ho was still in hiding at the end of the year.

Some 30 of the 60 prisoners arrested and charged in August and September 1992 for alleged involvement in a "spy" ring operated by the North Korean Government were sentenced to prison terms ranging from one year to life imprisonment (see *Amnesty International Report 1993*). Twenty-five others were given suspended sentences and released. Those jailed included writer and political activist Kim Nak-jung, who was sentenced to life imprisonment in February. A prisoner of conscience, he had advocated peaceful reunification through his writings, lectures and meetings and there was no evidence of espionage. Other prisoners of conscience included Choi Chin-sop, a journalist, and Lee Kun-hee, a secretary to a member of the National Assembly. They were convicted of belonging to an "anti-state" group and of passing state secrets to alleged spies, but there was no convincing evidence for this. The authorities failed to investigate reports that many of the prisoners arrested in this case had been held incommunicado and tortured during interrogation.

Dozens of political prisoners convicted under national security legislation in previous years remained in prison. Many of those arrested in the 1970s and 1980s had received long prison sentences for alleged contacts with North Korea and for espionage. There were consistent reports that many of these prisoners had been tortured during interrogation and convicted largely on the basis of their own coerced confessions. They included prisoners of conscience Kim Song-man and Hwang Tae-kwon, arrested in 1985 and serving sentences of life and 20 years' imprisonment respectively, and Chang Ui-gyun, who had been arrested in 1987 and sentenced to eight years' imprisonment. In April the UN Working Group on Arbitrary Detention determined that the detention of these three prisoners contravened both the Universal Declaration of Human Rights and the International Covenant on Civil and Political Rights.

The authorities refused to release two prisoners held since the Korean War (1950 to 1953) because they had consistently refused to sign a statement of "conversion" to anti-communism, renouncing alleged communist views. Kim Sun-myung and Ahn Hak-sop were North Korean soldiers at the time of their capture in 1951 and 1953 respectively. They were sentenced to life imprisonment on espionage charges, but appear to have been simply prisoners of war who were convicted after unfair trials. They appeared to be prisoners of conscience.

In October the Judicial and Legal Affairs Committee of the National Assembly reviewed the case of Kang Ki-hun after new evidence emerged to suggest that he had been wrongly convicted in December 1991 of aiding and abetting the protest suicide of a political activist (see *Amnesty International Report 1993*). The new evidence, however, did not satisfy legal criteria for a retrial and Kang Ki-hun continued to be held. His arrest and conviction were apparently politically motivated: he was a prisoner of conscience.

Virtually all those known to have been detained for political reasons during the year were allegedly subjected to lengthy periods of interrogation, sleep deprivation and threats by both the Security Division of the National Police Administration and the ANSP. Some prisoners said that they had been beaten and forced to do repeated physical exercises during interrogation.

The pacifist and human rights advocate, Kim Sam-sok, was stripped naked, sexually assaulted and beaten by officials of the ANSP after his arrest in September. He and his sister, Kim Un-ju, were arrested without warrant and held incommunicado for two days. Kim Sam-sok told his lawyer that he had been forced to make a false confession and that he had tried to commit suicide. Kim Un-ju said she had been deprived of sleep and slapped and shaken by interrogators who also made sexual threats. The two were detained under the NSL on suspicion of contacting and passing state secrets to "anti-state" groups in Japan with the aim of benefiting North Korea. Their trial had not concluded by the end of the year.

In November former political prisoner Mun Guk-jin brought a civil law suit against the government, claiming damages for torture inflicted when he was arrested in 1980 and 1986. Doctors have attested that Mun Guk-jin's current mental illness is a direct result of torture.

There were some 50 prisoners under sentence of death, most of whom were kept permanently handcuffed. There were no executions.

Amnesty International called for the release of prisoners of conscience, for an end to torture and ill-treatment and for impartial investigations into all torture allegations. In May it urged the government to ratify the UN Convention against Torture. Amnesty International also urged the government to amend the NSL and other laws used to detain political prisoners and it called on the authorities to review the cases of long-term political prisoners, many of whom had been tortured and convicted after unfair trials. In December Amnesty International urged the authorities not to carry out any executions and to commute all death sentences.

KUWAIT

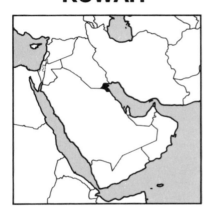

Hundreds of political prisoners, including possible prisoners of conscience, arrested in 1991 on charges of "collaboration" with Iraqi forces during the occupation of Kuwait, remained in custody. At least 89, some of whom appeared to be prisoners of conscience, were brought before the State Security Court during the year. After unfair trials 18 of them were sentenced to death, including one *in absentia*, and at least 39 were given prison sentences. Over 100 people, including 13 women, some of whom appeared to be prisoners of conscience, continued to serve prison terms imposed following unfair trials in 1991 and 1992. Four Iraqi nationals were reported to have been severely tortured, resulting in one death. The fate and whereabouts of at least 62 detainees who "disappeared" from custody in 1991 remained unknown. An Iraqi national was executed in May. This was the first

judicial execution in Kuwait since 1989. A second execution was carried out in December.

In August the Council of Ministers issued a decree ordering the dissolution of all unlicensed organizations, including one of the country's leading human rights groups, *al-Jami'a al-Kuwaitiyya lil-difa' 'an Dahaya al-Harb*, the Kuwaiti Association to Defend War Victims, which has been working on behalf of Kuwaitis missing and believed to be held in Iraq since 1991 (see **Iraq** entry). The government decree effectively ignored a resolution adopted by the National Assembly in December 1992 calling for non-governmental groups working on behalf of the missing Kuwaitis to be legalized. The Hostages and Missing Committee, a seven-member parliamentary committee with responsibility for following up cases of Kuwaitis held in Iraq, condemned the government's decision to close down these organizations. Its members resigned in protest at the National Assembly's failure to support their efforts to have the government's decision overturned.

Hundreds of political prisoners, including possible prisoners of conscience, remained held following their arrest in 1991 on suspicion of "collaboration" with Iraqi forces during the occupation of Kuwait (see *Amnesty International Report 1993*). During the year at least 89 of them were brought before the State Security Court, the majority on charges relating to "collaboration with the enemy". The trial proceedings fell short of international standards for fair trial: among other things, some defendants were denied access to lawyers before trial and some evidence accepted by the court was withheld from the defence. In all 18 people were sentenced to death, including one *in absentia*; 39 received prison terms ranging between two years and life; and 27 were acquitted. Among those convicted were Samir Ahmad Samara, a Palestinian, who was sentenced to life imprisonment, and Zuhair 'Umar Salah Mahmud, a Jordanian national, who was sentenced to 15 years in prison. Defendants were denied the full right of appeal available to defendants in ordinary criminal cases. There was no information available about the precise number of defendants still awaiting trial at the end of 1993.

Eleven Iraqis and three Kuwaitis appeared before the State Security Court on

5 June, charged with involvement in an alleged Iraqi government plot to assassinate the former US President, George Bush, during his visit to Kuwait in April. The defendants were not allowed access to lawyers before the trial. The prosecution asked for the death penalty to be imposed on the 11 Iraqis and one of the Kuwaitis. Before the trial, the US Government justified an air strike on Baghdad by stating that its investigations provided compelling evidence of an Iraqi intelligence assassination plot. The verdict had not been announced by the end of the year.

One hundred and two political prisoners, including 13 women, continued to serve prison terms in Kuwait Central Prison following their conviction on charges of "collaboration". Some appeared to be prisoners of conscience. Fifty-nine had been sentenced by the Martial Law Court in 1991 and the others by the State Security Court in 1992 after trials which did not satisfy international standards for fair trial (see *Amnesty International Reports 1992* and *1993*).

Four Iraqi nationals were reported to have been abducted by Kuwaiti forces on 28 August near the Iraqi town of Safwan, close to the Iraq/Kuwait border. They were alleged to have been severely tortured during interrogation before being returned to the Safwan area two days later. One of the four, Ma'add Zahir, was reported to have died as a result of the torture.

The cases of seven policemen implicated in the torture of a Sri Lankan detainee in June 1992, said to have been referred to the Criminal Court, remained unresolved. The detainee, Colompurage Asoka Pathmakumara, died before reaching hospital (see *Amnesty International Report 1993*).

The fate and whereabouts of at least 62 Palestinians, Jordanians, Iraqis and other nationals who "disappeared" in custody between February and June 1991 remained unknown at the end of the year (see *Amnesty International Report 1993*). Among them were 'Awatif Qasim Muhammad 'Ali al-Maliki, a young Iraqi woman who had "disappeared" at the end of February 1991, and 'Ali Daifallah, a Palestinian who had "disappeared" in May 1991 together with his son, Muhammad.

'Abd al-Rahman Hassan Khafi, an Iraqi national sentenced to death by the State Security Court in July 1992, was executed in May after his sentence was upheld by the Court of Cassation and ratified by the Amir, Shaikh Jaber al-Ahmad al-Sabah. He had been convicted of membership of the pro-Iraq *Hizb al-Tahrir al-'Arabi* (Arab Liberation Front) and of killing a Kuwaiti border guard. This was the first judicial execution known to have been carried out in Kuwait since 1989. Kamal Matar, a member of the *bidun* (stateless Arab) community, was executed in December following his conviction for murder.

During the year 18 people were sentenced to death, including one *in absentia*, by the State Security Court. They were convicted of "collaboration" (see above) after proceedings which failed to conform to international standards for fair trial. Their sentences had not been ratified by the end of the year. They included 10 Jordanians, six Iraqis and one Kuwaiti woman, Siham Ibrahim Hussain 'Ali. A Kuwaiti man was sentenced to death by the Criminal Court in August after being convicted of rape. Another man was sentenced to death in December after being convicted of murder.

In addition to requesting information about other unresolved cases, Amnesty International sought further information about the legal basis for the arrest in December 1992, and continued detention without trial, of 'Abd al-'Aziz Su'ud al-'Ali, a *bidun* and former member of the Kuwaiti armed forces.

Amnesty International continued throughout the year to press for the fair trial or release of all political prisoners, for steps to be taken to clarify all "disappearances" and to investigate all torture allegations and deaths in custody. Amnesty International also called for the commutation of all death sentences.

In July Amnesty International publicly criticized the unfairness of trials before the State Security Court, and urged the government to review all sentences already passed by the court, including death sentences. Amnesty International also expressed concern that the 14 people charged in connection with an alleged plot to assassinate George Bush (see above) might not receive a fair trial in view of statements by the US and Kuwaiti governments which appeared to undermine the defendants' presumption of innocence.

Amnesty International published a report in September, *Iraq: Secret detention of Kuwaitis and third-country nationals,* which highlighted the cases of 140 people believed to be detained in Iraq since the end of the Gulf conflict (see **Iraq** entry). The organization publicly urged the Kuwaiti Government to make available immediately all documents left behind by Iraqi occupying forces which related to the arrest of Kuwaitis and third-country nationals by Iraqi forces, and to provide a complete list of all those who it believed remain in detention in Iraq.

Throughout the year the Kuwaiti authorities failed to address the substance of any of Amnesty International's concerns and requests for information. In July the Minister of Justice publicly denied Amnesty International's claims that trials before the State Security Court were unfair.

Kamilov, Khayriddin Kasymov and Khurshed Nazarov, were arrested in early January in Osh, southern Kyrgyzstan, reportedly by Kyrgyz law enforcement officials. They were forcibly returned to Tadzhikistan, where they were detained and reportedly tortured by Tadzhik officials (see **Tadzhikistan** entry).

Amnesty International continued to call on the government headed by President Askar Akayev to abolish the death penalty. In March Amnesty International wrote to the Minister of Internal Affairs expressing concern about the forcible repatriation of the three Tadzhik journalists and calling on the authorities to ensure that their treatment of asylum-seekers conformed to international standards.

KYRGYZSTAN

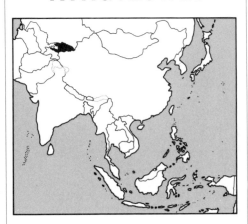

LAOS

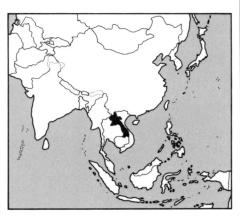

Four death sentences were commuted. Three journalists fleeing from Tadzhikistan were arrested and forcibly repatriated: they were detained and reportedly tortured subsequently.

A new Constitution entered into force in May. It incorporates a number of human rights guarantees found in the principal international human rights instruments.

The death penalty remained in force for 15 peacetime offences and others in time of war. No death sentences or executions were reported, but four people who had been under sentence of death at the beginning of 1993 had their sentences commuted to 20 years' imprisonment during the year.

Three journalists who had fled from neighbouring Tadzhikistan, Akhmadsho

Three prisoners of conscience continued to be held throughout 1993. One long-term prisoner of conscience died in custody. Three untried political detainees were released from "re-education" but continued to be restricted. Three other political prisoners continued to serve sentences of life imprisonment after an unfair trial.

In February the National Assembly approved the appointment of Nouhak Phoumsavanh as President. At the same time it endorsed the formation of a new government, which involved extensive ministerial changes.

Three prisoners of conscience continued to be held in the northern province of Houa Phanh. Thongsouk Saysangkhi, Latsami Khamphoui and Feng Sakchittaphong had been sentenced to 14 years' imprisonment in November 1992 after a trial that failed to meet international standards for fairness. Despite official charges against them which included preparing for rebellion, Amnesty International believed that they were detained for peacefully advocating a multi-party political system (see *Amnesty International Report 1993*). According to unofficial sources they were transferred early in the year from Sop Hao Central Prison to "Re-education" Camp 7. They were reportedly held initially in harsh conditions in a dark cell. In August they were moved to a different location within the camp with improved conditions. However, all three were reported to be suffering from chronic medical conditions and no medical facilities were available in the camp.

In April prisoner of conscience Thuck Chokbengboun died after an illness. He had been detained in "re-education" camps without charge or trial for almost 18 years, often in harsh conditions, and had been ill for a long time. In March he was transferred from Sop Pan "Re-education" Camp in Houa Phanh province to a government hospital in Vientiane, the capital, for medical treatment. He died three weeks later.

In January three untried political prisoners were moved from the Sop Pan camp to a village to which they were restricted. Ly Teng, Tong Pao Song and Yong Ye Thao, who had been held in "re-education" camps without charge or trial since 1975, were moved to a village in Sop Hao, Houa Phanh province. They had been under police investigation in 1992 in connection with alleged killings in the 1970s (see *Amnesty International Report 1993*). Their freedom of movement was restricted and they were prohibited from leaving the village.

Three other political prisoners, Pangtong Chokbengboun, Bounlu Nammathao and Sing Chanthakoummane, remained in detention at the Sop Pan camp. Before being sentenced to life imprisonment after an unfair trial in 1992, they also had been detained without charge or trial for more than 17 years (see *Amnesty International Report 1993*).

According to unofficial sources, Khamsone Vongnarath, a Lao student detained in 1992, was released in early 1993. He had been forcibly taken back to Laos from Moscow in December 1992 (see *Amnesty International Report 1993*).

Amnesty International continued to call for the immediate and unconditional release of prisoners of conscience and the fair trial or release from detention or restriction of other long-term political prisoners. In August Amnesty International published a report, *Laos: Freedom of expression still denied, multi-party advocates and political prisoners sentenced after unfair trials.* The report detailed the organization's concerns about prisoners of conscience and other political prisoners. By the end of the year no response had been received from the Lao authorities about any of these concerns.

LATVIA

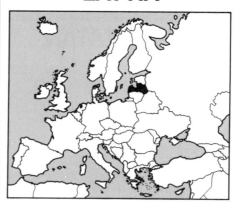

One person was executed.

In June the first parliamentary elections since the restoration of Latvia's independence in 1991 were held. In July the new parliament, the *Saeima*, reinstated the 1922 Constitution of the Republic of Latvia and chose Guntis Ulmanis as President and Head of State. He nominated Valdis Birkavs as Prime Minister.

In April Andres Serguts was executed following the rejection of his petition for clemency. He had been sentenced to death in July 1992 on two counts of premeditated murder under aggravated circumstances. Two other death sentences, both passed the previous year, were commuted. No prisoners were reported to be under sentence of death at the end of the year.

Throughout the year Amnesty International asked the Latvian authorities to confirm the number of people under sentence of death, but received no reply. Amnesty International appealed for commutation of all death sentences, including that passed on Andres Sergunts, and urged the authorities to consider the complete abolition of the death penalty.

In January the organization published a report entitled *The Baltic States: Time to abolish the death penalty.*

LEBANON

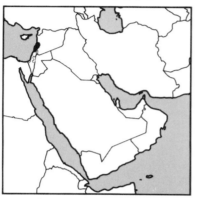

Dozens of people were arrested on security grounds: some were held without charge or trial before being released uncharged but others were brought to court. Those arrested included possible prisoners of conscience. New reports of torture and ill-treatment were received. Nine people were killed by government forces during an apparently peaceful demonstration. The fate of thousands of people who had been abducted by armed groups in previous years remained unclarified. One death sentence was passed but had not been carried out by the end of the year.

The Lebanese army continued to extend its deployment and bring under government jurisdiction territory previously controlled by various armed militias. However, a "security zone" along the Lebanese/Israeli border extending northwards to the Jezzine region remained under the control of the South Lebanon Army (SLA) militia and Israeli armed forces. *Hizbullah*, the main active militia opposing the SLA and Israeli troops inside Lebanon, controlled areas of south Lebanon. Syrian forces remained deployed throughout most of the country, particularly in the centre and north, with the agreement of the Lebanese Government.

In July, following increased clashes between Israel, the SLA and *Hizbullah*, Israeli forces bombarded extensive areas of south Lebanon for a week and *Hizbullah* fired rockets into northern Israel. Israeli officials indicated that the bombardment was aimed at forcing civilians to leave the area and to put pressure on the Lebanese Government to prevent *Hizbullah* from carrying out attacks against Israel. About 130 Lebanese and Palestinians, including civilians, as well as two Israeli civilians were killed in the attacks before a cease-fire agreement was reached. Amnesty International called on both sides to end any deliberate targeting of civilians.

Dozens of suspected political opponents were arrested by government forces and Syrian personnel stationed in Lebanon. They included possible prisoners of conscience. In March about 40 supporters of General Michel 'Aoun, a former military leader who was ousted in 1990 by Lebanese and Syrian forces, were arrested in connection with the distribution of leaflets opposing the Syrian presence in Lebanon. Most were released shortly afterwards, but eight remained in incommunicado detention for several weeks. Four of them were later released without charge. The other four, Michel al-Haje, Pierre Najm, 'Imad Shahin and Georges Za'anni, were charged and then released. Amnesty International could not confirm if they were brought to trial.

Elie Mahfoud, a lawyer and President of the *Mouvement du Changement*, Movement for Change, an organization which supports General 'Aoun, was arrested in July and held for about a week. He was released without charge. His arrest was reportedly connected to a statement he had made about the existence of political prisoners in Lebanon.

Dozens of alleged supporters of General 'Aoun and others were detained in October and December, some by Syrian personnel. They included 'Ubad Zwayn, who was reportedly beaten severely while being interrogated for three days in October in two Syrian detention centres in Lebanon and then released. A complaint about his allegations was submitted to the Lebanese authorities, but no response was received.

In April and May, in a clamp-down on the press during which three newspapers were temporarily closed, four journalists and a cartoonist were charged before the Publications Court with various offences in connection with articles published in the newspapers. Proceedings against two were

194

suspended in July, but the trials of the others had not been concluded by the end of the year. All faced sentences of up to three years' imprisonment if convicted.

At least five members of the Lebanese Forces (LF), a Christian militia, were reportedly arrested in August on suspicion of having spread negative propaganda about the Israeli bombardment of south Lebanon in July. Three were released without charge but two of them – Georges al-'Alam and Georges Shehadeh – were detained for interrogation and in September were charged with killing seven military personnel in previous years. Initially, security sources reportedly said that they would not be charged as the crimes were covered by the General Amnesty Law of 1991, but the Public Prosecutor held that the crimes had been committed for personal and vindictive motives and hence were not covered by the law. Both men were apparently still in custody at the end of the year. No information was received about 20 LF members who had been awaiting trial for state security offences at the end of 1992 (see *Amnesty International Report 1993*).

In November Samir Nasr, a possible prisoner of conscience, was detained in the Ministry of Defence and charged in connection with alleged links between the Guardians of the Cedar, a political party, and Israel. He complained of ill-treatment, including blows to the face and threats. His trial began in December.

Four supporters of General 'Aoun who had been arrested in November 1992 (see *Amnesty International Report 1993*) were released in January. They and eight others faced charges including distribution of leaflets. Their trial was postponed indefinitely in April.

New reports of torture and ill-treatment of detainees were received, including the cases of 'Ubad Zwayn and Samir Nasr. In one case a man deported from a European country was allegedly beaten and given electric shocks after being arrested in Beirut several times between February and April, possibly by Syrian officers stationed in Lebanon.

In September government forces killed nine people and injured about 30 others during an apparently peaceful demonstration in Beirut organized by *Hizbullah* to protest against the signing of the Declaration of Principles between Israel and the Palestine Liberation Organization (PLO). All

demonstrations had been banned in July. The government set up an investigation into the incident but no details of its methods or findings were known.

In April Bassam Saleh al-Muslah was sentenced to death on conviction of raping and murdering a seven-year-old girl in January. The execution was not carried out.

As in previous years the SLA held over 200 prisoners at any one time in the Khiam detention centre in the "security zone" in south Lebanon. About 30 men and women were released from the centre during the year. Most detainees were suspected of being members of armed groups opposing Israel and the SLA, and many were believed to have been tortured during interrogation. The detainees were held outside any legal framework and without access to their families or the International Committee of the Red Cross. Amnesty International continued to be concerned that some or all of those detained at Khiam might be held as hostages.

In June *Fatah*, the main faction of the PLO, released 78 members of the Fatah Revolutionary Council, a Palestinian group headed by Abu Nidal. They had been held in the context of clashes between the two groups in Palestinian refugee camps in Lebanon. Twelve members of the Fatah Revolutionary Council apparently remained in detention in the 'Ain al-Helwah camp at the end of the year. At least two had been sentenced to death by a PLO court, but their sentences were not carried out.

Little information was received about the fate of thousands of people who had been taken prisoner by armed groups since 1975. They included Palestinians, Syrians and other nationals, although the large majority were Lebanese. Butros 'Atmeh, a Lebanese Christian who had been abducted in Tibnin in August 1992 (see *Amnesty International Report 1993*), was released in March. The fate of another man abducted at the same time remained unknown. No information was received about the fate of Butros Khawand, a member of the Political Bureau of the Phalange Party, who had been abducted in September 1992 (see *Amnesty International Report 1993*). Of four Israeli soldiers still missing in Lebanon since 1982 and 1986, at least one, Ron Arad, may have been alive and secretly held by Iranian Revolutionary Guards in Lebanon or held in Syria.

Dozens of people were deliberately

killed, apparently for political reasons, but there was rarely sufficient information to determine those responsible. In March *Hizbullah* released Elias al-'Asmar and the body of Naji Kan'an. Both were SLA members who had been taken prisoner in November 1989. Naji Kan'an's killing while in custody had been announced shortly after his capture. In April and November, Yunes 'Awad and Mou'in Shabayleh, both senior *Fatah* officials, were killed by unknown assailants.

Amnesty International called for the release of any prisoners of conscience and sought information about arrests, including clarification of the procedures by which Syrian personnel stationed in Lebanon may detain people. It also called for impartial and thorough investigations into allegations of torture and the killings of demonstrators in September, asking for the official guidelines on opening fire to be reviewed to ensure their consistency with international standards. In April the organization urged the authorities to commute the death sentence on Bassam al-Muslah.

Amnesty International sought information from the governments of Lebanon, Iran and Syria about the fate of several people who went missing in Lebanon in previous years, fearing that they might have been killed or be held as hostages, but received no response.

In an oral statement to the UN Commission on Human Rights in February, Amnesty International called for the release of detainees in Khiam as well as SLA members and Israeli soldiers, who may be held as hostages. It also called for their protection against any form of ill-treatment.

LESOTHO

At least seven trade unionists who appeared to be prisoners of conscience were detained for short periods. Peaceful demonstrators were assaulted by police. Three prisoners remained under sentence of death.

In March Lesotho citizens voted in the first democratic elections to take place for 23 years. The opposition Basotholand Congress Party won all 65 National Assembly seats and formed a new government, headed by Prime Minister Ntsu Mokhehele, to replace the former military rulers.

Lesotho adopted a new Constitution and Bill of Rights.

The government ordered few inquiries into cases of human rights violations reported in previous years, effectively giving impunity to those members of the security forces responsible for political killings and torture in the past.

Police used provisions of the Internal Security Act (1984) which restrict meetings and demonstrations to prevent workers from airing grievances about pay and working conditions. In August lawyers challenged these provisions, on the grounds that they contravened constitutional guarantees. In late August parliament amended the relevant section of the Act, removing the requirement for meeting organizers to obtain prior police permission.

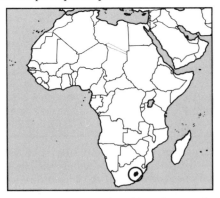

In July police forcibly dispersed a peaceful march in the capital, Maseru, organized by members of the Construction and Allied Workers Union of Lesotho (CAWULE). Police assaulted the marchers with batons, and some marchers were injured by flying tear-gas canisters. The General Secretary of CAWULE was detained for several hours and charged with contravening the Internal Security Act. The case had not concluded by the end of the year, pending the outcome of the August legal challenge to the Internal Security Act. In August, six branch officials of the Lesotho Amalgamated Clothing and Textile Workers' Union were detained for up to 48 hours then released on bail pending charges which were subsequently dropped.

In July, two soldiers convicted of the 1986 murder of two former government ministers and their wives (see *Amnesty International Report 1992*), one of whom faced the death penalty, had their sentences confirmed. Their appeal hearing was short and did not allow for full review of the case or consider the torture allegations made by the appellants during their trial. Two other prisoners remained under sentence of death.

Amnesty International raised with the newly elected government its continuing concerns about past human rights violations, and urged the new government to provide safeguards in law and practice against future human rights abuses.

LIBERIA

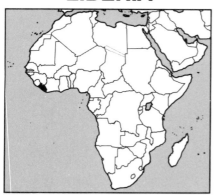

All parties to the continuing civil war were responsible for deliberate killings of civilians. Forces loyal to the interim government in Monrovia massacred 600 people – mainly women, children and old people – in June. Two soldiers were reported to have been executed after conviction by court-martial.

Fighting continued in the first half of the year between the multinational forces of the Economic Community of West African States (ECOWAS) Ceasefire Monitoring Group – known as ECOMOG – and the National Patriotic Front of Liberia (NPFL), headed by Charles Taylor. The ECOMOG forces were supported in the field by the Armed Forces of Liberia (AFL), the former national army under President Samuel Doe, which was reinstated by the Interim Government of National Unity in Monrovia in 1992. They were also supported by the United Liberation Movement for Democracy in Liberia (ULIMO), an armed group founded in 1991 by former AFL members.

By May ECOMOG forces had taken control from the NPFL of key installations outside Monrovia, the capital. Hundreds of civilians died when ECOMOG forces bombed and strafed NPFL areas, and thousands fled. ECOMOG aircraft made a number of attacks on border posts in Côte d'Ivoire and on international aid vehicles and their occupants. In May ECOWAS stopped all international aid agencies from entering NPFL-controlled territory from Côte d'Ivoire, accusing them of smuggling arms and fuel to the NPFL. Aid was not resumed until August and was then obstructed by continued disagreement over its distribution. Hundreds of civilians in NPFL territory were reported to have died from malnutrition and disease. In December aid agencies withdrew from Lofa County in northwest Liberia after their refugee camp at Vahun was looted by ULIMO troops.

On 25 July a peace agreement was signed by parties to the conflict, under the aegis of ECOWAS, the Organization of African Unity (OAU) and the UN in Cotonou, Benin. It provided for a cease-fire and disarmament, to be supervised by an expanded ECOMOG force and the UN, for the release of prisoners, and for the establishment of a joint transitional government until elections in 1994. The agreement contained no specific human rights guarantees and no mechanisms for monitoring the human rights situation or investigating human rights violations. It provided for an amnesty which could be interpreted to benefit those responsible for human rights violations, war crimes or crimes against humanity.

In August the first members of the UN Observer Mission in Liberia (UNOMIL), in all expected to number 600, started to arrive. In late December the ECOMOG force was expanded by the arrival of the first troops from countries in eastern and southern Africa. However, by the end of the year none of the warring factions had begun to disarm; cease-fire violations were occurring, including the movement of troops and the obstruction and looting of humanitarian assistance; and hundreds of prisoners had not been released. Members of a joint transitional government had been named but disagreement continued over the appointment of key ministers.

New armed factions emerged which were not party to the peace agreement. In October the Liberian Peace Council, a new armed group mostly comprising members of former President Samuel Doe's Krahn ethnic group, took control of parts of southeastern Liberia from the NPFL. In November and December another new armed group, the Lofa Defense Force, contested control with ULIMO of several towns in Lofa County.

Forces supporting the Interim Government carried out hundreds of extrajudicial executions. Although ECOMOG troops were not implicated directly in these killings, they were alleged to have been involved in some individual instances of abuse. In January ECOMOG soldiers beat and injured a British Broadcasting Corporation journalist in Monrovia, John Vambo, apparently because he had criticized ECOMOG in his reports. In September the Criminal Court refused a writ of *habeas corpus* in the case of Peter Bonnah Jallah, detained without charge or trial by ECOMOG since November 1992 on suspicion of involvement in the October 1992 attack on Monrovia by the NPFL. The court accepted that he was held as a prisoner of war, despite the terms of the peace accord.

Although ECOMOG disarmed and expelled AFL and ULIMO troops from Monrovia in March following complaints of harassment and looting, AFL and ULIMO soldiers continued to detain, beat and rob civilians and to kill those suspected of supporting the NPFL as they took over NPFL areas. AFL soldiers were identified as responsible for the extrajudicial execution in January of Brian Garnham, manager of a research laboratory near Robertsfield. The Interim Government set up a committee of inquiry which included the Minister of National Defense, and in April five soldiers were charged with disciplinary offences. An AFL court-martial dismissed charges against one and the four other cases had not proceeded by the end of the year.

ULIMO reportedly executed eight of its fighters in February for looting and harassing civilians. However, other ULIMO abuses went unpunished. In February, 13 elders at Haindi were held responsible for the drowning of a ULIMO commander, and extrajudicially executed. Towns and villages were burned as ULIMO contested control of Lofa County in March. Those summarily executed included 14 young men in Zorzor suspected of supporting the NPFL. Refugees who fled to neighbouring Guinea were reportedly either forcibly returned to Liberia or executed in Guinea after perfunctory investigations by an illegal tribunal of Liberian exiles based in Macenta and apparently linked to ULIMO. In July ULIMO was alleged to have extrajudicially executed as many as

300 members of the Lorma ethnic group in Voinjama who opposed their control of the town. In October ULIMO fighters reportedly killed large numbers of people from the Kissi ethnic group in Foya district. In November, after thousands of refugees had fled from fighting in Sierra Leone into Lofa County, ULIMO forces reportedly took prisoner about 300 of them, on suspicion of being supporters of the Revolutionary United Front, an armed group in rebellion against the Sierra Leone government and in alliance with the Liberian NPFL. In December about 20 people in neighbouring Guinea were killed in attacks by ULIMO on villages suspected of supplying NPFL combatants.

In September a UN inquiry found that the AFL had been responsible for the extrajudicial executions of nearly 600 unarmed civilians – mostly women, children and elderly people – at displaced people's camps near Harbel in June. Immediately after the massacre the Interim Government, the AFL and ECOMOG claimed that the NPFL was responsible, despite NPFL denials. The UN Security Council called for an investigation into the killings and the UN Secretary-General established a Panel of Inquiry which visited Liberia in August. The investigation concluded that the AFL, not the NPFL, had planned and carried out the killings, and that there had been a deliberate attempt to implicate the NPFL and to cover up the AFL's responsibility. The panel called for a criminal investigation and prosecution of those responsible. However, the Interim Government requested further evidence from the Panel of Inquiry before proceeding with charges against three AFL soldiers named in the Panel of Inquiry's report, and no one had been brought to justice by the end of the year.

In December, 800 captured NPFL fighters held by the Interim Government at Monrovia Central Prison were reported to be suffering severe malnutrition and medical neglect; five were said to have died. Most had been held since being taken prisoner during the NPFL attack on Monrovia in late 1992. The Interim Government ordered an internal investigation but its outcome was not known by the end of the year.

Two unnamed soldiers were reportedly executed in January after being convicted of looting by an AFL court-martial.

NPFL forces also continued to detain, beat and kill civilians deliberately, accusing

198

them of supporting rival armed groups. When ECOMOG forces took Buchanan in April, civilians who refused to flee with the NPFL were apparently killed by NPFL soldiers. In May, in an attack on Fasama, a town under ULIMO control, about 200 civilians were reportedly killed indiscriminately by NPFL soldiers. In August and September there were reports of NPFL attacks on Liberian refugees in camps close to the border in Côte d'Ivoire or as they returned to tend their crops in southeastern Liberia. Several were reportedly killed. In October the NPFL was accused of killing civilians in the course of conflict with ULIMO for control of Lofa and Bong Counties. In November the NPFL detained UN aid workers for several days, accusing them of spying. They were released uncharged.

In October Sierra Leonean Revolutionary United Front forces were reported to have killed civilians in Lofa county on suspicion of supporting opposing forces. Also in October Liberian Peace Council fighters reportedly killed civilians in Sinoe County in the southeast who refused to join them and, in December, nine church ministers in Greenville after accusing them of being "anti-Krahn".

Following the Harbel massacre in June, Amnesty International made a renewed appeal to all parties to the conflict to respect human rights and observe international humanitarian standards. The organization urged all sides to issue clear public orders to their troops not to kill or torture prisoners or non-combatants.

In December Amnesty International publicly called for those responsible for human rights abuses during the conflict to be brought to justice and for effective measures to protect human rights to be incorporated into the peace process.

LIBYA

Five prisoners of conscience held since 1973 continued to serve life sentences. Scores of suspected government opponents, some of them accused of participating in an alleged military revolt, were arrested during the year. Over 500 other suspected government opponents arrested in previous years, including possible prisoners of conscience, continued to be held apparently without charge or trial. Seventeen political prisoners continued serving sentences imposed after unfair trials. The use of torture by security forces continued to be reported. Summary executions were reported in October.

UN sanctions banning air travel and arms sales and restricting Libya's diplomatic presence abroad, which were imposed in April 1992, were still in place at the end of the 1993. The sanctions were imposed in the light of the Libyan Government's refusal to hand over two Libyan nationals to British or US authorities who wished to bring them to trial. The two men were accused of planting the bomb which destroyed a civilian airliner in flight in 1988 over Lockerbie in the United Kingdom, killing 270 people. The Libyan Government, which does not have an extradition treaty with either country, in effect refused to hand over the two men claiming that they would not receive a fair trial.

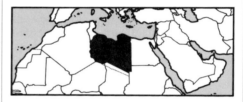

In June and again in September the Libyan leader, Colonel Mu'ammar Gaddafi, called publicly for the country's legislature to introduce judicial punishments of amputation for repeated theft and flogging for prostitution and adultery. Amnesty International considers both punishments to constitute cruel, inhuman and degrading treatment. Colonel Gaddafi also called for the scope of the death penalty to be extended to punish people found guilty of drinking alcohol and those deemed to be "heretics". Such changes in legislation had not been effected by the end of the year.

Between January and October, scores of suspected government opponents were arrested in Tripoli, Benghazi and other cities. All those arrested were alleged members or supporters of banned Islamist opposition groups; many of them had fought against Soviet forces in Afghanistan between 1979 and 1989. Most remained in secret unacknowledged detention at the end of the year, apparently without charge or trial. Among them was 'Ali Haroun al-Twati al-Badri, a sergeant-major in the police force arrested in January and believed to be held in a secret detention centre in al-Hawwari district of Tripoli. In another case, a high-school student, 'Imad al-Saqr, was arrested in June in Tripoli and was believed to be held in Abu Salim Prison.

In October scores of military and police personnel as well as civilians were arrested following an alleged military revolt in Misrata and Bani Walid. It was not possible to obtain information regarding their fate and whereabouts by the end of the year. However, among them were reportedly nine colonels, including Muhammad 'Abdul-'Ati al-Buma, Muhammad al-Nahaysi and al-Muftah al-Qarrub.

Five prisoners of conscience, all suspected members of the prohibited Islamic Liberation Party, continued to serve life sentences in Abu-Salim Prison in Tripoli (see Amnesty International Reports 1991 to 1993). They included al-'Ajili Muhammad 'Abdul-Rahman al-Azhari, an engineer arrested in Tripoli in 1973.

In June approximately 400 people, among them possible prisoners of conscience, were detained in various places along Libya's border upon their return from a pilgrimage to Mecca in Saudi Arabia. The pilgrims had made their way to Mecca by land or sea, contradicting government claims that Saudi Arabia, which had complied with the UN ban on air travel, had closed its doors to all Libyan pilgrims. The pilgrims were held for two to three weeks without charge or trial, apparently as a punishment for contradicting government claims.

Over 500 political prisoners, including possible prisoners of conscience, were still detained without charge or trial at the end of 1993. The majority had been held incommunicado since their arrest in previous years.

Most were detained between January 1989 and May 1991 during a crack-down on outlawed Islamist groups (see Amnesty International Reports 1992 and 1993). Among them were 'Abdul-Naser al-Bashir Abu-Lseyen, a doctor who was arrested in January 1989 at his home in Suq al-Jum'a, and 'Abdul-Salam al-Duwadi, a secondary school teacher and preacher in a mosque in Sibrata, who was arrested the same month after dawn prayers.

Around 80 others still held had been arrested between 1974 and 1986, most of them following an armed clash in May 1984 at Bab al-'Aziziya between the security forces and members of the opposition National Front for the Salvation of Libya (see previous Amnesty International Reports). They included Rahil al-Gaddafi Yusuf al-Bar'asi, a professor at Gar-Yunis University in Benghazi, and 'Abdul-Mun'im Qasem al-Najjar, a sociology lecturer at the University of Tripoli. Both were believed to be held in Abu-Salim Prison in Tripoli.

Seventeen government opponents sentenced to life imprisonment after unfair trials in previous years remained in Abu-Salim Prison in Tripoli (see Amnesty International Reports 1991 to 1993). 'Abdullah Menina, arrested in Benghazi in May 1984, remained in detention despite having been tried and acquitted in 1985 (see previous Amnesty International Reports).

Two political prisoners, 'Abdul-Hadi Ghafir and Fahim al-Tajuri, held since 1984 and 1989 respectively, were released in July. According to reports, neither had been formally charged or tried.

Torture and ill-treatment by the security forces continued to be reported. Among the victims were said to be scores of people arrested in the aftermath of an alleged military revolt in October (see above). There were allegations that officers who led the revolt were summarily executed, but this could not be confirmed by the end of the year.

In December a prominent government opponent "disappeared" in Cairo, Egypt, following his reported abduction by Libyan government agents. Mansur Kikhiya, a former Minister of Foreign Affairs, was in Cairo to attend the General Conference of the Arab Organization for Human Rights, during which he was re-elected to its Executive Board. The Egyptian authorities launched an investigation into his "disappearance", but the outcome and the fate and whereabouts of Mansur Kikhiya were not known by the end of the year.

In January the government invited Amnesty International to visit Libya. Amnesty International welcomed this initiative but before setting a date for the visit requested information about some of the many concerns and cases it had raised with the government over several years. No response had been received by the end of the year.

During the year Amnesty International continued to appeal for the immediate and unconditional release of all prisoners of conscience and for the fair trial or release of the hundreds of other political prisoners. In July the organization publicly appealed to the government not to introduce the judicial punishments of amputation and flogging, or to extend the scope of the death penalty. In December Amnesty International sought assurance from Colonel Gaddafi that Mansur Kikhiya had not been abducted and taken back to Libya.

LITHUANIA

Two people were executed.

In February Algirdas Brazauskas won Lithuania's first direct presidential elections. Adolfas Slezevicius was confirmed as Prime Minister by parliament in March.

Lithuania became a member of the Council of Europe in May and signed the European Convention for the Protection of Human Rights and Fundamental Freedoms. It had not ratified this instrument by the end of the year.

In June parliament repealed Article 122 (part one) of the Criminal Code under which homosexual acts between consenting adult males were criminal offences punishable by imprisonment.

Two people were executed following rejection of their petitions for clemency by President Algirdas Brazauskas. Vladimir Ivanov and Valentinas Laskys were sentenced to death in July and August respectively, both for premeditated murder under aggravated circumstances. It was not clear whether appeals against the sentences were heard in either of the cases. Two other men were believed to be still under sentence of death at the end of the year. Information from official sources indicated that another nine death sentences were passed during the year, all of which were commuted.

In July Amnesty International asked the authorities whether anyone had been imprisoned under Article 122 (part one) at the time of its abolition, and if so, whether they had been released. No reply had been received by the end of the year.

In July Amnesty International wrote to the Minister of National Defence raising again its concern about the punitive length of alternative service – 24 months compared to 12 months for military service (see *Amnesty International Report 1993*). No reply had been received by the end of the year. There were no reports of people imprisoned for refusing to perform military service on grounds of conscience.

Amnesty International appealed for the commutation of all the death sentences that it learned about during the year. In its letters to the authorities the organization asked whether the condemned prisoners' internationally guaranteed right to have their convictions and sentences examined by a court of higher jurisdiction had been respected. No reply was received. Amnesty International also urged the authorities to consider the complete abolition of the death penalty. In May the Procurator General informed the organization that it was "too early" for Lithuania to abolish the death penalty for exceptionally serious and cruel crimes.

In January the organization published a report entitled *The Baltic States: Time to abolish the death penalty.*

LUXEMBOURG

At least two criminal prisoners were held in prolonged isolation.

In November the Luxembourg Government published the report of the Committee for the Prevention of Torture (CPT) a committee of experts set up under the European Convention for the Prevention of Torture and Inhuman or Degrading Treatment or Punishment. In the report of its visit to Luxembourg in January the CPT criticized the use of prolonged solitary confinement for disciplinary purposes as "unacceptable".

At least two prisoners were kept in prolonged isolation in Schrassig prison. In April Jean-Marie Sauber was ordered to be placed in isolation for eight months for disciplinary reasons. Satko Adrovic was released from solitary confinement in August after completing eight and a half months of a 12-month punishment for attempting to escape. A number of other prisoners spent periods of up to six months in isolation.

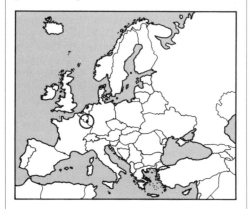

Prisoners placed in isolation spend 23 hours a day in their cells and are transferred for one hour a day into another cell, open to the outside but covered with a wire mesh, where they exercise alone. Amnesty International is concerned that prolonged isolation may seriously damage the physical and mental health of prisoners and may constitute cruel, inhuman or degrading treatment or punishment.

The organization expressed its concern about the use of prolonged isolation in Schrassig prison in several exchanges of correspondence with the Luxembourg authorities. In his replies the representative of the Procurator General responsible for prisons described solitary confinement as a necessary disciplinary measure, the use of which was allowed by law.

MACEDONIA
(THE FORMER YUGOSLAV REPUBLIC OF)

Information came to light about the reported beating and other ill-treatment of ethnic Albanian prisoners in 1992. Ethnic Albanian refugees from Serbia were forcibly returned to that country, despite fears that they would be at risk of serious human rights violations there, and after some were allegedly ill-treated by Macedonian police.

In January UNPROFOR, the UN peace-keeping force in the former Yugoslavia, deployed a small contingent of troops in Macedonia, aimed largely at deterring the spread of conflict from neighbouring Serbia. A monitoring mission of the Conference on Security and Co-operation in Europe (CSCE) had been established in 1992. In April, following months of controversy over use of the name "Macedonia", to which Greece objected, the republic was admitted to the UN under the temporary name of "The Former Yugoslav Republic of Macedonia". Continuing opposition from Greece, Albania and Cyprus also prevented Macedonia from being admitted as a member of the CSCE, although it was granted observer status.

Information came to light in February about an incident which had occurred in December 1992. A group of about 20 ethnic Albanian criminal prisoners was transferred from Idrizovo prison near Skopje to a prison in Skopje itself. In Skopje, during several hours of questioning which took place over two days, the prisoners were reportedly punched, kicked and beaten all over their bodies by police, who included officers of the state security service. Some prisoners who sought medical care did not receive it until several days later.

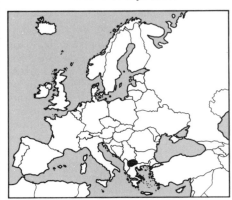

In August at least 47 refugees from Serbia, all ethnic Albanians, were forcibly returned to Serbia. These were largely men of military age from Kosovo province in Serbia, many of whom might have fled the Federal Republic of Yugoslavia (FRY) to avoid military service. Some of them were allegedly ill-treated by Macedonian police. It was not known what became of them after they were returned to the FRY.

In March Amnesty International wrote

202

to Prime Minister Branko Crvenkovski calling for an investigation into the alleged assault on ethnic Albanian prisoners in Skopje. No reply had been received by the end of the year. In September the organization appealed to the authorities not to forcibly return ethnic Albanians to the FRY, on the grounds that they would be at risk of human rights violations there. It expressed concern that no serious examination was being made of individual cases, and that the men were being returned without regard to their possible fate upon return.

MALAWI

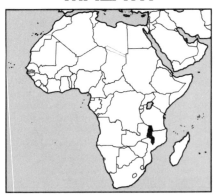

For the first six months of 1993, while Malawi was still a one-party state, members of pro-democracy groups were subject to death threats, violent attacks and arrest. Several returning exiles were detained without charge. Political prisoners were subjected to ill-treatment and harsh prison conditions. After a referendum in June, when Malawi adopted a multi-party system, major political reforms resulted in releases and in charges against government opponents being dropped. All long-term political prisoners were released, including a prisoner of conscience who had been imprisoned for 11 years. The Preservation of Public Security Act was amended to remove powers of indefinite detention without trial. There were no executions; executions were suspended while the cases of up to 120 prisoners under sentence of death were to be reviewed.

In December Malawi acceded to the International Covenant on Civil and Political Rights and to the International Covenant on Economic, Social and Cultural Rights.

A referendum in June on whether to retain the one-party state or reintroduce a multi-party system resulted in a two-thirds majority in favour of a choice of political parties. During the referendum campaign international observers noted substantial intimidation of pro-democracy advocates by government supporters in the ruling Malawi Congress Party (MCP), the paramilitary Malawi Young Pioneers (MYP) and the police and security forces. Many opposition supporters were beaten, threatened or arrested and several returning exiles were detained. After the referendum, the government formally ended the one-party state after 29 years by repealing Section 4 of the Constitution to allow for opposition parties. At the same time an amnesty was declared for all exiles and political prisoners. In August the government revoked the ban on Jehovah's Witnesses, in force since 1967 (see *Amnesty International Report 1987*).

In October the government suspended the "Traditional Courts" which had jurisdiction over political offences and all cases involving the death penalty. The trials before these courts had failed to meet international standards for fair trial. The government, in consultation with the six opposition parties, enacted a series of legislative reforms in November affecting human rights. In particular, an interim Bill of Rights was added to the Constitution, and the Preservation of Public Security Act was amended to end indefinite detention without charge or trial. The first multiparty elections were scheduled for May 1994 and the position of Life-President was abolished. During the illness of Dr H. Kamuzu Banda in late 1993 his presidential duties were carried out by a Presidential Council consisting of the new Secretary General of the MCP and two cabinet ministers. In December the MYP was forcibly disarmed by troops led by junior officers.

In the first months of 1993 a number of prominent pro-democracy activists were arrested, held for several days or weeks and either charged with political offences such as sedition or detained illegally without charge. They included, in January, Bakili Muluzi and Chakakala Chaziya, leaders of the United Democratic Front (UDF), who were held for two weeks; Alice Longwe, the wife of pro-democracy activist the Reverend Aaron Longwe who had been arrested for several months in 1992 (see

Amnesty International Report 1993), who was held overnight; and the Reverend Peter Kaleso, who was held for 11 days after addressing an Alliance For Democracy (AFORD) rally. Shyley Kondowe, Robert Khembo and John Banda, all members of the Malawi Democratic Party (MDP), an opposition group formed outside Malawi, were arrested on their return from South Africa in February. Shyley Kondowe and John Banda were released on bail at the end of March and Robert Khembo was released in mid-April. He was rearrested almost immediately after criticizing the government in radio interviews and held until after the referendum. Exiles returning from Zambia were also arrested in February and April, including Edmond Jika of the United Front for Multi-Party Democracy and Kaphwiti Banda of the UDF. They were held without being tried until around the time of the referendum. Many of those arrested were held incommunicado in Maula Prison in Lilongwe or Chichiri Prison in Blantyre where prison conditions were harsh. Under the terms of a general amnesty shortly after the referendum in June, people who had returned from self-imposed exile abroad and had been arrested prior to the referendum were released uncharged, sedition and other charges against other government opponents were dropped, and all pro-democracy advocates who had been arrested in the referendum campaign were released.

Multi-party campaigners also received threats of violence, some were harassed by police, others were beaten by MYP vigilantes, and a number had their homes or property attacked.

Chakufwa Chihana, a trade unionist and leader of the AFORD opposition group, who was convicted of sedition and sentenced to two years' imprisonment with hard labour in December 1992 (see *Amnesty International Report 1993*), had his conviction upheld after appealing to the Supreme Court in March 1993. However, his sentence was reduced to nine months' imprisonment with hard labour, and he was released on 12 June just before the referendum, but too late to participate in it.

On 24 January, long-term prisoner of conscience and lawyer Vera Chirwa was released. She had been abducted from Zambia in 1981 with her husband, Orton Chirwa, and convicted of treason after an unfair trial in a Traditional Court (see *Amnesty International Reports 1983* and *1984*). Her husband, a former Minister of Justice and also a prisoner of conscience, died in prison in October 1992. By the end of 1993 the authorities still had not complied with calls for an inquest into his death.

Other long-term political prisoners were released after the referendum. They included Gwanda Chakuamba Phiri, a former MYP commander, who was released in July after serving 13 years of a 22-year sentence for alleged sedition. In October he was made Secretary-General of the ruling MCP and became a Chairman of the Presidential Council for two months during President Banda's illness. Fred Kazombo Mwale, a nephew of President Banda who had been detained without charge since 1991, was also released in July. Nelson Mtambo, Sydney Sonjo and Ntwana Mlombwa, who had been imprisoned since the mid-1960s for alleged involvement in an unsuccessful armed rebellion, were among the last known political prisoners to be released: they were freed in October. Focus Gwede, a former Head of Special Branch (the security police), was sentenced to death in 1977 for treason (see *Amnesty International Report 1978*). This was later commuted to life imprisonment. He was also freed in October.

In September police opened fire on unarmed sugar workers in Chikwawa (southern Malawi) killing at least one person and injuring others. No inquiry was announced and it appeared that the police could still kill people with impunity.

Several death sentences were imposed by Traditional Courts but there were no executions. In October the government suspended all current death sentences – almost 120 – which were under appeal. Traditional Courts were suspended and were due to lose their jurisdiction over capital and other major crimes. Over 400 capital criminal cases which were awaiting trial by Traditional Courts were to be returned to the ordinary courts.

Amnesty International called for the release of pro-democracy supporters arrested during the referendum campaign and other prisoners of conscience. Amnesty International published two reports: in May, *Malawi: Preserving the one-party state – human rights violations and the referendum*; and in September, *Malawi: Amnesty International's recommendations for permanent protection of basic human rights following the pro-democracy vote.* The organization recommended that safeguards be included in the Constitution to guarantee internationally recognized human rights, in particular the rights to freedom of expression and association, the right to a fair trial within a reasonable time and the prohibition of torture. Amnesty International also recommended the abolition of indefinite detention without charge or trial, improvements in adherence to human rights standards by the police force and the ratification of international human rights treaties.

Amnesty International representatives, whose request to visit Malawi had been refused in April, visited the country in November for the first time in over 20 years. They met members of the government, opposition parties, lawyers, religious and human rights groups to discuss human rights.

Amnesty International wrote to the government in December welcoming the human rights improvements since the June referendum and pressing for further safeguards to protect human rights in the Constitution, laws and practices of the security forces.

MALAYSIA

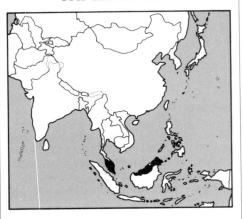

All seven prisoners of conscience who had been detained without charge or trial under the Internal Security Act (ISA) were released but restricted. Sixty of the 74 communists who had been detained without charge or trial under the ISA since 1989 were also reported to have been released. Caning continued to be widely used as a punishment for some 40 crimes. At least 12 people were sentenced to death and at least six people were executed.

In November the legislative assembly of Kelantan state, which is dominated by the opposition *Parti Islam se-Malaysia*, Islamic Party of Malaysia, approved laws for Muslim offenders which prescribed amputations for theft and stoning to death for adultery. However, for these laws to take effect in Kelantan, the Malaysian federal Constitution would have to be amended. Prime Minister Mahathir Mohamad, head of the National Front federal government, said that it would be difficult to enforce strict Islamic laws in Malaysia's multiracial and multi-religious society.

Seven prisoners of conscience who had been detained without charge or trial under the ISA on suspicion of advocating the secession of the state of Sabah from Malaysia were released from detention but had restrictions imposed on their freedom of movement. Abdul Rahman Ahmad and Benedict Topin were released in June, Vincent Chung, Wenceslous Damit Undikai and Albinus Yudah were released in November and Jeffrey Kitingan in December. Ariffin Haji Hamid was also reported to have been released, but the date was not disclosed. Sixty of the 74 communists who had been detained without charge or trial under the ISA since they voluntarily renounced their involvement in armed opposition and surrendered to the authorities in December 1989 (see *Amnesty International Report 1993*) were also reportedly released, but their identities were not disclosed.

In August the federal Justice Minister introduced a bill in Parliament to extend the use of caning by making it a mandatory penalty for the crime of breach of trust. He said that the aim was to deter the increasing number of "white collar" crimes. Caning continued to be widely inflicted as a supplementary punishment to imprisonment for some 40 crimes including drugs offences, rape and attempted rape, kidnapping, firearms offences, attempted murder, causing grievous injury, child abuse, robbery and theft. For instance, S. Silvaratnam, a waiter, was sentenced in January to 10 years' imprisonment and six cane strokes for grievously injuring two men. In February Sulaiman Musa, an unemployed man, was sentenced to five years in prison and six strokes of the cane after being convicted of raping two teenage sisters. Amnesty International believes that caning constitutes cruel, inhuman or degrading punishment prohibited by international law.

At least 12 people were sentenced to death, nine of whom were convicted of drugs offences and three of murder. The Supreme Court confirmed the death sentences on three people. At least six people were executed, including three Filipinos and two Pakistanis who had reportedly been tortured in custody and convicted of drugs offences in Sabah state after unfair trials. One of the executed Filipinos, Hassim Escandar, was sentenced to death despite the failure of the prosecution to present its key witnesses in court and the denial of any opportunity for Hassim Escandar's counsel to examine the witnesses. Amnesty International received no further information about five other Filipinos imprisoned and under sentence of death in Sabah state after unfair trials (see *Amnesty International Report 1993*).

In June Amnesty International published a report, *Malaysia: Death of an innocent? Death penalty accused presumed guilty.* This criticized the law under which a mandatory death penalty is imposed on people convicted of drug-trafficking because it places the onus on the accused to prove their innocence rather than on the state to prove their guilt. This contravenes a basic principle of Malaysian jurisprudence and also contravenes numerous international legal safeguards which state that the accused has the right to be presumed innocent until proved guilty.

Amnesty International appealed during the year for the release of prisoners of conscience and called for the prompt trial or release of other political prisoners arbitrarily detained under the ISA. It called for the commutation of all death sentences and an end to the use of caning as a punishment.

MALDIVES

At least 22 possible prisoners of conscience were arrested in the run-up to presidential elections. Over 30 political prisoners arrested in previous years, including some prisoners of conscience, were released.

In October President Maumoon Abdul Gayoom was re-elected for his fourth term as President. In the Republic of Maldives, parliament elects a presidential candidate by secret vote and puts its choice to the people to ratify in a referendum. Three candidates stood in the parliamentary vote in August. The candidate who came second, Ilyas Ibrahim, had fled the country earlier.

At least 22 supporters and associates of Ilyas Ibrahim were arrested between April and September. They appeared to be possible prisoners of conscience. Some were convicted of attempting to assist Ilyas Ibrahim to take power by irregular means. Don Didi, a woman arrested in June, was sentenced in late August to 10 years' banishment after being convicted of using black magic on Ilyas Ibrahim's behalf. Mohamed Saleem, a member of parliament, was arrested in September. He was released after 15 days, but then rearrested and placed under house arrest, apparently without charge or trial. In October all those held in connection with Ilyas Ibrahim were reportedly transferred to house arrest.

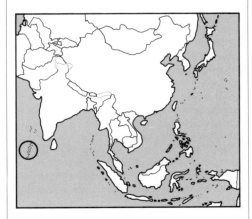

Ilyas Ibrahim was tried *in absentia* in September for allegedly breaking his ministerial oath and violating the Constitution, and sentenced to over 15 years' banishment.

Over 30 prisoners arrested in previous years – some prisoners of conscience and other political prisoners sentenced after unfair trials – were released by order of the President or because they had served their sentences. Among them was prisoner of conscience Mohamed Nasheed, who had spent 18 months in solitary confinement before being sentenced to three years' imprisonment for withholding information on an alleged conspiracy against the government in 1990. Four other prisoners sentenced after unfair trials in the same conspiracy case had been released in May. They were Mohamed Shafeeq, Abdullah Muaaz Ahmed, Mohamed Khaleel and Ilyas Hussein.

Six remaining prisoners of conscience from a group of seven arrested in March 1990 for distributing leaflets alleging vote-rigging were released by the end of the year.

Released prisoners reported that police had ill-treated them in pre-trial detention. Political prisoners and others are commonly held in police custody at Dhoonidhoo detention centre, where they may be held for months in solitary confinement, sometimes in handcuffs, and subjected to other forms of cruel, inhuman or degrading treatment.

Amnesty International learned during the year that seven Sri Lankan Tamils imprisoned in connection with a failed coup attempt in 1988 (see *Amnesty International Report 1989*) had been held in chains at Gamadhoo prison island until the middle of 1993. They were transferred to Sri Lanka in November.

In June Amnesty International published a report which documented over 30 cases of prisoners of conscience or other political prisoners sentenced after unfair trials since 1990. Amnesty International urged the government to release all prisoners of conscience, ensure that all other political prisoners received fair and prompt trials, and take steps to prevent ill-treatment and torture. There was no response from the government. In October Amnesty International expressed concern about the arrests of supporters of Ilyas Ibrahim and sought information about their cases. The government responded by saying that they had all contravened the Constitution and laws of the country and had been sentenced accordingly, but gave no details.

MALI

Eight suspected opponents of the former transitional government arrested in July 1991 remained in detention without trial throughout the year. Former President Moussa Traoré and three senior security officials were sentenced to death. There **were reports that the army extrajudicially executed at least 20 civilians and summarily executed a soldier accused of theft.**

The government resigned in April following violent student demonstrations. President Alpha Oumar Konaré appointed a new Prime Minister whose government included members of opposition political parties. A new Ministry for Human Rights was created but later abolished in a government reshuffle in November.

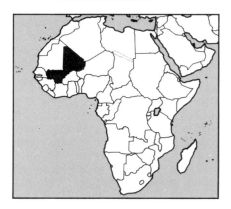

The government and the *Mouvements et fronts unifiés de l'Azawad* (MFUA), the Azawad Unified Movements and Fronts, an umbrella organization of Tuareg opposition groups, continued to implement the April 1992 peace agreement (see *Amnesty International Report 1993*). In February an agreement was signed providing for the integration into the national army of an initial group of 600 former Tuareg rebels. In May the President granted an amnesty to 10 Tuareg prisoners apparently convicted during the conflict between the government and armed Tuareg rebels. A few days later, Rhissa Ag Sidi Mohamed, the leader of the *Front populaire de libération de l'Azawad* (FPLA), the Popular Front for the Liberation of Azawad, who had opposed the April 1992 peace agreement, publicly renounced rebellion. However, the north remained unstable because of widespread banditry. Plans for the voluntary repatriation of an estimated 160,000 Tuareg and Moors who had taken refuge in neighbouring countries during the conflict were delayed. Later in the year, there were renewed attacks by armed groups against civilians, including representatives of non-governmental organizations operating in the north. It was unclear, however, whether these attacks were launched by politically motivated groups or by armed robbers.

Major Lamine Diabira, a former Minister of the Interior, and seven other army officers arrested in July 1991 were detained without trial throughout the year. They had been accused of plotting to overthrow the transitional government which came to power after General Moussa Traoré was overthrown in March 1991 and were initially detained incommunicado and without charge. In June they were charged with conspiracy and attempting to overthrow the government by force but were not brought to trial. Further evidence became available during the year which suggested that Major Lamine Diabira had been detained solely because he had sought the prosecution of officers he claimed were responsible for abuses committed by General Moussa Traoré's government.

In August the security forces detained six black Mauritanians near Kayes in southwest Mali, ostensibly on suspicion of armed robbery. Two of them, Mamadou Bocar Bâ and Lam Moussa, were representatives of a refugee organization based in Senegal, on an authorized visit to meet Mauritanian refugees. They were reportedly arrested solely because they were black Mauritanians and were released uncharged after 14 days. During 1993 several other black Mauritanians were reportedly detained and it was not clear whether any remained in detention at the end of the year.

In December the authorities announced that a plot to overthrow the government had been foiled. This statement, however, was later disclaimed by the government who said that four soldiers had been arrested for unauthorized contact with General Moussa Traoré's former aide-de-camp, detained since July on charges of embezzlement. The soldiers were not known to have been charged by the end of the year.

The trial of General Moussa Traoré and 32 former government ministers and officials ended in February (see *Amnesty International Report 1993*). General Moussa Traoré and three senior security officials were convicted by the High Court in Bamako on charges of murder and grievous bodily harm. They were convicted in relation to the killing by the army of 106 pro-democracy demonstrators in the days before the government was overthrown in March 1991. The 29 other defendants were acquitted. General Moussa Traoré and the three officials were sentenced to death. They lodged an appeal on points of law to the Supreme Court, but their sentences were confirmed in May. Their plea for clemency had not been considered by President Konaré at the end of the year. The four men faced further charges of embezzlement of public funds, together with General Moussa Traoré's wife, his eldest son and other former government officials. Judicial investigation of these charges continued but a trial date had not been set by the end of the year. No other death sentences were known to have been passed.

There were reports that at least 20 civilians who had recently returned to Mali in accordance with the peace agreement were extrajudicially executed by the army in Adat Malene and Amaskore, near Goundam, in January. Three Tuareg were reported to have been killed by soldiers in December as they returned to Mali from a refugee camp in Mauritania, but the circumstances of the deaths were unclear. The soldiers said that the Tuareg had been shot while resisting arrest on suspicion of banditry. A commission of inquiry composed of security officials and representatives of Tuareg groups was reported to have been established, but its conclusions had not been made known by the end of the year. There were also reports that at least seven black Mauritanian refugees were extrajudicially executed in the region of Kayes in separate incidents between June and November.

In August in Kidal, a soldier was reported to have been summarily executed by colleagues in public without any form of trial. The soldier, a former Tuareg rebel who had recently been integrated into the national army, was alleged to have been involved in armed robberies in Kidal. It was not known whether an official investigation was carried out into this summary execution.

Armed Tuareg groups were also responsible for deliberate killings of civilians. For example, in February members of the FPLA abducted Mohamed Oudd Obeid, an Arab trader from Gao, who was later found strangled in a well. He reportedly supported a different Tuareg faction, the *Front islamique arabe pour la libération de l'Azawad* (FIAA), the Islamic Arab Front for the Liberation of Azawad. Later that month, in reprisal, members of the FIAA

208

intercepted a convoy led by MFUA vice-president Aghatam Ag Alassane, who was on his way to meet Rhissa Ag Sidi Mohamed, the FPLA leader. Aghatam Ag Alassane was held briefly but other captured members of the convoy, including members of the FPLA, were held for longer periods before being released.

In March Amnesty International urged President Konaré to exercise presidential clemency by commuting the death sentences imposed on General Moussa Traoré and the three others if they were confirmed on appeal. The President told the organization that its concerns would be considered.

MAURITANIA

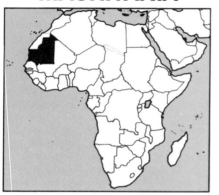

There were reports of torture and ill-treatment by the security forces. An amnesty law was introduced to give immunity from prosecution to perpetrators of major human rights violations from 1989 to 1992.

The situation in southern Mauritania, bordering on Senegal and Mali, remained tense. More than 60,000 black Mauritanians who had fled or been expelled in 1989 or 1990 (see *Amnesty International Reports 1990* and *1991*) remained in Senegal and some in Mali. Although there was no official reason why they could not return, many refused to do so because of reported harassment and killings of black Mauritanians and because they felt their status in Mauritania would be unclear. At the time of expulsion, their identity papers had been confiscated and had not been reissued.

In January the Special Court of Justice, which had been established in 1978, was abolished. It had passed death sentences without any right of appeal and had convicted people on the basis of confessions made under duress. In October 1992, the President of the Special Court of Justice had rejected a complaint by lawyers on behalf of nearly 200 families of the "disappeared" (see *Amnesty International Report 1993*).

In May the government enacted a total amnesty for all members of the security and armed forces for all offences committed during a three-year period from 1989 to 1992. During that time, more than 400 black Mauritanians had been extrajudicially executed, thousands had been arbitrarily detained for lengthy periods without charge or trial and many others had "disappeared". The authorities said the amnesty law was a contribution towards national reconciliation but they took no steps at all to investigate or resolve the cases of the "disappeared" or other victims of gross violations.

In March there were protests when an army colonel implicated in torture visited France for military training and Mauritanian human rights activists publicly called on the French authorities to bring him to justice. However, no investigations or other legal proceedings were initiated against him either by the French or Mauritanian authorities and he was able to return to Mauritania.

There were several reports of arrests, torture and killings of members of Mauritania's black population in the south, but few details were available. It appeared that the abuses may have been racially motivated. In February seven black Mauritanian villagers from Tektaké Ferlo were arrested by members of the gendarmerie, apparently as opponents of the government. They were all reportedly tortured before one escaped, three were released and three were transferred to prison in Sélibaby. In similar circumstances, M'Baye Ba, from Kalinioro village, was arrested in late February or March and reportedly tortured at the police station at Ould Yengé before being transferred to prison in Sélibaby. He and the three others from Tektaké Ferlo were all apparently freed in return for substantial payments to a local judicial official.

In June, Mamadou Bodiel Tall, a Senegalese national, died shortly after he was reportedly tortured and robbed by Mauritanian security forces at their military encampment near the Senegal border. He apparently drowned when he tried to swim the Senegal river after escaping; when he got into difficulties Mauritanian soldiers allegedly stopped him returning to the Mauritanian side. His body apparently bore evidence of torture.

In response to Amnesty International's appeal for an inquiry into the death in August 1992 of Dia Hamath Atoumane (see *Amnesty International Report 1993*), the authorities told Amnesty International that neither he, nor others detained with him, had been tortured – although they did not explain how they had reached this conclusion.

Amnesty International was very concerned by the amnesty granted in May to those responsible for mass killings and "disappearances", as it appeared likely to prevent relatives of those who "disappeared" or were killed obtaining clarification of their fate, as well as providing legal immunity against prosecution for the perpetrators of these gross abuses. Amnesty International criticized the amnesty and continued to urge the authorities to appoint an impartial and independent inquiry into the "disappearances" and other violations and to hold those responsible to account.

In an oral statement to the UN Sub-Commission on Prevention of Discrimination and Protection of Minorities in August, Amnesty International included reference to its concerns in Mauritania.

MAURITIUS

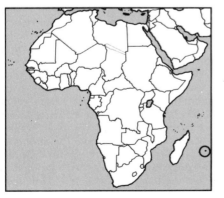

There were reports that police officers were responsible for beating prisoners. Four people were sentenced to death but there were no executions.

In September the Attorney General announced that the government was drafting constitutional amendments which would limit the rights of people arrested for drugs offences. The proposals were not made public, but were reported to include denying suspected drugs offenders access to lawyers and removing their right to bail.

As in previous years, there were reports that police officers were responsible for beatings. In January Iqbal Chamroo needed two days' hospital treatment after he was hit on the head while being searched by plainclothes anti-drugs officers in Pleine Verte. He submitted a complaint to the police but it was not known if any action had been taken by the end of the year. In May police officers at Plaine Magnien detained and severely beat Basdeo Appadu. After his family learned of his ill-treatment and intervened on his behalf, he was taken to hospital where he required an operation. An internal police investigation led to the arrest of five police officers but it was not known if they had been charged or brought to trial by the end of the year.

The authorities did take action against police officers implicated in brutality in previous years. In September, two police officers were charged with causing injuries leading to the death of Eddie Labrosse in June 1992 (see *Amnesty International Report 1993*). Apparent attempts by senior police officers to cover up police wrongdoing during the course of the investigation led lawyers in June to urge that a commission of inquiry into police brutality and corruption be established. The authorities rejected the request.

In July the Judicial Committee of the Privy Council (JCPC) in London, the highest court of appeal for Mauritius, freed Radha Krishna Kunnath, an Indian national sentenced to death for drug-trafficking in 1989. The JCPC ruled that he had been unfairly tried because language interpretation had not been available during his trial (see *Amnesty International Reports 1990* and *1991*).

Four prisoners were convicted of drug-trafficking and sentenced to death during the year. In December the Supreme Court rejected the appeals of two women – Zaheeda Banoo Hussain and Shameer Bano Naseerudin – who had been sentenced to death in May. There were no executions.

Amnesty International urged the government of Prime Minister Anerood Jugnath to commute all death sentences and abolish the death penalty.

210

MEXICO

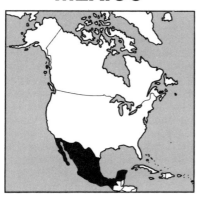

Dozens of people detained on account of their peaceful political activities, including members of indigenous communities, were prisoners of conscience. Frequent torture and ill-treatment by law enforcement agents continued to be reported. The whereabouts of hundreds of people who had "disappeared" in previous years remained unknown. At least nine people were reported to have been extrajudicially executed.

The government adopted constitutional changes and modifications to the Penal Code, purportedly to help fight serious crimes including drug-trafficking. Human rights organizations expressed concern that these changes – including the extension of the maximum period for pre-judicial detention from 24 to 96 hours – could undermine defendants' right to a fair and prompt trial.

Governmental human rights bodies, such as the National Human Rights Commission and similar offices at state level, continued to receive hundreds of complaints, and issued dozens of recommendations to the relevant authorities regarding cases of human rights violations. Virtually none of the recommendations concerning gross human rights violations were fully implemented.

Dozens of people, including Indian peasant activists, were arrested for their peaceful political activities. On 6 June the Chiapas state police carried out violent raids on the Tzeltal and Tzotzil Indian communities of Chalam del Carmen, Río Florido, Nuevo Sacrificio, Edén del Carmen and El Carrizal. Children, women and men were beaten, and scores of houses

were destroyed during the raids. Twenty-three peasants – including two children aged 14 and 15, and three elderly people aged 80, 90 and 102 – were arbitrarily arrested, apparently solely for their peaceful political activities, and transferred to *Cerro Hueco*, a prison in Tuxtla Gutiérrez. All those imprisoned were tortured and ill-treated to force confessions to crimes they did not commit (see below). On 25 June the elderly prisoners were released uncharged and the children were transferred to a juvenile detention centre. Another eight people, against whom charges were suspended, were released in September, but 10 remained in prison awaiting trial at the end of the year on a range of charges, including murder.

Prisoner of conscience Manuel Manríquez San Agustín, an Otomí Indian and human rights activist, was sentenced on appeal to 23 years' imprisonment in April. He had been detained in Mexico City, the capital, in 1990 on false charges of murder based on a confession extracted from him under torture; he remained in prison at the end of the year. Pablo Molinet, a poet imprisoned in Salamanca, Guanajuato state, in 1992, was also sentenced on appeal to 23 years' imprisonment in November. He had been charged with murder based on confessions extracted from him under torture. There were indications that he may have been targeted because of his literary activities (see *Amnesty International Report 1993*).

Two prisoners of conscience were released uncharged in July. Gerardo Rubén Ortega Zurita and José Cruz Reyes Potenciano had been arrested in 1992 in connection with their peaceful attempts to oppose police harassment of members of the gay and lesbian communities in Mexico.

There were frequent reports of torture by law enforcement agents, particularly the state judicial police, throughout the country. The most common methods reported were beating, near-asphyxiation with plastic bags, forcing alcohol into the nose, and the application of electric shocks. Confessions extracted under duress continued to be admitted as evidence in courts, and medical treatment for detainees who had been tortured was frequently unavailable.

Juan Carbajal Sáenz was held incommunicado after his arrest by the judicial police in Mexico City in February. He was beaten, water was forced into his nostrils and he received electric shocks to the testicles. He was eventually sentenced to nine years' imprisonment in September after being convicted of robbery despite a lack of evidence and his production of a medical certificate indicating the injuries he had sustained under torture. Thirteen members of the Tzotzil indigenous community of San Isidro el Ocotal, Chiapas state, were also tortured after being detained by army personnel in March. They were held incommunicado for two days during which they were beaten, subjected to semi-asphyxiation with plastic bags and mock executions to make them confess to a murder. They were released uncharged, but those responsible for the torture were not brought to justice. The 23 Tzeltal Indian peasant activists arrested in Chiapas in June (see above) were also held incommunicado and brutally tortured for three days by being beaten, by having alcohol forced into their nostrils, and with electric shocks. They were forced to sign statements in Spanish, which some could not understand, and charged with murder and other crimes. Domingo López Gómez, aged 102, required hospital treatment as a result of injuries sustained under torture when he was released in late June. No action was taken to investigate their torture allegations or bring to justice those responsible. Nor were those responsible for the torture of six Mixe and Zapotec Indian activists from La Trinidad Yaveo, Oaxaca state, in 1992, and Amir Aboud Sattar in 1991 (see *Amnesty International Report 1993*), brought to justice in 1993.

Little progress was reported in investigating hundreds of "disappearances" which had occurred mostly during the 1970s and early 1980s. An investigation into the 1988 "disappearance" of José Ramón García, a political activist, did confirm the participation of government officials in his abduction (see *Amnesty International Report 1993*), but his fate and whereabouts remained unknown.

Omar Ricardo Mendoza Palacios, a 13-year-old, and three other youths, were killed in suspicious circumstances in May by the judicial police in Mexico City. The police said the four were killed during a gun battle with police, but eye-witness reports that the victims were unarmed when shot at close range were supported by forensic evidence. Those responsible had not been brought to justice by year-end.

Five other people, all suspected drug-traffickers, were reported to have been extrajudicially executed in June by members of the army in Mesa de la Guitarra, Chihuahua state. The five were said to have been detained three days earlier and tortured before being killed. Some of the soldiers alleged to be responsible were arrested, but their legal position was unclear at the end of the year. No one had been brought to justice by the end of the year in connection with the 1992 killing of Tomás Diego García, a Mixe Indian from La Trinidad Yaveo, Oaxaca state (see *Amnesty International Report 1993*).

Amnesty International continued to call for full and impartial investigations into alleged human rights violations, and to urge the authorities to bring to justice those responsible for torture, "disappearances" and other grave violations. In June Amnesty International published a report, *Mexico: The persistence of torture and impunity*, which set out in detail the steps needed to bring an end to torture. Amnesty International's Secretary General held a meeting with Mexico's Ambassador to the United Kingdom in London in November, during which he expressed the organization's concern about continuing human rights violations in Mexico, including the rise in reports of arbitrary imprisonment and torture of indigenous peasants in rural areas of Chiapas. He reiterated calls for the effective implementation of Amnesty International's recommendations.

MOLDOVA

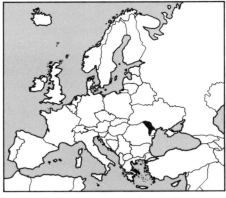

The situation of 15 people on death row remained unclear. Six political prisoners in the self-proclaimed Dnestr Moldovan

Republic (DMR) faced a trial that appeared to fall short of international standards of fairness. One of them was sentenced to death.

In January parliament defeated a proposal by President Mircea Snegur to hold a referendum on unification with Romania. This issue had provoked tension with the DMR which, unlike other parts of Moldova, had not been historically part of Romania. The DMR, which is not recognized internationally, continued to consolidate its own parallel government structures during the year.

Moldova acceded to the International Covenant on Civil and Political Rights and the International Covenant on Economic, Social and Cultural Rights in January. In May it acceded to the four Geneva Conventions of 1949 and their 1977 Additional Protocols.

As of February, 15 prisoners under sentence of death had not been executed as the country lacked its own executioner and facilities (see *Amnesty International Report 1993*). They were all still on death row at the end of the year.

The trial of six people arrested by the DMR authorities in 1992 opened in April. Ilie Ilaşcu, Alexandru Leşco, Tudor Petrov-Popa, Andrei Ivanţoc, Petru Godiac and Vladimir Garbuz were charged with murdering two DMR officials and planning other violent political acts during the period of armed conflict between DMR and Moldovan forces in 1992. Earlier, charges had been dropped against a seventh man, Ştefan Urîtu (see *Amnesty International Report 1993*). At least four of the men had been members of a party supporting unification with Romania.

All the defendants except Vladimir Garbuz refused to recognize the jurisdiction of the DMR and denied the charges, withdrawing their confessions and claiming that they had been made after beatings, threats and intimidation. At least one defendant had previously described being refused access to a lawyer of his own choice for almost two months, during which time he was allegedly subjected to a mock execution on four occasions. Three of the charges against them carried a possible death sentence. The trial concluded in December, with guilty verdicts against all six. Ilie Ilaşcu was sentenced to death, and the others received terms of imprisonment of from two to 15 years.

Amnesty International sought further information about people under sentence of death in Moldova, and continued to urge that all death sentences be commuted.

The organization called on the DMR authorities to take all necessary steps to ensure that Ilie Ilaşcu and his co-defendants received a fair trial. It also urged them not to impose the death penalty in this or any other case in the territory they control and to commute the death sentence passed on Ilie Ilaşcu.

MONGOLIA

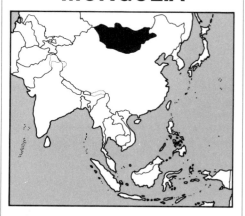

At least one death sentence was passed.

In June President Puntsalmaagiyn Ochirbat was re-elected in Mongolia's first direct presidential elections. Nominated by opposition parties, he defeated the candidate of the ruling Mongolian People's Revolutionary Party.

Amendments to the criminal code which came into force in August reduced the number of offences punishable by death to five: premeditated murder, aggravated rape or rape of a minor, and three anti-state offences involving violence. The offences for which the death penalty was abolished included treason.

One death sentence was reported. The true figure was probably much higher, but official statistics for death sentences and executions during the year were not available.

Amnesty International continued to call on the authorities to commute all death sentences and to take steps to abolish the death penalty.

MOROCCO AND WESTERN SAHARA

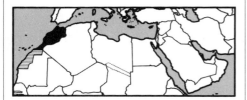

Over 450 political prisoners, including more than 140 prisoners of conscience and probable prisoners of conscience, were serving sentences imposed after unfair trials in previous years. Over 100 people were arrested during the year for political offences; many of them were released uncharged but some were sentenced to up to 20 years' imprisonment after unfair trials. Torture and ill-treatment continued to be reported: at least three people allegedly died as a result of beatings. Hundreds of Sahrawis and Moroccans who had "disappeared" in previous years were believed to be still held in secret detention centres. Formerly "disappeared" Sahrawis released in 1991 continued to be subject to restrictions on their freedom of movement and expression. One prisoner was executed. One man was sentenced to death and over 150 prisoners remained on death row.

Direct and indirect elections for the National Assembly, the first for nine years, were held in June and September. The centre-right parties which have dominated the government during the past 20 years won a majority; however, an alliance of the two main opposition parties increased its seats.

Morocco ratified the UN Convention against Torture in June, and in November a Minister for Human Rights was appointed.

The UN-sponsored referendum on the future of the Western Sahara, postponed from January 1992, had still not taken place by the end of the year (see *Amnesty International Reports 1992* and *1993*). However, the cease-fire agreed between the *Frente Popular para la Liberación de Saguia el-Hamra y Rio de Oro*, Popular Front for the Liberation of Saguia el-Hamra and Rio de Oro, (known as the Polisario Front), and Morocco continued in force and observers from the UN Mission for the Referendum in Western Sahara (MINURSO) remained in place.

More than 450 political prisoners, including over 140 prisoners of conscience and probable prisoners of conscience, remained in prison at the end of 1993. Most had been imprisoned after unfair trials in previous years after being convicted of offences against state security, membership of illegal organizations, distributing leaflets or disturbing public order. Conviction had usually been secured solely on the basis of confessions allegedly extracted under duress. They included people arrested after demonstrations and riots in 1984 and 1990, supporters of illegal Marxist and Islamist organizations, and people sentenced to five years' imprisonment after allegedly making remarks critical of King Hassan II (see previous *Amnesty International Reports*).

Abdessalem Yassine, leader of the banned Islamist organization *al-'Adl wa'l-Ihsan*, Justice and Charity, remained under house arrest without charge or trial at his home in Sale. His lawyer was allowed to visit him. Two leading members of *al-'Adl wa'l-Ihsan* who tried to visit him in August were detained briefly.

Two prisoners of conscience were released in July by royal amnesty. Noubir Amaoui, secretary general of the *Confédération démocratique du travail*, Democratic Labour Confederation, had been sentenced in April 1992 to two years' imprisonment for defamation (see *Amnesty International Report 1993*). Driss Ghenimi, the regional secretary of the *Union générale des travailleurs marocains*, General Union of Moroccan Workers, had been sentenced to five years' imprisonment in May 1992 after members of a rival trade union alleged that he had insulted the King. Defence lawyers had walked out of the court after being refused permission to call witnesses.

Over 100 people were arrested in June and September after demonstrations in a number of towns against alleged election fraud. Most demonstrators were released uncharged but in Bouznika, Benahmed and Tifelt demonstrators were charged with unauthorized demonstrations and damage to public buildings. Six remained in detention awaiting trial at the end of the year.

Trials frequently fell short of international fair trial standards. Six Sahrawis arrested after demonstrations in Assa in September 1992 were sentenced in July to 20 years' imprisonment in two trials in the

214

Rabat military court. They were convicted of offences against external state security for possessing Polisario flags; three of them were also convicted of burning vehicles. The trials were held *in camera* and the defendants, who stated in court that they had been beaten by police, were not allowed full defence rights.

Thirteen students from Oujda, who had been arrested in December 1992, were sentenced in January to up to one year's imprisonment on charges of participating in unauthorized demonstrations and spreading false information to disturb public order. They stated during their trial that they had been forced to sign police statements under torture, without having been allowed to read them. In February eight were acquitted on appeal, one had his sentence reduced to six months and one had his sentence raised to 18 months' imprisonment.

The new limit of six days *garde à vue* (incommunicado) detention (for offences not related to state security) introduced in 1990 appeared to be generally respected, except in Western Sahara where detainees were frequently held for several months in illegally prolonged *garde à vue* detention. Other provisions in the same law providing for medical examinations to be available for all detainees and for families to be promptly informed of an arrest appeared to be generally disregarded. Torture and ill-treatment continued to be widespread in Western Sahara. Elsewhere beatings and deprivation of food and sleep were reported in police and gendarmerie stations. Demonstrators arrested in June in Bouznika stated that they were beaten by police immediately after arrest and marks of beatings were recorded by the investigating judge. However, no further investigations appear to have been made into the allegations.

At least three people died in custody allegedly as a result of ill-treatment. Mustapha Hamzaoui died in Khenifra Police Station shortly after his arrest in May. Relatives and other observers, including doctors and representatives of Moroccan human rights organizations, stated that bruises could be seen on his body. A second autopsy ordered by the Khenifra authorities was carried out without a family representative being allowed to be present. It found that death was the result of suicide. The family and the *Organisation marocaine des droits de l'homme*, Moroccan Human Rights Organization, lodged a charge of homicide against persons unknown. This was brought to court in September but the case was adjourned and had not been heard by the end of the year.

Hundreds of people of Western Saharan origin and Moroccans who had "disappeared" after arrest in previous years remained unaccounted for and were believed to be still alive in secret detention. They included Faraji Mohamed-Salem Bueh-Barca, who "disappeared" in Laayoune in 1976 at the time of a Polisario Front attack. Abdelhaq Rouissi, a trade union activist who "disappeared" in 1964, was reported to be still alive, although seriously ill, in secret detention.

More than 300 Sahrawis released in 1991 after up to 16 years in secret detention continued to be severely restricted in their freedom of movement and association. Some were rearrested in 1992 and 1993 and held in secret detention for several months; others were expelled from Western Sahara to towns in Morocco. Neither the survivors of "disappearance" nor the families of the 81 people known to have died in previous years in the secret detention centres of Tazmamert, Agdz, Qal'at M'Gouna and Laayoune were known to have received any compensation from the government. No inquiry has been held into how such secret detentions were allowed to take place and no one has ever been brought to justice for perpetrating these abuses.

One prisoner was executed during the year. Mohamed Tabet, a former police commissioner and district official in Casablanca, was sentenced to death in March by the Casablanca Criminal Court for rape, debauchery and violence against over 1,000 women. He was executed in August in the first known execution since 1982. Three other police officers, who were convicted of covering up his offences after a charge was lodged by victims in 1991, were sentenced to up to 20 years' imprisonment. A policeman was sentenced to death in December after being convicted of raping handcuffed young boys. More than 150 other prisoners who had been sentenced to death in previous years, some of them in the 1960s, remained on death row. They included 14 political prisoners sentenced between 1979 and 1985.

In the framework of the Western

Saharan settlement, Amnesty International called on the Moroccan Government to ensure that no Sahrawi was imprisoned for the non-violent expression of opinion. The organization urged the UN to amend and widen the mandate of MINURSO so that it could monitor alleged human rights violations and take appropriate action to address them.

Amnesty International welcomed the government's ratification of the UN Convention against Torture and called for safeguards enshrined in the Convention to be implemented immediately in order to stop torture and ill-treatment. The organization also called for the unconditional release of all prisoners of conscience, for the release of all those who remained "disappeared" and for the commutation of all death sentences. It welcomed the releases of Noubir Amaoui and Driss Ghenimi and the appointment of a Minister for Human Rights.

In May Amnesty International delegates were allowed to visit Morocco for the first time since 1990. They held talks with the *Conseil consultatif des droits de l'homme* (CCDH), Human Rights Advisory Council, a government-appointed body which includes representatives of political parties, professional bodies and two human rights groups. The organization subsequently sent the CCDH and the government the names and details of 80 Moroccans and 485 Sahrawis who were believed to have "disappeared" after arrest and a list of 159 prisoners of conscience and possible prisoners of conscience. In December the CCDH told Amnesty International delegates it would examine the lists and stated that victims of "disappearance" and former inmates of Tazmamert and their families would be given free legal assistance to seek compensation.

Amnesty International published a report in February, *Morocco: Continuing arrests, "disappearances" and restrictions on freedom of expression and movement in Western Sahara*; and another in April, *Morocco: Breaking the walls of silence – the "disappeared" in Morocco*.

In oral statements to the UN Commission on Human Rights in March and to its Sub-Commission on Prevention of Discrimination and Protection of Minorities in August, Amnesty International included reference to its concerns in Morocco. In April Amnesty International submitted information about its concerns in Morocco

and the Western Sahara for UN review, under a procedure established by Economic and Social Council Resolutions 728F/1503, for confidential consideration of communications about human rights violations.

In a letter sent in January, the President's office of the Sahrawi Arab Democratic Republic denied cases previously raised by Amnesty International of detention of prisoners of conscience, long-term incommunicado detention, torture and deaths in custody of political opponents which had been reported between 1976 and 1991 in the camps near Tindouf in Algeria under the control of the Polisario Front. In its February report on Morocco (see above) Amnesty International made public these concerns.

MOZAMBIQUE

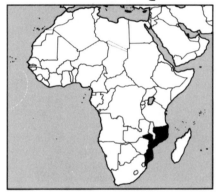

A year of peace, following the October 1992 agreement to end the 16-year civil war, brought a great improvement in the human rights situation. Nevertheless, there were reports of security personnel causing deaths which may have been extrajudicial executions: it was not clear whether any of the deaths were properly investigated. The armed opposition detained people in violation of the peace agreement and failed to account for others whom it had detained before October 1992. It was also reported to have summarily executed one of its own members.

Both President Joaquim Chissano and Afonso Dhlakama, leader of the armed opposition *Resistência Nacional Moçambicana* (RENAMO), Mozambique National Resistance, repeatedly affirmed their commitment to peace, despite violations of the

216

peace agreement which was monitored by UNOMOZ, the UN Operation in Mozambique, (see *Amnesty International Report 1993*). There was greater freedom of movement, although restrictions continued in RENAMO-controlled areas. Roads were repaired and mines removed, facilitating the distribution of food and seeds. Thousands of refugees were repatriated from neighbouring countries under the protection of the Office of the United Nations High Commissioner for Refugees: thousands more returned spontaneously. There were various initiatives to increase awareness of civil and political rights.

A major set-back was the delay in demobilizing the two armies and various paramilitary forces, which should have been completed by April, but was delayed until late November. There were several demonstrations by government soldiers, some involving violence, in support of pay demands. Unemployed former soldiers and deserters from both sides' armies and paramilitary groups turned to armed banditry, joining others who had done so in previous years.

Deep distrust between the government and RENAMO led to frequent disputes. From March to June RENAMO boycotted meetings of the commissions set up to implement the peace agreement. Each side accused the other of setting up paramilitary groups which could be used to overturn the peace process or election results. The government transferred thousands of former soldiers into a new paramilitary police unit and there were allegations that RENAMO had set up a secret battalion.

However, by October, after meetings between President Chissano and Afonso Dhlakama and a visit by UN Secretary-General Boutros Boutros-Ghali, a new timetable was agreed for demobilization and the formation of a unified army in time for elections in October 1994 (originally elections had been set for October 1993). Agreement was also reached on extending state administration to RENAMO-controlled areas and on the composition of the electoral commission and commissions to monitor the police and security services. The parties also assented to a UN proposal for the deployment of 128 UN civilian police monitors: about half were deployed by the end of the year.

In July Mozambique acceded to the International Covenant on Civil and Political Rights and its Second Optional Protocol, aiming at the abolition of the death penalty (Mozambique had abolished capital punishment in 1990).

Under the terms of the peace agreement the government had released all political prisoners in 1992 (see *Amnesty International Report 1993*). There were few reports of new political arrests. RENAMO alleged that government forces arrested two of its members in Tete province in July. These and other violations of the agreement were investigated by the Cease-Fire Commission.

There were several reports of deaths in custody, or during security operations, which may have been extrajudicial executions.

Several people were reportedly killed and at least one was feared to have "disappeared" after the government suppressed a mutiny by members of the Presidential Guard in late March. The guards had reportedly kidnapped a senior officer to back their demands for better pay and conditions. Unofficial sources said that the day after the guards had been confined to their barracks at Magoanine, outside Maputo, the capital, commandos entered the barracks, shooting randomly, wounding some guards and killing others, including Agostinho Pedro from Nampula province.

Hundreds of guards were reportedly arrested and held for about a month before being released and sent to their home towns or villages. Of about 200 held in the Machava Civil Prison, Maputo, at least three were said to have received no treatment for bullet wounds. Six others, all suspected leaders of the mutiny, were reportedly confined in one cell with their hands bound except at meal times. One of these, Alberto Gomes, was reported to have been whipped. He was subsequently removed from the prison and apparently "disappeared". Former soldiers demanded a commission of inquiry to investigate the March incident which, they claimed, resulted in the death or "disappearance" of several, possibly over 30, guards. No such inquiry took place before the end of the year.

RENAMO alleged that Ossufo Buanamassari died in June on Mozambique Island, Nampula province, after police arrested and beat him for failing to show his identity card. The Cease-Fire Commission investigated the incident and ordered that the case be submitted to the commission monitoring the police, but this did not begin work until December 1993.

Juma Francisco Maulane, who had been convicted of burglary, died of bullet wounds in Maputo Central Prison in August. Initially, the authorities claimed that he had committed suicide in his cell: subsequently, they said he had been shot while trying to escape. No judicial inquiry appeared to have been carried out to establish the circumstances of his death.

Reports of abuses by RENAMO included the failure to account for people detained by its forces before the peace agreement entered into force and the apparent deliberate killing of one of its own officers. The peace agreement called for the release of prisoners by both sides, but RENAMO freed none, maintaining that those it had captured were living freely in RENAMO-controlled areas. Among those missing was Sandra Francisco Galego, who was abducted in Tete province in 1986 when she was 14 years old. In May the family of Tiago Salgado, a former government soldier who had joined RENAMO in 1991, accused RENAMO of deliberately and arbitrarily killing him earlier in 1993. In July RENAMO confirmed the death: it said that Tiago Salgado had been arrested on suspicion of spying for the government and was killed when trying to escape.

RENAMO also detained some 50 people in June and July in an apparent attempt to back its claim that the peace accords allowed it, and not the government, to administer RENAMO-controlled areas. RENAMO accused the detainees of hunting or cutting wood without obtaining RENAMO's permission. Over 20 people, including Aurelio Manhiça, a National Assembly deputy, and Luis Mondlane, a Presbyterian minister, were held in Salamanga, south of Maputo, and a similar number of woodcutters were detained in Manica and Sofala provinces. The detainees were released in August.

Amnesty International wrote to representatives of the government, RENAMO and the UN, and to others involved in the peace process, to propose ways of strengthening human rights protection. It made inquiries and expressed concern about reports of extrajudicial executions by government forces and urged that human rights education be included in training courses for the unified army. It also informed RENAMO of its concerns about captives held by RENAMO.

217

MYANMAR

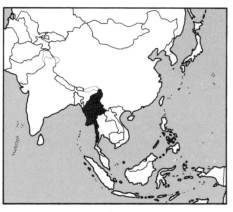

Hundreds of government opponents remained imprisoned, including dozens of prisoners of conscience, despite the release of some 2,000 others in the last 20 months, and at least 40 new political arrests were made. Some of those held were detained without trial, but most had been sentenced after unfair trials. Persistent human rights violations continued to be reported from many parts of the country, with members of ethnic minorities particularly targeted. The violations included arbitrary seizure of civilians to serve as military porters or labourers, ill-treatment and extrajudicial executions.

Myanmar remained under martial law and the ruling State Law and Order Restoration Council (SLORC), chaired by General Than Shwe, continued to refuse to convene the People's Assembly elected in 1990 and to suppress political opposition, freedom of expression and association.

Armed groups, representing different ethnic minorities, continued to oppose the government mostly in the east, although by the end of 1993 the SLORC controlled most of the country. Thousands of Mon and Karen civilians were reportedly forcibly relocated from their villages by the army, which frequently resorted to ill-treatment, torture and killings during the resettlements. Human rights violations by the army were widespread and systematic in the context of counter-insurgency activities.

On 1 January the official news media announced that the SLORC had commuted all death sentences to life imprisonment, benefiting at least 31 prisoners under

218

sentence of death. It was also announced that all sentences of more than 10 years would be reduced to 10 years.

On 9 January a National Convention to establish principles for drafting a new constitution was convened by the SLORC in Yangon, the capital. Almost 700 delegates attended, 120 of them elected members of the People's Assembly including some 90 from the National League for Democracy (NLD), which had won the 1990 elections. The Convention, to be reconvened in January 1994, met intermittently throughout the year. In September Aung Toe, the Chief Justice, set out "basic principles on which the fundamental principles of the state should be based", one of which was "participation of the Defence Services in the leading role in the country's national politics".

Hundreds of political prisoners, at least 70 of them prisoners of conscience, remained behind bars; most had been convicted under laws which criminalized peaceful political activity and allowed unfair trials. Despite the abolition of military tribunals in 1992, dozens of political prisoners who had been sentenced to long prison terms after unfair trials by such tribunals were still held.

Among the prisoners were leaders and organizers of the NLD and most other opposition parties. Twenty-nine members-elect of the People's Assembly, arrested from 1990 onwards, were still imprisoned at the end of the year. Other prisoners, from every part of Burmese society, included Buddhist clerics, community leaders, university and high school students, writers, civil servants, doctors, lawyers and workers' leaders.

Among the prisoners of conscience were NLD leader and 1991 Nobel Prize winner Aung San Suu Kyi, who has been held under house arrest since 1989; U Kyi Maung, an NLD member-elect of the People's Assembly, who was sentenced to two 10-year prison terms by military tribunals in 1990 and 1991; and Nai Tun Thein, Nai Ngwe Thein, and Nai Bala, three central executive committee members of the Mon National Democratic Front (MNDF), who were arrested in December 1991 and sentenced to 14-year prison terms in late 1992.

Over 700 political prisoners were released during the year. They included U Thumingala Linaryar, a prominent Buddhist monk, U Hla Wai, a leader of the Democratic Party for a New Society (DPNS), and Aung Din, a student leader, all prisoners of conscience. However, many released prisoners were still subject to surveillance by military intelligence agents and other restrictions on their freedom, such as being forced to report daily to the local authorities.

There were at least 40 new political arrests during the year. In the run-up to the National Convention in January, 14 people were arrested for distributing leaflets critical of the political process. Among them were Shwe Htoo, Yi Myint and Moe Kyaw Oo, who were reportedly sentenced to three years' imprisonment. In August Dr Aung Khin Sint and his assistant, Than Min, both leading NLD members, were arrested for writing and distributing letters to National Convention delegates. In October they were both sentenced to 20 years' imprisonment.

Over 20 prisoners, including prisoners of conscience, were sentenced to prison terms after unfair trials. Nay Lin, youth organizer for the Federation of Trade Unions in Burma (FTUB), was reportedly sentenced to seven years' imprisonment in January for putting up posters calling for the release of Aung San Suu Kyi. He was one of several trade unionists arrested in the run-up to the National Convention. Fazal Ahmed, a Muslim member-elect of the People's Assembly from Rakhine (Arakan) State and a member of the National Democratic Party for Human Rights, was reportedly sentenced to two years' imprisonment in March. Prisoner of conscience Ma Thida, a writer and doctor arrested in August, was sentenced with nine others to 20 years' imprisonment in October.

Political prisoners were held in poor conditions, sometimes amounting to cruel, inhuman or degrading treatment. Conditions were particularly harsh in Insein, Thayet and Tharawaddy prisons, where hundreds of political prisoners were held. Students and young people appeared to be particularly targeted for torture and ill-treatment in detention. Prisoners were routinely shackled, deprived of food and water, held in extremely overcrowded cells with poor sanitation and rarely received any medical treatment.

Members of ethnic minority groups – such as the Mon, Karen, Shan and Kayah groups who make up one third of the population – continued to be targeted by government forces in the context of their counter-insurgency campaigns. Women and children were particularly vulnerable to grave human rights violations, including rape and murder, as they were frequently left behind in their villages after the men had fled from military advances. Troops routinely entered villages, burned houses, stole livestock and crops and evicted villagers from their homes.

Members of ethnic minorities were routinely seized in their villages and fields by the military, accused of supporting insurgents, and severely beaten or subjected to other forms of torture. A 75-year-old woman from Papun township in Kayin State was publicly beaten in February by soldiers because she could not speak Burmese, and so could not answer their questions. In October the army accused a man from Hlaingbwe township of being an insurgent, covered his head with a plastic bag, and then poured hot water into it, causing near-suffocation.

Scores of members of ethnic minorities were extrajudicially executed by soldiers. In January troops from the 99th Regiment reportedly entered a village in Thaton district in Kayin State and seized four young farmers, dressed them up as insurgents, photographed and then killed them. The victims included 17-year-old Maw Da. The soldiers allegedly shot the four in the back of the neck and left the bodies behind for the villagers to bury. Troops then burned seven houses and ordered all the villagers to relocate to another area. Patrols from the nearby barracks confiscated livestock and commandeered porters and other unpaid labourers to work at the army camp.

Thousands of members of ethnic minorities were arbitrarily seized by the military and forced to serve as porters carrying army supplies, or as unpaid labourers building roads and army camps or working on commercial projects. Porters were held in army custody for periods ranging from a few days to a few months, and some were taken into forced service as many as 20 times in one year. Porters, who received little or no food and water, frequently fell ill from malnutrition and malaria, but received no medical attention and were forced to continue work, sometimes until they collapsed and were left behind or simply killed by troops. Elderly men and women, schoolchildren and pregnant women were among those conscripted. A woman from Hlaingbwe township, Kayin State, was forced to carry ammunition for seven days in March with her 70-year-old husband, whom she said was often beaten because he could not manage his load. He died five days after being released. Another man from Hlaingbwe township was reportedly stabbed to death by troops in August because he could not carry his load.

Dozens of porters and labourers were said to have died from exhaustion and neglect, or were shot or beaten to death by soldiers when they became too weak to carry their loads, or were killed for disobeying orders or trying to escape. Female porters were raped by soldiers.

Scores of porters were reportedly ill-treated if they were unable to carry their loads, could not speak Burmese well, or attempted to escape. Typically, they were kicked with army boots or beaten with fists, rifle butts or bamboo sticks. In February a Karen woman who had been held for one month was kicked with boots and beaten with a rifle butt because she could not lift her load of mortar shells and rice. In August a Karen man from Hlaingbwe township was kicked repeatedly in the back with army boots because he had slipped and fallen in mud; he said that he was still being treated for internal injuries two months later.

In mid-January forced repatriations of Burmese Muslim refugees from Bangladesh to Myanmar were suspended. Some 260,000 refugees had fled to Bangladesh by the first half of 1992 and several thousand had been repatriated without the protection of the UN High Commissioner for Refugees (UNHCR) (see *Amnesty International Report 1993*). Repatriations later resumed with UNHCR involvement, and by late November it was reported that some 50,000 refugees had been repatriated since September 1992. In November the UNHCR and the SLORC signed a Memorandum of Understanding which stipulated that "UNHCR will be given access to all returnees; that the returnees will be issued with the appropriate identification papers and that the returnees will enjoy the same freedom of movement as all other nationals".

In previous years armed opposition groups had tortured, ill-treated or summarily executed prisoners. Amnesty International was not able to investigate fully all

220

such allegations but was concerned by reports that two prisoners were being held incommunicado by one faction of the All Burma Student Democratic Front (ABSDF) and might be at risk of torture or execution. In February Amnesty International wrote on their behalf to General Bo Mya, President of the Democratic Alliance of Burma (DAB), which acts as an umbrella organization for many armed opposition groups including the ABSDF. There was no response but in May the two men were reportedly sentenced to 10 years' imprisonment by a form of military tribunal for allegedly "traitorous" activities.

The UN Special Rapporteur on Myanmar submitted an extensive report to the UN Commission on Human Rights in February, detailing human rights violations in Myanmar. In March the Commission adopted a resolution on Myanmar which extended the mandate of the Special Rapporteur for another year and strongly urged the Myanmar Government to restore respect for human rights and fundamental freedoms. It called on the SLORC to consider lifting emergency measures and to cooperate fully with the Commission and the Special Rapporteur. On 6 December the UN General Assembly adopted without a vote a resolution which welcomed recent improvements made by Myanmar but also "deplored the continued violations of human rights".

In October Amnesty International published a major report, *Myanmar: The climate of fear continues, members of ethnic minorities and political prisoners still targeted*, which described how members of political parties and ethnic minorities lived in an atmosphere of fear which pervaded the whole country. Amnesty International appealed to the government to release prisoners of conscience, to ensure fair and prompt trials for all other political prisoners and to release civilians arbitrarily seized against their will by the military to serve as porters or labourers. While Amnesty International welcomed releases of political prisoners, the commutation of death sentences and the abolition of military tribunals, it called on the authorities to stop arbitrary detention, torture and extrajudicial executions.

In oral statements to the UN Commission on Human Rights in March and the Working Group on Indigenous Populations in August, Amnesty International included reference to its concerns in Myanmar.

NEPAL

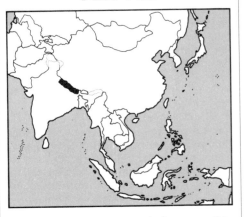

Hundreds of people, including possible prisoners of conscience, were detained during a series of opposition strikes and demonstrations and held without charge or trial for up to several weeks. Torture and ill-treatment of imprisoned demonstrators and other prisoners was reported. There was one reported "disappearance". At least 24 people were reportedly killed by police in circumstances suggesting that they may have been victims of extrajudicial executions.

Legislation to provide compensation for torture victims was drafted, but had not been passed by the end of the year. The draft bill set an upper limit for compensation but it did not define torture as a crime or require that perpetrators be brought to justice.

A committee was established in August under the Home Minister to review the cases of prisoners convicted of criminal offences under the previous government who may have been falsely charged for political reasons. It had not finished its work by the end of the year.

Over 1,000 people were arrested in June and July during a series of nationwide strikes and demonstrations called by the main opposition party, the Communist Party of Nepal (United Marxist-Leninist) (CPN-UML), in alliance with other opposition parties. Some of the demonstrations were violent, with stone-throwing, arson and destruction of public and private property. According to the police, about 1,280 people were arrested between 24 June and 4 July 1993, of whom 150 were charged with breaking the curfew or public order offences. Most of the others, including hundreds of possible prisoners of conscience, were held in administrative detention without charge or trial under the Public Offences Act, which permits up to 35 days' detention, and then released.

Under the terms of a nine-point agreement reached between the CPN-UML and the government of Prime Minister Girija Prasad Koirala in August, the detained demonstrators and strikers were released and any charges against them withdrawn.

The parliamentary Foreign Affairs and Human Rights Committee established five teams to inspect jails, police stations and the offices of government attorneys in the five development regions. Their findings were not known at the end of the year.

There were several reports of ill-treatment and torture in police custody, including beatings of detainees held during the demonstrations and rape and attempted rape of women prisoners in both 1992 and 1993. Amnesty International does not know of a single case in which a police officer has been prosecuted for torture.

Manikala Rai was allegedly raped and subjected to other torture by five police officers at a Kathmandu police station in December 1992. The authorities, however, took action only against one sub-inspector, who was dismissed from the police force in January. The police department said he had not been prosecuted because there had not been conclusive medical evidence of rape.

Teelu Ghale was reported to have been tortured at the Hanuman Dhoka police station in Kathmandu and at the Bhaktapur police station in September. Police apparently attempted to extort money from her, beat her, subjected her to electric shocks on her wrists and attempted to rape her. When required by the Supreme Court to respond to a *habeas corpus* petition, the police denied she was in custody and transferred her to Bhaktapur police station, where she was further abused and denied food for two days. In early October police took Teelu Ghale to the District Court and charged her with selling one gram of heroin; they told the Supreme Court that she had been arrested only on the day that she was charged. However, the Supreme Court ordered an investigation and found that she had indeed been arrested in September. Contempt of court proceedings were initiated against the police officers

concerned but had not concluded by the end of the year. No action was known to have been taken regarding her torture.

There were numerous complaints of prisoners being beaten by police, including reports from Kathmandu, Lalitpur, Bhaktapur, Rolpa, Ilam, Rukum, Lamjung and Morang. Victims included people detained in connection with the strikes and demonstrations, and street children. The police denied that detained demonstrators had been beaten. Other forms of torture reported included beatings on the soles of the feet, having pins pushed under the finger nails and electric shocks.

One person reportedly "disappeared" in police custody during the June demonstrations. Pravakar Subedi went missing from his student hostel in Kathmandu on 25 June. His brother later saw a photograph in a magazine which he believed showed Pravakar Subedi, injured, being carried into custody by four police officers. The police had not traced him by the end of the year.

At least 24 people were reported to have died in circumstances suggesting that they may have been victims of extrajudicial executions. They included at least 21 people who were reportedly killed when police opened fire on opposition strikers and demonstrators in June and July in circumstances that did not appear to justify the use of lethal force. The government acknowledged 16 deaths. Under the terms of the agreement between the government and the CPN-UML, relatives of the deceased were paid compensation by the government. However, no independent inquiry was held into these shootings to establish whether the police officers responsible had acted within the law. Two other people were killed in August when police opened fire on a crowd gathered outside Barahathawa police station, Sarlahi District, protesting against the arrest and torture of three youths. The crowd had reportedly thrown stones at the police station before the firing started. The Home Ministry said it had investigated the incident, but it had not made its findings known by the end of the year.

In June police in Katari reportedly opened fire on a group of some 60 Tibetans who had crossed the border into Nepal on their way to India. Jemyang Kelsand died after being shot in the head. A government spokesman said that the Tibetans had

222

attacked the police first, but other reports suggested that the police had opened fire after two children threw stones at them. The Home Ministry said it had investigated the incident, but the findings were not made public. No independent inquiry was held.

Amnesty International urged the government to ensure that all reports of torture and killings by the police are promptly, thoroughly and independently investigated. It called also for the introduction of adequate safeguards against torture and ill-treatment of prisoners.

In November an Amnesty International delegation visited Nepal and met the Prime Minister and other government ministers and officials. Amnesty International expressed concern about the climate of impunity and called on the authorities to bring to justice those responsible for human rights violations. The government said it was committed to upholding human rights and that police had been required to open fire on demonstrators in order to maintain law and order. The police responded to six individual cases of alleged torture, death in custody and "disappearance" reported in 1992 and 1993 which Amnesty International had raised, and denied that the human rights violations described had taken place. The Prime Minister said the government would examine Amnesty International's recommendations for human rights safeguards.

NETHERLANDS
(KINGDOM OF THE)

A further report of police ill-treatment was received from the Netherlands Antilles, a Caribbean country forming part of the Kingdom of the Netherlands.

Gerardo E. Chong was arrested in November 1992 having twice escaped from the police earlier the same day. He alleged that he first escaped after a police officer menaced him with his truncheon and threatened to shoot him. In the second incident he admitted that he hit one of the officers with an iron bar before escaping in a police car. During his subsequent arrest he was shot and wounded slightly in the head. He alleged that in the police station five or six officers beat and throttled him as he lay manacled on the floor. He claimed

that medical evidence supported his allegations of police ill-treatment.

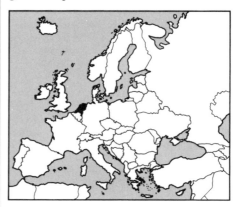

In May the Netherlands Antillean Government provided further information to Amnesty International about two deaths in custody in previous years (see *Amnesty International Report 1993*). Henry K. Every died as a result of an injury to the chest caused by crushing. Leroy Neil died of peritonitis while being interrogated by the police; previously he had shown clear signs of illness, such as vomiting and diarrhoea.

In October Amnesty International wrote to the Minister of Justice of the Netherlands Antilles expressing concern about the allegations of ill-treatment made by Gerardo E. Chong and the conduct of the inquiries into the two deaths in custody.

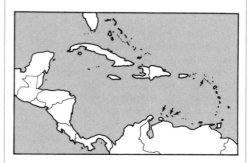

Also in October Amnesty International wrote to the Minister for Netherlands Antillean and Aruban Affairs in The Hague. The organization had previously written to the Minister of Justice of the Netherlands Antilles in December 1992 regarding the findings of the Commission of Inquiry into alleged unlawful and violent behaviour by the police (see *Amnesty International Report 1993*) but had received no response.

Amnesty International was not aware whether any of the Commission's recommendations had been implemented or whether disciplinary or criminal action had been taken against police officers involved in unlawful actions. Amnesty International considered that the Commission's report showed that the fundamental human rights and freedoms of the citizens of the Netherlands Antilles had been endangered. Accordingly, Amnesty International requested the Minister for Netherlands Antillean and Aruban Affairs to exercise his discretionary power, under Article 43 of the Charter of the Kingdom, to intervene in order to safeguard these rights. In December the Minister replied that it had been agreed with the Minister of Justice of the Netherlands Antilles to thoroughly update police training. He expressed the hope that the new training program would " ... drastically improve police officers' relations with the public, and thus also with prisoners".

In December the Minister of Justice of the Netherlands Antilles informed Amnesty International of the steps the government intended to take to implement the recommendations of the Commission of Inquiry and to increase compliance with international standards. These included reforms to the Codes of Criminal Procedure and the Prison System, a bill recently introduced in Parliament establishing a complaints commission to examine police conduct, and the planned reorganization of the police force.

NEW ZEALAND

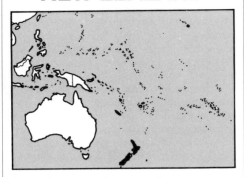

Several inmates in two prisons were reportedly ill-treated by prison officers.

Prison officers were reported to have ill-treated inmates in Mount Crawford Prison in Wellington and Mangaroa Jail, near Hastings, during the year.

Several inmates of the remand wing at Mount Crawford Prison alleged that some prison officials subjected them to cruel, inhuman or degrading treatment, including verbal abuse and physical brutality such as being beaten while handcuffed. Between June and August, seven officers from Mount Crawford Prison were suspended and one of them was dismissed after an independent inquiry by private investigators appointed by the Justice Department. The inquiry report, which was submitted to the Justice Department, identified 44 instances of ill-treatment over a 30-month period. Eighty per cent of the complaints were of alleged assault.

Similar complaints from inmates at Mangaroa Jail came to light in June and July. Some Mangaroa Jail prison officers, known as "designated hitters", were used by the prison authorities to beat inmates. The complaints included prolonged assaults lasting several days, the abuse of confidential information to harass or degrade inmates, and the neglect of care, especially of suicidal inmates. Twelve prison officers were dismissed by the Department of Justice in June after an official investigation into allegations of cruelty at the jail. However, the investigation had not led to criminal prosecutions of any Mangaroa Jail staff by the end of the year.

A second independent investigation into the management of Mangaroa Jail found the same instances of ill-treatment of prisoners and added that there was evidence of similar practices in other prisons. The second report, which was made public in July, recommended the setting-up of an independent prison complaints authority, a review of prison staff recruitment and improved training. The Justice Minister stated that many of the report's recommendations would be implemented.

In September Amnesty International wrote to the authorities about the reported incidents of ill-treatment at Mount Crawford Prison and Mangaroa Jail. Amnesty International asked what steps the government had taken in response to the allegations of cruelty and called on it to ensure that prisoners' rights were fully respected. The government replied in November, stating that the New Zealand prison system had embarked on "far-reaching reforms".

NICARAGUA

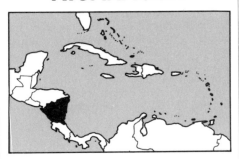

Members of the police and army were implicated in several possible extrajudicial executions of former rebels, but few steps were taken to investigate or bring to justice those responsible for human rights violations. There were allegations of ill-treatment by police and the army in response to political violence. Armed political groups committed numerous deliberate and arbitrary killings and other abuses.

There was growing division between President Violeta Barrios de Chamorro and factions of her own party, the *Unión Nacional Opositora* (UNO), National Opposition Union. In January several UNO factions broke away from the ruling coalition, officially declared themselves to be in opposition and boycotted the National Assembly. They accused the President of "co-governing" with the opposition *Frente Sandinista de Liberación Nacional* (FSLN), Sandinista National Liberation Front, and maintaining Sandinista control over the army. An all-party "national dialogue" initiated in September collapsed after one group of UNO deputies accused another of corruption when they switched allegiance to form a pro-government majority with the FSLN in the National Assembly.

In August the US Government suspended economic aid to Nicaragua, accusing Nicaragua of "harbouring terrorism" and of failing to establish effective civilian control over the armed forces, resolve property claims by US citizens, and prosecute those allegedly responsible for human rights abuses. This followed the discovery in late May of a weapons cache said to belong to a faction of the demobilized Salvadorian armed opposition, together with documents suggesting the existence of an international kidnapping ring involving Latin American and European armed opposition groups.

In September President Chamorro announced a series of reforms to the armed forces and said that General Humberto Ortega would relinquish office as head of the army in 1994 and that there would be changes to the military intelligence hierarchy. The measures were vociferously challenged by the armed forces, prompting renewed controversy about the role of the military.

The Supreme Court failed to issue a ruling, due in January, on a challenge to a provision of the penal code which could result in the imprisonment of people solely on the basis of their homosexuality (see *Amnesty International Report 1993*).

There was continued violence by rival armed groups of ex-combatants: *recontras*, (former members of the Nicaraguan Resistance (NR) or "*contra*" who had fought against the previous Sandinista government); and *recompas*, (mainly ex-army members). Against a backdrop of political polarization, economic deprivation and growing lawlessness, both groups of ex-combatants refused to give up their arms, despite a demobilization program which had been initiated under international supervision following the end of the armed conflict and the election of President Chamorro in 1990. In August a delegation of about 40 government officials, including two vice-ministers, was taken hostage by a *recontra* group in Quilalí, Nueva Segovia region. The group's demands included the removal of General Ortega. In reprisal, a *recompa* group took over 30 people hostage the next day in UNO headquarters in Managua, the capital, among them Vice-President Virgilio Godoy. The group demanded the release of the government officials held hostage in Quilalí. All hostages were released unharmed following mediation efforts involving national human rights groups.

Both groups carried out dozens of deliberate and arbitrary killings and other abuses, particularly in the northern regions of Jinotega and Matagalpa. On both sides there was evidence in some cases of collusion by different branches of the government, and in the majority of cases the authorities failed to investigate and prosecute those responsible.

Among the victims of abuses committed by *recontra* groups were members of agricultural cooperatives, such as Patricio Montano Téllez and his sons, Demetrio and David, who were reportedly tortured and killed in San Martín, Juigalpa region, in January. Also targeted, according to certain sources, were FSLN supporters, including Juan Dávila Pérez and two of his children, who were murdered in Waslala, Matagalpa region, in February.

Apparent political killings attributed to *recompa* groups included the murder in February of the president of the *Partido Nacional Conservador*, National Conservative Party, Miguel Rivera Rocha. In November three former army officers were found guilty of the November 1992 killing of a prominent landowner, Arges Sequiera Mangas (see *Amnesty International Report 1993*). However, the accused were tried *in absentia* and had not been apprehended by the end of the year.

The President signed an amnesty law in September granting immunity from prosecution to members of rearmed groups who had committed "political" crimes before 28 August. The law had originally been approved by the National Assembly in August, but was subsequently amended so as to benefit those responsible for the August hostage-takings. Although some groups disarmed under the terms of the amnesty, several *recontra* and *recompa* groups remained active at the end of the year and the army launched special operations in the north with the stated intention of eliminating them.

Earlier, in July, when army troops reclaimed the town of Estelí which had been occupied by a *recompa* group, dozens of civilians were killed or wounded. There were widespread allegations that soldiers had used excessive and disproportionate force against unarmed civilians.

Members of the army and National Police were implicated in several killings of former NR members in 1993 and previous years. A farmer from Pantasma, Jinotega region, who had demobilized from the NR in 1990, was reportedly killed in August by an army lieutenant, who was already facing charges of homicide and had been confined to barracks by the *Auditoría Militar*, military tribunal. Witnesses to the killing said they had been threatened by the lieutenant; neither the killing nor the threats were apparently the subject of a judicial investigation.

In March the *Comisión Tripartita*, Tripartite Commission, made up of representatives of the government, the Catholic Church and the *Comisión Internacional de Apoyo y Verificación* (CIAV), International Commission of Support and Verification – a body of the Organization of American States – published its findings on 10 killings of former NR members, including three killings allegedly committed by the army between 1990 and 1992 and one by the police in 1991. The Tripartite Commission said that Miguel Centeno Valenzuela had been shot dead in cold blood by two members of the National Police in December 1991. Proceedings against the officers allegedly responsible had been opened by the military tribunal in late 1992, but the two did not appear to have been detained and no progress was reported. The Commission also found a series of irregularities in the preliminary police investigation, including falsification of the testimony of witnesses.

Regarding the killing of former NR member Harold Benavides Cortéz in February 1991, the Commission revealed that the two army officers allegedly responsible had been released without charge in May 1991, after a military tribunal investigation which had taken testimony only from other soldiers.

The Commission found that in other cases civilians and *recompa* forces had killed former NR members but had escaped prosecution because in all but one case official investigations had been negligent and had involved a police or military cover-up. The Commission recommended prosecution of those allegedly responsible for the killings. However, in a report in December the Commission criticized the lack of compliance with its recommendations and documented further cases of killings involving government forces. It also called for the scope of military jurisdiction over investigations into abuses to be restricted.

Evidence continued to come to light of police and army complicity in *recompa* abuses. In one of the cases investigated by the Commission, CIAV observers and other witnesses reportedly saw army members collaborating with *recompa* forces who had held a police delegation captive in Wamblán, Matagalpa region, in December 1991 and had executed the local chief of police, a former NR member. Investigations into the case were not opened until late 1992, and did not result in the prosecution of those allegedly responsible.

226

No progress was made in the case of Jean Paul Genie Lacayo, a 17-year-old shot dead in 1990 by escorts of General Ortega. An appeal presented by relatives to the Supreme Court in 1992 challenging military jurisdiction over the case was rejected in December (see *Amnesty International Report 1993*).

Incidents of ill-treatment by police were reported, often in the context of labour conflicts or violence by armed groups. Many of those arrested or involved in disturbances during a transport workers' strike in September sustained injuries as a result of apparent excessive force by police. Nine FSLN youth activists detained in connection with disturbances in Portezuelo in September claimed to have been beaten on arrest and in police custody. The *Centro Nicaragüense de Derechos Humanos* (CENIDH), Nicaraguan Centre for Human Rights, lodged a formal complaint but no official investigation was undertaken. There were also isolated cases of ill-treatment of criminal suspects, including the beating of a minor, Ricardo José Sabogal Viales, in October, by the National Police in Managua. Again, CENIDH's complaint to the authorities appeared not to produce any official response.

Three former Spanish citizens of Basque origin who had been granted Nicaraguan citizenship were summarily expelled from Nicaragua in May. Javier Larreategui Cuadra, Sebastián Etxaniz and Francisco Azpiazu were detained on 25 May in connection with the discovery of an arms cache in Managua two days earlier. They were held by police beyond the legal limit of 72 hours and then expelled to Spain against their will on 30 May, despite an order from a judge that they should be released and should remain in Nicaraguan territory and despite fears that they would be at risk of torture or ill-treatment in Spain, where they were wanted for serious crimes linked to the activities of an armed Basque separatist group. After five days in custody on arrival in Spain, during which they were not physically ill-treated, the men were transferred to prison in Madrid under judicial investigation.

In June Amnesty International asked the government to obtain guarantees that the three men expelled to Spain would not be subjected to ill-treatment there and to clarify the apparent procedural irregularities. The authorities replied that the three had obtained their Nicaraguan nationality fraudulently, that procedures for their expulsion had been entirely in accordance with national laws, and that the government could take no position with regard to the risk of human rights violations in another sovereign country.

In August Amnesty International publicly condemned the taking of hostages by *recontra* and *recompa* groups, calling for their immediate and unconditional release. In October the organization wrote to President Chamorro voicing concern that the September amnesty law would perpetuate the impunity with which both governmental and non-governmental forces had been allowed to commit deliberate and arbitrary killings and other abuses since she took office. It expressed dismay that the law's scope was extended following the August kidnappings so as to allow those responsible to benefit. In connection with the occupation of Estelí, the transport workers' strike and the political violence in August, Amnesty International called for preventive measures to be taken to avoid human rights abuses, including steps to ensure that the use of force by law enforcement officials conformed to international standards and that human rights violators were brought to justice. In a detailed reply in December, the President argued that the amnesty law was necessary to prevent further violence and to encourage those who had taken up arms to return to civilian life.

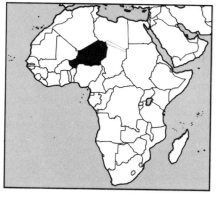

NIGER

Some 70 members of the Tuareg minority ethnic group detained without charge or trial from August 1992 onwards were released in April and Tuareg rebels released all their prisoners. Two Tuareg may have been extrajudicially executed. Peaceful demonstrators were detained briefly.

President Mahmane Ousmane came to power in April following multi-party presidential and parliamentary elections and ending the transitional period set up by a National Conference in 1991. A cease-fire between government forces and Tuareg insurgents had been in effect during the election period.

More than 20 people still held hostage by the Tuareg rebel organization, the *Front de libération de l'Aïr et de l'Azawad* (FLAA), Liberation Front of Aïr and Azawad, were released by 12 April. Negotiations between the new authorities and the FLAA led to a three-month renewable truce in June which was subsequently renewed for the rest of the year. Also in June the government lifted the state of emergency which had been imposed in April 1992. However, disagreement among the Tuareg rebels about the truce led to the creation of two new groups. In October the three rebel factions came together again for negotiations with the government, but these were broken off in November. No acts of violence by armed rebels were reported from June onwards.

In July, soldiers mutinied in several army barracks, mainly with economic demands, but also in protest against the truce signed with the FLAA, which apparently confined them to barracks. The mutineers took some 11 officials hostage, including the Deputy Chief of Army Staff, and the Prefect of Tahoua, but all were released by 13 July. The mutineers apparently went unpunished.

A commission set up by the National Conference to examine past political crimes and human rights violations concluded its work by presenting its findings to the new Prime Minister, Mahamadou Issoufou, in line with provisions of the new Constitution. The commission's work was incomplete, as it had not investigated most of the allegations of human rights abuse reported to it. It had only completed investigations into five cases, all concerning corruption. Parliament apparently refused to renew the commission's mandate because it considered that the normal courts were competent to deal with any outstanding cases. No new prosecutions for past human rights violations were initiated as a result of the commission's findings,

but the secrecy surrounding the commission's recommendations made it impossible to establish if this was for political reasons. When two army officers were prosecuted in November 1992, the government had ordered their release the day after they were sentenced to 10 years' imprisonment. The work of the commission had been hampered by the arbitrary arrests of leading Tuareg in 1992, which provoked the commission's chairman to go into exile for eight months (see *Amnesty International Report 1993*). The High Court of Justice, a special court set up in 1991 to try former government and security officials, and which allows no right of appeal to those convicted, remained in place, but heard no cases during the year.

On 2 April the authorities ordered the release of remaining Tuareg prisoners held for political reasons, believed to number about 70. They were among more than 200 Tuareg arrested by the army from August 1992 onwards (see *Amnesty International Report 1993*). Some had been held outside any legal framework. Many appeared to be prisoners of conscience, imprisoned solely because they were Tuareg, with no evidence that they were involved in the Tuareg rebellion. Of 31 Tuareg prisoners who were held at the main prison in Niamey, the capital, on 2 April, 11 were taken hostage by other prisoners who demanded that they too should be released. On 23 April, some 900 prisoners, including criminal suspects, convicted common law prisoners and the 11 remaining Tuareg detainees, escaped from prison in Niamey.

Demonstrations and marches in Niamey were broken up by the security forces on several occasions and resulted in a series of arrests. It seemed that the security forces intervened on the grounds that the demonstrations had not been authorized, although in all but one case they appeared to be peaceful until the security forces intervened.

Fourteen organizers of a demonstration protesting against disruption in education were held in custody for 24 hours in January and then released. They were charged with responsibility for damage caused when the security forces intervened. They had not been brought to trial by the end of the year.

At least eight leading members of the former sole political party, the *Mouvement national pour la société de développement-*

Nasara (MNSD-Nasara), National Movement for a Society in Development, were arrested on 13 August after a march. The eight were not charged but were reportedly kept in custody on the personal orders of the Minister of Justice. On 19 August a court ordered their release on the grounds that their arrest had been illegal.

In September, a member of the MNSD-Nasara was held briefly by the mayor of a village near Maradi for playing music which he considered to be insulting to the authorities. Ten members of the MNSD-Nasara, who apparently assaulted the mayor while demanding the release of their colleague, were sentenced to three years' imprisonment on charges of assault. Five others were acquitted.

Two Tuareg killed near Agadès in December may have been victims of extrajudicial execution, on account of their ethnic origin. The two market gardeners were travelling to market when soldiers opened fire on them. The incident took place in the context of increased tension when the truce between the government and Tuareg rebel organizations was not renewed.

Amnesty International appealed for the release of all prisoners of conscience and welcomed the releases of Tuareg detainees.

NIGERIA

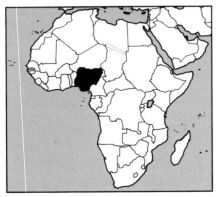

Hundreds of critics and opponents of the government, including journalists, human rights activists and trade unionists, who were detained, mostly without charge, were prisoners of conscience. More than 40 people arrested in 1992 in connection with religious riots remained held without trial. Several dozen members of the Ogoni ethnic group were extrajudicially executed by security forces. At least 26 people were sentenced to death, most after grossly unfair trials before special tribunals; some death sentences were subsequently commuted and no executions were reported.

Although transition to civilian rule was due to be completed in August, a military government remained in power at the end of the year.

In January a two-chamber National Assembly was inaugurated and a Transitional Council chaired by Chief Ernest Shonekan was established to run day-to-day government affairs until the return to civilian rule scheduled for 27 August. However, its powers were severely restricted and the National Defence and Security Council, headed by President Ibrahim Babangida, effectively retained political control. Candidates of the only two political parties allowed (which had been established by the military government), the Social Democratic Party (SDP) and the National Republican Convention (NRC), contested a presidential election on 12 June. Although it was evident that Chief Moshood Abiola of the SDP had been successful, on 23 June President Babangida annulled the results of the election, citing malpractices. International observers, however, judged that the election had been fair.

The refusal to announce the results of the election led to protest both at home and abroad. The military authorities responded by introducing repressive new laws, suppressing the news media and detaining critics and opponents. They repealed legislation providing for transition to civilian rule. President Babangida maintained, however, that his military government would relinquish power as scheduled. On 26 August he resigned and appointed an Interim National Government headed by Chief Shonekan, which undertook to organize a fresh presidential election and to hand over power to an elected civilian government by March 1994. On 17 November, however, following a High Court ruling that the Interim National Government was illegal and strikes in protest against increased domestic fuel prices, the military once again intervened. Chief Shonekan was forced to resign and was replaced as head of state by former Defence Minister General Sani Abacha, who dissolved the National Assembly and all other elected bodies and banned the two political parties. He established a predominantly military Provisional Ruling Council and subsequently appointed a Federal Executive Council composed largely of civilians. The new military government promised a constitutional conference in early 1994.

On 5 May the government promulgated the Treason and Treasonable Offences Decree No. 29 of 1993, under which anyone whose actions or views were deemed "capable of disrupting the general fabric" of Nigeria could be sentenced to death. The decree was suspended on 21 May, after national and international protest, but was not repealed.

In July Nigeria acceded to both the International Covenant on Civil and Political Rights and the International Covenant on Economic, Social and Cultural Rights.

Journalists, human rights activists and trade unionists were among hundreds of prisoners of conscience detained during the year.

In the months preceding the June presidential election dozens of journalists were arrested. Malam Aliyu Hayatu, editor of the independent *Reporter* newspaper, was arrested in March and charged with "inciting public disturbances with intent to endanger public peace" for criticizing the military authorities. He was released on bail but was not tried. The newspaper was closed. There were further arrests of journalists following the military authorities' decision to annul the results of the presidential election, including four editors of *Tell* magazine who were arrested in August. On 16 August the military authorities promulgated a decree which proscribed several newspapers closed the previous month; the ban was lifted in November.

After the military authorities failed to announce the election results, the Campaign for Democracy (CD), an alliance of pro-democracy groups, called for a week of protest in early July. Hundreds of people were arrested during demonstrations in Lagos and other towns, and more than 100 people died in clashes with security forces. It appeared that in some cases the security forces opened fire indiscriminately. Among those arrested were three leading CD members: its chairman, Dr Beko Ransome-Kuti, also President of the Committee for the Defence of Human Rights; Femi Falana, a lawyer and President of the National Association of Democratic Lawyers; and Chief Gani Fawehinmi, a prominent human rights lawyer. All three had been arrested

previously. They were charged with sedition and conspiracy. Although bail was granted, the authorities continued to detain them under legislation allowing administrative detention of security suspects for renewable periods of six weeks. They were freed in late August, shortly after the Interim National Government came to power. At the same time Chief Shonekan announced that detained journalists were to be released.

Three staff members of the Civil Liberties Organisation (CLO), a non-governmental human rights organization affiliated to the CD, were also arrested in early July. The CLO had been a particular target for harassment since the beginning of the year. Wale Shittu, Femi Adenuga and Emmanuel Nweke were arrested by police in Lagos, charged with sedition and released on bail after a month, but were not tried.

Joseph Akinjala, Deputy Secretary General of the National Union of Petroleum, Energy and Gas, was arrested in August and held for several days after threatening to call a strike if President Babangida did not leave office on 27 August.

There were further arrests of CD members and supporters during September and October. Most were released uncharged after a short time. Dr Beko Ransome-Kuti was again arrested in October, together with more than 20 others, including his daughter, Morenike Ransome-Kuti, a lawyer, Olusegun Mayegun, former president of the National Association of Nigerian Students, and Chima Ubani, CD General Secretary. They were released shortly afterwards but 17 of them, including Dr Ransome-Kuti, were charged with unlawful assembly and disturbing the peace; their trial was adjourned until 1994.

Ken Saro-Wiwa, N.G. Dube and Kobari Nwiee, prominent members of the Movement for the Survival of the Ogoni People (MOSOP), were arrested in Port Harcourt in Rivers State in June. They were charged with unlawful assembly, seditious intention and seditious publication. They were released on bail after several weeks but had not been tried by the end of the year. The Ogoni community has campaigned against environmental damage and inadequate compensation for destruction of land and crops by oil companies.

In June there were reports that more than 40 members of the Kataf ethnic group, arrested during 1992 in connection with

230

religious riots, were still held without trial (see *Amnesty International Report 1993*). Seven had been acquitted by Civil Disturbances Special Tribunals in late 1992 and early 1993 but remained in Kaduna Prison. Sixteen others, against whom charges had been withdrawn or whose trials had been adjourned, also remained held and at least 21 others remained in detention without charge or trial.

Nine army officers, convicted after a grossly unfair trial in connection with a coup attempt in April 1990, remained held (see *Amnesty International Report 1992*). At least three other soldiers remained held in connection with the coup attempt. One had been acquitted and two appeared to be held without charge or trial.

There were reports of ill-treatment by police both of pro-democracy activists and criminal suspects. In August Morenike Ransome-Kuti (see above) was beaten by police in her home in Lagos. Okey Uzoho, a leading member of the NRC, was beaten when arrested by police on 20 November; he was subsequently admitted to hospital.

Prison conditions remained extremely harsh and amounted in some cases to cruel, inhuman or degrading treatment. In October the CLO reported that eight prisoners under sentence of death in Kirikiri Maximum Security Prison were held in appalling conditions. Held in small, dark cells with no toilet facilities, they were rarely able to wash and one mentally ill prisoner was chained to a wall in an isolation cell.

The security forces extrajudicially executed dozens of members of the Ogoni ethnic group in Rivers State. In April security forces were reported to have opened fire on peaceful demonstrators in Biara; 11 people were injured. Shortly afterwards, further shooting by the security forces at Nonwa resulted in one death. In early August at least 35 members of the Ogoni ethnic group, including children, were killed in Kaa by armed men, some in uniform. Although local officials claimed that the incident was an ethnic clash between the Ogoni and neighbouring Andoni people, there was evidence implicating the security forces.

Several hundred other people were reported to have died between July and September in violent clashes between members of the Ogoni and Andoni communities. There were further allegations that the security forces were implicated in aggression against the Ogoni community. There was no official investigation into any of these killings.

Seventeen prisoners, all but two from the Kataf community, were sentenced to death in February and March after grossly unfair trials before two Civil Disturbances Special Tribunals in Kaduna. They were convicted of culpable homicide in connection with the riots in Kaduna in May 1992. Some of them, including Zamani Lekwot, a retired army general, had already been tried for unlawful assembly and released. They were immediately rearrested and charged with culpable homicide on substantially the same evidence, with no right of appeal to a higher court. Convictions and sentences were referred to the military government. In March a High Court in Lagos granted a temporary injunction restraining the government from executing Zamani Lekwot and others sentenced to death. The case was subsequently referred to the Supreme Court. However, in August President Babangida commuted the death sentences to five years' imprisonment.

Five others were reported to have been sentenced to death in March and April by a Civil Disturbances Special Tribunal in Bauchi, in connection with religious riots in Bauchi State in 1991.

Four other death sentences were reported, including two passed in October by a Robbery and Firearms Tribunal in Benue State. No executions were reported.

In September a High Court in Maiduguri, Borno State, granted refugee status to 244 Chadians arrested in 1991 and 1992. The court also ruled that their arrests and detention at a military camp had been illegal, and granted an injunction restraining the federal government from deporting them. Over 200 Chadians had been illegally deported in 1992; at least three were tortured to death or extrajudicially executed by the Chadian authorities (see *Amnesty International Report 1993*).

Amnesty International repeatedly urged the government to release pro-democracy activists who were prisoners of conscience. In February and March the organization urged the government to commute the death sentences imposed on Zamani Lekwot and others convicted after unfair trials before Civil Disturbances Special Tribunals. Amnesty International called for the release of Ken Saro-Wiwa and other members of the Ogoni ethnic group and, following killings by the security forces in Rivers State in May and August, called for an independent inquiry and for immediate steps to be taken to prevent further killings. No replies were received from the government.

PAKISTAN

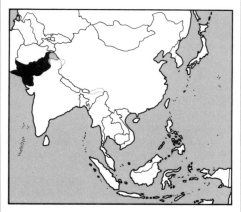

Several prisoners of conscience charged with blasphemy remained in prison while new blasphemy cases were registered against others on account of their peaceful political opinions or religious beliefs. Over 200 possible prisoners of conscience were among hundreds of people arbitrarily detained during army operations in Sindh Province. Several cases of unacknowledged detention in police custody were investigated by the courts. Hundreds of people were reportedly tortured in police or military custody. Sentences of flogging and amputation were passed. Over a dozen deaths were reported which the authorities alleged were "encounter" killings but which appeared to be deaths after torture or extrajudicial executions. Fifty-seven people were sentenced to death, some by special courts which failed to meet international standards. One execution was reported.

After months of political uncertainty, President Ishaq Khan and Prime Minister Mian Nawaz Sharif resigned in July. Moeen Qureshi was appointed to form an interim government. General elections for the national and provincial assemblies took place in October. The leader of the Pakistan People's Party (PPP), Benazir Bhutto, was sworn in as Prime Minister on 19 October. The PPP candidate,

Farooq Leghari, was elected President in November.

In September the government announced plans to establish a National Human Rights Commission to investigate human rights violations, but no further developments were reported by the end of the year.

Army operations initiated in May 1992 to combat criminal and political violence in Sindh continued. The police and military enjoyed legal immunity for acts deemed to have been committed "in good faith".

An ordinance promulgated in September extended the death penalty to cover drug-trafficking.

Eight charges of misrule and corruption filed against Benazir Bhutto after her dismissal as Prime Minister in August 1990 were still pending. Her husband, Asif Zardari, was acquitted of the tenth charge in the 12 cases against him and was released on bail in February after 28 months in prison.

Blasphemy laws, which carry a mandatory death penalty, continued to be used to harass or detain people for their political or religious beliefs. Dr Akhtar Hamid Khan, a Muslim poet in his seventies and founder of the Orangi Project, a development program, was charged with blasphemy in two separate cases. He was reported to have been falsely accused by traditional Islamists whose businesses had been adversely affected by the self-help training program his project offered to the poor. Dr Khan remained at liberty but under threat of imprisonment as a prisoner of conscience.

Gul Masih, a Christian who had been sentenced to death in 1992 for blasphemy, remained in jail (see *Amnesty International Report 1993*). He was a prisoner of conscience. Three other Christians were arrested in May in Gujranwala, Punjab, accused by their Islamist neighbours of writing blasphemous statements on a mosque's walls. One of them, a 13-year-old boy, was released on bail in November.

Several members of the Ahmadi religious minority were prisoners of conscience. Abdul Qadeer, Mohammad Haziq Rafiq Tahir, Mohammad Ilyas Munir and Nisar Ahmad were arrested in 1984 and falsely accused of murder during the martial law period (1977 to 1985). Sentenced to 25 years' imprisonment after an unfair trial by a military court, they were still in prison at the end of 1993. Scheduled hearings of their appeals to the Lahore High Court were repeatedly postponed. At least 60 Ahmadis were charged for using verses from the Koran during their peaceful religious activities: one was sentenced to three years' imprisonment and two were charged with blasphemy.

At least four journalists who had reported an incident in which excessive force was allegedly used by police against student demonstrators in January were detained and reportedly beaten on the orders of a police deputy superintendent. They lodged complaints but the police officers involved were not brought to justice. Several other journalists were imprisoned in tribal areas after trials which contravened tribal court regulations and international fair trial standards. Sailab Mahsud, who was arrested in South Waziristan by the Tribal Agency there after he had compiled a report on a tribal leader charged with drugs offences who had escaped from detention, was sentenced to 16 years' imprisonment in October; however, he was released in mid-November. Afzal Afzaal was released from a jail in a tribal area in October after two weeks of a three-year sentence when he reportedly paid a large sum of money to the local tribal area authorities and undertook not to report "false news stories".

G.M. Syed, a possible prisoner of conscience, continued to remain under house arrest on sedition charges (see *Amnesty International Report 1993*).

Over 200 possible prisoners of conscience were among hundreds of people arbitrarily arrested during army operations in Sindh. Most were supporters of the *Mohajir Qaumi Mahaz* (MQM), Mohajir National Movement. Dozens of them were reportedly detained solely because they were relatives of MQM activists being sought by the authorities. Many of those detained were tortured to extract information or to force them to change their political allegiance. Many were held in secret detention without charge or trial for up to six months. In March *Radio Pakistan* reported a government decision to withdraw charges against 835 detainees. By the end of the year it was not known if any of them had been released.

At least two cases of unacknowledged detention were reported, but the actual number was believed to be much higher. In January, four police officers were arrested after an inquiry confirmed that they had kept two men and five women in unacknowledged detention and tortured them at Gulshan-i-Iqbal police station in Karachi.

Torture in the custody of the police, the paramilitary and the armed forces continued to be widespread and systematic, frequently leading to deaths. Scores of victims included political prisoners, criminal suspects and ordinary citizens from whom the police wanted to extract bribes.

Police arrested dozens of women reportedly to rape them. Those resisting rape were reportedly charged with the Islamic offence of *Zina* (adultery) under which release on bail is not permitted. As the law does not provide effective safeguards against the arbitrary use of this charge by the police, scores of women, some of whom had been detained in previous years, remained in jail pending a judicial hearing of the *Zina* cases against them. Also detained were women who had gone to the police to report incidents of rape, but were then held in custody on grounds of confession to illegal sexual intercourse.

Few police officers accused of rape were brought to trial. However, three police officers at Tando Ghulam Haider in Hyderabad district, Sindh Province, were each sentenced to 10 years' imprisonment and 10 lashes for arresting eight members of the Bheel tribe in October 1992 and raping the women. However, they were subsequently acquitted by the Supreme Appellate Court on technical grounds.

Bonded labourers were reportedly tortured with police complicity in hundreds of private camps run by rural landlords or factory owners. A camp was discovered in March when two women escaped after 16 years of incarceration, reporting torture and ill-treatment of the inmates and gang-rapes of several women.

Sentences of flogging were reportedly delivered in at least 12 cases: nine men were sentenced for sexual offences and three men for drugs offences. When hearing appeals filed in previous years, the Supreme Court increased two men's sentences from 10 to 30 lashes and the Federal Shari'a Court, hearing appeals within its Islamic jurisdiction, acquitted one man but upheld sentences of 10 and 50 lashes on two other men. Two men were reportedly flogged in September in the tribal areas. Each received five lashes after a tribal court convicted them of drug-smuggling. They had no right of appeal.

A man reportedly detained in bar fetters in Hyderabad Central Jail for eight years without trial was released in July by a High Court order. It was not known if the authorities took any action against those responsible for his illegal detention and ill-treatment.

In January a man and a woman who had reportedly stolen money from a hospital fund received sentences of amputation of a hand from a Special Court for Speedy Trial in Multan, Punjab. Their appeal before a higher court remained pending.

Over a dozen deaths were reported which the authorities alleged were "encounter" killings but which appeared to be deaths after torture or extrajudicial executions. Nazir Masih, a Christian, died in May in Faisalabad, Punjab, after police reportedly beat him for refusing to give them alcohol. In July a young handicapped man arrested with several other villagers in Mirpur Khas, Sindh, was reportedly tortured to death when he failed to pay a bribe the police demanded for his release.

No members of the security forces involved in the killings were brought to justice. In most cases, the police refused to register a 'First Information Report' – on the basis of which an official investigation is carried out – by the victim's family.

New information was received about a "disappearance" which had occurred in November 1991. Allah Rakhio, a customs inspector, had "disappeared" after being detained by the army. No government action was known to have been taken to establish his fate or whereabouts.

Following the apparent "disappearance" of a young man arrested as a criminal suspect, the Lahore High Court ruled in March that a police officer at Phalia police station, Lahore, should be brought to justice. A bailiff instructed by the court to search the police officer's private residence found the prisoner detained there. An official investigation was promised but was not carried out.

In May the government informed Amnesty International that following a court order, a case had been registered against the station house officer accused of the extrajudicial execution of Mohammed Yusuf Jakhrani after his arrest during a police and military operation in June 1992 in Kandhkot, Sindh (see *Amnesty International Report 1993*). However, no investigation was known to have taken place. In three other cases the government reportedly undertook to investigate police and military involvement in allegedly unlawful killings, but no investigation was known to have been carried out.

The courts imposed 57 death sentences during the year. Special Courts for the Suppression of Terrorist Activities sentenced 22 men to death for murder or kidnapping; Special Courts for Speedy Trial sentenced 18 people to death for murder or rape; and ordinary lower courts sentenced 14 people to death for murder, blasphemy or sexual offences. In February a lower court sentenced Nasrin Bibi to death by stoning for alleged bigamy. She remained in jail until July when the Federal Shari'a Court acquitted her.

Appeal courts acquitted eight prisoners sentenced to death by lower courts and commuted three other death sentences to life imprisonment. The Supreme Appellate Court commuted another two sentences to life imprisonment and imposed the death penalty on two men acquitted of a murder charge by a lower court. In February the Sindh High Court ordered the suspension of a planned execution of a man whose appeal was still pending. At the end of the year, several hundred prisoners remained under sentence of death.

No death sentences upheld by the Supreme Court were reported to have been commuted by the President. In September, one man was hanged in Quetta. Dozens more prisoners were reportedly awaiting execution in various prisons, including 15 women in Multan Jail, Punjab.

In January Amnesty International published a report, *Pakistan: Arrest and torture of political activists*, in which it expressed concern about the mass arrests of PPP activists in November and December 1992. In August the organization expressed concern about the detention of Salamat Masih and two other Christians on charges of blasphemy, and in June Amnesty International urged the government to investigate the "disappearance" of Allah Rakhio and clarify his whereabouts. In September Amnesty International welcomed the decision of the interim government to establish a National Human Rights Commission but recommended an extensive review of

234

existing institutions for more effective human rights protection. It also called upon all the political parties running for election to make clear their commitment to the protection of human rights. In November Amnesty International urged the government to release Sailab Mahsud. An Amnesty International report published in December, *Pakistan: Torture, deaths in custody and extrajudicial executions*, revealed a pattern of widespread and systematic torture, including rape, in custody. Amnesty International urged the new government to investigate past torture cases, and to enforce safeguards against the use of torture.

PANAMA

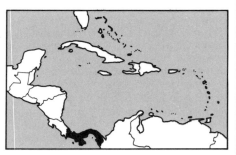

A political party leader whose detention was alleged to be politically motivated remained imprisoned. There were reports of ill-treatment by the police of protesters and detainees. A number of security force personnel were convicted of human rights abuses carried out under previous administrations.

In the run-up to the first elections since the US invasion, scheduled for May 1994, there were widespread allegations of corruption and improper use of the courts to undermine political opponents. In response, and in an attempt to assure a fair and free electoral context, Panama's political parties entered into a pact, undertaking to refrain from using the courts and other institutions as mechanisms for persecution or repression and to avoid violence and intimidation in the lead-up to the elections.

Controversy continued as to the identities, numbers and manner of death of those who lost their lives during the US invasion in 1989. The USA has repeatedly said that a relatively low number of civilian casualties were caused inadvertently when US troops

were trying to take control of or neutralize military targets. However, some human rights groups in Panama and abroad claim that civilian areas considered supportive of Panama's then *de facto* leader, Defence Forces Chief Manuel Noriega, were intentionally targeted during the invasion, that many non-combatants died, and that they were buried in unmarked graves in order to obscure their identities and numbers. In October the Inter-American Commission on Human Rights of the Organization of American States decided to admit petitions filed on behalf of some 300 Panamanians seeking compensation from the USA for non-combatant deaths and injuries and property damage which they said were caused by US troops during the invasion.

In January Panama acceded to the Second Optional Protocol to the International Covenant on Civil and Political Rights, aiming at the abolition of the death penalty.

After being held in untried preventive detention for a period far exceeding the standard penalty of six months to a year provided for the fraud with which he had been charged, Jaime Simons was eventually transferred to house arrest in December on grounds of ill-health (he suffers from prostate cancer). A founder member of Manuel Noriega's political party, Jaime Simons had been arrested by US forces in 1989. Trial proceedings against him were finally initiated in his absence – he was judged too ill to attend – on 13 December, but suspended the following day to allow the authorities to carry out further inquiries. There were allegations – which were difficult to assess – that his continued detention and the authorities' long refusal to transfer him to house arrest had been politically motivated (see *Amnesty International Report 1993*).

Three leaders of the so-called Dignity Battalions, a disbanded paramilitary group allegedly responsible for human rights violations under Manuel Noriega's government, were released in September after serving almost four years in prison on charges of having "threatened the legal personality of the state" (see *Amnesty International Reports 1992* and *1993*).

Police allegedly used excessive force in breaking up peaceful demonstrations by trade unionists, families of victims of the US invasion, and indigenous peoples, leading to a number of injuries and one known death. In May a member of the Ngob-Buglé indigenous group died from his injuries after police in Chiriquí province forcibly dispersed indigenous demonstrators calling for complete demarcation of indigenous lands. Investigations into the killing had apparently not been completed by the end of 1993.

In June former President Manuel Solís Palma, and four former military officials, were found guilty of having established the so-called Dignity Battalions. It was not clear whether all were present for their trial or whether they had been formally sentenced and jailed by the end of the year. Also in June the courts made the first award to victims of human rights abuses during Panama's two decades of military rule, ruling that the Panamanian Government should pay damages to demonstrators beaten in 1984 by the police.

In October Panamanian magistrates sentenced Manuel Noriega and two others to 20 years' imprisonment for the 1985 torture, murder and beheading of an outspoken opponent of his administration, Hugo Spadafora (see *Amnesty International Reports 1986, 1988, 1990* and *1991*). Seven others were acquitted. Manuel Noriega, who was serving a lengthy jail sentence in the USA for drug-trafficking and money-laundering, was sentenced *in absentia*. The courts also ruled that Manuel Noriega was to be tried *in absentia* for the summary execution of a rebel army major who had led a 1989 coup attempt against him (see *Amnesty International Report 1990*).

In November, three officers of the Panamanian National Guard were found guilty of murdering Colombian priest Hector Gallego. He had "disappeared" in Veraguas province in 1971 after being arrested by the National Guard, commanded at that time by Panama's then ruler, General Omar Torrijos. The three convicted officers had apparently not been sentenced by the end of the year.

PAPUA NEW GUINEA

Dozens of suspected supporters of an armed secessionist group on Bougainville Island were extrajudicially executed by government forces, some after being tortured, and at least 11 reportedly "disappeared". Torture and ill-treatment continued to be reported throughout the country. Serious human rights abuses were reportedly committed by the secessionist group on Bougainville.

Armed conflict on Bougainville continued between the Papua New Guinea Defence Forces (PNGDF) and the secessionist Bougainville Revolutionary Army (BRA). In February government troops entered the provincial capital, Arawa, and Prime Minister Paias Wingti called for the unconditional surrender of Bougainville rebels. Despite an agreement to restore essential services to Bougainville, delivery of food and medicine to the island continued to be obstructed by the PNGDF.

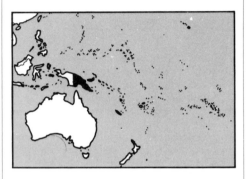

In May an Internal Security Act was passed by parliament. The Act grants the Head of State power to order the arrest of members of organizations deemed to "support terrorism" and gives the security forces extra powers to arrest without warrant and detain suspects without charge for up to 20 days. Faced with mounting criticism on human rights grounds, the Prime Minister agreed to review the Act in October. The government proposed an amendment to the Constitution which would reverse the legal presumption of innocence, but this had not been enacted by the end of the year.

Dozens of suspected BRA supporters were extrajudicially executed by government troops on Bougainville, some after being tortured. In January, six men, including Rodney Soguwan and Alex Solomon, were shot dead in cold blood when government troops intercepted their boat off Bougainville, according to a seventh man, Moresi Tua, who was shot and wounded but managed to escape. He said the soldiers, who were in a patrol boat, shot one man dead and then shot the others when they jumped into the sea to try and escape.

In late January Ellen Divai was killed by a mortar bomb fired by the PNGDF, which also injured eight other people travelling in a truck towards Arawa township. There was apparently no official investigation into the incident.

Ken Savia, a leading member of the independence movement in Bougainville, reportedly "disappeared" after being seized by government troops who raided Arawa General Hospital on 13 February. Eye-witnesses said that the following day he was seen tied to the back of a military truck and being dragged along the road. Ken Savia was subsequently reported to have been killed by government soldiers. Ten other people, including a nine-year-old girl and a three-month old baby and their mother reportedly "disappeared" after being seized by troops at the hospital during the raid. The government failed to provide any information about the "disappearance" of Ken Savia and the other 10 people.

In January and September the government stated its commitment to pay compensation for the killing of two Solomon Islanders, Jacinta Popo and Peter Kamaraia, during a raid by government troops in 1992 (see *Amnesty International Report 1993*).

Torture and ill-treatment by the security forces continued to be reported on Bougainville and in other parts of Papua New Guinea. Suspected BRA supporters were the principal victims on Bougainville. On mainland Papua New Guinea, the main victims were villagers involved in disputes over logging operations, and criminal suspects.

On Bougainville, staff and patients from the Arawa Hospital were reportedly seized by PNG soldiers and beaten after government troops raided the hospital in February. In September a girl from Luagua village in South Bougainville was reportedly raped in public by a government soldier.

On the mainland, at least three incidents of ill-treatment and harassment reportedly occurred in Morobe province. Inhabitants of Kaiapit village said that police from Goroka entered the village in January, lined up young men and threatened to "blow them up", fired their weapons, pushed gun barrels into the mouths of those who protested, and beat others with gun butts and barrels. The Eastern Highlands Police Commissioner said he would conduct a full investigation into the incident, but it was not known whether this had taken place by the end of the year.

Vere Tau, a probation officer at Gabagaba village in Central province, alleged that he was beaten in Boroko police station in February. He said he was punched on the face, kicked and beaten with a baton. He was charged with insulting a police officer, a charge later dismissed at the district court. There was no known official investigation into the allegations of ill-treatment.

In June police in the capital, Port Moresby, reportedly arrested and beat three people from Bougainville, whom they accused of being BRA supporters. There were apparently no grounds for the allegations against the men, who were then charged with driving under the influence of alcohol.

In September a police riot squad reportedly detained Gewai Dusty Zamunu, a village leader and environmental activist in Morobe province, interrogated him about his opposition to a logging operation in Sowara village, and severely beat him. He was released after he appeared before a magistrate on 20 September.

The BRA was responsible for human rights abuses on Bougainville. BRA members reportedly assaulted and raped civilians and subjected others to death threats. Amnesty International condemned these abuses and called upon the BRA to respect human rights and basic international humanitarian standards.

In June Amnesty International representatives met the Minister of State for Bougainville to discuss the human rights situation on Bougainville.

In November Amnesty International published a report, *Papua New Guinea: "Under the Barrel of a Gun" – civil conflict and human rights on Bougainville, 1991 to 1993*. It described a pattern of extrajudicial execution, torture and other violations by the PNGDF on Bougainville. The report also documented serious human rights abuses by the BRA. It urged the government to initiate thorough and impartial investigations into human rights violations in Bougainville, and to bring suspected perpetrators to justice.

Amnesty International also urged the government to permit direct access to Bougainville by international human rights and legal organizations to monitor human rights.

PARAGUAY

Torture and ill-treatment of criminal suspects, including juveniles, by the police continued to be reported. An army colonel was imprisoned briefly for denouncing corrupt practices by senior army commanders. Important new evidence emerged about the torture, killing and "disappearance" of political prisoners during the past administration of General Alfredo Stroessner.

In May presidential and congressional elections were held. Juan Carlos Wasmosy of the ruling Colorado Party was elected the country's first civilian president since 1954. International observers criticized military intervention in the electoral process after a senior army commander said the armed forces would not accept an opposition victory. In his inaugural speech, President Wasmosy pledged his government to respect human rights.

In January Paraguay accepted the jurisdiction of the Inter-American Court of Human Rights.

New reports were received of torture and ill-treatment in police stations and detention centres. The victims included children and other young people. In April, 16-year-old Blas Américo Villalba, who was accused of armed robbery, testified before an investigating judge that he had signed a confession under torture. He said he had been arrested in March and taken to the police Intelligence Department where he was beaten and kicked in the stomach. He also alleged that plastic bags had been placed over his head while he was given electric shocks, and that he had been threatened with death. His co-defendant, 19-year-old Luis Ferreira Martínez, told the

investigating judge that he had been taken by three police officers to a wooded area on the outskirts of Asunción where he was tortured and threatened with death. In June Blas Américo Villalba died of wounds received in what police described as an armed confrontation after he had escaped from a juvenile detention centre. Judicial authorities failed to conduct thorough investigations into these and other allegations of torture and continued to accept as evidence confessions allegedly made under duress.

Army Colonel Luis Catalino González Rojas was rearrested in January and held in the military prison of Peña Hermosa in the Chaco region. Colonel González had been arrested in September 1992 after opening investigations into corruption within the armed forces and provisionally released in October pending the military court's verdict (see *Amnesty International Report 1993*). In January the Supreme Military Court acquitted him of charges of defamation and slander but sentenced him to 90 days' "disciplinary arrest" for having publicly denounced the involvement of his superiors in corrupt practices. He was released in February, before the expiry of his sentence.

Judicial investigations into torture and deaths in custody of political prisoners under General Stroessner's administration continued, despite efforts by alleged perpetrators to block the trials. In May the Supreme Court of Justice rejected a petition presented by defence lawyers acting for Pastor Coronel, the former head of the *Departamento de Investigaciones de la Policía* (DIP-C), Police Investigations Department. The petition argued that charges against Pastor Coronel for the torture of opposition activist Bienvenido Cáceres in 1982 should be dropped because the statute of limitations had expired. The Supreme Court confirmed the Appeal Court's ruling that the statute of limitations should only apply from the day that General Stroessner was overthrown in February 1989.

Detailed evidence substantiating allegations of widespread human rights violations by the military and police during the period of General Stroessner's rule (1954 to 1989) continued to emerge from police records confiscated by judicial officials in December 1992. The confiscated archive material included meticulous records of

238

the arrest, torture and murder of political prisoners. It also showed that the police had continued to monitor the activities of opposition leaders after General Stroessner was overthrown in 1989. Further archive material was uncovered in early 1993 from other branches of the security services, including the Interior Ministry's Technical Office for the Repression of Communism, which again provided evidence of human rights violations. Arrest warrants were issued against the senior officers of the Technical Office, but they had not been detained by the end of the year. Under provisions of the 1992 Constitution, relatives of "disappeared" prisoners and victims of torture gained access to the security services' records. The information acquired was used to substantiate formal charges against leading members of the former Stroessner administration.

In May a criminal court judge ruled that former President Stroessner, who remained in exile in Brazil, was in contempt of court for deliberately failing to appear before the court to answer charges relating to the deaths in custody of brothers Rodolfo and Benjamín de Jesús Ramírez Villalba. The brothers were detained in 1974 and accused of plotting to assassinate General Stroessner. They were severely tortured and held chained and incommunicado in the DIP-C for 22 months. Both were believed to have been killed by DIP-C officials in 1976, although their bodies were never found. In November the criminal court judge investigating the "disappearance" of the Villalba brothers sought the extradition of General Stroessner from Brazil.

The archive material also provided proof of collaboration between the military governments of Paraguay, Uruguay, Argentina, Chile and Brazil during operations to combat "subversion" in the 1970s and 1980s. In March relatives of Gustavo Edison Inzaurralde Melgar and Nelson Santana Escotto, both Uruguayans, presented a formal criminal complaint against Paraguayan, Argentine and Uruguayan security officials for the illegal detention, torture and kidnapping of the two men in 1977. DIP-C documents showed that both men had been arrested in Asunción in March 1977 on suspicion of membership of an illegal left-wing organization. In May 1977 the prisoners were handed over to Uruguayan and Argentine army intelligence officers who secretly took them to

Argentina. Their whereabouts remain unknown. The criminal court judge issued arrest warrants against several former high-ranking Paraguayan police and military officers in connection with the arrest, torture and "disappearance" of the two men and summoned the Argentine and Uruguayan intelligence officials to testify. However, they failed to appear.

Amnesty International called for the release of Colonel González Rojas. The organization continued to call on the government to set up independent investigations into allegations of torture and to ensure that past human rights violations were thoroughly and impartially investigated.

PERU

At least 4,000 political prisoners, including some 200 prisoners of conscience and possible prisoners of conscience, awaited trial or were tried under judicial procedures which fell short of international standards. Forty-nine people "disappeared" and 27 were extrajudicially executed. Torture was frequently reported. The authorities failed to clarify thousands of past cases of human rights violations. The scope of the death penalty was widened. The armed opposition continued to commit widespread abuses, including torture, deliberate and arbitrary killings and hostage-taking.

The clandestine *Partido Comunista del Perú (Sendero Luminoso)* (PCP), Communist Party of Peru (Shining Path), and *Movimiento Revolucionario Túpac Amaru* (MRTA), Túpac Amaru Revolutionary Movement, continued to commit widespread armed attacks, although these diminished in number following government counter-insurgency successes. Imprisoned leaders of the PCP, including its president, Abimael Guzmán, reportedly wrote to President Alberto Fujimori in September and October requesting talks leading to a "peace accord"; the President rejected the requests. Active sectors of the PCP subsequently indicated that the armed campaign would continue.

In January the newly elected *Congreso Constituyente Democrático* (CCD), Democratic Constituent Congress, commenced work, following the suspension of constitutional rule in April 1992. It was charged with drafting a new Constitution. The CCD immediately passed a resolution stating that all decree laws issued during 1992, including anti-terrorism decrees, would remain in effect until they were revised or revoked by Congress.

Also in January, the CCD established a *Comisión de Derechos Humanos y Pacificación*, Human Rights and Pacification Commission, to investigate alleged human rights violations. The Commission, which received complaints of hundreds of human rights violations, publicly appealed to the judicial authorities to investigate them.

In November the CCD amended existing anti-terrorism legislation to allow writs of *habeas corpus* to be filed before the courts, repealed provision for the accused to be tried *in absentia* and permitted lawyers to represent more than one defendant at a time. However, procedures retained in the legislation still fell short of international standards.

In March the government renewed agreements with the International Committee of the Red Cross allowing it access to all prisons administered by the Ministry of Justice (see *Amnesty International Report 1993*).

The new Constitution, which came into effect in December, upheld the right to life although it extended the scope of the death penalty to include the crime of "terrorism". This extension violated the American Convention on Human Rights, ratified by Peru in 1978, which requires that states do not extend the scope of the death penalty. The Constitution also made provision for military courts to try civilians accused of "treason and terrorism".

In May dissident army general Rodolfo Robles alleged in a signed statement that a "death squad" existed within the army's intelligence services. He accused the squad of responsibility for the massacre in Lima, the capital, of 14 people in November 1991 (see *Amnesty International Report 1992*) and the killing of a lecturer and nine students abducted in July 1992 from La Cantuta University (see below). President Fujimori acknowledged to journalists in July that a "death squad" possibly continued to operate within the security forces, but no investigation into the allegation was known to have been initiated.

In November the UN Special Rapporteur on extrajudicial, summary or arbitrary executions published a report on Peru which strongly criticized the government for its failure to investigate and bring to justice those responsible for gross human rights violations.

Some 200 prisoners of conscience and possible prisoners of conscience were believed to be held at the end of the year. All were detained on terrorism-related charges which appeared to be politically motivated. The majority had not been brought to trial.

In May Rómulo Mori Zavaleta, an active member of the *Partido Unificado Mariateguista*, a legally registered left-wing political party, and his nephew, Wagner Cruz Mori, were each sentenced to 20 years' imprisonment. Both were convicted of assisting an MRTA member to find a doctor to treat an injured colleague. They were prisoners of conscience.

Several prisoners of conscience were freed. They included Magno Sosa Rojas, a journalist, who was freed in February after five months' imprisonment (see *Amnesty International Reports 1992* and *1993*). In March, 11 members of a peasant organization from San Ignacio, Cajamarca department, were released after eight months in prison.

At least 2,000 prisoners charged with "terrorism" remained held with no sign as to when judicial procedures in their cases would begin – ostensibly because of lack of resources on the part of the authorities. Many of them had been charged before new trial procedures were introduced in May 1992. In 1992 and 1993 hundreds of other prisoners were brought before secret civilian and military courts under procedures which fell far short of international standards. For example, the lawyer representing Dr Luis William Polo Rivera, accused of being a leading PCP member, had reportedly been given access to his client only once – for 10 minutes in November 1992 – before trial. In January the secret military appeal tribunal confirmed Dr Polo's life sentence and reportedly refused his lawyer access to the evidence on which he had been convicted.

In May a civilian lower court judge examined the case of Juan José Cholán Ramírez, a prisoner of conscience who was accused by the army of having links with the MRTA. The judge reportedly concluded that army personnel had obtained his confession under torture, that police had refused him access to a lawyer, and that there was insufficient evidence on which to prosecute him. Despite these conclusions, and in compliance with the law which requires all terrorism-related cases to be heard by a secret high court, the judge sent Juan José Cholán for trial before the Chiclayo High Court.

"Disappearances" and extrajudicial executions continued to be committed by the security forces, although on a lesser scale than in previous years. Forty-nine "disappearances" reported during the year remained unclarified. For example, two students, Rony Guerra Blancas and Milagros Flor Túpac González, reportedly "disappeared" on 10 and 11 February respectively after their abduction in the city of Huancayo, Junín department, by civilians believed to be linked to the army. Justiniano Najarro Rua "disappeared" in July after he and his 14-year-old nephew were detained in San Juan de Miraflores, Lima, by two armed men who identified themselves as police. Both were driven to an unknown destination from where the nephew was subsequently released. Almost without exception, *habeas corpus* petitions filed in favour of these and other victims of "disappearance" were rejected by the courts on the grounds that the security forces denied their detention.

Some progress was made in the investigations into the "disappearance" of a lecturer and nine students from La Cantuta University in July 1992 (see above and *Amnesty International Report 1993*). In April a congressional commission and the military justice system both opened separate investigations into the case. In June Congress rejected a majority report of the commission, which found the army responsible for the "disappearances", adopting instead the minority report which absolved the army. In

July and November unmarked graves containing remains of the "disappeared" victims were discovered near Lima. Following excavations ordered by the Public Ministry, keys and clothing retrieved from the graves were identified by relatives of the victims. In December the Minister of Defence announced that the military investigator into the case had ordered the arrest of at least four implicated officers; and a civilian prosecutor filed charges of kidnapping, enforced disappearance and aggravated homicide against 11 officers. However, by the end of the year it was not clear whether those responsible would be brought to trial before a military or civilian court.

Twenty-seven people were reported to have been extrajudicially executed by the security forces. On 21 August, four hooded and heavily armed men, two of them in police uniform, reportedly detained Teófilo Núñez Quispe in Huancan district, Junín department, and took him to an unknown destination. Two days later his body was found in the nearby city of Huancayo.

Ten settlers, among them three boys, were reported to have been extrajudicially executed on 10 September in Delta, Chanchamayo province, Junín department, by members of a civil defence patrol linked to the army. The victims were said to have been hacked to death with machetes and axes. Thirteen members of the patrol identified by witnesses were detained by the police, but nine were subsequently released by an examining judge.

Members of the security forces were convicted for illegal killings in three cases following international pressure to bring those responsible to justice. However, in the vast majority of alleged extrajudicial executions the perpetrators were not brought to justice. In February the Supreme Council of Military Justice upheld the 10-year term of imprisonment imposed on army lieutenant Javier Bendezú Vargas in connection with the massacre of 15 peasants in Santa Bárbara in July 1991, but acquitted him of aggravated homicide. Two soldiers implicated in the massacre and convicted of rape, aggravated homicide and abuse of authority, had their convictions quashed (see *Amnesty International Reports 1992* and *1993*).

In March the Supreme Council of Military Justice upheld the six-year prison sentence imposed on former lieutenant Telmo Hurtado for the massacre of 69 peasants in

Accomarca in August 1985 (see *Amnesty International Reports 1986, 1990* and *1993*).

In November, three police officers were each sentenced by a civilian court to 18 years' imprisonment, and two others to five and six years' imprisonment respectively, for the unlawful killing of brothers Rafael and Emilio Gómez Paquiyauri and student Freddy Rodríguez Pighi in June 1991 (see *Amnesty International Report 1992*). Three other officers accused of having been directly implicated in the killings were acquitted. The five who were convicted appealed against their convictions but their cases had not been heard by the end of the year.

Torture and ill-treatment were frequently reported. In March the bodies of Alberto Calipuy Valverde and Rosenda Yauri Ramos were found in Angasmarca district, Santiago de Chuco province, La Libertad department. The military reportedly acknowledged that both had died as a result of ill-treatment in the Angasmarca military base. A judicial investigation was reportedly opened into the case by a military court, but nobody had been brought to trial by the end of the year.

Juan Abelardo Mallea Tomailla, a prisoner of conscience, was reportedly tortured on 21 July by members of DINCOTE, the anti-terrorism branch of the Peruvian National Police, and forced to sign a self-incriminating document. He had been arrested in Lima on 10 July, on suspicion of having links with the PCP.

Hundreds of civilians were deliberately and arbitrarily killed by the PCP, many of whom were first tortured and ill-treated. Members of the security forces who surrendered or were otherwise *hors de combat* suffered the same fate. On 18 August the PCP detained and hacked to death at least 62 men, women and children in the province of Satipo, Junín department. The PCP accused the indigenous communities of setting up army-controlled civil defence patrols. Herminia Barboza Oré, a community leader in the neighbourhood of Cruz de Mopute, San Juan de Lurigancho, Lima, was reportedly shot dead in her home by the PCP on 21 August.

The MRTA also committed human rights abuses, although on a lesser scale. In February the body of David Ballón Vera, a businessman who had reportedly been held hostage for five months by the MRTA, was found with two bullet wounds in his head and bearing signs of torture.

Amnesty International appealed to the authorities to investigate thoroughly and impartially the thousands of cases of human rights violations perpetrated since early 1983. With few exceptions the authorities failed to bring to justice those responsible.

In January and June Amnesty International urged the President and members of Congress not to widen the scope of the death penalty and appealed for its abolition in the new Constitution. In February the organization submitted to Congress recommendations for the protection of human rights to be incorporated in the new Constitution.

In May Amnesty International published a report, *Peru: Human rights since the suspension of constitutional government*, which detailed extensive human rights abuses by the government and the PCP and MRTA. The organization urged the government to end human rights violations and bring anti-terrorism legislation into line with international standards.

Amnesty International condemned deliberate and arbitrary killings and other abuses by the armed opposition and urged such forces to respect human rights and basic humanitarian standards.

Amnesty International urged President Fujimori to ensure that allegations of extrajudicial executions made by dissident army general Rodolfo Robles were the subject of a full, impartial and independent public inquiry.

In oral statements to the UN Commission on Human Rights in February and to its Sub-Commission on Prevention of Discrimination and Protection of Minorities in August, Amnesty International included reference to its concerns in Peru. In March Amnesty International submitted information about its concerns regarding torture in Peru to the UN Committee against Torture, pursuant to Article 20 of the UN Convention against Torture. In April Amnesty International submitted information about its concerns in Peru for UN review under a procedure established by Economic and Social Council Resolutions 728F/1503, for confidential consideration of communications about human rights violations.

242

PHILIPPINES

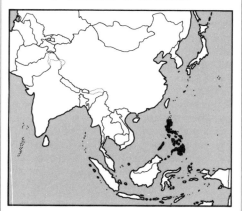

At least 65 people were reported to have been extrajudicially executed and at least 14 people reportedly "disappeared" in police or military custody. Some political prisoners were released, but more than 300 remained in prison, among them possible prisoners of conscience, and there were new arrests. Some of those detained were reported to have been tortured or ill-treated. Legislation restoring the death penalty was signed into law in December.

The government continued to face armed opposition from the communist New People's Army (NPA), the Moro National Liberation Front (MNLF), and other groups seeking independence for predominantly Muslim areas of Mindanao. Armed opposition groups committed grave human rights abuses, including deliberate and arbitrary killings and hostage-taking.

Despite a stated commitment to peace by both parties, talks between the government and the National Democratic Front, an umbrella opposition organization including the NPA, were repeatedly stalled over the question of venue and no talks had been held by the end of the year. The government held talks with MNLF leaders in October and these resulted in a provisional cease-fire.

In September the chief of the armed forces said that military counter-insurgency activities would be stepped up and the government announced that responsibility for the counter-insurgency campaign would not be handed over to the Philippine National Police (PNP), formally under civilian authority, until the end of 1994.

The official militia, the Citizen Armed Force Geographical Unit (CAFGU), engaged in counter-insurgency operations and continued to recruit members from unofficial vigilante groups. CAFGU members were implicated in numerous reports of extrajudicial killing and other human rights violations. Despite mounting national and international pressure for the CAFGU to be dismantled, President Fidel Ramos said in June that the CAFGU was still needed in "critical areas" where the NPA remained active. In October the President approved an armed forces proposal to demobilize 11,000 CAFGU members over the next two years.

In February President Ramos issued Administrative Order 40, specifying that military or police commanders would be held responsible for disciplinary or criminal offences by their subordinates. The order states that security force members accused of criminal offences must be immediately discharged from service and the case referred to a civilian court. Nevertheless, effective investigation of alleged human rights violations and related prosecutions continued to be obstructed by the security forces. This included intimidation of judges, lawyers, witnesses and complainants; and refusal of access to information, personnel and military premises. In April church leaders publicly protested that a police officer convicted in August 1992 of murdering Domingo Peralta, a farmer, and his three children, remained at large. The officer, who was sentenced to double life imprisonment, was allegedly being protected by police officials.

Investigations by the official Commission on Human Rights (CHR) continued to be impeded by cumbersome and lengthy procedures, and by the CHR's practice of placing the burden of proof on complainants, despite the risk of reprisals or their lack of resources.

At least 65 people were victims of apparent extrajudicial execution by government and government-backed forces. Among those killed were members of farmers' and peasants' organizations, and human rights advocates. Environmental activists and members of tribal communities were particularly targeted.

In the heavily militarized regions of northern Luzon, several people were reported to have been extrajudicially executed, including 18-year-old Boy Gonzalez in June and Jovito Tuldog in September. Both men were residents of Calabigan, Kalinga-Apayao, and were reportedly killed while in the custody of the 50th Infantry Battalion of the Philippine Army. Jovito Tuldog was stabbed and his body bore marks of torture. He was shot in the face at point-blank range.

Chris Batan, a human rights worker and tribal activist, was shot dead in February in Sadanga, Mountain province, also in northern Luzon. Eye-witnesses identified the killers as members of a local CAFGU unit and filed a complaint with the provincial prosecutor. By September two of the suspected perpetrators were held under "technical arrest" in Tococan, Bontoc Province, but no court proceedings had been initiated. One of the suspects was, however, released in December. In Butuan City on the southern island of Mindanao, another tribal activist, William Rom, was hacked to death with machetes in July by armed men also identified as CAFGU members.

Harassment, including death threats, beatings and interrogation by military and military-backed forces, was widespread. The victims included human rights advocates and others critical of government policy. In June Sonny Boy de la Peña and Edwina Bodozo Joromo, both peasant organizers in Cebu, received death threats they believed were sent by CAFGU members. In July the two reported being fired at by CAFGU members; they subsequently left their homes in fear of their lives.

Clovis Nazareno, a journalist in Bohol province whose writings are frequently critical of government policies, was subjected to threats and ill-treatment by military and police officials. In June he filed a complaint with the provincial prosecutor after being beaten by a police officer. The complaint was dismissed in July after witnesses failed to testify, reportedly for fear of violent reprisals.

At least 14 people reportedly "disappeared" after being abducted by government or government-backed security forces. Among them was Romeo Legaspi, a journalist and publisher in Olangapo City, Zambales province. He was abducted in January by armed men believed to be linked to the police force. Romeo Legaspi had previously been threatened by local police, about whom he had written a critical article in a local newspaper. A *habeas corpus* petition was filed with the Supreme Court, but the fate and whereabouts of

Romeo Legaspi remained unknown at the end of the year. Three others, Andrea Basabe Espra, Teofanes Areja and Cresencio Caburnay, who "disappeared" in February, were found in April in the custody of the PNP in Bogo, Cebu.

An estimated 350 political prisoners, including possible prisoners of conscience, remained in detention. Most were accused of supporting the armed opposition and charged with illegal possession of firearms or other criminal offences. Among the possible prisoners of conscience was Leonardo Belleza. A former prisoner of conscience, he was released on 15 January and rearrested on 22 January in Leyte province on a murder charge. It appeared that the real reason for his arrest, however, was his human rights activism. Leonardo Belleza was one of a group of farmers from Leyte who were charged with rebellion in 1988 after publicizing human rights violations (see previous *Amnesty International Reports*). Another possible prisoner of conscience was Divine Grace Castillon, daughter of a peasant organizer, who remained in detention more than three years after being arrested without warrant by soldiers in Lapu-lapu City, Cebu, in October 1990. She was accused of belonging to an NPA assassination squad and charged with robbery with homicide but no date had apparently been set for her trial.

Jaime Tadeo, a possible prisoner of conscience, was released on parole in August 1993, after more than three years in prison. Chairman of the Peasant Movement of the Philippines, he had been convicted in 1987 on a charge of misappropriation of funds originally brought against him under the administration of former President Ferdinand Marcos. He had been taken into custody in May 1990. Jaime Tadeo had been an outspoken critic of government policy and had been threatened by men believed to be linked to the security forces a day before his arrest.

There were new reports of torture or ill-treatment of political detainees. Suspected NPA sympathizers in rural areas were beaten after being apprehended by soldiers or paramilitaries at their homes or while working in their fields. In August Emily Absalon, the 13-year-old daughter of a suspected NPA member, was reportedly raped by two CAFGU members in Rizal, Occidental Mindoro. The suspected perpetrators were subsequently arrested and remained in

244

detention at the end of the year pending a court hearing.

The death penalty, abolished by the 1987 Constitution, was restored in December. The legislation provided for capital punishment for "heinous crimes", including murder, drug-trafficking, kidnapping or serious illegal detention, rape and arson.

Deliberate and arbitrary killings of civilians by NPA members continued to be reported. The victims included five men in Negros Occidental province, who were reportedly shot in front of their families in May.

In August an NPA representative in the Manila area said that NPA "hit squads" would execute up to 10 known criminals and kidnap others in the ensuing months, although it was not known whether the plan was implemented.

In Mindanao, MNLF separatists were allegedly responsible for bomb attacks in several cities, including Zamboanga and Cagayan de Oro, resulting in dozens of people being injured. The MNLF also claimed responsibility for taking 22 people hostage for two weeks on Basilan Island in August.

Throughout the year, Amnesty International appealed to the government to conduct independent and impartial investigations into all reports of extrajudicial executions and "disappearances" and called for those responsible for such abuses to be brought to justice.

Amnesty International called for the release of all prisoners of conscience and for all other political prisoners to be tried promptly and fairly, or released. It urged the government to dismantle militia forces widely alleged to be responsible for human rights violations and to prohibit the use of vigilante groups in counter-insurgency operations. It appealed to the government and to members of Congress not to reinstate the death penalty.

Amnesty International condemned hostage-taking and deliberate and arbitrary killings by armed opposition groups and called for them to cease such abuses and respect basic humane standards as required by international law.

In an oral statement to the UN Working Group on Indigenous Populations in July, Amnesty International included reference to its concerns in the Philippines.

POLAND

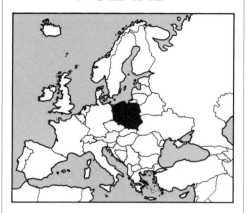

At least eight conscientious objectors were imprisoned for refusing to perform military service and were considered prisoners of conscience. One person was sentenced to death.

Poland ratified the European Convention for the Protection of Human Rights and Fundamental Freedoms in January.

At least 40 people were tried before military courts for refusing to perform military service on grounds of conscience. Requests made by members of the Roman Catholic Church to perform alternative service are usually refused because the authorities consider that personal convictions in such cases should be overridden by the fact that the Church does not object to military service.

Piotr Dawidziak and Piotr Krzyżanowski, conscientious objectors to military service, began serving one-year prison sentences in February. They were both released in August. Radosłav Jamrozik began serving a one-year prison sentence in April.

Four other conscientious objectors were imprisoned in August, October and November. Roman Gałuszka was released from prison in April after serving a sentence imposed in 1992 (see *Amnesty International Report 1993*).

One person was sentenced to death for murder in May. However, there have been no executions in Poland since 1989.

Amnesty International called for the release of prisoners of conscience. The organization also called on the Polish authorities to commute the death sentence and to abolish the death penalty.

PORTUGAL

There were reports of torture and ill-treatment by police and prison officers. Judicial and administrative inquiries were very slow but a few cases of alleged ill-treatment came to trial during the year.

All the reports of torture and ill-treatment concerned people who had been detained on suspicion of having committed criminal offences. Officers from all law enforcement agencies were accused of ill-treating detainees: *Polícia Judiciária* (PJ), Judiciary Police; *Polícia de Segurança Pública* (PSP), Public Security Police; and the *Guarda Nacional Republicana* (GNR), Republican National Guard. Prison officers were also alleged to have ill-treated criminal suspects. Some of the allegations referred to incidents in previous years. In many cases the complainants were released without charge. The most common forms of ill-treatment alleged were repeated kicks, punches and beatings with truncheons. Detainees also reported threats of assault, including sexual assault.

In March Pedro Leitão Pereira, a student from Oporto, was stopped in the street by two PSP officers. They accused him of being a fugitive whom they had pursued earlier. According to his statement, he gave them his identity papers and an account of his movements and offered to go to the police station. The police, however, took him down an alley-way and assaulted him with truncheons, injuring his legs and head, before allowing him to go. He required hospital treatment for injuries consistent with his allegations. He presented a formal complaint to the 12th Squadron of the PSP. An investigation was opened but had not concluded by the end of the year.

In February 1992 Francisco Carretas and a friend alleged that they were assaulted by GNR officers in Charneca da Caparica, near Almada. In a complaint to the authorities, Francisco Carretas stated that the officers took them to the GNR post in Almada where they were beaten with truncheons, kicked, punched and threatened, and then took them to a nearby wood where they were again kicked and punched. One officer threatened to assault Francisco Carretas sexually. He was then released. Photographs showed extensive bruising and other injuries to his back, buttocks and legs. A military judicial investigation was opened but no progress was reported by the end of 1993.

Numerous inquiries into allegations of torture and ill-treatment remained unresolved. Some had been open for many years. However, judicial decisions were reached in some cases.

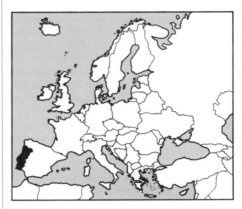

Both civil and military prosecuting officers stated during the year that inquiries into the injuries and subsequent death of Domingos do Couto had been closed at the request of the commanding officer of the northern military region. Domingos do Couto had died in hospital in 1984 having alleged that four days earlier GNR officers had severely beaten him with truncheons, causing injuries to his chest and heart (see *Amnesty International Report 1993*). The prosecuting officers did not explain how or by whom his injuries had been inflicted in custody, nor the circumstances of his subsequent death.

In March a court in Setúbal found one PSP officer guilty of abusing his authority and causing serious injury to Alexandre Gravanita. Alexandre Gravanita, a Portuguese citizen born in Angola, had been kicked, punched and racially abused in a PSP station in Setúbal in 1991 (see *Amnesty International Report 1993*). The PSP officer was sentenced to one year's imprisonment and fined. A second officer was convicted of giving false testimony and sentenced to eight months' imprisonment. Both sentences were suspended for three years. The officers appealed against their sentences.

In May six GNR officers were charged in Almada with causing physical harm to Paulo Manuel Ferreira Portugal. He alleged that GNR officers had assaulted him in August 1991 causing injuries to his head, jaw,

246

eyes and back (see *Amnesty International Report 1993*).

In June a court in Caxias acquitted the former governor of Linhó Prison and seven guards on charges of causing serious bodily injuries to prisoners. The charges were based on allegations of systematic beatings of prisoners following the death of Mário Manuel da Luz in a punishment cell in June 1989. The prison governor had earlier been forcibly retired following a disciplinary inquiry into allegations of ill-treatment. The Public Prosecutor appealed against the verdict of the Caxias court (see *Amnesty International Reports 1990* to *1993*).

Amnesty International urged the authorities to ensure that detainees were not tortured or ill-treated. The organization asked for information about inquiries into allegations of ill-treatment and the progress of any judicial or administrative proceedings.

In December 1992 the Ombudsman announced an inquiry into the PJ. In February Amnesty International asked him to include in his inquiry two cases of alleged torture and ill-treatment by the PJ which were unresolved from previous years: those of Isidro Albuquerque Rodrigues, who was arrested in June 1990 (see *Amnesty International Reports 1992* and *1993*), and Orlando Correia, who was arrested in September 1992 (see *Amnesty International Report 1993*). The result of the Ombudsman's inquiry was not known at the end of the year.

In November the UN Committee against Torture considered the Portuguese Government's Initial Report on its compliance with the UN Convention against Torture. The government replied to the Committee's questions on its report and supplied information on some specific cases of alleged torture and ill-treatment. In its conclusions the Committee welcomed government efforts to implement the Convention but regretted that, despite these efforts, ill-treatment and sometimes torture in police stations continued. It also criticized the frequent delays and length of inquiries into such allegations and considered that those responsible were not always brought to justice. It believed that this situation, as well as the lightness of sentences for people convicted of torture and ill-treatment, created "an impression of relative impunity for the authors of these crimes which is highly prejudicial to the application of the provisions of the Convention".

QATAR

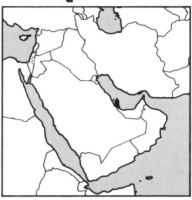

Two prisoners of conscience were arrested and held without trial for several weeks.

M.V. Babu and Samuel Philip, both Indian nationals, were arrested in Doha in January, reportedly after holding a Christian prayer meeting in a private house. Such meetings are illegal under Qatari law.

Amnesty International expressed concern about the arrest and detention of the two men to the Minister of the Interior in the government headed by the Amir of Qatar, al-Shaikh Khalifa Ibn Hamad Al Thani, and called for their immediate and unconditional release. The authorities responded that a decision to deport the two men had been "taken in view of the breach of Qatari Visa Law No. 3 of 1963 by the named persons. This law authorizes the concerned authority in the country to effect immediate deportation of any foreigner who does not comply with it ... no criminal charges were brought against them under Qatari criminal law."

ROMANIA

Five men were imprisoned solely because of their homosexuality and were considered prisoners of conscience. There were reports of torture and ill-treatment by the police. Two Roma were killed in racial violence with the apparent acquiescence of the police. The authorities failed to clarify a "disappearance" case.

In April a National Minority Council was established to advise the government and parliament on ethnic minorities. Representatives of the ethnic Hungarian minority left the council in September in protest over what they said was the government's failure to provide effective guarantees for minority rights.

In July the Law on the Reorganization of the Judiciary came into force. The independence of the judiciary was compromised by this law's criteria for the appointment and grading of judges. Furthermore, under this law the Ministry of Justice and presidents of courts have excessive power potentially to interfere with the work of the judges. The new law also maintains the powerful role of prosecutors and retains military courts as a parallel system of justice. Complaints of police abuse can be made only to the military prosecutor and the Ministry of Interior.

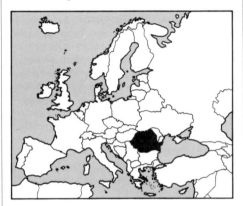

Romania acceded to the (First) Optional Protocol to the International Covenant on Civil and Political Rights in July. In October Romania became a member of the Council of Europe. In the same month it signed the European Convention for the Protection of Human Rights and Fundamental Freedoms and the European Convention for the Prevention of Torture and Inhuman or Degrading Treatment or Punishment, but had not yet ratified these instruments by the end of the year.

In January Milorad Mutaşcu, aged 22, and Mirel Ciprian Cucu, aged 17, were arrested near Timişoara for private, consensual sexual relations. Mirel Ciprian Cucu was charged under Article 200, paragraph 1, of the Penal Code which prohibits sexual relations between people of the same sex at any age. He was released to await trial after two months' detention. Milorad Mutaşcu was charged under the same article, paragraph 2, for homosexual relations with a minor, although a heterosexual relationship between people of the same ages would be lawful. He was released in May pending trial. There was no evidence of coercion or exploitation in the relationship and both men were treated as adults in terms of police procedure and preventive detention. In June the Timişoara Court sentenced Mirel Ciprian Cucu and Milorad Mutaşcu to suspended sentences of one and two years' imprisonment respectively.

In December information came to light that three more men were serving prison sentences solely because they had engaged in consensual homosexual relations. Marius Aitai, a 22-year-old prisoner in Gherla prison, had been sentenced in 1992 to two years and six months' imprisonment for having sexual relations with another prisoner. In two separate cases in 1993, Cosmin Hutanu, aged 21, had been sentenced to one year and two months' imprisonment, while Ovidiu Chetea, aged 20, had been sentenced to one year and six months' imprisonment.

In February Viorel Baciu was reimprisoned in Botoşani following the decision of the Supreme Court of Romania to reject an extraordinary appeal. He had been arrested in 1988, tried for murder and rape and sentenced to 10 years' imprisonment. Allegedly, he had been prosecuted and convicted on false charges because of his father's religious beliefs. Information about the torture of Viorel Baciu and other detainees in Suceava came to light in 1991 (see *Amnesty International Report 1992*). In 1992 the General Prosecutor, considering the charges to be groundless and illegal, filed an extraordinary appeal and suspended the prison sentence. The Supreme Court rejected this appeal on the basis of Viorel Baciu's confession, although it had reportedly been obtained under torture.

There were many reports of torture and ill-treatment of detainees, often in order to force a confession. In some cases victims who complained were later intimidated.

In June Andrei Zanopol was beaten by two officers in front of his home in Galaţi and later in a police station. For five days after his arrest the local prosecutor refused him access to his lawyer. He received medical treatment from a doctor who reportedly refused to give him a certificate. Later Andrei Zanopol was released and charges of alleged bribe-taking were dropped.

Costel Covalciuc was arrested in Dorohoi

248

in June and sentenced to three months' imprisonment for threatening his wife with a knife. On the sixth day of his detention he died in suspicious circumstances. Witnesses who saw his body in the morgue before the autopsy said that his hands were smeared with blood and his body was covered in bruises. After an official investigation, the authorities said that Costel Covalciuc had not been ill-treated and that his death resulted from heart spasms, possibly induced by abstinence from alcohol.

Information became available on a number of cases of homosexual men, or men suspected of being homosexual, who allegedly had been tortured or ill-treated by police in 1990 and 1992. Their actual or suspected sexual orientation appeared to have influenced such treatment. In one such case, Doru Marian Beldie, aged 19, had been arrested in June 1992 for allegedly forcing a minor to have homosexual relations. In the 17th District police station in Bucharest he had reportedly been beaten with truncheons on his hands and feet for several hours in order to force him to sign a confession. Subsequently, he was charged under Article 200, paragraph 2, of the Penal Code and sentenced to four years and six months' imprisonment.

The number of investigations into police abuses which resulted in charges or convictions was extremely small. This atmosphere of impunity particularly encouraged further acts of racial violence against the Roma community. At the end of the year no one had yet been charged for the attack on the Roma in Bucharest in 1992 (see *Amnesty International Report 1993*). Until criminal proceedings are completed the victims of the attack cannot file for compensation.

In September police officers failed to protect two Roma who were killed and some 170 Roma who were forced to abandon their homes during racial violence in the Transylvanian village of Hădăreni. Two Roma brothers, Pardalian and Lucian Repa Lăcătuş, who were allegedly responsible for killing a Romanian during a fight, were arrested by police when they tried to escape from a burning house. Two armed police officers failed to protect them from a crowd of Romanians and ethnic Hungarians who beat and kicked them to death. A third Roma burned to death in the house. Some 45 police officers later failed to protect the Roma community of the village

who were forced to flee as the crowd set alight another 12 houses and vandalized four more. Some of the Roma were later reportedly ill-treated and harassed by the police when they returned to collect their belongings. Four Roma families were reportedly threatened with death by other inhabitants if they returned to the village. In November residents of Hădăreni threatened to attack the Roma community again if the village council's decision to expel 21 families was not carried out. No one had been charged for the killings, destruction of property or the alleged ill-treatment of Roma by the end of the year.

Amnesty International repeatedly called for investigations into reports of torture and ill-treatment. The organization also repeatedly called for the abolition of Article 200, paragraph 1, of the Penal Code which allows for prosecution and imprisonment of adults engaging in consensual homosexual acts in private. In March Amnesty International called for a review of Viorel Baciu's case and for a full and impartial investigation into allegations of torture and ill-treatment by police in Suceava.

In April Amnesty International called for the immediate release of Milorad Mutaşcu from prison. In May it published a report, *Romania: Continuing violations of human rights*. In September it urged President Ion Iliescu to ensure that the inquiry into the killing of Roma in Hădăreni would be prompt, thorough and impartial. In November the organization urged him to take all necessary measures to protect the Roma from further acts of racial violence and to stop their forcible expulsion from Hădăreni. In December Amnesty International called on the President to release the three men who had been imprisoned solely because they had engaged in consensual homosexual relations.

The Ministry of Justice informed Amnesty International in January that its inquiry into the "disappearance" of Viorel Horia (see *Amnesty International Reports 1992* and *1993*) had concluded that he had not been detained following the events of 13 to 15 June 1990 and that the police had thoroughly investigated his whereabouts. Amnesty International pointed to errors in official records of people who were detained with Viorel Horia and to another statement from a witness who saw the boy in the military base. In April the government informed Amnesty International that the investigation into the deaths of Andrei Frumuşanu and Aurica Crăiniceanu (see *Amnesty International Report 1993*) would be completed in April or May. No one, however, had been charged in connection with their killing by the end of the year. Most government replies about reports of torture and ill-treatment stated that official investigations had not established any illegal use of force by law enforcement officers. However, in one case the authorities confirmed that three police officers had been charged with the ill-treatment of a man in Borş. Amnesty International asked the government for more information on the investigations, and particularly on the methods used.

RUSSIA

At least two men were jailed for refusing on conscientious grounds to perform compulsory military service, but were later given suspended sentences on appeal. They were prisoners of conscience. Scores of possible prisoners of conscience were believed to have been released following the amendment in April of a law punishing consensual, adult homosexual acts. There were numerous allegations of ill-treatment in police and military custody, and in the armed forces. At least six people were said to have died following such ill-treatment. New legislation reduced the scope and application of the death penalty, but over 500 people were under sentence of death during the year and at least one was executed. Asylum-seekers who faced serious human rights violations in their home countries were said to be among those expelled from the Moscow area in October.

Political life was dominated by the conflict between President Boris Yeltsin and parliament over the pace and direction of reforms, and over the division of powers between the legislature and the executive.

249

After months of disagreement President Yeltsin dissolved parliament in September, and called fresh elections for both houses of a remodelled bicameral legislature. Some parliamentarians resisted these moves, and the tense situation culminated at the beginning of October in armed clashes in Moscow. Over 100 people died before government forces regained control, and the Vice-President and parliamentary speaker were among those arrested for "organizing mass disorders". President Yeltsin declared a two-week state of emergency in the city, and almost 10,000 people without residence permits were expelled from the Moscow area. Elections to the new-style parliament took place in December.

Legal moves aimed at strengthening human rights continued. In February Russia acceded to the 1951 Convention relating to the Status of Refugees and its 1967 Protocol, although officials acknowledged that lack of resources hampered its implementation.

In April an amendment to the law against sodomy (Article 121 of the Criminal Code) decriminalized consensual adult homosexual acts, and government sources reported that all those convicted solely of such activity would be released.

The scope and application of the death penalty were also reduced by criminal code amendments in April. Article 73 (which carried a possible death sentence for "especially dangerous crimes against the state committed against another working people's state") was abolished, and men over 65 and all women were exempted from the death penalty. However, the amendments also widened the grounds for which the death penalty could be imposed for premeditated murder. The amendments increased from 11 to 13 the number of "aggravating circumstances" under which a death sentence could be passed. In July new legislation introduced the right to trial by jury in capital cases.

After years of discussion a new constitution was finally passed following a referendum in December. Among its provisions was the right to a civilian alternative to compulsory military service for conscientious objectors. However, by the end of the year the necessary legislation to introduce such an alternative had still not been passed.

The lack of such a law had already resulted in the imprisonment of at least two

250

conscientious objectors earlier in the year, although the previous constitution had also guaranteed the right to an alternative service. In separate trials in Moscow, pacifists Aleksandr Chizhikov and Oleg Astashkin received sentences of 12 and 24 months' imprisonment respectively for refusing their call-up papers. Both were given suspended sentences on appeal and released – Aleksandr Chizhikov in May just over a month after his trial, and Oleg Astashkin in June, after more than seven months under arrest.

Scores of possible prisoners of conscience were believed to have been released following the decriminalization in April of consensual homosexual acts between adult men. The Interior Ministry had reported in July that there were still 73 men imprisoned solely for such activity, but the stigmatization of offenders continued to make it difficult to obtain details about individuals and about the progress of releases.

Numerous allegations of ill-treatment indicated that beatings in police and military custody, and of conscripts in the armed forces, were systematic and widespread. At least six people were said to have died following such ill-treatment. For example, a member of an investigatory commission set up following the deaths of four sailors from the Pacific Fleet in January reported that the four had suffered from malnutrition, and died after being forced to perform heavy manual tasks. Two were said to have been beaten shortly before their deaths. One of the dead, Seaman Danilov, had apparently had to have his fingers amputated after being compelled to work outdoors in freezing temperatures without gloves, and to have been beaten by other recruits with a crowbar before hospitalization. Press and other sources have long reported that conscripts faced beatings, sometimes fatal, and other ill-treatment by longer-serving recruits, and that this practice was frequently condoned by those in authority.

Ill-treatment in custody was also reported to be widespread and after the October events in Moscow scores of people were said to have been beaten following detention by police or army units. Amur Yusupov, for example, reported that five policemen kicked him and beat him with their fists and truncheons in the security unit of the Moscow Hotel on 8 October. He also reported that the police called an ambulance only after he had signed a statement to say he had no complaints against them. Amur Yusupov received hospital treatment for concussion and a fracture of the left shoulder blade.

According to the Interior Ministry, 505 prisoners were under sentence of death at the end of August, but no statistics were known to have been issued for the full year. At least one execution took place after a petition for clemency by Kazbek Kokayev, sentenced to death for murder in 1990, was turned down in May.

Among those expelled from the Moscow area in October were said to be a number of asylum-seekers from republics of the former Soviet Union who faced serious human rights violations if returned to their home countries. Others, who did not have residence permits because of delays in processing their asylum applications, alleged that police officers extorted large sums of money from them in order not to deport them from Russia.

Amnesty International called on the government to release all people imprisoned for their conscientious objection to compulsory military service, and urged the introduction of a civilian alternative of non-punitive length. It welcomed decriminalization of consensual adult homosexual acts, and sought assurances that all those imprisoned for such activity had been released.

Amnesty International repeatedly expressed concern about allegations of ill-treatment, urging that all such reports be investigated swiftly and impartially, with the results made public and any perpetrators brought to justice.

The organization welcomed the reduction in the scope and application of the death penalty, but throughout the year continued to urge the authorities to commute all death sentences and to take concrete steps towards total abolition.

Amnesty International called on the authorities to ensure that no asylum-seekers were returned to countries where they could face human rights violations, and that their cases were considered thoroughly and swiftly in the light of international standards on the protection of refugees.

RWANDA

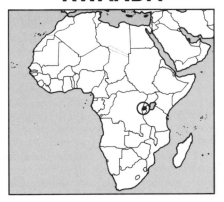

At least 300 unarmed civilians were reported to have been extrajudicially executed by members of the security forces and allied gangs. At least three detainees "disappeared" from custody. Opponents of the former ruling party and human rights activists were subjected to death threats and attacks apparently carried out by members of the security forces or militias linked to them. At least one prisoner of conscience was held during the year and other arbitrary, short-term arrests of possible prisoners of conscience were reported. There were reports of torture and ill-treatment of detainees in custody. An armed opposition group was responsible for human rights abuses, including the deliberate and arbitrary killing of as many as 300 civilians.

In April the coalition government set up in 1992 extended its term of office for a further three months in order to complete peace talks between the government and the armed opposition Rwandese Patriotic Front (RPF). Prime Minister Dismas Nsengiyaremye repeatedly accused President Juvénal Habyarimana of obstructing the peace talks and condoning political violence. In July the conflict resulted in the replacement of Dismas Nsengiyaremye as Prime Minister by Agathe Uwilingiyimana.

The peace talks, which began in 1991, culminated in the signing of a peace agreement on 4 August in the Tanzanian town of Arusha and the cessation of hostilities.

The government and RPF signed a series of protocols in the months leading up to the agreement. Some of the protocols, in particular the Protocol relating to the Rule of Law, signed in August 1992, included provisions for the protection of human rights. Article 15 calls for the establishment of an independent national commission of inquiry to be responsible for monitoring human rights violations and Article 16 calls upon the signing parties to set up an international commission of inquiry to investigate human rights violations committed during the conflict. However, no such inquiry was initiated by the end of the year. A power-sharing protocol allocated six posts to the RPF in a 22-member broad-based transitional government, to be formed after concluding the peace agreements.

The August peace accord provided for the appointment of Faustin Twagiramungu, leader of the *Mouvement démocratique de la République* (MDR), Republican Democratic Movement, as Prime Minister to head a broad-based transitional government, until elections scheduled to take place in early 1995. This government was to be formed after a UN peace-keeping force had been deployed in the country. However, although by the end of the year most of the UN forces had arrived, the transitional government had not yet been formed.

An International Commission of Inquiry composed of representatives of foreign non-governmental human rights organizations visited Rwanda in January at the invitation of local human rights groups to investigate human rights violations. Soon after its visit, the commission announced that widespread human rights abuses had been committed by the security forces and government officials, as well as by supporters of extremist Hutu parties. The government denied that government officials were responsible for extrajudicial executions.

The UN Special Rapporteur on summary or arbitrary executions visited Rwanda in April. He reported that members of the security forces and government officials had been implicated in the deliberate and arbitrary killings of at least 2,300 civilians, as well as other human rights violations, since the beginning of the conflict with the RPF in October 1990. He stated that members of the security forces, militias allied to the *Mouvement républicain national pour la démocratie et le développement* (MRND), National Republican Movement for Democracy and Development – the former single ruling party – and the RPF had been

252

responsible for human rights abuses.

A series of violent demonstrations was held in the capital, Kigali, by supporters of the MRND and its main political ally, the *Coalition pour la défense de la République* (CDR), Coalition for the Defence of the Republic, soon after the government and the RPF signed a power-sharing protocol in January. MRND and CDR gangs loyal to President Habyarimana attacked homes belonging to members of opposition parties which supported the protocol and the peace talks. By the end of January violence had spread to at least eight prefectures and more than 80 people had been killed. The violence was exacerbated by the breakdown of a short-lived cease-fire agreement on 8 February.

Soon after the International Commission of Inquiry left Rwanda in January, there was a new wave of extrajudicial executions by the security forces and militia gangs belonging to the MRND and CDR, who were believed to be armed by the security forces, in which over 300 people were reported to have been killed throughout the country. The victims included at least 19 suspected opponents of the MRND and CDR who were said to have been killed within Kigali military barracks in mid-February. The body of one, a Ugandan national, Kituku Hayidarusi, was found by his family two days after his arrest on 12 February: it reportedly bore marks of beatings and gunshot wounds. At least 17 other corpses of people known to have been arrested by soldiers were reportedly deposited at Kigali hospital morgue while other prisoners were reportedly used to bury some execution victims in various cemeteries in Kigali. Most were said to have been shot in the head. Relatives of the victims generally did not initiate official inquiries, apparently for fear of reprisals by soldiers.

In November, 38 people, including officials of the MRND, were shot dead and others wounded following an attack by unidentified assailants in four villages in the northern demilitarized zone. Another similar attack took place on 29 November in Mutara village in Gisenyi prefecture, where 17 people including women and children were killed. The killings occurred in the run-up to local elections. A unit of the UN Observer Mission to Uganda and Rwanda (UNOMUR) carried out a preliminary investigation into the killings: it confirmed that they had occurred but was unable to determine who was responsible.

Three students at the Seventh Day Adventist University of Mudende, Gisenyi prefecture, "disappeared" after being arrested by two soldiers and a police officer in February. The whereabouts of Alphonse Nkunzurwanda, Céléstin Palimehutu and Emmanuel Hakizimana remained unknown despite inquiries by their colleagues, local human rights groups and others to which the authorities apparently did not respond.

Members of political parties opposed to the President were subjected to death threats and assaults apparently by the security forces. The victims included Sylvestre Kamali, the MDR's head in Gisenyi prefecture, who was attacked several times by men believed to be members of the security forces. On one occasion his family home in Gisenyi town was destroyed by fire. A second house owned by the family in Kigali was twice invaded by unidentified armed men in February. In addition both Sylvestre Kamali and his wife were subjected to death threats from men claiming to be members of *Interahamwe*, a clandestine armed group reportedly linked to the President.

Human rights activists, in particular those who had assisted the International Commission of Inquiry, received death threats and were also subject to assault by members of the security forces and local government officials. Ignace Ruhatana, a leading member of a human rights organization known locally as "KANYARWANDA", was attacked and injured in May by men believed to belong to the security forces. Muhikira, a Tutsi whose son had assisted the commission as an interpreter, was reportedly forced to commit suicide when armed Hutu gangs, accompanied by members of the local police, surrounded his home and ordered him either to come out and be killed by them, or to kill himself. The local police did not intervene to save Muhikira's life.

On 14 November Alphonse-Marie Nkubito, a state procurator and president of a local human rights organization, was seriously injured by a grenade: it was thrown at him by unidentified men as he entered his home in Kigali.

At least one government critic was imprisoned as a prisoner of conscience. Janvier Africa, a journalist for *Umurava* newspaper, was sentenced to two and a half years' imprisonment in July by the

High Court in Kigali for insulting the Head of State. He had been arrested in September 1992 after alleging publicly that President Habyarimana had been involved personally in organizing "death squads" (see *Amnesty International Report 1993*). He was held throughout the year in Kigali Central Prison where he was reported to have received death threats.

Other journalists charged in 1992 were not brought to trial. It appeared that three journalists and a human rights activist, Fidèle Kanyabugoyi, who were provisionally released in April 1992 (see *Amnesty International Report 1993*), were not brought to trial. It was unclear whether charges against them had been dropped.

Several dozen members of the Tutsi ethnic group were apparently arbitrarily detained in Gisenyi prefecture during February. Most of them, including Epiphanie Mukeshema and Fulbert Rubayiza, appeared to be prisoners of conscience detained solely on the basis of their ethnic origin. They were released after a few days without charge. Also in February, about 12 students studying at the Institute St. Fidèle near Gisenyi town were arrested and detained for a few days on suspicion of complicity with the RPF. It was believed that they were detained because of their membership of opposition political parties.

Twelve people, including Cyriac Munigatama and Emmanuel Niyonshutu, were arrested in February by soldiers at a roadblock in Gitarama and accused of trying to join the RPF. They were detained in Kigali Central Prison, where some of them were beaten. They were released without charge after a few days. Their allegations of ill-treatment were not known to have been investigated.

In March Amnesty International learned that a soldier had been tried and sentenced to one year's imprisonment for the allegedly accidental shooting of Antonia Locatelli, an Italian missionary who had been killed in February 1992 during widespread disturbances in Bugesera region. However, there was apparently no independent investigation into the related killing of some 300 Tutsi (see *Amnesty International Report 1993*), although Fidèle Rwambuka, a local mayor and regional MRND representative, was suspended from his post in February 1993 for his alleged involvement in the Bugesera killings. He was murdered in August by unidentified men, amid allegations

that he was killed to prevent him from revealing official complicity in the killings.

The RPF was also responsible for human rights abuses. In February members of the RPF reportedly shot dead several unarmed civilians at a camp for displaced people close to the Ugandan border, when the inmates refused to cross into Uganda. A few weeks later, the RPF was reported to have deliberately and arbitrarily killed 300 Hutu supporters of the CDR and the MRND in Ruhengeri town, apparently in reprisal for attacks against Tutsi by the security forces and Hutu gangs.

Amnesty International continued to press the government to investigate reports of extrajudicial executions, "disappearances" and torture which had occurred since October 1990 and bring those responsible to justice. It urged the authorities to end arbitrary arrests and release all prisoners of conscience. The government was not known to have initiated or conducted any impartial inquiries into the reports of killings.

Amnesty International also called on the RPF to prevent deliberate and arbitrary killings of unarmed civilians and captured combatants and to respect human rights and basic humane standards.

SAINT VINCENT AND THE GRENADINES

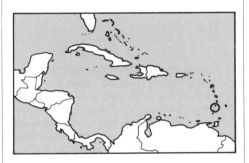

The death penalty for juvenile offenders was abolished. Three new death sentences were imposed. Seven people were under sentence of death but no executions were carried out.

On 5 August Parliament passed an amendment to the Criminal Code raising

254

the age at which a death sentence may be imposed to 18 years at the time of the crime. In October 1989 the law had been changed to allow death sentences to be passed for anyone over 16. Saint Vincent and the Grenadines acceded to the Convention on the Rights of the Child in October.

Three people were sentenced to death between July and October after being convicted of murders committed in 1991 and 1992. There were no executions. At the end of the year there were seven people on death row.

In December Amnesty International wrote to the Prime Minister, James Mitchell, welcoming the abolition of the death penalty for juvenile offenders but urging the government to change the law to end the mandatory nature of the death penalty as a first step towards the total abolition of the death penalty. The organization also called for the commutation of all current death sentences.

SAUDI ARABIA

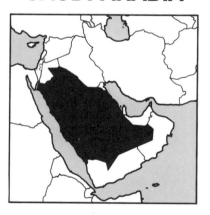

Scores of people were arrested for their political, human rights or religious activities. Some were prisoners of conscience. Over 400 Iraqi refugees were arrested following clashes in a refugee camp during which at least nine refugees were shot dead by camp guards; at least 30 of those arrested were still held at the end of the year. At least 28 people, among them prisoners of conscience, who had been arrested in previous years and held without charge or trial or sentenced after unfair trials, were released. Reports of torture continued to be received and at least two detainees died allegedly as a result of

torture or ill-treatment. The judicial punishments of flogging and amputation continued to be imposed. At least 80 people were executed.

In August King Fahd bin 'Abdul 'Aziz appointed a 60-member *Majlis al-Shura*, Consultative Council. The establishment of the council was part of a series of reforms announced in 1992 (see *Amnesty International Report 1993*). In May the Committee for the Defence of Legitimate Rights (CDLR) was founded in Riyadh by six prominent Sunni Muslim religious scholars and professionals. Its stated aims were the "alleviation of injustice ... and the defence of human rights decided by the *Shari'a* [Islamic law]". In response, the council of senior *'Ulama* – the highest religious authority in the kingdom – stated that the country had no need for human rights organizations since it was ruled in accordance with the *Shari'a*. Negotiations aimed at securing improved rights for the country's Shi'a Muslim minority were held during the year between the authorities and Shi'a Muslim leaders. Under part of the agreement reached, all known Shi'a Muslim prisoners of conscience and political prisoners were released (see below).

Between May and September, over 20 members and supporters of the CDLR were arrested and detained. They were prisoners of conscience. At least 16 were academics or staff members at King Sa'ud University in Riyadh. Among them was Professor Muhammad al-Mas'ari, the CDLR's spokesperson, who was arrested in May at his living quarters on the university campus by officers of *al-Mabahith al-'Amma*, General Intelligence. He was held incommunicado without charge or trial and allegedly tortured by being deprived of sleep for prolonged periods. He was released in November. Dr 'Abdullah al-Hamid, a founding member of the CDLR, was arrested at his house in June. A writer and lecturer, he had been summoned on more than one occasion by the authorities, apparently in attempts to persuade him and other CDLR founding members to disband the committee. He was held incommunicado without charge or trial until his release in September. The remaining CDLR supporters or members were released in October. Among them was Dr Ahmad al-Tuwaijri, a well-known poet and former dean of the College of Education at King Sa'ud University. He was arrested in September reportedly after signing a petition calling for the release of Muhammad al-Mas'ari.

The arrest of Christian worshippers for the peaceful expression of their religious beliefs continued (see *Amnesty International Reports 1992* and *1993*). In June and October, at least nine nationals of the Philippines were arrested in Riyadh and Abha following their participation in prayer meetings. Among them was Robinson Azucena Articulo, an office manager, who was arrested in June and held in Malaz prison in Riyadh. It was not known whether the detainees were still held at the end of the year.

Between April and September, scores of suspected government opponents were arrested by *al-Mabahith al-'Amma*, mainly in the province of al-Qasseem. They had allegedly distributed audio cassettes and literature criticizing government policies and corruption within the ruling family. All were said to be followers of *Salafiyya*, a fundamentalist Sunni Muslim doctrine. It was not known whether they remained in detention at the end of the year.

Over 400 Iraqi refugees were arrested following a protest in Rafha refugee camp in March. The majority were released shortly after, but at least 30 of them continued to be held at the end of the year. Among them was Farazdaq Wahab 'Abdul-Majeed, a bus driver from the Iraqi city of Kut, who was arrested after being wounded during the protest.

The protest began after news reached the camp that the Saudi Arabian authorities had refused to admit an Iraqi family seeking asylum on the border between Iraq and Saudi Arabia. It reportedly started peacefully, but became violent after one of the protesters, Jabbar Muhammad Karim al-Etaym, a taxi driver, was shot and killed by camp guards. Some of the refugees then occupied the camp's educational facility, which was set on fire, reportedly resulting in the deaths of four of its employees. The disturbances were subsequently quelled by army personnel, who reportedly fired into the protesters, killing at least eight more refugees. The government announced an investigation into the incident, but no details of its composition or findings were disclosed. However, the official news agency said in May that nine refugees had been killed during the March protest when guards opened fire to clear a path to the burning building.

At least 28 Shi'a Muslim prisoners of conscience and political prisoners were released (see above). Among them were five students from King Sa'ud University who had been held since 1989, and four alleged supporters of *Hizbullah fil Hijaz*, Party of God in Hijaz, who were serving prison terms imposed after unfair trials in late 1989 or early 1990 (see *Amnesty International Reports 1989* to *1993*).

New reports of torture and ill-treatment were received. Hussein al-Shuwaykhat, a 17-year-old student, died in January in *al-Mabahith al-'Amma* prison in al-'Awamiyya, Eastern Province. His body was returned to his family allegedly bearing marks of torture. He had reportedly been held without charge or trial since March 1991 on suspicion of theft. It was not known if an inquest or inquiry into his death was held.

Many Iraqi refugees were reportedly tortured or ill-treated following the protest in Rafha refugee camp (see above). One of them, Hussein al-Jizani, a former prisoner of war, was allegedly beaten to death by members of the armed forces two days after the protest. Fifteen Iraqi refugees who had apparently witnessed the incident were arrested and reportedly forced to sign a statement to the effect that Hussein al-Jizani had died of a heart attack.

The judicial punishments of flogging and amputation continued to be imposed. Mikhail Cornelius Mikhail, an Egyptian member of the Coptic Orthodox Church, received 500 lashes prior to his release and deportation to Egypt in January: he had been sentenced in October 1992 to seven years' imprisonment and 1,000 lashes on charges of blasphemy. At least five judicial amputations of the hand were carried out during the year. All the victims had been convicted of repeated theft.

At least 80 people were executed, all by being publicly beheaded. The victims included Egyptian, Pakistani and Saudi Arabian nationals who had been convicted of drug-trafficking, murder or rape. Three of them, two Saudi Arabians and an Egyptian, who had been convicted of murder and rape, were beheaded and then crucified in April in the city of Ha'il in Tabuk Province.

Amnesty International welcomed the release of prisoners of conscience and other political prisoners during the year but expressed concern about the arrests of others

256

for the peaceful expression of their political or religious beliefs. It called for the immediate and unconditional release of all prisoners of conscience. The organization urged the authorities to investigate thoroughly all deaths in custody, including those which had occurred in 1992 (see *Amnesty International Report 1993*), and all allegations of torture. It asked the government for details of the official investigation into the incident at Rafha refugee camp, but there was no response from the government to any of Amnesty International's appeals.

In July Amnesty International published a report, *Saudi Arabia: An upsurge in public executions*, and expressed grave concern that 105 people had been executed during a one-year period up to May, many of them apparently after unfair trials. It urged the government to take immediate steps to stop executions, reduce the number of capital offences and allow defendants access to defence lawyers during trials. The Saudi Arabian Ambassador to the United Kingdom, responding through the news media, stated that Amnesty International's opposition to the death penalty was tantamount to "contempt for the beliefs of all Muslims".

In September Amnesty International published a further report, *Saudi Arabia: Religious Intolerance; The arrest, detention and torture of Christian worshippers and Shi'a Muslims*. It reported the emergence of a clear pattern of discrimination against religious minorities, particularly since the Gulf crisis in 1990 and 1991. It also highlighted the detention without trial of hundreds of men, women and children solely for the peaceful expression of their religious beliefs, as well as the frequent reports of torture. Amnesty International urged the government to release all prisoners of conscience immediately and to enact legislation to combat religious intolerance.

SENEGAL

Over 250 political detainees were held without trial in connection with the activities of armed separatists in the Casamance region: all were released in mid-July. Many were reported to have been tortured by the security forces. Torture was reported to be frequent in police

stations elsewhere in Senegal. **The army was responsible for "disappearances" and possible extrajudicial executions in villages suspected of supporting the separatist movement and new information emerged about a massacre of villagers in 1992. Armed separatists in Casamance committed serious human rights abuses.**

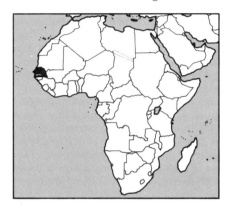

Armed conflict in the Casamance region between government forces and armed separatists belonging to the *Mouvement des forces démocratiques de Casamance* (MFDC), Movement of Casamance's Democratic Forces, escalated in the run-up to presidential and parliamentary elections in February and May. President Abdou Diouf was re-elected and subsequent negotiations between the government and the MFDC culminated in a cease-fire agreement in early July. There was much controversy surrounding the elections: the President of the Constitutional Council resigned before the results of the presidential elections were announced; and in May, the day after the parliamentary election results were announced, the Vice-President of the Constitutional Council, Maître Babacar Sèye, was murdered. His murder increased political tension: the leader and other members of the main opposition party, the *Parti démocratique sénégalais* (PDS), Senegalese Democratic Party, were accused of complicity; suspects, including a PDS member of parliament, were tortured in custody; and one leading suspect who initially implicated opposition leaders alleged later that it was actually a government envoy who had commissioned him to kill Maître Babacar Sèye, while trying to make the killing look as if the PDS had organized it.

The MFDC committed serious human rights abuses in the Casamance region, including deliberate killings of unarmed civilians. In a series of violent attacks at the time of the February elections, 28 people, both soldiers and civilians, including prospective voters and others involved in the elections, were killed by MFDC forces.

Some 256 prisoners, most of whom had been detained in late 1992 or early 1993, were held without trial in connection with the Casamance conflict. All were unconditionally released in mid-July after the cease-fire agreement. More than half had been held in Dakar, the capital, but were sent back to Ziguinchor, regional capital of Casamance, following their release. It appeared that many of them had been held unlawfully, in breach of existing detention procedures, but the secrecy surrounding their cases made this impossible to confirm. Few of them had legal representation. Amnesty International delegates who visited Senegal in June were denied access to them.

Many of the 256 were alleged to have been tortured. Both the army and the gendarmerie operating in the countryside of Casamance were reported to torture captives in order to obtain information about rebel movements. For example, Filidée Diédhiou, a hotel worker from Cap Skirring, was said to have been tortured by having molten plastic dripped on to his skin while he was detained for a week in January at a police station in Ziguinchor.

Torture was also reported in Dakar and other parts of the country. The most widely publicized case was that of Mody Sy, a PDS member of parliament, who was arrested on 20 May on suspicion of providing weapons for the murder of Maître Babacar Sèye the week before. He alleged that he was tortured at a gendarmerie post in central Dakar by being suspended between two tables and having electric shocks applied to his fingers and genitals. After a week he was transferred to Dakar's central prison, bearing scars which were consistent with his allegations. Despite widespread publicity, the authorities did not agree to his lawyers' request that he be medically examined until 11 June: even then, the results were not made public or apparently disclosed to the lawyers, and a formal complaint lodged on 28 July and an internal gendarmerie inquiry had made no progress by the end of the year.

In a related case, Ramata Guèye, a market seller, was arrested in July and tortured

over two days at the gendarmeries in Thiès and Pout before being released uncharged. She was seriously bruised, had a sprained thumb and some of her hair was pulled out. Her complaints of torture were also publicized but, as in Mody Sy's case, the authorities apparently failed to take any action against those responsible.

The army was responsible for "disappearances" and what appeared to be extrajudicial executions of villagers suspected of supporting the separatist movement in Casamance. Bruno Bassène, from Diakène village, reportedly "disappeared" after he was detained in January at a military check-point near Ziguinchor. A few days earlier he had apparently witnessed two extrajudicial executions near Diakène, when Théodore and Ignace Djivounouk were shot dead by government soldiers. Their bodies had then been tied, dragged some distance and mutilated. The cemetery at Diakène was later said to have been attacked by government forces when the two men were being buried.

Seven other men "disappeared" in January after being detained by soldiers at Dar Salam village. They included Ousmane Bassène, Daniel Tandeng and Gaston Manga. Following the July releases, it appeared that at least 24 other people had "disappeared": although they were reported to have been detained they were not among those freed.

New evidence emerged that government troops had killed at least 100 people at Kaguitt village in September 1992 (see *Amnesty International Report 1993*) following an attack there by MFDC separatists. Government soldiers had reportedly sealed off the village, rounded up all men and boys between the ages of 14 and 70, and killed them, either torturing them to death or extrajudicially executing them. Two others were taken away and "disappeared". The incident was surrounded by official secrecy and civilians were denied access to the village for some months after the incident. The authorities did not acknowledge that any unlawful killings had occurred and did not initiate any official inquiry.

Amnesty International expressed concern to the government about reports of torture, "disappearances" and extrajudicial executions and called for official action to halt such abuses. In June Amnesty International representatives visited Senegal and

258

met senior government legal officers and security officials. The authorities refused to provide any information about the detainees from Casamance and senior security officials would give no information at all.

In June Amnesty International published a short report, *Senegal: Opposition member of parliament tortured in police custody*, about the torture of Mody Sy and others and the authorities' complete failure to investigate torture allegations, in breach of the commitment to do so that they had given to the UN Human Rights Committee in 1992 (see *Amnesty International Report 1993*). Nor did the government investigate the reported "disappearances" or extrajudicial executions, despite appeals from Amnesty International.

In September the Minister of Justice told Amnesty International that the existence of "slips" or "unfortunate mistakes" did not indicate a practice of torture. He also stated that formal complaints by Mody Sy and Ramata Guèye were being investigated, although no details were available nor was any progress reported by the end of the year.

In November Amnesty International submitted a document to the authorities enumerating its concerns and urging them to ensure impartial inquiries into all allegations of torture and "disappearances". Amnesty International asked for details of the terms of reference of inquiries which were reportedly under way.

SIERRA LEONE

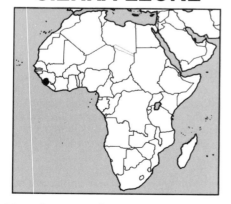

More than 300 political detainees, including prisoners of conscience, who had been held without charge or trial were released,

but more than 150 remained in detention at the end of the year. Conditions in prisons remained extremely harsh; deaths in custody from disease and malnutrition were common. People suspected of supporting rebel forces were tortured and ill-treated and captured rebels were extrajudicially executed by soldiers. Three people were sentenced to death for murder, but there were no executions. Armed opposition forces also committed serious human rights abuses.

On 29 April, the first anniversary of the coup which brought the National Provisional Ruling Council (NPRC) headed by Captain Valentine Strasser to power, the government announced the release from detention of former government ministers. It also announced amendments to legislation introduced in 1992, including the Treason and Other Offences (Special Military Tribunal) Decree, No. 12 of 1992, which established a special military court to try people involved in attempts to overthrow the government (see *Amnesty International Report 1993*). Trials before the tribunal would now be held in public and chaired by a High Court judge and those convicted would have a right of appeal to the Court of Appeal. The government also promised a return to a multi-party political system within three years and a National Advisory Council was established to draft a new constitution and prepare a transition to civilian rule.

Armed conflict continued in the south and east between government forces and the armed opposition Revolutionary United Front (RUF). It had begun in 1991 when the RUF invaded from neighbouring Liberia and continued after the NPRC took power in 1992. During the year, government forces recaptured most of the areas previously held by rebels. Captain Strasser announced a unilateral month-long ceasefire during December and offered an amnesty to rebel forces who surrendered, but rebel attacks continued. Both sides committed gross human rights abuses, including torture and killings of captured opponents. From June onwards hundreds of boys aged under 15 who had been enlisted into the Sierra Leone army were demobilized.

Several hundred people were being detained without charge or trial at the beginning of the year, mostly at the Central Prison, Pademba Road, in Freetown, the capital. They included former government ministers and officials arrested at the time of or immediately after the April 1992 coup and others arrested subsequently as suspected opponents of the NPRC. Some were prisoners of conscience. They were held under emergency legislation introduced in May 1992 which allowed indefinite administrative detention without charge or trial and from which there was no recourse to the courts. In April, 24 former politicians were released from prison but, like other detainees released in late 1992, they were placed under house arrest and remained so throughout the year. Commissions of inquiry which were established to investigate corruption by former government ministers completed their investigations but the government brought no charges against them.

Those held also included eight former prison officers who had been arrested in December 1992 for alleged involvement in a coup attempt (see *Amnesty International Report 1993*). They were held without charge or trial at the Criminal Investigation Department (CID) headquarters in Freetown until they were released in November. Two soldiers, Lieutenant M.A. Jalloh and Corporal S.S. Koroma, and a student, Sahid Mohamed Sesay, also accused of involvement in the coup attempt, were believed to be still held at Pademba Road Prison at the end of the year. Following international condemnation of the executions in December 1992 of 26 others accused of involvement in alleged coup attempts, the government said that it would make public the transcript of their trial before a Special Military Tribunal. It failed, however, to do this. In January, Chernor Ojuku Sesay, editor of *The Pool* newspaper, was held without charge for four days apparently because of an article criticizing the executions. He was beaten and kicked by a senior member of the NPRC while detained.

Seven people were arrested in early March on suspicion of plotting with former President Joseph Saidu Momoh to overthrow the government. They were held at CID headquarters in Freetown until 1 April when all but Ernest Allen, former Acting Permanent Secretary at the Ministry of Defence, were released. Ernest Allen was transferred to Pademba Road Prison and held without charge until 9 July when he and 85 other political detainees were released from the prison. Also released were

Adeline Koroma, a former government information officer, and K. Roy Stevens, a journalist, both held since May 1992, and Harry T.T. Williams, a former government minister, arrested in October 1992 who, like those released in April, was kept under house arrest.

In mid-October, 10 people were arrested after an independent newspaper, *The New Breed*, referred to allegations of government corruption previously reported by a foreign newspaper. Dr Julius Spencer, a university lecturer and the newspaper's director, Donald John, a journalist, and three others were charged with seditious publication and libel. They were released on bail in late October and had not been tried by the end of the year. Two other journalists were detained briefly in November. Paul Kamara and Sallieu Kamara, prominent members of the National League for Human Rights and Democracy and editor and deputy editor respectively of *For di People* newspaper, which had not appeared since stringent rules regulating the press were introduced by the NPRC in January, were arrested on 27 November. They were held for questioning for two days at CID headquarters in Freetown but were not charged.

Four British nationals of Vietnamese and Chinese origin were arrested in October in Freetown on suspicion of involvement in a plot against the government. They were charged with treason on 23 December but a preliminary investigation of their case before a magistrate's court was adjourned. A fifth person arrested shortly after the others was released uncharged on 30 December.

More than 150 detainees remained in Pademba Road Prison after the releases in July and arrests continued throughout the year. Most were held in connection with the armed conflict between government and rebel forces. About 20 had been held since 1991, when they were captured following the RUF invasion; others were arrested after the NPRC came to power. Large groups of civilians were detained, apparently indiscriminately, by soldiers as they retook areas previously held by rebels. For example, 27 farmers were arrested in January in Njaiama-Nimikoro, Kono District, Eastern Province, when, at the request of the military, they returned to their homes with their families after fighting had ceased. Although they were first held for

260

questioning in military barracks, no proper investigation into their alleged involvement in rebel activities appeared to have taken place. None had been captured during fighting and allegations that they might have supported or collaborated with rebel forces were unsubstantiated. Among those held at Pademba Road Prison accused of involvement in rebel activities were 16 boys under the age of 18, including one 14-year-old, Alhaji Kallon. He was among 154 political detainees freed from Pademba Road Prison on 12 November. A further 35 were released on 18 November. However, more than 150 political detainees remained held without charge or trial at the end of the year.

Torture and ill-treatment of suspected rebels and their supporters by soldiers in the war zone were common. Captives often had their arms bound tightly behind their backs, sometimes resulting in paralysis of the hands and arms. Several detainees in Pademba Road Prison had serious injuries to their arms; others had scars from bayonet wounds inflicted by the military forces who had initially detained them. There were also reports of torture and ill-treatment by security forces in areas of the country not affected by armed conflict. For example, in late August a pregnant woman, Ramatu Kanu, was reported to have died at a village in Tonkolili District, Northern Province, after being beaten by two soldiers who were searching for her husband. He too was later beaten by the soldiers. Police subsequently investigated the incident but it was not known whether those responsible were prosecuted.

Conditions in prisons throughout the country were extremely harsh. In March more than 70 prisoners who had been arrested as vagrants in Freetown in December 1992 died from starvation and neglect in Magburaka Central Prison, Mafanta, Tonkolili District. Thirty-three people died in early May after 62 people arrested in connection with a murder were locked in a small police cell in Kenema, Eastern Province. Official inquiries into both incidents were announced and several police officers in Kenema were subsequently suspended. However, the conclusions of the inquiries had not been made public by the end of the year. Although the incidence of prisoners' deaths at Pademba Road Prison was significantly lower than in previous years, deaths from disease and malnutrition still

occurred. In October the government announced that major improvements to the country's prisons were to be undertaken.

At least three people were sentenced to death for criminal offences. It appeared that soldiers may also have been sentenced to death by military courts, but no details were available. In April a High Court in Freetown sentenced three men to death for murder. No executions of condemned prisoners were carried out.

In Eastern and Southern Provinces, soldiers extrajudicially executed those captured in the conflict between government and rebel forces. Rebels captured on the battlefield were summarily killed; others were executed publicly, often by beheading, without any form of trial. For example, in January soldiers who had retaken Koidu in Kono District, Eastern Province, admitted to journalists that captured rebels were summarily executed. Three rebels captured in Koidu, one bleeding heavily from a gunshot wound, were bound and beaten. Two died as a result; the other was stabbed to death. In April a man and a woman captured while laying mines were reported to have been publicly mutilated and executed by soldiers in Daru, Kailahun District, Eastern Province.

Rebel forces also committed human rights abuses, including torture and deliberate and arbitrary killings of unarmed civilians. In August RUF forces were reported to have killed 21 people in Kailahun District. Sixteen members of the RUF and five civilians were reportedly executed by firing-squad after they were accused of plotting to overthrow the leader of the RUF, Foday Sankoh. Eight villagers, four men and four women, were reported to have been bound and shot by rebel forces in late October during a raid on the village of Ngieya, near the Liberian border, and in late December rebel forces were reported to have shot some 20 villagers when they attacked two villages in Pujehun District, Southern Province.

Amnesty International representatives visited Sierra Leone in early May. They visited parts of the country affected by armed conflict and also Pademba Road Prison where they saw 264 political detainees. In June Amnesty International published a report, *Sierra Leone: Political detainees at the Central Prison, Pademba Road, Freetown*, and called for a review of the cases of all political detainees held without charge or trial. When 86 detainees were released in July following a review of their cases by police and military authorities, the government said that rebels or those who collaborated with them would remain in detention while the armed conflict continued. Amnesty International welcomed the releases, but urged the government to review the cases of all political detainees in order to establish the grounds for their detention and to release those against whom no evidence of involvement in rebel activities had been found. In August Amnesty International drew attention to the cases of detainees under the age of 18 in its report, *Sierra Leone: Prisoners of war? Children detained in barracks and prison.* The government subsequently admitted that boys under 18 were held, but claimed that there were only eight. Amnesty International welcomed further releases of political detainees in November, but called again for a review of remaining cases. It also called for the early trial or release of those detained in connection with alleged coup plots in December 1992 and October 1993.

Amnesty International urged the government to take steps to prevent torture and extrajudicial executions and to ensure that all troops had clear orders not to kill prisoners. It also publicly condemned the deliberate and arbitrary killing of 21 people by the RUF in August, and called on the RUF to observe basic international humanitarian standards.

SINGAPORE

Two former prisoners of conscience continued to be subject to government orders restricting their freedom of expression and association. Criminal offenders were sentenced to caning. At least 26 people were sentenced to death and five were executed.

Restriction orders limiting freedom of association and expression continued to be imposed on Chia Thye Poh and Vincent Cheng, two former prisoners of conscience. A similar order imposed on another former prisoner of conscience, Teo Soh Lung, lapsed in June and was not renewed.

Caning, which constitutes a cruel, inhuman and degrading form of punishment, remained a mandatory punishment for

some 30 crimes, including armed robbery, attempted murder, drug-trafficking, illegal immigration and rape. For example, in September Muhamed Shah Jantan, a carpenter, was sentenced to 12 strokes of the cane and 14 years' imprisonment after being convicted of rape. There was no information about the damages claim made in court in March 1991 by Qwek Kee Chong, a convicted prisoner, for "grievous injury" caused by caning (see *Amnesty International Report 1992*).

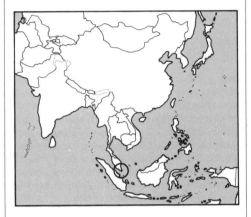

At least 26 people were sentenced to death, of whom 23 were convicted of drug-trafficking and three of murder. They included Yeo Poh Choon, who was convicted of drug-trafficking and sentenced to death in September by the Court of Criminal Appeal despite having been acquitted in July by the High Court on the same charge.

At least five people were executed. A Malaysian man was executed in February and two Hong Kong nationals were executed in July: all three had been convicted of drug-trafficking. Mohamed Bachu Miah and Mohamed Mahmuduzzaman Khan, both labourers from Bangladesh, were executed in July after being convicted of the murder of another Bangladeshi labourer. Mohamed Mahmuduzzaman Khan was executed despite a clemency petition to President Wee Kim Wee which included a signed confession by Mohamed Bachu Miah stating that he had been solely responsible for the murder.

Amnesty International urged the authorities to lift the restrictions on the two former prisoners of conscience, to end caning and to commute all death sentences.

262

SOMALIA

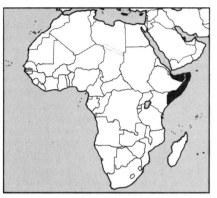

Hundreds of non-combatant civilians were deliberately killed by armed political groups and their supporters on account of their membership of a particular clan. Somali civilians, including children, were arbitrarily killed by UN peace-keeping and US troops, who detained dozens of people without charge or trial. Five women were summarily executed by stoning in the breakaway Somaliland Republic.

A UN military operation, "Operation Restore Hope", authorized by the UN Security Council in December 1992 to establish "a secure environment for humanitarian relief operations", sought to exert control in a country racked by civil war, famine and the absence of central government or rule of law. The multinational UN task force, UNITAF, led by US forces, reduced the number of deaths caused by starvation, but was only partially successful in securing peace between the Somali fighting groups or protecting relief workers and supplies. In March the 15 armed political groups of the main two rival Somali coalitions agreed to stop fighting and to set up a 78-member Transitional National Council (TNC) as a two-year interim political and legislative authority for the country. However, the TNC had not been established by the end of the year.

In May "Operation Restore Hope" handed over to a second UN Somalia operation, UNOSOM II, which was to last two years with US military backing. The UN Security Council authorized it to use force to end fighting in different parts of the country and to disarm and demobilize all armed Somali groups. It was mandated to establish a Somali police force and new

administrative, legal and judicial institutions, and to prepare a new constitution in conjunction with the TNC. It initiated a relief and reconstruction program, supplementing the activities of international relief agencies.

Increasing tension in the south of Mogadishu, the capital, between UN forces and General Mohamed Farah Aideed's United Somali Congress (USC) faction, the leading group in the Somali National Alliance (SNA) coalition, led to the killing of 23 Pakistani UN troops on 5 June. A UN Security Council resolution the next day authorized the investigation and detention for prosecution, trial and punishment of those responsible for the deaths. The UN Special Representative on Somalia declared General Aideed a wanted person in connection with the killings. This was followed by five months of bitter fighting in Mogadishu between UN forces and US supporting forces and General Aideed's armed supporters. Several hundred Somalis, many of them apparently unarmed and including children, were killed by UN and US troops. Somali gunmen killed over 70 UN and US soldiers, including 18 US soldiers in October during a UN operation to arrest SNA leaders. In response to international concern about the violence, the UN then reverted to seeking a political solution to the conflict with General Aideed, who had evaded capture. The UN Security Council rescinded its arrest order and established a new international commission of inquiry into the 5 June killings of UN troops. It also tried to reopen all-party reconciliation talks.

By the end of the year the Somali police force and courts were being re-established in some areas on the basis of the constitution and laws established at independence in 1960. The inter-clan fighting which had ravaged the country in 1991 and 1992 had mostly subsided, although areas of tension remained.

In the first four months of the year before the UNOSOM II operation, scores of defenceless civilians were arbitrarily killed on account of their clan origin during fighting between opposing clan factions in the southern port of Kismayu. On 2 January Sean Devereux, a British aid worker, was shot dead in Kismayu by unidentified gunmen, reportedly because of his criticism of massacres of unarmed civilians there the previous month by the Somali Patriotic

Movement (SPM). Killings of clan opponents from minority clans or sub-clans occurred throughout the year, particularly in Kismayu and Mogadishu. A pro-Aideed mob killed four foreign journalists on 13 June and General Aideed's USC militias reportedly killed several people suspected of spying for the UN.

Many of the hundreds of killings by UN peace-keeping and US troops appeared to violate human rights or humanitarian standards. In most cases, neither the UN nor the governments of the troops concerned carried out investigations in accordance with international standards. In March US military authorities investigated one death caused by shooting and decided not to bring charges. However, in April a US soldier was convicted by a court-martial in Mogadishu of aggravated assault on two Somali civilians. Canadian military investigators charged eight Canadian soldiers with criminal offences, including murder, torture and unlawful use of lethal force, in connection with two incidents in March. They had not been tried by the end of the year. A Belgian Ministry of Defence inquiry investigated reports of 31 killings and cases of ill-treatment of Somali civilians by its troops. According to its report in November, 13 cases were under judicial investigation, but no further details were known at the end of the year.

Some 20 civilian demonstrators were killed by Pakistani troops in Mogadishu on 13 June. The Pakistani authorities said their soldiers were returning fire against gunmen who were using civilians as "human shields". On 12 July US troops killed over 60 civilians, including elders and religious leaders with whom UN officials were negotiating. The troops said they had attacked what they believed was a command post of General Aideed, although this was evidently not the case. On 3 October scores of civilians were killed and some 700 wounded, about a third of whom were women and children, in gun battles between General Aideed's militias and US troops, who suffered 18 casualties in their search for SNA leaders. In all these cases, the investigations by the UN, US and Pakistani authorities to establish whether the killings by their forces were lawful or not, and whether they could have been avoided, failed to satisfy international standards for thorough, prompt and impartial investigations.

UN and US troops arrested hundreds of Somalis during the year, mostly in Mogadishu and particularly after the killing of 23 Pakistani UN troops on 5 June. Most were released after days or weeks, although some 400 alleged criminals were transferred from UN custody to Somali prisons and police stations. The UN began to establish new courts in August, but no detainees were known to have been tried by the end of the year. Of the 70 people arrested for political or security reasons in the conflict with General Aideed, most were held and interrogated in a special detention centre in the UN compound in Mogadishu. They included about 20 SNA leaders arrested by US troops in October. Detainees were denied access to relatives, although the International Committee of the Red Cross (ICRC) was allowed to visit all UN detainees. None was brought before a judicial authority, charged with an offence or allowed access to a lawyer. It was unclear whether they were detained in a law enforcement operation or were effectively prisoners of war. A UN spokesperson said they were being held in "preventive custody" for security reasons. By the end of the year all but eight had been released.

In March the UN Commission on Human Rights called for the appointment of an Independent Expert on Somalia. He was appointed in August but had not visited Somalia by the end of the year. In September the UN Security Council approved the establishment of a human rights office as part of UNOSOM II which would investigate human rights violations and train police, judges and prison officers. By the end of the year only limited steps had been taken to implement this human rights program. An Independent Jurist was appointed by the UN in December to review the UN detentions.

A Nigerian soldier in the UN force and a US serviceman, who were captured by General Aideed's militias in September and October respectively, stated that they had been ill-treated in custody. They were eventually given medical treatment and allowed visits by the ICRC, and were released in November. The bodies of some Pakistani, US and Nigerian soldiers killed in the fighting were mutilated by pro-Aideed mobs.

The breakaway "Republic of Somaliland" in the northwest, relatively untouched by the violence in the south, refused to join the proposed TNC. In May

264

clan and political groups elected Mohamed Ibrahim Egal as President to head a two-year interim administration. A new National Charter stated that Somaliland would abide by the Universal Declaration of Human Rights. It declared that legislation would be based on laws in force before General Siad Barre's coup in 1969 and on Islamic Law, but the administration did not legalize cruel, inhuman or degrading punishments such as flogging, which had been inflicted by courts earlier in the year.

Summary and extrajudicial executions took place in Hargeisa in Somaliland in January. On 8 January five women were stoned to death for adultery after being arrested by an Islamic group, taken into police custody and tried by an informal Islamic "court". They were denied legal representation, condemned to death, refused any appeal and publicly stoned to death the next day by the religious group which had arrested them. Somaliland officials did not intervene. Later, after local and international criticism, police arrested Sheikh Dahir Ahmed Yunis, the leader of the religious group, and 15 others involved in the incident, but released them later unpunished.

Amnesty International appealed to all Somali political groups, military and civilian, to commit themselves publicly to human rights objectives, end the abuses and support the rule of law. In April Amnesty International published a report, *Somalia: Update on a disaster – proposals for human rights*. It urged the UN to establish an international group of independent civilian advisers to implement international human rights standards, investigate human rights abuses by all parties, including UN and other foreign forces, and take prompt corrective action. It called for a public inquiry into human rights violations in Somalia over the past two decades, and for those responsible for extrajudicial executions and other deliberate and arbitrary killings and torture, to be brought to justice.

Amnesty International urged the UN to investigate thoroughly killings of civilians by UN forces and asked the governments of Belgium, Canada, Pakistan and the USA what steps they were taking in regard to allegations of abuses by their troops. It also called on the UN to ensure that no one was detained by UN forces contrary to the UN's own standards on the rights of detainees.

The UN wrote to Amnesty International in June rejecting allegations of disproportionate use of lethal force by UN troops and dismissed the proposal for UNOSOM to have civilian human rights advisers. In November the UN told the organization that it was striving to ensure adherence by UNOSOM to all international and humanitarian laws. It later provided some details of three incidents of killings by UN troops, the troops' rules of engagement and detention procedures, and the new UNOSOM Human Rights Office. The Canadian Government replied to Amnesty International in July about the investigations it had initiated, but at the end of the year Amnesty International had received no reply from the US, Belgian or Pakistani governments.

Amnesty International condemned summary executions by armed Somali groups and the executions in Somaliland.

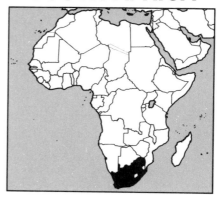

SOUTH AFRICA

Over 4,300 people were killed in political violence. Further evidence emerged of covert security force collusion in political killings. Prisoners of conscience were among hundreds of prisoners detained without trial under security legislation. Detainees were tortured by members of the police and army; at least 39 died in police custody in suspicious circumstances. Few of those responsible for human rights violations were brought to justice. Over 400 prisoners were under sentence of death but there were no executions.

Negotiations between President F.W. de Klerk's government, the African National Congress (ANC) and other political parties led to an agreement on a post-elections "Interim Constitution", which included a chapter on "Fundamental Rights", and was passed by the tricameral parliament on 22 December. In December the newly established Transitional Executive Council (TEC) began to monitor the conduct of key government departments prior to elections set for April 1994. A coalition of right-wing parties, including the Inkatha Freedom Party (IFP) and the Conservative Party, boycotted the negotiations from July and at the end of the year still refused to accept the new Constitution and to participate in the multi-party TEC.

In January South Africa signed the UN Convention against Torture and Other Cruel, Inhuman or Degrading Treatment or Punishment, but had not ratified it by the end of the year.

The level of political violence remained high, with over 4,300 people killed during the year. Attacks on train and taxi commuters continued, and apparently random shootings by unidentified attackers in passing vehicles constituted a new form of terror for township residents in the Vaal Triangle, East Rand and Natal. The pattern of these shootings, which often coincided with key events in the negotiations process, suggested that they were being perpetrated by a "third force" of professional killers, possibly consisting of elements within the security forces and other armed groups opposed to the peace process. In the East Rand there was evidence of police collusion with IFP supporters involved in conflict with ANC supporters.

Towards the end of the year right-wing parties, including the IFP, were stockpiling weapons and running paramilitary training camps in opposition to the new Constitution and the TEC.

The Azanian People's Liberation Army (APLA), the armed wing of the Pan Africanist Congress of Azania (PAC), maintained a policy of attacking police officers and were under suspicion in connection with attacks resulting in the deaths of more than 50 white civilians. More than 200 police officers died in politically motivated attacks, the majority in the context of political violence in the East Rand. In November APLA officials and the Minister of Law and Order held talks in Zimbabwe which aimed at a "cessation of hostilities".

International observers, who had been sent to South Africa under the August 1992 UN Security Council Resolution 772, helped to limit the level of violence, particularly during mass demonstrations which followed the assassination in April of South African Communist Party leader Chris Hani by right-wing conspirators.

The judicial commission chaired by Appeal Court Judge Richard Goldstone continued to investigate and report on incidents and issues relating to the political violence. In December the commission made public its evidence of a "hit squad" operating within the KwaZulu police. Lawyers were appointed as Police Reporting Officers under the 1991 National Peace Accord to investigate complaints against the police, but were hampered by insufficient resources, limited access to police files and financial dependence on the police.

Members of the security forces continued to commit extrajudicial executions and other human rights violations, despite some attempts by the authorities to make the police more accountable to local communities. For example, police fired indiscriminately into a crowd of peaceful demonstrators outside Protea police station, Soweto, in the aftermath of Chris Hani's assassination. Nine people were killed and around 240 injured. Elsewhere, the Bophuthatswana police brutally attacked peaceful demonstrators. In one incident in August they shot dead 14-year-old David Letsile without provocation.

The police were also implicated in targeted assassinations of political activists and members of the ANC's armed wing, Umkhonto weSizwe (MK), and in deaths in custody which appeared to be deliberate killings. In one case in April, six plainclothes police officers shot dead former MK member Khaya Simani in Nyanga township, Cape Town.

Members of the Internal Stability Unit, the former riot police, were repeatedly implicated in assaults, torture and extrajudicial executions of township residents in areas including Cape Town, Durban and the East Rand. Soldiers, too, were responsible for extrajudicial executions. In October the South African Defence Force (SADF) shot dead five youths aged between 12 and 17 during a night raid on a house in the Transkei "homeland" which they claimed was an APLA base. Post-mortem evidence showed that at least 70 shots had been fired into the bodies of the youths who were lying in their beds at the time. There had been no progress in the investigation

266

by the end of the year because the South African authorities refused to cooperate.

As in previous years, members of the security forces were granted impunity for human rights violations. In May the Ciskei "homeland" government decreed that 69 members of the Ciskei security forces who had faced charges arising from the September 1992 shooting in Bisho of unarmed demonstrators should be unconditionally indemnified against prosecution (see *Amnesty International Report 1993*).

The Goldstone Commission did not issue a final report on the June 1992 Boipatong massacre (see *Amnesty International Report 1993*). However, 31 residents of KwaMadala hostel were still on trial for the murders at the end of the year. During the trial evidence emerged indicating that the police had deliberately destroyed ballistic evidence.

There were no results from the official investigation into a high-level cover-up of police involvement in the 1988 murder of 11 people in Trust Feed, Natal (see *Amnesty International Report 1993*). The official committee responsible for the inquiry was dissolved and the investigation was referred to the Goldstone Commission, which said that it was not authorized to investigate incidents which occurred before 1990.

Clear evidence implicating senior military officers in covert "hit squad" assassinations emerged during the inquest into the 1985 assassinations of Matthew Goniwe and three other Eastern Cape political activists (see *Amnesty International Report 1986*). The inquest had not concluded by the end of the year.

In November General Oupa Gqozo, head of the Ciskei "homeland" government, and one other person were brought to trial before the Ciskei Supreme Court for the 1991 murders of two alleged coup plotters, Charles Sebe and Onward Guzana, after an inquest court ruled that they were responsible for the deaths. Both were acquitted in December.

An IFP member was sentenced to death in September for murders committed in the Port Shepstone area, Natal. The court ordered an investigation into allegations that members of the KwaZulu police had supplied the accused with weapons.

The security forces used special powers under the terms of the Public Safety Act in districts declared "unrest areas" to detain without charge hundreds of ANC supporters, particularly young men suspected of being members of so-called self-defence units. Lawyers, human rights monitors and relatives of detainees frequently reported that during the initial 24 or 48 hours of arrest and interrogation, the security forces denied them access to detainees. Compelling medical evidence of torture was submitted to the Supreme Court, which issued an injunction restraining the police from further assaulting the detainees.

The police also detained scores of people under permanent security legislation allowing 10 days' incommunicado detention. Those detained included leading PAC members and suspected members of APLA and of right-wing organizations.

Provisions of Bophuthatswana's Internal Security Act were repeatedly used within the nominally independent "homeland" to prevent political meetings, demonstrations, funeral processions and voter education workshops and to detain organizers and sympathizers. In August Thabo Sejanamane, coordinator for the human rights monitoring organization, Mafikeng Anti-Repression Forum, was detained in an apparent effort to hamper his work. At the same time five members of the Mafikeng ANC branch executive were detained when they attempted to organize a march through Mafikeng. The six, all prisoners of conscience, were released uncharged after almost a week in custody.

Officials of the Police and Prisons Civil Rights Union (POPCRU) from Pietermaritzburg were detained in March during a strike by prison warders, denied a bail hearing, and brought to trial two months later when they were acquitted of all charges and released.

There was widespread evidence of torture and ill-treatment of political detainees and criminal suspects by the police and, less frequently, members of the armed forces. In general, the government failed to react when torture was reported.

Some interrogation and torture sessions reportedly occurred outside police stations – in the open countryside or inside police vehicles. The police may have been attempting to evade the scrutiny of various organizations, including the International Committee of the Red Cross which had been granted access to all police stations in 1992. Dozens of residents of Bruntville and other townships in Natal who were detained in January and February complained of being subjected to electric shocks, beatings and other forms of torture while being interrogated by police in abandoned farm buildings in isolated areas.

At least 39 prisoners died in police custody in suspicious circumstances. Wellington Mbili died as a consequence of gunshot and hand-grenade injuries when the police took him to a remote area near Port Shepstone, Natal, allegedly to point out an arms cache. The police said they shot him when he attempted to throw a hand-grenade at them. He was handcuffed and guarded by three armed police officers at the time.

In several cases inquest courts found police officers responsible for torture or deaths of prisoners. In March an inquest court found a police officer criminally liable for the death of Bethuel Maphumulo in Protea police station in December 1990. A forensic pathologist representing Amnesty International observed the inquest. In November the officer was acquitted of Bethuel Maphumulo's murder.

Officers of a police weapons investigation unit known as the "Yankee Squad", based in the Vaal Triangle, were suspended following an investigation by a Police Reporting Officer into allegations of systematic torture. In November the same Police Reporting Officer's unit discovered electric shock and other torture equipment in police armoured vehicles in the East Rand.

Over 400 prisoners were under sentence of death, more than 300 in Pretoria and the remainder in the nominally independent "homelands". Fifty-four new death sentences were imposed. Two executions scheduled in Venda in May were halted after lawyers intervened. In June parliament debated a government proposal to end the moratorium on executions, which had effectively been in force since February 1990. Parliament voted to resume hangings but the government later said it would abide by the moratorium until constitutional negotiations had been completed.

Members of opposition organizations were convicted of killings and other acts of violence. It was not always clear if they had been acting on explicit orders from their organizations. In September, for instance, three ANC members were convicted of six murders in an April 1992 attack on a passenger bus in Umgababa, Natal. In October a former Conservative Party

parliamentarian and a member of an extreme white right-wing organization were sentenced to death for the murder of Chris Hani. Apart from targeted killings by members of opposition organizations, many people died simply because of where they lived. In Sundumbile, Natal, and Radebe Section in Katlehong township, deaths occurred when IFP supporters attempted to drive out non-IFP families. At the same time, Zulu-speaking township residents were targeted as suspected IFP supporters by ANC supporters.

Amnesty International representatives visited South Africa on five occasions to investigate human rights violations. Amnesty International called on the government to institute independent inquiries into cases of extrajudicial executions, torture, death threats and other forms of harassment. It also urged the government to suspend from duty security force members implicated in such violations and to bring perpetrators to justice. Government and police officials responded, for the most part, with denials of the alleged violations or by placing the onus of investigation on the Goldstone Commission.

In December Amnesty International appealed to the government and the TEC to implement specific urgent measures prior to the elections, including the establishment of locally supported police complaints investigation units, prompt and impartial action against perpetrators of human rights violations, and removal of all restrictions on freedom of assembly and association.

Amnesty International appealed to ANC officials to take disciplinary steps against executive members of the ANC branch in Khutsong, Carletonville, who had been implicated in acts of torture, assaults and killings against local members of the ANC Youth and Women's Leagues. In May an Amnesty International representative attended part of the proceedings of the ANC-appointed Motsuenyane Commission, which was investigating reports of human rights abuses by ANC officials in exile during the 1980s. The Commission's report, made public in August, found that torture and killings had been carried out by ANC personnel and identified alleged perpetrators. The ANC leadership accepted these findings and assumed collective responsibility for the abuses, but declined to discipline the perpetrators or remove them from

268

positions of authority. Instead, they called on the government to set up a "Commission of Truth" to inquire into all violations of human rights committed by all parties.

In oral statements to the UN Commission on Human Rights in February and to its Sub-Commission on Prevention of Discrimination and Protection of Minorities in August, Amnesty International included reference to its concerns in South Africa.

SPAIN

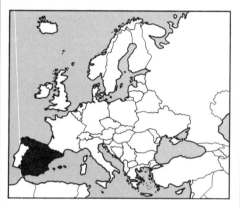

There were allegations of torture and ill-treatment by members of the security forces and the police. Trials of officers accused of torture and ill-treatment took place; several officers were granted amnesties.

The armed Basque group, *Euskadi Ta Askatasuna* (ETA), Basque Homeland and Liberty, and the *Grupos de Resistencia Antifascista Primero de Octubre* (GRAPO), First of October Anti-Fascist Resistance Groups, continued to attack the security forces and civilians. It was reported that 15 people, including civilians, were killed by ETA: others were injured and one was killed by GRAPO. In July Julio Iglesias Zamora, a Basque industrialist, was taken hostage by ETA; he was released in October.

Special legislation regarding armed groups remained in force. People suspected of collaborating with these groups can be held in extended incommunicado detention for up to five days by judicial order – two days longer than the normal limit – and are denied the right to designate their own lawyer.

In April the UN Committee against Torture considered the Spanish Government's periodic report on its compliance with the UN Convention against Torture and Other Cruel, Inhuman or Degrading Treatment or Punishment. In its conclusion the committee expressed "... concern at the increase in the number of complaints of torture and ill-treatment, at delays in the processing of such complaints and at the impunity of a number of perpetrators of torture".

In March Hamid Raaji, a Moroccan national, alleged that he had been racially abused and hit in the groin by municipal police officers in Valencia when they stopped him for an identity check. Four days later one of his testicles was removed in an emergency operation. The police officers were indicted on charges of causing him injury with menaces but they had not been brought to trial by the end of the year.

In August Carlos Viña Pena, a serving officer of the Civil Guard reserve, was involved in a motor accident in La Coruña. He and the other driver were taken by officers of the national police to the police station in Lonzas reportedly to make a statement. He claimed that a uniformed police corporal assaulted him in a corridor and later beat him with a truncheon in an interrogation room. Six other officers apparently witnessed the incident. Carlos Viña received hospital treatment and was released the following day. He later complained to the court in La Coruña and provided medical certificates and photographs showing severe bruising to his right shoulder, back, left arm and thighs.

In September Josu Caminos, a bank employee, was stopped by officers of the national police at a barricade in Pamplona. He claimed that when he asked why he had been stopped, officers kicked him and beat him with truncheons. As a result, he suffered increasingly severe breathing difficulties and eight days later was operated on to drain his right lung which had flooded with blood because of internal injuries.

In September Mohamed Hegazy and Raed Shibli were fined and sentenced to one month and one day's imprisonment for resisting arrest by Civil Guard officers; they were acquitted of injuring the officers. In 1991 both men had alleged they were severely beaten in a Civil Guard station in Ibiza following their arrest (see *Amnesty International Report 1992*). The court stated that their allegations of ill-treatment in the station had not been considered and would be heard separately.

In February three officers, including a senior inspector, of the *Ertzaintza*, the Basque state police, were charged with torturing Andoni Murelaga, an ETA member, in 1990. They were still awaiting trial at the end of the year.

In June a Civil Guard officer was found guilty of causing multiple injuries – including a burst ear-drum – to a trade union leader in Mallorca. Antonio Copete alleged that the officer had assaulted him in 1992 during a demonstration and when he was handcuffed and under arrest. The officer was sentenced to one year's imprisonment, disqualified from public office for one year and ordered to pay compensation.

In October a San Sebastian court acquitted five Civil Guard officers of torturing a suspected ETA member, Juan Carlos Garmendia, in 1982. The defendants were acquitted by a majority verdict of the judges on the grounds that the trial proceedings were not held within the legally prescribed time limit. The Prosecutor and the plaintiff appealed to the Supreme Court against the acquittals. One of the defendants, a senior officer, had been sentenced in 1987 to four months' imprisonment and four years' disqualification from holding public office for torturing another prisoner in 1982. He had not served any part of this sentence and had been promoted. In February the government granted the senior officer, and four other co-defendants, an amnesty on the 1987 sentence of disqualification, but he entered prison in May to serve the four-month sentence.

Amnesty International urged the authorities to ensure that all allegations of torture and ill-treatment were thoroughly and impartially investigated and to ensure that those found responsible were brought to justice.

In August, following the kidnapping by ETA of Julio Iglesias, Amnesty International publicly urged his immediate and unconditional release. Amnesty International stated its unreserved condemnation of abuses by armed political groups, such as hostage-taking and deliberate and arbitrary killings, which contravene international humanitarian standards.

269

SRI LANKA

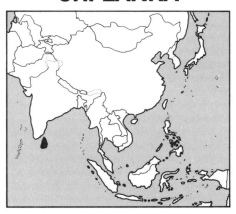

Thousands of suspected government opponents, particularly Tamils, were arbitrarily arrested. They included prisoners of conscience. Some were soon released but others were held for long periods in unacknowledged detention. Hundreds of other political suspects arrested in previous years continued to be detained without charge or trial throughout the year. Torture and ill-treatment in custody continued and over 25 "disappearances" were reported. Extrajudicial killings were reported in both the northeast and the south. The Liberation Tigers of Tamil Eelam (LTTE) were responsible for numerous human rights abuses, including executions of prisoners.

In May President Ranasinghe Premadasa was assassinated in the capital, Colombo, by a suicide bomber who the authorities claimed was a member of the LTTE. Lalith Athulathmudali, a leader of the opposition Democratic United National Front (DUNF), had been assassinated the week before, during an election rally. Prime Minister Dingiri Banda Wijetunga became President following President Premadasa's assassination. In May Provincial Council elections were held in all but the northeastern areas.

Armed conflict between government forces and the LTTE continued in the northeast. Military operations, particularly in the north, intensified in the second half of the year, with heavy loss of life on both sides as well as among the civilian population. The LTTE retained control of most of the Jaffna peninsula; control of much of the rest of the northeast was disputed between the LTTE and government forces.

270

In June the Emergency Regulations were revised: secret detention was prohibited and, for the first time, publication of all authorized places of detention was required. However, the authorities remained empowered to detain political suspects indefinitely without charge or trial, and in the northeast long periods of detention in police or military custody were still permitted. The additional safeguards provided under the regulations – such as the requirement that detentions be promptly notified to the Human Rights Task Force – were repeatedly flouted.

The mandate of the Presidential Commission of Inquiry into Involuntary Removals (PCIIR), whose role is to investigate "disappearances" since January 1991, was revised in September and extended for a further two years. The terms of reference were altered to enable the PCIIR to investigate cases more speedily. However, the government had taken no known action on the commission's findings and none of its reports had been published by the end of the year.

In October the government established a unit under a senior police officer to examine "disappearance" cases submitted to the government for clarification by the UN Working Group on Enforced or Involuntary Disappearances. According to the government, the unit would "initially" examine reported cases between 1983 and January 1991, using an administrative procedure which falls far short of international standards for the investigation of "disappearances".

Thousands of Tamil people, including prisoners of conscience detained solely on account of their ethnic origin, were arrested, especially in Colombo. Some were arrested by plainclothes officers during the night and driven away, blindfolded, in unmarked vehicles. Many were held in unacknowledged detention for days, or longer, before being released, sometimes on payment of a bribe. Some were brought before magistrates and released on bail; others were kept in custody without being charged and were still held at the end of the year.

There were successive waves of such arrests. They began in June, after the Provincial Council elections, and continued to the end of the year. They were apparently connected to investigations into the assassinations of Lalith Athulathmudali and President Premadasa, as well as to reports that LTTE suicide bombers were present in Colombo. Police, military and armed Tamil groups allied with the government were all reported to have participated in these arrests.

Some people were abducted in Colombo and were later found in police custody in Batticaloa in the east. For example, in November, Sinnathambi Meganathan, bodyguard to a Tamil member of parliament, who was seized by a group of plainclothes men while travelling on a bus in Colombo, was traced a week later; he was then released without charge. He had been beaten and had injuries all over his body, including burn marks on his feet. He said he had been given electric shocks to his thumbs. Before his release, he was reportedly forced to sign a statement saying he had not been ill-treated in custody.

The Eelam People's Democratic Party (EPDP), a militant Tamil group which acts in concert with government security forces, also reportedly detained people illegally early in the year. In January Tharmalingam Selvakumar, a former EPDP sympathizer, was abducted in Colombo by the EPDP and held for five days at their Colombo headquarters, where he was beaten. He said that several other Sinhalese and Tamil prisoners were also held there, some of whom had been tortured. Tharmalingam Selvakumar was handed over to police custody, where he remained until released by a court some 12 days later. He was repeatedly threatened with death after he filed a Supreme Court petition alleging violation of his fundamental rights by the EPDP and the police.

There were continued reports of arbitrary arrest in the northeast by the security forces and militant Tamil groups associated with them. In Batticaloa and Trincomalee districts, the security forces reportedly paraded hundreds of people before masked informants in order to identify suspects, with many then being detained for questioning. Most were released within a week. Others were detained solely because they were relatives of alleged LTTE members. Some prisoners were held in unacknowledged detention for several days; others for longer periods.

In the south, scores of members and supporters of opposition parties, particularly the DUNF, were reported to have been arrested and held for short periods in the run-up to the Provincial Council elections. They included possible prisoners of conscience. In Kandy, for example, 28 DUNF supporters were arrested after putting up posters and distributing leaflets in April. They were released on bail. Arrests and detention of Sinhalese people believed to have been connected with the Janatha Vimukthi Peramuna (JVP), People's Liberation Front, in the south from 1987 to 1990, continued to be reported, but their number was not known.

According to official figures, 2,348 people were in detention under the Emergency Regulations or the Prevention of Terrorism Act in August: 338 in detention camps, 518 in rehabilitation centres, 1,092 in prisons and 400 in police stations. Of these, the majority in police custody were Tamil, while most of those in detention camps and rehabilitation centres were Sinhalese. Of those in prisons, 889 were Tamil and 203 Sinhalese. No figures were given for those detained in military custody.

At Kalutara prison alone, 464 Tamil prisoners had been held for over 32 months without trial, and many of the Sinhalese in prisons and detention camps had also been held for well over two years without trial. M.G. Palitha, a Sinhalese arrested in November 1989 in Polonnaruwa, had been held without charge or trial for 35 months. In May the Supreme Court reportedly awarded him financial compensation for unjustified detention. Tamil detainees held in connection with the conflict in the northeast began to be referred for "rehabilitation" – a form of untried detention in a rehabilitation camp – and at least 40 had been subsequently released by August.

Over 25 "disappearances" were reported from the northeast. Sixteen people reportedly "disappeared" after being arrested by the army at Vannathi Aru, Batticaloa District, in February. The army announced an internal investigation into these "disappearances" but its findings were not known by the end of the year. In Mannar District, three men reportedly "disappeared" in July after police took them from a bus.

The discovery of a body burned on a tyre at Modera, Colombo, in August raised fears of a resumption of "death squad" killings (see *Amnesty International Report 1990*) by forces linked to the government. A notice by the body suggested that the victim was an LTTE member who had been sought by the police for alleged involve-

ment in the assassination of the President and whose identity had been publicized. Two other bodies were found in August in Colombo. They had been blindfolded, assaulted and shot in the head. No outcome of investigations into these deaths was known by the end of the year.

In the north, hundreds of civilians were reportedly killed by the security forces as they attempted to cross the Kilali lagoon from the Jaffna peninsula to the mainland. Some appeared to be victims of extrajudicial executions. The lagoon, which provided the only remaining passage from the peninsula to the mainland, was a prohibited zone under the Emergency Regulations and all craft crossing the lagoon were vulnerable to attack. In some cases, navy personnel reportedly boarded boats and deliberately killed civilian passengers even if they offered no resistance.

There were also reports that security forces summarily executed LTTE members who offered no resistance and could have been arrested. For example, in January, after villagers in Kaluwankerny had been screened by the Tamil Eelam Liberation Organization – a militant group which works alongside the army – soldiers summarily shot dead two men who they alleged had been collecting "taxes" for the LTTE.

Five remand prisoners, all apparently former JVP members, were killed by prison guards in suspicious circumstances at Mahara prison in September. The authorities said they were shot while trying to escape. However, post-mortem examinations were alleged to have revealed injuries caused by beatings with blunt weapons after the victims had been shot in the legs.

There were continued reports of harassment and death threats, including the delivery of wreaths, issued by the military to journalists in the south. Iqbal Attas, defence correspondent of *The Sunday Times* (Colombo), received repeated death threats after he criticized the number of casualties sustained and weaponry lost during military operations in the north in October.

Impunity remained a major obstacle to the long-term improvement of human rights: no perpetrators of "disappearances" were known to have been prosecuted and the few trials of alleged human rights violators that did take place had failed to reach any conclusion by the end of the year. In one case, the authorities transferred the initial hearings into the murder of 39 Tamil

272

men, women and children at Mailanthanai, Batticaloa District, in August 1992 (see *Amnesty International Report 1993*) from Batticaloa to Polonnaruwa, making it more difficult for witnesses to attend. The defendants, 23 soldiers, faced a total of 83 charges. In August warrants for the arrest of 10 witnesses were issued after they had failed to attend the court.

The LTTE was responsible for grave human rights abuses in the northeast. They held an unknown number of political opponents in unacknowledged detention and were responsible for numerous abductions of people who were held for ransom. They obtained money from the local populace under threat of violence and were reported to have executed people alleged to have betrayed the LTTE or to have committed criminal offences, as well as members of rival Tamil groups. In August it was reported that the former deputy leader of the LTTE, Mahattaya, and several of his supporters had been detained by the LTTE. At least one of Mahattaya's aides was later said to have been executed in November but the situation of Mahattaya himself and others remained unknown.

Some prisoners were released by the LTTE through the International Committee of the Red Cross, including seven civilians captured in an LTTE attack on an army camp at Janakapura in July and several policemen held captive since 1990.

Amnesty International continued to urge the government to implement key human rights safeguards which the organization had proposed in 1991 (see *Amnesty International Report 1992*). In February Amnesty International made public its assessment that many essential safeguards had still to be implemented and called on the government to move forward quickly on these. Amnesty International also continued to press for full investigation of all "disappearances", including those which took place before 1991, for all political prisoners to receive prompt and fair trials, and for a halt to arbitrary arrests. It called for information on official investigations into reported human rights violations to be made known, and continued to call for perpetrators of violations to be brought to justice.

Amnesty International condemned executions of prisoners and other grave abuses by the LTTE and called on the LTTE to cease such practices immediately and to account for the whereabouts of those detained by LTTE forces. Amnesty International also urged the LTTE to respect human rights and international humanitarian standards.

In an oral statement to the UN Commission on Human Rights in March, Amnesty International included reference to its concerns about extrajudicial executions and "disappearances" in Sri Lanka.

SUDAN

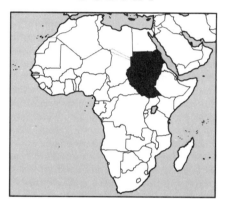

Hundreds of suspected government opponents were imprisoned. They included scores of prisoners of conscience. Most were detained without charge or trial for weeks or months. Torture was common and widespread, and some prisoners convicted of criminal offences were flogged. The fate of hundreds of prisoners who had "disappeared" in previous years remained unknown. Hundreds of people were extrajudicially executed in war-affected areas. All factions of an armed opposition group active in the south committed serious human rights abuses.

In October the ruling military National Salvation Revolution Command Council (NSRCC) announced its dissolution and replacement by a civilian government; Omar Hassan Ahmad al-Bashir remained President and the new government was mainly composed of the same officials. There was little change in the pattern of gross human rights violations established in previous years. In the war zones serious abuses were committed by all sides as armed conflict continued between the government and the Sudan People's Liberation Army (SPLA). By mid-1993, nearly three million people had been displaced in the south and adjacent areas of the north. In the Nuba mountains, the government forcibly evicted people from their homes and resettled them in so-called "peace villages" under the control of the army and the Popular Defence Force (PDF), a government-created militia.

All factions of the internally split SPLA were responsible for gross abuses of human rights. In a bitter factional war, opposing SPLA forces massacred civilians, often because of their ethnic origin, and killed dissidents as well as captured government soldiers.

Outside the war zones, the government suppressed all independent political activity. A state of emergency remained in force with political parties still banned. Between April and June there were mass arrests of members of traditional Islamic orders. In May the state took control of key mosques of the Ansar, Khatmiya and Ansar Sunna sects in the capital, Khartoum. In October the night curfew in force since 1989 was lifted in Khartoum. The Khartoum authorities continued to move people displaced from the war zones who were squatting around the capital to government-controlled camps away from the city.

In March the UN Commission on Human Rights appointed a Special Rapporteur on Sudan. In November he submitted an interim report to the UN General Assembly which concluded that "grave violations of human rights have taken place in Sudan".

Hundreds of people were arrested for political reasons, scores of whom were prisoners of conscience. Most were detained without charge or trial for a few weeks or months. They included members of traditional Islamic orders and banned political parties, trade unionists, civil servants, students, and people from the south and the Misseriya and Nuba communities. Most detainees were taken initially to secret detention centres known as "ghost houses"; some were subsequently moved to civil prisons.

At any one time, at least 100 political detainees were held in "ghost houses" and there were scores of other political prisoners in civil prisons. The practice of making suspected government opponents report daily to security offices, effectively a form of day-time detention, became increasingly widespread.

Several prisoners of conscience arrested in previous years remained in jail throughout the year, although some were released.

Ali Ahmad Hamdan, who had been arrested in May 1992, and two other members of the Ba'ath Arab Socialist Party (BASP), who had been arrested in December 1992, remained held without charge or trial. All three were apparently suspected of producing the underground newspaper al-Hadaf (The Target). At least four members of the banned Sudan Communist Party (SCP) who had been arrested in December 1992, including Farouq Ali Zacharia, an economist, also remained held throughout the year. Seven other SCP members arrested at the same time were released during 1993.

Journalists critical of the government or involved with underground opposition newspapers were among prisoners of conscience detained during the year. In January Mohamed Abdulsid, the Khartoum correspondent of the international daily Asharq al-Awsat, was arrested and held without charge or trial until March. Moatisim Sagiaroun and Ahmad Tutu, BASP members alleged to be journalists with al-Hadaf, were detained in March and remained held without charge or trial at the end of the year.

Over 90 people detained between April and June in northern and western towns were prisoners of conscience. The majority belonged to the Ansar religious order and the banned Umma Party. Some were released after a day, but most were held without charge for about six weeks. Others were detained for longer: they included two former cabinet ministers, Ibrahim al-Amin and Fadlallah Burma Nasir, who were arrested in mid-April and released in August and September respectively.

At least 15 people were detained in April after the authorities announced they had discovered a plot to organize acts of sabotage. Nine of them were shown on national television, shackled and bruised. Five other prisoners allegedly implicated in the plot were released between April and November, at least three of them on bail. The authorities repeatedly said that those detained in connection with the alleged plot would be tried, but no action had been taken by the end of the year.

Arrests of suspected government opponents continued throughout the year. In September the government took retaliatory action against several people who had met the UN Special Rapporteur. Twenty-nine women were arrested when trying to petition the UN official, two of whom were

274

dragged along the ground before being forced into police vehicles. All were released within hours. The Minister of Justice said that they had been arrested on the grounds that their gathering had been illegal.

In November at least 33 students were arrested after a student protest at Khartoum University turned into a confrontation with riot police. The students were detained without charge for several weeks. The authorities stated that only 17 students were held. The same month Sid Ahmad al-Hussein, the Deputy Secretary General of the banned Democratic Unionist Party (DUP) and a former cabinet minister, was arrested after a political meeting at Omdurman Ahlia University. The authorities announced that he would be charged with treason and espionage but he remained uncharged in detention at the end of the year.

In the war zones, the security services continued to arbitrarily detain suspected government opponents, particularly prominent or educated members of the Nuba community. For example, Hamid Yacoub was seized by security agents while on a bus and held incommunicado for two weeks in May. He was released only after a government minister intervened. In July Benjamin Loki Matayo, a priest, was detained by Military Intelligence officials in Juba. He remained in incommunicado detention without charge at the end of the year. In December over 60 members of the Misseriya ethnic group from South Kordofan were reportedly detained on suspicion of supporting the SPLA.

There was widespread torture by the army, other security agencies and the PDF. The victims included children. Detainees were frequently beaten when they were taken to "ghost houses" and torture during interrogation was systematic. Methods most often cited were beating, whipping and being forced to stand for long periods. For example, in March in Khartoum 13 school children who refused to join a government-created youth organization were reported to have been stripped and lashed with split bamboo canes and made to stand for several hours in the sun while detained by security officials.

Suspected government opponents arrested in the war zones were particularly at risk of torture in military detention centres. In the Nuba mountains, detainees alleged they had had bags containing chilli powder tied over their heads. In the south, there were reports that captured SPLA combatants were routinely tortured before being extrajudicially executed.

Children suspected of living on the streets in Khartoum were subjected to cruel, inhuman or degrading treatment after they were arbitrarily detained in round-ups. In May approximately 30 children under the age of 11 were reportedly beaten in a police station in south Khartoum after being detained.

Cruel, inhuman or degrading punishments, including flogging, were imposed by Public Order Courts after unfair trials. In September a senior judge revealed that punishments provided under Shari'a law had been imposed in secret in prisons: it was not clear whether these included limb amputations and executions. However, hundreds of people were flogged in public. The majority were from the urban poor, frequently petty traders and women convicted of brewing alcohol. For instance, Peter al-Birish, an Anglican bishop, received 80 lashes in July after being convicted of adultery. In November, eight men, among them three brothers of a prominent government opponent in exile, received 40 lashes after being convicted of consuming alcohol.

The fate of hundreds of people who "disappeared" in previous years remained unknown. The vast majority were civilians from the war zones. Evidence emerged in 1993 that Camillo Odongi Loyuk, a former soldier and administrator, had been beaten to death in custody in Khartoum in December 1992. The authorities stated in March that he had never been arrested, but it was known that he had been detained in Khartoum in August 1992.

There were no signs that a government-established committee of inquiry into hundreds of extrajudicial executions and the "disappearance" of 230 people in Juba between June and August 1992 was carrying out any work. Nevertheless, in the middle of the year official sources said that "the committee [had] found no evidence of improper action by the military courts or the army". No report was forthcoming by the end of the year and the committee did not appear to represent a genuine attempt to investigate human rights violations (see *Amnesty International Report 1993*).

Hundreds of civilians and prisoners were reported to have been extrajudicially executed during the year. For example, hundreds of villagers were killed during a prolonged offensive by government forces in the Nuba mountains which had begun in late 1992 and continued into 1993. In May, five prisoners held in el-Obeid prison were reportedly taken back to the Nuba mountains near Dilling and extrajudicially executed.

In the south, the army and PDF attacked villages and extrajudicially executed civilians in Bahr al-Ghazal and Upper Nile. In Bor, army patrols reportedly carried out a series of extrajudicial executions in the countryside around the town. In February, for instance, a young woman died after being captured and raped by soldiers. Her father, who was captured with her, was extrajudicially executed. In March PDF troops attacked villages around the railway line in northern Bahr al-Ghazal and allegedly killed civilians and raped scores of women. In another incident PDF troops abducted over 300 women and children, apparently intending to make them domestic slaves. Army units reportedly intervened to free the prisoners when the PDF attempted to take their captives back to northern Sudan.

All factions of the SPLA were responsible for gross human rights abuses, including deliberately killing deserters and torturing and killing captured government soldiers. In April, one of the factions, the Torit group, massacred about 200 Nuer villagers, many of them children, in villages around the town of Ayod. Some of the victims were shut in huts and burned to death. Others were shot. The killings were apparently in revenge for a massacre by troops belonging to the Nasir faction in 1991 (see *Amnesty International Report 1992*).

Amnesty International repeatedly appealed to the government to release all prisoners of conscience immediately and unconditionally, and to ensure that all political detainees were promptly and fairly tried, or released. It also expressed concern about torture, including floggings, "disappearances" and extrajudicial executions, and called for action to halt these abuses. In September Amnesty International published a report, *Sudan: The ravages of war – political killings and humanitarian disaster*, which called on all parties to the conflict to respect humanitarian law. The government failed to provide substantive responses to any of Amnesty International's appeals and dismissed the organization's criticisms as "distorted fiction". The government said that Amnesty International had no credibility because it had not visited Sudan recently.

Amnesty International also appealed directly to the SPLA to end deliberate and arbitrary killings and other abuses, to respect human rights and observe basic humanitarian standards. However, the SPLA apparently took no steps to end human rights abuses. In October a representative of the Torit faction dismissed Amnesty International's concerns about the SPLA's human rights record as "absurd".

In oral statements to the UN Commission on Human Rights in February and the UN Working Group on Indigenous Populations in July, Amnesty International included reference to its concerns in Sudan. Following submission of the UN Special Rapporteur's interim report, in December the UN General Assembly adopted a resolution expressing deep concern at serious human rights violations in the Sudan and called on the government and the SPLA fully to respect human rights.

SWAZILAND

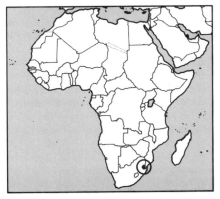

More than 60 people were briefly detained on account of their peaceful political activities and subsequently received suspended prison sentences. Most were ill-treated in custody. Army personnel and officially condoned paramilitary groups were implicated in ill-treatment and torture of detainees. A law allowing 60 days' administrative detention was repealed. Four death sentences were imposed and three others were commuted; no executions were reported.

276

National elections were held in October amid debate over the *tinkhundla* system of indirectly elected parliament. All party political activity remained prohibited under the King's Proclamation No. 12 of 1973 and the banned Peoples' United Democratic Movement (PUDEMO) called for a boycott of the elections. King Mswati III appointed Prince Mbilini Dlamini as Prime Minister in November. Pro-democracy activists advocating the legalization of political parties experienced renewed repression by police and vigilante groups loyal to the monarchy.

The Minister of Justice told the UN World Conference on Human Rights in June that no human right should be denied because the full enjoyment of other rights had not been achieved. However, following his return to Swaziland, the Ministry of Justice issued a statement in which it said that in developing countries, respect for human rights depends on the availability of economic and financial resources.

In August magistrates went on strike to oppose the government's appointment of a Special Committee to evaluate the work of magistrates and other judicial officers and to dismiss those found not to be performing their duties satisfactorily. Magistrates and lawyers objected to the establishment of the Special Committee on the grounds that it threatened the independence of the judiciary. Court proceedings were disrupted by the strike, which concluded with striking magistrates being heavily fined.

In September the King's Order-in-Council No. 1 of 1978, known as the 60-day detention law, was repealed. This order had allowed administrative detention without charge or trial for renewable 60-day periods of anyone deemed an opponent of the government. Also in September the Non-Bailable Offences Order of 1993 was issued. This denies bail to those held on a wide range of criminal charges, including contravention of Section 6 of the Public Order Act of 1963, a charge which could be misused to detain non-violent political activists.

Scores of government critics were arrested and charged with political offences during the year. For example, in March, 62 PUDEMO supporters were arrested in Nkhaba after attempting to meet to discuss the elections. They were confronted by an *impi* (paramilitary group) led by former Prime Minister Prince Bhekimpi Dlamini, as well as armed, uniformed government soldiers and plainclothes police. *Impi* members assaulted several PUDEMO supporters in full view of the police, but no charges were brought against those responsible despite formal complaints to the police by several of those assaulted. Fifty-six detainees, both men and women, were kept together overnight in the back of a police truck, without food, water or toilet facilities. All were charged under the 1973 Proclamation and released the following day on bail conditions that included a prohibition on further breaches of the 1973 Proclamation. Three members of this group were subsequently convicted of contempt of court after being arrested for further political activities. In August all 62 were convicted and sentenced to three-month suspended jail terms.

Four political activists, including former prisoner of conscience Dumisane Khosa, were arrested and charged under a new electoral law with "interfering with the elections", because they had distributed political leaflets. The cases against the four were dropped from the court register, but the charges remained and the four could still be prosecuted if their cases were rescheduled.

There were reports of soldiers assaulting and torturing a number of criminal suspects. In a separate case, PUDEMO regional secretary Professor Dlamini was seized by government soldiers loyal to Prince Bhekimpi in July, following repeated incidents of harassment by the police. During his interrogation, he was allegedly repeatedly threatened with being shot, and soldiers threatened to kill members of his family if he did not cooperate. He was released some 30 hours later but warned to leave the country or he would be killed. Both Professor Dlamini and PUDEMO laid charges of assault and abduction, but no official action was known to have been taken against the soldiers responsible.

Four death sentences were passed by the courts. In September the King commuted three death sentences which had already been confirmed on appeal. Seven people remained under sentence of death awaiting the outcome of appeals.

Amnesty International called for the withdrawal of charges against those peaceful political activists who could become prisoners of conscience if convicted, and for the amendment of laws affecting freedom of expression to bring them fully into conformity with international human rights standards. Amnesty International also urged the authorities to investigate all allegations of beatings and other ill-treatment of prisoners by the security forces or others acting with their acquiescence, and to bring to justice those found responsible for violating human rights. Amnesty International urged Swaziland to become a party to the African Charter on Peoples' and Human Rights and other relevant international instruments.

SWEDEN

A man died in custody after being severely ill-treated. The government expelled an asylum-seeker who risked grave human rights violations if returned to Peru.

Tony Mutka died in custody on 20 July, during his transfer from Hall prison, near Stockholm, to a distant hospital psychiatric unit. Wearing only his underpants, handcuffed behind the back, and with his legs in chains, he was transported from the prison lying on the floor of a van. One of the guards allegedly stood on his neck or head and shoulders during transport. He died of suffocation. Three of the four members of the prison staff involved in the transfer were charged. The three were convicted of misconduct and fined. The Prosecutor, who had sought convictions for gross misconduct and prison sentences, lodged an appeal.

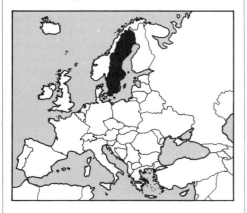

A Peruvian asylum-seeker, Mónica Castillo Páez, was expelled in August. She had fled to Sweden in 1990, but was refused asylum there, despite fears that she would be at grave risk if returned to Peru.

Her brother had "disappeared" after detention and was presumed dead and his lawyer had been maimed by a letter-bomb. Mónica Castillo Páez' cousin had been killed, allegedly by security forces, and she and her family had received threats from people thought to be acting with the support of the Peruvian security forces. The aircraft returning her to Peru made a scheduled stop in the Netherlands, where she was able to disembark and ask for asylum.

Amnesty International wrote to the government expressing concern about the death in custody of Tony Mutka. The organization urged the Swedish authorities not to forcibly return Mónica Castillo Páez to Peru.

SWITZERLAND

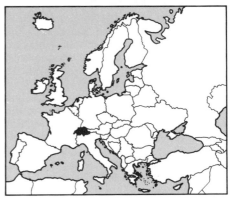

Scores of conscientious objectors to military service served sentences of imprisonment or compulsory work imposed by military tribunals. There were reports of ill-treatment in police custody.

In January the European Committee for the Prevention of Torture (ECPT), a committee of experts set up under the European Convention for the Prevention of Torture and Inhuman or Degrading Treatment or Punishment, published a report on its visit to Switzerland in 1991, with the government's response. The ECPT stated that it had received "numerous" allegations of ill-treatment in police custody and concluded that "the risk of being ill-treated in police custody cannot be dismissed". It made various recommendations to increase safeguards against ill-treatment, including the rights for all detainees in police custody to have access to a lawyer and to inform family or friends of their arrest.

278

Although a national referendum in 1992 had voted to introduce, in principle, a civilian alternative to military service, this was still not available during the year. However, draft federal legislation, covering the grounds on which conscientious objector status might be granted, admission procedures to civilian service and the nature and length of civilian service, was submitted to a national consultation between July and October. A revised text and the results of the consultation were due to be considered by parliament in 1994.

Meanwhile, under the Military Penal Code, refusal of military service remained a criminal offence. However, where a tribunal concluded that a conscript was unable to reconcile military service with his conscience because of "fundamental ethical values" he was sentenced to a period of work in the public interest and did not acquire a criminal record. Conscientious objectors failing to qualify for a sentence of compulsory work because, for example, the military tribunals considered that they opposed military service on political grounds, continued to receive sentences of up to 12 months' imprisonment.

Many sentenced conscientious objectors did not serve their sentences during the year. In several cantons moratoria were in force on the implementation of such sentences pending the introduction of legislation on civilian service. Some objectors sentenced to prison terms benefited from these, while others lodged appeals.

Nevertheless, a number of conscientious objectors entered prison: they were prisoners of conscience. Andrea Cadalbert began a three-month prison sentence in April for refusing military service. He had already completed initial military service training and eight refresher courses when he concluded that further military service was incompatible with his conscientiously held beliefs.

There were reports of ill-treatment in police custody, some of which referred to earlier years. It was reported that formal complaints rarely led to the conviction of police officers and that the police responded to medical evidence of injuries in a number of cases by stating that the injuries had been sustained while resisting arrest. Allegations of ill-treatment often concerned people of non-European ethnic origin.

In July Sidat Sisay, a Gambian national,

alleged to the federal authorities that he was ill-treated by Geneva airport police in January. He was in transit between the Gambia and the USA where he was due to receive urgent medical treatment for severe lower back pain and walking difficulties. On disembarkation at Geneva airport he was stopped by three policemen who accused him of carrying a forged passport and told him that he could not continue his journey. Sidat Sisay alleged that he was then ordered to strip naked in their office and was beaten and kicked on his back, leg and sides.

Sidat Sisay denied his passport was forged and was released after questioning by two officials. He said they confirmed the validity of his passport and advised that he be allowed to continue his journey, as scheduled, on a flight leaving the following morning. However, the next day the police and the airline concerned informed him his flight was cancelled, apparently because they believed there might be irregularities in his passport. He was held in an airport cell for two days, then put on a flight back to the Gambia.

The airline subsequently issued him with a refund ticket and he travelled to the USA in March. A medical report issued after his return home from Geneva recorded bruising to his lower back and chest and damage to his right knee, aggravating his existing medical condition. It concluded that his injuries were consistent with his allegations of ill-treatment. In November the Canton of Geneva's Justice and Police Department informed Sidat Sisay that an investigation had concluded that he had been subjected to a body search but not stripped naked or beaten. Sidat Sisay maintained his allegations of ill-treatment and offered to identify the police officers involved.

Amnesty International appealed for the release of prisoners of conscience and expressed concern that under the Military Penal Code people continued to be punished for refusing military service on grounds of conscience. It submitted comments to the Federal authorities on the draft legislation on civilian service, welcoming several of its proposals. The organization also sought information on the steps being taken to investigate allegations of ill-treatment and on the outcome of inquiries opened into such allegations.

SYRIA

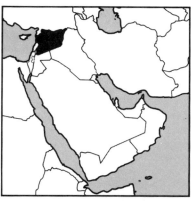

Over 500 long-term political detainees, including prisoners of conscience, appeared before the Supreme State Security Court (SSSC) whose procedures fall far short of international fair trial standards. Dozens of defendants were sentenced to lengthy prison terms; most hearings were still in progress at the end of the year. Several thousand other political prisoners, including prisoners of conscience, remained held. Some were serving prison sentences, but most were held without charge or trial under state of emergency legislation that had been in force for over 30 years. Other political prisoners continued to be detained beyond the expiry of their sentences. Torture of detainees continued to be reported. At least 14 people were executed.

In April the People's Council (parliament) passed a law to make it an offence punishable by death to produce or traffic in drugs. This took effect in July but no one was known to have been sentenced under it by the end of the year.

Trials of suspected government opponents before the SSSC, which began in 1992 (see *Amnesty International Report 1993*), continued throughout 1993. Over 500 long-term political detainees, including prisoners of conscience, appeared before the SSSC charged with membership of, or activities linked with, various unauthorized political parties and organizations. Some were charged with offences which carry the death penalty. All the defendants had been arrested between 1980 and 1992 and held without charge or trial. By the end of the year dozens had been sentenced to lengthy prison terms, but the cases of the others

were still in progress.

Those sentenced were all convicted of membership of or links with *Hizb al-'Amal al-Shuyu'i* (PCA), the Party for Communist Action, and were given prison terms ranging from three to 15 years. All were denied the right of appeal as the SSSC's verdicts are final. They included Rustum Ahmad Rustum and Malik al-As'ad, both prisoners of conscience, who were each sentenced to 15 years' imprisonment. Both had been detained since 1982.

Most of the defendants whose trials were still in progress were charged with having links with the PCA; *al-Hizb al-Shuyu'i al-Maktab al-Siyassi* (CPPB), the Communist Party Political Bureau; *Hizb al-Ba'th al-Dimuqrati al-Ishtiraki al-'Arabi* (ASDBP), the Arab Socialist Democratic Ba'th Party; *Hizb al-Ittihad al-'Arabi al-Ishtiraki fi-Suriya*, the Arab Socialist Union Party in Syria; *al-Tanzim al-Sha'bi al-Dimuqrati al-Nasiri*, the Nasserist Democratic Popular Organization; and Kurdish organizations. The defendants included prisoners of conscience such as Mufid Mi'mari, a teacher accused of supporting the CPPB, and Usama 'Ashur al-'Askari, a student charged for having links with the PCA. They had been held since 1980 and 1982 respectively.

Most of the defendants, including those who were convicted and sentenced, were represented by volunteer lawyers, although the majority of those charged in connection with the CPPB were said to have refused legal representation in protest against their trial before the SSSC. All had been denied access to legal assistance in lengthy pre-trial detention, including during interrogation by the SSSC prosecutor in preparation for the court hearings. The defendants first had contact with their lawyers during their initial appearance in court for questioning. Invariably, the lawyers had no prior access to their clients' files and were not aware of specific accusations brought against them. Access to this information was granted only after the defendants' first appearance before the court. In some cases lawyers were denied the right to meet their clients in private or to call defence witnesses. Access to the trial was mostly limited to defendants' relatives, but some sessions were attended by Amnesty International observers who visited Syria in May.

All those detained as suspected supporters of the ASDBP were referred for trial

AMNESTY INTERNATIONAL REPORT 1994

except Ahmad Suwaidani, a former diplomat and member of the Ba'th Party Regional Command who has been held without charge or trial since 1969. Similarly, those detained in connection with the CPPB were referred for trial with the exception of the organization's first secretary, Riad al-Turk, who remained in detention without charge or trial. In August he was reportedly allowed the first visit by his family since his arrest in 1980.

Several thousand other political prisoners, including prisoners of conscience, continued to be held. Ten of them, all prisoners of conscience, were serving prison sentences imposed in 1992 (see *Amnesty International Report 1993*) but the overwhelming majority were detained without charge or trial.

One of the 10 sentenced prisoners of conscience, Nizar Nayyuf, a sociologist serving a 10-year sentence, reportedly staged a hunger-strike in February in protest against conditions in Sadnaya Prison. He was said to have been transferred to Tadmur Prison where conditions are known to be particularly harsh. The other nine were believed to be still held in Sadnaya Prison at the end of 1993. They included Aktham Nu'aysa, a lawyer serving a nine-year sentence, who was reported to be in poor health.

Those who remained held without charge or trial included suspected members or sympathizers of unauthorized organizations, former government officials, members of professional associations, Palestinians and Lebanese nationals. Most of them had been held for many years.

Eight prisoners of conscience, all former members of the official Ba'th Party, including former government ministers, continued to be detained without charge or trial since their arrest between 1970 and 1972 (see previous *Amnesty International Reports*). All were said to be in poor health. One of them, Salah Jadid, a former Chief-of-Staff of the Syrian army and senior official of the Ba'th Party, died in custody in August in al-Mezze Military Prison after almost 23 years in detention. The authorities said he died of natural causes, although there was no independent autopsy or inquest into his death. Salah Jadid was the third prisoner in this group to die within nine months. The other two were Dr Nur al-Din al-Attassi, a former President of Syria, and Muhammad Rabah al-Tawil, a

former Minister of Interior, who died in December 1992 and April 1993 respectively, months after their release in August 1992. Six other prisoners of conscience from the same group were released in 1993, including Hakem al-Faiz and Kamil Hussain who had been detained since 1971.

Most uncharged political detainees were held for their alleged connections with *al-Ikhwan al-Muslimun*, the Muslim Brotherhood (see previous *Amnesty International Reports*). Most remained in incommunicado detention and their whereabouts were unknown. They included Muhammad Zahed Derkal, who was said to have been arrested in mid-1980 in the Abu Khair Mosque in Damascus. His whereabouts remained unknown until 1986 when former prisoners reported that he was held in Tadmur Prison. It was not known whether he was still held there. There was new information suggesting that Bara al-Sarraj, held since 1984 for alleged links with the Muslim Brotherhood, had been sentenced in 1989 to 20 years' imprisonment. No details about his trial or whereabouts were available.

Dozens of members of professional associations, notably doctors and engineers, were believed to be still held without charge or trial following their arrest in 1980 (see previous *Amnesty International Reports*). They included Tawfiq Draq al-Siba'i, a medical doctor who was arrested in Homs in 1980. His whereabouts were unknown. In May the SSSC concluded that the case against an engineer, Salim Khirbik, had elapsed and he was released.

Scores of Lebanese nationals and Palestinians arrested in previous years in Lebanon or Syria as suspected members of Lebanese and Palestinian political organizations remained held (see *Amnesty International Report 1993*). Most were held incommunicado and their whereabouts were unknown. They included a Lebanese national, Elias Yusuf al-Souri, who was arrested in 1980 in Beirut and has since been held in Syria.

Other political prisoners continued to be detained beyond the expiry of their sentences without further charges being brought against them. They included Mahmud Muhammad al-Fayyad, an army officer, whose 15-year prison sentence expired in 1985. He was believed to be in al-Mezze Military Prison.

Torture of political detainees reportedly remained common with methods including beatings on all parts of the body; *falaqa* (beatings on the soles of the feet); and *dullab* (the "tyre" method – hanging the victim from a suspended tyre and beating him or her with sticks and cables). Many of the defendants who appeared before the SSSC testified that they had been tortured in previous years and that confessions made during interrogation were extracted under duress. However, the court did not order medical examinations for such defendants or investigations into their allegations.

At least 14 people were executed. Nine had been convicted of rape and murder and five others, who were executed in May, had been convicted of setting fire to al-Hasaka Prison in March, causing the deaths of 57 inmates and injuring others. The speed with which the five were tried, sentenced and executed may have undermined the additional guarantees and safeguards required by international standards in death penalty cases.

New information was received suggesting that two political prisoners, Al-Hakam Karkoukli and Muhammad Jamal Tayyem, had been sentenced to death in 1980. No details were available about their trial or whether the sentences had been carried out.

Amnesty International continued to appeal for the immediate and unconditional release of all prisoners of conscience, for all other political prisoners to receive fair and prompt trials or be released, for impartial investigation of all torture allegations and deaths in detention, and for an end to the use of the death penalty. Unlike in previous years, Amnesty International received a number of replies from the Syrian authorities giving information in response to some of Amnesty International's queries.

In May two Amnesty International representatives visited Syria and observed some of the proceedings of the SSSC (see above). In meetings with government officials they urged the authorities to release all prisoners of conscience, drew attention to evidence of torture and other irregularities in the pre-trial detention of those being tried before the SSSC, and called for such defendants to be given fair trials or released.

Officials told Amnesty International's delegates that torture was not tolerated in Syria and that some members of the security forces were serving long prison sentences for having used torture, but no details were provided either of such cases or of any investigations into torture mounted by the Syrian authorities.

In an oral statement to the UN Commission on Human Rights in February, Amnesty International included reference to its concerns about arbitrary detention under the State of Emergency Law in Syria. In April Amnesty International submitted information about its concerns in Syria for UN review under a procedure established by Economic and Social Council Resolutions 728F/1503, for confidential consideration of communications about human rights violations.

TADZHIKISTAN

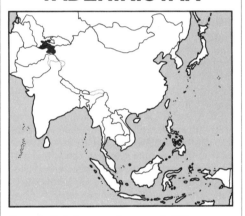

Extrajudicial executions and "disappearances" at the hands of pro-government forces continued on a large scale into early 1993, claiming the lives of scores of people who were targeted mainly because of their regional origin. Later in the year there were further "disappearances": the victims included political activists. One prisoner of conscience was conditionally released following trial, and two probable prisoners of conscience were convicted on allegedly fabricated charges of illegal possession of firearms. Four political prisoners were tortured in detention. At least six people were sentenced to death, including at least one political prisoner who may have received an unfair trial. Armed forces apparently subordinate to a self-proclaimed opposition "government-in-exile" were reported to have deliberately and arbitrarily killed captured government soldiers and civilians.

Armed conflict between government forces, who were supported by army units from Russia and neighbouring Central Asian states, and armed opposition groups continued sporadically throughout the year. The fighting was mainly in areas along the southern border with Afghanistan and in eastern Tadzhikistan. The government headed by Supreme Council Chairman Imamali Rakhmonov rejected appeals by foreign mediators for direct peace negotiations with the leaders of a self-proclaimed opposition "government-in-exile" formed in early 1993 in northern Afghanistan.

In June the Supreme Court banned four opposition parties and organizations linked to the previous coalition government which had resigned in November 1992 (see *Amnesty International Report 1993*). The ban was imposed on the Democratic Party, the Islamic Renaissance Party, and the *Rastokhez* (Renaissance) and *Lali Badakhshon* (Ruby of Badakhshan) organizations on the grounds that they had abandoned parliamentary methods to achieve their political goals, in favour of the violent seizure of power.

The wave of extrajudicial executions and "disappearances" which began after the capital, Dushanbe, fell to government forces in December 1992 at the climax of the civil war (see *Amnesty International Report 1993*) continued during January and February. Scores of people, mainly from the Pamir and Garm regions of eastern Tadzhikistan, were reportedly summarily executed or "disappeared" after being detained by forces of the People's Front of Tadzhikistan, a paramilitary group linked to the government. Extrajudicial executions and "disappearances" in Dushanbe were reported to have followed checks of identity papers on the streets and at the airport, and during house-to-house searches. Some people were reportedly executed on the spot, others were detained and their bodies found later in the street or the city morgue. The fate of others remained unknown. Isolated similar cases were reported later in the year in Dushanbe and in southern rural areas.

In April Democratic Party activist Ayniddin Sadykov "disappeared" after being taken from a bus in Dushanbe by armed men. In July member of parliament Saidsho Shoyev and his brother Siyarsho Shoyev "disappeared" after being seized by armed men from a Dushanbe street. In both cases the circumstances of the "disappearances" suggested that they were the work of forces operating with government complicity: the car used by the abductors of the Shoyev brothers was reportedly identifiable from its number plates as belonging to the Ministry of Defence.

Prisoner of conscience Bozor Sobir, a leading poet and former Democratic Party activist, was arrested in March. He went on trial before the Supreme Court in October and at the end of December was convicted of attempting to overthrow the government, attempting to inflame inter-ethnic discord and participating in unsanctioned demonstrations. He was given a two-year suspended sentence and was immediately released. He was acquitted of two other charges.

Two probable prisoners of conscience were sentenced to prison terms in March following separate trials on charges of illegal possession of firearms: there were grounds to believe that the charges had been fabricated because of their opposition political activities. Dzhumaboy Niyazov, a Democratic Party activist, was sentenced to seven years' imprisonment by the city court in Khudzhand, Leninabad Region, for illegal possession of cartridges for an automatic weapon. Nuriddin Sadiriddinov, a *Rastokhez* activist, was sentenced by the district court in Asht, Leninabad Region, to 10 years' imprisonment for illegal possession of a pistol and bullets. In both cases sources claimed that the firearms and ammunition had been planted during police searches of their homes.

Four political prisoners – Mirbobo Mirrakhimov, Akhmadsho Kamilov, Khayriddin Kasymov and Khurshed Nazarov – were tortured in pre-trial detention in investigation-isolation prison No. 1 in Dushanbe. All were reported to have been beaten during interrogation, as a result of which Khayriddin Kasymov was reported to have suffered a broken nose and had several teeth knocked out. Akhmadsho Kamilov was allegedly not allowed by his interrogators to sleep or to sit for long periods. Mirbobo Mirrakhimov had been the director of the state radio and television company under the previous coalition government and was charged with treason in the form of "conspiracy to overthrow the government", and defamation. Akhmadsho Kamilov, formerly director of national television, and Khayriddin Kasymov and Khurshed Nazarov, who were television journalists, were charged with "agitation and propaganda calling for the violent overthrow of the government" and theft of state property. They were arrested in January in neighbouring countries (Mirbobo Mirrakhimov in Turkmenistan and the three others in Kyrgyzstan) reportedly by local law enforcement officers, and forcibly returned to Tadzhikistan. They were still in pre-trial detention at the end of the year.

The death penalty remained in force for 18 peacetime offences as well as others in wartime. At least six people were sentenced to death. They included Adzhik Aliyev, a political prisoner and Islamic Renaissance Party activist, who was sentenced to death in August for crimes including treason, terrorism and murder following a possibly unfair trial. He was still awaiting the results of an appeal against his sentence at the end of the year.

Forces apparently subordinate to the opposition "government-in-exile" and based in the Kalai-Khumb district of the Gorno-Badakhshan Autonomous Region were reported in June to have deliberately and arbitrarily killed nine government soldiers whom they had taken prisoner. In July up to 200 civilian residents of the village of Sarigor, Khatlon Region, were reportedly deliberately killed by opposition forces based in Afghanistan who entered the village after overrunning a nearby border post.

Amnesty International continued to call on the Government of Tadzhikistan to investigate all reports of extrajudicial executions and "disappearances", and to bring those responsible to justice. In February Amnesty International wrote to Chairman Rakhmonov about statements by security officials indicating that security forces had been authorized to carry out summary executions. It urged the government to take all measures necessary to ensure that forces under government control were aware of and conformed fully to international standards on the use of force. Amnesty International also requested the government to confirm or deny media reports that illegal possession of firearms in certain circumstances had been made a capital offence. In a detailed reply received in June, the Chairman of the National Security Committee gave assurances that death sentences had not been passed on people found to be illegally in possession of firearms. He also asserted that the security forces used firearms only in self-defence or to protect the lives of others. However, he confirmed that the statements about which Amnesty International had expressed concern had indeed been made, albeit only as a warning against criminal activity. Amnesty International replied in July stating that even if intended only as a warning, such statements were unacceptable, since they could be interpreted as giving official authorization to summary executions.

Amnesty International called for the release of Bozor Sobir and for a judicial review of the cases of Dzhumaboy Niyazov and Nuriddin Sadiriddinov. It called on the government to ensure that detainees were not subjected to torture or any other form of ill-treatment. It called for a review of the case of Adzhik Aliyev on the grounds that he may not have received a fair trial. It urged commutation of all pending death sentences and continued to call for complete abolition of the death penalty.

In August Amnesty International wrote to the leaders of the Democratic and Islamic Renaissance Parties, as representatives of the self-proclaimed "Government-in-exile of the Republic of Tadzhikistan". Amnesty International expressed concern about the reported deliberate and arbitrary killings of captured government soldiers and civilian residents of Sarigor and made clear its total condemnation of such deliberate and arbitrary killings and hostage-taking. It called on the party leaders to ensure that all armed forces subordinate to or acting with the approval of the "government-in-exile" fully respect human rights and the basic humanitarian standards set out in the Geneva Conventions and other relevant international standards.

In May Amnesty International published a report, *Tadzhikistan: Hidden terror – political killings, torture and "disappearances" since December 1992*. The press centre of the Interior Ministry responded in June by denouncing Amnesty International as an organization whose main aim was "the publication and dissemination of slanderous material". Amnesty International published a further report, *Tadzhikistan: Human rights violations against opposition activists*, in October.

In an oral statement to the UN Sub-Commission on Prevention of Discrimination

284

and Protection of Minorities in August, Amnesty International included reference to its concerns in Tadzhikistan, including "disappearances" and political killings.

TAIWAN

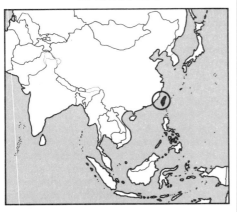

One possible prisoner of conscience was acquitted and one released at the end of his sentence. A conscript died as a result of torture in an army disciplinary unit. Prisoners under sentence of death continued to be held in conditions amounting to cruel, inhuman or degrading treatment. At least three people were executed.

A new cabinet led by Prime Minister Lien Chan was named in February by President Lee Teng-hui, who was re-elected Chairman of the ruling Kuomintang at a party congress in August. In January the Foreign Ministry issued a paper, *Report on Foreign Affairs*, which stated that rejoining the UN was one of Taiwan's "major diplomatic goals". Taiwan is not a party to any of the UN's treaties relating to the protection of human rights.

Chang Tsan-hung, a possible prisoner of conscience, was acquitted in March of charges of sedition and attempted murder for which he had been sentenced to 10 years' imprisonment in June 1992 (see *Amnesty International Report 1993*). The Taiwan High Court ruled that "no direct evidence could prove he resorted to violence and threats" in his advocacy of independence for Taiwan. He had been released on medical bail in October 1992. Chen Tzu-tsai, a prisoner of conscience, was released in November after serving a one-year prison sentence for illegal entry into Taiwan. He had returned to Taiwan

from the USA in 1991 despite being barred from doing so on account of his past political activities.

Chen Shih-wei, a conscript, died in July after being tortured by officers in an army disciplinary unit. There was no provision to allow him to apply for exemption from military service on grounds of conscience. He had reported to his unit for military service about 36 hours later than permitted. As a punishment, he was immediately assigned to the Li-Teh Training Unit, based on Green Island, where officers were apparently ordered to single him out for severe punishment. Chen Shih-wei was imprisoned, handcuffed and tortured for more than two days. He was then taken to hospital where he died four days later. Two officers were indicted on manslaughter charges and appeared before a military tribunal in October. The family of Chen Shih-wei was not allowed to make a statement before the tribunal. The trial had not been completed by the end of the year.

Prisoners under sentence of death continued to be subjected to cruel, inhuman or degrading treatment. They were forced to wear ankle shackles at all times, including during exercise periods. The Vice-Minister of Justice stated in July that shackles were necessary to prevent escape and suicide.

The Prison Law was revised in July to allow executions to be carried out by lethal injection; in the past they could only be carried out by firing-squad. According to unofficial reports, at least three people were executed by firing-squad during the year. Organs from the executed prisoners were used for transplants. Amnesty International feared that death-row prisoners were not in a position to give genuinely free consent to the use of their organs. The government did not publish detailed statistics on executions but indicated in May that all the prisoners whose death sentences had been upheld by the Supreme Court had been executed. The number of prisoners awaiting execution at the end of the year was not known.

There were fears that four citizens of the People's Republic of China who had applied for political asylum would be forcibly returned to China, despite being at risk of human rights violations there. However, in October the four were given permission to remain in Taiwan for 12 months and released from a holding centre. Three of them had been held for over a year. The four included Chang Kuo-chung and Wang Ching, who had been active in the 1989 pro-democracy movement in China. Both had fled to Taiwan in October 1989, but had been forcibly returned by the Taiwanese authorities and detained in China. They had returned to Taiwan again in September 1992.

In July Amnesty International published a report, *Taiwan: Ill-Treatment on "Death Row"*, in which it criticized the permanent shackling of condemned prisoners as an arbitrary additional punishment which constitutes cruel, inhuman or degrading treatment. Amnesty International also expressed concern about the use of organs from executed prisoners for transplant operations and about new legislation authorizing the use of lethal injections to carry out executions, both of which could lead to the involvement of medical personnel in executions. The organization urged the government to commute all death sentences and take steps towards abolishing the death penalty.

In August Amnesty International called on President Lee Teng-hui to order an independent and impartial investigation into the death of army conscript Chen Shih-wei. Amnesty International also urged the government to recognize the right to conscientious objection to military service and provide an alternative civilian form of service.

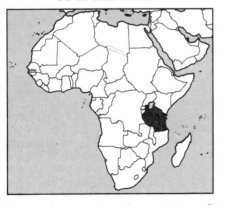

TANZANIA

Dozens of supporters of opposition political parties, some of them prisoners of conscience, were held for brief periods. Long-standing charges were dropped against a prominent political opponent of the government. Courts continued to impose cruel, inhuman or degrading punishments. At least three people were sentenced to death but no executions were reported.

In September, following months of debate about the creation of a Tanganyika government similar to the government of Zanzibar, the Union government, led by President Ali Hassan Mwinyi, announced that it would propose constitutional amendments to the 1964 union between Zanzibar and the mainland. The issue arose after it emerged in January that Zanzibar had secretly joined the Organization of Islamic Conference (OIC) in December 1992. In August Zanzibar withdrew from the OIC in an attempt to defuse the constitutional crisis.

There were widespread allegations that officials and supporters of the *Chama cha Mapinduzi* (CCM), Party of the Revolution, which retained control of government and administrative structures, had harassed members of opposition parties as they campaigned in the build-up to local government elections in November, the first elections under the multi-party constitution introduced in 1992.

In April militant Islamists destroyed three pork butcheries in Dar es Salaam. The authorities, accusing the *Baraza la Kuendeleza Koran Tanzania* (BALUKTA), the Quran Development Council of Tanzania, of involvement, banned the organization. Dozens of people were arrested, including prisoners of conscience, and held briefly. For example, 36 people who were arrested for demonstrating peacefully against the authorities' action in bringing charges against other BALUKTA members for allegedly destroying pork butcheries, were denied bail for periods ranging between one and two weeks before charges of holding illegal demonstrations were dropped. The 36, all prisoners of conscience, were then released.

In September at least 30 people were arrested in Zanzibar and Pemba after the Minister of Home Affairs instructed police to bring sedition charges against people abusing or insulting government leaders. The arrests followed a pattern established in previous years whereby the police arrest government opponents, charge them with sedition or a minor criminal offence, the courts deny bail for a brief period, ostensibly on the grounds that the accused might

286

interfere in police investigations, and the charges are subsequently dropped before the cases come to trial. Among those arrested after the minister's instructions were 10 people accused of organizing an illegal assembly and insulting Dr Salmin Amour, the President of Zanzibar. The 10, including Huwena Hamad, wife of Seif Shariff Hamad, a prominent Zanzibari leader and Vice-Chairman of the Civic United Forum (CUF), one of Tanzania's main opposition parties, appeared to be prisoners of conscience. They were released within days and it was not clear if charges remained outstanding at the end of the year.

Charges of illegally possessing government documents brought against Seif Shariff Hamad in 1989 were finally dropped in February. Seif Shariff Hamad had been released on bail in December 1991 (see *Amnesty International Report 1993*).

The courts continued to impose cruel, inhuman or degrading punishments in the form of caning. For example, in July Samil Walji from Dar es Salaam received six strokes of the cane after he had been convicted of trespassing with intent to commit an offence.

At least three men were sentenced to death for murder; two of them were militiamen from Singida convicted in the High Court of torturing and killing a prisoner arrested for rape in 1990. There were no reports of executions.

Amnesty International was concerned about the detention of prisoners of conscience, and about the use of caning and the death penalty.

THAILAND

An army conscript died after being beaten in custody and at least one person died and over 30 were injured as a result of police beatings of demonstrators. The fate and whereabouts of 21 people who went missing during the security forces' violent crack-down on pro-democracy demonstrators in May 1992 had still not been established by the end of the year; they may have been victims of extrajudicial executions. At least eight death sentences were imposed during the year but no executions were reported. Prisoners were reportedly held in conditions amounting to cruel, inhuman or degrading treatment, as were

asylum-seekers from Myanmar, thousands of whom were threatened with forcible return to Myanmar, where they would be at possible risk of human rights violations.

Prime Minister Chuan Leekpai, who had been elected in September 1992, continued to govern the country at the head of a five-party coalition. A law which empowered the supreme military commander to order troops to suppress demonstrations was repealed in March and a bill requiring prior Cabinet approval for military intervention in civil disturbances was passed by the Senate in July. Both pieces of legislation were enacted in the wake of the military's violent suppression of pro-democracy demonstrators in May 1992 in Bangkok, the capital, during which at least 52 people were killed and some 700 people injured (see *Amnesty International Report 1993*).

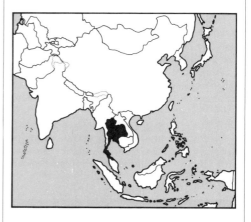

In a statement by the Thai Government to the UN World Conference on Human Rights in Vienna in June, Foreign Minister Prasong Soonsiri announced that his government was taking steps to accede to the International Covenant on Civil and Political Rights; however, at the end of the year accession to the treaty had not taken place.

Prominent social critic and Buddhist scholar Sulak Sivaraksa, who returned to Thailand to face charges of lese-majesty in December 1992, was formally charged in March, and his trial continued intermittently throughout the year. He would be considered a prisoner of conscience if convicted and sentenced to prison.

On 6 May Samphan Pinyoying, an army conscript, was severely beaten by a drill sergeant and later died in hospital. His wife stated that he had previously been in good health. The Army Commander-in-

Chief subsequently promised to investigate the death, and bring those found responsible to justice, but no further information emerged by the end of the year.

Ill-treatment of unarmed demonstrators by police was reported on several occasions, in at least one instance leading to the death of a demonstrator. In late February and March, protests broke out against the construction of the Pak Moon hydroelectric dam in Ubon Ratchathani province. Protesters, concerned that the dam would displace hundreds of people and harm the environment, were reportedly beaten by police with clubs during a demonstration in March. After conflict between those in favour of the dam's construction and those who opposed it, police allegedly attacked the anti-dam demonstrators. Three demonstrators were reportedly seriously injured and at least 30 others received minor injuries. The House of Representatives Committee on Human Rights and Justice investigated the incident, but in early April its Chairman stated that the evidence was too contradictory to lead to prosecutions. The Interior Ministry held its own investigation, the preliminary findings of which were that the police had not acted with excessive force. However, the final results of the Interior Ministry investigation were not known by the end of the year.

On 8 May Sa-ngiam Tomjai-od was severely beaten by police during an initially peaceful demonstration by thousands of farmers in Kamphaeng Phet province to demand that the government protect the falling price of rice. He died later that day in hospital of severe head injuries. His wife stated that she had witnessed police beating his head with a baton and kicking him in the face. Over 30 other demonstrators and police officers were reportedly injured during a clash between police and protesters. The Interior Ministry set up a committee to investigate the incident and the House of Representatives Committee on Justice and Human Rights also indicated that it would conduct an investigation. In early June the Interior Ministry committee found that the police were not guilty of killing Sa-ngiam Tomjai-od, but urged the Police Department to continue its attempt to identify those responsible for beating him. No further information regarding the results of the investigation was available by the end of the year.

The whereabouts of 21 people who vanished during the security forces' violent crack-down on the May 1992 demonstrations remained unknown; they may have been the victims of extrajudicial executions. In May, 36 relatives of people who were killed or went missing during the 1992 demonstrations filed a civil lawsuit against members of the government in power at the time of the demonstrations. In November, four parents whose sons had been killed in the May 1992 crack-down appeared at a court hearing and claimed that they had received inadequate compensation. However, no information about this case was available. An Interior Ministry committee had not made any progress in locating the missing 21 during the year, and most of their families had received no compensation. By the end of the year, the government had not made public the findings of a Defence Ministry investigation into the military's crack-down on the demonstrations, although the final report had been submitted to the government in July 1992.

A total of 285 prisoners were reported to be under sentence of death at the end of the year. At least eight death sentences were imposed during the year, four for heroin-trafficking and four for murder. No executions were reported.

There were continuing reports of criminal prisoners being held in conditions amounting to cruel, inhuman or degrading treatment, including the use of iron shackles, lack of medical care and overcrowding. Allegations of such ill-treatment focused on foreigners serving prison sentences for drug-trafficking, but in August the Interior Ministry denied that torture or ill-treatment occurred in Thai prisons.

Thai police continued to detain in harsh conditions asylum-seekers from Myanmar (Burma), particularly those who participated in demonstrations against the military government there and who refused to go to a "safe camp" run by the Thai authorities in western Thailand. Asylum-seekers were in many cases charged with illegal immigration and were routinely fined and sentenced to imprisonment for terms of several months in the Immigration Detention Centre (IDC) in Bangkok, then deported back to Myanmar. Prisoners in the IDC were routinely held in extremely overcrowded cells. There were continuing reports of asylum-seekers from Myanmar being beaten by IDC prison officials, although Amnesty

288

International was not able to confirm these allegations.

Almost 8,000 asylum-seekers from Myanmar belonging to the Mon ethnic group at Lah Loe refugee camp, Kanchanaburi province, faced forcible return to Myanmar. The Thai authorities announced plans to repatriate most of them to a site in Halakanee, Myanmar. If repatriated, they would be at possible risk of human rights violations (see **Myanmar** entry).

Amnesty International expressed its concern to the authorities about allegations of beatings of asylum-seekers by prison officials and conditions of detention which amounted to cruel, inhuman or degrading treatment at the IDC in Bangkok. The authorities responded by stating that the Burmese asylum-seekers were fighting among themselves, which necessitated the intervention of prison officials, who claimed that they did not ill-treat the detainees.

TOGO

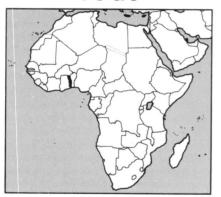

At least 50 people were extrajudicially executed by the security forces, who continued to perpetrate widespread human rights violations with impunity. Dozens of suspected government opponents were arrested, including possible prisoners of conscience; many were ill-treated and at least one reportedly "disappeared". In August, 21 prisoners died in detention, reportedly as a result of torture or ill-treatment. Two political prisoners were sentenced to prison terms after being convicted on the basis of evidence allegedly extracted under torture.

There was continued political instability as a result of tension between the Head of State, General Gnassingbé Eyadéma, and opponents of his administration. In January President Eyadéma unilaterally re-appointed Joseph Kokou Koffigoh as Prime Minister, asserting that the official period of transition agreed at a National Conference in 1991 had ended in December 1992. This undermined the power of the transitional executive body, *Haut Conseil de la République*, High Council of the Republic, which declared the appointment invalid. The new government formed by Prime Minister Koffigoh was increasingly criticized by *le Collectif de l'opposition démocratique*, the Collective of Democratic Opposition, known as COD-II, and a general strike which had begun in November 1992 continued until August. Independent human rights organizations came under pressure from the government, and opposition leaders and supporters, as well as journalists working for independent newspapers, were subject to intimidation and harassment by the security forces, and by supporters of the *Rassemblement du peuple togolais* (RPT), the Assembly of the Togolese People, headed by the President. RPT supporters were also attacked by opposition supporters in some areas. Over a quarter of a million citizens fled from Togo to seek refuge abroad.

General Eyadéma was returned to power in the presidential election of 25 August which was widely criticized as unfair. Gilchrist Olympio, an opposition leader and victim of an assassination attempt in May 1992 (see *Amnesty International Report 1993*), was prevented from standing in the election, and there were many reported irregularities in the voting. A special security force, set up in April to exclude members of the army, was given the task of keeping order during the elections, under the supervision of military advisers from France and Burkina Faso. Legislative elections had not taken place by the end of the year.

At least 50 people were extrajudicially executed by the security forces. They included at least 19 people who were shot dead on 25 January in Lomé, the capital, when the security forces opened fire without warning on a peaceful opposition demonstration in support of French and German government intervention in the political process in Togo. Five days later, apparently in reprisal for the killing of a soldier and a gendarme, the security forces again fired indiscriminately on civilians, killing at least five. In a related incident on 1 February, Date Issac Gbikpi-Benissan, the bodyguard of opposition leader Léopold Gnininvi, was killed by unknown assailants, believed to be members of the security forces. The Minister of Defence was ordered by General Eyadéma to open an investigation into the violence on 30 January. However, there was no evidence that an investigation actually took place.

At least 20 people, including soldiers and civilians, were summarily executed following an attack on the barracks of the *Régiment interarmes togolais* (RIT), Togolese Combined Regiment, on 25 March. The reason for the attack was unclear: some reports suggested that the attackers came from Ghana, others that it was a settling of scores within the barracks. Those executed included Colonel Eugène Koffi Tepé, deputy chief of army staff, who was apparently suspected of having instigated the attack, and three of his relatives. They were killed in the immediate aftermath by soldiers loyal to General Eyadéma. Over the next two days other soldiers were executed, apparently because of suspected complicity in the attack or because they were suspected of belonging to the clandestine Association of Democratic Servicemen, or because of their ethnic origin. Almost all of those targeted in this way came from ethnic groups such as the Ewe and Kotokoli, which formed a minority in the security forces dominated by members of General Eyadéma's own northern-based Kabyé ethnic group. One soldier, Yao Agbémavi Akiti, "disappeared" after he was reportedly questioned by his superior officers on 29 March. His body was later found in the mortuary of Lomé's main hospital, covered in knife wounds. Over 100 members of the security forces fled to Ghana and Benin, fearing for their safety.

There were several other reports of extrajudicial executions and attempted assassinations by the security forces. In February opposition activist Léopold Ayivi was shot and seriously injured by two armed men apparently linked to the security forces. In mid-April Bondja Bidjakine, from Naki-Ouest in northern Togo, was reportedly shot at point-blank range by soldiers pursuing villagers who had chanted slogans hostile to President Eyadéma during a public meeting. On 24 August, the eve of the presidential election, the deputy mayor of Lomé, Louis Amédome, was seriously injured and his motorcycle taxi driver killed when they failed to stop at a road-block manned by the security forces who apparently suspected Louis Amédome of having opposition sympathies. He was taken into custody and remained in detention without charge or trial at the end of the year. A statement by the authorities linked this incident with the discovery of an alleged coup plot the same day; the authorities said two men, who later escaped, had been intercepted at the border with Ghana in possession of a grenade and other materials.

Dozens of people were arrested by the security forces; many of them were ill-treated and at least one reportedly "disappeared". Most were not formally charged and were apparently arrested for their non-violent opposition to the government. At least 30 were reported to be still held, mostly without charge and apparently unlawfully, at the end of the year. Corporal Nikabou Bikagni, arrested in October 1992 (see *Amnesty International Report 1993*), appeared in court on 31 December charged with importing arms and ammunition but his trial was postponed. At least four people, apparently arrested solely because they were related to Corporal Bikagni, remained in detention without charge or trial in the civilian prison in Kara.

Over 40 soldiers and civilians were arrested following the attack on the RIT barracks on 25 March. Most of the civilians were reportedly released by July, but at least 15 soldiers were still detained at the end of the year, including Major Fondoumi, and Private Kokou Agbenya, who was reportedly severely beaten when arrested. They were held, incommunicado and apparently illegally, without being remanded by a judicial official, at various military locations.

Government opponents were arbitrarily arrested and detained, particularly in areas where there was strong support for the President and the RPT. Between March and May, five members of the Odanou family were arrested in the northern town of Korbongou, apparently because they supported the opposition. Four were released but Kanlou Odanou apparently "disappeared" in detention and was feared to be dead. Another member of his family, Landame Odanou, had apparently been held since September 1991 without charge or trial and reportedly remained in detention at the end of 1993.

On 26 August, at least 40 people, mostly opposition supporters, were arrested following violence the previous day in Agbandi, central Togo. They were taken to the Gendarmerie in nearby Blitta. It was not clear whether they had been involved in the election day violence but within 24 hours at least 21 of them died in custody, including four youths aged between 12 and 15, either at the Blitta Gendarmerie or at the hospital in nearby Sokodé. The authorities said that 15 of the prisoners had been poisoned by food brought to them by their relatives; a French police toxicologist who examined a sample of contaminated food sent to France by the authorities reportedly identified poison, but there was no examination of the bodies. Those who died were reported to have been assaulted in custody and then forced into a small cell, possibly causing asphyxiation. The remaining detainees were transferred to the Gendarmerie headquarters in Kara before being released on the orders of a magistrate. There was no impartial inquiry established into the deaths.

On 27 August, a relative of one of the detainees who had died, Kokou Okessou Mbooura, was arrested in Blitta and charged with attempting to administer a poison. However, it appeared that when he arrived in Blitta, at least 15 of the detainees had already died and others were seriously ill. Held in prison in Kara, he had not been brought to trial by the end of the year.

In November several journalists and others associated with independent newspapers were arrested and held in Lomé and Kara. Some appeared in court and were released, but Ali Akondo and Tampoudi Dermane remained in detention awaiting trial at the end of the year. Moudassirou Katakpaou-Touré, the editor of an independent newspaper, *La Lettre de Tchaoudjo* (The Tchaoudjo Letter) was brought to trial in December on charges of offending the President and libelling the President and the Minister of Defence. He was found guilty on both counts, fined and released, as the remainder of his sentence was suspended. He was a prisoner of conscience.

The use of torture by the security forces was reportedly widespread, with methods including severe beatings and electric shocks. Two men, Attiogbé Stéphane Koudossou and Gérard Akoumey, arrested in July in connection with bomb attacks in Lomé, were convicted by a criminal court in Lomé on the basis of confessions which they alleged had been extracted under torture during their pre-trial detention and which the court took no steps to investigate. They were sentenced to three years' imprisonment in September. Captain Charles Esso Pello, who had been arrested in July 1992 (see *Amnesty International Report 1993*), and was reportedly tortured with electric shocks, was apparently released on bail.

In May a Togolese opposition group in exile in Ghana was reported to be holding captive at least one person, Vincent Coco Adote Akouete-Akue. There were subsequent reports that he was beaten to death by former Togolese soldiers who had joined the opposition group and suspected him of being a spy.

Throughout the year, Amnesty International expressed concern to the government about a wide range of human rights violations – including extrajudicial executions, "disappearances", detention without trial, deaths in detention and torture – carried out with impunity by the security forces. In October the organization published a report, *Togo: Impunity for killings by the military*, focusing on the armed forces' involvement in human rights violations committed in 1993 and previous years. The report noted that soldiers appeared fully confident that, with President Eyadéma in power, they would not be held to account for human rights violations. Amnesty International called on the government to investigate persistent violations by the security forces and bring those responsible to justice.

TRINIDAD AND TOBAGO

An 11-year-old boy was flogged. There were attempts to resume executions but none were carried out. At least four people were sentenced to death. Fifty death sentences were commuted. At the end of the year there were just over 50 people on death row.

In April an 11-year-old boy was sentenced by a magistrate to receive a flogging of 20 strokes, in violation of national law and international standards prohibiting torture and cruel, inhuman or degrading punishment. He had pleaded guilty to a charge of being in possession of cocaine; he had, allegedly, been given a small sum of money to carry the drugs from one adult to another. The Corporal Punishment (Offenders not over Sixteen) Act allows offenders under 16 to be given six strokes with a tamarind or similar rod. The flogging was carried out immediately after sentencing, with a leather belt. The boy was therefore denied the right of appeal, already seriously restricted by this Act. Furthermore, the magistrate ordered the boy to be confined and to receive no visitors, not even his parents. The right for children deprived of their liberty to maintain contact with their family through visits and correspondence is enshrined in the UN Convention on the Rights of the Child, to which Trinidad and Tobago is a party. A court hearing seeking compensation and other redress for the boy, which was due to take place in May, was postponed several times and had not taken place by the end of the year.

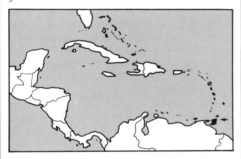

New death sentences were imposed and there were renewed attempts to resume executions. There have been no executions since 1979. Four men were sentenced to death in March, all for the murder of a businessman nearly four years before. Five prisoners, convicted of murder between 1977 and 1988, were issued with execution warrants during the year: Michael Bullock and Irvin Phillips were scheduled for execution in August; Ramcharan Bickaroo and Robinson LaVende, two of the longest-serving death row prisoners in the Caribbean, were to have been hanged in October; and Victor Baptiste was also to be hanged in October. However, all five were granted stays of execution by the High Court after constitutional motions were filed on their behalf, arguing that executions would infringe their constitutional rights. The motions had not been heard by the end of the year.

The appeals of Gayman Jurisingh, Peter Matthews and Faizal Mohammed, who were scheduled for execution in November 1992, were dismissed by the Court of Appeal in April (see *Amnesty International Report 1993*). They were granted conditional leave to appeal to the Judicial Committee of the Privy Council (JCPC) in London, which is the final court of appeal for Trinidad and Tobago, but their appeal was still pending at the end of the year. The decision in their cases also affected Brian Francois and Lal Seeratan, whose executions had been scheduled for December 1992 (see *Amnesty International Report 1993*).

A decision by the JCPC in the case of two Jamaican prisoners – that execution more than five years after sentencing would constitute "inhuman or degrading punishment or other treatment" and that sentences should be commuted to life imprisonment – was applicable to cases in Trinidad and Tobago (see **Jamaica** entry). In December the Attorney General announced that 50 prisoners who had been under sentence of death for over five years would have their sentences commuted. The 10 prisoners who had been scheduled for execution between November 1992 and October 1993 benefited from the ruling.

The Court of Appeal upheld the appeal of a death row prisoner sentenced for a murder committed in 1979. Bunny Brann was convicted in 1980 and then in 1985 and 1988 as a result of retrials following successful appeals. At his latest appeal the court ruled against another retrial on account of the time he had already spent in prison, the evidence against him and the cost of further proceedings; it ordered his release on 7 October. He had spent 13 years on death row. The court reserved a decision on his co-appellant, Donaldson Mottley. However, his was one of the 50 sentences commuted in December.

In May Amnesty International wrote to the Minister of Legal Affairs to express concern about the flogging of the 11-year-old boy and said he should be entitled to fair and adequate redress from the state, including financial compensation. The organization urged the government to ensure that those involved in the judicial process were fully informed of the provisions of current legislation; to amend the country's laws to reflect its obligations under international law; and to make these obligations widely known, especially to those involved in judicial procedures. Amnesty International urged the government to abolish corporal punishment and not to permit its use as a judicial punishment or to punish breaches of discipline in prisons.

Amnesty International appealed to the government to grant clemency to all prisoners under sentence of death and made specific appeals on behalf of prisoners whose executions were scheduled.

In August Amnesty International protested to Prime Minister Patrick Manning about statements reportedly made by the Minister of National Security shortly before the scheduled August executions. The Minister was quoted as having urged members of the public to protest against the actions of those who he said were "overly concerned with the rights of the criminal", apparently a reference to human rights lawyers who intervene in death penalty cases. He reportedly said, "when they file their motions to stop the hangings you must get up and let your voices be heard", which Amnesty International feared could lead to harassment or intimidation of lawyers and a reduction in the number willing to assist death row prisoners. Amnesty International drew attention to the requirements of the Basic Principles on the Role of Lawyers, adopted by the Eighth UN Congress on the Prevention of Crime and the Treatment of Offenders, and was further concerned that the Minister's strongly retentionist views could affect his review of cases carried out as Chairman of the Committee on the Prerogative of Mercy.

No replies had been received from the government by the end of the year.

TUNISIA

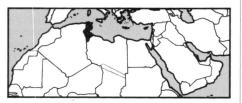

Hundreds of people suspected of sympathizing with illegal Islamist or left-wing opposition groups were arrested during the year. They included scores of prisoners of conscience. Other prisoners of conscience were among over 2,000 political prisoners serving sentences imposed after unfair trials in 1993 or previous years. Hundreds more people, many of them women, were detained or ill-treated apparently because of their relationship to suspected members of illegal parties. Released detainees and others had their movements restricted. Detainees were frequently held incommunicado for illegally prolonged periods: their arrest dates were falsified to conceal this. Torture and ill-treatment in the Ministry of Interior, police stations and other secret detention centres were widespread. Reports of cruel, inhuman or degrading treatment of prisoners were received from many prisons.

In April Tunisia made a declaration under Article 41 of the International Covenant on Civil and Political Rights (ICCPR), allowing communications from states concerning violations of that treaty, although it has not yet ratified either the (First) Optional Protocol (allowing communications from individuals concerning violations of the ICCPR) nor the Second Optional Protocol, aiming at the abolition of the death penalty. An Ombudsman was appointed to receive individual complaints about actions by any public body. However, neither he nor other human rights advisers in various ministries prevented or investigated serious human rights violations. They failed to provide details on the whereabouts and legal status of detainees held in illegally prolonged incommunicado detention and did not investigate cases of falsification of arrest dates and allegations of torture or ill-treatment.

Amendments to the legal code passed in November gave a broad definition of "terrorist" offences, including "inciting racial or religious hatred". The amendments made it possible to prosecute people for offences defined as "terrorist" committed in other countries, even if they are not recognisable crimes under that country's law. The period of preventive detention was reduced to a maximum of nine months for misdemeanours and 14 months for criminal offences.

There was new government action against human rights activists following the government's dissolution in 1992 of the *Ligue tunisienne des droits de l'homme* (LTDH), Tunisian Human Rights League (see *Amnesty International Report 1993*). In February, 18 human rights activists were arrested for setting up a national committee to defend prisoners of conscience. The committee's coordinator, Salah Hamzaoui, was held for two weeks; the others were released after a few hours. They were charged with forming an unauthorized organization, distributing leaflets and spreading false information. No trial had been held by the end of the year. The dissolution of the LTDH was quashed by a decision of the administrative court, but the league carried out no public activities during the year.

Hundreds of suspected sympathizers of the unauthorized Islamist organization *al-Nahda*, and scores of supporters of the *Parti communiste des ouvriers de Tunisie* (PCOT), Tunisian Communist Workers' Party, were arrested during the year. Many were held incommunicado (*garde à vue*) in pre-trial detention far beyond the 10-day legal limit. Arrest dates were consistently falsified to conceal this fact. Some of those arrested were released uncharged, but hundreds were sentenced to terms of imprisonment after unfair trials. Some were prisoners of conscience. Some detainees were reportedly held secretly in private houses immediately after their arrest.

In July and August dozens of suspected government opponents, including Tunisians resident abroad who had returned for their summer holidays, were arrested and kept in *garde à vue* detention for up to two months: many alleged they were tortured. They included Samir Moussa, who was arrested at Tunis airport in July and detained incommunicado until September when he was released uncharged. Salaheddine Zikikout, a student in France since 1988, was arrested on arrival at the port in Tunis, the capital, in early August and held incommunicado until late September, although his arrest date was falsified and recorded as 19 September. He was reportedly tortured.

Tawfik Rajhi, an academic resident in France since 1982, was arrested in July four days after his return to Tunisia for a visit. He was held incommunicado for 23 days and his arrest date was falsified. He was allegedly ill-treated and forced to sign a police statement which he had not read, and was then sentenced in August to two years' imprisonment and two years' *contrôle administratif*, administrative control (see below), on charges of membership of *al-Nahda* (subsequently reduced on appeal to eight months' imprisonment). He was

convicted solely on the basis of his confession. The court judgment failed to record either his prolonged incommunicado detention or his rejection of his confession. He was a prisoner of conscience.

Scores of prisoners of conscience sentenced in previous years remained in prison throughout the year. Seven were granted amnesties in January, including two pregnant women who had been ill-treated after their arrest in November 1992. Another, Moncef Ben Salem, a university professor, was released from prison in May after the completion of his sentence (see *Amnesty International Report 1991*) but restricted in his movements and denied a passport. People who visited his home were questioned by the police.

Some relatives of suspected government opponents were detained apparently to induce those being sought to give themselves up. For example, a teenage girl from Tajerouine was arrested in March in place of her sister who had been sentenced *in absentia* to eight months' imprisonment for membership of *al-Nahda* and for holding unauthorized meetings. The family was told that the teenager would be released when her sister surrendered. The sister did so the following day and was detained, whereupon the teenager was held incommunicado for a further four days and questioned about her sister's activities.

Critics and suspected opponents of the government were increasingly placed under administrative control when released from prison, even when it was not part of their court-imposed sentence. Those affected were required to report to a local police station regularly, sometimes as often as twice a day.

Trials of suspected government opponents violated international standards for fair trial. In several cases, defence lawyers complained that detainees had signed confessions after being tortured during illegally prolonged incommunicado pre-trial detention but such allegations were ignored by the courts, which failed to order investigations and accepted contested confessions as evidence of guilt. Hundreds were convicted under laws which restrict freedom of assembly, expression and association for allegedly belonging to an illegal organization, distributing leaflets, participating in unauthorized meetings, collecting funds for unauthorized organizations and other offences. Some were sentenced to prison terms solely for giving small sums of money for distressed families of political detainees.

Thirteen women students and teachers from Tajerouine were among the prisoners of conscience sentenced after unfair trials. They were tried in El Kef in February, convicted and sentenced to between six and eight months' imprisonment on charges which included distributing leaflets (although no leaflet was produced as evidence during the trial). Five of them were reportedly tortured and sexually harassed while in pre-trial detention.

In January, four men were sentenced to seven months' imprisonment for membership of an unauthorized organization and collecting funds: the money had been given to the sick mother of a detainee.

Naoufel Ziadi, General Secretary of the *Union générale des étudiants tunisiens*, General Union of Tunisian Students, and an outspoken critic of the government, was arrested in May after he had been sentenced *in absentia* to two years' imprisonment on drugs charges. The charges were based on accusations made by another detainee during interrogation and appeared to refer to another person with the same name. The conviction and sentence were upheld in June, even though the other detainee withdrew his accusation and there was no other evidence against Naoufel Ziadi. He was released on bail pending appeal.

Torture and ill-treatment of detainees remained common both in the Ministry of the Interior and at police stations. The methods used included beatings, especially on the soles of the feet, sometimes when the victim was suspended by the ankles; suspension for long periods in contorted positions, often accompanied by beatings; semi-suffocation with cloths drenched in dirty water or bleach; sexual abuse with sticks and other objects; and electric shocks. Women detainees, particularly those arrested in connection with *al-Nahda* or the PCOT, were sexually abused and threatened with rape.

One woman student who was held incommunicado for seven days at El Kef police station in February alleged that she was stripped and beaten by guards. At her trial, however, the court ignored a request by her lawyer that she be medically examined and she was sentenced to seven months' imprisonment for membership of the PCOT and illegal collection of funds.

Mounir Jaouadi, an *al-Nahda* supporter who was forcibly returned in January from Algeria, where he was seeking asylum, was detained incommunicado for two months in the Ministry of the Interior. He was beaten and severely tortured, and only allowed access to his family in March. When they saw him, his relatives barely recognized him: his face was bruised and he could hardly walk. Nine other Tunisians forcibly returned from Algeria in January and July were also allegedly tortured in incommunicado detention (see **Algeria** entry).

No further steps were known to have been taken to investigate eight deaths in custody in 1991 and 1992, despite compelling evidence of torture. The authorities refused to reopen investigations into the deaths of Rachid Chammakhi and others in 1991, and no details emerged of the investigation which the authorities had said would be reopened into the death in custody of Faisal Barakat in October 1991 (see *Amnesty International Report 1993*).

There were frequent reports of ill-treatment of prison inmates, including beatings, food deprivation, and detention in isolation cells. Some prisoners, including suspected members of *al-Nahda* jailed in 1992, were reportedly taken from prison to the Ministry of the Interior and tortured. Some political prisoners were also reportedly raped and beaten by criminal prisoners who were held in the same cells but their complaints were consistently ignored by prison staff.

Political prisoners were often reportedly denied medical treatment for injuries sustained as a result of torture in pre-trial detention or other ailments. Thameur Jaoua, who was arrested while in hospital recovering from a back operation in January, was severely beaten during 18 days in incommunicado detention and was apparently coughing blood in February. He was sentenced to 14 months' imprisonment in March for alleged membership of an illegal organization. His family was not allowed to take him medicine at Sfax Prison and no doctor visited him until April. In April the Public Prosecutor ordered an inquiry into his lack of medical care but its outcome had not been made public by year-end.

Despite repeated requests, the authorities provided no information about Kamal Matmati, who had "disappeared" after being arrested in Gabès in October 1991. He was believed to have required hospital treatment after being beaten in custody, and to have died in detention two weeks later, but this could not be confirmed.

Amnesty International continued to call for the release of all prisoners of conscience, for the fair trial or release of other political prisoners, and for thorough and impartial investigation of all allegations of torture and ill-treatment of prisoners. It continued to call also for full investigation of the deaths in custody which had occurred in 1991 and 1992. In June Amnesty International published a report, *Tunisia: Women victims of harassment, torture and imprisonment*, and called on the government to bring an end to the harassment and torture of wives and families of detainees.

In an oral statement to the UN Commission on Human Rights in February, Amnesty International included reference to its concerns about arbitrary detentions in Tunisia.

TURKEY

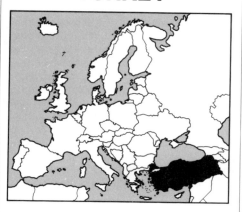

Hundreds of people were detained as prisoners of conscience. Some were soon released but others were sentenced to prison terms. Torture of political and criminal detainees in police stations was widespread and systematic, and there were at least 24 reported deaths in custody as a result of torture. At least 26 people reportedly "disappeared" in security force custody and scores of people were killed in the mainly Kurdish southeastern provinces and also in western Turkey, in circumstances which suggested that they had been extrajudicially executed by members
of the security forces. A death sentence was approved by a parliamentary judicial commission, the first such approval since 1984. An armed opposition group was responsible for more than 200 apparently deliberate and arbitrary killings of prisoners and other non-combatants.

Following the death of President Turgut Özal in April, Süleyman Demirel became President. He was succeeded as Prime Minister by Tansu Çiller.

State of emergency legislation was in force throughout the year in 10 southeastern provinces, where the nine-year-long conflict between government forces and the secessionist guerrillas of the *Partiya Karkeren Kurdistan* (PKK), Kurdish Workers' Party, grew fiercer in intensity. Over 4,500 people, including civilians, were killed during the year.

In November the UN Committee against Torture published a report after a three-year investigation which concluded that "the existence of systematic torture in Turkey cannot be denied".

Hundreds of people suspected of supporting Kurdish separatism were arrested, many of them at public meetings and demonstrations, and held for hours or days in police custody as prisoners of conscience. Most were released unconditionally or after being charged under various articles of the Turkish Penal Code (TPC). Article 8 of the Anti-Terror Law, which outlaws any advocacy of separatism, was increasingly used to prosecute and imprison people for the peaceful expression of their opinions. In July Kurdish writer Edip Polat began a two-year prison sentence. He had been convicted by Ankara State Security Court under Article 8 for publishing memoirs of his imprisonment in Diyarbakır during the mid-1980s. In September a warrant was issued for the arrest of 24 representatives of associations, trade unions and publications in Diyarbakır for allegedly expressing separatist views in a joint public statement they had made about the human rights situation in southeastern Turkey. Subsequently, Sadık Yaşar, Hanifi Yıldırım, Mehmet Tekin and Veysi Varlı were arrested and remanded in custody. Their trial had not concluded by the end of the year.

Torture by police or gendarmes (soldiers carrying out police duties in rural areas) continued to be reported from all parts of Turkey, particularly the major cities and the southeast. Detainees suspected of links with illegal armed organizations were held for up to 30 days in incommunicado detention, unprotected by even the most basic safeguards against torture. In July Mıtlık Ölmez was detained in the street by plainclothes police belonging to the Anti-Terror Branch. He was interrogated at Istanbul Police Headquarters for allegedly assisting the PKK: he said he was hung by the arms, given electric shocks to his fingers, tongue and penis, and had a truncheon repeatedly forced into his anus. As a result, his arms became partially paralysed. A medical examination two weeks later, by the State Forensic Medicine Institute, found injuries consistent with his allegations. His sister, Yıldız Ölmez, who was detained the same day, was allegedly tortured by being given electric shocks to her fingers and nipples; dragged around by the hair; forced to stand on one leg; sexually assaulted; and suspended in a crucifix position.

There were at least 24 deaths in custody apparently as a result of torture. Those who died included criminal suspects and people detained on suspicion of involvement with armed political organizations. Yücel Dolan was detained in Hazro, Diyarbakır province, in July. He was sent to Diyarbakır Gendarmerie Headquarters for interrogation. The same evening his father, Resul Dolan, the mayor of Hazro, was told that he was unwell. Two days later Resul Dolan found his son's body in the morgue of the state hospital, where it had been delivered by the gendarmerie. There was evidence of beating on the shins and feet, of a blow to the back of the head and of electric shock torture. There were also said to be injuries to the genitals. However, the family was told by the State Security Prosecutor that Yücel Dolan had died of a heart attack, although no autopsy report had been made available by the end of the year.

Baki Erdoğan was detained in August and interrogated at Aydın Police Headquarters for alleged membership of the illegal armed organization Devrimci Sol, Revolutionary Left. He died three days later, although this was apparently covered up for more than 24 hours. An autopsy report prepared by the local prosecutor and two medical practitioners described extensive wounds, but stated that Baki Erdoğan had died from tuberculosis and not as a result of the wounds. The Turkish Medical Council stated that the marks on his body were consistent with his having received electric shocks, being hung up by the wrists and subjected to falaka (beating on the soles of the feet). However, there was no official investigation into his death or that of Yücel Dolan and no action was taken against those responsible for their torture by the end of the year.

There were also reports of ill-treatment of inmates in prisons. Most related to occasions when police or gendarmes entered prisons during hunger-strikes and other protests by prisoners, or when prisoners were travelling to or from court in the custody of gendarmes. In February police and gendarmes entered wards in the hospital wing of Diyarbakır E-type prison and reportedly beat hunger-striking prisoners with sticks and truncheons. Seventy prisoners were treated in hospital for their injuries, including Müfit Eren, whose leg had been fractured; Hatip Karaaslan, who had an arm broken; and Emin Bahçeci, who sustained serious head wounds.

At least 26 people were reported to have "disappeared" in custody. In August Aysel Malkaç, a journalist for the newspaper Özgür Gündem (Free Agenda), "disappeared" shortly after leaving the premises of the newspaper in the Kumkapı district of Istanbul. According to the newspaper, eye-witnesses saw her being detained in the street, apparently by plainclothes police officers, but the Istanbul police authorities denied holding her. Another detainee reported having seen Aysel Malkaç at the Anti-Terror Branch of Istanbul Police Headquarters one or two days after her "disappearance" and stated that she appeared exhausted and had difficulty in walking. Since mid-1992, 11 journalists and distributors of the newspaper have been killed in circumstances giving rise to allegations of security force involvement.

Hundreds of people were victims of political killings, many in circumstances which suggested that they may have been victims of extrajudicial executions. Those targeted included journalists, members of the Demokrasi Partisi (DEP), Democracy Party, which campaigns for political rights for the Kurdish minority, and people who had been imprisoned for or interrogated about separatist offences, or whose relatives had joined the PKK's guerrillas. Ferhat Tepe, a journalist for Özgür Gündem, was abducted in Bitlis in July, reportedly by a man carrying a two-way radio, shortly after police had been looking for him at the office of his father, İsak Tepe, chairman of the Bitlis branch of the DEP. Subsequently, İsak Tepe reportedly received telephone calls from a person who said he was a member of the *Türk Osmanlı İntikam Tuğayı*, Turkish Ottoman Revenge Brigade, and whose voice reportedly resembled that of a local gendarmerie commander known to be critical of the DEP. İsak Tepe asked the police to investigate the gendarmerie commander, but was apparently told that the police could not interfere with the military authorities. Ferhat Tepe's body was found in a lake 360 kilometres away and buried as an "unknown person", although the case received wide publicity and the police had photographs of him. His body was exhumed and delivered to the family. A full autopsy was never carried out, but his father said that there were marks of torture on the body.

In September Mehmet Sincar, a DEP member of parliament, and Metin Özdemir, a local DEP official, were shot dead by three gunmen in broad daylight in a street in Batman. They had just attended the funeral of Habib Kılıç, chairman of the local branch of the DEP, who had been killed in a similar attack. Heavy police surveillance was lifted hours before the killing. Six days later Mehmet Sincar's family home in Kızıltepe, Mardin province, where mourners were gathered for his funeral, was attacked with a bomb. The assailants were not captured in spite of a heavy police presence around the house and throughout the town.

There were many credible allegations that security forces fired indiscriminately at the houses of unarmed civilians following clashes with PKK guerrillas in southeastern Turkey – particularly when members of the security forces had been killed in such clashes. During August, September and October such incidents occurred in Yüksekova in Hakkari province; Cizre, Çukurca and Dargeçit in Şırnak province; Sason in Batman province; and Lice in Diyarbakır province; resulting in more than 40 deaths. In October, 12 hours after an operation in which one guerrilla and a gendarmerie officer were killed in Altınova, Muş province, a large body of gendarmes returned to the town and allegedly burned 30 houses, apparently selecting in particular families whose sons or daughters had left to join the PKK. Animals

were killed and burned, together with foodstuffs and fodder. Inflammable material was thrown into the house of Nasır Öğüt – who died in the flames together with his wife and six children.

There were also allegations of extrajudicial executions in Istanbul and Ankara, the capital, in the course of police operations against the armed opposition group, *Devrimci Sol*. In August police from the Anti-Terror Branch of Istanbul Police Headquarters shot Mehmet Salgın, Hakan Kasa, Nebi Akyürek, 16-year-old Sabri Atılmış and Selma Çıtak at a café in the Okmeydanı district of the city. The police announced that those killed were armed members of *Devrimci Sol* who had fired on security forces. However, it appeared that no such clash had actually taken place, and one witness reported that Selma Çıtak, the cashier at the café, had attempted to surrender.

In November the Judicial Commission of the Turkish Grand National Assembly (TBMM) approved the sentence of death passed on Seyfettin Uzundiz, convicted of murder during the course of a robbery. This was the first such approval since 1984. At the end of the year the sentence was still awaiting ratification by the general assembly of the TBMM.

PKK guerrillas were responsible for over 200 deliberate and arbitrary killings. The victims included children, teachers, local politicians and other civilians; most of those killed were village guards and their families, and people suspected of collaborating with the security forces. In May a unilateral cease-fire called by the PKK came to an end when guerrillas abducted and killed 32 unarmed members of the security forces and four civilians near Bingöl. In August PKK guerrillas killed nine people whom they had taken prisoner from the village of Yoncalıbayir, Elazığ province. In October they killed 35 prisoners, including two juveniles, in the Çat district of Erzurum.

Amnesty International condemned these grave abuses and in June publicly urged the PKK to cease executions and other abuses. Amnesty International called on the leadership of the PKK to ensure that all PKK forces were instructed to respect human rights and basic international humanitarian standards.

In July Amnesty International published a report, *Turkey: Escalation in human rights abuses against Kurdish villagers.* The organization appealed for the release of prisoners of conscience; urged the government to initiate full and impartial investigations into allegations of torture, extrajudicial executions and "disappearances"; and called on both sides in the conflict in the southeast to abide by internationally accepted human rights and humanitarian standards. In October an Amnesty International delegate observed a court hearing in Istanbul of an action to close the Istanbul branch of the independent Turkish Human Rights Association. The trial concluded in December with an acquittal.

In an oral statement to the UN Commission on Human Rights in February Amnesty International included reference to its concerns about extrajudicial executions and "disappearances" in Turkey.

TURKMENISTAN

At least five government opponents were detained briefly by police to prevent them meeting visiting foreign dignitaries; they were prisoners of conscience. A government opponent detained on criminal charges was a possible prisoner of conscience. At least one person was believed to have been executed. A national of Tadzhikistan was forcibly repatriated: he was detained and reportedly tortured after his return to Tadzhikistan.

At least three opposition political activists were taken into police custody on 20 April and held for several hours to prevent them attending a meeting to discuss human rights with a delegation from the Conference on Security and Co-operation in Europe. Nurberdi Nurmamedov and Ak-Mukhammed Velsapar of the non-violent opposition *Agzybirlik* organization, both former prisoners of conscience (see *Amnesty International Report 1993*), and Murad Divanayev, of the unregistered opposition Democratic Party, were arrested at their homes in the capital, Ashgabat, and held at police stations for the duration of the scheduled meeting. On 18 August Nurberdi Nurmamedov, Aman Goshayev (also an *Agzybirlik* member) and Mukhamedmurat Salamatov, a former editor of an independent newspaper, were held in police custody for the duration of a brief visit to Ashgabat by a US congressman. Four *Agzybirlik* members – Ak-Mukhammed Velsapar, Khudayberdi Khalli, Yusup Kadyrov and Mamed Sakhatov – were arrested and held briefly for questioning after they met the congressman. All were prisoners of conscience.

In August Karadzha Karadzhayev was arrested on charges of embezzlement and slander which unofficial sources claimed were fabricated to punish him for opposition activities. He was tried in December and sentenced to three years' imprisonment, but was immediately released under an amnesty.

At least one person was believed to have been executed in 1993 for murder.

Mirbobo Mirrakhimov, a broadcasting executive who had fled Tadzhikistan, was arrested in January in Ashgabat, reportedly by Turkmen law enforcement officials. He was forcibly returned to Tadzhikistan. He was detained upon arrival in Tadzhikistan and was reported to have been severely beaten (see **Tadzhikistan** entry).

Amnesty International called on the government headed by President Saparmurad Niyazov to stop placing government opponents in short-term detention to prevent them exercising their fundamental human rights. It sought further information about the charges against Karadzha Karadzhayev. The organization continued to urge the authorities to abolish the death penalty. In March Amnesty International wrote to the Minister of Internal Affairs expressing concern about the forcible return of Mirbobo Mirrakhimov to Tadzhikistan.

In November Amnesty International published a report, *Turkmenistan: A summary of concerns about prisoners of conscience, ill-treatment and the death penalty.*

UGANDA

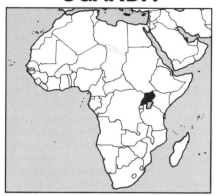

Journalists held briefly on sedition charges were prisoners of conscience. Treason charges against more than 30 prisoners, including possible prisoners of conscience, were dropped. Dozens of uncharged political prisoners were freed. Criminal charges were brought against others, but there were long delays in bringing them to trial. At least 30 suspected opponents of the government were briefly detained during military operations. There were reports of torture and ill-treatment of prisoners; in at least four cases the victims died. Prison conditions in some prisons amounted to cruel, inhuman or degrading treatment. The courts continued to impose sentences of caning. Members of the security forces were reportedly responsible for extrajudicial executions. At least 14 death sentences were passed and the Supreme Court confirmed seven death sentences. At least nine prisoners were hanged.

The scale of armed opposition to the government of President Yoweri Museveni in the north and the east continued to decline. This led to a reduction in military counter-insurgency operations and a consequent decline in human rights violations by the National Resistance Army (NRA). Rebel groups were responsible for human rights abuses.

The government continued to show reluctance to investigate human rights violations by NRA troops in rural areas. A commission of inquiry established in early 1989 into violations in Gulu District again appeared to have fallen into abeyance (see *Amnesty International Report 1992*). In September villagers and former victims of human rights violations that took place around Odudui and Dakabela in eastern Uganda in 1989 renewed demands that the soldiers responsible be brought to justice. The authorities were not known to have taken any action in response.

In one important case, however, two NRA soldiers were tried on charges arising from the deaths of 69 detainees at Mukura in Kumi District in July 1989 (see *Amnesty International Report 1990*). The soldiers, who had been arrested in May 1992 after a long period of official inaction, were detained without charge until April when 47 counts of murder were brought against them in the General Court-Martial. In November they were acquitted of murder, but one, Captain George Oduch, was sentenced to five years' imprisonment for "failure to execute his duties". The trial, which revealed significant inadequacies in the army's systems for carrying out investigations, implicated at least one other officer in the murder of the detainees. He had been detained in military custody until 1990 when he reportedly escaped.

In March the government announced the establishment of a judicial commission of inquiry into the administration of justice. The inquiry, which heard evidence relating to the mismanagement of investigations, prosecutions and trials in criminal cases, had not concluded by the end of the year.

In October the authorities brought sedition charges against three journalists who were held briefly as prisoners of conscience before being granted bail. Teddy Sseze Cheeye, editor of the *Uganda Confidential* newsletter, was detained for five days before being granted bail on charges of publishing and printing seditious material in an article alleging that senior government officials were guilty of nepotism in public appointments. In December he faced further sedition charges relating to an article published in August alleging that Janet Museveni, the President's wife, was implicated in a murder.

In October Hussein Musa Njuki, editor-in-chief of *The Shariat* newspaper, and Haruna Kanabi, a sub-editor on the paper, were held respectively for 11 days and nearly three weeks before being bailed on sedition charges after *The Shariat* carried an article criticizing the government and accusing government ministers of double standards. None of the three journalists had been tried by the end of the year.

300

There was, however, a reduction in the number of prisoners known to be facing the capital charge of treason. Treason charges preclude the granting of bail for 480 days and had been misused since 1988 to hold suspected government opponents for long periods without bringing them to trial (see *Amnesty International Report 1993*). Over 30 prisoners, among them possible prisoners of conscience who had been held for over three years, were released during the year after treason charges against them were dropped. In August, for example, the Minister of State for Defence announced that Martin Okello and eight other soldiers had been freed from military custody and would not face trial because "their human rights had been grossly abused by their long detention without trial". Detained in January 1990, the nine had been held without charge until March 1991 when they were charged with treason.

The authorities also reduced the number of political prisoners detained without charge by freeing dozens and bringing criminal charges against others. However, in at least one case in June treason charges were brought against a prisoner, Sergeant Kabanda, who had already been held for three years in military custody without charge or trial. He had not been tried by the end of the year. In February long delays in bringing soldiers to trial, many of them charged with capital offences, led to a riot in Luzira prison in which four prisoners were killed.

There were new arrests during military operations in eastern Uganda. In June, following attacks by the armed opposition Uganda People's Army (UPA) around Kachumbala in Kumi District, NRA soldiers briefly detained over 30 civilians, including children and elderly people. There were reports that some of those held were beaten but all were released after a few days.

In August over a dozen villagers from around Kanyum in Kumi District were briefly detained by NRA soldiers searching for the killers of a local official. The soldiers, who reportedly caned each of the men before releasing them, returned to the village the next day and bound Sam Esele in the manner known as *kandooya* or "three-piece" tying, a practice officially outlawed within the NRA, before caning him and setting him free. The authorities were not known to have taken any action against the soldiers.

There were several other reports of torture and ill-treatment by soldiers, members of paramilitary Local Defence Units (LDUs), police and prison officers. In some cases those reportedly responsible were arrested and charged but in others no action appeared to be taken. For example, in March a military intelligence officer in West Nile confined three men in a pit in a barracks near Koboko for five hours before beating them and setting them free. The incident was reported to local officials but they apparently took no action. There were several reports of NRA soldiers beating criminal suspects. In August a man was flogged to death by soldiers in Kalaki barracks in Pallisa for alleged gun-running. The local police arrested both NRA and LDU personnel who were then forcibly freed by soldiers from Kalaki barracks. In this case the authorities ordered the arrest of both the soldiers involved in the original incident and those who had freed them. In November the authorities arrested three NRA soldiers in Kabale after they deliberately burned a man in their custody.

There were widespread reports of police officers beating criminal suspects in what appeared to be a country-wide pattern. For example, in March 13 civilians suspected of murder were beaten by police at Aloi in Lira District. The commander of the police post, who threatened to detain journalists who learned about the incident, was subsequently arrested. It was not known if any other action was taken.

Torture and harsh prison conditions amounting to cruel, inhuman or degrading treatment, including grossly inadequate food supplies, reportedly led to the deaths of convicted criminal prisoners. For example, four prisoners reportedly died in Masafu prison in eastern Uganda – two in July and the others in August and September – where prison guards were also reported to have regularly beaten and tortured prisoners. Prison deaths in Kabarole in western Uganda, initially reported in July, led district officials to visit prisons in December. They reported that prisoners, who were being kept virtually naked in "appalling conditions", were malnourished and were receiving inadequate medical care. It was not clear if official investigations were conducted into individual deaths.

Courts at all levels – the High Court, magistrates courts and Resistance Committee (RC) courts – continued to impose sentences of caning for a wide variety of criminal offences including theft, attempted rape and giving false information to the police. Caning, which is provided for in the Penal Code, constitutes a cruel, inhuman or degrading punishment. The sentences passed down by RC courts, composed of locally elected councillors with no legal training, were particularly heavy. An 80-year-old widow from Namuganga received 10 strokes of the cane for stealing a hen in September.

With the decline in military activity in rural areas there was a reduction in the number of extrajudicial executions compared with previous years. However, in September, four suspected car thieves who were shot dead by NRA soldiers at Namanve near Kampala, appeared to be victims of extrajudicial execution. The accounts of witnesses raised fears that the killings were part of a "shoot-to-kill" warning to deter other car thieves. Although a police investigation opened immediately, there had been no arrests by the end of the year.

In March, nine men convicted of murder in previous years were hanged in Luzira prison. The Supreme Court dismissed the appeals of seven other prisoners who had been sentenced to death for treason, murder and aggravated robbery, while the High Court condemned at least 10 to death for a variety of offences, including treason. A man condemned to death in March had spent nearly nine years in prison on remand. The General Court-Martial sentenced four NRA soldiers to death for robbery with violence.

Armed opponents of the government abducted civilians and government officials and committed rape and deliberate and arbitrary killings. The District Administrator of Nebbi District was abducted in March by insurgents belonging to the Lord's Resistance Army who held him for two weeks in Gulu District and then set him free. Adolescent girls were particularly at risk of abduction by insurgents who often then raped them.

In April, five girls were abducted and raped by UPA insurgents in Kumi District; two were freed by NRA troops. Nine RC officials and villagers were deliberately killed by UPA insurgents in Kumi District in January, March and July. In the incident in July

insurgents surrounded a funeral in Kanyum and picked out six men who they then shot dead. Amnesty International condemned the abuses of human rights by armed opposition groups and urged them to abide by basic humanitarian standards.

During the year Amnesty International urged the government to review the cases of those charged with treason and to mount impartial and prompt investigations into reported extrajudicial executions. In May Amnesty International published a report, *Uganda: The death penalty – a barrier to improving human rights*, which expressed grave concern about the execution of nine men convicted of criminal offences and urged the abolition of the death penalty. In September the Minister of State for Defence announced that a review had been ordered of the cases of individuals, believed to number over 100, sentenced to death by army tribunals in previous years, because such courts were "illegal and incompetent" to try death penalty cases.

UKRAINE

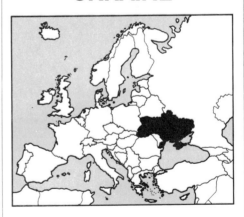

At least 78 people were sentenced to death, and at least one person was known to have been executed.

Tensions between parliament and the government over the pace of reforms continued. In September President Leonid Kravchuk took over direct control of the government after Prime Minister Leonid Kuchma and his cabinet resigned. New elections for both parliament and president were called for 1994.

A new draft constitution was published for discussion in October. It proposed,

302

among other things, limiting the application of the death penalty to premeditated murder only.

In December the Interior Ministry announced that 78 people had been sentenced to death by the Supreme Court during the year for premeditated, aggravated murder. However, no figures were given for the four other crimes which currently carry a possible death sentence, and no details were provided on the number of executions or commutations for 1993.

At least one execution came to light through unofficial sources, although the true figure was believed to be much higher. Aleksandr Yepikov had been sentenced to death for murder by a court in Donetsk on 29 January. His appeal was turned down by the Supreme Court on 15 May, but the exact date of execution was not known.

Amnesty International urged the authorities to commute all death sentences and to publish comprehensive statistics on the application of the death penalty, in line with international recommendations.

UNITED ARAB EMIRATES

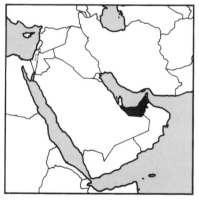

Four prisoners of conscience, all Indian nationals, continued to serve sentences imposed for allegedly insulting Islam, while six others, also Indian nationals, were released pending an appeal. Three foreign nationals, arrested for alleged anti-Islamic activities, also appeared to be prisoners of conscience. Two people were reportedly sentenced to the amputation of a hand and a foot. Two death sentences were confirmed by the Supreme Court and at least 11 people were executed.

Four prisoners of conscience, all Indian nationals resident in the United Arab Emirates (UAE), remained in prison on account of their involvement in a play staged at the premises of the Indian Association in Sharjah in May 1992. The play was considered by the authorities to be insulting to Islam and to the prophets Mohammad and Jesus (see *Amnesty International Report 1993*). The Court of Appeal confirmed the sentences of six years' imprisonment followed by deportation on two of the four, but in the other two cases – those of Monoy Mathews, the director of the play, and Kallarakkal Joseph Francis, an actor – it increased the term of imprisonment to 10 years, also to be followed by deportation. However, the Court of Appeal freed six others who had been arrested and sentenced with the four, and they remained at liberty although the Public Prosecutor's Office lodged an appeal against the Appeal Court's decision.

In May Shara Damkar, also an Indian national, was reportedly detained in Dubai in connection with alleged "anti-Islamic" activities after video cassettes, books and pamphlets promoting Hinduism were allegedly found in his possession. However, no further information about his case was available by the end of the year.

A British national and an Iranian national, both Christians, were reportedly arrested in separate cases for proselytizing. The former was reportedly sentenced to six months' imprisonment, but no information was available about the latter.

According to press reports, a UAE national and a Pakistani national were each sentenced in March to cross-limb amputation (the amputation of a hand and foot from opposite sides of the body) in the emirate of Fujairah after being convicted of piracy. It was not known whether the sentences were carried out.

At least 11 people were executed. A Bangladeshi national, who had been convicted of a murder in 1992, was executed in January. His sentence had been confirmed by the Supreme Court and then by the President of the UAE, al-Shaikh Zayed bin Sultan Al Nahayan. In May three UAE nationals and an Indian national were reportedly executed. In November five Indian nationals and a Pakistani national were also reported to have been executed, all for murder. The six executions in November were reportedly carried out in

Sharjah Central Prison.

In April the Supreme Court upheld the death sentences on two men who had been convicted by an Abu Dhabi court in July 1992 on charges of kidnapping and rape. It was not known whether the executions were carried out.

The Supreme Court upheld a further death sentence in December on a Yemeni national, Mashal Badr al-Hamati, who had been convicted of murder by a court in Abu Dhabi in 1991. He was 17 years old at the time of the offence. The case then passed to President al-Sheikh Zayed bin Sultan Al Nahayan for final confirmation. The prisoner had not been executed by the end of the year.

Amnesty International urged President al-Shaikh Zayed bin Sultan Al Nahayan to commute all death sentences and called for punishments such as amputation and flogging to be replaced with an alternative form of punishment which does not amount to cruel, inhuman or degrading treatment. Amnesty International also called for the immediate and unconditional release of all prisoners of conscience. The organization received a detailed response from the Ministry of Information and Culture concerning the Indian prisoners of conscience. This insisted that freedom of religious belief and worship are guaranteed in the UAE, but added that "it is the objective of our legal system that the practising of one fundamental human freedom does not impinge upon the practising of another." The Government of Sharjah also responded stating that "Blasphemy is an offence in this country and since the cases of the 10 Indians have been thrashed out in the courts of the land, we see no point in discussing this matter any further."

UNITED KINGDOM

Possibly unfair trials took place in Northern Ireland on the basis of uncorroborated confessions. Several people who were detained for deportation were ill-treated; one woman died as a consequence. Soldiers involved in disputed killings in Northern Ireland were brought to trial. Armed groups deliberately and arbitrarily killed civilians.

The level of violence increased in Northern Ireland as Republican and Loyalist armed groups carried out torture and killings: 83 people were killed in Northern Ireland by armed groups. The predominantly Catholic Republican armed groups, notably the Irish Republican Army (IRA), seek a unification of Northern Ireland with the Republic of Ireland. This aim is opposed by Loyalist armed groups from the Protestant community, notably the Ulster Defence Association (UDA) which also acts under the name of the Ulster Freedom Fighters (UFF), and the Ulster Volunteer Force (UVF).

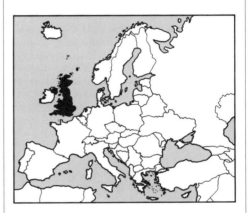

The Royal Commission on Criminal Justice in England and Wales issued its report in July (see *Amnesty International Report 1992*). Its recommendations included setting up a new investigative body on miscarriages of justice, retaining the right to silence but with advance disclosure of the defence case, and tightening up rules on the admissibility of uncorroborated confessions as evidence.

The government introduced legislation for England and Wales allowing courts to draw adverse inferences against defendants remaining silent during interrogation and trial. Similar legislation was introduced in Northern Ireland in 1988 (see *Amnesty International Report 1992*).

In May the European Court of Human Rights upheld the United Kingdom's (UK) derogation from the provisions of the European Convention which require that detainees are brought promptly before a judicial authority. In the case of *Brannigan and McBride v. UK*, the majority of the Court concluded that the UK could derogate from these provisions by authorizing the detention of people suspected of terrorist

304

offences for up to seven days without being brought before a judge.

Three former police officers charged with conspiring to pervert the course of justice in the "Guildford Four" case (see previous *Amnesty International Reports*) were acquitted in May after a jury trial. The trial of three former police officers charged with the same offence in relation to the "Birmingham Six" case (see previous *Amnesty International Reports*) was stopped in October when the judge decided that a fair trial would not be possible given prejudicial publicity.

In July four police officers were charged with attempting to pervert the course of justice in connection with the conviction in 1986 of four Ulster Defence Regiment soldiers for the murder of a Catholic civilian (see *Amnesty International Report 1993*). The police officers had not been tried by the end of the year.

In July the Home Secretary ordered the expulsion to Northern Ireland of John Matthews immediately after he had been released from detention when charges of involvement in a bombing in London were dropped. The Home Secretary said the grounds for expulsion were that John Matthews was "concerned with terrorism". The process whereby citizens can be excluded from Great Britain is secret.

Trials took place in Northern Ireland of young people charged with murder on the basis of uncorroborated confessions. In July the trial concluded of five people charged with murder in connection with the 1991 IRA killing of a police officer in Beechmount, Belfast. All five accused alleged that they had signed confessions after being subjected to ill-treatment and coercion. After the court heard evidence concerning the first defendant's interrogation, a deal was reached whereby he was acquitted and the remaining four defendants were convicted on lesser charges. The four were released having served two years in pre-trial detention. Eight people were tried in connection with a 1991 bomb attack on the security forces in the Ballymurphy area of Belfast (see *Amnesty International Report 1992*). In March, one of them was sentenced to 14 years' imprisonment for attempted murder; the trial of the seven others had not been concluded by the end of the year. Amnesty International sent lawyers to observe proceedings in both trials.

Several people being deported were ill-treated by police and private security firm officers. Jamaican-born Joy Gardner died after she was seized by police for deportation at her home in August. Tape was placed over her mouth and a body-belt tied around her waist restraining her arms behind her back. An independent post-mortem found that she had died as a result of a form of suffocation. The specialist police deportation unit and the officers involved were suspended, and the Metropolitan Police and the Home Office initiated inquiries into the police role in forcible deportations.

In July the inquest into the 1991 death in custody of Omasese Lumumba, a Zairian asylum-seeker, found that he had been unlawfully killed as a result of the "use of improper methods and excessive force in the process of control and restraint" by London prison officers. No disciplinary or criminal proceedings were brought against any of the prison officers involved.

During the year action was taken in relation to killings or attempted killings by soldiers in 1993 and previous years. In October a soldier was charged with the attempted murder that month of a mourner at the house of an IRA man who had blown himself up during a bomb attack in Belfast.

In June, one soldier was convicted of the murder of Karen Reilly and another soldier of the attempted murder of Martin Peake in September 1990 (see *Amnesty International Report 1992*). The trial in November of two soldiers charged with the 1990 murder of Fergal Caraher and the attempted murder of Míceál Caraher resulted in acquittals (see *Amnesty International Report 1991*). An Amnesty International delegate attended part of the trial.

The inquest into the 1986 death of Seamus McElwaine found that he had been shot dead by soldiers of the Special Air Service (SAS) regiment. The inquest found that he had been wounded and incapacitated, questioned by the soldiers, then, within five minutes, shot dead. The Director of Public Prosecutions requested a full report from the police. No prosecutions had been brought by the end of the year.

The inquest into the deaths of John McNeill, Peter Thompson and Edward Hale, who were killed by undercover soldiers in 1990 (see *Amnesty International Report 1991*), began in April, but was postponed after legal challenges were made against the government's issuing of Public Interest

Immunity Certificates. These certificates would have allowed army witnesses to testify behind screens and would have excluded certain evidence from oral testimony.

In September the European Commission on Human Rights declared admissible an application made by the families of three IRA members who were shot dead by the SAS in Gibraltar in 1988. The applicants argued that Article 2 of the European Convention (the right to life) required states to adopt clear, detailed rules strictly limiting the use of lethal force, and that the UK law was too vague to conform to Article 2. The applicants also contended that there should be an effective procedure for establishing the full facts but that the inquest procedure was inadequate.

The Northern Ireland authorities recalled Chief Constable John Stevens to investigate further alleged collusion between the security forces and Loyalist paramilitaries; the allegations had emerged during the 1992 trial of a military intelligence officer, Brian Nelson (see *Amnesty International Reports 1991* and *1993*).

Karamjit Singh Chahal, a Sikh asylum-seeker, remained in prison challenging a deportation order to India issued on "national security" grounds (see *Amnesty International Report 1992*). He had been detained without charge since August 1990.

Armed groups carried out deliberate and arbitrary killings and acts of torture. Loyalist armed groups claimed responsibility for killing 48 people, including 42 Catholic civilians. In January Patrick Shields and his son, Diarmuid, were shot dead and another son wounded in a UVF attack on their home. In August Sean Lavery, the son of a prominent member of Sinn Féin (widely considered to be the political wing of the IRA), was shot dead in the family home by the UDA/UFF. In September the UVF shot dead Jim Peacock, a prison officer. In October, seven people were killed and 11 injured when UDA/UFF gunmen sprayed machine-gun fire into a crowded pub. Fifty-seven men were hospitalized after being shot in the limbs as punishment; others were beaten.

Republican armed groups claimed responsibility for the killing in Northern Ireland of 14 members of the security forces and 21 civilians. In October an IRA bomb attack on a shop in the predominantly Protestant Shankill Road killed nine Protestants, including two children – seven-year-old Michelle Baird and 13-year-old Leanne Murray – and injured over 50 people. The IRA said it killed Aidan McGovern, a Catholic, in September for supplying building materials to the security forces. In June the Irish National Liberation Army killed John Murphy, a Catholic man who had worked for the Royal Ulster Constabulary, the Northern Ireland police force, until 1991. Three civilians were killed in IRA bomb attacks in England, including three-year-old Johnathan Ball and 12-year-old Tim Parry in Warrington in March. Armed Republican groups also carried out punishment beatings and shot 27 men in the limbs. For example, Damian McCartan and Edward Kane were shot and maimed by the IRA. Others were forced to leave Northern Ireland under threat.

In February Amnesty International published a report, *Northern Ireland: The Right of Silence*, which documented concerns about the application of the Criminal Evidence (Northern Ireland) Order 1988 and urged its repeal. In July Amnesty International published *Northern Ireland: Fair trial concerns in Casement Park trials*, about the trials of 41 people charged in connection with the murder of two soldiers during a funeral in Belfast in March 1988. It said that a wide-ranging independent inquiry should examine the cases of all those convicted in the Casement Park trials (see *Amnesty International Report 1993*). It also urged the government to refer immediately the cases of Patrick Kane, Michael Timmons and Sean Kelly to an appropriate judicial authority for further review.

Also in July Amnesty International wrote to the Home Secretary expressing concern that his labelling of John Matthews as a terrorist, based on secret information which could not be refuted, could make John Matthews a target for Loyalist armed groups in Northern Ireland.

In August Amnesty International urged the government to initiate an independent inquiry into the treatment of people being detained for deportation, as well as into the circumstances of the death of Joy Gardner, and the alleged ill-treatment of deportee Dorothy Nwokedi.

In November Amnesty International published *United Kingdom: Unlawful killing of detained asylum-seeker Omasese Lumumba*, which called for an independent inquiry into his death. The report also expressed concern about the government's handling of asylum claims and the detention of asylum-seekers, and urged the government to implement a series of specific recommendations.

Amnesty International urged the government not to forcibly deport Karamjit Singh Chahal to India where he would be at risk of serious human rights violations.

Amnesty International submitted its comments to the government on Draft Codes of Practice on the detention, treatment and interrogation procedures for suspects held under emergency legislation in Northern Ireland, which did not conform to international standards.

Amnesty International was concerned that the government's practice of issuing Public Interest Immunity Certificates in the context of inquests in Northern Ireland was being used to prevent the disclosure of information that was crucial to a full examination of killings in suspicious circumstances.

During the year Amnesty International publicly condemned human rights abuses by Republican and Loyalist armed groups and urged them to abide by minimum humane standards and to halt deliberate and arbitrary killings and torture.

UNITED STATES OF AMERICA

Thirty-eight prisoners were executed, more than in any other year since executions resumed in 1977. The victims included four juvenile offenders. More than 2,750 prisoners were under sentence of death in 34 states. There were reports of

torture and ill-treatment by police and prison officers and a number of officers were prosecuted.

Thirty-eight prisoners were executed, bringing the total number of executions since 1977 to 226. The state of Washington carried out its first execution for 29 years. Texas carried out 17 executions. Others were carried out in Virginia (five); Missouri (four); Florida (three); Arizona, Delaware and Georgia (two each); and California and Louisiana (one each).

Four juvenile offenders were executed during the year, in violation of international standards which prohibit the execution of people under 18 at the time of the crime. Curtis Harris, black, and Ruben Cantu, of Latin American origin, were executed in Texas in July and August respectively; Frederick Lashley, black, was executed in Missouri in July (he was the first juvenile offender to be executed in Missouri for over 60 years); and Christopher Burger, white, was executed in Georgia on 7 December (the last such execution in Georgia was in 1957). All were aged 17 at the time of their crimes and came from acutely deprived backgrounds.

Frederick Lashley and Ruben Cantu were both represented at their trials by lawyers who had never handled a death penalty case before. Curtis Harris and Frederick Lashley were tried before all-white juries after the prosecutor in each case had used peremptory challenges to remove all black prospective jurors.

Curtis Harris' execution took place days after the US Supreme Court had narrowly rejected an appeal in another case which claimed that a statute in force in Texas from 1976 until 1991 had been unconstitutional because it had not allowed a defendant's youth to be considered as a separate mitigating factor at the sentencing stage of a capital trial. The statute had been changed in 1991 to allow a broad range of mitigating factors to be considered, but this did not apply retroactively to prisoners, like Curtis Harris, who had been sentenced earlier.

Frederick Lashley, who had been abandoned as a baby, was convicted of the murder of his foster mother while under the influence of drugs. He had started drinking heavily when he was 10 and had been suicidal, requiring psychiatric care from an early age. He had been living on the streets at the time of the murder. His trial lawyer later stated: "Frederick's case was my first capital murder trial. At that time I had not received any training in death penalty litigation."

In January the US Supreme Court ruled that there was no constitutional right of appeal based on newly discovered evidence of innocence, where the original trial was free from procedural error. The ruling dismissed the appeal of Leonel Herrera, who was subsequently executed in Texas in May for the murder of a police officer. In 1992 his lawyers had presented new evidence alleging that his brother had committed the murder, but this was too late to be considered by the state courts. Three dissenting US Supreme Court Justices (out of nine) argued that "the execution of a person who can show that he is innocent comes perilously close to simple murder."

Several prisoners were executed despite evidence that they were mentally impaired. They included Robert Sawyer, who had a long history of mental illness and was mentally retarded – information his trial lawyer had failed to present to the jury. He was executed in Louisiana in March.

One prisoner was granted clemency: Bobby Shaw in Missouri, who also had a history of mental illness.

There were new allegations of torture and ill-treatment by police and prison officers across the country, and several officers were prosecuted.

In April, two Los Angeles police officers were convicted of federal civil rights charges arising out of the beating of black motorist Rodney King (see *Amnesty International Report 1993*) and sentenced to 30 months' imprisonment; two other officers were acquitted.

In June a Los Angeles police officer was charged with murder for the killing of John Daniels Jr, an unarmed black truck driver (see *Amnesty International Report 1993*).

In October, two former Detroit police officers, convicted of murder for the fatal beating of black motorist Malice Green in November 1992, were sentenced to prison terms of up to 18 and 25 years.

Other cases under investigation included that of Michael Bryant, black, who died in police custody in Los Angeles in March 1993. He was shot with a taser (an electric stun gun) after falling into a pool, and then "hogtied" – placed face-down in restraints with his hands and ankles tied

together from behind. A coroner found the cause of death to be acute cocaine intoxication and asphyxiation from restraint procedures. There were calls for a review of restraint procedures after another suspect died in police custody in Los Angeles in September after being "hogtied".

An investigation was also being carried out into the case of Johnnie Cromartie, black, who died in police custody of head and other injuries in New York in May. Reports alleged that two white police officers repeatedly kicked him while he was lying face down with his arms handcuffed behind his back.

In February the Chicago Police Board ordered the dismissal of a former station commander after finding that he had ill-treated a suspect in 1982; two others cited in the March 1992 hearings were suspended (see *Amnesty International Reports 1992* and *1993*).

Inquiries were conducted by the Treasury and Justice Departments into the handling of a 51-day stand-off between federal agents and members of an armed religious cult, the Branch Davidians, in Waco, Texas, which ended in a fire in which 75 cult members died, 25 of them children. Concerns were raised, among other things, about the use of CS gas which Federal Bureau of Investigation (FBI) agents pumped into the Branch Davidian compound for several hours during the final assault in April. The Treasury's report published in October was critical of the initial raid on the compound conducted by the Bureau of Alcohol, Tobacco and Firearms, in which several cult members and four federal agents were killed; however, the Justice Department cleared the FBI of any blame for events during the siege and the final assault on the compound. Murder and conspiracy charges were pending against several surviving cult members at the end of the year.

In May the Justice Department began an investigation into more than 40 deaths in jails in Mississippi between 1987 and 1993. This followed hearings in Mississippi in April in which civil rights groups questioned the state rulings of suicide in all cases, alleging that some of the deaths were suspicious and accusing jail officials of abusing inmates. Cases raised at the hearings included that of Andre Jones, a black youth found hanged in August 1992 (see *Amnesty International Report 1993*).

308

In December the Justice Department called for the closure of four Mississippi jails as a result of its investigation, and condemned substandard conditions in others that violated the Constitution. The Justice Department was still investigating the inmates' suicides at the end of the year.

There were allegations of gross medical neglect amounting to ill-treatment in the case of Steven Armstrong who died in the Moberly Correctional Centre, Missouri, in August. Several inmates alleged that the prisoner was left naked and without medication in a stripped punishment cell while suffering repeated epileptic seizures. Although health care management at the prison had changed since 1992, there had been previous deaths and allegations of inadequate health care at the institution. At the end of 1993 the prison's health care services were still investigating Steven Armstrong's medical care.

Hearings began in September in a civil suit brought by inmates of Pelican Bay Prison, a maximum security prison in California. The prisoners alleged a pattern of cruel treatment, including excessive use of force, sensory deprivation and denial of adequate medical and psychiatric care (see *Amnesty International Report 1993*). The trial ended in December and judgment was pending at the end of 1993.

The US Justice Department opened an investigation into the alleged widespread sexual abuse by guards of inmates at the Georgia Women's Correctional Institution (GWCI). The abuses, which reportedly continued until they were exposed in a lawsuit in 1992, included coercion of inmates into having sex with guards, forcing inmates into guard-run prostitution rings, and enforced abortions. Charges of rape and other sexual offences were pending against at least 12 employees and others had been dismissed from their jobs or transferred by the end of the year.

Damages were paid to six former inmates of the women's prison in Maryville, Ohio, who had been sexually abused by prison employees in previous years.

In July the Eighth Circuit Court of Appeals rejected an appeal by Leonard Peltier, a leader of the American Indian Movement convicted of the murder of two FBI agents in 1977. His appeal had argued that the prosecution had conceded since his trial that it did not know who had killed the agents and had changed its theory, put forward at trial, that Leonard Peltier had actually committed the killings. Other irregularities were also alleged (see previous *Amnesty International Reports*).

In June the US Supreme Court upheld the policy initiated by President George Bush in May 1992, and subsequently continued under President Bill Clinton, of forcibly returning all Haitians intercepted at sea outside US territorial waters to Haiti (see *Amnesty International Report 1993*).

Amnesty International made numerous appeals on behalf of prisoners sentenced to death, urging clemency in all cases. It condemned the execution of juvenile offenders and urged the Clinton administration to withdraw the US Government's reservation to Article 6 of the International Covenant on Civil and Political Rights – one of a series of international treaty provisions which prohibit the execution of juveniles.

Amnesty International also expressed concern about evidence of racial discrimination in the imposition of the death penalty in juvenile cases in Texas: seven of the eight juvenile offenders on the state's death row at the end of the year were black or of Latin American origin, and there was marked evidence in some judicial circuits of gross racial disparities in the sentencing of young offenders.

The organization also criticized the US Supreme Court's ruling in the case of Leonel Herrera (see above).

In April Amnesty International wrote to the US Attorney General about the Waco, Texas, incident. The organization expressed concern about the use of CS gas, which it pointed out could be lethal if used in massive quantities in occupied areas. It called for official inquiries to examine whether the action taken by law enforcement officials was in line with international standards, including the UN Code of Conduct for Law Enforcement Officials.

In June Amnesty International wrote to the US Justice Department welcoming its decision to investigate the alleged suicides in Mississippi jails, and referring to concerns it had raised in 1991 about alleged assaults of inmates at the Harrison County Jail, Mississippi.

Amnesty International wrote to the authorities about other allegations of ill-treatment in police custody or prisons, including the death of Johnnie Cromartie in New York; the allegations of medical neglect at the Moberly Correctional Centre in Missouri; and the alleged long-standing sexual abuse of inmates at the GWCI.

In February Amnesty International told the Justice Department it remained concerned by abuses of some inmates at the Montana State Penitentiary during the quelling by guards of a riot in September 1991 (see *Amnesty International Report 1993*). A number of Native Americans were among those allegedly ill-treated.

Amnesty International wrote to the California authorities about its concerns in the case of Geronimo ji Jaga Pratt, a former leader of the Black Panther Party serving a life sentence in California (see previous *Amnesty International Reports*).

In June Amnesty International wrote to the Governor of Illinois to inquire about alleged irregularities in the manner in which Manuel Salazar, a US citizen of Mexican origin, was returned from Mexico to stand trial on a capital charge in the USA, where he was subsequently sentenced to death. The organization was still seeking clarification at the end of the year.

In recommendations to the Executive Committee of the UN High Commissioner for Refugees, Amnesty International expressed concern about the US policy of forcibly returning all Haitian asylum-seekers directly to their country, without the possibility of having their cases heard.

URUGUAY

There were new cases of ill-treatment of detainees and prisoners, including children held in a remand prison. A man was shot dead by police on arrest. Three members of a former armed opposition group were killed in suspicious circumstances. The authorities again failed to take any **steps to clarify the fate of those who "disappeared" during the period of military rule or to bring to justice those responsible for human rights violations at that time.**

In June the Head of Military Intelligence was transferred from his post following allegations that military personnel had been responsible for the abduction in 1992 and possible "disappearance" of Eugenio Berríos, a former Chilean military agent who left Chile in 1991 when summoned to appear in court in connection with the 1976 killing of former Chilean Foreign Minister Orlando Letelier. Although investigations were opened before the civilian courts, at the end of the year the whereabouts of Eugenio Berríos had not been clarified.

Ill-treatment by police appeared to be frequent in poor areas of the capital, Montevideo, and other cities. A young man detained in March in the 3rd District police station of Montevideo was tortured with electric prods to make him confess to 14 counts of robbery. A judge confirmed the injuries and two electric prods were seized from the police station. Four police officers were later charged with abuse of authority and with inflicting injuries.

In other cases, those responsible for torture or ill-treatment were not brought to justice. In January a disabled man suffered a fractured jaw after reportedly being beaten and subjected to a mock execution at the 4th District police station in the department of Canelones. In August in the Police Headquarters in Montevideo, a young man was allegedly hooded, beaten and tortured with electric shocks in order to make him confess to a theft: on his release, a policeman warned him against reporting the incident.

There were reports of ill-treatment of prisoners in *Libertad* maximum security prison, near Montevideo. Judges from the Supreme Court who visited the prison in June and July reported that conditions were deplorable and provided forensic evidence of beatings of prisoners which was submitted to the Minister of the Interior. Similar information was given to the parliamentary Human Rights Commission by a group of public defence lawyers and also in a report published in August by a non-governmental working group established to study the country's prison system.

Judicial investigations were initiated after allegations that in March children

310

held at the Miguelete remand home had been beaten by guards. Fourteen of the 18 children examined bore marks of beatings and three were hospitalized. The director and five police officers were convicted of inflicting serious personal injuries in connection with the incident and the home was closed. In July the *Instituto Nacional del Menor*, National Children's Institute, which ran Miguelete, was ordered to pay compensation to the family of Rafael Berón Charquero, a 16-year-old who committed suicide allegedly after being ill-treated there in 1991 (see *Amnesty International Reports 1992* and *1993*).

Hugo César Almeida Figueroa was shot dead by police after being arrested in connection with a neighbourhood dispute in La Chacarita, a shanty town of Montevideo. Neighbours who said that they saw police beating the man after he had been hand-cuffed intervened on his behalf; in the ensuing struggle police fired several shots, fatally wounding Hugo Almeida. The judge investigating the incident found insufficient evidence to try the three policemen involved, but witnesses later presented a formal complaint before the courts.

Three members of the former armed opposition group, *Movimiento para la Liberación Nacional-Tupamaros* (MLN-T), National Liberation Movement-Tupamaros, which was active during the period of military rule (1973 to 1985), were killed in circumstances giving rise to suspicions that former or current military personnel might be involved. On 23 April Ronald Scarzella, a member of the *Movimiento por la Tierra* (MT), Movement for Land, an organization linked to the MLN-T, was found shot dead. A few weeks before, the MT had been the subject of threats and other acts of intimidation including an attack on its property. The day after his killing, Ronald Scarzella's widow received an anonymous telephone call threatening the life of one of her daughters. Neither this case, nor the killing, days later, of two other former MLN-T members, Ruben Larrosa and Francisco Martínez de Cuadro, had been clarified by the end of the year.

In September death threats were issued against street children and juvenile delinquents in leaflets distributed in Montevideo by the "Forces against Juvenile Delinquents", a clandestine group believed to include former police and military personnel. The leaflets said that children

caught stealing in the city's commercial centre would be killed, but no such killings were reported by the end of 1993.

The government took no steps to bring to justice those responsible for killings, "disappearances" and torture during the period of military rule, or to clarify the fate of the victims, although in 1992 the Inter-American Commission on Human Rights (IACHR) had called on the government to do this when ruling that the 1986 Expiry Law (see *Amnesty International Reports 1988* to *1992*) was incompatible with the American Convention on Human Rights (see *Amnesty International Report 1993*). The Uruguayan Government responded, jointly with the Government of Argentina, by seeking an "advisory opinion" from the Inter-American Court of Human Rights questioning, among other things, the IACHR's jurisdiction to comment on domestic legislation. In July the Court endorsed the IACHR's authority to find a state in violation of an international instrument to which it is a party.

An appeal court upheld the right of Sara Méndez to ascertain the identity of a 17-year-old she believes to be her "disappeared" son (see *Amnesty International Reports 1992* and *1993*). However, it concluded that the necessary blood and psychological tests could not be carried out without his consent; the young man and his adoptive parents continued to refuse such tests.

In February a Uruguayan member of parliament presented a formal complaint before a Paraguayan court, requesting clarification of the fate of two Uruguayan citizens who had "disappeared" in Paraguay in the hands of Uruguayan, Argentine and Paraguayan personnel in 1977 (see **Paraguay** entry). A senior Uruguayan army officer was summoned to appear before a Paraguayan court but had refused to do so by the end of the year. Documents relating to the "disappearances" of the two Uruguayans had been found in Paraguay in 1992 and revealed that a Uruguayan military intelligence officer had participated in their interrogation.

In June Amnesty International wrote to the Minister of the Interior to seek information about the investigation into the killing of Ronald Scarzella and to express concern about reports of ill-treatment of prisoners, including children. However, no response was received.

UZBEKISTAN

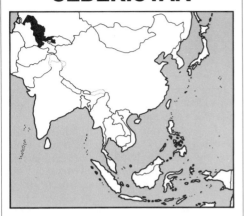

Several convicted prisoners of conscience received suspended prison sentences or were released under an amnesty. A probable prisoner of conscience already serving a prison term was tried on new charges and given an additional prison sentence. Two opposition activists arrested on firearms possession charges were probable prisoners of conscience. Government opponents were assaulted by unidentified attackers, possibly with official complicity. An opposition leader was feared to have "disappeared". At least four people faced the death penalty.

In January the Supreme Court suspended the activities of the opposition movement *Birlik* (Unity) for three months on the grounds that it intended to organize public demonstrations. Later *Birlik* was effectively outlawed after it failed to satisfy the terms of a March decree requiring all political organizations to re-register by 1 October. The main opposition party, *Erk* (Freedom), also reportedly failed to re-register. A ban on unauthorized public meetings and demonstrations imposed in 1990 remained in force.

Six men were convicted in August by the Supreme Court of "conspiracy with the aim of seizing power" (Article 54 of the Criminal Code). The charges arose from their activities as organizers of a non-violent social organization called *Milli Mejlis*, National Council (see *Amnesty International Report 1993*). They received suspended sentences of between one and five years' imprisonment. The suspended sentences resulted in the release of three defendants, Babur Shakirov and Khazratkul

Khudayberdi, who had been in pre-trial detention since August and December 1992 respectively, and Salavat Umurzakov, who had been held since May 1993. Two others, Olim Karimov and Otanazar Aripov, had already been released after spending several weeks in detention after their arrests in December 1992 and January 1993 respectively. All were prisoners of conscience. The sixth defendant, Abdulaziz Makhmudov, was not held in pre-trial detention.

Abdumannob Pulatov, a prisoner of conscience who had been abducted from Kyrgyzstan in December 1992 by Uzbek security officials (see *Amnesty International Report 1993*), was tried in the Supreme Court in January. He was charged with "infringement upon the honour and dignity of the President", under Article 191-4 of the Criminal Code. He was sentenced to three years' imprisonment but was immediately granted an amnesty and released. In February Vasilya Inayatova, a poet, was tried in the City Court of Tashkent, the capital, on the same charge and sentenced to two years' imprisonment. She was also immediately released under an amnesty.

Several opposition activists were detained for short periods, apparently to prevent them meeting visiting foreign dignitaries or travelling abroad. On 13 September, for example, Otanazar Aripov and at least one other person were taken into police custody to prevent them meeting a visiting US government representative.

Probable prisoner of conscience Pulat Akhunov, who was serving a sentence of 18 months' imprisonment for an allegedly fabricated criminal offence (see *Amnesty International Report 1993*), was charged in February with illegal possession of narcotics and assault on a prison guard. Unofficial sources alleged that these new charges were also fabricated. In August Pulat Akhunov was convicted by Andizhan Regional Court and sentenced to a further three years' imprisonment. In September he was sent to serve his sentence at a labour camp for especially dangerous criminals at Kyzylteppa, Navoi Region. Sources described conditions at this camp as the worst in Uzbekistan.

In November *Birlik* activists and probable prisoners of conscience Nosyr Zokhir and Akhmadkhon Turakhonboy-ugly were arrested separately on the same day after a single hand grenade was found in each of their homes in Namangan during police

312

searches. Unofficial sources alleged that security forces planted the grenades in order to fabricate criminal charges against these two men.

There were at least three further incidents which followed a pattern reported in 1992 in which government opponents were assaulted by unidentified attackers. There were allegations that the attacks were carried out with the complicity of the authorities. In May Shukhrat Ismatullayev, co-chairman of *Birlik*, suffered a fractured skull after three men hit him with iron bars in a Tashkent street. In September Shukrulla Mirsaidov, Uzbekistan's Vice-President until he resigned in 1992, was severely beaten in a Tashkent street by five men whom he alleged were government agents. In October Samat Muratov, first secretary of *Erk*, was seized from a street in the town of Karshi and driven to a rubbish dump, where he was beaten unconscious. Furthermore, in November three political exiles from Uzbekistan were attacked in their apartment in Moscow by suspected Uzbek government agents.

There was no news of Abdullo Utayev, leader of the unregistered Islamic Renaissance Party, who apparently "disappeared" after being detained in Tashkent in December 1992 by armed men believed to be government agents. The authorities denied holding him.

The Uzbekistan Criminal Code retained the death penalty for 19 peacetime offences as well as others in wartime. No new death sentences were reported, but one person convicted in 1991 and one convicted in 1992 were still under sentence of death at the end of 1993. The fate of two others convicted in 1992 and known to be under sentence of death at the beginning of 1993 could not be confirmed.

Amnesty International appealed to President Islam Karimov for the release of all prisoners of conscience, and for all possible steps to be taken to end attacks on opposition figures for exercising their fundamental human rights. It called for the repeal of Article 191-4 of the Criminal Code which appeared to place unwarranted restrictions on freedom of expression. Amnesty International called for a judicial review of Pulat Akhunov's criminal convictions and expressed concern that he had been placed in the Kyzylteppa colony deliberately to put him at risk of violence from fellow inmates. It sought further information on the charges against Nosyr Zokhir and Akhmadkhon Turakhonboyugly. It called on the authorities to clarify the whereabouts and legal status of Abdullo Utayev. Amnesty International continued to press the authorities to abolish the death penalty.

Amnesty International sought to send an observer to the trials of the *Milli Mejlis* organizers and of Pulat Akhunov. No reply was received to a request for official support for a visa application.

In June Amnesty International published a report, *Uzbekistan: Clampdown on dissent*, and in September it published *Uzbekistan: Clampdown on dissent – an update: prisoners of conscience on trial*.

VENEZUELA

Dozens of people were detained for their non-violent political or social activities. Torture and ill-treatment were widespread and at least one death in custody as a result of torture was reported. Scores of people, including a three-year-old child, were killed by the security forces in suspicious circumstances; some may have been victims of extrajudicial executions.

On 21 May, the Senate suspended President Carlos Andrés Pérez from office after the Supreme Court ruled that he should stand trial for alleged corruption. The Senate's President, Octavio Lapage, took over as Head of State until 5 June, when Ramón José Velásquez, a Senator, was elected by Congress as Venezuela's interim President until the end of the administration's term, in February 1994. Former President Rafael Caldera won presidential elections on 5 December.

Scores of people were injured and at

least one was killed when the security forces forcibly dispersed dozens of demonstrations – most of which were peaceful – held to protest against worsening economic conditions.

In February Venezuela ratified the Second Optional Protocol to the International Covenant on Civil and Political Rights, aiming at the abolition of the death penalty.

Scores of people, including human rights activists, political activists and Catholic priests, were arrested. They included prisoners of conscience. Fernando Arias Figueroa, a human rights activist, and two student activists, Jorge Luis López Colmenares and Rafael Enrique Flores Farfán, were all arrested in February, the latter two without warrants by the *Dirección de Inteligencia Militar* (DIM), Directorate of Military Intelligence, in the town of Valencia. All three were tortured (see below) and charged under military jurisdiction with attempted murder, despite a lack of evidence to substantiate such a charge. The students were released on bail in October, but Fernando Arias Figueroa remained imprisoned at the end of the year. He had not been brought to trial.

In March Mario Landino and seven other peasant activists, including Bari and Yucpa Indians, were detained by an army unit which raided their community of El Turpial, near the border with Colombia. The eight were reportedly arrested as a result of their peaceful activities on behalf of peasants' rights and were believed to be prisoners of conscience. Dozens of people, including at least 10 children, were beaten by soldiers during the raid and several houses were destroyed. Most of those detained were held incommunicado for several days and tortured before being released without charge. However, Mario Landino remained imprisoned under military jurisdiction at the end of the year. Those released subsequently received death threats.

In November at least 40 political or community activists, including Noel Acosta, a candidate for Zulia State's Chamber of Deputies, and two Catholic priests, Father Adolfo Rojas Giménez and Father Oscar Freitez, were arrested without warrant by the army on suspicion of plotting against the government. Most of those arrested were released without charge shortly afterwards but Noel Acosta, the two

priests and others remained in detention under military jurisdiction for several weeks.

Hundreds of people were detained under the *Ley de Vagos y Maleantes*, Law of Vagrants and Crooks, which permits administrative detention for periods of up to five years, without judicial appeal or review. Most of those arrested under this law were from the poorest sectors of the population and none had committed any punishable crime or criminal offence. Scores of those detained under this law were reported to have been tortured and at least one was extrajudicially executed in custody (see below). Most of those held for alleged involvement in the coup attempts of February and November 1992 (see *Amnesty International Report 1993*) were released after the charges against them were suspended, but dozens remained in prison.

Torture and ill-treatment by the security forces during criminal investigations were widespread and those responsible were able to act with impunity. At least one person died in detention as a result of torture. The police used various methods of torture to extract confessions from criminal suspects including beatings, suspension by the wrists or ankles for long periods, near-asphyxiation with plastic bags, electric shocks, and mock executions. Confessions allegedly obtained under torture continued to be accepted as evidence by the courts. State attorneys regularly failed to take effective action to investigate complaints of torture and official forensic doctors frequently avoided documenting cases of torture.

Medical treatment for detainees who suffered torture was mostly unavailable or grossly inadequate. Fernando Arias Figueroa, Jorge Luis López Colmenares and Rafael Enrique Flores Farfán were held incommunicado for six days following their arrest by the DIM in Valencia in February. During the first four days they were reportedly interrogated and beaten, suspended by the wrists for long periods, partly asphyxiated with plastic bags and water, subjected to electric shocks and mock executions, slapped on the ears and deprived of food and water. They were apparently forced to sign blank statements and were then transferred to prison under military jurisdiction and charged with attempted murder. They filed a formal complaint about their torture in March, supported by

314

medical evidence, but no action was known to have been taken against those responsible for their torture. Douglas Jesús Baptista León, a taxi driver, was arrested without warrant by members of the *Policía Técnica Judicial* (PTJ), Criminal Investigations' Police, in Caracas in September. He was held incommunicado at the PTJ's central headquarters and tortured by being suspended by the wrists, subjected to electric shocks and beaten on the body and head, which impaired his hearing. While in detention he was apparently seen by a district attorney who failed to document his condition. His relatives paid money to the police and he was released. Walter Alexander Del Nogal, a law student, was also reportedly tortured at the PTJ's headquarters in Caracas after he was arrested in October. The police beat him, suspended him by the ankles and partly asphyxiated him using a plastic bag with ammonia to make him admit to plotting against the government and incriminate others. He remained in prison without charge at the end of the year. Also in October, Freddy Ramón Alcarra Rangel died, seven days after his arrest, apparently as a result of beatings and blows to the head inflicted by warders of the PTJ detention centre in the *Retén de Catia* prison in Caracas.

In November Amnesty International representatives visited a PTJ detention centre at the *Retén de Catia* prison in Caracas where they had access to several torture victims. One, Richard Alves Medina, had been brutally beaten by the police after his arrest a few days earlier, sustaining a fractured arm, but had received no medical treatment. Other detainees had also sustained injuries under police torture. No action was taken by the authorities to bring to justice those responsible for the torture of 22 people, including a pregnant woman, in Valencia, Carabobo, in 1992 (see *Amnesty International Report 1993*).

Prison conditions continued to be extremely harsh, frequently amounting to cruel, inhuman or degrading treatment, and scores of prison inmates reportedly suffered torture or ill-treatment. The government publicly acknowledged the deteriorating conditions and increased risk to prison inmates due to overcrowding, bad sanitation and other factors, but took no effective action to address the problems. Scores of prisoners were killed in violent incidents, including protests against prison conditions. In June at least six prisoners were killed and more than 20 injured in the *Centro Penitenciario*, central prison, in Barcelona, Anzoátegui state, during violent clashes between inmates and guards after scores of prisoners were denied visits on Father's Day.

Scores of people were killed by the security forces in suspicious circumstances; some of them may have been victims of extrajudicial executions. They included Lisandro José Silva Piñago, a secondary school student, who was shot twice at close range by a police officer while he was queuing in a Caracas shop in June. The police officer said he thought the student was a thief. In September a three-year-old child was killed when members of the *Guardia Nacional*, National Guard, fired without provocation at a group of bystanders during a police raid in Caracas. Also in September, Sergio Rodríguez Yance, a human rights activist, was shot dead by a member of the Military Police during a peaceful student demonstration in Caracas. Official investigations were opened into the above cases but those allegedly responsible had not been charged or brought to trial by the end of the year.

Francisco Javier Méndez Cortéz was shot dead by the National Guard in November when he tried to seek help from the director of a prison in El Dorado, Bolívar state, after he had been beaten by prison guards. He was waiting to be released after having completed a sentence of 12 months' imprisonment under the Law of Vagrants and Crooks in September. His case did not apparently result in an official inquiry, nor did similar such killings in previous years. By the end of 1993, none of those responsible in 1992 for the massacre of at least 63 inmates in the *Retén de Catia* prison in Caracas or the killing of two Wayúu Indians had been charged or brought to trial (see *Amnesty International Report 1993*).

Amnesty International expressed concern to the government about the imprisonment of prisoners of conscience, torture and ill-treatment and possible extrajudicial executions and called for urgent action to remedy these abuses. In November Amnesty International published a report, *Venezuela: The eclipse of human rights*, which contained detailed recommendations for human rights safeguards. The report was released in Venezuela during the visit of an Amnesty International delegation which met the Foreign Minister, Interior and Justice Ministry officials and members of the Supreme Court, as well as representatives of the main political parties contesting the December elections, to discuss human rights. Those interviewed by the delegation, including representatives of Rafael Caldera's party, vowed to adopt measures to implement a repeal of the Law of Vagrants and Crooks. Earlier, in April, Foreign Minister Fernandó Ochóa Antich had visited the International Secretariat of Amnesty International in London and assured the organization of his government's commitment to ending human rights violations.

VIET NAM

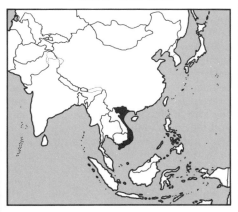

At least 60 prisoners of conscience and possible prisoners of conscience remained held throughout 1993. At least 13 prisoners of conscience were released, along with several other political prisoners who had been held without trial. At least nine political arrests were reported. Some political trials held during the year appeared to fall short of international fair trial standards. Eight prisoners were reported to have been sentenced to death but no executions were recorded.

In January the Criminal Code was amended to provide for the imposition of the death penalty on people convicted of smuggling or illegally transporting goods or currency across Viet Nam's border.

At least 13 prisoners of conscience were released, along with several other political prisoners who had been held without trial. Among the prisoners of conscience

released were Dominic Tran Dinh Tu, **315** the 87-year-old founder of the Catholic Congregation of the Mother Coredemptrix; Tran Mai, Dinh Thien Tu and Tran Dinh Ai, all Protestant pastors; Thich Duc Nhuan, a Buddhist monk (see *Amnesty International Report 1986*); and Stephen Chan Tin, a Catholic priest who had been under house arrest since 1990. Also released was Nguyen Si Binh, a nuclear engineer and businessman with US citizenship, who was a possible prisoner of conscience (see *Amnesty International Report 1993*).

However, more than 60 prisoners of conscience and possible prisoners of conscience known to Amnesty International remained in prison throughout 1993. The prisoners of conscience included Ngo Van An, a former teacher; Pham Duc Kham, a former army officer of the Republic of Viet Nam; Doan Thanh Liem, a lawyer; and Nguyen Van De, a Catholic priest. Dr Nguyen Dan Que, also a prisoner of conscience, was allegedly placed in solitary confinement in a camp in Dong Nai province. In April the UN Working Group on Arbitrary Detention ruled that the detention of Nguyen Dan Que was arbitrary and in violation of the Universal Declaration of Human Rights and the International Covenant on Civil and Political Rights (ICCPR).

Pham Hong Tho, Vo Van Pham and Nguyen Xuan De, all arrested in 1991, were convicted in May of "activities aiming to overthrow the people's government". However, it appeared that the real reason for their imprisonment was their advocacy of a multi-party political system and that they were prisoners of conscience. The People's Supreme Appellate Court of Danang confirmed their conviction and sentences of 13, 12 and six years' imprisonment respectively. It stated that they were guilty of "mobilizing propaganda to foment suspicion, eroding the confidence of the people in the Communist Party and the government".

At least nine Buddhist monks and lay Buddhists were arrested in Hue city and at the Son Linh pagoda near Vung Tau City in mid-1993, after public demonstrations in Hue city in May. Thich Tri Tuu, who was arrested in June, was charged with "disrupting security and public order" and sentenced to four years' imprisonment in November. Like the others, he belonged to the Unified Buddhist Church, which opposes the government-sponsored Viet Nam Buddhist Church, and was a follower of

316

Thich Huyen Quang, a prisoner of conscience under house arrest since 1982 (see previous *Amnesty International Reports*). All nine were sentenced to prison terms ranging from six months to four years and appeared to be prisoners of conscience.

In January it was reported that Pham Cong Canh and three others had been tried and sentenced to imprisonment in November 1992 for producing a film in violation of the government's policies and regulations. They appeared to be prisoners of conscience.

Several political prisoners were convicted after what appeared to be unfair trials. In March Doan Viet Hoat, an academic and prisoner of conscience, was sentenced to 20 years' imprisonment by the People's Court of Ho Chi Minh City after being convicted of activities allegedly aimed at "overthrowing the government" (see *Amnesty International Report 1993*). He was alleged to belong to an unauthorized organization formed in 1989 called *Dien Dan Tu Do* (Freedom Forum), to have published an unlicensed newsletter containing articles written abroad which were critical of the Vietnamese Government, and to have himself sent articles abroad for publication. Ten editions of the newsletter were said to have been issued by the time that Doan Viet Hoat was arrested in November 1990. In May 1992 *Saigon Giai Phong*, the official paper of the Ho Chi Minh City Committee of the Communist Party, publicly denounced him as the leader of a "reactionary group" and accused him of unlawful acts intended to overthrow the government. At his trial in March, which lasted less than two days, the presiding judge reportedly demonstrated a clear bias against the accused and acted in an intimidatory manner. Doan Viet Hoat was not allowed to choose his own defence lawyer. In April 1993 the UN Working Group on Arbitrary Detention ruled that the detention of Doan Viet Hoat was arbitrary and in violation of the Universal Declaration of Human Rights and the ICCPR, to which Viet Nam is a state party. In July Doan Viet Hoat's sentence was reduced on appeal to 15 years' imprisonment by the Supreme Court.

Six political prisoners convicted in May for setting off home-made bombs were allegedly not allowed to choose their own defence lawyers, in breach of international standards of fair trial. They included Tran Manh Quynh, a former Vietnamese army officer with US citizenship, who was sentenced to 20 years' imprisonment, and Le Thien Quang, another former army officer, who was sentenced to 15 years' imprisonment.

Eight people were reported to have been sentenced to death after being convicted of offences including smuggling, murder, drug-trafficking, arms theft and fraud. They included Wong Chi Shing, a Hong Kong resident and British national convicted of drug smuggling in May, and Tran Ngoc Minh, who was convicted of murder. Both were sentenced by the Supreme People's Court, from which there is no right of appeal to a higher tribunal, although prisoners under sentence of death may apply to the President for clemency. Wong Shi Ching's application for clemency was rejected in November. However, no prisoners were known to have been executed in 1993.

Amnesty International appealed for the release of prisoners of conscience, for the fair trial or release of other political prisoners and for the commutation of all death sentences. Amnesty International expressed concern to the government about the arrests of Buddhist monks and others and indicated to the authorities its wish to send a delegation to Viet Nam to discuss human rights. In December an official of the Ministry of Foreign Affairs said that the government was considering Amnesty International's initiatives.

In October Amnesty International published a report, *Socialist Republic of Viet Nam: Continuing concerns*, which reiterated its concerns about the imprisonment of prisoners of conscience, detention without trial, unfair political trials and the death penalty.

YEMEN

One long-term prisoner of conscience remained held. Over 300 suspected members or supporters of a militant Islamic opposition group were arrested following violent attacks in the south. Some were still held without charge or trial at the end of the year. Scores of people detained in late 1992, among them possible prisoners of conscience, were released. A group of at least 20 government opponents, most of

whom had been convicted after unfair trials, remained in prison. Torture and ill-treatment were widespread and the judicial punishment of flogging was frequently carried out in the northern provinces. A Somali refugee was killed in circumstances suggesting that he may have been extrajudicially executed, and at least five political activists were killed or were targeted for assassination in attacks suggesting the involvement or complicity of some officials. No steps were taken to clarify the fate of several hundred people who "disappeared" in previous years. Over 30 people were executed and hundreds of people were under sentence of death.

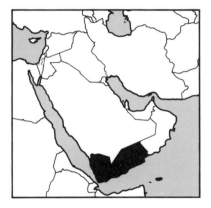

Parliamentary elections were held in April and a coalition government was formed by the three main parties. The Council of Representatives elected a Presidential Council and General 'Ali 'Abdullah Saleh was reconfirmed as its Chairman.

The Penal Code and the Code of Criminal Procedures of unified Yemen had not been promulgated by the end of the year and the legal systems of the former People's Democratic Republic of Yemen (PDRY) and the former Yemen Arab Republic (YAR) remained separate.

Mansur Rajih, a prisoner of conscience, remained under sentence of death after more than 10 years' imprisonment (see *Amnesty International Report 1993*). 'Ali 'Abdul-Fattah Hashim, a prisoner of conscience held on charges of apostasy since April 1992, was released in June.

Over 300 suspected members or supporters of Islamic Jihad, a militant Islamic opposition group, were arrested in January, May and August, following bomb attacks, killings and attempted assassinations in the provinces of Aden, Hadhramaut, Lahj

and Abyan. In Aden, scores of people were arrested in January following bomb attacks on the city's two main hotels. Most were held only briefly, but 14 were charged with "forming armed gangs". In July, six of the 14 escaped from al-Mansura prison in Aden. A suspected member of Islamic Jihad was subsequently arrested and charged with helping the detainees to escape. The nine remaining prisoners, including Shahab 'Abdo Sa'id Sayf, a public sector employee, were still detained without trial and without access to legal counsel at the end of the year.

In May over 20 people were arrested in al-Qutn Directorate in Hadhramaut province, following the killing of two army officers and a soldier at a check-point. Some were released, but 10 were tried before al-Qutn Court of First Instance on charges of premeditated murder and acts of terrorism. There were procedural irregularities during pre-trial detention, including denial of access to defence counsel until shortly before the trial, and some of the defendants were allegedly tortured during interrogation (see below). Two were sentenced to death, five received prison terms ranging from five to 10 years, and three were acquitted. Appeals were pending against all the sentences. In December, seven other suspected Islamic Jihad detainees were tried in al-Hutta Directorate in Lahj province on charges of planning the assassination of the province's Deputy Governor. Their trial had not been concluded by the end of the year. In Abyan province, scores of people were arrested in August following the attempted assassination of a member of the Political Bureau of the Yemeni Socialist Party (YSP), one of the three main parties in government. Most were released shortly after; it was not known how many remained in detention at the end of the year.

All the detainees who were known to be still held at the beginning of the year in connection with the December 1992 riots were released by February (see *Amnesty International Report 1993*). Among them were 20 people who were acquitted by the Sana'a Court of First Instance. During their trial, all stated that they had been tortured to extract confessions. They included Muhammad 'Ali Hatem al-Ru'ud, a 15-year-old high school student.

At least 20 government opponents, among them possible prisoners of conscience, remained in prison. They had

318

been arrested at different times during the 1980s and most had been convicted after unfair trials. At least one was held despite having been tried and acquitted. All were suspected members of the former National Democratic Front (NDF), the main opposition group in the former YAR (see previous *Amnesty International Reports*). Two members of the former NDF were released during the year.

Torture and ill-treatment of detainees remained common and widespread, particularly in police stations and at *al-Mabahith al-Jina'iyya* (Criminal Investigations) centres. The methods used included beatings all over the body, electric shocks, threats of rape and "Kentucky Farruj" (suspension from a metal bar inserted between the hands and knees which are tied together). 'Ali Yahya Muhammad Qina'i, a farmer from Zabeed, al-Hudaida province, was arrested in September and held in *al-Mabahith al-Jina'iyya* centre in al-Hudaida city. He was allegedly tortured with "Kentucky Farruj" to force him to give false testimony in a murder case. Two fellow inmates who testified before a representative of the Public Prosecution that 'Ali Yahya Muhammad Qina'i had been tortured were themselves allegedly tortured as punishment. 'Abdullah 'Ali 'Abdullah al-Dhabibi, a member of the Civil Guard who was arrested in October by police from al-Thawra police station in Sana'a, the capital, was allegedly tortured to force him to confess to drug-smuggling. He sustained broken ribs and injuries to his head.

Several suspected members of Islamic Jihad were reportedly tortured. 'Ali Muhammad 'Umar 'Abdullah al-Kurdi was reportedly beaten in front of other detainees in al-Mansura prison in August. Other Islamic Jihad suspects were reportedly ill-treated and threatened with rape, and two of those held in Hadhramaut province were allegedly raped.

Public floggings as a judicial punishment were frequently imposed in the northern provinces. Between January and October in Sana'a alone, at least 865 people were flogged in al-Sab'in Public Garden. In al-Hudaida city, 44 people were flogged in October.

A Somali refugee, 'Abdul-Rahman Du'ala 'Abdul-Rahman, was the victim of a possible extrajudicial execution in September in al-Kud refugee camp in Abyan province. He was killed when members of

al-Amn al-Siyassi, Political Security, fired indiscriminately into a group of refugees who were trying to prevent two women from being removed from the camp at night. No judicial investigation was known to have been carried out into the incident.

There were several political killings and attempted assassinations in circumstances suggesting the involvement or complicity of the authorities. The victims were mostly members of the YSP. Some of the perpetrators were reportedly known to the authorities, but no attempts were made to apprehend them. Among the victims was Kamil Muhammad al-Hamid, a nephew of 'Ali Salem al-Bidh, Secretary General of the YSP. He was shot dead in October in Aden while in the company of two of 'Ali Salem al-Bidh's sons who were said to have been the intended targets.

A parliamentary inquiry into the killing of demonstrators in December 1992 (see *Amnesty International Report 1993*) was concluded in January. It found that the military and security forces were not responsible for the killings, although it urged the authorities to compensate the victims' families.

The fate of hundreds of detainees who "disappeared" in previous years in the former PDRY and YAR remained unknown (see previous *Amnesty International Reports*).

Over 30 people were executed after being convicted of premeditated murder and highway robbery. The executions were carried out in public in Sana'a, and other cities. Among the victims was Nasser Munir Nasser al-Kirbi, who was only 13 years old. He was executed with three others in Sana'a in July following their conviction for murder and highway robbery. Hundreds of people remained under sentence of death.

Amnesty International urged the government to release prisoner of conscience Mansur Rajih immediately and unconditionally. It called for a judicial review of the cases of political prisoners sentenced after unfair trials, details of which were published in August in an Amnesty International report, *Yemen: Unlawful detention and unfair trials of members of the former National Democratic Front*. In August the authorities again denied that any political prisoners were being held in Yemen.

In response to an invitation from the government, Amnesty International in July submitted its initial comments on unified Yemen's draft Penal Code, Code of Criminal Procedures and other legal reforms. It urged that all such legislation conform to international human rights standards.

In October Amnesty International urged the fair trial or release of suspected members or supporters of Islamic Jihad. It also urged the government to establish an inquiry into new allegations of torture. Amnesty International continued to urge the government to clarify the fate of hundreds of detainees who had "disappeared" in previous years.

In December Amnesty International called on the government to set up an inquiry into the death of a Somali refugee and all politically motivated killings. It also appealed to the Presidential Council not to ratify death sentences.

YUGOSLAVIA
(FEDERAL REPUBLIC OF)

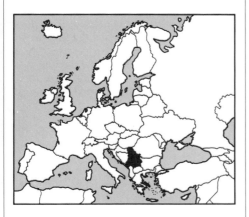

There were numerous reports of police ill-treatment and torture. The majority of victims were ethnic Albanians in Kosovo province but they also included Serbian and Montenegrin political opponents of the government. At least three people died following ill-treatment in detention by police. Some 30, and probably more, ethnic Albanians sentenced to prison terms of up to 60 days for non-violent political activity were prisoners of conscience. Over 90 other ethnic Albanians were detained on charges of seeking the secession of Kosovo by violence. By the end of the year 18 of them had been sentenced to up to five

years' imprisonment, often after unfair trials. Some were prisoners of conscience. About 25 people, mainly Muslims from Montenegro, "disappeared" on the border with Bosnia-Herzegovina.

On 1 June the federal President, Dobrica Ćosić, was ousted after he lost a vote in the federal Parliament. Opposition to him was led by deputies of the *Socijalistička Partija Srbije* (SPS), Socialist Party of Serbia, and the ultra-right-wing *Srpska Radikalna Stranka* (SRS), Serbian Radical Party. A new federal President, Zoran Lilić, was appointed on 25 June.

Elections were held for the Serbian parliament in December after the Serbian President, Slobodan Milošević, dissolved parliament. The SPS increased its representation in the parliament but failed to win a majority over the opposition parties.

Around 450,000 refugees from Bosnia-Herzegovina and Croatia remained in Serbia and Montenegro. The majority were Serbs who had arrived in 1991 or 1992. Non-Serbs continued to leave some areas of Serbia and Montenegro, particularly Muslims from the Sandžak region and Croats and Hungarians from Vojvodina, who continued to suffer threats or attacks on their property by supporters of extremist Serbian parties, although less frequently than in 1992.

Economic sanctions against Serbia and Montenegro, which had been imposed by the UN in 1992 because of their involvement in the wars in Croatia and Bosnia-Herzegovina, were strengthened in April. The sanctions, in combination with high military expenditure, had a drastic effect on the economy.

The long-term monitoring mission of the Conference on Security and Co-operation in Europe (CSCE) in Kosovo, the Sandžak and Vojvodina was forced by the federal government to close down in July. The government also refused to allow the UN Special Rapporteur on the former Yugoslavia to set up an office in Belgrade, the capital.

Ethnic tension in Kosovo persisted and there were a number of shooting incidents involving ethnic Albanians and police in which several police officers and more than 12 ethnic Albanians were killed in disputed circumstances. Tension increased after the departure of the CSCE mission in July, with a new wave of arrests and political trials of ethnic Albanians. *Lidhja*

320

Demokratike e Kosovës (LDK), the Democratic League of Kosovo, the main ethnic Albanian party, continued to call for Kosovo's independence from Yugoslavia.

Almost daily reports were received of ill-treatment of ethnic Albanians by police in Kosovo. Victims were commonly arrested and held for periods ranging from a few hours to several days in police stations where they were beaten or otherwise ill-treated. Systematic searches were often carried out on the pretext of searching for hidden arms or draft evaders. These sometimes involved large-scale police actions against whole villages or parts of towns. In other cases identity checks in the street were followed by ill-treatment and detention. Political and human rights activists were often deliberately targeted. For example, Sami Kurteshi, an activist in the Council for the Defence of Human Rights and Freedoms, an ethnic Albanian human rights group, was arrested in July during a raid on the Priština office of the group. He was taken to a police station where he was severely punched and beaten about the body with truncheons, including on his genitals and the soles of his feet. Schools organized privately by ethnic Albanians, who rejected the curricula and education in the Serbian language laid down by the Serbian authorities, were targets for police raids in which directors, teachers and pupils were reportedly ill-treated.

Some of those arrested in Kosovo were beaten so severely by police that they required hospital or other medical treatment. For example, Selajdin Braha, an ethnic Albanian, was arrested in Prizren in August and beaten so severely that police took him to hospital where he was treated and held under guard until the following afternoon, when he was returned to the police station for further interrogation.

One detainee, Arif Krasniqi, died as a result of ill-treatment in police custody in August. Following his death, in the first known instance in recent years, two policemen were sentenced in December to three years' imprisonment for causing his death; they were released pending appeal.

Police were reportedly responsible for numerous other cases of ill-treatment in a variety of circumstances throughout Serbia and Montenegro. In Belgrade on the day of the ousting of President Ćosić, 1 June, supporters of one of the main opposition parties, the *Srpski Pokret Obnove* (SPO),

Serbian Renewal Movement, clashed with police in demonstrations around the federal parliament building. One policeman was killed and 16 policemen and at least 32 demonstrators were injured. Some of the demonstrators were allegedly beaten by police as they tried to flee the area. Some hours later police arrested about 30 people at the headquarters of the SPO, including the party leader, Vuk Drašković, and his wife Danica. They were beaten by police as they were taken from the office to waiting cars. Later medical examinations confirmed that they were also repeatedly beaten in the first few days of detention and that, among other injuries, Vuk Drašković received head injuries and Danica Drašković injuries to her spine. Both were released on 9 July. Criminal charges against them were dropped.

Ljubiša Petrović, a 65-year-old refugee from Bosnia-Herzegovina and a local activist in the Democratic Party, was arrested in Čajetina on 12 August. He was beaten by police and charged with "obstructing officials" before being released that evening. A doctor reportedly confirmed injuries apparently consistent with him having been beaten. Ljubiša Petrović died five days later; the autopsy confirmed the injuries although it did not state that they had been the cause of his death. No action was known to have been taken by the authorities to investigate the alleged beating or prosecute those responsible.

In Montenegro a number of police officers were investigated for allegedly ill-treating people in their custody, including Boro Bojanić, who died in custody in September.

Some 30 ethnic Albanians, and probably more, were sentenced to up to 60 days' imprisonment for non-violent political activity: they were prisoners of conscience. For example, Hysen Matoshi, Naim Canaj and Muharrem Hoda, all political activists, were each imprisoned for 40 days for organizing a concert to celebrate Albania's national day in November.

A number of men were sentenced to terms of imprisonment for avoiding military service. It was not clear, however, whether they included individuals who had refused to undertake military service on grounds of conscience.

Between July and September some 90 ethnic Albanians were arrested on charges of being members of organizations which the authorities said were seeking Kosovo's secession by violent means. Many of them were local political activists or former political prisoners, including former prisoners of conscience. By the end of the year at least 18 had been brought to trial and sentenced to up to five years' imprisonment. Some were prisoners of conscience. None was accused of having used violence. Many of the defendants were convicted partly on the basis of confessions and other statements which they alleged had been extracted under torture during pre-trial detention. The trials were also unfair in other respects: for example, lawyers were apparently denied access to their clients following arrest and during part of the investigation.

About 25 men, mostly Muslims from towns in Montenegro but also non-Muslim refugees from Bosnia-Herzegovina, "disappeared" after they were abducted from a train travelling between Belgrade and Bar in February. This occurred as the train travelled on a 10-kilometre section of track which passes through Bosnia-Herzegovina but in territory under the control of Bosnian Serb forces. The abductors, alleged by some sources to be paramilitaries who also operate on Yugoslav territory, boarded the train when it stopped and were allegedly assisted by Serbian police and Yugoslav Army soldiers who had been travelling on the train to identify the victims. The Yugoslav, Serbian and Montenegrin authorities all condemned the abductions and said there would be an investigation, but no outcome had been announced and the victims remained "disappeared" at the end of the year.

In June the federal criminal code, which previously allowed the death penalty for crimes such as "genocide" and "war crimes", was brought into line with the federal Constitution of April 1992, and the death penalty was removed. However, the death penalty could still be imposed under the republican criminal codes of Serbia and Montenegro for "aggravated murder". No death sentences were passed or executions carried out during the year.

Amnesty International appealed to the Yugoslav authorities for independent and impartial investigation of all allegations of "disappearance", torture and ill-treatment and called for the perpetrators of such abuses to be brought to justice. It called also for the immediate and unconditional release of prisoners of conscience and for other political prisoners to receive fair and prompt trials or be released. In September Amnesty International publicly urged the Yugoslav Government to allow the CSCE long-term mission to return to Yugoslavia. Amnesty International delegates were refused permission to visit Yugoslavia for research purposes in October but an Amnesty International observer was able to attend the trial of three ethnic Albanians in Prizren in November.

In oral statements to the UN Commission on Human Rights in February and to its Sub-Commission on Prevention of Discrimination and Protection of Minorities in August, Amnesty International included reference to its concerns in Yugoslavia.

Amnesty International welcomed the establishment by the UN of an *ad hoc* international tribunal to try individuals responsible for committing serious violations of humanitarian law in the territory of the former Yugoslavia since 1 January 1991 (see **Working with international organizations**). The organization appealed to the Yugoslav authorities to do all possible to bring an end to human rights abuses by Bosnian Serb forces whom they supported. It also renewed appeals for the investigation of "disappearances" committed by forces under the control of the Yugoslav Army during the war in Croatia in 1991 (see *Amnesty International Report 1992*).

ZAIRE

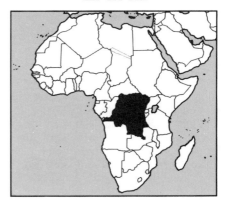

Hundreds of unarmed civilians were extrajudicially executed by soldiers, some when troops attacked protesters, others in reprisal for actions by civilians or when

soldiers rioted. Scores of political opponents of President Mobutu Sese Seko were detained without trial: many of them were prisoners of conscience. Hundreds of soldiers involved in riots or suspected of opposing the President were also detained without charge or trial. Torture and ill-treatment of prisoners were widespread. New "disappearances" were reported and the fate of scores of political opponents of the government who "disappeared" in previous years remained unknown.

Political violence escalated as the struggle for power between President Mobutu and his opponents continued, paralysing the economy and leading to a near-total breakdown in law and order. The security forces, which remained under the control of the President and his allies, periodically rampaged through towns and cities, looting and killing unarmed civilians with virtual impunity. Politically motivated intercommunal disturbances in parts of the country resulted in thousands of deaths.

In January armed soldiers rioted in the capital, Kinshasa, and a series of strikes against the President brought the city to a standstill. In February Belgium, France and the USA called on President Mobutu to hand over executive power to opposition leader Etienne Tshisekedi, who had been appointed Prime Minister by a National Conference in 1992 (see *Amnesty International Report 1993*). The President rejected the demands and announced that he had dismissed Etienne Tshisekedi. Troops loyal to the President sealed off the People's Palace to prevent a meeting of the High Council of the Republic, the transitional legislative body elected by the National Conference, and troops held members of the Council prisoner for three days. No action was taken against the soldiers.

In March President Mobutu revived the former one-party National Assembly and appointed Faustin Birindwa as Prime Minister. The High Council refused to recognize his appointment. For the remainder of the year, there was a political stalemate between the two legislative bodies and the two Prime Ministers heading rival government structures, but effective power remained in the hands of the President and the army.

In April Faustin Birindwa's government ordered soldiers to raid the homes of Etienne Tshisekedi and his cabinet on the pretext of recovering government property. Several civilians were wounded in the attacks.

Etienne Tshisekedi's government continued to call for civil disobedience and workers' strikes to force President Mobutu to relinquish power. It also asked the UN to send a peace-keeping force to the country. The UN Secretary-General sent an envoy to Zaire in mid-July and September, but there were no apparent improvements in the situation. The Organization of African Unity also tried to mediate without success.

Intercommunal violence led to thousands of deaths in Shaba and North Kivu regions, apparently instigated or condoned by the regional authorities.

In Shaba region, gangs made up of members of the indigenous population attacked members of the Luba ethnic group originating from West and East Kasaï regions, killing more than 500 people between mid-1992 and mid-1993. Sources in Shaba region alleged that the violence had been encouraged by former Prime Minister Nguz a Karl-i-Bond and Shaba's governor, with the aim of driving supporters of Etienne Tshisekedi, himself from West Kasaï, out of Shaba. In December the two Shaba leaders declared the region autonomous from central government.

In the southeastern parts of North Kivu region, members of the Nyanga and Hunde ethnic groups attacked Banyarwanda, people of ethnic Rwandese origin, from March onwards. About 7,000 people, mostly Banyarwanda, were reported to have been killed by mid-August: the killings were said to have been incited by Nyanga and Hunde chiefs who control local government, and condoned by the regional governor. Although the governor and his deputy were suspended by the President at the end of July, those responsible for the killings were not brought to justice.

There were also reports of serious human rights violations in the northeastern part of North Kivu region, near the border with Uganda, in the aftermath of armed clashes between government soldiers and rebels calling themselves "Lumumbists". Government troops reportedly committed extrajudicial executions of unarmed civilians, set villages on fire, looted property and raped women villagers. The rebels were also reported to have deliberately killed civilians and looted property.

Rioting troops in Kinshasa killed nearly 1,000 people, many of them unarmed civilians, in late January. Soldiers from Kokolo military barracks in Kinshasa and from the *Centre d'entraînement des troupes aéroportées* (CETA), Airborne Troop Training Centre, rioted after being paid in new five million zaire notes declared illegal by Etienne Tshisekedi, which many traders refused to accept. The *Division spéciale présidentielle* (DSP), Special Presidential Division, was sent in by President Mobutu to quell the disturbances, but turned its fire on armed soldiers and unarmed civilians indiscriminately. At the same time they also attacked known opponents of the President; many civilians were shot dead in their homes. French troops evacuated foreign nationals after the French Ambassador was shot dead. Several hundred soldiers suspected of involvement in the Kinshasa riots were reportedly arrested and detained by the DSP at Tshatshi military barracks. There were fears for the detainees' safety: there had been no further information about them by the end of the year.

Berthos Kibassa, the son of opposition leader Kibassa Maliba, was among the civilians executed extrajudicially at the end of January. Soldiers believed to belong to the DSP launched an unprovoked rocket attack on the house of Kibassa Maliba, then entered the building and burned Berthos Kibassa's body. Other members of the family were severely injured.

About 52 unarmed men, women and children were reportedly shot dead – and many others injured – on 22 February by members of the DSP in Kinshasa's Kimbanseke district. The attack was reportedly in reprisal for the killing of a soldier by a group of civilians. As in previous incidents no investigation was known to have occurred and no action was apparently taken against the soldiers responsible.

On 4 July at least four men were shot dead and an 11-year-old boy was stabbed to death by soldiers loyal to President Mobutu who tried to prevent the main opposition party, the *Union pour la démocratie et le progrès social* (UDPS), Union for Democracy and Social Progress, from holding a rally at Kinshasa's principal sports stadium.

Scores of President Mobutu's opponents were detained in a wave of arrests which began in March. Those held included trade unionists and journalists. Most were prisoners of conscience. Most of those detained were held incommunicado for several weeks at security force detention centres, then moved to Kinshasa's Makala Central Prison. None were charged and all were believed to have been released within four months.

Several UDPS members were arrested in late March, including Placide Mukendi, Martin Lukulungu and Lambert Tshitshimbi Katombe, a former army colonel and security adviser to Etienne Tshisekedi. They were all released untried by the end of July.

At least 18 members of the *Union Sacrée*, Sacred Union, a coalition of opposition political parties including the UDPS, were arrested in April and held without charge or trial for up to several months. Joseph Olenga Nkoy, an aide to Etienne Tshisekedi, was detained for just over two months and reported to have been tortured at the Kinshasa headquarters of the National Gendarmerie, known as the "Circo".

At least five trade union leaders were arrested following a strike by civil servants in May. They included Kuku Gedila and Ngandu Tshilombo, leaders of the *Confédération démocratique du travail* (CDT), Democratic Labour Federation. All prisoners of conscience, they were held for up to three months in cells below the Procuracy building in Kinshasa.

People working for independent newspapers were also targeted. In March and April independent newspaper vendors in Kinshasa were attacked by members of the security forces, who confiscated or destroyed many of the newspapers. Kenge Mukengeshayi, editor-in-chief of *Le Phare* newspaper, was one of at least eight journalists who were arrested. He was detained in April by security police. In April the High Court ordered his release, but he was immediately redetained by order of the Procurator General. He was released untried in June.

Further arrests of President Mobutu's critics occurred from October onwards. Those arrested included Ferdinand Chimanuka, a member of the *Parti démocrate et social chrétien* (PDSC), Christian Democratic and Social Party, and president of an opposition coalition in Kivu. He was released in December by the Supreme Court which ruled that he had no case to answer. Other detainees, including Déo Kambale, a

324

leading UDPS member, were released, but it was not clear at the end of the year how many remained in custody.

More than 50 soldiers arrested in January 1992 (see *Amnesty International Report 1993*) in Kinshasa continued to be held incommunicado without charge or trial. There were fears for their safety.

Torture and ill-treatment of prisoners were widespread. Political detainees were frequently beaten by members of the security forces, either at the time of arrest or while in custody. Kalala Mbenga Kalao, a journalist working for *Tempête des tropiques*, was brutally assaulted by the soldiers who arrested him in August after his newspaper published statistics indicating that members of President Mobutu's ethnic group comprise 70 per cent of the officers in the Zairian Armed Forces. He was first detained in a school building taken over by the Civil Guard, then transferred to a military security service detention centre. He was released without trial in September.

There were also reports of detainees being subjected to electric shocks, whipping and rape. The authorities, including the judiciary, failed to investigate claims of torture.

"Disappearances" of suspected government opponents continued to be reported. At least five people, including Emile Nkombo, a UDPS official, reportedly "disappeared" after being seized by members of the security forces on 4 July at Kinshasa's principal sports stadium when the UDPS was trying to hold a rally there. The fate of dozens of people who "disappeared" in previous years remained unknown and it was feared that they had been extrajudicially executed in secret (see previous *Amnesty International Reports*).

Conditions in Zaire's prisons and detention centres were so harsh they amounted to cruel, inhuman and degrading treatment. Dozens of deaths from starvation and medical neglect were reported in Kinshasa's central prison of Makala, and also in other prisons around the country. In some prisons, such as Bukavu Prison, locally made leg-irons which were welded around the prisoner's ankles were used as restraints, causing serious injuries to the victims.

President Mobutu commuted all death sentences to life imprisonment in November. No executions or new death sentences were reported during the year.

Amnesty International repeatedly expressed concern to President Mobutu about human rights violations by the security forces and called for the release of prisoners of conscience and for an end to torture, "disappearances", extrajudicial executions and other human rights violations. In September Amnesty International published a report, *Zaire: Violence against democracy*, and called publicly for an end to the cycle of abuse and the introduction of effective human rights safeguards in Zaire. President Mobutu's office said that the report contained "tendentious allegations", but failed to respond to any of the cases cited.

After considering communications concerning human rights violations in Zaire under a procedure established by the Economic and Social Council Resolutions 728F/1503, in March the UN Commission on Human Rights adopted a resolution deploring "the continuing serious violations of human rights" in Zaire and decided to consider the question again publicly at its 1994 session.

ZAMBIA

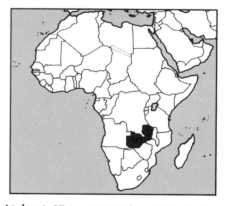

At least 27 government opponents were detained without charge or trial for up to two months. They were prisoners of conscience. One was later tried and sentenced to a prison term. There were reports of prisoners being ill-treated; at least two prisoners died after reportedly being beaten in custody. Suspected criminals were shot dead in circumstances suggesting they had been extrajudicially executed. At least three prisoners were sentenced to death, but there were no reports of executions.

In early March President Frederick Chiluba declared a state of emergency on the grounds that a document outlining plans to overthrow the government had been found at the headquarters of the opposition United National Independence Party (UNIP). UNIP sources said that the document, entitled *Zero Option*, was not party policy and contained policy options which had been rejected. With the declaration of a state of emergency, the Preservation of Public Security Regulations came into effect: they provide for indefinite detention without charge or trial. The emergency, and the powers of administrative detention it introduced, were lifted in May.

A Commission on Human Rights was established in May to investigate allegations of human rights abuses under both the previous and current governments.

At least 27 senior members of UNIP were detained without charge or trial in the days after the imposition of the state of emergency. Several were released within a few days, but at the end of March at least 15, all prisoners of conscience, remained in detention. Seven of them were freed in late April, including Rabbison Chongo and Rupiah Banda, who had both been ministers in the UNIP government defeated in multiparty elections in 1991.

In late May detention orders against the remaining eight were revoked shortly before the state of emergency was lifted. However, they were immediately rearrested and charged with various political offences before being released on bail. Three were charged with offences related to sedition and brought to trial; one, Bweendo Mulengela, a newspaper editor, was sentenced in October to nine months' imprisonment for possession of seditious material, a charge that arose from possession of the *Zero Option* document. He was granted bail pending an appeal which had not been heard by the end of the year. The trial of Henry Kamima, the former director of intelligence, and another former official opened in October but had not concluded by the end of the year. The two men were charged with retaining classified documents without authority. In November the trial of three other former detainees charged with a treason-related offence began, but it had not concluded by the end of the year. One of the three was Major Wezi Kaunda, chair of the UNIP committee on security and son of Kenneth Kaunda,

Zambia's President until 1991.

There were persistent reports of police ill-treatment of prisoners. At least two of the UNIP detainees alleged they were physically ill-treated. Cuthbert Nguni, a member of parliament, claimed that he was blindfolded, stripped naked and interrogated without a break for 39 hours during which he was hit on the back and made to do physical exercises. Henry Kamima alleged that he was tied to a chair and kicked on the shins while under interrogation. The allegations were investigated by the Commission on Human Rights, but it had not reported its findings by year-end.

At least two prisoners suspected of criminal offences died after they were reportedly beaten in police custody. Smart Siame and Matthew Mhango both died in January while in the custody of police in Lusaka. In each of the cases, which were unrelated, police accounts of their deaths differed from those of witnesses and family members. Inquests into the deaths had not been held by the end of the year. In general there were considerable delays in the opening of inquests; an inquest into the death of Dickson Zulu, who died after being beaten in police custody in August 1992, finally opened in April.

Police shot dead at least 13 criminal suspects, in some cases in circumstances which suggested they may have been extrajudicially executed. In at least two incidents suspected criminals were shot dead, according to the police, after they tried to escape while leading police officers to hidden stolen goods. In February the Minister of Home Affairs reaffirmed comments he had made in August 1992 making clear he was authorizing police to "shoot to kill" armed robbers (see *Amnesty International Report 1993*).

At least three prisoners were sentenced to death for murder and aggravated robbery. The total number of prisoners facing the death sentence remained at over 200. There were no reports of any sentences being carried out or commuted.

After the imposition of the state of emergency, Amnesty International called for the release of all those in detention considered to be prisoners of conscience, and expressed its opposition to administrative detention procedures which provided for indefinite detention without charge or trial. The organization also called for all death sentences to be commuted.

326

ZIMBABWE

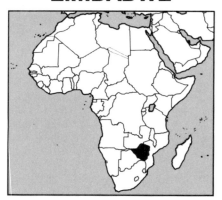

At least four people were killed by police in circumstances suggesting that they may have been extrajudicially executed. At least two people were sentenced to death but 37 others had their sentences commuted and there were no executions.

In November the Constitution was amended so that death sentences could no longer be challenged on the grounds that delays before execution or the conditions in which death-row prisoners were held could be considered inhuman or degrading punishment. In June the Supreme Court had commuted the death sentences on four prisoners to life imprisonment on the grounds that the delay in carrying out their sentences violated the constitutional ban on inhuman or degrading punishment. Following this ruling, the death sentences on 33 other prisoners were also commuted to life imprisonment.

There were reports during the year of killings by the security forces which appeared possibly to be extrajudicial executions. In February, four people, including a 10-year-old boy, were killed at Dalny gold mine, west of Harare, when police opened fire on demonstrators protesting at mineworkers' conditions. There were wide discrepancies between police and eye-witness accounts of the incident: police alleged that they had opened fire only after protesters used violence to try to disarm police; eye-witnesses said the demonstration had been peaceful. An investigation was ordered but no results were made public by the end of the year.

The authorities took no steps to investigate the mass graves discovered in 1992 at Antelope Mine near Kezi: the graves were believed to contain the remains of victims of extrajudicial executions carried out by the army between 1983 and 1985 (see *Amnesty International Report 1993*). They also failed to clarify the fate and whereabouts of Rashiwe Guzha, who "disappeared" after being reportedly kidnapped by officials of the Central Intelligence Organization (CIO) in 1990 (see *Amnesty International Report 1993*). The cases of Shepard Chisango, an army lieutenant who died in military custody in 1991, and Miria Chizhengeya, who died in police custody in 1992 (see *Amnesty International Report 1993*), remained unresolved.

Action was taken, however, in some cases of past human rights violations. A CIO official and a youth leader belonging to the ruling Zimbabwe African National Union-Patriotic Front (ZANU-PF) were sentenced to six years' imprisonment in April for the attempted murder in 1990 of Patrick Kombayi, a prominent member of the opposition (see *Amnesty International Report 1993*). In July an inquest opened into the death of Happy Dhlakama, who was allegedly beaten to death in police custody in Mutare in July 1990. It was adjourned several times and had not been completed by the end of the year. During 1993 it was learned that a police officer had been sentenced to four years' imprisonment in connection with the death in custody of Clever Magwera, who died in a police station in Kadoma in March 1991.

At least two people were sentenced to death but there were no executions.

Amnesty International urged the government of President Robert Mugabe to ensure that all cases of death in custody in previous years and killings by police were urgently and impartially investigated. The government responded by referring to progress in investigations into some cases. Amnesty International welcomed the commutation of 37 death sentences but expressed concern about the constitutional amendment. It called on the government to take steps to abolish the death penalty.

APPENDICES

AMNESTY INTERNATIONAL VISITS 1993

DATE	COUNTRY	PURPOSE	DELEGATE(S)
January	Brazil	Research	- Staff member of International Secretariat
January	South Africa	Research/Observe inquest	- Derrick Pounder (UK) - Two staff members of International Secretariat
January/February	Malaysia	Research	- Staff member of International Secretariat
January/February	Venezuela	Research/Discuss Amnesty International's concerns with government authorities	- Two staff members of International Secretariat
February	Ukraine	Research/Discuss Amnesty International's concerns with government authorities	- Joseph Middleton (UK) - Staff member of International Secretariat
February	Belarus	Research/Discuss Amnesty International's concerns with government authorities	- Joseph Middleton (UK) - Staff member of International Secretariat
February	South Africa	Observe inquest	- Peter Vanezis (UK)
March	Trinidad and Tobago	Research	- Staff member of International Secretariat
March	Austria	Research	- Staff member of International Secretariat
March/April	Pakistan	Research	- Two staff members of International Secretariat
March/April	former Yugoslavia	Research	- Staff member of International Secretariat
April	Germany	Research	- Staff member of International Secretariat
April	Luxembourg	Research	- Staff member of International Secretariat
April	USA	Research	- Staff member of International Secretariat
April	Tunisia	Research	- Staff member of International Secretariat
April	Bolivia	Observe trial	- Edgardo Carvalho (Uruguay)
April/May	Algeria	Discuss Amnesty International's concerns with government authorities/Research	- Secretary General of Amnesty International - Staff member of International Secretariat
April/May	former Yugoslavia	Research	- Staff member of International Secretariat
May	Sierra Leone	Research/Discuss Amnesty International's concerns with government authorities	- Wesley Gryk (USA) - Staff member of International Secretariat
May	Syria	Observe trial/Research	- Najib Hosni (Tunisia) - Staff member of International Secretariat
May	Argentina	Research	- Two staff members of International Secretariat
May	Bolivia	Research	- Two staff members of International Secretariat
May	Brazil	Research	- Two staff members of International Secretariat
May	United Kingdom	Observe trial	- Maryam Elahi (USA)

DATE	COUNTRY	PURPOSE	DELEGATE(S)
May	South Africa	Observe inquest/Research	- Staff member of International Secretariat
May	Israel/Occupied Territories	Research/Discuss Amnesty International's concerns with government authorities	- Allan Huglstad (Denmark) - Staff member of International Secretariat
May	Morocco	Discuss Amnesty International's concerns with government authorities/Research	- Deputy Secretary General of Amnesty International - Two staff members of International Secretariat
May/June	Japan	Research/Discuss Amnesty International's concerns with government authorities	- Staff member of International Secretariat
June	Israel/Occupied Territories	Research/Discuss Amnesty International's concerns with government authorities	- Staff member of International Secretariat
June	Senegal	Research/Discuss Amnesty International's concerns with government authorities	- Djibril Abarchi (Niger) - Stephen Ellis (UK) - Staff member of International Secretariat
June	Croatia	Research/Discuss Amnesty International's concerns with government authorities	- Alain Bovard (Canada) - Staff member of International Secretariat
June	Guatemala	Discuss Amnesty International's concerns with government authorities/Research	- Roger Clark (Canada) - Carlos Salinas (Chile) - Guadalupe Rivas (Mexico) - Staff member of International Secretariat
June	Denmark	Research	- Staff member of International Secretariat
June/July	Bulgaria	Research/Discuss Amnesty International's concerns with government authorities	- Staff member of International Secretariat
June/July	Romania	Research/Discuss Amnesty International's concerns with government authorities	- Staff member of International Secretariat
June/July	Egypt	Discuss Amnesty International's concerns with government authorities/ Research	- Secretary General of Amnesty International - Two staff members of International Secretariat
June/July	Jamaica	Observe trial	- Fritz Kodagoda (Sri Lanka)
June/July	Croatia	Research	- Staff member of International Secretariat
June/July	Peru	Research	- Two staff members of International Secretariat
July	Ethiopia	Research/Discuss Amnesty International's concerns with government authorities	- Willy Mutunga (Kenya) - Staff member of International Secretariat
July	Switzerland	Research	- Staff member of International Secretariat
July	Brazil	Research	- Linda Rabben (USA)
July	Cambodia	Research/Discuss Amnesty International's concerns with government authorities	- Roger Clark (Canada) - David Chandler (USA)
July/August	Indonesia	Research	- Staff member of International Secretariat
July/August	Albania	Research	- Jan Jansen (Netherlands)
August	Sri Lanka	Research/Discuss Amnesty International's concerns with government authorities	- Staff member of International Secretariat

DATE	COUNTRY	PURPOSE	DELEGATE(S)
August	USA	Research	- Staff member of International Secretariat
August/ September	South Africa	Research	- Rod Morgan (UK) - Staff member of International Secretariat
September	Egypt	Observe trial	- Christopher Avery (USA) - Staff member of International Secretariat
September	Germany	Research	- Staff member of International Secretariat
September	Israel/Occupied Territories	Research/Discuss Amnesty International's concerns with government authorities	- Two staff members of International Secretariat
September/ October	Turkey	Research/Observe trial	- Staff member of International Secretariat
September/ October	United Kingdom	Research/Observe trial	- Two staff members of International Secretariat
October	Hong Kong	Research/Discuss Amnesty International's concerns with government authorities	- Christopher Avery (USA)
October	Burundi	Discuss Amnesty International's concerns with government authorities	- Franca Sciuto (Italy) - Staff member of International Secretariat
October	northern Iraq	Research	- Staff member of International Secretariat
October	Turkey	Observe court hearing	- Daniel Bethlehem (UK)
October	Jordan	Research/Discuss Amnesty International's concerns with government authorities/ Observe trial	- Staff member of International Secretariat
October	northern Cyprus	Research/Observe trial	- Staff member of International Secretariat
October	Yemen	Research/Discuss Amnesty International's concerns with government authorities	- Staff member of International Secretariat
October/ November	Nepal	Research/Discuss Amnesty International's concerns with government authorities	- Three staff members of International Secretariat
October/ November	Venezuela	Discuss Amnesty International's concerns with government authorities/Research	- José Antonio Martín Pallín (Spain) - Two staff members of International Secretariat
November	Republic of Korea	Research/Discuss Amnesty International's concerns with government authorities	- Two staff members of International Secretariat
November	Malawi	Discuss Amnesty International's concerns with government authorities/ Research	- Two staff members of International Secretariat
November	Turkey	Research/Discuss Amnesty International's concerns with government authorities	- Curt Goering (USA) - Staff member of International Secretariat
November	Mexico	Research	- Staff member of International Secretariat
November	United Kingdom	Observe trial	- Robert Robertson (Canada)
November	Hungary	Research/Discuss Amnesty International's concerns with government authorities	- Staff member of International Secretariat
November	Jamaica	Research/Discuss Amnesty International's concerns with government authorities	- Rod Morgan (UK) - Staff member of International Secretariat

DATE	COUNTRY	PURPOSE	DELEGATE(S)
November	Federal Republic of Yugoslavia (Kosovo province)	Observe trial	- João Nabais (Portugal)
November/ December	China	Research	- Staff member of International Secretariat
November/ December	Antigua Barbados Dominica Puerto Rico St Christoper & Nevis St Lucia St Vincent	Research	- Staff member of International Secretariat
November/ December	Morocco	Research/Discuss Amnesty International's concerns with government authorities	- Two staff members of International Secretariat
December	Colombia	Research	- Staff member of International Secretariat
December	Israel/Occupied Territories	Research/Discuss Amnesty International's concerns with government authorities	- Staff member of International Secretariat

APPENDIX II

STATUTE OF AMNESTY INTERNATIONAL
Articles 1 and 2

As amended by the 21st International Council, meeting in Boston, USA, 6 to 14 August 1993

Object and Mandate

1. The object of AMNESTY INTERNATIONAL is to contribute to the observance throughout the world of human rights as set out in the Universal Declaration of Human Rights.
In pursuance of this object, and recognizing the obligation on each person to extend to others rights and freedoms equal to his or her own, AMNESTY INTERNATIONAL adopts as its mandate:

To promote awareness of and adherence to the Universal Declaration of Human Rights and other internationally recognized human rights instruments, the values enshrined in them, and the indivisibility and interdependence of all human rights and freedoms;

To oppose grave violations of the rights of every person freely to hold and to express his or her convictions and to be free from discrimination by reason of ethnic origin, sex, colour or language, and of the right of every person to physical and mental integrity, and, in particular, to oppose by all appropriate means irrespective of political considerations:

a) the imprisonment, detention or other physical restrictions imposed on any person by reason of his or her political, religious or other conscientiously held beliefs or by reason of his or her ethnic origin, sex, colour or language, provided that he or she has not used or advocated violence (hereinafter referred to as "prisoners of conscience"); AMNESTY INTERNATIONAL shall work towards the release of and shall provide assistance to prisoners of conscience;

b) the detention of any political prisoner without fair trial within a reasonable time or any trial procedures relating to such prisoners that do not conform to internationally recognized norms;

c) the death penalty, and the torture or other cruel, inhuman or degrading treatment or punishment of prisoners or other detained or restricted persons, whether or not the persons affected have used or advocated violence;

d) the extrajudicial execution of persons whether or not imprisoned, detained or restricted, and "disappearances", whether or not the persons affected have used or advocated violence.

Methods

2. In order to achieve the aforesaid object and mandate, AMNESTY INTERNATIONAL shall:

a) at all times make clear its impartiality as regards countries adhering to the different world political ideologies and groupings;

b) promote as appears appropriate the adoption of constitutions, conventions, treaties and other measures which guarantee the rights contained in the provisions referred to in Article 1 hereof;

c) support and publicize the activities of and cooperate with international organizations and agencies which work for the implementation of the aforesaid provisions;

d) take all necessary steps to establish an effective organization of sections, affiliated groups and individual members;

e) secure the adoption by groups of members or supporters of individual prisoners of conscience or entrust to such groups other tasks in support of the object and mandate set out in Article 1;

f) provide financial and other relief to prisoners of conscience and their dependants and to persons who have lately been prisoners of conscience or who might reasonably be expected to be prisoners of conscience or to become prisoners of conscience if convicted or if they were to return to their own

countries, to the dependants of such persons and to victims of torture in need of medical care as a direct result thereof;

g) provide legal aid, where necessary and possible, to prisoners of conscience and to persons who might reasonably be expected to be prisoners of conscience or to become prisoners of conscience if convicted or if they were to return to their own countries, and, where desirable, send observers to attend the trials of such persons;

h) publicize the cases of prisoners of conscience or persons who have otherwise been subjected to disabilities in violation of the aforesaid provisions;

i) investigate and publicize the "disappearance" of persons where there is reason to believe that they may be victims of violations of the rights set out in Article 1 hereof;

j) oppose the sending of persons from one country to another where they can reasonably be expected to become prisoners of conscience or to face torture or the death penalty;

k) send investigators, where appropriate, to investigate allegations that the rights of individuals under the aforesaid provisions have been violated or threatened;

l) make representations to international organizations and to governments whenever it appears that an individual is a prisoner of conscience or has otherwise been subjected to disabilities in violation of the aforesaid provisions;

m) promote and support the granting of general amnesties of which the beneficiaries will include prisoners of conscience;

n) adopt any other appropriate methods for the securing of its object and mandate.

The full text of the Statute of Amnesty International is available free upon request from: Amnesty International, International Secretariat, 1 Easton Street, London WC1X 8DJ, United Kingdom.

AMNESTY INTERNATIONAL
NEWS RELEASES 1993

15 January
Brazil: Indigenous communities face human rights violations; the authorities fail to act

19 January
Pakistan: Political activists and journalists arrested and tortured

21 January
Bosnia: Rape and other human rights violations are still widespread

3 February
Racism: Police in Europe are guilty of human rights abuses

10 February
Australia: Justice system is weighted against aboriginal people

12 February
Sri Lanka: Despite government promises, gross human rights violations continue

19 February
Sudan: Mass killings, ethnic displacement and other gross human rights violations continue

23 February
Morocco: Amnesty International denounces neglect of human rights concerns in Western Sahara

2 March
Algeria: Human rights violations increase under state of emergency

8 March
Women: Amnesty International urges protection for women activists

15 March
Togo: Security forces are still allowed to act with impunity

17 March
Japan: Government is failing to protect those fleeing persecution

25 March
UN **World Conference on Human Rights:** Human rights at risk of being undermined, says Amnesty International

26 March
USA: Executions of juvenile offenders are imminent

30 March
Japan: Amnesty International fears further executions

1 April
Baltic states: Amnesty International launches a campaign against the death penalty

7 April
Morocco: Amnesty International calls on governments to halt "disappearances" once and for all

8 April
India: Amnesty International calls for access to investigate human rights abuses throughout India

16 April
China: Amnesty International calls for fundamental reforms to end torture

19 April
UN **World Conference on Human Rights:** Conference could turn back clock on human rights, says Amnesty International

21 April
UN **World Conference on Human Rights:** Open letter to Heads of State and Government from Amnesty International's Secretary General calls for action to drive the Conference forward

21 April
Chad: Hundreds of deaths underline broken promises of reform

23 April
War crimes: The international war crimes tribunal for the former Yugoslavia must be fair, just and effective

28 April
Bangladesh: Serious human rights violations continue

30 April
Somalia: Update on a disaster – Amnesty International makes proposals for human rights

5 May
Tadzhikistan: Hidden human rights tragedy is taking place

7 May
Brazil: Amnesty International fears sabotage of judicial proceedings after massacre

12 May
Indigenous peoples: Indigenous peoples are still at risk around the world

18 May
Malawi: Human rights violations threaten referendum

19 May
Guatemala: Violations of the past continue

26 May
Egypt: Grave human rights violations escalate amid political violence

27 May
Israel and the Occupied Territories: Amnesty International is extremely concerned at the situation in the occupied Gaza Strip

28 May
Azerbaydzhan: Hundreds of hostages held in the Karabakh conflict – civilians continue to pay the price

1 June
UN **World Conference on Human Rights:** World Conference on Human Rights is a "Slap in the face of humanity", says Amnesty International

4 June
China: Authorities crack down on protests in Tibet

14 June
UN **World Conference on Human Rights:** Secretary General of Amnesty International to speak at the world's biggest post-card display collage in Vienna

14 June
UN **World Conference:** Nobel Peace Prize winners boycott opening of World Conference on Human Rights

17 June
UN **World Conference:** Human rights organizations protest as Myanmar speaks at World Conference

18 June
Myanmar: Burmese Nobel prize winner still a prisoner on her birthday

21 June
UN **World Conference:** First week "week of shame", says Secretary General of Amnesty International

24 June
UN **World Conference:** Amnesty International makes delegates walk over 13,000 appeal letters and says "Stop trampling on human rights!"

24 June
UN **World Conference:** Amnesty International spells out agenda for action on human rights

29 June
Maldives: Political prisoners, including prisoners of conscience, are still held after three years

1 July
Saudi Arabia: Public executions reach shocking proportions

1 July
Kuwait: Amnesty International fears imminent executions and is concerned that defendants in Bush assassination case will not get fair trial

6 July
USA: More juvenile offenders face execution following Supreme Court ruling

8 July
Amnesty International Report 1993: Governments are playing politics with people's lives

13 July
India: Government fails to accept Amnesty International's proposed visit to Bombay

22 July
Taiwan: Prisoners on death row suffer cruel, degrading and inhuman treatment

28 July
Indonesia: Systematic abuse in Aceh province in the name of "restoring order"

3 August
Georgia: Human rights violations alleged during the conflict in Abkhazia

9 August
Laos: Amnesty International calls for release of prisoners of conscience and review of unfair trial

12 August
Sierra Leone: Children are detained in rebel war

336

14 August
Amnesty International's International Council Meeting (ICM): ICM looks to changing human rights violations

18 August
Japan: Amnesty International calls on new Prime Minister to address human rights concerns

20 August
Angola: Action is needed to stop human rights abuse in bloody civil war

23 August
Trinidad and Tobago: Amnesty International urgently appeals to government to halt tomorrow's executions

26 August
Yemen: Political prisoners are still behind bars

8 September
Iraq: Gulf war detainees are held as prisoners of conscience

8 September
Iraq: Scores of prominent Sunni Arabs arrested and are at risk of abuse in custody

14 September
Saudi Arabia: Christians and Shi'a Muslims suffer persecution

16 September
Zaire: Thousands of people are murdered or tortured as Zaire faces worst human rights crisis since the civil war

23 September
Egypt: Grossly unfair mass trials and death sentences are a travesty of justice

29 September
Sudan: Human rights violations are at the heart of the famine

1 October
Refugees: International protection of refugees is threatened by powerful governments

5 October
Togo: Massive human rights violations continue despite political reform

7 October
Council of Europe: Amnesty International urges historic Council of Europe summit to live up to 44-year-old pledge

8 October
Myanmar: Climate of fear is all-pervasive amid ongoing human rights violations

11 October
Francophone Summit: End impunity for violators of human rights, appeals Amnesty International

12 October
Yugoslavia: Human rights violations continue in Kosovo as authorities deny Amnesty International access to the region

14 October
North Korea: Thousands have suffered systematic torture, summary executions and detention during 30 years of human rights violations

18 October
Commonwealth: Amnesty International renews calls to heads of government to do more to promote and protect human rights

19 October
Organization of American States (OAS): OAS must tackle "disappearances" and political killings, says Amnesty International

20 October
Campaign against political killings and "disappearances": Amnesty International launches a major campaign to end the bloodshed and terror

26 October
Afghanistan: Hundreds of Afghan asylum-seekers risk forcible return

28 October
Algeria: Hundreds are sentenced to death and more than 20 executed after unfair trials

29 October
Burundi: Amnesty International delegates return from Bujumbura with reports of killings following the coup

4 November
United Nations: Progress is stalled on UN High Commissioner for Human Rights

10 November
Venezuela: Human rights are eclipsed by rising instability and violence

11 November
Egypt: UN Committee against Torture examines Egypt's appalling torture record

15 November
Portugal: Torture and ill-treatment by police continue; authorities fail to bring perpetrators to justice

17 November
Iran: Serious human rights violations continue amid political and religious repression

19 November
Papua New Guinea: Torture and killings continue on Bougainville; government turns a blind eye

23 November
Iraq: Amnesty International calls on UN to set up human rights monitoring urgently

7 December
Pakistan: Amnesty International calls on new government to stop torture, political killings and "disappearances"

9 December
South Africa: Human rights abuses jeopardize prospects for free and fair elections

9 December
Human rights in the 90s: Amnesty International's Secretary General sets an agenda for action

15 December
India: "Disappearances" persist in Jammu and Kashmir and in Punjab

15 December
United Nations: Amnesty International welcomes UN resolution on High Commissioner for Human Rights

16 December
Bahrain: Citizens are turned away at airports and forced into exile

AMNESTY INTERNATIONAL AROUND THE WORLD

There were 4,349 local Amnesty International groups registered with the International Secretariat at the end of 1993, plus several thousand school, university, professional and other groups in over 80 countries around the world. In 53 countries these groups are coordinated by sections, whose addresses are given below. There are individual members, supporters and recipients of Amnesty International information (such as the monthly *Amnesty International Newsletter*) in over 150 countries and territories.

SECTION ADDRESSES

Algeria:
Amnesty International,
Section Algérienne,
BP 99 Garidi, Kouba,
16051 Alger

Argentina:
Amnistía Internacional,
Sección Argentina,
Avenida Colón 56,
6º Piso, Oficina "A",
Córdoba 5000

Australia:
Amnesty International,
Australian Section,
Private Bag 23, Broadway,
New South Wales 2007

Austria:
Amnesty International,
Austrian Section,
Wiedner Gürtel 12/7, A-1040 Wien

Bangladesh:
Amnesty International,
Bangladesh Section,
GPO Box 103, Ramna,
Dhaka 1000

Barbados:
Amnesty International,
Barbados Section,
PO Box 872, Bridgetown

Belgium:
Amnesty International,
Belgian Section (*Flemish branch*),
Kerkstraat 156, 2060 Antwerpen 6

Amnesty International,
Section belge francophone,
9 rue Berckmans, 1060 Bruxelles

Bermuda:
Amnesty International,
Bermuda Section,
PO Box HM 2136, Hamilton HM JX

338

Brazil:
Anistia Internacional,
Seção Brasileira,
Rua Fernando Machado 991,
Porto Alegre, R.S. 90010321

Canada:
Amnesty International,
Canadian Section
(*English-speaking branch*),
214 Montreal Rd, Suite 401, Vanier,
Ontario, K1L 8L8

Amnistie Internationale,
Section canadienne francophone,
6250 boulevard Monk,
Montréal, Québec H4E 3H7

Chile:
Amnistía Internacional,
Sección Chilena,
Casilla 4062, Santiago

Colombia:
Señores,
Apartado Aéreo 76350,
Bogotá

Côte d'Ivoire:
Amnesty International,
Section Ivoirienne,
04 BP 895, Abidjan 04

Denmark:
Amnesty International,
Danish Section,
Dyrkoeb 3, 1166 Copenhagen K

Ecuador:
Amnistía Internacional,
Sección Ecuatoriana,
Casilla 17-15-240-C, Quito

Faroe Islands:
Amnesty International,
Faroe Islands Section,
PO Box 1075, FR-110, Tórshavn

Finland:
Amnesty International,
Finnish Section,
Ruoholahdenkatu 24 D,
00180 Helsinki,

France:
Amnesty International,
Section Française,
4 rue de la Pierre Levée,
75553 Paris, Cedex 11

Germany:
Amnesty International,
German Section,
Heerstrasse 178, D-53111 Bonn

Ghana:
Amnesty International,
Ghanaian Section,
PO Box 1173, Koforidua E.R.

Greece:
Amnesty International,
Greek Section,
30 Sina Street, 106 72 Athens

Guyana:
Amnesty International,
Guyana Section,
c/o PO Box 10720, Palm Court Building,
35 Main Street, Georgetown

Hong Kong:
Amnesty International,
Hong Kong Section,
Unit 3C, Best-O-Best Commercial Centre,
32-36 Ferry Street, Kowloon

Iceland:
Amnesty International,
Icelandic Section,
PO Box 618, 121 Reykjavík

India:
Amnesty International,
Indian Section,
13 Indrapastha Building,
E 109 Pandav Nagar,
Delhi 110092

Ireland:
Amnesty International,
Irish Section,
Sean MacBride House,
8 Shaw St, Dublin 2

Israel:
Amnesty International,
Israel Section,
PO Box 14179, Tel Aviv 61141

Italy:
Amnesty International,
Italian Section,
Viale Mazzini 146, 00195 Rome

Japan:
Amnesty International,
Japanese Section,
Daisan-Sanbu Biru 2F/3F,
2-3-22 Nishi-Waseda,
Shinjuku-ku, Tokyo 169

Korea (Republic of):
Amnesty International,
Kyeong Buk R.C.O. Box 36,
706-600, Daegu

Luxembourg:
Amnesty International,
Luxembourg Section,
Boîte Postale 1914,
1019 Luxembourg

Mauritius:
Amnesty International,
Mauritius Section,
BP 69 Rose Hill

Mexico:
Sección Mexicana de Amnistía Internacional,
Apartado Postal No. 20-217, San Angel,
CP 01000 México DF

Nepal:
Amnesty International,
Nepalese Section,
PO Box 135,
Bagbazar, Kathmandu

Netherlands:
Amnesty International,
Dutch Section,
Keizersgracht 620, 1017 ER Amsterdam

New Zealand:
Amnesty International,
New Zealand Section,
PO Box 793, Wellington 1

Nigeria:
Amnesty International,
Nigerian Section,
PMB 59 Agodi, Ibadan, Oyo State

Norway:
Amnesty International,
Norwegian Section,
Maridalsveien 87, 0461 Oslo 4

Peru:
Señores,
Casilla 659, Lima 18

Philippines:
Amnesty International,
Philippines Section,
PO Box 286, Sta Mesa Post Office,
1008 Sta Mesa, Manila

Portugal:
Amnistia Internacional,
Secção Portuguesa,
Rua de Campolide 105, 1º Dto,
1000 Lisboa

Puerto Rico:
Amnistía Internacional,
Sección de Puerto Rico,
Calle Robles No 54-Altos,
Oficina 11, Río Piedras,
Puerto Rico 00925

Senegal:
Amnesty International
Senegalese Section
c/o International Secretariat
1 Easton Street
London WC1X 8DJ
United Kingdom

Sierra Leone:
Amnesty International,
Sierra Leone Section,
PMB 1021,
Freetown

Spain:
Amnesty International,
Sección Española,
Apartado de Correos 50.318,
28080 Madrid

Sweden:
Amnesty International,
Swedish Section,
PO Box 27827,
S-115 93 Stockholm

Switzerland:
Amnesty International,
Swiss Section,
PO Box,
CH-3001 Bern

Tanzania:
Amnesty International,
Tanzanian Section,
PO Box 4331,
Dar es Salaam

Tunisia:
Amnesty International,
Section Tunisienne,
48 Avenue Farhat Hached,
3ème étage,
1001 Tunis

United Kingdom:
Amnesty International,
British Section,
99-119 Rosebery Avenue,
London EC1R 4RE

United States of America:
Amnesty International of the USA (AIUSA)
322 8th Ave,
New York,
NY 10001

Uruguay:
Amnistía Internacional,
Sección Uruguaya,
Yi 1333 Of. 305,
Montevideo

Venezuela:
Amnistía Internacional,
Sección Venezolana,
Apartado Postal 5110,
Carmelitas 1010-A,
Caracas

COUNTRIES AND TERRITORIES WITHOUT SECTIONS
BUT WHERE LOCAL AMNESTY INTERNATIONAL GROUPS EXIST
OR ARE BEING FORMED

Albania	Gambia	Pakistan
Armenia	Gaza Strip and West Bank	Papua New Guinea
Aruba	Georgia	Paraguay
Bahamas	Grenada	Poland
Benin	Hungary	Romania
Bolivia	Jamaica	Russia
Bulgaria	Jordan	Singapore
Cameroon	Kazakhstan	Slovakia
Central African Republic	Kuwait	Slovenia
Chad	Kyrgyzstan	South Africa
Costa Rica	Lesotho	Taiwan
Croatia	Lithuania	Thailand
Curaçao	Macau	Togo
Czech Republic	Malaysia	Ukraine
Dominican Republic	Mali	Yemen
Egypt	Malta	Zambia
Estonia	Moldova	Zimbabwe
Fiji	Mongolia	

Amnesty International groups in Sudan have ceased activities following the banning of all political parties, trade unions and non-governmental organizations including the Sudanese Amnesty International Organization, under which the Sudanese groups were officially registered in Sudan.

INTERNATIONAL EXECUTIVE COMMITTEE

Ross Daniels/Australia
Celso Garbarz/Israel
Liz Jenkins/United Kingdom
Menno Kamminga/Netherlands
Mardi Mapa-Suplido/Philippines
Gerry O'Connell/Italy
Marie Staunton/United Kingdom
Tracy Ulltveit-Moe/International Secretariat
Susan Waltz/United States of America

SELECTED INTERNATIONAL HUMAN RIGHTS TREATIES

States which have ratified or acceded to a convention are party to the treaty and are bound to observe its provisions. States which have signed but not yet ratified have expressed their intention to become a party at some future date; meanwhile they are obliged to refrain from acts which would defeat the object and purpose of the treaty.

(AS OF 31 DECEMBER 1993)

	International Covenant on Civil and Political Rights (ICCPR)	Optional Protocol to ICCPR	Second Optional Protocol to ICCPR aiming at the abolition of the death penalty	International Covenant on Economic, Social and Cultural Rights (ICESCR)	Convention against Torture and Other Cruel, Inhuman or Degrading Treatment or Punishment	Convention relating to the Status of Refugees (1951)	Protocol relating to the Status of Refugees (1967)
Afghanistan	x			x	x(28)		
Albania	x						
Algeria	x	x		x	x(22)	x	x
Andorra							
Angola	x	x		x		x	x
Antigua and Barbuda					x*		
Argentina	x	x		x	x(22)	x	x
Armenia	x*	x*		x*	x*	x*	x*
Australia	x	x	x	x	x(22)	x*	x*
Austria	x	x	x*	x	x(22)	x	x
Azerbaydzhan	x			x		x*	x*
Bahamas						x*	x*
Bahrain							
Bangladesh							
Barbados	x	x		x	x(28)		
Belarus	x	x		x			

	International Covenant on Civil and Political Rights (ICCPR)	Optional Protocol to ICCPR	Second Optional Protocol to ICCPR aiming at the abolition of the death penalty	International Covenant on Economic, Social and Cultural Rights (ICESCR)	Convention against Torture and Other Cruel, Inhuman or Degrading Treatment or Punishment	Convention relating to the Status of Refugees (1951)	Protocol relating to the Status of Refugees (1967)
Belgium	x		s	x	s	x	x
Belize					x	x	x
Benin	x	x		x	x	x	x
Bhutan							
Bolivia	x	x		x	s	x	x
Bosnia-Herzegovina	x*			x*	x*	x*	x*
Botswana						x	x
Brazil	x			x	x	x	x
Brunei Darussalam							
Bulgaria	x	x		x	x(22)(28)	x*	x*
Burkina Faso	x					x	x
Burundi	x			x	x*	x	x
Cambodia	x			x	x	x	x
Cameroon	x	x		x	x	x	x
Canada	x	x		x	x(22)	x	x
Cape Verde	x*			x*	x		x
Central African Republic	x	x		x		x	x
Chad						x	x
Chile	x	x		x	x	x	x
China					x(28)	x	x
Colombia	x	x		x	x	x	x
Comoros							
Congo	x	x		x		x	x
Costa Rica	x	x	s	x	x*	x	x

	International Covenant on Civil and Political Rights (ICCPR)	Optional Protocol to ICCPR	Second Optional Protocol to ICCPR aiming at the abolition of the death penalty	International Covenant on Economic, Social and Cultural Rights (ICESCR)	Convention against Torture and Other Cruel, Inhuman or Degrading Treatment or Punishment	Convention relating to the Status of Refugees (1951)	Protocol relating to the Status of Refugees (1967)
Côte d'Ivoire	x			x		x	x
Croatia	x			x	x	x	x
Cuba					s	x	x
Cyprus	x	x		x	x(22)	x	x
Czech Republic	x*	x*		x*	x*	x*	x*
Denmark	x	x	s	x	x(22)	x	x
Djibouti						x	x
Dominica	x*			x*			x
Dominican Republic	x	x		x	s	x	x
Ecuador	x	x	x*	x	x(22)	x	x
Egypt	x			x	x	x	x
El Salvador	x	s		x		x	x
Equatorial Guinea	x	x		x		x	x
Eritrea						x	x
Estonia	x	x		x	x		x
Ethiopia	x*			x*		x	
Fiji						x	x
Finland	x	x	x	x	x(22)	x	x
France	x	x		x	x(22)	x	x
Gabon	x			x	s	x	x
Gambia	x	x		x	s	x	x
Georgia							x
Germany	x	x*	x	x	x	x	x
Ghana	x					x	x

	International Covenant on Civil and Political Rights (ICCPR)	Optional Protocol to ICCPR	Second Optional Protocol to ICCPR aiming at the abolition of the death penalty	International Covenant on Economic, Social and Cultural Rights (ICESCR)	Convention against Torture and Other Cruel, Inhuman or Degrading Treatment or Punishment	Convention relating to the Status of Refugees (1951)	Protocol relating to the Status of Refugees (1967)
Greece				x	x(22)	x	x
Grenada	x			x			
Guatemala	x	x*		x	x	x	x
Guinea	x			x	x	x	x
Guinea-Bissau				x		x	x
Guyana	x	x*		x	x	x	x
Haiti	x					x	x
Holy See						x	x
Honduras	s	s	s	x	x(22)	x	x
Hungary	x	x		x		x	x
Iceland	x	x	x	x	s	x	x
India	x			x			
Indonesia				x	s		
Iran (Islamic Republic of)	x			x		x	x
Iraq	x			x			
Ireland	x	x	x*	x	s	x	x
Israel	x			x	x(28)	x	x
Italy	x	x	s	x	x(22)	x	x
Jamaica	x	x		x		x	x
Japan	x			x		x	x
Jordan	x			x	x	x	x
Kazakhstan							
Kenya	x			x		x	x
Korea (Democratic People's Republic)	x			x			

	International Covenant on Civil and Political Rights (ICCPR)	Optional Protocol to ICCPR	Second Optional Protocol to ICCPR aiming at the abolition of the death penalty	International Covenant on Economic, Social and Cultural Rights (ICESCR)	Convention against Torture and Other Cruel, Inhuman or Degrading Treatment or Punishment	Convention relating to the Status of Refugees (1951)	Protocol relating to the Status of Refugees (1967)
Korea (Republic of)	x	x		x		x	x
Kuwait						x	x
Kyrgyzstan							
Lao People's Democratic Republic							
Latvia	x	x		x	x		
Lebanon	x			x			
Lesotho	x			x		x	x
Liberia	s			s		x	x
Libyan Arab Jamahiriya	x	x		x	x		
Liechtenstein					x(22)		x
Lithuania	x	x		x		x	x
Luxembourg	x	x	x	x	x(22)	x	x
Macedonia (the former Yugoslav Republic of)							
Madagascar	x	x		x		x	
Malawi	x*			x*		x	x
Malaysia							
Maldives							
Mali	x			x		x	x
Malta	x	x		x	x(22)	x	x
Marshall Islands						x	x
Mauritania							
Mauritius	x	x		x	x	x	x
Mexico	x			x	x		
Micronesia (Federated States of)							

AMNESTY INTERNATIONAL REPORT 1994

	International Covenant on Civil and Political Rights (ICCPR)	Optional Protocol to ICCPR	Second Optional Protocol to ICCPR aiming at the abolition of the death penalty	International Covenant on Economic, Social and Cultural Rights (ICESCR)	Convention against Torture and Other Cruel, Inhuman or Degrading Treatment or Punishment	Convention relating to the Status of Refugees (1951)	Protocol relating to the Status of Refugees (1967)
Moldova	x*			x*			
Monaco					x(22)	x	
Mongolia	x	x		x			
Morocco	x			x	x*(28)	x	x
Mozambique	x*		x*			x	x
Myanmar (Burma)							
Namibia							
Nauru							
Nepal	x	x		x	x	x	x
Netherlands	x	x	x	x	x(22)	x	x
New Zealand	x	x	x	x	x(22)	x	x
Nicaragua	x	x	s	x	s	x	x
Niger	x	x		x		x	x
Nigeria	x*			x*	s	x	x
Norway	x	x	x	x	x(22)	x	x
Oman							
Pakistan							
Panama	x	x	x*	x	x	x	x
Papua New Guinea						x	x
Paraguay	x			x	x	x	x
Peru	x	x		x	x	x	x
Philippines	x	x		x	x	x	x
Poland	x	x		x	x(22)	x	x
Portugal	x	x	x	x	x(22)	x	x

	International Covenant on Civil and Political Rights (ICCPR)	Optional Protocol to ICCPR	Second Optional Protocol to ICCPR aiming at the abolition of the death penalty	International Covenant on Economic, Social and Cultural Rights (ICESCR)	Convention against Torture and Other Cruel, Inhuman or Degrading Treatment or Punishment	Convention relating to the Status of Refugees (1951)	Protocol relating to the Status of Refugees (1967)
Qatar							
Romania	x	x*	x	x	x	x	x
Russian Federation	x	x		x	x(22)	x*	x*
Rwanda	x			x		x	x
St Christopher and Nevis							x
St Lucia							x
St Vincent and the Grenadines	x*	x		x		x*	x
Samoa						x	
San Marino	x	x		x			
São Tomé and Príncipe							x
Saudi Arabia						x	x
Senegal	x	x		x	x	x	x
Seychelles	x	x		x	x	x	x
Sierra Leone				x	s	x	x
Singapore				x		x	x
Slovakia	x*	x*		x*	x*	x*	
Slovenia	x	x*	s*	x	x(22)*	x	x*
Solomon Islands				x			
Somalia	x	x		x			x
South Africa				x	s*	x	x
Spain	x	x	x	x	x(22)	x	x
Sri Lanka	x			x			
Sudan	x			x	s	x	x
Suriname	x	x		x		x	x

	International Covenant on Civil and Political Rights (ICCPR)	Optional Protocol to ICCPR	Second Optional Protocol to ICCPR aiming at the abolition of the death penalty	International Covenant on Economic, Social and Cultural Rights (ICESCR)	Convention against Torture and Other Cruel, Inhuman or Degrading Treatment or Punishment	Convention relating to the Status of Refugees (1951)	Protocol relating to the Status of Refugees (1967)
Swaziland							x
Sweden	x	x	x	x	x(22)	x	x
Switzerland	x			x	x(22)	x	x
Syrian Arab Republic	x			x			
Tadzhikistan						x*	x*
Tanzania	x			x		x	x
Thailand							
Togo	x	x		x	x(22)	x	x
Tonga							
Trinidad and Tobago	x	x		x			
Tunisia	x			x	x(22)	x	x
Turkey					x(22)	x	x
Turkmenistan							
Uganda				x	x	x	x
Ukraine	x	x		x	x(28)		
United Arab Emirates							
United Kingdom	x			x	x	x	x
United States of America	x			s	s		x
Uruguay	x	x	x*	x	x(22)	x	x
Uzbekistan							
Vanuatu							
Venezuela	x	x	x*	x	x	x	x
Viet Nam	x			x			
Yemen	x			x	x	x	x

	International Covenant on Civil and Political Rights (ICCPR)	Optional Protocol to ICCPR	Second Optional Protocol to ICCPR aiming at the abolition of the death penalty	International Covenant on Economic, Social and Cultural Rights (ICESCR)	Convention against Torture and Other Cruel, Inhuman or Degrading Treatment or Punishment	Convention relating to the Status of Refugees (1951)	Protocol relating to the Status of Refugees (1967)
Yugoslavia (Federal Republic of)	x	s		x	x(22)	x	x
Zaire	x	x		x		x	x
Zambia	x	x		x	x	x	x
Zimbabwe	x			x		x	x

s – denotes that country has signed but not yet ratified

x – denotes that country is a party, either through ratification, accession or succession

* – denotes that country either signed or became a party in 1993

(22) denotes Declaration under Article 22 recognizing the competence of the Committee against Torture to consider individual complaints of violations of the Convention

(28) denotes that country has made a reservation under Article 28 that it does not recognize the competence of the Committee against Torture to examine reliable information which appears to indicate that torture is being systematically practised, and to undertake a confidential inquiry if warranted

SELECTED REGIONAL HUMAN RIGHTS TREATIES

(AS OF 31 DECEMBER 1993)

ORGANIZATION OF AFRICAN UNITY (OAU)
AFRICAN CHARTER ON HUMAN AND PEOPLES' RIGHTS (1981)

Algeria	x	Gabon	x	Rwanda	x
Angola	x	Gambia	x	Saharawi Arab	
Benin	x	Ghana	x	Democratic Republic	x
Botswana	x	Guinea	x	São Tomé and Príncipe	x
Burkina Faso	x	Guinea-Bissau	x	Senegal	x
Burundi	x	Kenya	x	Seychelles	x
Cameroon	x	Lesotho	x	Sierra Leone	x
Cape Verde	x	Liberia	x	Somalia	x
Central African Republic	x	Libya	x	Sudan	x
Chad	x	Madagascar	x	Swaziland	
Comoros	x	Malawi	x	Tanzania	x
Congo	x	Mali	x	Togo	x
Côte d'Ivoire	x	Mauritania	x	Tunisia	x
Djibouti	x	Mauritius	x	Uganda	x
Egypt	x	Mozambique	x	Zaire	x
Equatorial Guinea	x	Namibia	x	Zambia	x
Eritrea		Niger		Zimbabwe	x
Ethiopia		Nigeria	x		

x – denotes that country is a party, either through ratification or accession
This chart lists countries which were members of the OAU at the end of 1993.

ORGANIZATION OF AMERICAN STATES (OAS)

	American Convention on Human Rights (1969)	Inter-American Convention to Prevent and Punish Torture (1985)		American Convention on Human Rights (1969)	Inter-American Convention to Prevent and Punish Torture (1985)
Antigua and Barbuda			Haiti	x	s
Argentina	x(62)	x	Honduras	x(62)	s
Bahamas			Jamaica	x	
Barbados	x		Mexico	x	x
Belize			Nicaragua	x(62)	s
Bolivia	x(62)	s	Panama	x(62)	x
Brazil	x	x	Paraguay	x(62)	x
Canada			Peru	x(62)	x
Chile	x(62)	x	St Christopher and Nevis		
Colombia	x(62)	s	St Lucia		
Costa Rica	x(62)	s	St Vincent and the Grenadines		
Cuba					
Dominica	x		Suriname	x(62)	x
Dominican Republic	x	x	Trinidad and Tobago	x(62)	
Ecuador	x(62)	s	United States of America	s	
El Salvador	x	s			
Grenada	x		Uruguay	x(62)	x
Guatemala	x(62)	x	Venezuela	x(62)	x
Guyana					

s – denotes that country has signed but not yet ratified
x – denotes that country is a party, either through ratification or accession
(62) denotes Declaration under Article 62 recognizing as binding the jurisdiction of the Inter-American Court of Human Rights (on all matters relating to the interpretation or application of the American Convention)
This chart lists countries which were members of the OAS at the end of 1993.

COUNCIL OF EUROPE

	European Convention for the Protection of Human Rights and Fundamental Freedoms (1950)	Article 25	Article 46	Protocol No. 6*	European Convention for the Prevention of Torture and Inhuman or Degrading Treatment or Punishment (1987)
Austria	X	X	X	X	X
Belgium	X	X	X	s	X
Bulgaria	X	X	X		X
Cyprus	X	X	X		s
Czech Republic	X	X	X		X
Denmark	X	X	X	X	s
Estonia	s			s	
Finland	X	X	X	X	X
France	X	X	X	X	X
Germany	X	X	X	X	X
Greece	X	X	X	s	X
Hungary	X	X	X	X	X
Iceland	X	X	X	X	X
Ireland	X	X	X		X
Italy	X	X	X	X	X
Liechtenstein	X	X	X	X	X
Lithuania	s				
Luxembourg	X	X	X	X	X
Malta	X	X	X	X	X
Netherlands	X	X	X	X	X
Norway	X	X	X	X	X
Poland	X	X	X		
Portugal	X	X	X	X	X
Romania	s				s
San Marino	X	X	X	X	X
Slovakia	X	X	X	X	s
Slovenia	s			s	s
Spain	X	X	X	X	X
Sweden	X	X	X	X	X
Switzerland	X	X	X	X	X
Turkey	X	X	X		X
United Kingdom	X	X	X		X

s – denotes that country has signed but not yet ratified

x – denotes that country is a party, either through ratification or accession

Article 25: denotes Declaration under Article 25 of the European Convention, recognizing the competence of the European Commission of Human Rights to consider individual complaints of violations of the Convention

Article 46: denotes Declaration under Article 46 of the European Convention, recognizing as compulsory the jurisdiction of the European Court of Human Rights in all matters concerning interpretation and application of the European Convention

* Protocol No. 6 to the European Convention on Human Rights: concerning abolition of the death penalty (1983)

This chart lists countries which were members of the Council of Europe at the end of 1993.

SELECTED STATISTICS

AMNESTY INTERNATIONAL MEMBERSHIP

At the beginning of 1994 there were more than 1,100,000 members, subscribers and regular donors in over 150 countries. There were 4,349 local Amnesty International groups registered with the International Secretariat, plus several thousand school, university, professional and other groups in over 80 countries.

PRISONER CASES AND RELEASES

At the end of September 1993 Amnesty International was working on 3,507 Action Files and cases featuring over 8,960 individuals, including prisoners of conscience and other victims of human rights violations. During the year action began on 856 new cases. A total of 922 cases involving the release of prisoners of conscience and possible prisoners of conscience was recorded.

URGENT ACTION APPEALS

During 1993 Amnesty International initiated 551 actions which required urgent appeals from the Urgent Action Network. There were also 318 calls for further appeals on actions already issued. Members of the Urgent Action Network were therefore asked to send appeals on 869 occasions. These actions were on behalf of people in 86 countries.

The 551 new actions were issued on behalf of people who were either at risk or had been victims of the following human rights violations: torture – 179 cases; political killing – 100 cases; "disappearance" – 76 cases; judicial execution – 95 cases; death threats and other threats to safety – 130 cases; and legal concerns such as detention without trial, incommunicado detention and arbitrary arrest – 108 cases. (These categories are not mutually exclusive; more than one concern may have been featured in an action.) Other concerns included ill-health, deaths in custody, *refoulement* (forcible repatriation) of asylum-seekers, flogging and forcible exile.

REGIONAL ACTION NETWORKS

Amnesty International's Regional Action Networks deal with human rights abuses in every country of the world. During the year, 2,417 Amnesty International local groups participated in the Regional Action Networks, which worked on the cases of thousands of victims of human rights violations.

AMNESTY INTERNATIONAL FUNDING

The budget adopted by Amnesty International for 1993 was £12,755,700. This sum represents slightly less than one quarter of the estimated income likely to be raised during the year by the movement's national sections. Amnesty International's national sections and local volunteer groups are responsible for funding the movement. There is no central fund-raising program and no money is sought or accepted from governments. The donations that sustain Amnesty International's work come from its members and the public.

RELIEF

During 1993 the International Secretariat of Amnesty International distributed £219,854 in relief (financial assistance) to victims of human rights violations such as prisoners of conscience and recently released prisoners of conscience and their dependants, and to provide medical treatment for torture victims. In addition, the organization's sections and groups distributed a further substantial amount, much of it in the form of modest payments by local groups to their adopted prisoners of conscience and dependent families.

Amnesty International's ultimate goal is to end human rights violations, but so long as they continue it tries to provide practical help to the victims. Relief is an important aspect of this work. Sometimes Amnesty International provides financial assistance directly to individuals. At other times, it works through local bodies such as local and national human rights organizations so as to ensure that resources are used as effectively as possible for those in most need. When Amnesty International asks an intermediary to distribute relief payments on its behalf, it stipulates precisely the intended purpose and beneficiaries and requires the intermediary to report back on the expenditure of the funds.